D1422667

Kept in the Dark

Kept in the Dark

The Denial to Bomber Command of Vital ULTRA and other Intelligence Information during World War II

John Stubbington

Pen & Sword
AVIATION

First published in
Great Britain in 2010
By Pen and Sword Aviation
An imprint of
Pen and Sword Books Ltd
47 Church Street
Barnsley
South Yorkshire
S70 2AS

ISBN 978-1-84884-183-3

Typeset in 10/12pt Palatino
by Mac Style, Beverley, E. Yorkshire

Printed and bound in Great Britain
by CPI Antony Rowe, Chippenham, Wiltshire

Pen and Sword Books Ltd incorporates the imprints of Pen and Sword
Aviation, Pen and Sword Maritime, Pen and Sword Military, Wharncliffe Local
History, Pen and Sword Select, Pen and Sword Military Classics and Leo
Cooper.

For a complete list of Pen & Sword titles please contact
PEN & SWORD BOOKS LIMITED
47 Church Street, Barnsley, South Yorkshire, S70 2AS, England
E-mail: enquiries@pen-and-sword.co.uk
Website: www.pen-and-sword.co.uk

CONTENTS

Acknowledgements 11

Foreword 13

Preface 15

Chapter One: Introduction 18
What this book contains 21
Security Classifications and Grades 26
Definitions 26

Chapter Two: Signals and Intelligence 28
The Polish Contribution 28
Prevailing Attitudes 29
Pre-War and Soon Afterwards 30
  Signals Intelligence up to Autumn 1940 32
  Changes during the Winter of 1940–41 35
  Changes during 1941 and 1942 39
  Changes during 1943 47
  Changes during 1944 – pre-D-Day 50
  Changes during 1944 – post D-Day 52

Chapter Three: Economic Warfare 56
Industrial Intelligence Centre 56
  Industrial Air Targets: Registration and Attack 57
  Intelligence Directorate for MEW 59
  Post-September 1938 60
Responsibilities of MEW – From 1939 61
  The Starting Position 62
  Through 1940 64
  Estimation of German Industrial Capacity and Vulnerability 65
Bombing as an Instrument of Economic Warfare 69
  Who Settled Bombing Policy 70
  Limitations of Night Bombing 72
  Developments at that Time 73
The German Oil Industry and Supply 74
German Transportation Systems 77
  An Analysis by the British Railway Research Service 77
  Other Statements by MEW about German Transportation 79
Economic and Operational Bombing Priorities – 1942 81

Chapter Four: Issues with the Bombing Offensives **84**
Prior Appointments for Sir Arthur Harris 84
Build-Up of the 8th USAAF in the UK 86
Strategic Target Selection 89
  POINTBLANK and OVERLORD 90
  The Final Phase.. 98
  Oil or Transportation 104
Precision versus Area Bombing 107
  Air Navigation 110
  Bombsights 117
  The Pathfinder Force.. 118
  The Required Damage Effect.. 122
  Circular Error Probable 125
  Bomber Command Accuracy 127
  The 8th USAAF Experiences 129
  Precision Bombing 135
  Summary 139
  Postscript 140

Chapter Five: Signals Intelligence within the Service Ministries **141**
Signals Intercept, Cryptanalysis and Intelligence.......................... 141
Relationships between GC & CS and Ministries........................... 145
  Admiralty 145
    The Battle of the Atlantic 146
  The War Office 152
  The Air Ministry 152

Chapter Six: Air Ministry Intelligence.................................... **156**
Introduction 156
Organisation Changes during the War 157
  From Pre-war to the End of 1940.................................... 158
  From January 1941 to August 1943 160
  From September 1943 to the End of the War 161
Specific Functions and Sections 163
  Special Liaison Duties 164
    Function and Development 164
    Current Archive Records... 167
  Photographic Reconnaissance 168
    Background 168
    Photographic Interpretation 170
  Aircraft Production and Airfield Intelligence........................ 170
    The Purpose 170
    Aircraft Production Intelligence in Peacetime..................... 171
    Aircraft Production Intelligence in Wartime....................... 172
    Dissemination of Aircraft Production Intelligence 173
    Airfield Intelligence 174
    Post-War Comments 175
  Intelligence Appreciations and Summaries 177

Order of Battle and Dispositions 177
    Methods of Work.. 178
    The Fighting Value of the GAF 179
    The Use of ULTRA within AI 3(b) 181
Target Intelligence 182
    The Use of ULTRA within AI 3(c)... 183
    The German Aircraft Industry 185
Bomb Damage Assessment.. 187
    Early Appreciations of the Bombing Offensive......................... 188
    MEW Damage Reports... 190
Enemy Transportation System 191
    Overview 191
    Air Intelligence Effort.. 192
    The Contribution of ULTRA Material.. 194
    Intelligence Reports from MEW 196
Liaison with the USAAF 198
    General Information Exchange 198
    Intelligence Exchange 199
Air Signals Intelligence and Organisation 200
    DDI 4's Responsibilities 201
    Internal.. 202
    Responsibilities to Other Air Intelligence Sections.................. 204
    Air Sigint Appreciation 205
    Dissemination of Air Sigint by the Air Ministry 206
Scientific Intelligence 208
    Policy.. 208
    Working Methods... 209
    Specific Topics... 211
Joint Intelligence Staff (Air) and AI (JIS) 213
    Function and Organisation... 213
    The Use of ULTRA by the JIS 214

Chapter Seven: Operational Intelligence at HQ Bomber Command 216
Introduction 216
Target Intelligence and Damage Assessment............................... 216
    Pre-Incendiary Period.. 217
    The Development of Fire Attack.. 217
        Strategic Bombing 219
        Pre-D-Day Operations 221
        Post-D-Day and Final Strategic Bombing.............................. 222
        V-Weapons and Operation CROSSBOW 225
Directive Targets.. 230
    CSTC Target Lists.. 230
Enemy Air Defence Intelligence 233
    Tactical Sigint Support.. 234
    Enemy Fighter and Air.. 236
    100 Group Bomber Support RCM and Night Intruders 238

Application of Intelligence Material.. 241
High-Grade Intelligence... 242
Photographic Reconnaissance.. 243
Planning Conferences.. 244
The Morning Conference 244
The Afternoon Conference... 246

Chapter Eight: Signals Intelligence within the 8th US Army Air Force in the UK **248**
Arrangements for the 8th USAAF.. 248
Activation in February 1942 249
Photographic Intelligence 250
Arrangements for Target Intelligence 251
Development of Strategic Operations.. 254
POINTBLANK.. 254
Combined Operational Planning Committee 259
Formation of the USSTAF 260
Inception and Development... 261
Tactical Air Intelligence 263
Relocation to France... 268

Chapter Nine: The Value of Signals Intelligence to the Combined Bombing Offensive **270**
The Linked Routing Protocol 271
Tactical Intelligence.. 273
Strategic Target Selection 276
Isolation of the Ruhr 277
Background 278
Transportation Attacks – Early 1945.. 278
Typical ULTRA Evidence 280
Failure to Use Special Intelligence... 281

Chapter Ten: Post-War Bombing Surveys and Other Reports **283**
Introduction 283
The US Strategic Bombing Survey... 285
Introduction 285
Armaments... 287
Overview 287
Armoured Vehicles... 289
Motor Vehicles 290
Weapons and Ammunition.. 291
The Aircraft Industry 293
The Steel Industry 295
Oil Targets 296
Transportation.. 299
Background 299
Post-OVERLORD 301

The Final Stage 302
Economic Effects of Air Attacks on Transportation 303
Overall Effects of the Bombing Offensive 305
The British Bombing Survey Unit Report 306
The Results of the Area Offensives.. 307
The Results of the Offensive against Oil Plants 310
Military Effects.. 310
Industrial Effects.. 312
The Results of the Offensive against Transportation.................................. 313
The Major Cause of the Transportation Crisis... 315
Reports by German Military and Civilian Officials..................................... 316
Military Reports... 316
Civilian Reports... 317
Albert Speer 318

Chapter Eleven: The Final Analysis **321**
Introduction 321
Changing British Political Thinking.. 323
Towards the End of the War.. 323
Subsequent Historical Analyses.. 325
Lack of Knowledge about Bomber Capabilities... 331
Evaluation and Selection of Targets 332
Power Groups... 337
Ministry of Economic Warfare 338
The Oil Lobby 340
Directorate of Bomber Operations... 342
Handling of Signals Intelligence... 346
General Aspects of the Strategic Air War 350
Contribution of the Bomber Offensive to the War...................................... 352

Afterword **357**

Appendix A: Bombing Targets for 1942 – MEW **359**

**Appendix B: Examples of RAF Y-Service Sigint against KG 40/Fw 200
Operations**.. **362**

**Appendix C: Established Officer Strength of the Air Intelligence
Directorate**.. **367**

Appendix D: Air Intelligence Organisation – 14 January 1941 .... **370**

Appendix E: Air Intelligence Organisation – July 1942 .... **372**

Appendix F: Air Intelligence Organisation – April 1944 .... **375**

Appendix G: Bomber Command Intelligence Organisation – End of War..... **378**

Appendix H: Jockey Committee Report **381**

Appendix I: Air Ministry Weekly Intelligence Summaries............................ 383

Appendix J: Bomber Command andthe U-boat Campaign:April
1942–March 1943 386

Appendix K: Extracts from Decrypts giving Effects of Air Attacks on
German Transportation 390

Appendix L: Overview of DDI 4 Activity 393

Appendix M: Distribution of GC&CS Air Sigint Intelligence Reports....... 405

Appendix N: Whitehall and the British Bombing Survey................................ 408

Appendix O: The End of the Third Reich, 1944–1945.................................... 414

Appendix P: The Oil Factor in German War Effort.. 417

Appendix Q: Airborne Intercept of Enemy R/T.. 427

Appendix R: Comparison with Dowding 429

Postscript 432

Abbreviations and Glossary... 433

Bibliography.. 436
The Bombing Offensive.. 436
Intelligence Support.. 437

Index... 439

Plate Section
1. Bletchley Park Mansion, courtesy of the Bletchley Park Trust
   Lancaster dropping a 4,000lb Cookie and 30lb Incendiaries (lWM CL 001404)
2. No. 5 Group raid on *Tirpitz*, 12 November 1944 (TNA Air 24/299)
3. Focke-Wulf 200 *Kondor*
   Focke-Wulf aircraft factory at Bremen (TNA Air 40/253)
4. PR Image of Radar Site at Auderville, taken on 22 February 1941
   Plan of V-2 launch site in Normandy (TNA Air 40/2887)
5. Wurzbzirg Ground Control Radar (TNA Air 41/10)
   Schweinfurt ball bearing factory map, issued October 1943 (TNA Air 40/253)
6. US War Department press release, 30 October 1945 (TNA Air 48/194)
   Total German Armament Production, 1940–45 (TNA Air 48/194)
   88mm Anti-Aircraft Flak gun in Field Deployment
7. Percentage Distribution of Armaments Production (TNA Air 48/194)
   RAF Lancaster and 22,000lb TALLBOY (IWM Ref. CH 015375)
8. German Aircraft Production 1939–1944 (TNA Air 48/194)
   A schematic plan of an underground lubricating oil plant at Porta,
   Westphalia (TNA Air 8/1019)

Acknowledgements

I wish to acknowledge the generous and effective assistance that has been provided to me during the research, drafting and editing of this book. In no order of precedence, I am particularly grateful for the extensive advice and guidance from:

- Sir Arthur Bonsall, KCMG, CBE, Director of GCHQ 1973–78; senior member of the Air Section at Bletchley Park throughout WW2.
- Professor Jack Dixon, who trained as an RAF pilot at the end of WW2 and subsequently graduated from Merton College, Oxford, before emigrating to Canada.
- John Gallehawk, a previous curator of the Archives at the Bletchley Park Trust and author of many Intelligence documents.
- Sqn Ldr Dick Green, CEng, with shared experience from relevant Air Intelligence appointments.
- Dr Phil Judkins, Chairman of the Defence Electronics History Society.
- Air Vice Marshal John Main, CB, OBE, FREng.
- John Nichol, RAF Historical Society.

By no means least, I acknowledge and appreciate the help from many members of the staff at The National Archives and Peter Elliott at the RAF Museum Library over a long period of research.

I also appreciate the tolerance of my wife Valerie during that long period of research and drafting when there were many other things that had comparable or higher importance in the whole scale of life outside the scope of writing a book.

*   *   *

The National Archives (TNA) at Kew has been a major source of the official historical material, from which extensive reference has been drawn both within the bibliography and the footnotes. Where direct reference has been made in footnotes or elsewhere, the source has been identified by reference to The National Archives folder number.

The Harris Archives at the RAF Museum, Hendon, has been a source of valuable records of correspondence between Sir Arthur Harris and the Prime Minister, other senior members of the Air Ministry and Government departments.

The Bletchley Park Archives has been a unique source of ULTRA Highlight Reports and some other Intelligence material that are not held in The National Archives at Kew.

*   *   *

Whereas the archive evidence used in this book has the validity of Official Records, the conclusions drawn from that evidence and the bibliography on some matters related to the conduct and performance of various Government and Air Ministry departments and staff are the sole responsibility of the author, unless otherwise supported by source material designated in the footnotes.

Foreword

This book, by Wing Commander John Stubbington, whose career in the Royal Air Force centred on Intelligence and Electronic Warfare, is a masterly and original thesis on the Allied Strategic bombing offensive against Germany in World War 2. It analyses the different but complementary bombing strategies pursued by the British and the Americans. The broadly accepted current arguments have been that the USAAF went for industrial targets by daylight 'precision' bombing whereas Bomber Command conducted night area bombing of city targets. These 'myths' are turned on their head and show – for the first time, for me at least – the truth of the matter. We had known since the Battle of Britain that the 'Trenchard Doctrine' was potentially doomed to failure, because we did not have the weapons to deliver the crushing blows against the German war industry and because we underestimated the astonishing vitality of German morale.

Wing Commander Stubbington has shown that the American 'precision' bombing was not so precise as was claimed. Yet he proves beyond contention that the Allied strategic bombing of the German heartland contributed immensely to ultimate victory. He does this by analysing the aims, the methods, the results, the evaluation of damage done by various methods – and his conclusions are to this reader beyond cavil. He demonstrates that oil, one of the so-called 'panacea' targets pooh-poohed by Harris, was in fact not all that vital for the German war effort – but for reasons different from Harris's. Oil was essential to the German military, but not to the war industry. His conclusion that the real damage to Germany's capacity to wage war was delivered by the strategic bombing campaign against the transportation systems, especially railways and canals, with the consequent inability to move raw materials and finished products, is totally convincing. This became increasingly critical as the German war industry was dispersed and the need for transportation between factories escalated. Aviation and motor fuels were finished products from the war industry but they had no value when they were in the wrong place.

The other dominant thrust of the book is the contribution of Intelligence to the conduct of the strategic bomber offensive. Here we enter a disturbing feature of the bureaucratic mentality and ethos at their worst. It is disturbing because at war, when the fate of nations and peoples is at stake, men – even high-ranking air force officers and government civilians whose sole motive should be that of duty – are driven by questionable forces which actually inhibit co-operation. The lack of co-operation between government and military offices blocked the exchange of Intelligence between different levels of the service and, even more incredibly, prevented the passing of important Intelligence to Bomber Command relating to the German Air Defence system and to Target Selection and Damage Assessment. These 'crimes' were relatively widespread and went uncorrected throughout the war. They contributed to the lengthening of the war and are a damning indictment of some of the people who occupied high offices in Whitehall at the time. They remind us of the intrigues and pettiness which inhabited the Air Ministry during the Battle of Britain.

In sum, this book, supported as it is by the most painstaking research and the most scrupulous standards of scholarly objectivity, makes for one of the most masterly examinations of the whole question of the strategic bombing of Germany in World War 2. If there have been any doubts in people's minds about the **absolute necessity of the Allied strategic bombing offensive** and the ways in which it was carried out, this book provides the conclusive answers to them.

Professor Jack Dixon
Victoria, Canada

Preface

The immediate background to the research behind this book goes back over four years. It may actually be the culmination of a career of twenty-five years within the Royal Air Force and then twenty years of professional and commercial work within the UK defence industry. The continuing theme through my career has been an association in a wide variety of ways with Intelligence, its collection and its application to military requirements.

Some fifteen years ago I became increasingly interested in the outstanding work by Tony and Margaret Sale to rescue Bletchley Park from the predations of developers and their subsequent salvation of a most valuable National Asset. That struggle continues with no support from the British government. However, in 2008, English Heritage provided funding to help the Bletchley Park Trust with repairs to the roof of the mansion, and the local Milton Keynes Council matched that support. In 2009, English Heritage has provided further funding support.

There has been a great deal of literature published over the post-war years that has addressed the facts – and sometimes the myths – relating to the decryption of ENIGMA and the provision of the ULTRA reports. But hardly any of that literature has recorded the way in which ULTRA was applied to the planning, implementation and assessment of the bombing campaigns. I had discussion some four years ago with Simon Greenish, the Director of the Bletchley Park Trust, about the need to address the ways in which some of the output of the Park was used to support strategic bomber operations during World War 2.

That initial discussion led into an extensive search of evidence both at the National Archives and at the Park. The information within that evidence formed the basis for my book published in August 2007 that described the work of the Bletchey Park Air Section and the provision of intelligence for the Combined Bombing Offensive by RAF Bomber Command and the 8th US Army Air Force during 1943–45. On the way, that research embraced the absolutely vital work done by the Y-Services to intercept the enemy signals messages; and also by No. 100 (Bomber Support) Group to provide Radio Countermeasures in direct support of bomber operations.

That earlier research did not embark on a study of the politics or the policy conflicts surrounding the strategic bombing campaigns but it did raise unexpected questions. Throughout virtually all of the war, those bombing campaigns were the only means of attacking the enemy's war economy and armament production. Indeed, without those campaigns there would have been no external pressures to restrict and ultimately to overcome the enemy's capability to produce armaments and to sustain the conflict. The approval of those campaigns and their implementation were subject to many important and often contradictory factors: strategic and tactical operational considerations, political priorities, target selection and professional judgement by the air commanders.

For most of that extended period, Bomber Command had the support of the British government and the people – notwithstanding some genuine minority objections. However, my research began to reveal activities within the UK political and military hierarchies that were disturbing. The continuing and deeper research started to reveal serious conflicts in policy driven not by the arguments on facts, but the clash of personalities and rivalries. In those covert and sometimes very overt clashes, the truth of the matters was of little consequence. This then began to reveal that, in several aspects of fundamental importance to the strategic bombing campaigns, there was a profound and widespread level of ignorance of the facts particularly among some of the top decision makers and their advisors.

In the search for any explanation or justification for that state of affairs, the key element may be that strategic bombing was a completely new military concept. There were no records of previous campaigns. The earlier doctrine of strategic bombardment that had been developed after World War 1 may have been theoretically correct, but the undisputed fact is that the resources were not made available. The reasons rest within the political mood for appeasement and the failure of the Air Council to adequately examine the concept of strategic bombing and its vital prerequisites. The rules for conducting such campaigns were evolved on the basis of events as they took place during World War 2. Of that there is no doubt. The performance of bomber operations for the first 2–3 years of the war was consistently far less than had been expected and proclaimed. The one factor that was consistently present was the courage and the effort of the bomber aircrews and their ground support services.

Those serious shortcomings both in understanding and in aircraft capability led to a growing sense of disappointment at the very top of the political and military command chains. There were many criticisms of the bombing campaign in those first 2–3 years and it was at times possible that Bomber Command would have been fragmented. In that adverse light, the leadership and drive of the Commander in Chief Sir Arthur Harris from February 1942 onwards were unequalled not only in keeping the Command together but in progressively building a truly awesome capability. But it is clear that there was a continuous lobby of dissent within Whitehall. That dissent came from uninformed perspectives of what was actually possible with the resources that were available, combined with personal or committee impressions of how the campaigns should be conducted. The common denominator was that none of that dissent had first-hand experience of controlling a strategic bomber offensive.

Within the internal stresses and conflicts in Whitehall there was another issue that has become apparent. The policy for handling and disseminating intelligence within and from the Air Ministry was flawed. The flaw related particularly to the provision of signals intelligence to the Home Air Commands. The Air Ministry policy was that signals intelligence for those commands would flow from the Ministry and not from the producers of the data. That would have been very reasonable, except that the Ministry had no facility for handling the mass of data that came from the various grades of signals intelligence. Also, the Ministry was inadequately aware of the detail of air operations being separately conducted by Fighter Command and Bomber Command. The political powers in Whitehall were closely interested in those operations that were taking place in every sense over their heads. This may well have created pressure for the Air Ministry and a need to be 'seen to be doing something'. In contrast, signals intelligence support for overseas air commands flowed directly from Bletchley Park. Those operations were largely 'out of sight' for the Whitehall warriors and the archives show that those air commands were able to benefit from that timely intelligence. The same was true for the Army and particularly for the Navy. The availability and use of signals intelligence – and this includes the high-grade ENIGMA and ULTRA material – within the context of the bombing campaigns has hardly figured in the official histories, except for the History of British Intelligence in the World War 2. That history was written long before public release of any of the evidence and it does not address the politics surrounding the use of that information within Whitehall.

It may be concluded that Sir Arthur Harris was fighting on two Fronts: one over Germany and one in Whitehall. Much the same had been true for Sir Hugh Dowding at Fighter Command before and during the Battle of Britain. His subsequent reward for that victory was to be relieved of command in circumstances that can only be described as scandalous. The reward for Sir Arthur Harris and the whole of Bomber Command when their job was done was to be subjected to criticism and vilification, which has dominated subsequent analyses and literature. The official history of the bombing campaign was subjected to prolonged obfuscation and suppression within Whitehall over a period of 16 years. The other two dominant official records were the 'Despatch on War Operations 'and the 'British Bombing Survey Unit Report'; both were withheld for over 50 years. The proliferation of many unofficial documents that address the bombing campaigns variously contain substantial details, but hardly any touch upon the way in which intelligence was used or denied. There has been substantial debate and argument between various authors about many of the most visible operations; for example, the raids on Berlin, Cologne, Hamburg, Nuremburg, Peenemunde, Schweinfurt, Dresden and many others. There has been substantial study and debate about many of the strategic bombing decisions taken along the way as the war progressed. That mass of literature has at different times contained many attempts to rewrite the history and to revise the perceived outcome of the bombing campaigns in the context of the contribution to the ultimate Allied victory. Some of that literature has reflected post-war attitudes back into wartime decisions and drawn conclusions which are invalid.

There has been almost a complete absence of any analysis of the realities and distinctions between 'precision' and 'area' bombing, another cause of massive controversy and widespread ignorance. A complete darkness has covered the politics, the policy conflicts, the personalities and the jealousies that embraced and smothered the use and abuse of signals intelligence within the planning and conduct of those strategic bombing campaigns. This book uncovers some of that contentious and covert history and throws light onto topics that have remained largely undisturbed. What is revealed is not flattering to some of the departments and some of the personalities.

John Stubbington
Trinity Hill, Medstead

CHAPTER ONE

Introduction

'It is a riddle wrapped in a mystery inside an Enigma; but perhaps there is a Key.'

Sir Winston Churchill, 1939

In the long history of warfare, never had so much information about the warring plans and capacity of the enemy been available to the ultimate victor during the conflict as the Allied powers had about the Axis coalition in World War 2. Allied traditional intelligence operations – commando forays, the work of resistance groups in enemy-occupied territory, spying activities by secret agents and aerial reconnaissance, for example – were often remarkably sophisticated and successful during the war. Nevertheless, the crème de la crème of clandestine operations and achievements was in the field of Signals Intelligence (Sigint) and particularly in solving of codes and ciphers (cryptography) and thereby 'reading the enemy's mail.' Never has an adversary had the opportunity to peruse so systematically and thoroughly the most secret communications of an enemy, sometimes even before the rival addressee received the message.

Where this book starts?

The material that this book contains goes to the very heart of British and Allied Intelligence during WW2, in the specific context of the planning, control and implementation of the bombing offensives against Germany. The initial bombing campaign from the UK was conducted by Bomber Command alone from the start of WW2, until joined by the 8th US Army Air Forces (USAAF) from the late summer of 1942. RAF Bomber Command and the USAAF jointly conducted the major Combined Bombing Offensive from the spring of 1943 through to the end of the war in Europe in May 1945.

There is a great deal of significance associated with the years prior to the declaration of war on 3 September 1939, related substantially to the prevailing politics within UK through the 1930s and the failure to make preparations for the looming conflict with Germany – that time which was described by Sir Winston Churchill as 'The Gathering Storm'. In that period many actions were not taken and many opportunities lost, the cost of which did not become clear even for several years after the war had started. British Intelligence in general was one of the casualties of that pre-war neglect. There was however very notable wisdom and foresight within much of the work conducted by the 1930s Industrial Intelligence Committee (IIC). The Director was Major Desmond Morton, who had very close contact with Churchill through those contentious years in the 1930s. The committee was subsumed into the newly created Ministry of Economic Warfare (MEW) in the autumn of 1939. Morton, subsequently Sir Desmond Morton, became the Prime Minister's personal representative on security and Special Intelligence material throughout the war.

The cryptographic work conducted assiduously over more than a decade by the Polish Intelligence Service and made available to British Intelligence in the summer of 1939 (see Chapter 2) was the catalyst for the successful Sigint attack on the German ENIGMA encrypted message traffic through most of WW2. That Sigint attack was mounted primarily from Bletchley Park by the organisation known as the Government Codes and Ciphers School (GC & CS). Whatever the strategic importance of ENIGMA and the subsequent high-grade decrypted and translated messages that were known as ULTRA, it must be appreciated that there was an enormous mass of medium and low-grade enemy signals traffic that was also subjected to extensive monitoring and intercept by British and Allied Sigint organisations. Credit must also be given to their German counterparts who were deriving valuable information from British and Allied signals traffic. The extent of this intercept was unprecedented in military, political and economic history. It set the foundation for what has subsequently become an accepted global fact of life, with immeasurable dividends for many nations to this present day and probably for as long as people, organisations and governments continue to use electro-magnetic message communications that are transmitted into the ether.

The Sigint organisations in WW2 were one of the primary means of providing intelligence to military, political and economic staffs. It was those military, political and economic staffs that should have been responsible for the appreciation of what the Sigint material contained and what it meant, in conjunction with the other sources of intelligence, and then making their decisions and taking actions. It will be seen that for a variety of reasons GC & CS at Bletchley Park did become deeply involved with the task of 'appreciating' much of the Sigint information, because of the complexity of the encrypted signals traffic, the decryption of those messages and the collective context of the multiple independent signals sources.

Arising from the research conducted in the course of preparation of the preceding book, at Bib. B28, there are sound arguments based on official archives that the handling of some Intelligence was faulty throughout most of WW2. There are separate arguments that some other departments within Whitehall were influenced by parochial and personal attitudes that interfered with the selection of strategic targets and the planning and implementation of the bombing offensives. Those arguments are at the core of the rationale and detail of this book. In order to appreciate and understand the context for those arguments, this book will take account of the different departments that had various responsibilities for handling Sigint and the associated intelligence products as they were applied to the conduct of the bombing campaigns during 1940–42 and the Combined Bombing Offensive during 1943–45. The following diagram shows a brief overview of those key departments within Whitehall and an indication of their relationships, together with the connections to the principal Air Commands and the various intelligence sources such as photographic reconnaissance, attachés, agents and prisoners of war:

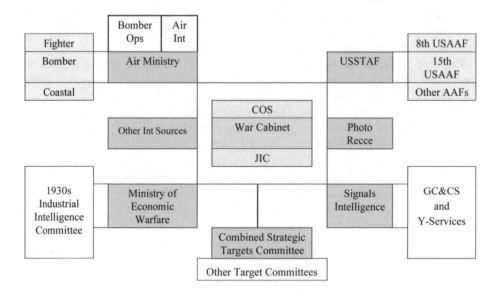

Within the diagram above, it should be noted that the Ministry of Economic Warfare did not form until the start of the war in September 1939. The Combined Strategic Targets Committee (CSTC) did not form until October 1944, but a variety of separate Target Committees were in place beforehand. These departments and functions are described and discussed in later chapters.

On the way through these many and varied paths it will be shown that there were overt and covert conflicts of policy, opinion and personality that collectively diverted or obstructed the provision of the 'best intelligence support' for the strategic bombing operations.

In some departments within Whitehall, even some elements of the Air Ministry, and within Washington there was a culpable failure to properly understand and appreciate the operational capabilities and limitations of the RAF and USAAF bomber forces. Perhaps that may be excused by the fact that 'strategic bombing' against enemy industrial targets was a novel form of warfare. It had been tried in a few previous conflicts, starting with some bombing in World War 1, but never in the magnitude of operations that progressively emerged from both sides of the conflict in WW2. One absolutely critical element of all bombing operations was the ability – or much more frequently the inability – to locate and attack specific targets. Within that context, the uninformed use of the terms 'precision' and 'area' bombing was widespread and gave rise to equally uninformed expectations of the effects of such bombing.

Quite apart from the extensive and complex methods of collecting, decrypting, translating and reporting the various types of Sigint traffic, which have been very well described and examined in a variety of published books (see the Intelligence Support bibliography) the crucial issues for this book are:

1. Did Bomber Command receive the best Intelligence support?
2. How was Intelligence used to support the planning, control and implementation of the bombing campaigns against Germany?

It should be clearly understood that Sigint was only one part of the collective Intelligence jigsaw. Not even the high-grade ULTRA material could always be used safely as a sole source, and the risk of using sole source material remains as much a problem today as it did in WW2. The critical trick here was to understand that vulnerability. The political and military use of the collective Intelligence involved many of the departments within Whitehall. The responsibilities and activities of these departments, with regard to the use of Intelligence for the bombing offensives, are described and discussed within Chapters 2–9, including the two major operational air commands – Bomber Command and the US Strategic Air Force Europe (USSTAF), the latter controlling the 8th and 15th USAAFs.

What this book contains
The following paragraphs provide a short introductory guide to the successive Chapters and the Final Analysis:

Chapter 2, Signals and Intelligence: Recognition is given to the invaluable contribution from the Polish Secret Service during the 1930s and the presentation of that work to British Intelligence. Whitehall had many different attitudes towards intelligence in general and Sigint in particular. The common denominators were a collective lack of any real understanding of the processes that were involved; in some areas an unwillingness to recognise the benefits; and entrenched positions that were a legacy of WW1. Perhaps the Admiralty was the exception to that generalisation, based upon the experience of exploitation of Naval Sigint during WW1. The Chapter recounts the emerging changes in attitudes towards Signals and Intelligence from the immediately pre-war days in 1939 to the autumn of 1944, as the Allies were then penetrating into enemy-occupied territory in western Europe.

Chapter 3, Economic Warfare: Sadly, much of the foresight of the IIC did not seem to transfer into the MEW when that Ministry was formed. It may be that no Ministry can just be created and immediately deliver sensible performance; there must be some period of internal organisation and training. The Ministry was however immediately responsible for all measures designed to undermine the enemy's economic structure and lead to its ultimate collapse. But the extent of the German rearmament programme had been profoundly ignored during the 1930s by much of Whitehall. It is no surprise that many of the appreciations of the German armaments capacity and production were so wrong. Whitehall was content to regard the system through a veil of inherited or commonsense assumptions and an absence of fact. The MEW became an instant authority on strategic target selection but was poorly equipped with internal resources and correct information; and had little understanding of the operational capabilities of the bomber forces. The long-term problem was that this largely disguised the impact of the bombing offensives and in turn led to critical and incorrect assessments of the performance of RAF Bomber Command and the 8th US Army Air Force (USAAF).

Chapter 4, Issues with the Bombing Offensives: The RAF and subsequently the USAAF strategic bomber forces were expected to deliver unrealistic results. That expectation came from both military and political authorities who shared a profound ignorance of the realities. The basic problem arose from many sources but initially from a combination of totally inadequate aircraft, installed equipment, aircrew training; and intelligence relating to the enemy air defence capability and to target selection. The operational tactics of bombing raids evolved but were handicapped by the absence or denial of intelligence. The common factor underlying all those sources was to a lack of understanding about the conduct of a strategic bombing offensive against a capable enemy who controlled an entire continent. Such a campaign had never previously been conducted and the understanding had to be gained by hard battle experience and equally painful assessment of the results. There were many mistakes in the policy and decision making chain but the most important issue was bombing accuracy. That mistake prevailed throughout the war and has remained a matter of intense debate ever since. There was a widespread belief that the bomber forces could deliver 'precison bombing'. The outstanding opponent of that largely uninformed belief was Sir Arthur Harris, the Commander-in-Chief (CinC) of RAF Bomber Command. For most of the war he held the view that his command delivered 'area bombing', recognising that the resources to deliver 'precision bombing' at night against an effective enemy air defence in all manner of weathers were not available. The USAAF came into the war in 1942 with the confident claim that it would deliver 'precision bombing'. The USAAFs' own post-war analyses showed that the claim was hollow within the intensity of air combat over Germany and the occupied territories. This chapter examines the differences and shows that 'precision bombing' was hardly ever deliverable by either of the bomber forces.

Chapter 5, Signals Intelligence within the Service Ministries: There were serious difficulties concerning the functions of Signals Intercept, Cryptanalysis and Intelligence production. The essence of the fundamental controversy revolved around misconceptions of the separate tasks and the 'ownership' of the signals products that were being generated. This became even more fractious when using the terms 'cryptography' and 'intelligence'. The relationships between GC & CS and the three Service Ministries differed significantly and are separately examined in this chapter, with particular note of the distinction between the Admiralty and the Air Ministry.

Chapter 6, Air Ministry Intelligence: The Air Intelligence branch was a small fledgling at the start of the war. As the war developed, that Branch grew from an initial staff of 40 people to a Directorate with over 700 people. Somewhat like the MEW, it was difficult to expand rapidly and remain cohesive. The organisational changes were substantial and tended to be responsive to external changes and pressures. The recruitment of staff with the necessary skills and personalities was an acute problem; most of the new staff had no military background and were given a one-week training course. Chapter 6 provides a detailed description of the development of the Directorate and then looks at particular internal Deputy Directorates and Sections that had functions which directly related to the provision of intelligence for the bombing offensives. The outstanding example of how the task could be done well was within the Scientific Intelligence section. One of the key problems within Air Sigint was a fundamental policy that resulted in the Home Air Commands being denied valuable operational intelligence. That denial did not happen for the overseas commands, nor for the USAAFs. It became a matter of the utmost importance and was a long-standing legacy from attitudes that came from an earlier time.

Chapter 7, Operational Intelligence at HQ Bomber Command: The work of the Command Intelligence Section was vital to the daily decision making and planning of bomber operations that were to be flown that same night. That work had to embrace everything from target intelligence and selection, the disposition and capability of the enemy air defence system, and finally to raid analysis and damage assessment. By no means least was the weather forecast which often became the determining factor in the target selection for that night. The time pressure was intense and unremitting on a 24-hour-a-day basis. The CinC was a demanding figure and required information to be available. This chapter provides a description of that work and the associated evolution of raid planning and tactics that formed the core of the Morning and Afternoon Conferences.

Chapter 8, Signals Intelligence within the 8th USAAF in the UK: The USAAF came into the war in Europe with practically no Intelligence assets. During the initial build-up of the 8th AAF – under command of General Eaker during 1942 – there was massive transfer of intelligence material from the Air Ministry and the creation of an internal USAAF organisation to handle that material on a 24-hour-a-day basis. The USAAF was able to make significant initial contributions with photographic reconnaissance aircraft and the production of maps. However, the conduct of daylight operations and the policy of 'precision bombing' demanded a level of target information that was not initially available. This gave rise to several specialised US agencies whose opinions did not always coincide with each other or with British opinions. Those conflicts impacted on the selection and agreement of strategic targets and this continued throughout 1943–45 with special impact on the high priority targets. Chapter 8 describes the processes for target intelligence and raid planning that were necessary for the daylight operations. It then describes the creation of the US Strategic Air Force (USSTAF) – otherwise known as WIDEWING, at Bushey Park – under command of General Spaatz with particular attention to the Operational Intelligence Division.

Chapter 9, The Value of Signals Intelligence to the Combined Bombing Offensive: The full contribution of Signals Intelligence to the winning of WW2 is still emerging slowly, over sixty years after that conflict ended. There was a carefully segregated dissemination system that limited the flow of ULTRA to selected political leaders and military commanders. That service did not exist for the CinC of Bomber Command. The research conducted in the course of preparation of this book has shown that some departments within Whitehall and Washington were influenced by parochial and personal attitudes that interfered with the selection of strategic targets and the planning and implementation of the bombing offensives. It is very debatable whether or not the MEW, the oil barons and the panacea target lobbies were correct in their strategic target selections. Harris was not the only commander who doubted the accuracy of some of those selections. The inescapable fact remains that during the late autumn and early winter of 1944, the Whitehall target selection staffs and the Combined Strategic Targets Committee (CSTC) obstructed the strategic bombing from attacking enemy transportation services and may consequently have extended the war by several months. The wider consequences for the timing of the eventual collapse of German military capability and the subsequent location of the Iron Curtain across the Eastern Front cannot be measured. Chapter 9 provides an assessment of these factors.

Chapter 10, Post-War Bombing Surveys: The US and the UK authorities recorded the effects of the strategic bombing operations in their separate post-war Bombing Surveys. There was a great deal of difference between the official national attitudes towards that survey work being undertaken. Within the US, the work had immediate Presidential approval and funding well before WW2 in Europe came to end. Within the UK, there was considerable reluctance from the Prime Minister and a deplorable shuffling of papers between Whitehall departments with a variety of delays and obstruction. Eventually, months after the war in Europe had ended, the Chief of Air Staff (CAS) became so exasperated that he gave his own approval for some survey work to start. The risk was twofold; that the German post-war building clearance and reconstruction work would erase the visible evidence of the effects of the strategic bombing operations, with their consequential impact upon the German war industry and upon the outcome of the war; and that the German officials and records would disappear.

The British Bombing Survey Unit (BBSU) was born under most contentious circumstances and was seriously deprived of resources and support from other Whitehall departments. Those departments had had major involvement with the formulation of policy and target selection for the bombing offensive. The BBSU reported that Intelligence weaknesses were due to the methods that were used by Political, Military and Intelligence staffs in appreciating the information, whose appreciations were often coloured by pre-conceived ideas or by wishful thinking.

The interim US Strategic Bombing Survey (USSBS) Report was placed into the public domain at the end of October 1945. The BBSU Report was not released into the public domain until 1998, which raises many questions about the unrecorded story of the BBSU and the surrounding bureaucratic controversy. The results of the bombing surveys and the associated politics are examined in Chapter 10.

Chapter 11, The Final Analysis: The strategic bombing offensive in Europe was a completely new style of conflict. It had never been used before and has never been used since, apart from the final few months of WW2 against Japan. Within the overall context of the planning and targeting of the bombing offensive, it will be shown that there were several influential power groups in Whitehall, each with their own ambitions and objectives but not all focussed exclusively on the primary task of securing victory. In the latter few months of the war there was a notable change in the British political thinking about the effects of strategic bombing. It may be that some were uncomfortable with what had been accomplished and may have regretted their personal association with the acrimony, decisions and the bombing directives. The policy behind those directives was from the very highest level of Allied Command, namely the Allied political leaders. It will also be shown that there was a very strong lobby that was anxious to distance itself from the facts and the ultimate price that many bomber aircrew had paid for that overwhelming contribution to the Allied victory. Much of the time in May–July 1945 was devoted to party politics in preparation for the General Election within the UK. Very few of the post-war and subsequent analyses have given informed consideration to the content and use or misuse of the Intelligence that was available to support the bombing offensives.

The progressive release of wartime records into the current public domain has revealed material that was simply not available to the public when most of the Official Histories were compiled. Another inter-related set of issues is apparent within some other publications, written over the intervening six decades, where the texts attempt to bring post-war judgements and values into an analysis of wartime decisions. The Total War situation during WW2 was created not by the bombing offensives but as a consequence of the British and Allied political decisions made in the face of the uncompromising and brutal Axis threat to Western and World democracy. In that context, strategic bombing was an instrument of political conflict and foreign policy.

In the end there is an unavoidable fact that continues to have resonance into the 21st century. Within the context of Western democracy and the associated high-level chains of command leading from prime ministers and presidents, as it was then and as it remains today, no military campaign will have ultimate approval if the prevailing political leadership and will is lost. The conclusions that this book reaches about the availability and use of intelligence within the hot-bed of Whitehall politics and personalities during the bombing offensives are not flattering. Some readers may wonder if that has changed today.

Appendices: There are nineteen separate Appendices which cover specific topics that do not need to be within the main body of the book, but which provide supporting detail for various activities and analyses.

This material in this book has been derived from an extensive research survey of:

- Official documents, reports, minutes and letters currently available in the public domain, many of which carried the highest security classifications at their time of origin during WW2. The various Departments of State, the Air Ministry, Bomber Command and other related organisations, issued those original papers.
- A wide variety of published literature, including the Official Histories of British Intelligence, Signals Intelligence and the Strategic Air Offensive during 1939–45.

The conclusions are those of the author alone and do not represent any official or otherwise published position. The author's career is briefly summarised on page 439.

Security Classifications and Grades

The early successes against the encrypted ENIGMA messages were soon followed by others that would give Allied intelligence and commanders valuable insights into German intentions and capabilities. Unfortunately, there were drawbacks. Intelligence can be of use only if it is placed in the hands of those who understand its significance. A carefully segregated intelligence distribution system was evolved for use outside of Whitehall that kept the information from the ENIGMA decrypts down to a limited number of senior field commanders, using a dissemination service that lay outside of normal intelligence channels. Churchill was adamant about restricting this information to the fewest number of recipients because a single revelation reaching enemy ears could destroy this major source of intelligence permanently.

The intelligence product from the German and subsequently the Japanese ENIGMA signals message traffic became known as ULTRA and the original British security classification was MOST SECRET. The term Special Intelligence was used as an exclusive general cover-name for these decrypts that were made available to the Allies by successful cryptanalytic attacks on the enemy's higher-grade enciphering systems.[1] The classification TOP SECRET was subsequently introduced when US addressees were involved in order to have a shared classification. The code word BONIFACE was used in some contexts to imply that the source of the information was an agent. In many documents and correspondence, the security designation CX/MSS was used where the CX designation implied an agent and the MSS designation was Most Secret Source.

Signals intelligence (Sigint) derived from the decryption of medium and low-level signals traffic was known as PEARL. There was a massive amount of other Sigint from multiple sources either in voice, then known as Radio Telephony (R/T), or in Morse or unencrypted codes, then known as Wireless Telegraphy (W/T). It should be noted that ENIGMA was transmitted as Wireless Telegraphy and that the interception of that traffic was therefore known as W/T Intercept. Chapter 6 has more detail, under Special Liaison Duties.

Definitions

Bletchley Park had other names. It was often referred to as 'Station X' without any indication of location. The official designation was the Government Codes and Ciphers School (GC & CS). These names and titles are commonly regarded as one and the same thing.

In some historical records the term 'Y-Service' has been used to mean the Signals Intercept Stations that received ENIGMA traffic and conducted signals traffic analysis on some of those enemy radio networks. In other historical records, the term 'Y-Service' has been used to mean those stations which intercepted and reported the lower grade Radio Telephony (R/T) and Wireless Telegraphy (W/T) enemy radio signals. Neither of these meanings is complete. In yet other records, the term has been used to mean both functions, which is more correct. In this book, the term 'Y-Service' embraces the combined functions of the separate Air Force, Army, Navy and Diplomatic Y-Services as well as the

---

1. Bib. B35, HW 11/1, General Preface, p. 9.

(UK) Radio Security Service; but the majority of the detail within this book relates specifically to work conducted by the RAF Y-Service.

The term 'cipher' was spelt 'cypher' during WW2. The spelling 'cipher' is used in this book.

Throughout the archive reports and other historical records of WW2 that have been researched in the preparation of this book, in the context of the enemy industry, economy and armed forces and the selected bombing targets, there is the use of either of the two terms 'Communications' and 'Transportation'. In both cases, the intended meaning is practically identical and generally includes the aggregate means of transport of finished goods, raw materials, personnel and their equipment. It embraces railways, roads, ships and waterways and in a small minority of cases, air transport. To avoid possible confusion, this book uses only the term 'Transportation'. Where there may be need to refer specifically to 'communications' in the sense of 'information exchange', whether that is by telephone, teleprinter or radio broadcast, etc., then such use is specifically identified.

As a general practice, calendar dates throughout the book are abbreviated; for example, 5th November 1942 will be shown as 5 Nov 42.

CHAPTER TWO

Signals and Intelligence

'There is nothing new except what has been forgotten.'

Marie Antoinette

This chapter provides an overview of the political and military attitudes and developments in the pre-war period and the emerging issues as the war developed. This is described in three sections.

- The most vital element was the invaluable work done by the Polish secret service during the 1930s with their initial detection and exploitation of the German ENIGMA machine.
- There is a summary of the understandings within Whitehall and the Service Ministries about Sigint, with particular emphasis on the different attitudes of the various departments.
- The Industrial Intelligence Committee (IIC) in the pre-war period and the creation of the Ministry of Economic Warfare (MEW) at the start of the war. MEW would have an important part to play with regard to the bombing offensives.

Perhaps not surprisingly, it will be seen that there was a substantial lack of knowledge and a marked divergence of attitudes. Perhaps that was not surprising? The subject of Sigint was quite new to many departments, some of which would subsequently become major players – not necessarily informed players – in the appreciation and application of that material.

Given those various attitudes and understandings, there are several key issues that arose with specific regard to the bombing offensives. These issues included the politics of strategic target selection; the misconceptions about navigation and target detection; and the general ignorance within most of the Whitehall departments, including the Air Ministry, about precision bombing and what was actually possible during operations. These related issues are discussed in Chapter 4.

The Polish Contribution

The breaking of the German high-level codes began with the efforts of the Polish secret service in the inter-war period, starting in the late 1920s. By creating a copy of the basic German enciphering machine – the so-called ENIGMA machine – the

Poles were able to read German signals traffic through the 1930s with varying degrees of success. However, shortly before the Munich Conference in September 1938, the Germans introduced additional rotors into their enciphering machine and by mid-September 1938, darkness closed over that German message traffic.[1]

The Poles nevertheless continued their work and, after the British guarantee to Poland in March 1939, they passed to Great Britain what they had thus far achieved. On 25th July 1939, in the Pyry Forest near Warsaw, the Poles met with Commander Denniston and Dillwyn Knox and revealed the extent of their knowledge about the ENIGMA machine and its use by the Germans. Soon afterwards, a Polish reconstruction of an ENIGMA machine was carried in a diplomatic bag from Warsaw to Paris by Captain Bertrand, Head of the Cryptological Section of the French General Staff.[2] That machine was then carried to Victoria Station in London and handed over to Colonel Stewart Menzies, then Deputy Head of the British Secret Service. The Polish contribution to ENIGMA decryption and the massive benefits that accrued to the Allies throughout the Second World War were encapsulated within the pre-war peacetime intention of the Polish General Staff:[3]

In the case of a threat of war, the ENIGMA secret must be used as our Polish contribution to the common cause of Defence and divulged to our future Allies.

The Poles and the French had continuing co-operation. This came to a climax in September 1939 when a small group of Polish code-breakers led by Colonel Langer, Head of the Polish Cipher Bureau, and fifteen of his staff who had initially escaped from Poland to Romania, arrived at the Château de Vignolles in France. The location became known by the codename *PC Bruno*.

Building on what they had learned from Poland and France, the staff at Bletchley Park with key people such as Knox, Welchman and Turing, and the Polish group at Vignolles via a secure teleprinter link, broke into some of the German multi-rotor codes early in 1940, just before the German offensives against Norway, the Low Countries and France. The equally important role of Denniston was to have recruited many of the staff.

Prevailing Attitudes

This section will look at the prevailing attitudes towards Sigint and Intelligence in general within Whitehall and the Service Ministries during the pre-war period and through until after the Normandy Invasion in June 1944, with a primary interest in Intelligence related to the bombing offensive. The reader should note that this does not attempt to provide a comprehensive analysis of this subject but is intended to portray the broad culture that existed. This subject will recur through later chapters of this book, looking then from the different perspectives of the various key commands and departments.

---

1. Bib. B10, p. 39. Polish work within their Operation WICHER on early ENIGMA codes was of incalculable value.
2. *ENIGMA: The Battle for the Code* p. 44, by Hugh Sebag-Montefiore.
3. Bib. B10, p. 50. Within Ch. 1, 'The Glow-lamp Machine' there is comprehensive history of these covert and complex arrangements.

Pre-War and Soon Afterwards

In the years before the war several bodies within the structure of British government shared the responsibility for intelligence. They were far from forming a single organisation. They had evolved on different lines, within different departments and with no one authority directly supervising them all. Indeed, the war had been progressing more than twelve months before co-ordination between some of these bodies even began to take place.

'If you want peace, be prepared for war'. There is no lack of evidence to the effect that Great Britain's neglect of this ancient maxim applied as much to the overall intelligence preparations as to the rearmament programme. The comparatively new business of Sigint was an infant prodigy within Whitehall. Let it not be forgotten that the business of listening to other people's messages was hardly new: the Japanese Navy did it operationally during the Russo-Japanese War of 1904–5 and the Admiralty did it quite effectively during World War 1. Indeed, Sir Francis Walsingham was extremely good at reading other people's messages for Queen Elizabeth in the 16th century. Perhaps Marie Antoinette's point quoted in this chapter's heading is relevant?

In 1937, the Wireless (Y) Intercept Committee realised that in the event of war the small number of Service signals intercept stations – the Y-Stations – would be fully occupied with military traffic and it was therefore arranged for the General Post Office to erect and staff the first of several intercept stations to target Axis diplomatic signals traffic for the Foreign Office. In 1938, a specialised commercial section was added to the civil side of GC&CS to scan and select foreign signals traffic for the Industrial Intelligence Centre.

The amount of intelligence obtained from Sigint sources during the war progressively became massive, far more on many subjects than was in the event required. Rightly so; all contingencies had to be contended for, even the most trivial and unlikely proving invaluable on occasions. But conversely, it was not unknown for information to be requested for which the relevant data had not been considered worth recording at all. In some cases, 'usable' intelligence was deliberately not used either on the grounds of security or because of political considerations.

The predominance of Sigint as a source of intelligence concerning not all, but most, subjects directly connected with politics, naval, military and air operations had not been foreseen prior to or even during the early stages of the war.[4] Ministries and Commands were initially handicapped by the lack of appropriate organisations and resources for handling this intelligence. Gradually some of those handicaps were overcome, but in other quarters the lessons were never learned. Some of the more enthusiastic disciples came to rely excessively on the high-grade ULTRA Sigint, unaware of or ignoring the fact that it was but one source in a catalogue of various intelligence sources. It was always risky to assume that the absence of an ULTRA reference to 'something' meant that the 'thing' did not exist.

---

4. Bib. B2, *The Official History of British Sigint*, Vol. 2, Ch. 15II. The author of this history was Frank Birch, a long-established and very well-respected member of the signals intelligence service before, during and after the war.

Some of the shortcomings in the treatment of Sigint were also due to the then prevailing attitude towards intelligence work as a whole. It was in most quarters regarded as a job that any person of average ability could perform, even as a 'secondary duty'.[5] But experience was to show only too clearly that, in the exploitation of Sigint, the capability of the intelligence officer was often as important as the intelligence itself. Among the then regular service officers, that was not an understatement. The path of the signals intelligence officer was beset with obstacles and pitfalls.

Very few people in the Ministries understood Research or how to do it and most regarded it as a bore. The mention of Research therefore tended to provoke the instinct of self-preservation. The most common reaction when up against something new that was not understood was to state that it was not worth doing, so Research was often despised as unrealistically academic. Alternatively, lip service was paid but little or nothing was actually done; the term was also misused to imply that some Research was being done, for example, flipping through a diary or consulting a card index.[6]

One major shortcoming was indeed the initial lack of adequate data recording systems. The Ministries' intelligence sections in most cases lacked the necessary awareness, staff and expertise. It was not enough just to keep a copy of the original signals message. There had to be an appreciation of what that message meant, as distinct from what it said, and the context of one message in the assembly of related messages. For example, to place reliance on one message was akin to listening to only one statement in a conversation between multiple parties. That became the function of the specialist; and such people were in very short supply. Faulty recording and cataloguing was a serious problem. A card index in unskilled hands could become a cemetery rather than a store.

Ill-conceived notions and an ingrained attitude of mind often hampered collation and the working-up of information. There was a tendency to be content with trundling investigation along well-known 'tramway' lines such as 'order of battle' and 'location', to the neglect of emerging and unfamiliar lines of investigation. And this was compounded to a very large extent by the official attitudes that impaired and often obstructed the development of new lines of intelligence investigation on the basis of privilege and prejudice concerning 'who may do what'.

These problems were themselves exacerbated by the robust and very inflexible security regulations that surrounded the production and handling of the high-grade ENIGMA signals traffic and the subsequent ULTRA Sigint products that were generated for use by the Ministries and some Command staffs. The meaning of these codewords has been provided in the section above entitled 'Definitions'. It will be shown later that just one of these security problems was the isolation of the high-grade material both in itself and in the staff who were indoctrinated into the decryption and intelligence production stages. This was to exacerbate a most

---

5. Author's Note: This 'subordination' of Intelligence continued long after the end of WW2.
6. Bib. B2, Vol. 2: 'The Intelligence Contribution to the War in the West', p. 671, Footnote (1).

critical and long-lasting problem, namely the separation between intelligence producers and intelligence users. Experience later in the war was to show that the careful handling and fusion of high, medium and low-grade signals traffic became a significant benefit to the overall intelligence production and operational application process, without compromising the security of any particular source.

But this awareness and knowledge did not exist, and arguably could not have existed, in the early stages of the war. The emergence of Sigint as a recognised and accepted major source of intelligence took many years and demanded the breaking down of many old-style preconceptions and traditions. Sometimes that culture adapted more easily, but in some cases it was unyielding and gave rise to serious conflicts relating to the dissemination and interpretation of Sigint within the Ministries and also between the Ministries and field commanders.

There is a separate but no less important issue and that concerned the personnel security vetting process at that time. To say that the process was imperfect is probably too kind. It was in some respects no more than a façade. The 'old school tie' and 'who knew who' contributed to some of the major security breaches through the war; and these were breaches at the top of the 'system'. The Cambridge Four and the Fifth Man represent such fundamental flaws in the security vetting system as to be almost unbelievable.

Harold 'Kim' Philby informally led the Cambridge spy ring during the 1930s. Soon after the start of the war, he and his friends rapidly secured jobs in British Intelligence and the Foreign Office where they had access to top-secret information. They spent their working lives passing valuable information to the Soviet Union. John Cairncross, the 'Fifth Man', was spotted by Anthony Blunt at Cambridge and introduced to Guy Burgess. He was recruited to the Communist party in 1937 and became a member of the Communist Party cell at Trinity College. He later worked in the Foreign Office alongside Donald MacLean. As an example of his high-level access to classified information, he took the minutes of a top-level meeting on 20 Apr 41 that was chaired by Lord Hankey and attended by 'C' with senior representatives from each of the three Services and GC & CS. That meeting discussed the security of UK Sigint channels. He transferred to Bletchley Park where he worked in Hut 3 during 1942/43, at the centre of ULTRA analysis and dissemination. Late in 1943, he moved into the Secret Intelligence Service (SIS) in London. He had been providing data to the Russians, at least during his time at Bletchley Park. His information about British and American atomic weapons programmes are thought to have been at the foundation of the Soviet atomic weapons programme.

Signals Intelligence up to Autumn 1940
From the start of the war in September 1939 to the Fall of France in the summer of 1940, Sigint was a small player in the overall context of Intelligence. But let it not be overlooked that intelligence as a total service was in a poor state during this period. It has been recorded that British Chiefs of Staff (COS) took their earliest and most crucial decisions regarding the German invasion of Norway on the basis of information that was 'little better than that of the newspaper reader'.[7]

---

7. Bib. B1, Vol. 1, Ch. 4, p. 137.

As an example of our appalling ignorance, we had no idea about the facilities at the small Norwegian ports where it was expected to land troops and supplies. Those supplies required wharves, cranes and storage facilities. Such facilities did not exist because the local Norwegian ports primarily served their fishing fleets; and the coastal steamers had their own derricks for moving cargo for that very reason.

However, Sigint made a major improvement in the spring of 1940 when the German forces made substantial use of ENIGMA during their Norwegian operations; GC&CS broke the Yellow key very quickly. That high-grade signals traffic was carrying GAF and Army operational signal communications and also information about Naval operations that concerned the enemy air and land campaign. Most importantly, it gave insight into the German intentions but it could not be properly exploited either by Whitehall or GC&CS.

It had not been foreseen that the Germans would make use of radio traffic for operational purposes at high echelon levels of command. That did not happen in World War 1 and, as late as 1939, GC&CS had feared that the outbreak of war could be followed by the imposition of radio silence for all except tactical signals traffic. The breaking of the GAF ENIGMA Yellow key revealed that neither GC& CS nor the Whitehall departments were equipped to handle the subsequent decrypts efficiently. The textual content of the traffic eluded the GC&CS staff's ability to make intelligent interpretation. The secure communication services between Bletchley and Whitehall were inadequate. The volume of material overwhelmed the Whitehall intelligence departments. And if that was not enough, the security arrangements which were in force for safeguarding the ULTRA material added delay and confusion. The then Commander in Chief (CinC) of RAF Bomber Command, Sir Richard Peirse, was not included on the approved list of recipients of ULTRA. Nor was Sir Hugh Dowding, CinC Fighter Command, who might have needed it more; he was not included on the list until October 1940. Indeed, later in 1941, when Mr Churchill required that Air Marshal Peirse should be included on the list, the Head of MI6, Sir Stewart Menzies, did not sanction that requirement.[8]

The general failure to read or make intelligent appreciation of the ULTRA material at that time was reflected in an observation by the CinC Home Fleet, who said:

It is most galling that the enemy should know just where our ships always are, whereas we generally learn where his forces are when they sink one or more of our ships.[9]

The German Navy had been reading the main British Naval Ciphers at least to a limited extent since 1938. The most glaring example of this was probably in early June 1940, when the *Gneisenau* and the *Scharnhorst* sank the aircraft carrier HMS *Glorious*, homeward bound during the evacuation of Narvik. Knowledge of the evacuation operation itself was held to a very small number of UK staffs; neither

---

8. Bib. B11, Bennett, p. 57.
9. Bib. B14, Ch. 4, p. 141.

GC & CS, RAF Coastal Command,[10] nor even the Duty Officer in the Admiralty Operational Intelligence Centre (OIC) knew of the operation.[11] The Admiralty heard the news of this loss in a German broadcast; such was the poverty of intelligence at that period.

There was no improvement in operational intelligence during the campaign in France. In the 14 days preceding the German invasion, the records of the Cabinet and the Chiefs of Staff continued to be headed 'The Netherlands and Belgium'. The War Office daily intelligence summary for the 24 hours to 11.00 on 8th May stated that there was no sign that an invasion of France was imminent.[12] The Germans had changed the ENIGMA Red key for GAF General traffic and it was not until the end of May that GC & CS was able to read that material on a regular basis. ENIGMA messages were then being decrypted and interpreted at a rate of about 1,000 signals each day, with the most important messages being passed directly to the British Expeditionary Force (BEF) and the Air HQ in France. But it still proved impossible to make much immediate operational use of the material. Much of this was because GC & CS was unable to interpret the mass of abbreviations, map and grid references, codenames, pro-formas and military jargon. Sadly, much of the material reached the commanders in France too late to be useful. There was another serious problem: it had very limited circulation at the field HQs and it was presented under the cover of an agent report, most probably being seen in the field with the degree of scepticism that was often associated with 'agent reports'.[13]

The volume of German signals traffic had overwhelmed the BEF's intelligence organisation in the first few days of the invasion. It was unable to make use of that material because it could not read the German Army medium- and low-grade codes. The rapid tactical moves that were largely enforced by the German advance caused major disruptions to signal communications within the BEF. The Intelligence staffs were dispersed between separate elements and ceased to have any effective contribution. The recorded evidence was destroyed before the evacuation from Dunkirk. Subsequent analysis by GC & CS and MI8 was conducted through the second half of 1940, based on intercepts being made in the UK. With hindsight, it may be seen that the BEF was already in such serious military trouble that Sigint would have had little effect on the outcome.

It was a rather different story regarding the German air operations, because a good deal of tactical signals traffic was passed in plain language or with codes that had already been broken. The intelligence obtained from those messages gave a clear idea of the course of the battle across the whole front. Thus, for

---

10. ADM 186/798, pp. 63, 129.
11. ADM 233/84, NID 02297/40, DNI Minute of 11 June 1940.
12. WO 106/1644, WO Daily Intelligence Summary No. 248 of 8 May 1940.
13. The material sent to the BEF and Air HQs in France was copied to a Mission at the French High Command. The Germans captured several HQs but they found no evidence that ENIGMA had been compromised. Some French staffs were co-operating with GC & CS and the Polish code-breakers up to the middle of June 1940; that information was never divulged to the Germans (Bib. B14, Vol. 1, Ch. 4, Footnote to p. 145.

example, the GAF broadcasts of 'bombing safety lines' enabled a determination of the rate and the extent of German advances; and the rapid collapse of the French defences. But little of this material dealt with the small sector of the front that was covered by the BEF, and even that was soon lost because of the inadequate signal communications between the Y-detachments and the various BEF and Air HQs' locations in a very mobile situation.

Photographic reconnaissance continued to function from French airfields after the BEF's field Sigint had closed down. Much of that reconnaissance was visual and severe losses were incurred. The Air Component Blenheims left for England on 20th May; the Lysanders remained in France, but by 22 May it was virtually impossible to operate. Thereafter, 212 Squadron Spitfires remained with the Back Component in the UK until the middle of June. During that time, apart from regular tactical reconnaissance sorties, these Spitfires undertook damage assessment tasks for Bomber Command against strategic targets in the Ruhr.

At the end of the campaign when the BEF was trapped at Dunkirk, it was the Y- organisation in the UK that helped to control the jamming of German Stuka dive-bomber radio communications and supplied critical information to the RN forces at Dover controlling the evacuation from the beaches. It was also a Y-Station that provided the single reference to Hitler's decision to stop the German panzer advance on the canal line outside Dunkirk on 24 May. It is impossible to determine where that Y-station was or even if the operational importance of the intercept was recognised in the stress of the situation.

It is interesting how the practices regarding Sigint dissemination varied between the RAF home commands. There is specific reference in Feb 40 to instructions drawn up at HQ Coastal Command for the organisation and functions of a Y-Section at the Command HQ.[14] It may perhaps be assumed that this was driven by the close co-operation between Coastal Command and the Admiralty. Later, there was discussion in Sep 40 about the study of German air navigation M/F beacons being done at HQ Bomber Command.[15] These beacons at the time had great value for bomber operations, but it was decided that the work should remain with the RAF Y-Service at Cheadle and that a direct secure line be set up between the Beacon Control section and Bomber Command. As it happened, the subsequent complexity of the beacon callsigns and the transmitted frequency changes were better handled by the Y-Service. Also in September 1940 there was Y-Service evidence from RAF Kingsdown that the German Y-Service was intercepting the R/T traffic used by Fighter Command,[16] and later in November the Air Section at GC&CS reported on the information that was being gained by the enemy from RAF inter-squadron radio communications. Fighter Command then agreed to use voice codes for inter-squadron radio communications.

Changes during the Winter of 1940–41
By the end of 1940, GC&CS had increased in size four-fold but had become poorly organised. The senior staffs had little training or experience in

---

14. Air 40/2890, AI 4 Internal Records, Q 1224 of 19 Feb 40.
15. Ibid. Q 1223 of 28 Sep 40.
16. Ibid. Q 1222 of 10 Sep 40, 5 Nov 40 and 7 Nov 40.

administration and organisation. The scope and the nature of the work were evolving almost on a daily basis as the intensity of the struggle to decrypt the ENIGMA material showed promise in various directions. New sections had to be created in response to these unpredictable opportunities; others arose because of activity outside of GC & CS, often within the single Services. Many sections were isolated from other sections because of the prevailing security regulations with regard to the high-grade material. Conversely, the small sections such as the Air Section suffered from serious shortages of staff because of the very high priority rightly given to ENIGMA work.

The personnel at Bletchley came from a wide variety of backgrounds, mostly non-Service, and they thrived on the broad nature of creative anarchy that existed within GC & CS. The staff at GC & CS recognised no frontiers in their Research activities; no division of labour within previously constructed frameworks, and they invaded into the territory of 'appreciation' that was regarded as sacrosanct by the Ministries. This was anathema to the rigidity of military practice and thinking. There was profound difficulty in distinguishing and compromising between the multiple conflicts of priority, products, personality and organisation.

This resulted in contentious debate and exchange of views among the three Services and GC & CS, with initially an attempt to involve the Joint Intelligence Committee (JIC). That foundered in the face of opposition from the Head of the SIS. But a committee formed of the three Heads of Service Intelligence and the Head of SIS met during February and March 1941 and reached agreement on broad principles:

- Exploitation of all forms of Service Sigint must remain under the control of the Services,
- Cryptanalysis must continue as an inter-service activity under the control of GC & CS.

The revised terms of reference established that the Chiefs of Staff were ultimately responsible for the co-ordination of Y-activity and cryptanalysis. These decisions in early 1941 brought to an end the misunderstandings arising from inadequate high-level direction of Sigint policy. Although disagreements did arise later, the broad system proved to be adequate for maintaining relations between GC & CS and the Service Ministries as the volume of Sigint increased through the war.

But there was continuing resentment about specific topics, notably that GC & CS remained in charge of the distribution of the results of cryptanalysis. The Admiralty typically took a very direct approach to this, perhaps being guided by their experience during the final years of World War 1.[17] It appointed an Assistant Director of the OIC (ADIC) to be responsible to the Director of Naval Intelligence for the co-ordination of work by the Naval Section at GC & CS and for subsequent action to be taken by the Naval Intelligence Division (NID) on the material provided from GC & CS. This appointment of a Captain, RN, was based in the OIC in Whitehall but required frequent visits to Bletchley, supplemented of course by the regular secure telephone and teleprinter contacts. The Admiralty

---

17. Bib. 14, Vol. 1, Ch. 9: 'Reorganisation and Reassessment: Winter 1940–41', p. 274.

approach resulted in Naval ENIGMA being tackled separately in Hut 8 rather than Hut 6; and its being reported by the Naval Section, rather than Hut 3. The outcome was totally successful and the Admiralty and GC & CS remained in close contact and agreement through the remainder of the war.

But the same was not true for the Air Ministry and the War Office.[18] Both continued to resent and chafe against the large measure of control that GC & CS had over the Sigint effort; and to complain through their advisers at GC & CS about the supply and selection of ENIGMA decrypts that they were receiving. Neither of these ministries made an appointment in any way similar to that of the Naval ADIC. The closest that Air Intelligence came to this was the complete revision, in April 1941, of the functions of the Deputy Director of Intelligence (DDI 4) (see Chapter 6), which saw a major shift from 'geographical' to 'functional' specialisations. It is shown at Appendix E, although these changes were implemented from April 1941 onwards. But the very great difference between DDI 4 and the Admiralty ADIC was the absence of responsibility for co-ordination between air operations and the analysis work at GC & CS.[19]

With specific regard to the War Office, the Military Intelligence directorate continued to conform more closely to the Admiralty style than to the revisions implemented within Air Intelligence, except that there never was a War Office section that equated in any way to the OIC. The task of Military Intelligence was primarily to provide intelligence to the Operations Directorate of the War Office and the General Staff. The Army Commands in all the active theatres post-1940 held their own Intelligence staffs and, from March 1941, they received Sigint directly from GC & CS via the Special Liaison Units (SLUs). This reflected the long-established tradition and relationship between the War Office and the overseas commands. One of the key aspects of the Military Intelligence work was selecting and training field intelligence officers for the fighting commands. This saw the formation, in 1940, of the Army Intelligence Corps from which there arose a better recognition of the value of strategic and tactical operational intelligence.

There was another factor at work during this period. The SIS was becoming remote from its principal customers – the Service Ministries and the Foreign Office – and there was growing indifference about the SIS intelligence products within the Ministries.[20] This may have had its roots in the pre-war government economy and SIS inactivity in the eastern Mediterranean, the Middle East and North Africa where much of the conflict was taking place in late 1941 and through 1942. But the relationships with the European and Scandinavian countries were also inadequate, with notable exceptions such as Poland and Norway. The situation in France had become fractious, because of the split between de Gaulle's Free French and the SIS attempts to revive intelligence contacts with Vichy France. The SIS was becoming isolated and their dependence on the Air Force and the Navy for transport support had short shrift. Transport loomed large

---

18. Ibid. p. 274.
19. Author's Note: From the available records, it would seem that DDI 4 hardly ever went to Bletchley, even though the Air Section – otherwise known as AI4 (f) at GC & CS – was part of his staff.
20. Ibid. p. 275.

because the SIS was being driven back into the UK as its base for operations. In fact, the Navy provided an MTB flotilla, but not until 1942. The RAF provided a special flight, No. 419 (Special Duties) Flight from July 1940 and then No. 138 (Special Duties) Squadron from the spring of 1941. The Government did not help because of the internal organisational rivalries and indifference to the SIS activities, with no sense of urgency in response to SIS requests for resources.

Air Intelligence, from the Sigint point of view, began at the start of 1941 to issue a series of bulletins to the air commands, which bulletins were reported to have been 'of crucial importance to the conduct of air operations in all theatres of the war'.[21] But it has subsequently become very apparent that these bulletins suffered from a range of problems that would not have been capable of disclosure at the time when Bib. B1 was published in 1981; and may well not even have been appreciated by the authors at that time? The release of ULTRA material into the public domain was only in the early stages; even at the time of writing in 2008/09 there is still WW2 material that has not been released. The nature of these problems within the Air Intelligence bulletins has been documented within Bib. B28.

The Y-station at Cheadle, supported by cryptanalysis in the Air Section at GC&CS, identified and reported by direct telephone to Fighter Command the W/T communications of GAF aircraft engaged in bombing, reconnaissance and anti-shipping operations. When the GAF began its heavy attacks against the UK, Cheadle was joined in this reporting by Hawkinge (later Kingsdown) which led the Home Defence Units (HDUs) in intercepting the R/T of the GAF single-seater fighter aircraft. It was found that Hawkinge and the HDUs could not solve the codewords and map grids used in the R/T, so their log books began to be sent to the Air Section in order that these problems could be solved. A new fighter sub-section was created in Dec 40 within the Air Section which produced a corrected version of the R/T in the form of a daily diary which was sent to Hawkinge for their guidance.

The US began to make a contribution, if as yet an insignificant one, during the winter of 1940–41 to items of intelligence for Whitehall's appreciations. Discussions between the two countries about defence programmes, equipment and staff plans went back at least to 1937, but before 1940 those discussions had rarely extended to intelligence matters, except informally between the two navies.[22] Early in 1940, in the interests of the SIS counter-espionage work within the US and with the approval of the President, there was closer intelligence liaison between the British and US authorities. There was an exchange of liaison officers: Colonel Stephenson was appointed by 'C' as the SIS representative in Washington and Colonel Donovan was appointed as the President's envoy to London. There was great significance to the latter appointment because the key purpose behind Donovan's visit to the UK in the summer of 1940 was to assess the determination and the ability of the UK to continue the war against Germany, both of which were doubted by the US COS. At the end of August, during the 'Standardisation of Arms' talks in London about supply and defence programmes and staff plans,

21. Ibid. p. 285.
22. Bib. B1, Vol. 1, Ch. 9, p. 311.

the Prime Minister and the President agreed in principle to the pooling of information. The US Army representative outlined the progress his Service had been making against Japanese and Italian ciphers and formally proposed to the UK Chiefs of Staff that the time had arrived for a free exchange of intelligence.[23]

Changes during 1941 and 1942

One of the challenges that continued through this period stemmed from the increasing ability of GC&CS to break and read various German ENIGMA traffic. Having increased four-fold in staff numbers from the outbreak of war to the start of 1941, GC&CS had expanded further to about 1500 by early 1942. It was then clear that this expansion would have to continue at a still more rapid rate, with the immediate impact on recruiting suitable staff, providing working and domestic accommodation – and creating an organisational and administrative structure to cater for the increasing variety of tasks. Before the end of the war, the staff numbers had exceeded 10,000.[24]

Early 1941 saw the Fighter sub-section within the Air Section at GC&CS becoming increasingly involved with GAF air defence communications of great interest to Bomber Command. The intercept logbooks from the RAF Y-Service stations were forwarded to the Air Section at Bletchley, which produced a daily diary of the radio traffic from 1 May 41 onwards. In quick succession, this had codeword solutions and by Sep 41 the first Codebook was available. But when the Fighter sub-section began to attach a summary of the air operations as reflected in the radio traffic, the Air Intelligence staff in London refused to condone this on the grounds that it did not fall within the scope of 'cryptography'. At this general period there were significant changes being made to the internal organisation of Air Intelligence. The RAF Deputy Directorate of Signals Y, which had been responsible for the study of enemy wireless traffic, their codes, ciphers and call signs and the production of intelligence from decodes, was transferred from the RAF Signals Directorate and re-designated as DDI 4 within Air Intelligence. The details are shown in Appendix E but these changes took place in April 1941. Through 1941 the Air Intelligence staff held firmly to the belief that only the Air Intelligence staff in London could judge what would be useful to the commands. Technical improvements in radio interception were coincidentally providing intercept opportunities from as wide as the south of Norway to the Spanish frontier, in all the zones where GAF air defence was operational on the Wetern Front.

In the course of research into the GAF fighter control system, the Fighter sub-section had built a database of valuable information concerning the enemy day and night fighter operational procedures. By Jan 42 it was able to show, by comparison of radio traffic on successive nights in which Bomber Command had used different raid plans, how the concentration of a bomber raid in time and space could saturate the GAF GCI system. In Mar 42, the Fighter sub-section

---

23. CAB 79/6, COS (40) 289th Meeting, 31 August 1940.
24. Bib. B31: This document provides a comprehensive summary of the total staff within the many various sections of Bletchley Park, largely based on the Weekly Returns that were instituted from March 1942.

issued a comprehensive report on GAF night-fighter control. However, this report did not go beyond the Air Ministry because another report was being prepared at the same time by ADI (Science). Air Intelligence did not consider the production of general intelligence reports to be a commitment of the Air Section.[25] The Fighter sub-section noted soon afterwards that on two bomber raids, on 12 and 17 Apr, the bomber losses were heavy. After these two raids, Bomber Command issued appreciations which the Air Section pointed out – to the Air Ministry – contained demonstrably false assertions about the way that the GAF had operated their fighters: Y-Sigint evidence had not been taken into consideration.[26]

The most important challenge confronting the Director was organisation of the work on the high grade ENIGMA system. The bottom line was to ensure the availability in GC&CS of enough people with the necessary skill and background, which only became available with time and experience. A relevant internal memo within GC&CS at that very time declared there was a need for permanent staff, not 'birds of passage', in relation to the military practice of posting staff at little or no notice. Gordon Welchman put it succinctly when he wrote:

Intelligence can be most unreliable if it is produced by someone without the necessary judgement and knowledge.[27]

The work involved the inter-related problems of:

- Interception of the signals traffic in the first place.
- Study of the W/T networks carrying that traffic (called Wireless Telegraphy Intelligence or WTI, later to be called Traffic Analysis or TA). This made subsequent decryption quicker and produced intelligence about the enemy which could continue to be available should the high-grade material become unreadable.
- Decryption of that traffic.
- Translation of the decrypts and reporting of the contents with the correct interpretation of German military terms.

> The concern was not with accumulating knowledge for its own sake, but to be able to use that knowledge to shorten the war. The ultimate objective was seen to be the provision of reliable operational intelligence to Commanders in the field who required information about the enemy intentions, dispositions and strengths.
>
> Against this was also the need for those Commanders to articulate their information requirements, with an understanding of the actual possibilities of signals interception, decryption and appreciation – and the elapsed time scales.

25. HW 3/105, p. 60.
26. HW 3/98, Ch. V, Radio Warfare, p. 10.
27. HW 14/40, 'W/T and BP' from Welchman to Commander Travis, dated 14 Jun 42.

It was crucial that the various Huts at Bletchley Park, each doing their own discrete pieces of the overall jigsaw, should develop better liaison with each other. By the middle of 1942 it was clearly demonstrated within Bletchley Park that a thorough collaboration had advantages for all concerned.[28] One of the first fruits of this collaboration was described in some detail. It concerned a German offensive in Libya that was expected to start on or soon after 25 May 42; that offensive may have been aimed at Tobruk.[29] In anticipation of that offensive the RED ENIGMA key would have priority over all other keys and within the RED frequencies the Mediterranean area would have priority. When the offensive started, the priority would shift to SCORPION provided it was reasonably current. In view of what was otherwise known or suspected of German intentions after the middle of June, GADFLY was expected to increase in priority and ultimately exceed SCORPION. *These codewords were used for different ENIGMA keys.* The outcome was that the advance analysis and appreciation was a definite benefit and the results amply justified the effort put into the preliminary discussions and planning.

But the need for liaison went far beyond the inner workings of Bletchley Park. Intelligence producers and the end-product users in the field needed liaison to close the overall Intelligence circle. In this very crucial aspect, it will be seen that Air Intelligence in Whitehall actively denied liaison between Bletchley Park and the home Air Commanders. It may be argued that Air Intelligence did not adequately understand how Bletchley Park worked and did not adequately understand what the Air Commanders required.

How strange that the overseas Air Commanders – and later the 8th USAAF in the UK – had that direct liaison with Bletchley Park via the SLUs without Air Intelligence involvement and gained great benefit from those liaisons.

This will be presented in later chapters.

This was just before the Air Section was allowed to issue the first BMP report on 1 Jun 42, the name being the combination of the first letter of the three principal originators: Bonsall, Moyes and Prior. Mr Bonsall went on after the war to become Sir Arthur Bonsall, KCMG, and Director of GCHQ between 1973 and 1978. These BMP reports are described in Bib. B28, Chapter 8. The Air Section had come to realise that their reports must combine intelligence from all available high, medium and low-grade Sigint sources. During the spring of 1942, the resources to prepare such reports were assembled and the style of report was investigated. The first of this new series of operational reports was issued on 1 Jun 42, to include the first RAF Bomber Command 1,000-bomber raid on 30 May. The security classification was usually Secret PEARL, which covered the use of information derived from decrypted medium and low-grade Sigint. Sometimes

---

28. Ibid; A MOST SECRET internal Bletchley Park paper entitled 'E-Priorities – A Liaison Problem' dated 11 Jun 42 and circulated to Hut 3, Hut 6, the Service Advisors and the W/T intercept organisation (Major Lithgow). This very important aspect of the development of work at Bletchley Park has been clarified by Sir Arthur Bonsall during the research for this book.

29. HW 14/37: CX/MSS/981/T6.

the classification went to Top Secret PEARL to cover high-grade material that may have been used as background but without being referenced; that happened more often after D-Day.

Much of the effort of analysis and production of the early BMP reports would still be misdirected or expressed in unsuitable form for the operational users. The principle reason was the official Air Intelligence policy that prevented direct contact between the Air Section and the operational users of the reports. The Air Section staff therefore had to make their own decisions on the content of the reports and tended to include too much data. Signals Intelligence was a rapidly evolving and increasingly important element of overall Intelligence; and there were too many independent parties associated with air signals intelligence, most of whom were insufficiently aware – or not aware at all – of the whole field of activity. The progressive co-ordination of collection, fusion, analysis and reporting had a long way to go. The BMP reports were thereafter prepared daily until the end of the war in Europe, initially with a small distribution list that included Air Intelligence, Fighter, Bomber and Coastal Commands. Eventually there were two editions of these BMP reports: BMP/N for night operations by Bomber Command and BMP/D for daylight operations by the 8th USAAF, with a total distribution to over 30 addressees.

The extent to which GC&CS was able to read GAF ENIGMA traffic must be taken into perspective. The GAF in the western theatre made little use of W/T except for tactical signal communications; and as a result there was little GAF ENIGMA material in this theatre. It was the GAF keys in other theatres that provided so much information on the movements of aircraft into and out of the western theatre. One of the GAF ENIGMA topics in the western theatre that did provide important intelligence was the breaking of the Fliegerkorps XII key in early 1942, to reveal the organisation of the enemy night-fighter system. The research into the German low-grade tactical codes and their R/T procedures – notably by the Air Section at GC&CS and at RAF Kingsdown – had a great deal to offer to the improvement of current or 'operational' intelligence. It provided Air Intelligence in London with the majority of information on which GAF order of battle assessments were based. This progressively had great benefit for RAF Bomber Command; and from mid-1943, for the conduct of the Combined Bombing Offensive with the 8th USAAF.

By the summer of 1942 GC&CS was regularly reading 22 different GAF ENIGMA keys and had at last broken into the German Army keys. In fact, the first Army key to be broken regularly was in use on the Russian Front, from June 1941. From November 1941, two of the main Army keys used in the Middle East were being read. Then there was the eventual success in December 1942 against the German naval 4-rotor key used for U-boat control; and coincident with but separately, success against the German Army high-level operational signal communications that used enciphered non-Morse transmissions from the *Geheimschreiber* machine. The challenge presented by *Geheimschreiber* was of a higher order even than the 4-rotor ENIGMA. In terms of intelligence value, these decrypts were often of more top-level strategic importance than was ENIGMA.

This led to the growing prestige of Bletchley Park and to the gradual erosion of the earlier barriers of jealousy and incomprehension between cryptanalysis and intelligence production, which had so handicapped previous work in both disciplines. The Service Intelligence staffs in London began to recognise and acknowledge that it was at Bletchley alone that the outputs of the German high, medium and low-grade signals traffic were being studied in close proximity. This was reflected in the provision to Bletchley of sensitive information concerning the future intentions of the Allied forces, which enabled the study of the Sigint material to be better prioritised onto the most important requirements of the various military Commanders.

Attention is drawn here to the comparative lack of ULTRA material that was thought by the Air Ministry to have value to the home air commands. In most of the overseas theatres of operation, the enemy was heavily reliant on radio communications because of the absence of landlines, for example, the Battle of the Atlantic, the North Africa campaign and even through the defence of Italy. During the early stages of the Combined Bombing Offensive from mid-1943, internal political, economic and military communications within Germany were largely conducted on telephones and teleprinters. Only when those landlines had been disrupted by the later stages of the bombing offensive was the enemy driven to use wireless for many internal communications; and that yielded the major access into ENIGMA for air defence, economic and industrial information. It was this factor that was represented as the reason why no Special Communications Unit (SCU) was created for Bomber Command to carry high-grade Sigint directly from GC&CS (Hut 3) until May 1944 (see Chapter 6, Special Liaison Duties).

But was that a correct assessment?

There is a letter dated 30 Apr 42 from Director Bomber Operations (DB (Ops)), then Air Cdre Baker, to CinC Bomber Command referring to the daylight raid on Augsburg.[30] The raid was a daylight operation by eight bombers against the MAN submarine diesel engine factory. That factory provided the engines for all U-boats built by Blohm & Voss; our Air Attaché in Berne subsequently reported on the extent of the damage and that a German civil engineer had estimated that it would be out of action for three months.[31] That raid had attracted a great deal of adverse visibility and was the subject of exchanges between the Prime Minister, MEW and CAS. The Minister of Economic Warfare, Lord Selborne, wrote to the Prime Minister to complain about the choice of Augsburg as a target. The Prime Minister spoke with the CinC, who provided a comprehensive response that set down the operational rationale for the raid; it was to mount a daylight low-level attack as a test case and he had had no need to advise MEW.[32] In that letter, the CinC noted that the complaint from MEW had taken no account of operational factors of which Selborne would have been unaware. The subsequent letter from Baker, on the instruction of CAS, was to tell the CinC that if he had any other

---

30. The Harris Archives, H53: MOST SECRET DB (Ops) 5060/DO dated 30 Apr 42.
31. Air 41/3507, 'The Contribution of Bomber Command to the Submarine Campaign' dated 8 Jul 42.
32. Air 41/3507, ATH/DO/5 dated 2 May 42, MOST SECRET to the Prime Minister.

special targets and would like to have up-to-the-minute information, then the latest intelligence would be made available without prejudice to security. The security classification of the letter from DB (Ops) dated 30 Apr 42 implies that high-grade intelligence material was available within the Air Ministry even then, but that it was not normally released to Bomber Command.

The Official History (within Bib. B1) reports that the home air commands were served with regular digests and appreciations from the Air Intelligence staffs, together with 'continuous discussions and direct contacts' with the Ministry. But these commands – Bomber, Fighter and Coastal – were held separately responsible for the application of that intelligence to the planning and conduct of their operations, on the principle that only they could combine the intelligence with their operational contact with the enemy. However, at least until the end of 1942, the commands had little success in discharging that responsibility. The reason, as was strongly represented by the Air Section at GC&CS, was that the arrangements in force for using the intelligence were too inflexible. The air commands needed more help to interpret the evidence; and this should have been solved by direct contact between GC&CS and the commands. But the Air Ministry maintained the belief that only the Air Intelligence branch could judge what would be useful to the home air commands.[33] Did the Air Intelligence staffs understand what would be useful to the home commands? There is serious scope for debate about the contention that:

> Bomber Command was not actually served
> with the Best Available Intelligence?

Air Intelligence had not foreseen the increasing scale of German bombing attacks into the UK in the spring of 1942; nor did the Home air defence forces derive much benefit from operational intelligence about the targets for these raids. In fact, the GAF was at pains to conceal the raids by the use of low-altitude approach and W/T silence.[34] The Air Ministry was surprised by the frequency of the raids. Intelligence had then lost the chief sources of information on enemy bombing intentions that had served so well during the Blitz through the winter of 1940–41. Those sources were: the manner of use of the 'radio beams' that provided guidance and target location data for the enemy bombers; their radio signals that had preceded the raids; and the beacon call signs and frequencies. It would be later in 1942 before the changes to the manner of use and the radiated frequencies, together with a new variant of X-Gerät, were resolved by ADI (Sci) and GC&CS.[35]

In parallel with those factors that related to German bombing of UK targets, there were other factors relating to RAF bombing of enemy targets. Bomber losses during the early daylight raids into Germany were heavy and unsustainable. The aircraft had inadequate defence against the enemy day fighters and Flak

33. Ibid. p. 237.
34. Air 41/49, The Air Defence of Great Britain, Vol. V, p. 53.
35. Bib. B15, Most Secret War, Ch. 28, 'The Baedeker Beams', p. 250–253.

defences; their bomb payload was too small; and the enemy was using early-warning radar. The only alternative was to adopt night bombing, but successful navigation and accurate target location was close to impossible with the primitive aids that were then installed on the bombers. The evolution of the bombing policy was then dictated by two dominant factors:

- The strategic considerations – partly predicated on pre-war doctrines; on the need to retaliate against the German raids into UK; and the fact that the bomber was the only offensive weapon available against the enemy war economy.
- The operational and technical limitations imposed by the aircraft types and equipment then available to Bomber Command.

The inevitable policy outcome was the adoption of area bombing, mostly against large and more easily located cities, with the option to select specific targets only when the night visibility permitted their identification. The persistent pressure from some quarters to concentrate on oil targets was to no avail, regardless of the arguments that were presented.

> Such targets became in effect 'targets of opportunity' with the consequence that repairs could usually be conducted after the attacks and the plant returned to use well before another raid was possible.

This had little aggregate impact on the overall enemy oil situation. During the early months of 1942, there was increasing pressure within the Chiefs of Staff to divert some of the bomber effort to long-range maritime reconnaissance, attacks on U-boats and air support for the land forces.[36] At this same time, the MEW was protesting loudly that Bomber Command disregarded the priority list of targets. It was in these contentious circumstances that the government again called on Mr Justice Singleton, this time to review the policy and practices surrounding the bombing campaign and to estimate the probable results that could be obtained over the succeeding 6, 12 and 18 months.[37] Singleton wrote in his report, delivered on 20 May 42, that the bombing should give priority to industrial areas rather than housing; and that there should be improved liaison between Bomber Command and the Target Committee.[38] The report recommended that Bomber Command must always have the final choice of targets in the light of vulnerability and feasibility. At that same time, there was pressure from the Air Ministry and the Chiefs of Staff to assign first priority for bombing to the enemy aircraft industry; this constituted another failure to recognise the operational inability to locate precise targets at night.

---

36. CAB 69/4, DO (42) 15 of 9 Feb 42; Cab 80/35, COS (42) 164 of 10 Mar 42.
37. CAB 79/20, COS (42) 114th Meeting of 10 Apr 42.
38. Bib. A4, Vol. 4, Appendix 17, dated 20 May 42; also in Air 8/1015, MOST SECRET, D.O. (42) 47.

Almost immediately afterwards, the CinC of Bomber Command requested permission to mount the first '1000-bomber raid' and this took place on the night of 30/31 May 42 against Cologne. The 8th USAAF did not attack targets in Germany until 1943.[39] The first raid into Germany by the 8th USAAF was when the 305th Bomb Group (BG) attacked the Navy yards at Wilhelmshaven on 27 Jan 43.

Concurrently, the German day-fighter and the night-fighter organisations continued to present a great challenge to the intelligence staffs. It was not until the middle of 1942 that Air Intelligence began to construct a realistic appreciation of the enemy air defence and night-fighter systems. It would seem that the Ministries in London had largely discounted some initial clues about the development of radar contained within the famous OSLO Report in November 1939.[40] It was Sigint that led the way into an understanding of the night-fighter threat and the ground organisation within the Kammhuber Line;[41] and the bulk of that Sigint was low-grade W/T and R/T with very little direct ENIGMA support. The Air Section at GC&CS was accomplishing this analysis with close support from the RAF Y-Service stations at Cheadle with its D/F Outstations and at Kingsdown with its Intercept Stations known as the Home Defence Units (HDUs). The Air Section had been pressing the Air Ministry to allow distribution of this information to the home air commands, but DDI 4 within Air Intelligence denied that request. The reason for that denial was that GC&CS had no remit to produce operational intelligence and that intelligence appreciations were made within Air Intelligence in Whitehall; this begged the premise that Air Intelligence had enough understanding of the Sigint material to make reasonable appreciations. This was not relaxed until after the first BMP report, issued on 1 Jun 42, after the '1000-bomber raid' on Cologne.

However, it should be understood that these BMP reports did not yield any sudden breakthrough in the operational application of intelligence. The style, content and format of the BMP reports went through many stages of improvement as the Air Section gained experience both in the preparation of the reports and in the nature of the material that was of most benefit to the operational users. It may not have been until the middle of 1943 when the Air Section was providing the RAF with 75 per cent of its intelligence on the GAF fighters, particularly the single-engine (S/E) fighters, that it became master of its trade. That was to continue throughout the last two years of the war. There have been arguments that the improvements would have taken place much more quickly had Air Intelligence not continued to obstruct direct exchange of information between GC&CS and the home air commands. That direct exchange did take place much more quickly between GC&CS and the 8th USAAF. Air Intelligence could not obstruct that process; and there is undoubted evidence that the 8th had greater benefit than did Bomber Command (see Chapter 8).

Another 'fly in the ointment' of intelligence collection and dissemination concerned the centralisation and co-ordination of photographic reconnaissance

39. Air 48/175 'The Effects of Strategic Bombing on German Transportation', p. 12.
40. Ibid. Ch. 8, pp. 69–71; Air 40/2572, Notes sent to Naval Attaché, Oslo: Nov 1939.
41. Bib. B28, Ch. 6, 'The German Night-fighter Organisation'.

operations. The key problem arose with bomb-damage assessment. This had been done within Bomber Command by No. 3 Photographic Reconnaissance Unit (PRU), formed at RAF Oakington on 16 Nov 40 with Spitfires and two Wellingtons and under the command of No. 3 Group. No. 3 PRU had developed specialised techniques to take photography for bomb-damage assessment and was well regarded by the CinC. It gave substance to the pre-war arguments by Sir Edgar Ludlow-Hewitt that Bomber Command must have a well-equipped PR unit (see Chapter 6). However, No. 3 PRU was transferred out of Bomber Command and back into No. 1 PRU at RAF Benson from 21 Aug 41. Bomber Command argued that it was then losing direct control over those specific PR operations and their priority, with immediate and adverse impact on planning the next days' operations; Air Marshal Portal was then CinC Bomber Command. This became and remained another source of argument between the Air Ministry and Bomber Command. However, by the autumn of 1942 No. 1 PRU had become too large and it was disbanded and formed into five new PR squadrons. No. 542 Sqn operating Spitfire PR IVs mainly from Mount Farm, and 543 Sqn operating Spitfire PR IVs from Benson flew bomb-damage assessment sorties. The PR XI, with the more powerful Merlin 61 engine subsequently replaced the PR IV, to overcome the disadvantage against the German Me 109G.

In comparison, the Army General Officer Commanding in Chief (GOCinC) Home Forces was allowed to retain control of a specialised Flight of aircraft, later No. 140 (Army Co-operation Squadron).[42] The 8th USAAF had its own PR units and photographic interpreters: those PR units were mostly operated within the structure of joint PR within 106 (PR) Wing and subsequently 106 (PR) Group; some of these interpreters were attached to the CIU and some were within the 8th USAAF Bomber Command HQ at Pinetree (see Chapter 8).

Changes during 1943

The GAF resumed its offensive against Britain on the night of 17/18 Jan 43 with a major raid on London. That offensive lasted through until the middle of the year. ENIGMA was providing good notice of the offensive by revealing the strengthening of the GAF bomber and fighter-bomber forces in France, but it also disclosed the GAF manpower shortages.[43] The intensity of the offensive never achieved the expectations of the German authorities. Among the many ENIGMA messages was the report that Goering had interviewed the commander of Luftflotte 3 about the failure of his aircrew to press home their attacks during the first half of Mar 43. There was also evidence in Mar 43 that the GAF was being supplied with new high explosive (HE) and incendiary bombs. On the strength of that information, the Prime Minister ordered that the air defences were to be brought to the highest state of readiness.[44] It was during this period that ENIGMA was gradually being combined with the medium- and low-grade W/T and R/T Sigint to yield increasingly valuable evidence of the intentions of the GAF.

---

42. Air 41/7, *Photographic Reconnaissance*, Vol. 2, p. 48.
43. CX/MSS/2175/T42; 2225/T28, 2277/T11 and 2388/T17.
44. Air 41/49, The Air Defence of Great Britain, Vol. 5, p. 189.

However, that information was rarely of immediate operational value because the process of interpretation, reporting into the Air Intelligence staff in London and the eventual availability to Fighter, Coastal and Bomber Commands was far too slow. The UK air defence radar service was widely deployed and gave better operational results, albeit handicapped by the German tactic of low-altitude approach to delay the point of initial radar detection of the incoming enemy bombers. The time delay in Sigint reporting through London provided the basis for the Air Section at GC&CS, in Apr 43, to press again for direct communication with the home air commands on matters that had a bearing on enemy air activity over the UK and in north-west Europe. Again this clashed with the Air Ministry official obstruction of any 'short-circuiting' of the intelligence protocol; but the outcome was a watered-down compromise that saw the centralisation of interpretation being done at RAF Kingsdown in Kent, one of the major RAF Y-Service stations.

The Air Operational Watch was eventually created within the Air Section at GC&CS in Jul 43. By Sep 43, tactical air Sigint was being directly reported to home air commands as part of the general build-up for Operation OVERLORD. It should be noted that this tactical Sigint contained:[45]

- Low-grade data on enemy bomber and recce operations,
- Enemy fighter Order of Battle data derived from R/T intercepts, but covertly augmented with ULTRA material that was then available to the Air Section,
- Immediate reporting of enemy fighter take-off and landings from bases in France.

The Air Operational Watch was to remain in existence until the end of the war. It provided great value during the preparations for OVERLORD in 1944 and the continuing strategic bomber offensive, with particular regard to the GAF fighter defences and tactics.

During 1943, Bomber Command was maintaining the continuous strategic bomber offensive on very much a nightly basis and with increasing USAAF support during the days. This was always subject to adverse weather, either over the target areas, or over the home airfields, insofar as recovery of the bombers after their raids into Germany. In Jan 43, the primary target for that offensive was determined by the UK War Cabinet to be the U-boat pens, in support of the Battle of the Atlantic (see page 146). However, from early Apr 43, it was clear that the raids against the U-boat pens were having inconclusive results. Bomber Command availed itself of the discretion about targets that was resident within the Casablanca Conference of the Allied Powers in Jan 43 and returned to the battle against the strategic targets within the area of the Ruhr. Those operations all fell within the scope of the POINTBLANK directive as issued later in May 43.

The region generally referred to as 'The Ruhr' included the densely built-up and heavily industrialised area not only of the Ruhr Valley but also of the upper valley immediately to the south. In extent, this region was some 40 miles from east to west and 25 miles from north to south, a total area of about 1000 square miles.

---

45. HW 50/32 'Army and Air Sigint Organisation for the Western Front.'

Economically and industrially this was by far the most important area in Germany, founded upon the coal deposits. Those coal deposits had given rise to a great concentration of steel production and associated heavy industries. At the peak of wartime effort, 61 per cent of Germany's total pig iron and steel production came from the Ruhr. The steel industry gave birth to two of the largest heavy engineering and armaments works in Europe – Krupps at Essen and Rheinmetall-Borsig at Düsseldorf. Out of the coal also came a most important internally produced material – synthetic oil. The ten synthetic oil plants in the Ruhr produced about 10 per cent of all oil supplies, including the imports from Romania, Poland and Hungary; and the most important element was aviation fuel. The Ruhr was the most strategically important target region in all of Germany.

The great intelligence challenges for the bombing offensive remained the same as they had been from the start of the war: strategic target selection and bomb-damage assessment. Photographic reconnaissance, and to some extent the night photography taken by the bombers, remained the dominant source of visual evidence on bomb damage. But the evidence so obtained was usually insufficient to permit firm conclusions on the complete value of the attacks. In the absence of reliable intelligence on these subjects, such as reports direct from Germany within Sigint or agent information, the effects of the visually recognisable damage on the enemy's economy and morale remained matters for assessment and speculation. The damage assessments in Whitehall were still being exaggerated, although there were increasingly determined efforts by the MEW and the Research & Experiments Department 8 (RE/8) to jointly improve the performance of their analyses.[46]

There was ENIGMA evidence showing the over-stretch of the GAF during 1942 and into 1943 and a decline in operational strength in the West. There was also an increase in fighter aircraft production through 1943 due to the influence of Speer. The evidence from Bomber Command showing the loss rates of the bomber aircraft and aircrews during the first six months of 1943 was showing an ominous increase in the performance of the GAF air defences, notwithstanding the increasing use of Radio Countermeasures (RCM) in support of those bomber operations from Oct 42 onwards. That was an electronic battle in which the Sigint services of both the UK and Germany were directly and continuously involved and has been described in Bib. B28. The Air Section at GC&CS together with the RAF Y-Service, predominantly at RAF Cheadle and Kingsdown, were at the heart of this electronic battle until the end of the war and their contribution was to become immeasurably more valuable when they eventually secured direct contacts with Bomber Command. An example of the operational value of that collective Sigint was seen from the ENIGMA evidence during the spring and summer of 1943 that reported:

- The redeployment of GAF resources to the West, at the expense of the Russian and Mediterranean Fronts.
- The redeployment of enemy fighter aircraft to German airfields, from bases in France, Belgium and Leningrad, in response to the increasing USAAF daylight raids.

---

46. Bib. B1, Vol. 2, Ch. 25, p. 516.

That information was used by Air Intelligence AI 3b in their assessments of GAF fighter strengths in north-west Germany through 1943 (see Chapter 6).

The authors of the history of the 8th USAAF drew attention to the under-estimates of day-fighter strength in the West. They suggested that had those errors been avoided, then the 8th USAAF may have realised sooner than it did that the casualties it was inflicting on the GAF day fighters and the damage to the aircraft factories were at best slowing down the increase in fighter production and front-line strength.[47] It is not possible however to conclude that there would have been any change in the strategic decision. There was unmistakeable evidence from ENIGMA and other sources to show that the GAF was giving the very highest priority to air defence of the Reich. The heavy bomber losses were the reason for the 8th USAAF stopping their deep penetration raids in October 1943, but the combination of the US daylight raids and the RAF night-time raids had forced the German aircraft industry to undertake the dispersal of their aircraft production facilities and some component factories. There were two consequences of that decision to disperse the aircraft industry:

• There was a reduction in the rate of increase in production, but the industry was then better able to withstand the bombing offensive when daylight raids were resumed in February 1944.
• There was an increasing dependence on transportation, which became critical as the war progressed through the last six months of 1944 and into 1945.

Bomber Command maintained the night raids without any break.

The Allies devised deceptive plans to confuse the enemy about any possible invasion plans. These plans included Operation BODYGUARD which was intended to persuade the enemy that the Allies would need 50 divisions for a cross-Channel invasion; that an invasion could well be mounted through the Balkans; or that the strategic bombing offensive would itself bring about Germany's collapse. However, there was ENIGMA evidence that General Rommel had been appointed to a command in the West – believed to be a response to the appointment of General Eisenhower as Allied Supreme Commander. In Dec 43, there was a decrypt of an appreciation by the German CinC West that the German Y-Service was continually intercepting signals that indicated Allied practice-landing exercises in the Portsmouth– Plymouth area.[48]

Changes during 1944 – pre-D-Day

There was a continuing increase in high-grade Sigint from before the start of 1944, which coincided with Germany's growing conviction that 1944 would bring the opening of the Second Front. An ENIGMA decrypt early in Feb 44 contained an Order of the Day issued from Hitler on 30 Jan 44 in which he stated that the Anzio landings were the first step in the Allied invasion plans for 1944.[49] Later in Feb 44, Sigint information showed the German Navy and Air Force conducting

47. Bib. B1, Vol. 2, Ch. 25, p. 523.
48. CX/MSS T33/79 dated 14 Dec 43.
49. DEFE 3/134, VI 5160 dated 30 Jan 44.

anti-invasion exercises along the Atlantic coast and around the Brittany peninsula.[50] There were many other important ENIGMA decrypts during the first five months of 1944 that provided ongoing detailed evidence of the German assessments of Allied intentions.

In the light of the ENIGMA evidence from late 1943 onwards, the Supreme HQ deception staffs drew up a more elaborate version of the original COSSAC plan for concentrating German attention on the Pas-de-Calais area and away from the Caen sector. This new plan became known as FORTITUDE and was approved on 23 Feb 44. In the Mediterranean the deception measures continued to conform to Plan ZEPPELIN, a part of the original Operation BODYGUARD. The intention was to demonstrate that the Allies might attempt a landing in the south of France, as a diversion from their larger deceptive 'intentions' to land in the Balkans. However, further ENIGMA decrypts in Mar–May 44 provided evidence that the Germans were increasingly suspecting that the main weight of an invasion would actually fall on Normandy. On 13 Apr 44 the decrypt of another German Army appreciation reported the move of the Allied Command HQ from London to Portsmouth and the presumption that the Allied invasion plans were well advanced.[51] There was also a very astute observation from the German Chief of Naval Operations, Admiral Meisel, in a meeting with the Japanese Naval Attaché in Berlin:[52]

that the Western Allies were bound to invade because they would wish to prevent a Russian penetration into central Europe.

From the middle of Apr 44 there was a marked increase in GAF reconnaissance operations along the south coast from Dover to Land's End, in Scotland and over the Home Fleet base at Scapa Flow. ENIGMA decrypts associated with this reconnaissance showed that Me 410 aircraft had been involved. There was a particularly pertinent Japanese report that GAF reconnaissance aircraft had detected 'a floodable sort of pontoon which could be sunk for use as a landing pier'.[53] No connection was made with the subsequent deployment of the Mulberry harbours.

There were two extremely important ENIGMA transmissions on 8 May 44:

- The Appreciation issued by the German CinC West General von Rundstedt in which he summarised his assessment of the prevailing and future situations. In that Appreciation he declared that it was essential for the Allies to capture large harbours and identified Cherbourg and Le Havre as having primary importance, but he held the view that the Allied landings could be anywhere from Boulogne to Normandy inclusive.[54]

---

50. Air Sunset 146 dated 19 Feb 44; ADM 223/318, Coastal Defence Report No. 4 dated 5 Mar 44.
51. DEFE 3/38, KV 848 and 965 dated 13 and 14 April respectively.
52. SJA 54 dated 15 Apr 44.
53. BAY/KV 146 dated 19 May 44.
54. KV 3763, shown in Bib.B1, Vol 3.2, Appendix 8, p. 794; and Hut 3 Archives: CX/MSS/T183/84 dd. 8 May 44.

- From Luftflotte (Air Fleet) 3, following Allied fighter attacks along the course of the Seine from Le Havre to Mantes, which declated:[55]

The view of Luftflotte 3 is that the landing is planned in the area Le Havre–Cherbourg.

Those ENIGMA decrypts were taken very seriously by Mr Churchill. In urgent exchanges with the Head of Special Intelligence and the British COS, it was concluded that there was no evidence to show that the German CinC West had accepted the specific view of Luftflotte 3. As time went on, from the end of Apr 44, the volume of ENIGMA decrypts progressively increased and there was some feeling within the Air Ministry that the evidence revealed German indecision rather than any firm conclusion.[56]

This aggregate ENIGMA evidence caused the Allied COS to authorise the implementation of Operation FORTITUDE SOUTH on 18 May 44, intended to demonstrate that the Allies would make an invasion into the Pas-de-Calais under General Patton after the initial landings in Normandy. Such were the levels of deception within the overall context of Sigint operations.

Within the volume of ENIGMA evidence prior to D-Day, it was clear that the strategic bomb damage to the railway network from West Germany and across northern France was a major problem for the German forces. Those ENIGMA reports showed that transportation was wholly dependent on improvised road transport.[57]

The Allied estimates of the German Air situation on D-Day were comprehensively reported in the JIC (44) 215 (O) paper dated 25 May 44.[58] The forecast of GAF aircraft available on the Western Front in the various sectors, including Germany north of 49°N, was 2,350. The S/E and T/E fighter forces were 900 and 650 respectively, of which 600 and 350 respectively were held within Germany. That estimate also reflected the ENIGMA evidence that the GAF was seriously short of combat-experienced formation leaders and crews; and that this was a major problem for the fighter forces.

Changes during 1944 – post D-Day

The primary focus of effort in the development of intelligence to support target selection, for the strategic bombing offensive during the second half of 1944 was the German oil industry. The Sigint provided testimony that was positive and unambiguous about the crucial significance of the state of the enemy's fuel supply.[59] That evidence was supported by PR. Probably the most crucial single item of intelligence was the ENIGMA message on 5 Jun 44 that reported the enemy's need to break into their strategic reserve of oil stocks. CAS immediately commented to

---

55. DEFE 3/155; KV 3242 dated 9 May 44; and Hut 3 Archives: CX/MSS/T178/86, 9 May 44.
56. Air Sunset 177 (AWL 2118 of 30 May 44).
57. Bib. B1, Vol. 3–2, Ch. 44, p. 85.
58. Ibid., Appendix 12.
59. Bib. A4, Vol. III, p. 229.

the Prime Minister on 8 Jun 44 that he believed that the strategic bombing should attack the synthetic oil plants as soon as they could be released from OVERLORD. On 20 Jun 44 the COS instructed the JIC to produce a fortnightly appreciation of the German fuel situation.[60] Soon afterwards, on 7 Jul 44, the Air Staff and the USSTAF set up a new working committee – the Anglo-American Oil Targets Committee. This committee was to supervise the oil campaign more scientifically and to reach quicker decisions on target priority for attack and reattack.

There was very considerable ENIGMA evidence that the Germans were deeply troubled by the offensive against their oil supplies. It became apparent for some time that they were abandoning the policy of concentrating production in large plants and had embarked on dispersal to multiple small self-contained plants. A special commission had been appointed to oversee and control the emergency repair programme for oil plants; this commission was headed by Geilenberg, one of Speer's deputies. Knowledge of this appointment initially came from an intercepted telegram dated 10 Jul 44. Certainly the construction of multiple small self-contained plants would have been a good countermeasure to the strategic bombing, but the other more dominant feature of dispersal was the associated priority demand for transportation to the places of use. The significance of transportation will become obvious later in this book. Through July, August and September there was continuing weight of evidence from Sigint to show the extent of the oil problem for German forces and that the dispersal into multiple small plants was not working as had been planned.

There is another aspect of the Sigint equation post D-Day that should be recorded. During the summer of 1944 the Germans began to make improvements to the security of the ENIGMA, FISH and their medium-grade ciphers. The first of the improvements was known as ENIGMA UHR. For much of that period through until the spring of 1945, GC & CS was able to maintain only a fragile grip on the expanding volume of encrypted Sigint. It was unable to read the medium-grade hand ciphers of the German Army and Air Force from Aug 44 until Feb 45. By the benefit of good fortune and the increasing bomb damage to internal communications, the Germans were unable to implement many of the planned improvements as quickly as had been expected; and one of the unintended consequences was that the number of active encryption keys diminished. This was particularly true for GAF keys and a bonus for the Allies was that GAF ENIGMA provided a more complete picture of the GAF's activities on all Fronts than at any previous period in the war – until 1 Feb 45, when the GAF introduced improved encryption and the volume of successful decrypts fell by almost 50 per cent, from about 1800 per day to about 1000.[61]

As an indication of the rapid increase in the overall workload at GC & CS during the last nine months of the war, the volume of Naval decrypts rose from about 10,000 per week at D-Day to about 15,000 per week in Aug 44; and to a peak of nearly 20,000 per week in the middle of Mar 45. The volume of decrypts that related to German Army operations, troop movements, resupply and tactical intentions were equally massive. The evidence of transport shortages was reflected in the

60. CAB 121/418, COS (44) 201st Mtg, 20 Jun 44.
61. Bib. B1, Appendix 15.

frequent urgent requests for resupply of ammunition, fuel and logistics support. Appendix K contains a few examples of these decrypted messages.

Later in this book it will be seen that there were very serious clashes of opinion throughout 1943, 1944 and into 1945 between Whitehall, the Air Ministry, the USSTAF, the Target Committees and eventually with the Supreme Headquarters, about the strategic targets for the bomber forces. The highest-priority targets at different times included the German aircraft production programme, oil, transportation, the U-boat bases, tanks, and many other lesser target sets as well as several 'panacea' targets. There are also major clashes of appreciation and analysis within many of the post-war publications, including the Official Histories. This book will address those clashes of opinion and their consequences in later chapters. The dominant theme has often been to criticise the policy of 'area' bombing, but usually without any appreciation or understanding of what that meant and why it was adopted. It is surprising that even Bib. A4 speaks of 'the general area campaign' without any attempt to explain and identify the selection of specific targets and aiming points.[62] That erroneous generalisation is repeated within Bib. B1, together with the emotional claim that 'Bomber Command flouted the Air Staff's instructions'.[63] Bib. B1 (at p. 518) goes even further to declare that 'Many of the synthetic oil plants were situated in isolated areas and were therefore good targets for instrumental bombing through cloud'. It has to be said that Bib. B1 may well be the authoritative Official History of British Intelligence in WW2, but it is certainly no authority on bombing practices and techniques. Regrettably in these areas it paints a picture that many other documents follow, but fails to portray what was operationally possible. Chapter 54 of Bib. B1 is open to the criticism that it focuses on the intelligence information within Whitehall yet makes serious criticisms of operational decisions and issues in which it has no comparable authority.

One saving grace within Bib. B1 may be the footnote (on p. 518) that records 'Much damage was done to transportation during Bomber Commands area attacks; and that was also true of benzol plants that were mainly in industrial areas'.[64] The point here is that those specific targets and many other targets were totally consistent with the bombing Directives. The manner of use of the term 'area' bombing displays a profound ignorance of the operational capabilities and the actual targeting process. Chapter 4 of this book discusses the specific subject of 'area' and 'precision' bombing by both Bomber Command and the 8th USAAF.

As the autumn 1944 bombing campaign proceeded, it was recognised within the intelligence material and by a few senior air staff officers that the vulnerability of German transport to air attack was a very real source of weakness. The aggregate evidence mostly from ULTRA, starting even before D-Day, showed that the strategic bombing of transportation was responsible for an increasing decline in the enemy's war production.[65] In August it was being reported that there was

---

62. Bib. A4, Vol. III, p. 57.
63. Bib. B1, Vol. 3–2, Ch. 54, p. 517.
64. Craven and Cate, Vol. III, p. 642.
65. Air 8/1019, COS Paper AO(46)1 dated 8 Mar 46, p. 55: Reference to the frequent representation of ULTRA evidence about oil to the Supreme Commander. Was this further evidence of the pressure from the oil committees?

a perceptible weakening of the transport system and that raw materials were being delayed. In a message of 20 Oct 44, Speer was quoted as saying that between 30 and 35 per cent of all armaments factories were at a standstill because of the destruction of traffic installations and the lack of prime power.[66] The prime power source was coal. From the end of Oct 44 the volume of such ULTRA information multiplied rapidly, and in parallel the enemy armed forces ENIGMA keys were also testifying to the mounting dislocation. By the turn of the year, the evidence to show the aggregate effects of the destruction of transportation not only on the enemy war production but also on military movements and supply was becoming overwhelming. Significantly in the offensive against transportation, the mines laid in the Danube during the summer of 1944 by RAF Wellingtons and USAAF Liberators of 205th Bomb Group operating from Foggia caused heavy losses to Axis shipping along the river. Very few tankers were able to pass and the consequent transport bottleneck proved a greater problem than the attacks on the oil refineries.[67] However, it will be seen that the CSTC was unmoved by such evidence and may even have discarded that evidence in favour of its predisposition towards oil.[68] That reference to the selective use of ULTRA evidence goes on to claim:

> What brought German industry down was the attack on the railway system, desultory though it was because of the opposition that was strenuously led by DB (Ops) (Bufton) and the MEW (Lawrence). What had been subsequently discovered is that Lawrence was sitting on scores of ULTRA reports that indicated that the whole German industrial system had started to break down by Sep 44 as a result of the paralysis of the railway system.

That claim is directly supported by Bib. A22 and is amplified within Appendix O. However, Bib. B1, Chapter 54, maintains the offensive against Bomber Command and the CinC but makes no reference to that abuse and misuse of the intelligence process within a Government department.

---

66. (1) DEFE 3/244; (2) Hut 3 Archives, CX/MSS/T347/46, 24 Oct 44.
67. Air 8/1019, COS Paper AO(46)1 dated 8 Mar 46, p. 60, Footnote 11.
68. Bib. A20, p. 147.

CHAPTER THREE

Economic Warfare

'Man prefers to believe what he wants to be true.'

Francis Bacon

This chapter will provide the background to the pre-war Industrial Intelligence Centre (IIC) and the creation of the Ministry of Economic Warfare (MEW) in the run-up to the Declaration of War in 1939. It will then describe the evolution of the MEW through the first few years of the war, with the intention of providing an overview of how that Ministry interacted with the bombing offensive.

Industrial Intelligence Centre

The Committee of Imperial Defence formed the IIC in the winter of 1929–30 to report on industrial developments and arms manufacturing in foreign countries and their preparedness to make war. It was administratively affiliated to the Department of Overseas Trade but received instructions from the Committee of Imperial Defence. From 1931 onwards the Director was Major Desmond Morton, who had very close contact with Churchill through those contentious years in the 1930s. Morton was one of the principal sources of information on German rearmament for Churchill during those 'years in the wilderness' when Churchill was opposing appeasement and advocating rearmament. Morton, subsequently Sir Desmond Morton, became the Prime Minister's personal representative on security and Special Intelligence material throughout the war.[1]

An early contact between the IIC and the Air Ministry was a letter from Morton to Wg Cdr Medhurst in 1934, saying that the IIC Reports and Memoranda would be sent to Medhurst as arranged at a previous meeting.[2] This was the start of a mutually beneficial and constructive exchange of information. An example of that exchange was a further letter providing initial estimates of the manufacturing man-hours required for different types of airframes and engines. As those estimates were improved, they would of course have had relevance to estimates of German aircraft manufacturing capacities.[3] This did

---

1. Bib. B32, Ch. 8; and PREM 7/14, personal letter from Morton dated 25 Sep 45.
2. Air 5/1154, IIC letter ICF/244 dated 12 Feb 34.
3. Air 5/1154, IIC letter ICF/439 dated 26 Sep 34.

indeed lead to an initial draft paper on the German Aircraft Industry that had been prepared in collaboration between the IIC and Air Intelligence.[4] The conclusions of that paper showed that the rate of aircraft construction in Germany could then have been about 320 airframes and 850 engines per month; but that it would have been unsafe to estimate an emergency capacity of less than 1000 complete aircraft per month if skilled labour was made available, given that the factories were then working at far less than their maximum capacities, i.e. on single-shift working.

An important point upon which Morton and Medhurst exchanged views was the damage that may be inflicted on both of their organisations if they were to publish conflicting data and estimates within the fields of industrial and economic affairs.[5] It may be assumed that they found mutual agreement to exchange their views on these topics prior to external visibility.

There is a fascinating description of the relationship between the IIC and the three separate Services during the 1930s, written by Morton after the war.[6] He had likened the relationship to that in the Book of Revelations 6, wherein were described the Four Horsemen of the Apocalypse. The black horse carried a rider with the scales, who was compared with the IIC.

The threat of war in 1936 was obvious, so obvious in fact that the main global insurance market – Lloyd's of London – had ceased trading in war cover on property by the end of the year.[7] But Chamberlain preferred a piecemeal approach, offering concessions on colonies, trade and credit in the hope that this would open the way to agreement on peace and security.

There are three topics within the overall history of the IIC that are regarded as having particular relevance to the subsequent issues that arose within the bombing offensives during WW2. These are:

• The selection and registration of Industrial Targets for Air Attack,
• The ground work for an Intelligence Directorate within the future MEW,
• The situation post-September 1938, after the miserable Munich Agreement.

Industrial Air Targets: Registration and Attack

A most significant paper that was prepared by the IIC during 1936 was 'Industrial Air Targets: Selection for Registration and Attack.'[8] The objective of the paper was to define 'objectives for air attack in war, other than the armed forces of the enemy and material in their charge'. In a highly industrialised country like Germany, an attack on industrial targets – which by definition included Transportation beside Works and Factories – involved selection from a vast number of targets. It was recognised that within those targets there would be those that were unsuitable for attack and others which probably would always suffer some damage. The candidate targets were grouped into Target Sets (the term 'target set' will be used

---

4. Air 5/1154, ICF/148 dated 10 Nov 36 – Secret.
5. Air 5/1154, ICF/548 dated 10 May 37 – Secret.
6. PREM 7/14, Personal letter from Morton to Medlicott, dated 3 Dec 48.
7. Bib. A23 Ch. 7, p. 203 and Reference 2.
8. Air 5/1154, ICF/548 dated 10 May 37.

throughout this book, to mean 'a number of targets all related to a single object or objective'), which included:

- Fuel and Power; coal, coke, oil and petroleum, electricity.
- Chemicals: General chemicals, Nitrogen, Explosives, Gases.
- Metallurgy: Mines, Non-Ferrous metals, Iron and Steel plants.
- Engineering: Armaments, Shipbuilding, Aircraft, Tanks, and Engines.
- Transportation: Roads, Railways, Inland waterways, Seaports and ships.

One point that has much significance is that German national oil wells could only provide a fraction of the country's wartime requirements for petroleum products and the derricks were widely dispersed in those oil fields. The paper recommended that these oil wells were not candidates for Registration at that time; see Appendix I, para. 4 of that paper. The refineries and storage tanks were however regarded as very favourable and vulnerable targets and that they should be registered. With regard to the synthetic petroleum plants, though vulnerable, they were individually small and hard to recognise from the air.

The Nitrogen industry was regarded as having major importance to the prospective German war economy. At that time there were two major plants that produced 80 per cent of the total national output; these were at Leuna-Merseburg and Oppau. The destruction of either of these was expected to have serious repercussions on a number of other industries.

A point that was later to have the most significance was that the nature of any attack on the Transportation target set must be closely governed by the actual strategic situation at the time. But it should be remembered that interference with transportation would have as great an economic as a strategic effect. The key targets in that set were:

a. Sea ports,
b. Specific locks on certain canals,
c. Specific railway objectives.

The exact objectives for b. and c. were a matter for further detailed study. It was foreseen that any attack on the railway system would demand a bomber force much larger than was then being considered at that point in time by the UK.

Factors that would have governed specific types of target as candidates for Registration included:

- Visibility: The degree of ease with which a target could be identified from the air.
- Vulnerability: The degree of damage that could be inflicted from the air.

The paper went on to examine the value of a specific target within any given target set; and to identify that, in a distributed or dispersed target set, there may be little real effect in destroying one specific target in isolation. It would therefore be necessary to identify the proportion of such target sets that would need to be destroyed in order to secure a serious reduction in collective output or value to the enemy. The chief factor outweighing all others in the selection of industrial targets for attack would be the actual strategic or economic situation that obtained at the time; and the associated priority that may be addressed to specific target sets.

Within the paper there were also the ingredients of what would later be known as 'area attack'. This was described as the aggregate damage that would be achieved in a crowded industrial area where important undertakings were in such close proximity that bombs missing the intended objective might well damage something else of comparable importance. Further, that in such areas, the more crowded the area then the greater the simultaneous and cumulative effect on both morale and material.

In conclusion, the paper went to great lengths to qualify that the prevailing strategic and economic situation would be of paramount importance and that no single target set could be predetermined to have first priority, or that any such attack(s) could be expected to have immediate decisive effects.

> There was no doubt that air attack on industrial targets would be an important operation in modern warfare; and that it therefore provided another means of exerting economic pressure on the enemy.

Intelligence Directorate for MEW

Under the instruction of the Economic Pressure Sub-Committee of the Committee of Imperial Defence, Morton was directed to draw up proposals for a Directorate of Intelligence within the then future concept of a MEW. That draft was circulated to other key departments in the Admiralty, the War Office and the Air Ministry for comment.[9] The draft contained sections that addressed:

- The Collection of Economic and Industrial Intelligence.
- The Statistics Sub-Section.
- The Collation of Intelligence, which included the 'Black List' and the 'Prize Court Section.'
- The Interpretation of Intelligence.
- The Intelligence Registry and Typing Staff.

On the basis of previous experience during World War 1, it was anticipated that the size of the Directorate could eventually rise to about 1000 persons.

That was followed in Apr 38 by a first draft of an Overseas Organisation to report to the future MEW Intelligence Directorate.[10] Morton had anticipated that Germany would be able to trade with a large number of countries, many across land borders, over which the UK would have no control. He saw that there was no time to be lost in creating an organisation that could provide economic and industrial information, much of it necessarily in a timely manner; and that such an organisation should be ready at the outset of war and not allowed to just take

---

9. Air 5/1154, ICF/968 dated 30 Mar 38.
10. Air 5/1154, ICF/968/S.1 dated 30 Apr 38.

shape as the war developed. A great deal of responsibility for collecting information would rest on diplomatic and consular staffs in foreign cities and ports; and on Dominion and Colonial Governments and their various Customs authorities.

There was Treasury approval for an initial increase in IIC staff in Sep 38, curiously coincident with but separate from the outcome of that flawed Munich Agreement between Chamberlain and Hitler.

Post-September 1938

As the pre-war crisis deepened and the 1938 Munich Agreement came and went, there was what could be called ambivalence in the mind of the bulk of the British Intelligence Services. It was not that the intelligence community was producing accurate assessments that were being filtered away from ministers by some unseen hand. On the contrary, the intelligence services themselves were often badly informed or even appeasement-minded. The three Service Intelligence Directorates alternated between underestimating and exaggerating German strengths. No effective central body existed to co-ordinate their assessments. The label 'blindness' seems appropriate to the way in which they failed to provide a balanced reading of German strengths and weaknesses.[11]

That 'blindness' was by no means confined to intelligence services. Ironically, it was the Chamberlain government, which for the most part had such an abysmal record in defence matters, and Mr Chamberlain in particular who forced an unwilling Air Ministry to invest substantial resources in air defence. On 1 Oct 38, Sir Warren Fisher of the Treasury reflected bitterly on the course of the rearmament program from 1935:[12]

> When I insisted on the insertion in the report of passages such as these [on the need to build up Britain's air defence system] the representative of the Air Staff acquiesced with a shrug of his shoulders. The Air Staff proposals were, of course, again quite insufficient [...] and their lack of imagination and foresight has been fully equalled by their incompetence in all practical matters, including strategic policy.

An Air Staff memorandum of June 1938 sets out the surprising unreality of its position and its lack of understanding of the conditions of air war:

> The speed of modern bombers is so great that it is only worth while to attack them under conditions which allows no relative motion between the fighter and its target. The fixed-gun fighter with guns firing ahead can only realise these conditions by attacking the bomber from dead astern. The duties of a fighter engaged in 'air superiority' fighting will be the destruction of opposing fighters [...] For these purposes

---

11. Bib. B32, Ch. 8, p. 179.
12. CAB 21/902, Letter from Sir Warren Fisher to Neville Chamberlain, dated 1 Oct 38, p. 4.
13. AIR 2/2964, 17 Jun 38, Air Staff Note on the Employment of two-seater and single-seater fighters in a Home Defence War; see also AIR 2/2964, 20 Jun 38, Minutes by DD Ops (Home).

it requires an armament that can be used defensively as well as offensively in order to enable it to penetrate into enemy territory and withdraw at will. The fixed gun fighter cannot do this.[13]

Only the spirited objections of Air Chief Marshal Sir Hugh Dowding, Commander in Chief of Fighter Command, kept the emphasis of British fighter production on Spitfires and Hurricanes and not on the two-seated Defiants.

As late as early 1940, some of the Air Staff tried to shut down the production lines of Spitfires and Hurricanes.[14]

Responsibilities of MEW – From 1939

It had been agreed before the war that the conduct of all operations of economic warfare should be in the hands of a single, independent Ministry, which was accordingly established on 3 September 1939. It then absorbed the functions and documentation of the preceding Industrial Intelligence Committee. The Ministers of Economic Warfare and their dates of appointment were:

- Rt Hon. Ronald H Cross, MP – 3 September 1939.
- Rt Hon. Hugh Dalton, MP – 15 May 1940.
- Rt Hon. Viscount Woolmer (later Earl of Selborne) – 22 February 1942.

The Ministry was made responsible for all measures designed to undermine the enemy's economic structure and lead to its ultimate collapse.[15] It advised on, and to a large extent directed, all possible measures to restrict the enemy's relations with the outside world and also provided reports and gave advice to guide the planning of the war. Its activities included control of contraband, restriction of enemy supplies and making recommendations for aerial attack on targets most likely to affect the enemy's economy. It was also responsible for control of the Special Operations Executive.

Also important in the work of the Ministry from the beginning of the war were three committees which included representatives of other interested departments; in particular the Admiralty, the Ministry of Shipping and the Board of Trade. A Contraband Committee made central assessment of the nature of cargoes intercepted by the Royal Navy and the Enemy Exports Committee considered particular cases arising from the embargo on enemy exports. In Jan 42 these two committees were amalgamated with the purely departmental Permits Committee to form the Blockade Committee, which continued until the end of the war. Finally

---

14. The suspicion exists that Dowding was removed from Fighter Command shortly after the Battle of Britain and never given another command because his success was a direct contradiction to pre-war doctrine. See Appendix P. Another suspicion was that the failure of the Night Fighter defence was the defining issue.
15. FO/371(2627), Note by the Foreign Office and MEW/Economic Advisory Branch, Ref. CR.317 dated 6 Feb 45.

there was a Black List Committee, which controlled a statutory list of the names of firms and individuals thought to be dealing with the enemy.[16-17] British firms were prohibited from trading with those on the list. It was a popular misconception that blockading Germany would by itself win the war just by stopping the flow of oil and essential war materials; even as late as Mar 40, Chamberlain was endorsing the war winning capability of the blockade as the 'main weapon'.[18]

Initially the Ministry was divided into four departments, but these soon increased in number and were divided into two branches known later in the war as the General Branch and the Enemy Branch, each under a director. The work of the two directors was at first co-ordinated by a director general, but in 1943 he himself became head of the General Branch, dealing with operational aspects of the Ministry's work. The Enemy Branch was put under the charge of the deputy director general. The Enemy Branch had developed in 1942 into a purely intelligence organisation and in Apr 44 it was transferred to the Foreign Office, under the title Enemy Branch, Foreign Office and Ministry of Economic Warfare. It remained at Lansdowne House, Berkeley Square with its own Establishments Department and with civil, not foreign, service grades. The work of the Enemy Branch principally involved the evaluation of economic intelligence, for example on potential bombing targets for the specific needs of its mainly service customers. The title of the branch was again changed to Economic Advisory Branch, Foreign Office and Ministry of Economic Warfare in Oct 44, and in Jun 45 it was dissolved.

The following sub-sections provide an overview of the:

- Political and Industrial Intelligence situation when the MEW was formed,
- Developments during 1940,
- The estimation of German Industrial capacity and vulnerability through the early and middle stages of the war.

The Starting Position

The proper study of foreign armament industries in peace-time should provide a sound basis for appreciating the capacities of those industries in wartime.

---

16. FO 935/19: Intelligence Priorities Committee: Third Meeting, 7 Jun 44. See related Loose Minute from Dr Noton to Mr Lawrence, within the MEW. Within the context of Economic Intelligence, the 'Black List' was a list of persons, places and things that were to be captured or occupied at once by Allied Forces during any advance to prevent destructive action by the enemy. This effectively became an obligation for Allied Field Commanders via the UK and US Chiefs of Staff. The procedure for Black List Targets was designated by JIC/849/44 dated 12 Jun 44.
17. FO 935/8: Combined Objectives Intelligence Committee – Black List Working Party. Minutes of 8th Meeting dated 13 Dec 44. The 21st Army Group reported that it was unable to fully comply with the Black List requirements because of the manpower situation.
18. A J P Taylor's *History of England – English History 1914–1945*, Ch. 13, p. 461.

That very reasonable expectation appeared in the Aircraft Production Intelligence section of the draft Air Intelligence Handbook, compiled at the end the war. It is an inescapable fact that this expectation was not satisfied prior to the start of WW2. Indeed, the extent of the German rearmament programme was profoundly ignored by some sections of the Government in Whitehall, which adhered to a policy of moderation, half-hearted measures and keeping things quiet.[19] Sir Winston Churchill was one of a few MPs who stood aside from this policy of appeasement and avoidance. The Labour Party had moved a Vote of Censure upon the Government in 1934 for bringing forward a proposal for a modest increase in the RAF; Mr Attlee had then said in the House of Commons:

We deny the need for increased air armaments.

At the time of the Munich Crisis in 1938, when the German rearmament programme was well advanced, there was a view in London that the British armaments industry was more flexible and more fertile than the German industry. This perhaps illustrates how profoundly naive was the wishful thinking of some departments within Whitehall; it is no surprise that their appreciations of the German armaments industry capacity and production were so wrong.

At the start of the war, the functions of MEW then included:

- Estimation of the enemy's capacity to keep his forces armed, equipped, provisioned and mobile.
- Identification of points at which his industry and transport were most sensitive to attack.
- Estimation of the limits that economics may impose on his ability to attack or defend in different theatres of war.

The complexity of these overall functions meant that MEW needed reliable methods of economic forecasting and a great store of accurate information. As it was, the methods did not exist and the information was not forthcoming. The fantasy world that some politicians were living in at that time does not speak well of the advice and 'guidance' that they were being given by the MEW. Despite the noble efforts of Morton and the IIC to deliver the organisation for economic and industrial intelligence that he had foreseen during 1936–38, the bottom line of the problem was the lack of suitable staff to undertake the immense amount of work to collect, collate and interpret the information. This reflected the ambivalent political opinions on appeasement or rearmament. Accurate information about the behaviour of the economy of the German Reich during the first years of the war was hardly ever available outside Germany. The pre-war data, that was substantially inadequate and in some cases incorrect, became increasingly outdated. Other sources of information were lost after the fall of France. Agents and Sigint provided few other compensating sources in the first years of the war. This changed later as ENIGMA yielded increasingly valuable information in the middle and final stages of the war.

---

19. Bib. B30, Vol. 1, 'The Gathering Storm', p. 170.

Through 1940

By the spring of 1940 there was a serious lack of credible information on the outputs and reserves of German war material. Early British estimates of enemy aircraft, tank and U-boat construction were too high; and indeed the estimates of aircraft and tank construction remained too high for several years. There was an unsatisfactory state of collaboration between MEW and the Air Ministry. This can only have been a consequence of the personalities then involved; that relationship had previously been good through most of the 1930s, viz. Morton and Medhurst. The estimated construction numbers for aircraft in 1940 were 13,300 by MEW; were 19,000 by the Air Ministry; but in fact were 10,826 of all types as given in official German statistics after the end of the war.[20] MEW was considerably better than was the Air Ministry. This latter quantity as known at the end of the war was remarkably close to the higher estimate from the IIC in 1936. [But see the later section on AI 3(b) etc and the Air Section.] One of the assumptions within these estimates was that the German aircraft industry would be working two-shifts in each 24-hour period. But information from France had revealed that in fact only one-shift working was taking place at that time; this appears not to have influenced the MEW or Air Ministry estimates.

Hitler had frequently issued directives demanding rapid economic adjustment to his military priorities, but the MEW weekly intelligence reports and the appreciations of the Joint Intelligence Committee (JIC) made no reference to them. For example, upon the attack on Poland in 1939, Hitler dropped naval construction as a first priority. In October 1939 he gave motor transport for troops priority over all other programmes. Munitions had become short after the Blitzkrieg against Poland and Hitler ordered that they be produced in greater quantities; in fact, by the third quarter of 1940, the rate had increased by 90 per cent compared with 1939.[21] In July 1940, Hitler made the decision that there would be an invasion of Russia in May 1941. He required that preparations be made for the invasion by way of Blitzkrieg, but he called for no major economic planning. The German aircraft industry did not respond adequately to Hitler's requirements at that time.

German concern about wastage of resources led, in March 1940, to the appointment of Dr Fritz Todt as Reichminister for Weapons and Munitions, primarily responsible for economising the consumption of scarce metals by the arms industry and with direct responsibility as Head of the new Ministry of Ammunition. In November 1940, Todt established a national committee to oversee the production of all guns and artillery, headed by Erich Mueller, the chief weapons designer from Krupps. London knew about Todt's appointment but had no reliable evidence about his objectives. His management paved the way for a subsequent expansion of armaments production under Albert Speer, who succeeded Todt after his death in Feb 42.

---

20. Bib. B1, Vol. 1, Ch. 7, Intelligence on the German Economy, p. 228.
21. Author's Note: This increase is reflected in Bib. A17, Ch. VIII, p. 186, which shows such an increase albeit with reductions in output from that point until the end of 1941. Production began to increase again after the appointment of Speer as Reichsminister for War Production in February 1942.

London did not detect the changes that were taking place in the adjustments to the German war economy, but continued to believe that the enemy economy was stretched from the outset. That was a false assumption based on an invalid appreciation of the German rearmament programme from 1936 onwards. That mistaken belief was at the root of subsequent gross errors in the appreciation of war productivity and led to multiple consequential errors, not least in under-assessing the effectiveness of the bombing campaign. It was one of the reasons why MEW continued calculating and recalculating when and where economic factors would constrain German military ambitions. There was practically no use made of economic intelligence to indicate Germany's forthcoming military moves; and the JIC complained about the lack of intelligence on German war production. If there is any other explanation for these failings, it could rest with the failure in Whitehall to appreciate the extent to which Hitler's strategy at that time rested on his faith in the Blitzkrieg concept.

The relationships between MEW and the three Service departments were at best uneasy. At the end of 1940, there had been a request from the Director of the Enemy Branch within the MEW that the three Service departments provide members of their staffs to work within the MEW. The idea was that this Service representation would provide a basis for improving the level of information exchange and thereby the acceptance of MEW estimates. This was not agreed by the Services. One of the reasons was the poor state of MEW's information about the enemy economy and the consequent failure for it to have any impact at the JIC, Joint Planning and Chiefs of Staff levels. But such views as the MEW did provide were most usually accepted, because it was the only Whitehall department with the responsibility to form an overall view of the German economy.

> There are sound reasons to challenge the credibility of those MEW appreciations; and equally sound reasons to question why they were usually accepted as correct.

The History of England 1914–1945[22] makes the claim that the MEW probably did more harm to Britain than to Germany. Perhaps all this is why the MEW seemed to be a Ministry without a mission, struggling to justify its existence. Withholding useful intelligence that it had from ENIGMA and which it should have employed could have been an attempt to display a veneer of indispensability. That is a commonly practised art and flourishes in a world where secrecy can be a cloak for mediocrity.

Estimation of German Industrial Capacity and Vulnerability

The major theme that ran through British estimates of German economic and industrial strength in the early and middle stages of the war was one of underestimating the reserve capacity that was available in the aggregate war production capacity of the enemy. This had two very significant consequences:

---

22. *The History of England 1914–1945* by A J P Taylor, p. 461.

- In the short term it led to over-assessments of war productivity based on the assumptions of manpower and machine utilisation.
- In the longer term it led to under-assessments of the effectiveness of the Strategic Bombing Offensive, as the reserve capacity in German industrial productivity was taken up after Albert Speer became Reichsminister for War Production early in 1942.

This largely disguised the impact of the bombing offensive and in turn led to critical and incorrect assessments of the performance of both RAF Bomber Command and the 8th USAAF. The period of greatest German war productivity was not actually reached until the middle of 1944, at the point where the bombing offensive was in fact having serious toll of the enemy's aggregate war production (see Chapter 10). The immediately post-war analysis of German war production by the US and the rather later analysis by the UK Survey Team were unambiguously clear that the bombing offensive had significantly damaged the German economic and industrial capacity.

Within the scope of Air Intelligence, one major aspect of assessment concerned the operational strength and production rates of enemy aircraft. This has been noted above, but the discrepancies between the Air and MEW estimates came to the attention of the Prime Minister particularly during the period before the Battle of Britain in the summer of 1940. The outcome of that crisis at the end of 1940 was the setting up of an independent study by Professor Lindemann and an impartial inquiry by Mr Justice Singleton. The Singleton Report was issued on 21 January 1941 and set down a rather general comparison between the strengths of the RAF and the GAF.[23] One of the elements within the scope of the report was the emerging evidence that was being derived from Sigint, particularly that being collected and organised at RAF Cheadle with support from the Air Section at GC &CS. This Sigint evidence had pointed to probable errors in the Air Intelligence assessments in September–October 1940; Air Intelligence did not accept the Sigint information at that time.[24] After the issue of the Singleton report, Lindemann paid special attention to the Sigint and call sign information. This gave rise to a particularly difficult and crucial period that focussed on the different methods that were being used to reach assessments of the Luftwaffe strength. A most critical factor was the number of aircraft in a German Staffel, the notional equivalent of an RAF Squadron. Was that number to be regarded as 9 or as 12? The outcome at the end of March 1941 was a proposal from the Chief of Air Staff (CAS) to the Prime Minister seeking approval of an estimate of Luftwaffe front line strength of 4,282 aircraft of various types, plus reserves of about 4,000.[25] This was very close to the numbers generated in the Singleton Report and it secured approval by Mr Churchill.

Similar discrepancies were in existence with regard to Army and Navy estimates; in both areas the MEW inputs were inconclusive. By the early months of 1941 there

23. Bib. B1, Vol. 1, Ch. 9, p. 301 [Do not confuse this report with the later report by Lord Justice Singleton into Bomber Operations, later in 1942].
24. Bib. B28, Ch. 8: Section on 'SALU', pp. 58–59.
25. Bib. 14, Vol. 1, Ch. 7, Intelligence on the German Economy, p. 228.

was growing recognition in Whitehall that the state of the German economy was not as critical as it had been represented in the summer of 1940. The attempted naval blockade had been unsuccessful, primarily because of land routes into Germany through Russia and Vichy France. Shipping from North Africa into Vichy France was supplying the Reich with large quantities of valuable commodities. At the same time, urgent goods of Russian origin or from the Far East were moving into the Reich at a rate of 1,700 tons per day; these goods included copper, rubber and tin. By March 1941, the German oil situation was seen to be comparatively strong; the earlier air offensive by Bomber Command against synthetic oil plants in Germany had been abandoned. The reasons went to the heart of the then insuperable problems within RAF Bomber Command regarding night navigation and target-location over hostile territory. Finding a 'small' target at night, often with cloud cover, with the primitive navigation aids available was at best unreliable. The bombing operations against oil targets through six months of the winter 1940/1941 were largely frustrated by poor weather and totally inadequate equipment, together with the higher priority that was accorded to the Battle of the Atlantic and the bombing of U-boat construction and support facilities.

The German synthetic oil industry was technically very impressive and it is well worth noting the basic processes. Coal contains the same constituents as petrol but in different proportions and the conversion of coal into petrol requires, in simplest terms, the addition of more hydrogen to the coal molecule. There were two main processes in use in Germany:[26]

- *Bergius Plants*: In this process clean coal is the raw material. It is ground into a paste with oil and then pressurised to about 3000 psi. Pure hydrogen at the same pressure is applied together with a catalyst. The oil is distilled off and the process is repeated with a different catalyst, yielding petrol as the end product. The quality of the petrol depends on the quality of the coal; bituminous coal yielding petrol suitable for aviation fuel.
- *Fischer-Tropsch Plants*: The raw material is coke that is gasified in water gas generators. It is then passed through a number of reaction vessels containing catalysts, which convert the gas into oil as a mixture of petrol and diesel. The petrol is of a low quality compared with the Bergius process and can only be used as a motor fuel. The diesel is of higher quality and the process also yields paraffin wax that is used to produce lubricating oil.

Germany had instituted trade agreements with the many occupied countries and the aggregate effect was that the inwards flow of goods and commodities began to exceed the German internal consumption.[27] Important new sources of raw materials had become available: nickel from Greece and Finland; chrome from the Balkan states; cobalt from Belgium and France; etc. There was then no shortage of coal, iron and steel. By no means least, the available manpower, from industrial workforces within occupied countries, alleviated the problem of German workmen being drafted into their own armed forces.

---

26. AHB II/70/143: Strategic Target System Dossier – Oil, STS/18 dated 9 Aug 44, by AI 3.
27. FO 837/441, Summary of Enemy Economic Developments No. 95, 14 July 1941.

Another ingredient of the aggregate industrial capability assessment by MEW was the quantity of German machine tools available to the industries. In 1941, MEW had estimated a quantity of 760,000; in fact, there were 1,840,000. Of the overall performance of German war industry, MEW confessed that 'only the most sketchy outline' could be discerned. The basic raw material for economic intelligence and analyses was then in general 'a variety of conflicting reports and statistics'.[28] No new source of economic intelligence information comparable with ENIGMA had been, or ever would be, uncovered; and the ENIGMA information did not start to show consistent dividends until 1942–43.

The politics of the German ball-bearing industry presented an outstanding example of incorrect assessment of the enemy war industry by the MEW. The persistent claim from the Whitehall committees was that 'the destruction of the ball-bearing industry would constitute a deadly blow to Germany's war economy'. There is a revealing letter that records the MEW organising the purchase of ball bearings from Sweden to a value of £1 million, to deny that quantity to Germany and to supplement stocks within the UK.[29] Much later, on 29 Nov 42, there was further pressure from Mr Lawrence within MEW for the Minister to write to the Secretary of State for Air suggesting that the time was then psychologically right for another round of the ball-bearing argument. That letter and others in the same context were classified MOST SECRET; and it was noted that Bomber Command had not been privy to the full MEW appreciation. *Who would have excluded Bomber Command and with what purpose?*

The USAAF bomber and crew losses during the daytime attacks on the Schweinfurt ball-bearing factories during the autumn of 1943 proved to be disastrous and contributed to the decision that the 8th USAAF suspend operations over Germany until they had adequate escort fighter protection. Harris responded to the DCAS Bottomley's letter of 17 Dec 43 with the view that he 'did not regard a night attack on Schweinfurt as a reasonable operation of war'.[30] The German reaction to the ball-bearing supply problem, under the admirable direction of Speer as Reichsminister for War Production, was to use their considerable engineering design skill to minimise the need for ball bearings in their various armament productions. The post-war bombing survey reports are very clear that ball-bearings never were a critical issue for Germany; stocks were high enough and imports remained sufficient until the design changes had reduced the need to levels that could be sustained. The Allied authorities and intelligence did not know at the time of the stocks of ball-bearings within the German industry and, with post-war hindsight, it can be seen that Bufton and the MEW were working on incorrect parameters. From examination of the records and personalities in the ball-bearing industry, the user industries and the testimony of war production officials, there is no evidence that the destruction of the ball-bearing industry would ever have had a critical effect on essential war production (USSBS Report). It is difficult to see other than that the MEW was wrong and that Harris was correct with regard to this 'panacea' target.

---

28. FO 837/441, Summary of Economic Developments, No. 119, 29 Dec 1941.
29. Air 40/1814, F/130/26 for the Secretary of State (Air) from MEW (undated, probably Mar 42).
30. Air 2/4477, Harris to Bottomley, dated 20 Dec 43, para. 2.

Bombing as an Instrument of Economic Warfare

'War is the continuation of politics by other means.'
Clausewitz – 'On War'

This section looks at the issues at the start and in first years of the war with regard to the determination of strategic bombing policy. The issues were:

- Who settled bombing policy?
- What were the limitations of night bombing?
- What were the policy developments in hand at that period?

In the late 1930s there was no clear perception of what was possible with the weapons of the time and with the weapons being developed. Admittedly, there was considerable difficulty in estimating capabilities with so little experience on which to draw. In 1938 the Joint Planning Committee conceded:[31]

> *In considering air attack we are faced with the difficulty that we lack the guidance of past experience in almost all the factors that affect it, and consequently the detailed methods of application and their effects are almost a matter for conjecture. We do not know the degree of intensity at which a German air offensive could be sustained in the face of heavy casualties. We do not know the extent to which the civilian population will stand up to continued heavy losses of life and property.*

Given that that was the case for air attack onto UK targets, it should be presumed that the same lack of knowledge obtained with regard to air attack onto German targets. It may also be presumed that there was substantial knowledge of how earlier Naval and Land battles had been fought and either won or lost; but it may perhaps be questioned whether that historical knowledge had direct relevance to the battles that would then be fought in WW2 with the weapons that were available.

By the end of 1940, experience of the results achieved by our bombing of Germany had led to a considerable revision of views as to the tactical possibilities and limitations of night bombing. It was revealed that navigation and identification difficulties prevented more than a small proportion of the sorties despatched from finding their primary targets; that the average aiming error in the face of increasing defences was greater than had been allowed for; and that the resistance of industrial plants to bombing was much greater than had been supposed. That led to the conclusion that:

- The destruction of specific industrial targets required a much greater weight of effort than had been supposed and could ony be hoped for on the rare occasions when exceptionally fine weather made the identification of small targets possible.

---

31. CAB 53/40, CAS 747 (JP), 15.7.38, CID, COS Sub Com., 'Appreciation of the Situation in the Event of War against Germany in April 1939,' p. 47.

- Under ordinary weather conditions the best that could be hoped for was the general blitzing of fairly large industrial areas, for which however the existing bomber force was probably not large enough. At any event it could not be employed effectively for this purpose, expect at close ranges, so that the maximum carrying capacity of the aircraft could be used.

That preceding paragraph is extracted from an MEW document dated 17 Jun 42.[32] The reader may wonder why that exceptionally sensible document had such little apparent impact on the higher levels staffs within Whitehall. It seems to identify very cogently many of the problems with target selection and night bombing.

Who Settled Bombing Policy

The Chiefs of Staff in conjunction with the War Cabinet determined the general objectives of strategic bombing policy. These determinations were revised from time to time in response to the shifting balance of the war and the assessed priorities of different threats. The changes were issued as Directives to Bomber Command and the 8th USAAF in the UK and to the 15th USAAF in the Mediterranean. The major determination of strategic bombing policy subsequently arose from the provisions and agreements of the Casablanca Conference in January 1943, followed by the subsequent issue in May 1943 of the POINTBLANK directive to Bomber Command and the 8th USAAF. Thereafter, the revised Bombing Directives reflected the political and military assessments of the emerging strategic and political objectives.

Those various Directives for the RAF and USAAF bomber forces were cognisant of the economic war against the German armaments production industry. They were issued by DCAS, but usually without any supporting rationale. The absence of that rationale was often a source of major argument. A particular problem was that the Directives often referred to Target Sets rather than specific targets. The Directives should have been lessons in clarity and precision; they were not. Neither were they Orders. All too often they were loosely worded and capable of several interpretations. This prompts the question, 'Who drafted the Directives?' What responsibility did the Director of Bombing Operations (DB (Ops)) have in this respect, acting as the staff advisor to CAS and DCAS on that very subject?

It is no justifiable defence to claim that the bomber forces were simply required to obey their orders, when those Directives left so much room for question and in many cases took no account of the prevailing operational conditions or the capabilities of the bomber forces.[33] Indeed, the Commanders of those bomber forces were properly entitled to take their operational decisions on target selection in the light of day-to-day operational factors. There was a far better dialogue and involvement when the bomber forces were subordinated to the Supreme Commander in the period March–September 1944 around the time of the Normandy invasion.

---

32. Air 40/1814, 'Bombing for Beginners', dated 27 Jul 42, p. 11.
33. See Ch. 4 with the discussion of the Issues concerning the Bombing Offensive.

But throughout the bombing offensives, the Commanders of the Bomber Forces retained the authority and the responsibility to overlay the Directives with their day-to-day operational judgements on the feasibility and effectiveness of the raids that they could deliver, in the light of the prevailing weather, the forces at their disposal and the enemy air defence threat along the planned route(s).

In comparison with the Army and the Navy operations, there were fundamental differences so far as strategic bombing was concerned. When Montgomery and Tedder undertook the battle against Rommel in the North African desert, the conflict was between military forces. When the Admiralty undertook the Battle of the Atlantic against the German U-boats, the conflict was between military forces, albeit that the Allied merchant shipping was the target of the German attacks and their objective was to strangle the UK economy. In neither case was Whitehall directly involved with the detailed conduct of those battles, other than in the provision of resources.[34] In neither case did those battles impact on the industrial war machine of the enemy. The German Army and Navy used the product of that industrial war machine; but the enemy industrial production capability was never the subject of the North African campaign or the Battle of the Atlantic. During the time in 1941–43 when the Admiralty and some Ministers were calling for the bombers to provide escorts for convoys, some of the operational facts get in the way. If a convoy was 4 hours flying time from, say, Cornwall, then how long would that bomber have over the convoy before it had to return to base for fuel. How many bombers would then be needed to provide continuous cover during the daylight hours for that one convoy. What about convoys outside of that radius. Doing the simple arithmetic, it is not difficult to see that much of Bomber Command would have spent a great deal of time in transit over water with little or no operational benefit.

The strategic bombing offensive was a completely new style of conflict. There had been sporadic bursts of aerial bombing against civilian targets even back into World War 1, but there was nothing that came even remotely close to the scale and impact of the Allied bombing offensive during WW2. This was Total War where the British and subsequently the American Air Forces were directly engaging the industrial war machine of the enemy as part of the Economic War. It may of course be argued that the Germans practised the same Total War with their blitz against UK targets; but with nothing like the weight and ultimate longevity, although that was not to be known in the early days of 1940–41.[35] The UK then stood alone against the Nazi military machine; Commonwealth assistance was heavily dependent on the merchant navies for transportation. The US was not then engaged.

The MEW expressed its views on the importance of economic targets and on the bombing policy that should be pursued at the Bomb Targets Information Committee and in continuous and informal contact with the Air Staff. There was

---

34. Author's Note: The point of this statement is that the Whitehall political machine was not involved with the conduct of those battles; but it is clearly recognised that the Naval Operations Centre during the Battle of the Atlantic was located in Whitehall.
35. Author's Note: My home city is Portsmouth, Hampshire. The records show that Portsmouth sustained 67 separate bombing raids between July 1940 and May 1944.

virtually no direct contact between the MEW and Bomber Command. In an MEW Paper there was a most interesting statement:[36]

> MEW loses touch with questions of bombing policy when they reach a level higher than the Director of Bombing Operations and that we are dependent upon him to resist in the higher levels any unsound tendencies to dilute, by-pass or emasculate policies which have been agreed between ourselves and the Air Staff as being unsound in the respects which are within our respective provinces.[37]

The distribution of that Paper is unknown; by association with related correspondence in the folder it is likely that it was addressed to the Secretary of State for Air Sir Archibald Sinclair, with a copy to Wg Cdr Morley in Bomber Operations 1.

Limitations of Night Bombing

The views expressed in this and the following sub-section on Current Developments are those represented by MEW in Feb 42.[38] This subject was at the core of the MEW policy and task. It is presented below in the current tense to emphasise the extraordinary value in that Paper.

> The sole merit of night bombing is that it enables large, slow and unescorted bombers to take the offensive in spite of fighter opposition and ground defences which would decimate them in daylight. It is obvious that the only targets that can be attacked effectively at night are areas, however great or small, and whatever they contain, into which it is possible to drop enough bombs to do effective damage. It is much less obvious what those targets may be. They vary from time to time in accordance with:
>
> - The season of the year, weather and moon conditions,
> - The aids to identification and their sufficiency to allow an economic proportion of bombs to impact within the target area,
> - The scale and form of attack to enable effective damage.
>
> These and other issues are operational problems to be answered by Bomber Command and the Air Staff, before they can form a view on whether or not a particular target is vulnerable to night bombing or not. Such targets may be too big to hurt, too small to hit, too hard to find, too well protected or too remote. But the better that MEW can understand the capabilities and limitations of the night bomber forces, then the less likely is it to waste time on examining impracticable projects or to exasperate the Air Staff and Bomber Command by proposing them. Whereas the limitations of other forms of warfare may be known, the limitations of night bombing are not known; the Air Staff may even not appreciate them.

---

36. Air 40/1814: 'Night Bombing as an Instrument of Economic Warfare', 4 Feb 42.
37. Author's Note: Bomber Operations was a Department in the Air Ministry; it was not at Bomber Command HQ.
38. Bib. A4, Vol. 4, Appendix 14: Memo from O L Lawrence to Lord Selborne, 4 Feb 42.

The results of night bombing against economic targets have not been negligible, though they have been patchy and less than the exaggerated hopes that have been placed on them. Night bombing has undoubtedly had a material effect on delaying submarine-building programmes, both in the building yards and (much more) by causing casualties and dislocation in the labour and organisation employed on the work. Night bombing has also had conspicuous success, under clear weather conditions, against certain relatively small towns. Other bombing attacks have not been negligible if judged by the standard of what should have been expected on the basis of operational data, rather than what had been expected from other positions.

Developments at that Time

The same excellent MEW Paper has the following content; sadly, the author of the paper cannot be determined but it is apparent that it was written for the Minister of Economic Warfare and may have been sent to the Secretary of State for Air. It has been impossible to identify any implementation of the proposals that were put forward. An extract from Section IV is as follows:

The MEW is making contributions where it is qualified to do so by collaborating on bomb-damage assessment and in the provision of technical advice from industrial contacts. The lessons to be learned from German bombing of this country are not being ignored. But over the last few months (last quarter of 1941 and January 1942) the attention of the Air Staff and Bomber Command has been practically monopolised by tactical and operational research with the view to improving methods and weapons and getting such improvements into service.[39] This has to some extent distracted attention from consideration of the objectives against which those improved methods and weapons are to be used. There is no doubt however that Air Intelligence and Bomber Operations recognise the importance of the economic targets and are alive to applying tactical and operational lessons in accordance with a coherent economic plan.

In the early part of 1941 an oil plan was prepared but not put into full effect owing to the rapid substitution of the Battle of the Atlantic directive. With the change in the strategic situation in June 1941, a new directive was issued based on the attack on transportation. It can now be seen that that directive suffered from the following problems:

- The precise objectives were too diffuse and were too difficult to satisfy with the operational resources available.
- The plan was too wide in scope and too lavish in alternatives, exacerbated by extensions that were grafted on afterwards by higher authorities.

---

39. Author's Note: At the time of the MEW Paper, Sir Arthur Harris had not arrived at Bomber Command and Sir Charles Portal had just assumed his responsibility as CAS.

The outcome was a lack of concentration of effort; partly caused by adverse weather, partly by strengthening enemy defences and partly by diversion to other objectives.

> *It is thought by some that Bomber Command tend to underestimate the importance of economic targets and the scale of attack needed to have an effect on them. The danger here is not so much that proper co-ordination will not be achieved between MEW, the Air Staff and Bomber Command in drawing up an effective and practicable plan for attacking economic objectives; but that such a plan will be rendered ineffective by subsequent amendments at a higher service or political level.*

The broad common sense of that MEW Paper was outstanding. The question that remains unanswered is: 'Why did it appear to remain buried for so long?' The proposal that MEW and Bomber Command should co-ordinate with the Air Staff was logical. But there is no evidence that Bomber Command ever saw this paper.

The records show co-ordination between MEW and the Air Staff, but not with Bomber Command.[40]

Did the Air Staff close ranks again and treat Bomber Command with the same arrogant attitude as was concurrently happening with Signals Intelligence?

And was that the same attitude as had been adopted towards Fighter Command and Sir Hugh Dowding during the Battle of Britain (see Appendix R).

The German Oil Industry and Supply

The significance of the German oil industry was to have major impact on the conduct of the Combined Bombing Offensive. Some background to the official estimates of oil production and supply may help to set the scene.

Pre-war assessments, not least by the IIC in 1936, had identified oil as a critical sector of the German economy. The Hankey Committee was set up in Oct 39 with the specific task of co-ordinating actions by different Government departments to deprive the enemy of his oil supplies. The Lloyd Committee was created at the same time, as a sub-committee to Hankey, to be responsible for assessments of the German oil position. It had based the early wartime estimates on pre-war data from the IIC and the SIS, including the secret storage capacity then thought to be available within Germany.[41] The Joint Planners within UK felt that, come June 1941, Germany's oil position would then have become so serious that she must

---

40. Author's Note: The co-ordination between the Air Staff and MEW can be widely seen, not least within the various Target committees and their working groups. Bomber Command was represented at some of those committee meetings, but that is quite different to being integrated into the working groups and contributing to the analyses of the basic material, the thinking processes and the subsequent recommendations to the committees, which could then often become *fait accompli*.

41. CAB 77/29, AO (46) 1 of 9 March 1946, quoting ICF/950 of 3 January 1938.

end the war, especially if oil supplies from Russia and Romania were denied use of the Danube for transport. There was an underlying belief within MEW that the whole German economy was 'taut' and subjected to authoritarian planning, with the assumption that the German industrial war machine was fully mobilised. This belief was later seen to be at serious variance with the facts. A summary of the Oil Factor as determined at the end of the war is provided at Appendix P.

As the war developed through the early phases and Germany's successes with territorial gains had expanded, the MEW estimates on the oil situation became more sober. The oil stocks were reinforced from acquisitions in occupied territories. In June 1940, the Hankey Committee refrained from forecasting when the balance between oil supply and demand would become critical to Germany and began to advocate air attack on the oil installations. Even more emphatically, the Lloyd Committee in June 1940 stressed the vulnerability of German oil installations to air attack and declared:

A more concentrated air attack on synthetic oil plants and a failure for any reason of the supply channels from Romania and Russia might cause a critical deterioration in their position.

NB. These Committee declarations failed to acknowledge or understand the basic operational limitations that constrained Bomber Command at that time: i.e. night navigation, target location and bomb aiming; and not least the weather and the German air defences.

Both the Hankey and Lloyd committees placed much weight at that time on a decisive attack at the earliest opportunity:

It is only by early action that we can obtain full value for our effort.

The force of the two committees' reports was that oil, as a single immediate weakness of the entire German economy, justified exceptional and concentrated assault. This was to play an important part in giving oil targets primary place in the British bombing directive of January 1941.[42] These oil committees had the ear of the Cabinet and therefore were able to exert considerable influence. This was to continue throughout the war and may well have contributed to the dominance of oil as a 'Whitehall target' for the duration of the bombing offensives. Those corridors of influence and power were dark and closed, certainly to Bomber Command.

At the same time, the MEW was reconsidering the estimates of German stocks of other basic raw materials and it was seen that their forecast rates of decline were not so rapid as had previously been suggested. During the summer of 1940 MEW had argued that these basic stock levels were limiting the expansion of German war production. But this also was revised considerably during the latter part of 1940. The acquisition of France and the Low Countries had augmented steel production by 50 per cent; French iron ores were under German control; Polish coal was added to German production and stocks of non-ferrous metals were seized from occupied territories. In September 1940, Romania had requested German help against other

---

42. Bib. 14, Vol. 1, pp. 158–162.

Balkan states and Russia. On 26 Sep 40, Whitehall received 'specific reports of the imminent arrival of German motorised units at Ploesti (a major oil producing area)' and more general reports 'of German personnel and material at other places in Romania'.[43] By October 1940, Germany had responded to those Romanian government requests and sent initial military missions to help Romania. This opened the door to Romanian oil resources. Curiously, at the end of September, Air Intelligence in London had 'doubted whether a German move into Romania was to be expected'.[44] This says something about the co-ordination of intelligence between the various departments. Indeed, there is evidence of a major intelligence failure at the strategic level at that time regarding the proper understanding of Hitler's intentions in South-east Europe, i.e. the failure to recognise that his moves into the Balkans and Greece were fundamentally defensive, to safeguard the availability of Romanian oil.[45] The MEW Intelligence Weekly recorded that the bulk of Romanian oil stocks, some 600,000 tons, had indeed been relocated during the period July–September 1941 as a safety precaution; and paid notable tribute to the tremendous feat of transportation so involved.[46] This can be seen to have strong correlation with the relative values of Oil and Transportation targets; oil was undoubtedly of great value to the military machine, but oil in the wrong place has no such value, as was seen during the Desert Campaign by General Rommel and subsequently during the Ardennes Offensive.

The critical factor concerning oil was in fact transportation to the places of use. In the MEW Weekly Intelligence Report No. 6, dated 19 Mar 42, there was reported evidence of a tacit admission by a German authority of a serious shortage of locomotives and wagons consequent upon the demands of the Russian Front. At that time, French locomotives were being overhauled at Mulhouse and sent to that Eastern Front. The overall transportation problem on that Front was exacerbated by the winter weather and the massive rail freight demands. The impact of the Russian war was indeed to become critical to the whole German war industry and economy.

The MEW estimates failed to move closer to reality because they continued to suffer from a more serious limitation. MEW did not understand the nature and peculiarities of the German economy as a system. Indeed, even at the start of 1942, it did not merely lack reliable information about the German economic policy; it did not even recognise that the study of these subjects was central to intelligence work on economic problems. It was content to regard the system through a veil of inherited or commonsense assumptions.[47] In particular, it still assumed that the German economy and the war industry capacity were under stress from a shortage of oil and raw materials.

In Apr 42, the Prime Minister approved the formation of a Technical Sub-Committee on Axis Oil. This became known as the Hartley Committee, which subsumed the work of the Hankey and Lloyd committees. It reported through

---

43. CAB 80/19, COS (40) 783: Resumé No. 56.
44. Air 40/2321, Minute of 29 September 1940.
45. Bib. 14, Vol. 1, Ch. 8; Strategic Intelligence during the winter of 1940/41, p. 260.
46. CAB 115/444; MEW Intelligence Weekly, Report No. 8, dated 11 Apr 42.
47. Bib. 14, Vol. 1, Ch. 7, Intelligence on the German Economy, p. 246.

the Joint Intelligence Sub-Committee to the COS. The final and most important oil committee was the Joint Oil Targets Committee, set up in Jul 44, and subsequently subsumed into the Combined Strategic Targets Committee.

In fact, the German war industry in the spring of 1942 was not centrally planned and the production was based on the premise of Blitzkrieg to be waged against individual enemies, rather than a prolonged war of attrition. That change in the German industrial philosophy and management did not occur until after Albert Speer was appointed Reichsminister for War Production in February 1942; the MEW appeared then to be faintly dismissive of his authority.[48] The German war production did not reach its highest capacity until the second quarter of 1944.

German Transportation Systems

An Analysis by the British Railway Research Service

There was a most constructive Paper produced in July 1940 that provided an assessment of the efficacy of air attack on German transport movements by rail and water.[49] Military staffs had never before faced that problem. The author, from the Railway Research Service, made the very prescient point that attacks on and damage assessment of the transport target set would demand new techniques in economic intelligence collection and appreciation,[50] for example:

- What action was being taken by the enemy authorities?
- Collection and interpretation of aerial reconnaissance.
- Intelligence reports from secret sources, agents and Sigint.
- Press and other news messages from enemy and neutral sources.
- Bomber aircrew reports and Raid analyses.

On the basis of bomber raids already then conducted, the Paper drew attention to some salient factors regarding certain key areas: Hamm, Osnabrück, Soest and Schwerte. These were the four rail entries and exits from the Ruhr and Wuppertal valleys to Eastern and Central Germany, as well as the North Sea ports. In short, these four junctions with their yards, locomotive running sheds, wagon repair sheds, coal dumps, etc, were the transport keys to the Ruhr and formed the bottlenecks to Germany's capacity to maintain the war effort for as long as the

---

48. CAB 115/444; The MEW Intelligence Weekly, Report No. 6, 19 Mar 42, p. 8.
49. Air 19/149; 'Air Interference with German Transport Facilities' by C E R Sherrington, from the Railway Research Section, dated 26 Jul 40. There was a supplementary Paper on the same subject issued on 9 Aug 40.
50. Air 19/149; MEW (Hugh Dalton) to SofS Air (Archibald Sinclair) dated 24 Jun 41: The Railway Research Service had been set up pre-war by the UK Railways Regions and was working for several Governments departments; half-funded by the MEW. The letter responded to a request from CinC Bomber Command (Sir Richard Peirse, at that time) for a Railways expert to be attached to Command HQ. The individual requested was Mr Brant. The CinC had been getting railway advice direct from the Railway Research Service; this had clearly ruffled some departmental feathers within the MEW!

Ruhr was the main industrial area.[51] A fifth important traffic artery was the Dortmund-Ems Canal.

There was no comparable geographical lay-out in Britain, France, Belgium or Italy; and its vulnerability was well recognised in German transport circles before the war. It was for that reason that Hamm was the first yard to be provided with well-equipped air raid shelters in 1937.

The Paper went on to describe that it was physically impossible to work a large railway marshalling yard under air attack in the hours of darkness, because adequate light was necessary for the continuous movement of locomotives and wagons. Congestion at a nodal yard would react rapidly on as many as 150 other railway centres up to 600 miles distant. The primary objective of any air attack must be to create congestion; that may have been even more effective than actual damage.

A large yard such as Hamm was seen as the centre of a clock with lines radiating out. The suggestion of cutting individual main lines was merely substituting a series of impossibly small and unilluminated targets for a large 'area target' that would need to be illuminated in order to function. In the case of Hamm, the yard is nearly 4 miles long and one half mile wide. When yards become congested, as happened at Ruhrort in the winter of 1939/40 because of adverse weather, 50,000 wagons were immobilised and normal working was not resumed for two weeks.

One consideration that was easily lost from sight within the Whitehall corridors was that effective bomb damage to a factory may well place that factory out of use for weeks or even months; but that was only one factory. Bomb damage to a nodal marshalling yard is quite different in nature; it affects the supply of raw materials and the distribution of finished products to and from multiple factories for 24 hours each day. Yard congestion is cumulative and it increases in a progressive fashion unless traffic flow is halted. Even if the bomb damage could be repaired within a few days. the effects would be widespread across all services using that yard.

The subsequent Supplementary Paper from the Railway Research Service expanded on the general principles and made particular note of the flexibility that was inherent in the overall German and European transportation systems. Whereas the option to use alternative means of transport may well have been available, it was always necessary to assess the implications. Reliance on road transportation for bulk freight would have been subject to motor vehicle capacity and fuel supplies, the latter usually dependent on bulk deliveries by rail; and this opened the directly associated problem of bulk fuel and oil movements from the refining and distribution plants. The main problem with overall transport flexibility was the presence of unavoidable bottlenecks quite apart from air attack and bomb damage. Certain sections of rail track had limitations on speed that reflected back to running traffic. Junctions with crossing track had inescapable flow limitations; as the traffic volume increased,

---

51. Author's Note: The analysis behind this Paper was exactly the sort of work that Morton and the IIC had been recommending in 1936, but was apparently never done until mid-1940. Ref. to p. 20 above.

the impact of any delay or blockage escalated. In the period just before the Paper was issued, there were examples of the widespread effect of congestion at those nodal points:

- All exports by rail from Denmark to Germany were reported to have been stopped for three weeks from 24 Jun 40.
- Butter, fruit, vegetables and potatoes from Holland had to be stopped because the German railway could not receive the trains.

In those summer months the rail traffic conditions should have been at their easiest, whereas into the autumn the traffic would increase significantly as raw material, especially coal, became the dominant freight. The Paper concluded that if air attacks on transport facilities were continued into the winter, then more valuable effects would have arisen with the shortening daylight hours and increasing rail traffic volume.[52]

Other Statements by MEW about German Transportation

In response to a request for information for Dominion Prime Ministers, a summary was prepared which covered the principle issues as seen at the end of 1940.[53] This summary reported on the German occupation and control of the Rumanian oilfields, but emphasised that the benefits could not be realised without the provision of a greatly increased number of oil tank wagons and Danube river barges, the latter being handicapped by the freezing of the river during the winter of 1940–41. Bombing attacks against targets that were then within range of the available aircraft had been achieving most successful results in dislocating the railway, seaports and inland waterway transportation services. That dislocation was evident from the restrictions that were placed on certain classes of goods in order to facilitate the passage of important freight. Even so, there was evidence of difficulties in the distribution of heavy goods such as coal and steel. The bombing of the German transport system had a formidable effect on the level of assistance that Germany could give to Italy.

Correspondence between MEW and the Secretary of State for Air during mid-41 addressed a request from Bomber Command via the Chief of Air Staff for Mr Brant, an official from the Railway Research Service, to be attached to Bomber Command to advise on transport targets. The position from MEW was that Mr Brant was part of a team working on the continental transport system; and that it was essential for economic intelligence and the study of air attack that transport should not be considered in isolation from other economic activities. The outcome

---

52. Author's Note: The Railway Research Service's Paper on vulnerability of the German transport system set out and explained a number of important factors; but the overriding factor was the impact of traffic congestion at the main marshalling yards. Such congestion had impact on all freight notwithstanding the allocation of priority status; priority freight may in fact be delayed less than other freight, but it would still be delayed. No evidence has been found to show how the conclusions of that Paper were used within the MEW, if in fact it was used at all.

53. Air 19/150; MEW OLL/MMJ dated 4 Dec 40.

was that Mr Brant was made available to Bomber Command on a part-time basis, by arrangement directly between the Air Staff and the Railway Research Service. The Minister of Economic Warfare, Mr Dalton, accepted that arrangement. The significance of this perhaps minor issue at that time was the importance subsequently attached to German transportation in general and the railways in particular, during the increasing intensity of bombing in preparation for D-Day in the spring of 1944, the Allied advances into Germany later in 1944 and through to the end of the war. Mr Brant was then a member of the CSTC Transportation sub-committee, created late in 1944, which provided significant advice and assessment of the enemy railway service during the period of intense argument and disagreement about the relative importance of transportation targets versus oil targets.

There are many instances where the importance of transportation was identified and emphasised by members of MEW through to and including the Minister in those early years of the war; and that recognition was clearly conveyed to the War Cabinet and the Air Staff. An example is the paper written in Jun 43 to assess the importance of the inland waterways in Western Germany.[54] This paper highlights the deliberate policy of the German government to divert as much commercial and industrial traffic as possible to the waterways in order to keep the railways free for military movements, where speed of movement was most important. The paper concluded that any bombing action to drive traffic back from the waterways on to the railways would present a serious conflict of alternatives. The key point was that unless rail transport could be provided for fuel and raw materials which had been loaded as a matter of policy on to the waterways, then the industrial undertakings must rapidly come to a standstill for lack of supplies. That pressure on rail traffic would then have unforeseeable consequences for military plans.

It is apparent from later years during WW2 that the earlier recognition of the value of transportation targets had become submerged under the weight of the powerful oil lobby within Whitehall.

Yet another – and perhaps most telling – paper from MEW addressed Air Attacks on Enemy Transportation Targets.[55] That paper examined the strategic importance of Transportation to the German war industry and war machine. In particular, it discussed the vital importance of locomotives and rolling stock. The huge distances that Germany needed to address at that time included, for example: the Ruhr to Rostov was 1,948 miles; an Army Division being transferred from Stalingrad to Rennes, i.e from the Eastern Front to the Western Front, had to move 2,688 miles. These distances were compared with ocean distances for the UK within the context of the Battle of the Atlantic. In addition, the destruction of one locomotive was related to an effective reduction in enemy war production, in terms of material not being delivered to the effective place of consumption, of 3,750 tons. In other words, the loss of locomotives was just as effective as the destruction of material or finished products. The vital argument within that MEW

---

54. Air 40/1815: 'Inland Waterways in Western Germany' dated 1 Jun 43, from MEW to Bomber Operations.
55. Air 40/1814: MEW Tn.1.c dated 1 Dec 42.

paper was that Transportation by rail and waterway had the same strategic importance to Germany as did merchant shipping to the UK. It will be seen later in this book that the same argument was valid in 1944/45, notwithstanding that the transit distances for German transportation had then reduced substantially but had increased in diversity as a consequence of the dispersal of vital industries in response to the strategic bombing offensive.

> There was no Champion for Transportation as there was for Oil, until the Deputy Supreme Commander took up the challenge in the spring of 1944 in preparation for the OVERLORD landings and the subsequent Allied advance through the occupied countries and into Germany.

Economic and Operational Bombing Priorities – 1942

Immediately after the Paper on 'Bombing as an Instrument of Economic Warfare', available in Air 40/1814, there was a flurry of correspondence between MEW and Bomber Operations in the Air Ministry. The most relevant exchange for the purpose of this book was the MEW concept for the conversion of economic priorities into operational priorities.[56] The bases for that conversion were as follows:

- The targets must be within a range that will ensure the maximum economy of effort.
- The outstanding tactical factor for 1942 would be the use of GEE, which was being seen by MEW as a potential 'war winner' if it should prove to be capable of supporting effective blind bombing in all weathers.[57]
- To avoid heavy casualties, large concentrations of bombers over heavily defended targets were to be avoided during moon-periods.[58]

With those principles in mind, the perception by MEW was that maximum results would be obtained by the following methods:

- During dark periods and regardless of weather, the conduct of blind bombing with the aid of GEE over large area targets.
- During moon periods, avoiding the use of bomber concentrations, the visual aiming of bombs against 'specific or semi-specific' targets.

---

56. Air 40/1814: 'Bombing Priorities–1942' dated 7 Feb 42, from MEW to Bomber Operations.
57. Author's Note: This was not to be. GEE was not able to support blind bombing with anything like enough accuracy except against large area targets: see the following section on 'Precision v. Area Bombing'.
58. Author's Note: This did not sit well with bombing tactics as they evolved. The operational benefits of concentration were powerful against the German night-fighter 'Himmelbett' GCI system and had an overwhelming effect on enemy air defences in general, air raid precautions and fire brigade resources.

For such a programme, two distinct types of target would be required:

- Large and continuously built-up areas which provide a basis for the use of GEE and a sufficient surrounding area of urban development to ensure that 'overs' and 'unders' would pay some dividend.
- Key industrial targets or highly specialised towns that were of such a size that they could be attacked by blind bombing on single raids. To accommodate the changes in weather, even during a single sortie, there should be a choice of targets to allow a 'precise' attack under optimum conditions and an alternative less-precise target for non-optimum conditions.

Thereafter, there were two appendices that provided 'Targets for Area Attack' and 'Specific and semi-specific targets, including alternative targets'. The details of those targets are contained within Appendix A of this book.

Soon afterwards a Loose Minute from Mr Lawrence within MEW sent to Colonel Vickers, another member of the Bomb Targets Information Committee, outlined a bombing policy that reflected the proposals in the earlier Paper, dated 4 Feb 42. Quite specifically, it also noted that the Leuna hydrogenation plant had been added to the target lists:

> at the personal request of the Secretary of State.[59]

It went on to say that certain diversions for politico-economic reasons were already contemplated; for example, the Defence Committee had already instructed that some attacks should be made on important industrial targets in Occupied France. Similar diversions should also be expected in the case of other Occupied Territories, but in each case it was believed that:

> The intrinsic economic value of the targets selected when combined with the indirect economic consequences on morale would fully justify such diversions from the economic warfare aspect.

In quick order afterwards there was continuing correspondence, this time sent to Air Intelligence 3c, on the Steel Production capacity of German Europe. That Loose Minute, while addressing the importance of the Ruhr from a steel production point of view, also drew attention to the even more important factors of coke and coking coal which would probably be damaged by attacks on the steel plants.[60] A separate Loose Minute dated 30 Mar 42, also sent to AI 3(c), addressed in detail the economic importance of Stuttgart and the satellite towns, with identification of the separate industries and factories. Attention was drawn to the concentration of important manufacturers for various armaments in the district, with the projection that any serious

---

59. Air 40/1814: Loose Minute (p. 3) from Lawrence to Vickers, dated 26 Feb 42 – 'Bombing Policy.'
60. Air 40/1814: Loose Minute from MEW/Objectives Department to AI 3(c) dated 12 Mar 43.

dislocation would have rapid and far-reaching results on the supply of military equipment for the Russian Front. At that same time, in Apr 42, there was a revealing agreement within a Cabinet Office paper prepared by Lord Cherwell which included the statement:[61]

The dehousing by bombing of the German working-class population with the object of lowering their morale and the will to fight became official British policy.

Later in 1942 there was a further flurry of correspondence within Whitehall following the decision by CinC Bomber Command to suspend pamphlet-dropping operations, on the grounds that this reduced the weight of bombs that could be carried. The Vice Chief of Air Staff (VCAS), Sir Wilfred Freeman, wrote to the CinC on 29 Sep 42 to explain that he was very anxious that this decision should not get to the War Cabinet.[62] He anticipated that the Foreign Secretary Mr Eden would sway the Cabinet 'with his persuasive tongue' and get a ruling that a definite number of bomber sorties would be allocated to pamphlet dropping. This was no more than another example of political diversions that had been anticipated within the MEW paper on the Bombing Policy.

Another matter that gained high visibility within Whitehall was the bold daylight bombing raid on Augsburg, flown at low-level by Lancasters. The Minister for Economic Warfare wrote to the Prime Minister about the planning of the raid, to complain that it had no relation to the Intelligence on which it should have been based.[63] Here is another example of Bomber Command not being provided with Intelligence that had a direct impact on planned operations. In his reply to a sharp question from the Prime Minister, the CAS defended the operation and observed that had the MEW been involved in the planning then there would have been a great deal of debate and delay which may well have compromised the paramount security and urgency of the operation.

It may be seen that there was growing divergence between the political, economic and operational aspects of the bombing offensive; most probably Bomber Command was never made aware of the MEW thinking on this issue.

---

61. *Echoes of War – The Story of H2S Radar* by Sir Bernard Lovell, Ch. 10, p. 105.
62. Harris Archives, H16, VCAS to CinC dated 29 Sep 42.
63. Harris Archives, H53, MEW to PM dated 27 Apr 42 'MOST SECRET'.

CHAPTER FOUR

Issues with the Bombing Offensives

'What hath Night to do with Sleep.'

John Milton, 1637

This section of the book raises issues that had major importance with regard to the bombing offensives. These issues recur many times throughout this book, but the intention here is to provide an initial picture that will show what these issues were and how they arose. They were:

- Relevant prior appointments held by Sir Arthur Harris,
- The Build-Up of the 8th USAAF in the UK,
- Strategic Target Selection,
- Precision versus Area Bombing.

Prior Appointments for Sir Arthur Harris

In 1936, as Deputy Director of Plans in the Air Ministry, Harris was working against what he argued was misguided political opinion. Several years earlier in 1932, the Prime Minister Mr. Baldwin had proclaimed that 'the bomber will always get through'.[1] That was before the advent of Radio Direction Finding (RDF). In 1936 Harris produced a document that proved to be remarkably prescient: France was ruled out as a strong ally and Germany was expected to seize Holland, Belgium and France. That paper developed the argument that area attacks on German cities were the only tangible way to reduce the German war industry; and that a bomber force with heavy aircraft designed to provide superiority in range and bomb load was essential. But the standards of equipment and training for navigation, target marking and bomb aiming were poor; Harris had realised this many years earlier when he was in Iraq in 1924.[2] Sadly, in the light of the government appeasement policy and general financial stringency at

---

1. Bib. A9, p. 8.
2. Bib. A8, p. 55.

that time, no progress was made. This may also have been a consequence of the low level of technical understanding by most of the upper echelon of the RAF in those days.[3] These views were later reinforced by Sir Edgar Ludlow-Hewitt in 1938, then CinC Bomber Command, when he told the CAS that he was unable to forecast when Bomber Command would be ready for war. He had then said, of Harris, that:

He has an exceptionally alert, creative and enterprising mind balanced by long practical experience together with energy and force of character to give his ideas practical shape and realisation.

The most significant point through those pre-war years and into the wartime years was the persistent talk of 'precision bombing' as if it was a realisable fact. The results of training exercises showed with absolute clarity that 'precision' was no part of the operational inventory, either with regard to bombing or to navigation. But that did not stop the Air Staff assumption that an average bombing error at night, from high altitude in moonlight conditions, would be the same as by day, namely 300 yards.[4] That was a surprising, critical and mistaken assumption. It was completely invalid, both by day and by night. It led to wholly erroneous expectations of the ability of Bomber Command to successfully attack small targets. Those false expectations gained wide acceptance within Whitehall and contributed to bombing policies that were operationally unrealisable, with consequent and unjustified criticism being aimed at Bomber Command. This is discussed in greater depth within the section on Precision v. Area Bombing later in this chapter.

During the early phases of the war, Sir Arthur Harris – to become the CinC of Bomber Command from February 1942 – held two appointments where the various failings of intelligence and the MEW estimates would have been very visible to him. From September 1939 to November 1940, he was Air Officer Commanding (AOC) No. 5 Group within Bomber Command; and, perhaps more importantly, from Nov 40 to May 41 he was Deputy Chief of Air Staff. To what extent did the memory of those early intelligence and estimation failures and their operational consequences, largely predicated on the inadequacies of the overall Intelligence 'system', remain with Sir Arthur Harris as the war developed? It was very clear that he held serious reservations about Intelligence and that might have been well justified at the time. The continuing problems with Intelligence and dissemination as the war evolved would have reinforced those reservations. We shall never know if that would have changed had he been indoctrinated – 'enwised' as it was known at the time – into the ULTRA material and subsequently given access to relevant high-grade intelligence during his three and a half years as CinC Bomber Command. That question must always remain unanswered and the consequences will always remain contentious.

---

3. Ibid.
4. Bib. A5, p. 35 (Noble Frankland).

> No CinC of Bomber Command in WW2 was given security clearance for ULTRA.

This remains a most curious situation. Sir Arthur Harris did however see some ULTRA material, directly from the hand of Sir Winston Churchill on a STRICTLY PERSONAL basis.[5] Sir Charles Portal also once provided him with ULTRA material during their long and contentious argument through the winter of 1944.[6] A senior commander such as Harris who had TOP SECRET clearance could reasonably have had occasional access to compartmented intelligence within the context of 'need to know'. That could have occurred for Harris from time to time when he met with the Supreme Commander and staff at the HQs in France after OVERLORD. But that is quite different from having routine access to and receipt of such compartmented material.

Sir Arthur Harris confirmed in a videotaped interview taken in 1982 that he had never been informed of the ENIGMA material.[7] There is a faint impression from some discussions during the research for this book that Sir Arthur Harris may have been regarded as a security risk. If in fact that was ever the case, then it would be reasonable to examine more closely the rather flawed security vetting procedures and the privileged methods of some appointments that had allowed the Cambridge Four to move so quickly into the highest security circles without impediment. There can be no doubt that Sir Arthur was a most loyal servant to the King and the country, notwithstanding that he ruffled feathers in many departments. By way of comparison, later in the war, the Commanding Generals of the USSTAF and the 8th USAAF were given access to ULTRA; but it was noted that General Spaatz advised General Eaker not to take that clearance because he would then not be permitted to fly on operations over Germany.

When Harris became CinC Bomber Command in February 1942 he inherited the policy of 'area bombing' that had been accepted by Churchill, the Air Staff and the former CinC Sir Charles Portal. There was nothing else available at that time, and that remained the case through to the end of the war against targets where there was no visual identification and in the face of the GAF air defence system.

Build-Up of the 8th USAAF in the UK

General Eaker took up his duties as Commanding General and initially established his headquarters at RAF Bomber Command HQ, High Wycombe, where the 8th USAAF was activated on 22nd February 1942. His HQs subsequently relocated in the immediate area to Wycombe Abbey School for Girls and became known as

---

5. The Harris Archives, H65 dated 30 Sep 44: Harris to Churchill regarding an ULTRA report.
6. The Harris Archives, H84 dated 8 Jan 45: Portal to Harris, p. 5. The ULTRA items in the dossier are not recorded. It is important to note that in his reply to Portal, Harris recorded that he had not seen those items before – see H84, ATH/DO/4 dated 18 Jan 45; they were returned to Portal under the cover of that same letter.
7. Bib. A6, AFHS Journal No. 31, 2004, p. 126.

Pinetree, close enough to allow the two Commanders to share daily conferences. In January 1944, the US Strategic Air Force (USSTAF), Europe, was formed at Bushey Park and incorporated both the 8th and the 15th AAFs. General Spaatz was appointed Commanding General of the Strategic Air Force and General Doolittle took command of the 8th.

Airfield construction was carried out on a massive scale. Initially 75 airfields, mostly pre-war purpose-built RAF bases, were reallocated to the 8th. Eventually, the 8th used 250 airfields. Even in the summer of 1943, the continuing build-up was suffering from accommodation problems within the UK. Not only was there very serious congestion at airfields within south and south west England, it was also necessary to disperse Units to Scotland and Northern Ireland and that impacted on operational readiness.[8]

The highest level planning for the build-up of the 8th in the UK was declared in a statement from General Stratemeyer to Air Vice Marshal Foster in Washington, dated 5 Feb 43, for the CAS in London. The details included the following numbers:

	30 Jun 43		31 Dec 43		30 Jun 44	
	Groups	U.E.	Groups	U.E.	Groups	U.E.
Heavy Bombers	18	1080	37	2220	45	2700
Fighters	7	700	15	1500	25	2500
Totals*		2716		5532		9088

* Within the Total numbers, all aircraft types are included: Heavy, Medium and Light Bombers; Dive bombers; Fighters; Observation and Troop Carriers. (U.E. = Unit Establishment).

The delivery of bomber aircraft for the 8th had begun in June 1942, with the arrival of four B-17 E/F groups and two B-24D Liberator groups. However, the build-up of the 8th had been handicapped by the more pressing need during mid-1942 to equip the 12th AAF to support Operation TORCH, the invasion of North Africa in November 1942. The first B-17 bombing raid from a UK airfield by the 8th AAF was on 17 Aug 42 against a target in France. The bombing offensive against U-boat bases and construction yards then secured high priority and remained the primary main focus of the 8th until Jun 43. Many of these earlier raids were flown at altitudes between 20,000 and 25,000ft and were relatively easy targets for flak and fighters. During this period there was growing concern within the 8th about the morale of the bomber crews, due to 'the failure to build them up to what they knew to be the requisite proportions if they are to continue to exist and do a worthwhile job'.[9] They knew that they were going down as a result of combat losses that were not being made good.

---

8. Air 8/1053, ACAS(P)/407/2 dated 25 Jun 43.
9. Ibid., Gen Eaker to Gen Andrews, dated 27 Feb 43.

There were many other problems that impacted on the build-up of the 8th. By no means least was the shortage of shipping capacity across the Atlantic for all the associated groundcrews and the multitude of bomber components and spares. A message dated 4 Mar 43 identified that there was some progress on that problem; it was forecast that in April/May/June 43 there was expected to be a movement of 51,000 AAF air and groundcrew personnel to the UK.

In Apr 43 there was a message from the RAF Delegation in Washington to advise that the US had made immediate diversions of Groups scheduled for the 8th AAF.[10] The diversions had been made on a Presidential Directive to the War Department; the 380th Heavy Liberator B.24 Group together with Mitchell B.25 medium bombers and Thunderbolt P.47 fighters had been reassigned to the south-west Pacific (Australia), in response to a request from General MacArthur.

In May 43, after a series of successful attacks into Germany by Bomber Command and the 'magnificent US bombing of Kiel', the CinC Bomber Command had earnestly requested CAS to urge the USAAF to enter into the offensive against Germany in force.[11] In that cipher telegram there was the statement:

If the US had one thousand Forts and B.24s here now or shortly [...] that sorely needed help would do so much to ease the single-handed battle that Bomber Command has fought to date over Germany.

In Oct 43 the 9th USAAF was relocated from the Mediterranean to UK to become the basis for the Tactical Air Force in preparation for the D-Day landings. The 9th Air Division, formerly the IX Bomber Command, joined the 8th USAAF.

In December 1943 there was continuing concern in London about the availability of heavy bombers from the US to adequately support the POINTBLANK directive and to prepare for OVERLORD.[12] The accommodation problems had then been overcome and airfields were ready. The root of the problem was the competing political and military pressure from other theatres, particularly from the Mediterranean for the 15th AAF and the Pacific. There was at that time the thought in London that there was a shortage of airfields in the Mediterranean theatre that were suitable for operating the heavy bombers against German targets within the scope of POINTBLANK, as distinct from targets in Italy. The impact was that the forecast operational strength of the 8th had been reduced from 1968 heavy bombers to only 1400.

The US had suggested a possible compensation by establishing two crews per aircraft to increase the utilisation of the aircraft. But that would never have compensated for bomber losses and battle damage on operations; the RAF had questioned whether there was even a need for two pilots per crew? The RAF had previously reduced their bomber crew complement to one pilot with great savings in training resources and no loss of operational efficiency.[13] The US Air

---

10. Ibid., TROON 114 31 Mar 43 MOST SECRET CYPHER to CAS.
11. Ibid., Harris to CAS, MOST SECRET CYPHER A.136 dated 15 May 43.
12. Air 8/1053, WEBBER W 1538 24 Dec 43, IMMEDIATE MOST SECRET to RAFDEL Washington for General Arnold.
13. Ibid., p. 2, para. 6.

Staff in Washington had replied by saying that their belief was that the primary German targets were fighter aircraft production facilities and those targets could be attacked from Italy; that airfields were ready and suitable; and that General Spaatz would have the authority, when he assumed the appointment of Commanding General of the USSTAF in Jan 44, to relocate Bomb Groups as he saw fit.[14]

At peak strength, the 8th USAAF eventually had more than 200,000 officers and men; 40 heavy bomb groups, 15 fighter groups and 2 photo reconnaissance groups. At peak operating periods, a typical mission would have 1400 heavy bombers, escorted by 800 fighters.

Strategic Target Selection

'Quot homines, tot sententiae' – So many men; so many opinions.

The dogmatism of the pre-war Air Staff had hindered the development of a broadly based concept of air power in Great Britain. At the outbreak of war, Britain possessed a bomber force that was incapable of surviving daylight operations in the face of German opposition and could not find its targets at night. The British Official History of the Strategic Bombing Offensive – Bib. A4 – put that part of the overall context of the air war succinctly:

Air superiority is not simply a question of being able to use an air force. It is a question of being able to use it effectively. From the point of view of the bombers, for example, it is not simply a question of getting through. It is a question of getting through and doing effective damage.[15]

This is not to argue that strategic bombing did not play a major role in the eventual Allied victory in WW2. Its success, however, was very different from that envisaged by its pre-war advocates.

A persistent and unresolved question throughout the strategic bombing offensive, even from 1940 but increasingly strident from 1944, was whether Oil or Transportation represented the most effective collective target set. There were of course other major target sets that justifiably gained first priority from time to time, notably the U-boat bases and their industrial support facilities during various periods in the Battle of the Atlantic; at other times, the GAF fighter production industries; armour and artillery, etc. From time to time various so-called 'panacea' targets were advocated, purporting to offer a quick solution but never delivering their promise. In Chapter 10 there is an overview of the results of the bombing offensives as seen by the post-war bombings surveys; in Chapter 11 there is discussion of the changing political attitudes; and a concluding examination of the issues that surrounded the selection of strategic targets.

There is perhaps one German statement on this subject that has high significance. It was made very soon after the night raids on Hamburg on 24/25

---

14. Air 8/1053, MARCUS 1965 dated 31 Dec 43, MOST SECRET from RAFDEL to CAS.
15. Bib. A4, Vol. 1, 'Preparation', p. 21.

and 27/28 Jul 43 and the complementary daytime raids by the 8th USAAF on 25 and 26 Jul 43. The aggregate effect of those raids, which were 'area bombing with high concentration', was seen by some very senior German officials and officers to be:[16]

> so catastrophic that a further 5 or 6 such raids would cripple the will to sustain armament manufacture and war production.

Hamburg was in a sense the nearest that 'area bombing' came to a final solution. But it should be noted that the bombing accuracy was very far from 'precision'; the second raid, on 27/27 Jul 43, was marked by the Pathfinder Force using H2S without any visual checks and the marking had an average error of 2 miles from the prescribed aiming point. The subsequent bombing was exceptionally well concentrated and did enormous damage.[17] History was to show that the Allies were neither operationally equipped nor politically prepared to maintain that scale of attack and that German war production recovered magnificently.

This section discusses the issues related to:

- POINTBLANK and OVERLORD,
- The Final Phase,
- Oil or Transportation.

POINTBLANK and OVERLORD

The policy and agreement between the UK and US at Casablanca in January 1943 was that command of the combined bombing offensive, in preparation for OVERLORD, would be assigned to the Supreme Commander in order to secure the most favourable situation for the landings in Normandy. That assignment of the bombing campaign, particularly the attacks on transportation in France, Belgium and West Germany, was seen in many influential quarters in Whitehall and Washington as a wasteful diversion from strategic attacks on Germany. This arose in no small part through the maze of staffs and committees that were directly and indirectly concerned with the formulation of the bombing policy, plans and strategic target selection.

The most important internal conflict within Whitehall during the last quarter of 1943 concerned the US/UK planning for OVERLORD and the associated use and control of the heavy bomber forces. Those bombers were the sole means of attacking the German homeland, within the context of the Casablanca agreement and Operation POINTBLANK. It was obvious that the planned assignment to directly support OVERLORD would have adverse consequences for the operations against strategic targets in Germany. The preliminary view of the Combined Chiefs of Staff was that this 'preparatory period for OVERLORD' would be a short phase, perhaps only two weeks of heavy tactical bombing with the main fight for air supremacy taking place over the beaches. It is of course now well known that this 'preparatory period' became three months, with three key objectives:

---

16. Bib. A4, App. 37, p. 378.
17. Bib. A9, Ch.17, p. 192.

- The subjugation of the GAF tactical fighter and fighter-bomber forces.
- The denial of effective use of the railway systems within northern France, Belgium, Holland and western Germany.
- Softening the fortifications that Germany had built along the Channel coast.

The immediate purpose of these attacks was to dislocate the enemy lines of transport, in order to prevent reinforcements and resupply of German forces engaging the beachheads and the early Allied penetrations into northern France. Harris and Spaatz, the commanders of the strategic bomber forces, disputed that. They felt that the strategic attacks into Germany represented the best means of supporting the Allied landings. It became a prolonged debate on the overall bombing policies. The view that railways were 'economical and responsive' targets had primarily arisen from the successful offensive against the Italian railways during 1943; and this had been presented at a meeting on 2 Feb 44 as being ' based on the result of much operational experience and is concurred by the Air Staff'.[18] That was concurred with at the time by the railway authorities of the Ministry of War Transport; however, there was a most significant footnote to this situation.[19]

But there was a very different position adopted by the Enemy Objectives Unit (EOU) within the US Office of Strategic Services, set up to provide targeting information for the 8th USAAF. The EOU held that 'damage to railway transport could under most circumstances be absorbed in the general enemy economic system without producing effects on the fighting qualities of the enemy.' In general, the EOU was not prepared to support anything but the most specialised target systems. It has been separately recorded that the EOU had a high opinion of itself and its egotism made it a bitter opponent of those who disagreed with its ideas.[20] With respect to attacks on transport, where the immediate impact was most important, the EOU held that anything less than 100 per cent was practically useless. This EOU belief was later to become a dominant feature of the arguments between the SHAEF, the Target Committees and the staffs of the strategic bomber forces. An example of the depth and longevity of feeling within the EOU may be seen from the statement at the end of Dec 44: 'It is the EOU's opinion that the rail program is ill conceived, not supported by intelligence and only remotely relevant to the requirements of the Army groups in the West.'[21]

---

18. Air 10/3855, Ch. 4, p. 15.
19. Ibid., Ch. 4, p. 15, Footnote 1: Both during this period and afterwards, many of the technical and economic experts whose advice was sought on various occasions were expressing themselves differently on the same problems. This had the effect of lowering confidence in the value of 'expert advice.' The Railway Research Service, connected with the MEW, had at that time taken the view that the tactical plan to cut railway routes leading to the planned assault areas in Normandy was adequate. Later, they advocated an alternative policy of using heavy and widespread bombing of railway centres (CAS's meeting, 25 March 1944).
20. Bib. A20, Ch. 5, p. 100; and 'The Collapse of the German War Economy' by A C Mierzejewski.
21. Air 20/4819: CSTC Transportation Targets – EOU/EWB, American Embassy, 22 Dec 44 – A Dissenting Opiion, para. 2.

In the continuing build-up to D-Day, alternative proposals for the use of the strategic bomber forces were tabled in March 1944 by the USSTAF, for the 8th USAAF in the UK and the 15th USAAF in the Mediterranean. These proposals had prior support from the Intelligence Directorate and the Bomber Operations branch within the Air Ministry in London. The enemy target systems then advocated were:

- The GAF, then believed to have been seriously damaged by attacks on the aircraft factories.
- The synthetic oil industry.
- Tank and MT factories, munitions, synthetic rubber, etc.

Railways were dismissed as being unsuitable for strategic air attack. It was argued that over two thirds of the aggregate railway freight was coal, coke, construction materials, iron ore and iron & steel products; and that any reduction in this freight would have no immediate impact on the fighting troops. But no orders were issued to implement those proposals and it fell to the CAS Air Chief Marshal Portal in Whitehall to resolve the increasingly acrimonious issues. CAS expressed the clash of views as follows:[22]

> On the one hand there is a school of thought which says that a bomb on Germany is worth x times as many anywhere else. At the other end of the scale, there are those who think that every bomb we can drop should be aimed at Transportation to hinder the German build-up.

The responsibility was heavy. CAS encouraged these different views to be openly debated until 25 March, when he convened a meeting of all the Army and Air commanders and the Intelligence staffs. It was readily agreed that the GAF was the over-riding priority target. Neither the Intelligence staffs nor the MEW experts suggested that the Oil Plan would yield immediate results in the field. It was agreed that oil represented a profitable target system but not as profitable as the railways from the point of view of the forthcoming OVERLORD operation. The meeting concluded that there was no suitable alternative to the Railway Plan.

That decision was immediately transmitted to the Combined Chiefs of Staff who, on 27 March 44, directed that control of all air forces – not just the bomber forces – should pass to the Supreme Commander General Eisenhower from where it was delegated to his Deputy Supreme Commander, Air Chief Marshal Tedder.[23] Tedder's position had been declared as follows:

> The Transportation Plan is the only plan offering a reasonable prospect of disorganising enemy movement and supply in the time available, and of preparing the ground for imposing the tactical delays which can be vital once battle is joined. It is also consistent with POINTBLANK.
>
> Since attacks on Railway centres have repercussions far beyond the immediate targets, attacks on such centres within the Reich will certainly assist in creating the

---

22. Air 10/3866, Ch. 4, p. 16.
23. Bib. B28, Ch. 2, The Combined Bombing Offensive, p. 9.

general dislocation required for OVERLORD. Moreover, since the Railway system is the one common denominator of the whole enemy war effort, it may well be that systematic attack on it will prove to be the final straw.

This resonates well with the earlier MEW view, expressed on page 80.

> It was to prove to be a singularly prophetic pronouncement.

The Supreme Headquarters was not the only body that saw transport as a most vulnerable asset. General Rommel, one of the senior German generals in charge of the defence of France, argued that the German Army must defeat any invasion attempt on the beaches before the Allies could consolidate a holding on land. He held the view that Allied air superiority would deny German ground movements and resupply, by striking at the transportation networks.

SHAEF's first Directive on 17 Apr 44 to the strategic bomber forces stated that the targets were:

- The GAF, particularly the fighter forces and their industrial support; this was fully supported by General Spaatz who felt passionately about Allied air superiority as a prerequisite for the invasion, but he would have wanted oil as the other priority.
- The railways, to destroy and disrupt those transportation services particularly affecting the enemy's movement towards the OVERLORD lodgement area.

The next round of argument on this agreed plan was from the Defence Committee of the UK War Cabinet. The plan was challenged on two grounds: that it would not seriously affect the enemy's mobility; and that it would result in major civilian casualties in France and Belgium.[24] The (UK) Defence Committee therefore reserved the right to veto attacks on any individual targets. Churchill was not prepared to see a situation where French opinion became hostile; and he was not prepared to disclose the OVERLORD plan to General de Gaulle. An initial estimation of casualties that was put before the Defence Committee came from DB (Ops) (Air Cdre Bufton); see p. 94. This was seen to be misleading and the estimate was revised, but the cat was then out of the bag. General Eisenhower acknowledged the political concern about civilian casualties but he was not prepared to compromise the military plan.[25] Eisenhower did think of resignation

---

24. Air 20/5307: see Minutes of War Cabinet Defence Committee Meetings dated 13 and 26 Apr 44.

25. Author's Note: Churchill clearly held the view that the future Allied strategy would be either to mount an invasion in Normandy, or the US would withdraw to concentrate on the battle in the Pacific. The latter option was obviously a major worry for Churchill because the weight of the European war would then have remained solely with the UK and the Commonwealth. The threat of a German invasion of UK was still present, especially if the US was to reduce its commitment in Europe. In the

but that was not related to the bombing strategy or to the Transportation Plan; it was related to the political interference by Whitehall in connection with possible French casualties arising from bombing French railway targets.[26] Ultimately, this matter was decided between the two Heads of Government; President Roosevelt declared that he was not prepared to intervene in military decisions in Europe from his office on the East coast of the US and Churchill accepted that position.

We see here the various levels of Whitehall 'committee management' of the strategic bombing offensive. DB (Ops) and MEW supported the alternative Oil Plan and held that the Transportation Plan had little or nothing to recommend it. That Whitehall opposition was regrettably characteristic, not least from DB (Ops) (Bufton) who tended to reject bombing policy plans other than those prepared by Bomber Operations. The records seem to show that this was a problem with almost all of the players; they all thought their own plan was best and dismissed others. There was a strong vein of self-interest present in the Allied hierarchy. Churchill himself had condemned the RAF Air Staff for their 'jealousies and cliquism' earlier in the war. In that context, the appointment as CinC Bomber Command was a sought-after prize: the analogy of Caesar and the Senate may be drawn to Sir Arthur Harris and the Air Staff – and within the Ides of March (1944?).

Bufton was a very persistent opponent and it may be asked whether his primary task really left him the time to be so controversial? His initial estimates of French casualties arising from the attack on transportation were extravagant and caused much controversy within the UK War Cabinet. AVM Kingston-McCloughry, Head of Air Planning with the AEAF, placed much responsibility for that error on Bufton. Even after the Commanders Meeting on 25 Mar 44, chaired by Portal, Bufton continued to believe that he knew better than Portal, Eisenhower and Tedder. He presented yet another alternative plan from Bomber Operations, submitted on 10 Apr 44, which he argued would have prevented the earlier acceptance of the Transportation Plan. He then produced a further modified version of that plan on 2 May 44, which was strongly attacked by Tedder at a meeting on 3 May. This was less than five weeks before the actual Normandy invasion. Bufton may have been better employed to develop the strategy that had been agreed by the Commanders, rather than continually diverting their attention with counter-arguments. History was to show that the Transportation Plan achieved major benefits for the Allied landings and the subsequent penetration across France and into Belgium.

With Eisenhower in ultimate charge of the strategic bomber operations through the pre- and post-invasion period, in accordance with the principles of the Casablanca Conference, Bufton had little influence. But he persisted with his

---

event of such an invasion of UK, it is difficult to see how the US would have responded when they had no bases to operate from. The US itself had no risk of invasion by Axis Forces.

26. The Harris Archives, H16: MOST SECRET: VCAS to CinC Bomber Command dated 12 Jan 43. The War Cabinet had previously endorsed area-bombing attacks on the French Atlantic coast against the U-boat bases, notwithstanding the casualties. It is interesting how political expediency changes.

arguments within the Air Ministry. He prepared a paper that was put before DCAS on 20 Jul 44.[27] He argued that the Air Staff was unable to ensure that bombing priorities that had been determined by the Air Staff were being followed by SHAEF. He went further to suggest that Bomber Command was confused and uncertain as to who was actually in control. The CinC, Harris, had no such confusion. At the request of CAS, Bufton provided another paper for CAS to place before the Chiefs of Staff, recommending that the control of the strategic bombers should revert to CAS. He argued that Eisenhower was primarily concerned with the land battle. He also recommended that General Spaatz, as the Commanding General of the US Strategic Air Forces Europe, should become Deputy Chief of Air Staff (US). That was all well above the role of an Air Cdre in the Air Ministry, even as the Director of Bomber Operations. That paper was first considered on 23 Aug 44.[28] Unsurprisingly, Portal and the Air Staff were unanimous in their support for the control of Bomber Command reverting to the Air Staff; but had the Air Staff actually shown any previous real authority over Bomber Command? The jury is still out on that charge.

The paper was held over for the forthcoming Combined Chiefs of Staff Conference in Quebec, in Sep 44. The Casablanca Conference, in Jan 43, had originally determined that control of the strategic bombers would revert to the Air Staffs when the Allied invasion into France was secure. By Sep 44, that had been achieved quite regardless of Bufton's arguments. Bufton was not easily set back. In a formal comment on a JIC Intelligence Report in Jan 45 he argued that the Supreme Headquarters was 'exceeding their powers' when requesting over-riding priority for air attacks aimed at delaying German movements on the Eastern Front.[29] He went on to declare that:

They (the Supreme Headquarters) cannot be properly considered to be in a position to decide whether it is more important to the war as a whole to delay those (German) movements to the Eastern Front rather than press home attacks on oil. The Supreme Commander should now be empowered to demand over-riding priority for emergency needs of the land battle only.

Within four days of that Minute to ACAS (Ops), Bufton had received the TOP SECRET ULTRA report from AI 3(e) that specifically recommended that very action (see Chapter 7, p. 232). What arrogance from Director of Bomber Operations in the Air Ministry to presume greater appreciation and knowledge of the war as a whole than a Four-Star Field Commander in the Supreme Headquarters and the Joint Intelligence Sub-Committee within Whitehall.

So what did those Bufton papers really accomplish, other than to raise the visibility of their author and distract the senior commanders with controversial arguments. There is an illuminating and patronising post-war comment from Bufton, stating that the staff of Bomber Operations:

27. Bib. A26: P271, Footnote 140 – from the Bufton papers, 3/51, dated 20 Jul 44.
28. Bib. A26: P271, Footnote 145 – from the Bufton papers, 3/51, dated 23 Aug 44.
29. Air 20/3218: Minute from DB Ops to ACAS (Ops) dated 25 Jan 45, commenting on JIC (45) 31 (0).

*had agreed among themselves that we would have forgiven CinC Bomber Command
everything had he put an extra 15 per cent of Bomber Command effort on precise
targets.*[30]

Against that should be set the beliefs and perceptions of Sir Arthur Harris when
he said in one of the series of letters to and from the CAS (Portal) during late 1944
and into 1945:

*My main difficulty over Bufton is that he ignores what is the major and essential
part of his job while spending his time trying to run my Command, but without the
responsibility. He makes no serious attempt to consult or agree with me or my staff
and is therefore a great handicap.*[31]

However, from the enemy point of view, an appreciation in mid-May 1944 by the
German CinC West, Field Marshal von Rundstedt, warned that the Allies were
aiming at the systematic destruction of the railway system and that the attacks had
already hampered supply and troop movements. A German report on 3 Jun 44,
dealing with the attacks on the railways, declared that:

*The systematic destruction that has been carried out since March of the entire
(Railway) network – not only of the main lines – has most seriously crippled the
whole transport system.*

During this same phase of the war, the threat to UK from the German long-range
V-1 and V-2 weapons was increasing and became regarded by the British
government as a serious menace. By the end of 1943, Intelligence had clarified the
Allied understanding of the V-1 programme and was forming a view on the
emerging V-2 programme. Bomber effort against the associated launch sites,
many of which were in northern France, came primarily from the Tactical Air
Forces with limited support from Bomber Command and the 8th USAAF. The
overall effort was known as CROSSBOW. This was a modest diversion for the
strategic air forces, with specific attacks on massive concrete installations in the
Pas-de-Calais and against the development site at Peenemünde. The great value
of those attacks should never be underestimated, but they were modest within
the overall scale of strategic bombing effort. They certainly reduced the danger
to London and may also have had significant benefit for the D-Day invasion.

Meanwhile, the 15th USAAF was attacking targets from the Mediterranean
bases. The target sets for the 15th included as first priority the support of the
Armies engaged in the Battle for Italy; then targets within the POINTBLANK

---

30. Author's Note: Air Cdre Bufton was Director Bomber Operations during 1942–45.
 This statement was in a letter dated 7 Sep 72, within the Bufton Archives at Churchill
 College, Cambridge. It creates an impression that Bomber Operations had a
 patronising attitude towards the CinC; but the responsibility was to advise and
 recommend, not to make command decisions. It was always for the CinC to take the
 most difficult decisions; that was and remains the challenge of command.
31. The Harris Archives, H 84, Harris to Portal, ATH/DO/4 dated 24 Jan 45.

Directives; and, to a minor extent, 'political targets' in the south-east of Europe related to the Balkan and Bulgarian situations. In direct support of the OVERLORD preparations, the 15th was also directed to targets such as the aircraft factories around Vienna and the railway centres in the south east of France and southern Germany. At the start of May 44, the decision was taken to attack the railway centre at Ploesti; the attack was by a large number of heavy bombers to increase the survivability of the bombing force against the expected strength of the German fighter defences. The weight of attack was deliberately extended to other adjacent 'tactical targets', which included the oil refining installations. That fortuitous attack on the oil at Ploesti became very important, which the Chiefs of Staff Mediterranean (COSMeD) recognised in their next routine directive COSMeD 117, issued on 30 May 44. That directive placed oil as the second priority target set for the 15th USAAF; and the later COSMeD 124 issued on 6 Jun 44 moved oil to first priority. The 15th USAAF subsequently played a very significant part of the overall execution of the attack on oil as the war moved into the final stages.

The subsequent total bombing effort of Bomber Command and the 8th USAAF in the three months preceding D-Day was 187,000 tons, distributed between the following target sets:[32]

Target Set	Tonnage
GAF	31,913
Transportation targets	62,888
Long-Range Weapon Installations	11,081
Coastal towns	11,788
Towns	52,121
Oil	3,834
Other targets	12,904

Harris had not been convinced that the bombers could hit the smaller targets, but the railway marshalling yards were not small and the transportation attacks achieved far better results than he had been prepared to offer. It is important to recognise why that was:

- There was favourable weather,
- Targets were often well within range of the *Oboe* system and therefore target marking by PFF was often better than was the case over Germany,
- Targets had not been previously attacked and generally had only light air defence resources,
- It was possible to obtain good photographic images for damage assessment soon after the attacks, better and quicker than was usually the case from German targets,

---

32. Air 10/3866; British Bombing Survey Report, Ch. 11.

- There was also a high political demand to minimise civilian casualties and the bomber crews were ordered to abort their attack if there was poor target identification.

It should not be overlooked that the Tactical Air Forces played a great part in these overall attacks, with particular impact on bridges, open lines, moving trains and small stations.

Intelligence information indicated that the pre D-Day attacks on railway targets had been extremely effective. After D-Day and until the early part of August, when the heavy bomber attacks on railways in western Germany and the occupied countries diminished, the targets were selected on a day-to-day basis in the light of intelligence on enemy movements.

During that period of six months or more, the proportion of Bomber Command's effort that was applied to strategic targets in Germany fell to only 30 per cent. The CinC frequently emphasised this aspect of the targeting policy and he held firm to the belief that the primary task of Bomber Command was to deliver strategic attack onto German military, economic and industrial targets. Those targets may well have required precision attack – but Harris knew and understood that this was not possible with the bombing capability at his disposal. What became possible in France in good weather and at short range, during the spring of 1944 before the D-Day invasions, did not carry into Germany in bad weather and at longer range in the face of a determined enemy air defence capability. That was the key fact that was not appreciated by so many of the Whitehall and Air Staff critics of the bombing offensive – and many of the post-war historians. It is also debatable whether or not the MEW was correct in its strategic target selection. Harris was not the only commander who doubted the accuracy of some of those selections by the MEW and later by the CSTC.

The Final Phase
On 16 Sep 44 the Combined Chiefs of Staff transferred control of the strategic bomber forces back to the joint command of the RAF Chief of Air Staff in London and the Commanding General of the USAAF in Washington, General Arnold. Executive responsibility was delegated to the Deputy CAS Air Marshal Bottomley and to the Commanding General of the USSTAF, General Spaatz. In effect, what then happened was that control of the strategic bombing offensive changed from the unified command of the Supreme Commander to the fragmented command structure that had existed before the preparations for D-Day. General Arnold doubted whether this structure could 'obtain the maximum use' of the strategic bomber forces; and he could not understand why no attention had been given to maintaining the priority attack on the enemy transportation system. Portal's reply to Arnold demonstrated a complete lack of appreciation of the strategic implications of transport, which had become abundantly clear on the evidence of the French campaign.[33]

Two further changes to the air situation on the Western Front also took place. The enemy lost much of his previously very good air raid early-warning system

---

33. Bib. A5, p. 144.

as he retreated back towards Germany. This became significant as the intensity of the strategic bombing against targets in Germany increased from Aug 44 and onwards. Coincident with this retreat, the Allies were able to provide ground stations for navigation and bomb aiming systems that were much closer to the targets in Germany than had been possible from within UK. This had a direct benefit to navigation and bomb aiming accuracy.

The three air commanders who had primary responsibility for the strategic bombing offensive, namely Bottomley, Spaatz and Tedder, agreed on the wording of a new Bombing Directive that was very much a compromise. It was issued on 25 Sept 44, with the following target priorities:

- First priority – Oil.
- Second priority – Transportation; Tank and Ordnance depots; MT plants and depots.

Very soon afterwards, the CTSC was formed to study specific target sets and to recommend priorities – but not to make policy! Noble Frankland gave a post-war impression of the CSTC, as follows:

> An international committee which is not executive can at best produce a compromise and at worst can degenerate into a propaganda platform. Most of the members were convinced advocates of the Oil Plan. The committee was jealous of protocol. When the Transport Plan threatened to extend into the strategic sphere, it was seen by the CSTC as a threat to the Oil Plan and the Deputy Supreme Commander Tedder was seen to be exceeding his authority.[34]

The forces of contention were too powerful to produce an incisive and concentrated bombing policy. The conviction that oil was a war-winning target was too strong to ignore. The intelligence about oil had high visibility because a separate Cabinet Committee had previously handled it. The counter-claim that transportation was an essential target to support the armies and to cripple the German war economy could not be rejected. The debates within the CSTC bear witness to the deadlock. The Directive was creating a situation that Tedder described as a 'patchwork quilt'.[35]

This was quickly followed by DCAS with the release of the executive order for Operations HURRICANE I and HURRICANE II.[36] The objective of those operations was to mount a concentrated attack on vital areas within the Ruhr; this was consistent with the intentions of the Supreme Commander and was also intended to demonstrate overwhelming Allied air power to the German leaders and the people. HURRICANE I was conducted from 14 Oct 44; HURRICANE II was heavily dependent on visual bombing conditions, primarily for the 8th USAAF, and was in fact cancelled in Feb 45.

---

34. Bib. A5, p. 146 and Footnote (4) – AHB IIG/86/6, CSTC Minutes.
35. D/SAC/H20, Part III, Encl. 71A. memo by Tedder on 'Air Policy to be adopted with the view to Rapid Defeat of Germany', dated 25 Oct 44.
36. Air Ministry CMS/608/DCAS dated 13 Oct 44; to Bomber Command, SHAEF and USSTAF.

The enemy oil production for Sep 44 was estimated at only 25 per cent of the usual monthly quantity. The enemy's oil position was made even worse when the Russians over-ran major refineries on the eastern Front. The Intelligence view at that time was very optimistic and DB (Ops) in the Air Ministry had put forward a paper in which he said that:

The strategic air forces now have an opportunity, within a few weeks, of bringing the war to an end through the attack on enemy oil supplies alone.

The key element of the strategic bombing offensive in the Final Phase was the continuous disagreement between Whitehall and the Supreme Headquarters at Versailles as to whether oil or transportation targets should have higher priority:

- The CSTC issued their appreciation on 13 Oct 44, which ruled out 'the feasibility of an overall attack on enemy transportation', either against strategic targets within Germany or tactical targets in close proximity to the land battle. The CSTC advocated that the Tactical Air Forces should attack the German railway system; with specific support from Bomber Command to use the very large Tallboy and Grand Slam bombs against particular targets. Notwithstanding the Bombing Directive issued by DCAS on 25 Sep 44 from Whitehall, there had been no specific transportation targets selected by the CSTC for attack.
- On 21 Oct 44, the Combined Chiefs of Staff called for a complete re-examination of the targeting policy. The CSTC maintained the Whitehall view and replied to the effect that nothing should be done to lower the priority of oil targets.

The Deputy Supreme Commander, in his paper dated 25 Oct 44, said that the various types of air operations should fit into a single comprehensive pattern and not something of a 'patchwork quilt'. He was firmly convinced that the 'common denominator' to the whole German war effort was the rail, road and waterway transportation systems. That conviction was predicated on his battle experiences in North Africa, around the Mediterranean and during OVERLORD. He had the view that the distinction between strategic and tactical bombing targets had become purely academic; a target set such as transportation could embrace both strategic and tactical objectives. Transportation was the only target that could not be dispersed or put underground; indeed, the dispersal of the German war industry made transportation even more critical. That was probably the most significant contribution to the endless arguments about bombing policy. Accepting that the oil plan was a key to the enemy road transport and air operations, he argued that the attack on railways was a necessary complementary part of the bombing offensive. He ended his paper with the statement:

That the execution of a co-ordinated campaign against transportation systems in western Germany would rapidly produce a state of chaos which would vitally affect not only the immediate battle in the west but also the entire German war effort.

Harris maintained his view that bombing policy was not just a matter of strategy, but it also had to reflect tactical factors such as the weather and the enemy opposition. He had always understood that the heavy bombers had to attack what they could, which was by no means the same as what they should. This had significant distinction between Bomber Command operations and those of the 8th USAAF. By late 1944, the USAAFs had massive long-range escort fighter cover for their operations into Germany. In contrast, Bomber Command relied on the RCM and Intruder operations of 100 (Bomber Support) Group.

Immediately afterwards, on 26 Oct 44, there was a crucial meeting at the Supreme Headquarters. The purpose was to determine future strategic bombing policy and targeting. The outcome was that transportation targets were restored to second priority, above tank and ordnance depots, MT plants and depots. The key areas for railway attacks were designated as the Ruhr and the Frankfurt-Mannheim zones. Subsequently, the British Chiefs of Staff in conjunction with their US colleagues in Washington went further and deleted ordnance and armoured vehicle depots; but added that when the weather was too bad for precision attacks, the strategic bombing should attack industrial areas relating either to Oil or to Transportation installations.

Notwithstanding the authority of that decision, it continued to be challenged particularly by the CSTC in Whitehall and the EOU of the US Department of Economic Warfare, who felt that any attack on Transportation directly constituted a reduction of attack on oil. It is specifically noted that the CSTC was unanimous in believing that attacks on oil would prove the best means of expediting the defeat of the enemy 'within the next few weeks'; the CSTC had no real concern with enemy transportation as a principal target set.

However, Tedder's definition of a 'common denominator' did have impact. The CSTC Working Committee (Transportation) was formed soon afterwards within Whitehall. It should also be recorded that membership of that committee included representatives from all the main players – but not from Bomber Command! The first report was a comprehensive plan for the attack on the German Transportation System.[37] That report contained some very sound material:

- In view of the weather probabilities, the greater part of the attack would have to be under non-visual conditions and target selection must reflect that situation.
- Optimum interdiction effect would be achieved by heavy damage to marshalling yards and other nodal junctions, but that this effect had to be sustained by continuous pressure and kept under careful review.
- That much of the attack on transportation within the Ruhr would be associated with the attack on oil plants; and that aiming points and direction of bombing runs must reflect that aspect of joint attacks.
- That the German inland waterway system in the west was a major carrier of raw materials that were vital to the enemy war effort.

In that period, Tedder issued a decisive TOP SECRET advisory Note to all Army Group and Tactical Air Commanders.[38] The Note set down the policy underlying

---

37. Air 20/4819: CSTC Working Committee (Transportation) Report dated 7 Nov 44 (Top Secret).
38. Air 20/3218, DSC/TS 100 dated 23 Nov 44, distributed to all Army and Air Force Commanders, for Action.

the strategic bombing operations, in order that no opportunity would be lost in co-ordinating the actions of the Strategic and Tactical Air Forces. The dominant factor was that the attacks on oil and on transportation were of equal stature and represented the most effective methods of contributing to the Land Campaign and achieving the final defeat of Germany. The Note clearly identified that the co-ordinated attacks on rail and water transport had played a major part in the success of the Land Campaign hitherto; and that far-reaching results would be achieved by similar operations against transport within Germany. A 3-page Appendix identified the important railway and water transport targets; they were to be complementary to the attacks on oil. They were calculated to disrupt the whole system of enemy transport, to delay and disorganise the supply and reinforcement of the enemy armies, to disorganise his war production and generally weaken the central control of the whole German war machine.

The weather did indeed take a hand and during September/October/November it was very poor and the opportunities for visual precision bombing of the oil and transportation targets were very few. In fact, two of the largest oil installations – at Leuna and Poelitz – were particularly difficult for day and night raids from UK airfields because of the required depth of penetration into hostile airspace. At the start of December, 47 enemy oil production installations and depots were again operational. There was a strong fear in some planning circles in Whitehall that oil had been subordinated to transportation targets.[39] DB (Ops) (Bufton) had criticised a SHAEF Enemy Transportation Weekly Summary (No. 16) that had been written by Major Ezra, a transportation expert on the G-2 staff at SHAEF. Bufton declared that it had been written against a 'rather limited background' and that the inferences drawn from the *facts* 'are by no means agreed by our own Intelligence or by MEW'.[40] That Minute further declared that the newly created CSTC Transportation Sub-committee would 'bring the SHAEF Weekly Summary into line'. The CSTC had no room for dissenting voices. This became crystal clear in an immediately post-war review of operations by the Transportation Sub-committee.[41]

---

39. Air 20/4819: 'The Attack on German Transport – A Dissenting Opinion' by the US EOU/EWD, dated 22 Dec 44. An example of the depth and longevity of feeling within the EOU may be seen from the statement: 'It is the EOU's opinion that the rail program is ill conceived, not supported by intelligence and only remotely relevant to the requirements of the Army groups in the West.'

40. Air 20/4819, TOP SECRET Minute 30554 from DB Ops to DCAS and ACAS (Ops) dated 14 Dec 44.

41. Air 20/3377: 'Review of Operations of the Working Committee (Transportation), Oct 44–May 45', 14 Jun 45. It should be noted that this final Review of Operations omitted direct or indirect reference to certain TOP SECRET sources of information – see Air 20/4819, Loose Minute Z/611 dated 15 Jun 45 from Mr Wood, EAB4 at the Foreign Office, to Air Cdre Bufton. Mr Wood was Chairman of the Transportation Sub-Committee of the CSTC. Those sources may well have been the ULTRA material about enemy transportation that had been set aside by the CSTC. Subsequent Minutes within Air 20/4819 provide excellent illumination of the deep and bitter controversy that surrounded transportation target selection. The Minute dated 21 Jun 45 from BOps1 to DB (Ops) commented on the differences of opinion about certain

But in Dec 44, the situation was dramatically brought to a head by the German counter-offensive in the Ardennes from 17 Dec 44. The Allied military response was to direct a large part of the strategic bomber effort to attacks on railways and nodal points in the transportation network that served the enemy offensive.

After the Ardennes offensive had concluded in the Allies favour, there were further specific operations against transportation targets. The first was Operation CLARION, conducted on 22 Feb 45, which was dedicated one-day all-out attack by the strategic bomber forces against railway targets throughout Germany.[42] Immediately after CLARION, there was a call from the Supreme HQ for a similar operation against the Ruhr. The JIC in London had issued a report that favoured an all-out attack on rail and canal transportation to deny coal distribution.[43] Not only had coal production in the Ruhr fallen by 50 per cent, from 18 million tons in mid-44 to 9 million tons in Feb 45, but the Germans had also lost the coalfields in Upper Silesia to the Russians. The railway system had only three weeks stock on hand. The JIC had estimated that further severe disruption to coal distribution would cause the German war effort to collapse within 'a few weeks.' DB (Ops) in the Air Ministry took the view that this would not amount to a clash 'between our strategic requirements and those in support of our armies in the west.' Starting from early March 1945, the task of crippling the railway system in the Ruhr was undertaken as a priority. The task included the destruction of main railway centres in the Ruhr zone and the cutting of main lines leading north, east and south. The plan was prepared by the CSTC Communications (Transportation) Working Party.

Throughout this final phase of the war from Oct 44 through to the ceasefire in May 45, and even from Jan 45 when oil production had fallen most seriously, the CSTC maintained its unrelenting pressure for attacks to be made against oil targets whenever there was the opportunity for visual bomb aiming. In operational terms, such conditions were indistinguishable from those required for precision attacks on railway targets. The British and US Chiefs of Staff had previously stated at the end of Oct 44 that when such conditions did not obtain, that area attacks against industries related to oil and transportation were to be undertaken. In fact, the records show that from early Mar 45 the majority of the strategic bombing effort was used against transportation targets. This coincidentally gave rise to yet further argument within Whitehall, when the Director of Transportation (Maj-Gen McMullen) wrote to Air Cdre Bufton to object to, 'the undesirability of unnecessarily damaging railway facilities [...]

---

aspects of the Review and that much of the bitterness and general ill-feeling at the time had been left out. There was a specific comment 'that sleeping dogs should now be allowed to lie'. Much of that argument applied as much to the main CSTC and not just the Working Committee; there was specific reference to the opinions of the US EOU – the reader may see Footnote 118 on p. 46. A separate Minute in reply from DB (Ops) dated 22 Jun 45 acknowledged those omissions, but said that he did want another round of argument; and regarded the Review as an acceptable history of the attack on transportation.

42. Air 10/3866; The BBSU Final Report, Part 6 'The Final Phase', p. 26.
43. JIC Report dated 1 March 1944: 'The Effects of Interrupting the Export of Hard Coal from the Ruhr to the rest of the Reich.'

which we shortly require to use'.[44] The CSTC had many voices. But it must be recognised that in those final weeks of the war in Europe, notwithstanding the gravity of the Allied concern about the German National Redoubt, there were very legitimate reasons to look forward to the post-hostility situation and the need for transportation in all forms.

After Sep 44, the strategic bomber attack on oil, railways and cities within Germany aggregated to 73 per cent of the total effort of the heavy bombers until the end of the war. The balance of 27 per cent was used in many various ways:

- There was continuing tactical support to the armies, bombing field targets in the immediate land battle area, not least during the Ardennes Offensive.
- An important target set that was attacked at the turn of the year 1944/45 was the U-boat base support and production facilities; this became so important as the submarine threat intensified, with new style U-boats. Early in Feb 45, U-boats became fifth on the list of target priorities. The best estimates that could be made on the loss in production of Type XXI and XXIII boats from Sep 44 onwards was about 80, or some 45 per cent of the total number produced in that period.[45]
- Attacks were mounted as necessary against GAF aircraft factories, particularly those associated with the Me 262 twin-engine jet fighter and also against aircraft parked on airfields.

Finally, from April, the primary task of the bomber forces was to assist the army in the latter stages of the occupation of Germany.

Oil or Transportation

The persistent question – oil or transportation? – will recur throughout this book. There were powerful committees in Whitehall that studied the German oil industry and the military requirements. The primary pre-war committee was the IIC; then there were the Hankey and Lloyd committees. In 1942 the Hartley Technical Sub-committee on Axis Oil was formed, replacing both the Hankey and Lloyd committees. The Joint Oil Targets Committee was created in Jul 44, which in turn was subsumed into the Combined Strategic Targets Committee from Oct 44 onwards. The point here is that oil had strong champions within the Whitehall 'committee culture' from pre-war days and throughout the conflict.

At the end of Oct 44, the CSTC estimated that German oil production had risen in October to 30 per cent of the pre-attack level, compared with 25 per cent in September. The committee had then drawn the following conclusions:

- Heavy bombers were not effective in attacks on small oil storage facilities.
- Benzol plants were very difficult to hit because they were small and hidden in urban areas.
- The USAAF blind bombing was not as accurate as had been hoped.
- The Allies had much to learn about the size and type of bomb to produce the required result.

---

44. Air 20/4819: BM/Tn.1.c/CSTC dated 12 Apr 45.
45. JIC Report dated 1 March 1945: Ch. 27, p. 158 (Check date of Report).

But in the final analyses of the post-war bombing surveys by the UK and the US teams (see Chapter 10) a common theme was that oil was not the most critical element from the German military point of view. The more critical element that affected the entire military and war production supply chains was the progressive shortage of transportation. However, this was not supported by the CSTC. There is a most illuminating Minute within the file BC/S.24990/1 that reports on the CSTC meeting just before 22 Nov 44.[46] The CSTC committee had then decided that no specific transportation targets would be allotted for the Ruhr, but instead there would be area attacks against principal centres of population with the aiming points arranged to cover rail facilities. For that reason, the CSTC assigned the following descending order of target priorities:

- Specific oil plants,
- Area attacks on Ruhr towns where damage was incomplete,
- Special transportation targets such as viaducts and canal embankments,
- Attacks against marshalling yards with routes leading to and from the Ruhr.

It was curious that the CSTC should have assigned a higher priority to area attacks on towns than to transportation targets at that stage in the war. This continued to be the case even through to the beginning of Mar 45, when railway marshalling yards in the Upper Rhine and Kassel areas were given no priority, but included under the list of 'Alternate Weather and Filler Targets'.[47] If the CSTC distaste for transportation targets was in anyway whatsoever part of a 'turf war' in Whitehall, it should be noted that the SHAEF Main HQ produced an Army Intelligence Review of the strategic bombing priorities as at 19 Feb 45.[48] Paragraph 1 of that Review, under the heading 'Enemy Transportation Situation' stated that:

Present evidence clearly indicates that the enemy's overall transportation situation is rapidly worsening as a result of bombing, loss of Silesian hard coal and the dislocation caused by the economic readjustment necessary as a result of the loss of the Silesian industry; the biggest single blow at German economy since the war began. It has already been pointed out that the enemy has now become almost entirely dependent on the Ruhr for such things as coal and steel; and in consequence the RUHR transportation services have assumed vital importance to the enemy.

Most recent intelligence has further emphasised the seriousness of the enemy's coal situation throughout Germany and has disclosed difficulty in maintaining present output from the Ruhr owing to attacks on rail and water outlets, and difficulty in distributing and using these most economically. The shortage is having an immediate effect on the enemy's transport potential itself.

---

46. Air 14/1206 'Intelligence on Directive Targets – General', Minute 34 dated 22 Nov 44 from Int.1 to the CIO at Bomber Command.
47. Ibid., Minute No. 41 dated 4 Mar 45 from Gp Capt. Plans to CinC Bomber Command. There is a handwritten footnote to that Minute by Sir Arthur Harris. It reads: 'I note that denial of all aviation fuel to the enemy was celebrated by him with the first large scale air attacks over here for years!'.
48. Air 14/1206, Encl 87A: Top Secret Summary by the Assistant Chief of Staff (G-2) dated 19 Feb 45.

There seems to be little doubt therefore that the entire enemy industrial output is in grave jeopardy as a result of increasing inability within the transportation system, especially those services leading to the Ruhr. It seems therefore all the more urgent that as much effort as possible should be directed against the Ruhr transportation services.

Some of the relevant ULTRA high-grade Sigint information is shown within Appendix K. The CSTC did not seem to want to hear that evidence. But a CSTC Target Priority signal early in Apr 45 reported that transportation attacks had 'denied the enemy use of synthetic fuel from plants in the Ruhr'.[49] No mention was made of the other principal elements of the war industry.

This leads to the actual evidence upon which the CSTC based its recommendations on relative priorities between various target sets from Oct 44 onwards. There is no doubt that the high-grade ULTRA material was a most powerful input to the aggregate intelligence appreciations on oil. But there was compelling evidence also from ULTRA that the real problem was often not the lack of oil but the inability to deliver stocks to the operational users.[50] That inability did not stop with oil. Ammunition, guns, rations for the troops and fresh troops to relieve battle-weary units were all subject to transportation problems. This had been a critical issue for the Afrika Korps during and after Alamein, where the real problem was the length of the supply line across the desert and the failure of the Italians to secure shipping between Italy and North Africa.[51] This same issue also arose during:

- The German assault on Russia, then closely coupled with the bitter winter weather,
- The Allied advances into German-occupied territories after D-Day, when the French railway system had been extensively disabled,
- The Ardennes Offensive when the enemy's tactical transportation was so shattered as to leave isolated 'islands' of supplies that could not be moved to the operational battle units,
- And finally, when the 'Isolation of the Ruhr' was completed in Mar 45.

The intelligence was correct, albeit incomplete, but the economic appreciations were wrong.

---

49. Air Ministry Signal MSW.467 issued on 4 Apr 45, para. 5d.
50. Air 14/1220, Minute to DDI 3 dated 31 Jul 42 which specifically refers to 'a general undercurrent of MSS evidence of fuel supply difficulties [...] chiefly to aviation fuel and gas oil requirements of the GAF. The flexibility of the Axis oil industry is such that there is no possible question of its being unable to meet the GAF's needs in any product.'
51. Bib. B35, HW 11/4: North Africa 1941–43, which has comprehensive data on these Supply and Transport problems.

But was that all that was wrong? There is evidence to show that MEW had disregarded ULTRA evidence that established the existence of coal shortages, lack of electric power and substantial falls in industrial output; indeed that the whole German industrial system had started to break down by Sep 44 as a result of paralysis of the railway and the inability to move raw materials and products into and between factories and users. This will be examined later in Chapter 7, pp. 230–233, from the point of view of the Bomber Command archives; and in Chapter 10, from the points of view within the post-war bombing survey reports, pp. 298–302 and p. 315.

Precision versus Area Bombing

The ongoing arguments and debates about 'precision' versus 'area' bombing invariably fail to make any definition of what these terms really meant or what was really possible. They are often used in an ethical context to imply that 'precision' was good and 'area' was bad; and therefore that Bomber Command was 'bad' because it usually delivered 'area bombing' unlike the USAAF which consistently claimed to deliver 'precision bombing'. Such a distinction is intellectually and operationally invalid without a careful and informed definition of these terms and an equally careful and informed appreciation of the actual operational capabilities of the Allied bomber forces in Europe during WW2.

The initial wartime experiences showed with great clarity that, in order to avoid extinction, Bomber Command would have to operate at night; with aircrews that were largely untrained; and with aircraft that were both unsuitable and ill equipped. The navigational failures that were revealed early in the war were a direct consequence of many years of neglect, by a largely pilot-dominated air force. This point is covered in more detail under 'Air Navigation' later in this chapter. Some thought may have been given to bombing at night but very little as to how the bomber could be navigated to the target area and nothing as to how the target would be located and identified; see the passage on the earlier concerns of Sir Arthur Harris in 1936, on page 84. The sad truth of this became officially inescapable after the Butt Report was released on 18 Aug 41. One of the devastating conclusions was that on average only one bomber within three got within five miles of the target; and, in poor conditions, that could fall to one in fifteen. There is no doubt that the earlier impressions that circulated and gained substance within Whitehall about the effectiveness of night bombing would have sowed the seeds of hope; and may well have reaped the bitterness of disappointment when the facts became apparent. There was great reluctance among some to accept information that conflicted with long-held beliefs and probably wishful thinking.

> It is noted that the Trenchard doctrine of strategic bombing was unsupported by navigation and bombing aids. The Germans, however, did not rely on strategic bombing but they did have the Radio Beam bombing aids.

There is evidence that at least a few members of the Air Ministry were aware of the uncomfortable truth about the absence of accuracy in bombing at quite early stages in the war. A letter from Wg Cdr Dewdney in AI 3c (Air Liaison) to Wg Cdr Scott in AI 3c has some very pertinent details.[52] Dewdney had visited the Bristol Aircraft Factory after it sustained heavy bomb damage; the purpose was to assess and agree with the senior staff the extent of damage and the vulnerability. Within that letter are the following details about bomb impact point accuracy:

> *With a 600 yards aiming error and accurate identification of the works, it would be necessary to drop 100 tons of bombs to 'write off' a single workshop. If aircraft can only be sure of getting within 2,000 yards of the target and are unable to see it, the figure goes up to something like 800 tons. Obviously in the latter case, there would be a considerable amount of collateral damage to other workshops.*
>
> *The recent indiscriminate bombing of Bristol was directed towards the centre of the town, some four miles away from the aircraft factory. There was serious consequential impact upon aircraft production:*
>
> - *Five dispersal sites were hit with damage to material stores.*
> - *Many of the workers homes were damaged and (workers) were absent from the factory.*
> - *Many of the workers could not get to work due to the absence of transport.*
> - *All contractors' staff that were doing building work within the factory were withdrawn to repair residential property damage within the town.*

These separate points will be seen to have relevance to later sections of this book.

Within this vexed subject of 'precision' and 'area bombing' there is also the need to appreciate the different operational tactics of Bomber Command and the USAAFs. The RAF bombers were lightly armed and flew at night, usually at medium altitude and without fighter escort. They did not fly in formation other than within a bomber 'stream' and an important element of the tactics was to avoid contact with enemy fighters.[53] On the other hand, the USAAF bombers were heavily armed and operated in daylight at medium/high altitude. It was not feasible to avoid contact with enemy day fighters. The objective in these daylight raids was to fly in close defensive formations and to accept air-to-air combat. The initial USAAF bomber losses were heavy and they became unaffordable, leading to the suspension of deep penetration raids over Germany until the introduction of the long-range US escort fighters.

There is good reason to believe that within the Air Staff in the period 1941–1943 there were many senior officers who genuinely believed that Bomber Command could deliver 'precision' bombing against selected elements of the German war

---

52. Air 14/1652: AI 3c (Air Liaison) letter dated 16 Jan 42.
53. Author's Note: To that effect, the increasing and eventually massive use of Radio Countermeasures (RCM) from Oct 42 onwards was to minimise detection by the German Air Defence system and their night fighters. The success of that strategy is undeniable, even in the face of the huge increase in effectiveness of the German Air Defence system. Without that RCM support, night bombing operations would have become unaffordable.

industry – specific factories, ball bearing works, oil plants, electric power generating stations, etc – and thereby expedite the end of the war. The resources that were becoming available to Bomber Command by the end of 1943 were indeed far better both in terms of aircraft, navigation aids and the weight of bomb load, but they did not provide the means of 'precision bombing' except under favourable visual conditions.

No. 100 (Bomber Support) Group had then just been formed to provide specialist RCM support for the bomber raids. But it must be recorded that in parallel with these improvements, there were matching improvements in the capability of the enemy air defence system. The average operational loss rate of Bomber Command through the first six months of 1944 exceeded 6 per cent per bombing raid. The Commander of the German Night Fighter Forces in that period, Generalleutnant Schmid, recorded that:

The task of forming a picture of the emerging air situation during a bomber raid using supporting RCM was one of the most exciting and difficult functions of command.

Those senior RAF officers who advocated 'precision' bombing should have known that Bomber Command could not deliver such an operational capability. Whether that advocacy was a defence mechanism against criticisms from the Government and the other armed forces, or whether it was a widely held but mistaken view, it represented a fundamental failure of professional knowledge.[54] It may indeed be argued that any criticism or liability flowing from the bombing policy should rest ultimately with Government and the Chiefs of Staff for failing to provide the bomber forces with the operational capability to discharge their politically and militarily approved missions. This argument would appear to have continued resonance in the 21st century.

At the root of the issue is the imperative to clearly define what 'precision' and 'area' really meant at that time. There were many inter-related factors, the more important of which are as follows:

- Air Navigation accuracy.
- Bombsights and Target Location.
- The Pathfinder Force (PFF).
- The required Damage Effects.
- Circular Error Probable (CEP).

These factors are discussed below, followed by a comparison with the USAAF experiences and results, leading to a definition and conclusion.

---

54. Bib. A8, p. 126: The Butt Report that was prepared through the autumn of 1941 had clearly identified the ineffectiveness of bombing at that time and also identified potential improvements. The findings concluded that only one in three bombers got within five miles of the intended target. In the Ruhr, where targets were more difficult to find, the proportion was one in ten. Whereas the detailed figures may not have been entirely accurate, they demonstrated the 'supreme importance of improving navigational methods.'

Air Navigation

The first and perhaps most important element in the WW2 bombing accuracy equation was accurate knowledge of where the bomber really was in relation to the target or the aiming point. Another and perhaps just as important element was the imperative to maintain track and time keeping throughout the whole mission, in order to achieve concentration of the bomber force en-route and over the target. Any straggler was more likely be acquired by the enemy air defence system and shot down. This became increasingly important after the raids as the bombing force returned to airfields in the UK.

The evolution of the aircrew category of the 'Navigator' was a lengthy process and a brief overview is appropriate. Although the need for non-pilot aviators had been recognised before WW1, it was 1916 before the Royal Flying Corps (RFC) formally recognised them as 'Flying Officer (Observers)' and 1917 before the Royal Naval Air Service (RNAS) followed suit with its Observer Officers. In Apr 18 these men were absorbed into the RAF, with the Army-style flying 'O' badge. Post-war policy dictated that the only professional aircrew would be pilots, other crew stations being occupied by ground tradesmen who would fly on a part-time basis as gunners, much of their training being provided at squadron level. This situation began to change in 1934 when the trade of the, still part-time, corporal observer was introduced, supported by a formal, if short, training course. In 1937 a navigation element was added to the Air Observer School syllabus and the flying 'O' badge was reinstated for students on completion of the course. Previously the exclusive preserve of pilots, in May 38 the Observer was made responsible for navigation – in war but, oddly enough, not in peace. From Jan 39 Observers were ranked as sergeants and employed on a full-time basis and in May 39 their responsibilities were extended to cover navigation in both war and peace.[55]

These changes were the result of Bomber Command's gradual acceptance of the fact that it was unrealistic to expect a pilot to act as navigator while simultaneously flying his aeroplane, especially at night and/or in cloud; and that misemploying ground tradesmen as aircrew on a part-time basis would simply be unworkable in war. With the introduction of more advanced aircraft with more sophisticated tactics, more complex electronic equipment and operational roles, then the function of the Observer within a crew became increasingly specialised during the first three years of WW2. There were, for instance, few similarities between the airborne duties of observers flying in Halifax bombers; and those who flew in maritime strike Beaufighters, Mosquito night fighters or Catalina flying boats. To cater for these differences, in the summer of 1942, the Observer was superseded by the Air Bomber and the Navigator, the latter having a number of role-related sub-specialisations. This change was marked by the introduction of a single-winged 'N' badge, although a dispensation permitted anyone previously entitled to wear the old 'O' badge to continue to do so once he was no longer eligible for employment as aircrew. That said, many of the old hands declined to give up their hard-won flying 'O's.

---

55. A brief summary from *Observers and Navigators* by courtesy of Wg Cdr C G Jefford, MBE, BA.

Air Navigation was never an end in itself. It was a team effort that also required the pilot to accurately fly the required heading, height and airspeed and the air gunners to search for and report identifiable ground features and to check drift. There should be no illusion that air navigation was easy either by day or especially by night. There were initially three main methods of navigating:[56]

- *Map reading*. This was based on noting distinctive features on a map and then recognising any of them on the ground. The opportunity to conduct en-route navigation by visual fixes was totally dependent upon the ability to see the ground clearly from the aircraft, in fact to 'observe'. At any time that could be denied by cloud or haze and at night was subject to moonlight and/or starlight. One of the Student Exercises for a budding 'navigator' was 'Locating Position after a 10-second Glimpse of the Ground through a Cloud-gap'. That exercise was based on a conceptual flight from Hornchurch-Munster-Kassel and return to base. Through the cloud-gap the student would have seen the ground for 5 miles in all directions. On the available map that was represented by a circle of 5/8th-inch radius. The official Notes on night map-reading stated that a definite pin-point 'ensures that the position will be known to a mile or so throughout the next fifty miles of the flight' and to 'circle down-moon of the area when searching for a target'.
- *Dead Reckoning (DR)*. The basic practice of Dead Reckoning was fraught with multiple errors, of which the most important were wind velocity – the combination of wind speed and direction – and the outside air pressure. The measured air speed of the aircraft depends on an accurate setting for outside air pressure and this will vary with altitude; any errors in air speed will generate errors in DR. The wind velocity is difficult to forecast with certainty and at heights increasing above 10,000ft the wind speed may often be within the range 50–100kt and, in the absence of any visual fixes, that can lead to considerable errors – see Bib. A33, Chapter XII, paragraphs 60 and 80. It is a simple geometric truth that a 1-degree error in aircraft heading will lead to a 1-mile error in position after 60 miles of flying.
- *Position lines*. A position line is any line such that a navigator knows that he may be *somewhere* along that line. Using three or more position lines would progressively reduce that error into the so-called 'cocked hat'. An aid to night navigation was the 'Bubble' sextant for astronomical navigation – as described in detail within Bib. A33, Chapter VII. There were 24 important Air Navigation Stars identified 'for night travelling and for preventing blunders in the air'. Astro navigation provided only a position line and the accuracy of that line was dependent on a variety of factors; under average conditions that could provide a 'band of position' some 10 miles wide along the determined line.

---

56. Air Navigation: Notes for Instructors and Students (6/41) Wt.8167-2742. There was a series of related Notes that addressed different aspects of Air Navigation. These Notes complemented Bib. A33, which was the Official RAF Publication on the whole subject of Air Navigation.

It must be recognised that night navigation over Germany and the Occupied Territories, even with visual fixes as and when they were possible and radio or radar navigation aids as they later became available, was a major challenge. It was closely coupled with the experience of the navigator. What could perhaps be achieved in benign training did not always carry into the rigours of combat and battle damage. Many budding navigators sadly never had the benefit of extended experience because of the bomber loss rates.

In order to achieve any degree of bombing accuracy, it was necessary for each bomber to fly an approach path that intersected either with the target, with any calculated offset aiming point or with target marker flares; and simultaneously to accommodate the wind speed and direction, which often varied at the intermediate altitudes between the bomber(s) and the target. How was that to be achieved operationally with bomber forces often numbered in hundreds of aircraft, without the risk of multiple collisions. Having an extended stream of bombers fly over the target area was an invitation to the German day and night fighters and to the anti-aircraft artillery (Flak) to take easy pickings. The RAF tactical response at night was bomber concentration, a lesson that had been well learnt in earlier phases of the bombing offensive long before the USAAF bombers operated in Europe from Aug 42 onwards. However, a concentration of bombers all attacking a 'precision target' simply cannot all be in the right place to deliver precision bombing. The same was true later with the USAAF bomber formations in daylight, where the bomb fall would reflect the formation spacing. Both of these operational tactics inevitably resulted in dispersion of the bomb fall around whatever was the aiming point, without prejudice to errors in locating the aiming point. This will be discussed later in this chapter.

For night bombing, the advent of radio and radar navigation aids of various types and the introduction of the Air Position Indicator offered great improvements compared with the initial options in 1939–41 of map reading with fleeting visual fixes, dead reckoning and astro navigation. Those radio and radar aids included GEE, *Oboe*, H2S and G-H. They all had their own inherent errors. In the case of those which used ground stations located in England or latterly within reoccupied territories on the continent, the errors were generally proportional to the distance from the ground-stations out to their maximum ranges of 350 miles or more, depending on the altitude of the bomber or the target marking aircraft. The following sub-sections very briefly decribe the introduction and use of the various radio and radar navigation aids.

GEE
When GEE was first introduced into bomber operations early in 1942, the primary benefit was that it offered the means to check ground position throughout the mission. The extent of the practicable operating range from the fixed ground stations was reported as 400 miles at 15,000ft; and at that range, the nominal ground position error ellipse was 3 miles in range and half a mile in bearing even on the most favourable location along the extended orthogonal from the GEE ground station baseline.[57] Keeping in mind the uncertainty of weather forecasts

---

57. Ibid. Main Report, p. 4, para. 4k. The introduction of GEE was not straightforward.
    On 13 Feb 42, a flare-dropping trial (CRACKERS) was flown by 3 Group. This

and the extent of evasive actions at any time through the night bombing missions, this was an immense help compared with the previous DR and occasional visual glimpses of the ground. The consequence was that the bomber had a much higher probability of maintaining the planned route and, crucially, the planned Time Over Target (TOT).

It was clearly recognised at least by Bomber Command that GEE was a valuable navigation aid – but it did not have sufficient accuracy for 'blind bombing' against 'precision' targets.[58] Trials had demonstrated that it was reasonable to expect a mean position error over the Ruhr of 1200 yards and, with skilful use, it was possible to achieve reasonable results against large targets at comparable ranges. These 'large targets' would need to have dimensions well in excess of 1200 yards in both the along-track and across-track aspects.

> There was no reasonable prospect of achieving 'precision bombing'.

The Prime Minister had specifically asked the CinC to provide a comparison between the Luftwaffe attack on Coventry that had used the *Knickebein* radio beams for navigation and the first GEE-guided attack on Essen early in Mar 42. In reply, Sir Arthur Harris had set down the comparative weight of those two raids and had made clear that the bomb dispersion of the GEE-guided attack corresponded very well with the expected GEE error at that range.[59] There was no reason why the War Cabinet and the Air Staff should not have been fully aware of that operational fact.

GEE eventually became vulnerable to radio countermeasures as the enemy acquired knowledge of the system; as indeed did the German *Knickebein* beams.[60]

---

exposed serious deficiencies in ground station operations and communications. These matters had been constantly raised by Bomber Command and by HQ No. 60 Group, but the Air Ministry had taken no remedial action. The trial had demonstrated the serious inaccuracies under operational conditions and aircrew confidence was being damaged. The CinC suspended all further GEE operations; there were major repercussions within the Ministry and within 48 hours the necessary communication and monitoring services had been installed. A further operational trial was flown on 19 Feb 42, with considerable success. On 21 Feb 42, the CinC issued a General Directive on the form of future GEE bombing operations.

58. Air 24/243: Bomber Command 'Memo on the Introduction of GEE' dated 31 Mar 42; Appendix 4 – A Trials Report by 115 Sqn, with the Operational Research Section at HQBC.

59. Air 41/3507, ATH/DO/5 dated 13 Mar 42, PERSONAL & SECRET to the Prime Minister.

60. The scientific intelligence work by ADI (Sci) – Dr R V Jones – against the *Knickebein* beams was extensively helped by RAF Y-Service intercept activity and the ULTRA reports, backed up by other sources including photo reconnaissance. This is described in Bib. B15, Chs 11 and 16. The RCM used against the *Knickebein* beams was known as ASPIRIN and against the *X-Gerät* beam system was known as BROMIDE. But attention is drawn to the German side of that story as recorded by Dr Price in the RAF Historical Society seminar on Electronic Warfare, in April 2002. The RCM may

One of the incidental aspects of that work was the extent of the bureaucratic resistance within Whitehall to the very concept of 'beam navigation.' The Air Ministry view was that 'All our own pilots were laboriously trained in navigation and they found their way to their targets very well' – Bib. B15, p. 102. That sad but widely held misconception in Jun 40 remained solid for a long time, even after the Butt report was issued on 18 Aug 41and the subsequent Singleton Report in May 42. Notwithstanding that resistance, the RAF was directed to set up an organisation to deal with those beams. This was No. 80 Wing under the command of Wg Cdr Addison – who later became AOC No. 100 (Bomber Support) Group.

By no means least, GEE provided valuable help with homeward navigation to tired aircrews, because the position accuracy improved as the range from the UK ground stations reduced. The loss rate from crashes in the UK had been a formidable part of the total losses and this was progressively reduced.[61]

OBOE

The advent of *Oboe* saw further improvements in accuracy but the limitation of *Oboe* was that a single pair of ground stations could support only one aircraft at a time; and it took about 10 minutes per aircraft to acquire the *Oboe* signal data and to reach the required bomb or flare release position. The great strength of *Oboe* was its use by the Pathfinder Force (PFF); and particularly by PFF Mosquitoes that could operate at an altitude up to 30,000ft. That had two significant benefits; it extended the line-of-sight range from the ground stations to beyond 400 miles and therefore the effective radius of *Oboe* operations; and at that altitude the Mosquitoes were largely well above the effective performance of the German fighters. Using *Oboe*, the PFF obtained errors of several 100s of yards for marker flares; but that degree of accuracy demanded favourable conditions and much lower altitudes – see Bomber Command Accuracy on p. 127. At those lower altitudes the effective range from the ground stations was progressively reduced. It has to be noted that the sky-marking flares were not stationary and they drifted with the winds at intermediate altitudes. Flares must be distinguished from Ground Markers, which are static after falling to earth. The choice of target(s) during the raid planning stage was influenced by the suitability of the navigation aids and the forecast weather. *Oboe* came to be the preferred option when the weather was clear enough for Ground Marking or Target Indicators (TIs) to be delivered by the PFF and visually tracked by the following bomber force.[62] On a cloudy night when sky-marking was required, it was

---

have been less effective than had been assessed by British intelligence, partly because the Germans had anticipated this and had taken precautions to transmit 'spoof beams'. But German bomber aircrew were worried that RAF night-fighters would use the *Knickebein* and the *X-Gerät* beams as a homing aid for attacks on the bombers. Some of the German aircrew did not use the beams when they were over the UK because of that fear. The RCM did therefore have good effect, perhaps for a different reason than expected and claimed at the time. The truth here may be a combination of both these arguments.

61. Bib. A1, Appendix A, p. 67.
62. Harris Archives, H42, ATH/DO/4 dated 16 Jun 43.

necessary to select an 'area target' because of the drift of the flares with the prevailing wind.

It should also be noted that the Germans introduced RCM against *Oboe* later in the war.[63] That information came from ENIGMA intercepts and was based on CX/MSS/B52 and CX/MSS/S145. The enemy organisation within IV GAF Sigs Regt 351 was described in the report; another comment was that one of the RCM transmitters was of very high power for the short ranges that were involved.

H2S

The development of the airborne radar H2S gave a different dimension to the air navigation task. H2S was fully contained within the bomber and therefore had no range limitation from any ground station. Large-scale production of H2S started in the spring of 1943 but there was high political pressure to provide H2S equipments not only for Bomber Command, with particular priority for the PFF, but also for the 8th USAAF. One of the aircraft installation problems was that the base of the H2S radar scanner was fixed to the fuselage and therefore shared all pitch and roll movements with the aircraft. That had serious effects on the cathode ray screen display that the operator used, especially in bad weather when the need for the H2S was highest and the aircraft was subject to turbulence. The solution was to develop a radar scanner with roll stabilisation and scan distortion correction. The programme agreed at a meeting on 5 Nov 43 was that the PFF should have 300 operational H2S Mk IIIA aircraft by July 1944, with Main Force aircraft being equipped from Aug 44.[64] The development of that stabilised scanner with suitable aircraft installation design into the Lancaster became a series of disasters. In Jan 45, Bomber Command had to resort to ad hoc squadron modifications to achieve any progress. That chapter of disasters was but one of the problems that confronted Bomber Command.

The degree of success obtained from the operational use of H2S with non-stabilised radar scanners rested very largely on the skill and experience of the navigator and his ability to interpret the image on the cathode ray screen. That image often had little correlation with map or visual images and would vary with the direction and slant angle to the radar-illuminated ground in front of the aircraft. The best ground areas were those with marked radar contrast, such as coastal and harbour features, rivers, lakes, etc. It was virtually impossible to identify a specific aiming point within a particular target area; the best that could usually be done was to estimate the position of that aiming point by reference to other cues that could be correlated either to a map or visually.[65] Not surprisingly, it was found that bombing accuracy was better with visual identification of the target following an H2S check than with the blind use of H2S alone.

The first 'blind bombing' raid of any appreciable size that was made by Bomber Command aircraft, all independently equipped with H2S, was on the night of 17/18 Nov 43 against Mannheim/Ludwigshaven. It was determined

---

63. HW 13/44, 'Radar Interception & Countermeasures' dated 14 Jan 45 (TOP SECRET ULTRA).
64. *Echoes of War – The Story of H2S Radar*, by Sir Bernard Lovell, Ch. 24, p. 202.
65. Bib. A1: Appendix A 'Radio Aid, to Navigation and Bombing', paras 71–86.

that 50 per cent of the bombs dropped on that raid fell within 1½ miles of the aiming point. H2S was never precise enough except against an isolated and compact target; it was no use over the Ruhr except when coupled with offset datum points and some visual cues within the immediate target area.[66]

The introduction of H2S Mark III, working in the 3cm radar band, offered better radar screen images and allowed the identification of smaller features. The Mark III equipment was used initially by the PFF from early 1944. The downside of H2S was the vulnerability to detection and tracking by the enemy Y-Service and the use of that detection to alert and direct enemy night-fighters.[67] The operational need for H2S was to diminish after the reoccupation of France. It was then possible by late 1944 to deploy the other radar systems' ground stations closer to the edge of the Western Front than had been possible from the UK. But the horrible delays in providing the stabilised radar scanner had serious adverse impact when attacking targets deeper into Germany.

LORAN

All aircraft of Bomber Command were to have been fitted with LORAN, but trials had shown that it had limitations in comparison with GEE. Operational trials had shown that the positional errors were in excess of the claimed theoretical error of 2 miles. The decision was made to confine LORAN to Nos. 5 and 8 (PFF) Groups, and the heavy aircraft within No. 100 Group. The benefit was the significant operational range available with the sky-wave (SS LORAN), but it was easy to jam.

G-H

The eventual introduction into service of G-H was the best system and from the latter months of 1944 was used by Bomber Command during daylight formation raids, often through 10/10ths cloud cover, with considerable success – notably against synthetic oil and benzol plants in the Ruhr. But it should be noted that the navigation and target location accuracy that was then being achieved still amounted to average radial errors of several hundreds of yards.[68] That should not be confused with actual bomb impact accuracies which were further distributed around that target location error.

The radar navigation systems that became available to the RAF and USAAF bomber forces throughout WW2 certainly provided great improvements in navigation, ultimately in totally 'blind conditions' deeper into Germany. But they never did allow 'precision' bombing, unless the target or aiming point could be acquired and tracked visually in the final stages of the bomb run.[69]

---

66. Harris Archives, H42, ATH/DO/4 dated 16 Jun 43.
67. Bib. B28, p. 40 and Air 14/745.
68. Bib. 1: Appendix B 'The Development of Bombing Techniques', paras 71–77.
69. Author's Note: This does not mean and may not be interpreted to mean that 'precision' bombing was not achieved using other methods: for example, low level visual bombing by ground-attack tactical aircraft; or high-level precision bombing by specialist squadrons under visual conditions using the very large TALLBOY and GRAND SLAM bombs, that had such different penetration shock effects on the targets than did the normal HE penetration or impact burst bombs.

The appreciation and operational tactics associated with target marking activities evolved with experience. For example, in Nov 44 there had again been criticism of the choice of targets selected by CinC Bomber Command. The question in point concerned an attack on Cologne on the night of 31 Oct/1 Nov, rather than attacking another target in the Ruhr. There was 10/10th cloud cover up to 10,000/12,000ft and full moonlight across the whole region. The CinC was not prepared to risk a deeper penetration than Cologne. In the internal Air Ministry autopsy after the operation, DB Ops had written that sky-marking could be effected using *Oboe* alone but that it was better for the target to have a good H2S radar response. The reason was that *Oboe* marking may not be continuous especially as a large number of *Oboe* failures were being experienced. Conversely, AOC 8 Group (PFF) reported that H2S marking in the centre of the Ruhr had been found unreliable.[70]

It is noted that another great advantage of the general improvements in navigation was the track and time keeping of the main force bombers. This was a collective benefit to survival; not least by securing maximum screening by the RCM that was provided from the end of 1943 by No. 100 Group against the German radar systems. That RCM support was carefully planned around the intended routes and times of the Main Force bomber streams. If those routes and times were not maintained, then the effectiveness of the RCM support would reduce.

Bombsights

Bomber Command was equipped with a variety of bombsights that had progressive improvements as the war continued. The early Mark II Course Setting Bombsight required an accurate determination of wind, the sighting of the target at a range of 2½–3 miles and a steady flight during the bomb run.

The Mark XIV Bombsight, initially brought into service during 1942, offered marked increase in accuracy and a skilled crew could achieve an average bomb error of 150 yds from an altitude of 20,000ft under benign conditions and with visual tracking of the target. But in operational practice under combat conditions, the errors increased up to 2000 yards.[71] In this same letter, AOC 5 Group was urgently requiring the installation of the Mark XIV bombsight across the bomber force, but he fully recognised that navigation remained the biggest problem. He advocated the use of offset datum points and then a timed run to the bomb release point. This would minimise the problem of target obscuration by smoke and debris and also simplify the tasks of the pilot and the bomb aimer.

The Stabilised Automatic Bombsight began service with No. 5 Group in the spring of 1943 and eventually proved itself to be extremely accurate, albeit after a long in-service development programme. There was a Private and Personal letter from CinC to CAS in April 44 protesting that it had taken 'four years to get a tactically practicable bomb sight into full use'.[72] When 617 Sqn towards the end

70. Air 20/3218, 5/634, DB Ops to CAS dated 3 Nov 44.
71. The Harris Archives, H51, RAC/DO/3/Air dated 20 Apr 43: from AOC 5 Group to CinC Bomber Command.
72. The Harris Archives, H98, BC/S.27600/4/Air dated 21 Apr 44.

of the war used the Mark IIA version of this bombsight, average errors of 80 yds were being obtained from a bombing height of 20,000ft by their experienced aircrews. The use of any of these bombsights demanded visual acquisition and identification of the target by the start of the bomb run, well before bomb release.

The Pathfinder Force

The concept and the somewhat contentious creation of the RAF Pathfinder Force (PFF) through 1941–42 has been well documented and this book has no intention of repeating that history. There was considerable difference of opinion between major personalities about the need for; the possible manner of conducting what was initially named as Target Finding Force (TFF) operations; and the potential effect on morale of the bomber aircrews at large. In many respects, the proposed creation of a TFF would have mirrored the Luftwaffe and the KG 100 specialist unit that operated over the UK using the *Knickebein* beams, transmitted from fixed ground stations in Germany and France. The reader's attention is drawn to the earlier comments, within the description of GEE, about that episode.

It is a matter of recorded history that the CinC Bomber Command was not convinced about the initial proposition and did indeed resist the formation of the TFF, later to become the PFF. The CinC favoured the use of the best squadron crews to lead the attacks by squadron and later, when cameras became available to record bombing results, that the best squadrons be selected as Lead Squadrons for the Main Force during the following months. At that point in time the Command did not have any operationally tested and proven radar navigation aids. GEE was in the process of introduction into service and the early experiences were mixed; this has been briefly portrayed in the Air Navigation section above. The policy arguments between the CinC, the CAS and Gp Capt. Bufton (initially Deputy Director and then as Air Cdre, Director of Bomber Operations) about the TFF and PFF may possibly have sown some of the seeds for the policy and personality clashes as the war and the bombing offensive developed. A comment by AOC 3 Group (Air Marshal Baldwin) concerning Bufton was that:

> Perhaps he (Bufton) had allowed his suspicions of Group and Operational Commanders to get the better of him!

The subsequent operational achievements of the PFF are sincerely acknowledged. This section of the book very briefly addresses the contribution of the PFF to bombing accuracy within the context of 'precision versus area' bombing operations. Air Vice Marshal D Bennett was to become AOC No. 8 (PFF) Group. He had been closely associated with the formation of Ferry Command to fly aircraft from Canada to the UK; he had flown operational bombing missions and had been shot down over Norway in 1942. He walked out to Sweden.

The operational objective of the PFF was to mark the required target(s) with coloured flares. The actual position of those flares could then be designated in relation to the required target(s), if necessary, and the following main bomber force would aim either at the flares or at a specified offset aiming point. Some techniques used ground-marker flares with the codewords PARAMATTA or NEWHAVEN, otherwise known as Target Indicators; others used airborne sky-marker flares, with the codeword WANGANUI.[73] The latter would be used when there was cloud cover of the target(s) or smoke obscuration; but such flares were never stationary – they were falling and drifting with the wind; and the wind vector may be quite different between the bomber and the flare altitudes. When a bomb aimer was using a sky-marker flare(s) as his aiming point, that flare was initially well above the real target and the bomb would still have some forward carry in its ballistic path. This aspect of the PFF operation is discussed in the reference.[74] There was a great deal of concern and assessment of the accuracy of flares and their delivery by the PFF. Major matters related to accurate timing of flare release and the subsequent arrival of the Main Force bombers; the Recommended Air Speed and altitude for those bombers, with particular regard to the cruise speed and the speed loss with open bomb doors; and the importance of maintaining the correct aircraft heading.

The concept of a Master Bomber was introduced later in the war against important targets, initially advocated by AVM The Hon. Cochrane of 5 Group during the summer of 1943. That task required the Master Bomber to remain over the target area and issue directions for additional markers and/or bombing offsets as the raid developed.

The practice of low-level target marking also gained some value and notoriety. Partly that was because one of the main enthusiasts was AVM Cochrane and an accomplished exponent was Gp Capt. Leonard Cheshire, VC. No. 5 Group had always had a certain individuality and no lack of skill. Low level target marking was difficult and dangerous but it could be very effective when the weather and visibility conditions were suitable.

The operational use of flares by the PFF was not simple. The following text shown below in italics is extracted from the pre-flight briefing for a raid on Essen during the night of 4/5 Jan 43:[75]

Four Mosquitoes of PFF and 30 Lancasters of No. 1Group will carry out a blind bombing attack with the aid of navigational and sky-marker flares. The Mosquitoes will operate in two sections of two aircraft; both pairs will carry out exactly the same procedure. The first from 1936 to 1940 hours and the second from 1938 to 1942 hours.

Preliminary warning flares (Green steady) will be released by the first pair at 1936 at a position approximately 5150N 0657E, four minutes before the Sky-marker flares which indicate the point of bomb release. Secondary warning flares will be dropped at 1938.The release-point flares themselves (Green with Red stars) will be dropped at 1940. The whole procedure will be repeated two minutes later by the second pair of

---

73. Air 14/2082: No. 5 Group/101/49, BC/S.23746/5/Ops 1(b), dated 2 Feb 43.
74. Air 20/4735, HQ PFF (No. 8 Gp) to DB (Ops), dated 26 Jul 43; this highlights the problem of wind drift. It was noted as a matter of simple fact that with a 60kt wind, the flare will drift one mile in one minute. In separate correspondence there was just as much concern about the imperative for accurate time keeping by the Main Force bombers to minimise bombing errors created by flare drift.
75. Air 14/2984, Briefing Details of Attacks by PFF and main Force – 3/4 Jan to 19/20 Feb 43.

Mosquitoes, whose release-point flares will be dropped at 1942 hours; these release-point flares will burn for two minutes. At that time White marker flares will start to burn for the emergency use of latecomers, who should approach them on the correct heading (170° magnetic) but should release their bombs about 2 miles short of the flares at the start of their burning period – increasing by a further mile for every minute later.

The Lancasters are to approach the release-point flares on an exact heading of 170° magnetic. When on this heading, the preliminary Green flares should be exactly on the port beam at a distance of five miles and the secondary Red flares should be to port and slightly ahead at a distance of 2½ miles. Each Lancaster will carry 1x4000lb GP Bomb which is to be dropped when exactly over the release-point flares; and ten containers of 4lb Incendiaries, which are to be released ten seconds after the HE bomb on the same heading. All aircraft are to maintain 20,000ft over the defended areas. The success of this operation depends on accurate timing.

The purpose of outlining that pre-flight briefing was to demonstrate the basic process of marker flare release and the subsequent actions by the bomber force; there is nothing extraordinary about that example. It was a small simple raid but it shows the most critical factors: flare release point accuracy, the correct heading of the main force bomber aircraft and precise timing. All of these factors demanded a high level of skill and there is no allowance for the distraction of combat or the effect of the winds on the actual position of the sky-marker flares.

Within the same folder Air 14/2984, there are many other examples of pre-flight briefing details; subsequent post-flight analyses made on the basis of night photography taken at the time; and later PR to disclose damage effects. These analyses did not make good reading but their purpose was to examine what actually happened and to recommend improvements in PFF and bombing techniques, as operational experience was gathered. The sort of problems that arose included:

- *H2S and Ground Marking Attack – Turin 4/5 Feb 43.* It had been hoped that well-placed Target Indicating markers would overcome the tendency for the main weight of attack to be offset from the aiming point. Visibility was good. The evidence showed that the TI markers were scattered and that the bombing followed that scattering, with the weight of attack falling on the Western edge of the town some two miles West of the aiming point. It was determined that the initial undershoot of the TI markers was a consequence of incorrect allowance for forward throw; and there was successive 'creep back' of subsequent markers.
- *H2S and Sky Marking Attack – Wilhelmshaven 18/19 Feb 43.* Visibility was reported as excellent and crews claimed to have had no difficulty in recognising the area; but there was a very strong westerly wind (60–80 mph) at the operational height. The evidence indicated that the weight of attack fell almost entirely in open country 2–6 miles west of the target, with negligible damage in the town. Only 4 out of the 13 H2S aircraft found it possible to home onto the aiming point, and those 4 crews also checked the position visually. The key problem was that the marker aircraft were not on schedule. The first markers were closest to the aiming point and then there was a progressive displacement to the west-southwest. This was compounded by enemy smoke screens and dummy markers, the visual effect of which was aggravated by

moonlight reflections. Another problem related to the use of H2S was that new construction work in the area may have generated an unexpected echo that was uncorrelated with the available maps.

Harris expressed his view about Schweinfurt as a target in a letter dated 9 Jan 44, to the Under-Secretary of State for Air and to Bottomley.[76] Harris wrote that Schweinfurt was a small, well-defended target which was difficult to locate at night; not only did Bomber Command lack the navigation and bombing aids to locate and attack that target, but he doubted if the PFF could position the visual bombing flares with sufficient accuracy. After further exhortation from the Air Staff, Harris did order a night raid on Schweinfurt on 24/25 Feb 44 that followed a daylight raid by the 8th USAAF on 24 Feb 44. The raid was not a success. The PFF first visual target marker aircraft reported no trouble in marking the aiming point but subsequent markers were short of the target and spread back to the south-west.[77] That tendency to 'creep back' was a known problem. There was one further raid on the night of 26/27 Apr 44 by 215 Lancasters and eleven Mosquitoes. That was also unsuccessful; the low level target marking was inaccurate and strong winds disrupted the Main Force timing over the target.

'Creep back' was a rather persistent problem in the bomb impact points as the raids developed. There was a tendency for bombers that were following the leading aircraft to aim towards the rear either of the marker flares or the fires from the immediately preceding bombs; the effect was that the bomb impact point tended to moved backwards away from the true aiming point or target. Training and practice reduced this problem but the visual distraction of multiple fires, not least decoy fires lit by the enemy, was always a problem. The PR Interpretation Report N.128 dated 28 Jun 43 is an example of the analysis that was conducted by the CIU into the enemy use of decoy fires.[78] These problems could not be eliminated, whether they arose as a direct consequence of decoys or as target identification errors when other bombs or flares had fallen in the wrong place.[79]

Target marking techniques were a subject of constant review and improvement. During May and Jun 44, Sir Arthur Harris and AOC 5 Group discussed the use of Mosquitoes for low-level offset marking of targets in the Ruhr – backed up by Lancasters.[80] The point was made that even the Mosquito was rather too vulnerable to light flak at low altitude where there was heavy searchlight

---

76. Air 2/4477, Harris to Under Secretary of State for Air and to DCAS, 9 Jan 44, p. 3, para. 12.

77. Air 25/156, Directorate of Bomber Operations Monthly Summary, March 1944, p. 4, para. 8.

78. Air 24/257, Bomber Command Intelligence Reports – July 1943. The PR report N.128 was an analysis of decoy fires used during the raid on Duisburg on the night of 12/12 May 1943.

79. The Bomber Command Navigation Bulletins provided advice and instruction; the emphasis was on the 'team effort' not least to keep checking the Estimated Time of Arrival at turning points, etc. The Bulletin No. 4 dated Aug 43, at p. 2, gives attention to this sort of mistake.

80. Air 14/1206: RAC/DO/2/Air dated 4 Jun 44: from AOC 5 Gp to CinC Bomber Command.

coverage. Gp Capt. Cheshire had suggested that a better aircraft would be a single seat long-range fighter, such as a Mustang or Typhoon. Cheshire thought that such an aircraft would allow accurate low-level marking and that this would be particularly useful beyond the range of the ground-based navigation aids such as *Oboe*, albeit subject to weather conditions en-route and in the target area. This was very much associated with the improved techniques of the Master Bombers, who could then use PFF Lancasters to back-up these low-level markers. Arrangements were made between Bomber Command and the USAAF for the loan of a Mustang to experiment with low-level target marking; a better option was seen to be the P-38 Lightning, which carried a two-man crew and had two engines with contra-rotating propellers that gave much better flight stability and better range.[81]

Even late in the war, the operational use of target marking was not without problems as the political and military need for increased bombing accuracy became more intense. Sir Arthur Harris wrote to the CAS in response to a draft bombing policy from the Deputy Supreme Commander Tedder:[82]

> *Area bombing must enter into any scheme because in bad weather we have to use sky-markers and we must have a large target within Oboe or G-H range. In those conditions we necessarily paint with a large brush.*
>
> *There is however another aspect of bombing which it is always difficult to impress or to keep impressed upon those outside the immediate Command; and that is the decisive effect of weather and tactical factors on what can be done at any given moment. Taking account of the altitude ceilings of our bombers and the winter cloud formations with high icing indices, it is often impossible to go where one wants to go.*

Given the statistical pattern of Bomb Impact Points there would have been perhaps many occasions when a single bomb scored a direct hit on the intended target, but this cannot be claimed as an example of 'precision bombing'. It was no more than a matter of chance. There is however absolutely no doubt that the PFF provided the means of significantly improving average bombing accuracy.

The Required Damage Effect

In making decisions on the type of bomb(s) to be used on any particular raid, there was always the requirement to gauge the characteristics of the target and its vulnerability to different types of munitions. This was handicapped by inadequate knowledge both of the target structures and of the effects of different munitions; the science of bomb effectiveness was quite immature. There were some studies and papers that examined the effects of different munitions, taking account of the gathering weight of experience from raids into the UK from German bombers and from PR and other intelligence on the effects of raids into Germany. The Allied use of concentrated incendiary attacks was in part predicated on the experience gained from a Luftwaffe attack late in 1941 on

---

81. The Harris Archives, H51, RAC/DO/2/Air dated 22 Jul 44 from AOC 5 Group to CinC Bomber Command.
82. The Harris Archives, H55: ATH/DO/4 from Harris to Portal, dated 1 Nov 44.

Southampton, in which thousands of incendiaries were dropped which effectively ignited and gutted an extensive area of the city.[83]

The subject of Required Damage Effects was complex and included factors such as:

- With the variety of air-dropped munitions that were available to the bombing offensive, what was the performance of a given type of bomb: blast, fragmentation, incendiary, etc. What blast air pressure would be generated at a given distance from detonation?
- What degree of accuracy was required to have the desired effect on a given target: different target structures have different vulnerabilities; what blast effect was required to collapse a wall or a roof on a given type of structure, or to penetrate through a number of floors in a building?
- How many bombs of a given type were required to have the desired effect on a given target.
- What were the relative merits of High Explosive versus Incendiary? This was the subject of much debate, sometimes acrimonious, between the various authorities; and decisions had to be taken on the stock levels of different bomb types.

There were hardly any informed answers to these questions.[84] In practice, the decisions on bomb loads often became a combination of High Explosive (HE) and Incendiary; what proportional mix would be applied for a given raid and how would that mix be disposed across the bombing force for the raid? The choice was often constrained by the availability of different munition types at the bomber stations when the raids were planned. Within the HE category there were several options:[85]

- General Purpose (GP): This was the standard type of bomb at the start of the war with various weights between 20lb, the usual 500lb and 1000lb options; and the less common 4000lb option. The GP bombs suffered from the same deficiency; too much metal and too little explosive. With a few exceptions, they all failed to distinguish themselves. At an Air Ministry meeting chaired by DCAS in Dec 40 it was determined that an improved bomb was required and this became known as the Medium Capacity (MC) bomb.
- Medium Capacity (MC): There were several manufacturing options for the bomb case – either welded, forged or cast. In general they had a 50/50 Charge/Weight ratio except for the cast case which had a lower 40/60 Charge/Weight ratio. The 500lb and 1000lb options gave satisfactory performance and the 1000lb version became the preferred choice by Bomber Command from 1943.

---

83. The Harris Archives, H53: DB (Ops)/4212 dated 21 Mar 42, to CinC Bomber Command.
84. Bib. A20, p. 74: Albeit in the context of desert warfare, Zuckerman noted 'There was practically no objective evidence about the effectiveness of any of the bombs or weapons used.'
85. Bib. A31, Ch. 3.

- High Capacity (HC): Driven in part by the effectiveness of the German parachute mines, the Air Ministry adopted the HC bomb. This appeared in the spring of 1941 in the form of the 4000lb 'blockbuster' or otherwise known as the 'Cookie'. It had a high 70/30 Charge/Weight ratio. There were initial problems with use of Amatol high explosive which had been developed during World War 1. This was progressively replaced with Cyclonite, Torpex, Amatex and Minol as high explosive technology improved. Minol was developed by adding aluminium powder to the high explosive main filling, which increased the blast effect and boosted the incendiary side effects.

The 4000lb Cookie used in conjunction with Incendiaries became a standard heavy bomber payload. It was also used with the Mosquito that could carry a Cookie to Berlin. During Jan–Apr 45, over 1500 Cookies were dropped on Berlin from Mosquito aircraft including one period of 36 consecutive nights. The Mosquito could reach Berlin in two hours at 27,000ft. The Lancaster took four hours on the outward journey alone at less than 20,000ft which significantly increased its exposure to the enemy air defences.[86] Over 68,000 Cookies were dropped by Bomber Command and the USAAF before the end of WW2.

There was yet a further challenge associated with the selection of bomb payloads, against the actual uplift capacity of the bomber. This arose because of the design of the various bombs and their loading points in the aircraft bomb bays. The problem was expressed by AOC 5 Group in a report to the CinC.[87] Whereas the Lancaster could carry a bomb-load of 14,000lb to short range targets in the Ruhr, the standard combination of one 4000lb 'Cookie' and 12 Small Bomb Containers with incendiaries amounted only to 7,600lb. In effect the Lancaster was carrying not much more than half of the possible weight of bombs. This did improve over time with the development in 1944 of the Aimable Clusters for various types of incendiary bombs.

The 4000lb HC bomb design gave rise to the 8,000lb and 12,000lb versions. The 12,000lb variant was used by 617 Sqn with modified Lancasters for high-altitude specialist bombing, sometimes with low-level target marking. By Jun 44 these 12,000lb MC bombs were overtaken by the 12,000lb TALLBOY and later by the 22,000lb GRAND SLAM bombs designed by Dr Barnes Wallis, capable of carriage only by the modified Lancasters of 617 Sqn and, later, also by 9 Sqn. Very briefly, these heavy bombs were intended to penetrate deeply in the ground before detonation and generate shock waves. These bombs were spin-stabilised and they demanded accurate aiming and impact.[88] The first TALLBOYs were used operationally on the night of 8/9 Jun 44 against the Saumur railway tunnel between Tours and Angers in France to stop the forward movement of a panzer unit by train, only a few days after the initial D-Day landings. They were dropped from altitudes between 6,000 and 10,000ft and blocked the tunnel for several

---

86. Author's note: Perhaps the use of Mosquitoes with 'Cookies' would have ben an alternative option for the Battle of Berlin, noting the high loss rate of the four-engined heavy bombers.

87. The Harris Archives, H51, RAC/DO/2/Air dated 10 May 43.

88. Bib. A31, Ch. 6, pp. 139–142.

weeks. That led to an Air Staff decision to increase the manufacture quantity but there were occasions later through 1944 when the available stocks could not support the operational need. One such instance was the delay of the attack on *Tirpitz* in Nov 44. Eventually, 854 TALLBOYs were dropped on targets as diverse as V-Weapon storage sites, U-boat pens, viaducts, oil depots and finally Hitler's retreat at Berchtesgaden.

Circular Error Probable

The dominant factor ultimately became the Circular Error Probable (CEP) of a bomb falling on an identified aiming point. The CEP denoted the radius of a disc around the aiming point within which 50 per cent of the bombs will impact. In operational practice, the statistical pattern of the CEP tended towards an ellipse rather than a circle with the major axis of the ellipse along the ground track of the bomber on the final bombing run.[89] The aiming point may be the whole target, or a selected piece of the target in the case of a dispersed industrial plant or a large railway marshalling yard. In some cases, there may be two or more aiming points within a large area target, selected so as to cover as much of the target as possible.[90] When multiple aiming points were planned, care had to be taken with regard to the sequence of attacks to minimise the obscuration of later aiming points by smoke and debris from the first attacks.

There are a multiple ingredients in the CEP factor, which include but are not limited to:

- Altitude, speed and ground track of the bomber in relation to the target.
- The flight stability of the bomber at the point of bomb release; in anything other than still air, the aircraft will exhibit random uncommanded pitch, roll and yaw movements that will induce accelerations that are inextricably conveyed to the bomb at the point of release.
- Prevailing wind speeds and direction at the intermediate altitudes below the bomber.

The time of flight of a typical HE bomb would be in excess of 35 seconds from a release altitude of 20,000ft. When bombing through cloud, the associated air turbulence would also disturb the path of the bombs. Just as an example, the following Table provides a typical indication of the wind speed and direction changes at various altitudes below the bombing height:[91]

Height above Ground (ft)	2,000	6,000	10,000	15,000	20,000
Wind Vector (Direction/ Speed-kt)	230°/20	240°/25	250°/30	260°/40	270°/50.

---

89. See Ch. 7: 'Post D-Day and the Final Stages.'
90. See Ch. 7. The section headed 'Post D-Day and Final Strategic Bombing' shows direct reference to this statistical pattern and the use of multiple aiming points, from the Bomber Command Target Intelligence records – Air 20/10189.
91. Air 24/257: Bomber Command Navigation Bulletin No. 5, Sep 43.

It is noted that the Incendiaries had quite different ballistic characteristics to those for the HE bombs; quite simply, they would have different impact points and would be more scattered by the prevailing winds.[92] A specific example is as follows, comparing the ballistics of the 4000lb 'Cookie' Bomb and the 4lb Incendiary when dropped together from an altitude of 18,000ft at an airspeed of 220kt, even without regard to dispersion in flight. (see Plate 1)

Direction of Flight:	Undershoot	Time Delay for Coincidence
Downwind	1007 yd	7.3 seconds
Upwind	1960 yd	25.1 seconds
Crosswind	1556 yd	Not applicable

The Undershoot is the lesser distance that the incendiary will carry forward after release against the nominal path of the Cookie. The Time Delay for Coincidence refers to the release time of the incendiary after the release of the Cookie to achieve nominal coincidence of impact point on the ground, and this will vary significantly with the intermediate winds during the fall of the incendiary. It may be seen from the image below that the incendiaries would disperse in a random fashion. This sort of ballistic problem with incendiaries was a source of great concern, especially when incendiaries were the preferred munitions for some attacks. An associated problem was 'incendiary clustering' which remained serious, at least through until Apr 44.[93] This was reported by CinC Bomber Command to CAS as a major problem causing untold bomber losses through having to make repeat attacks because of the unpredictable ballistics of the incendiary bombs.

Improvements were examined and trials were flown, for example with the Type 'J' 30lb incendiary bomb. This had been first designed in 1942 but it had a protracted development record; it produced a 'jet' of flame and was very effective when dropped in conjunction with MC/HC bombs. It was not used until Apr 44 and the results were inconclusive. The Type 'J' was supplied and dropped in Aimable Clusters, each holding 14 incendiaries. There was also the development later during 1944 of a cluster container which could hold one hundred and six 4lb incendiaries. The cluster container had a conventional bomb tail and had ballistics that were more comparable to an MC/HC bomb. It would be detonated at a low altitude and the individual incendiaries would be dispersed. That also minimised the risk of the small 4lb incendiaries hitting other bombers after they were scattered from higher altitudes. But it will be seen that incendiaries and their unpredictable ballistics did not fit the concept of 'precision' bomb delivery.

Another feature that was used to help reduce errors was the 'Roman Candle', a small 3lb tracer flare that could be fitted to the tail of the bomb and fused so as to burn from a few seconds after bomb release.[94] This was useful with delayed

92. Air 20/4735, Night Bomb Aiming (1943).
93. The Harris Archives, H98, BC/S.27600/4/Air dated 21 Apr 44, from CinC to CAS.
94. Ibid., Loose Minute from B Ops 2(a) to DB (Ops), dated 17 Jul 44.

fuse bombs; it allowed the bomb to be visually tracked down to the impact point and for corrections to be made by the following bombers, assuming that they also had adequate visual conditions and were not handicapped by smoke or debris from preceding attacks.

Bomber Command Accuracy

The Butt Report was released on 18 Aug 41 and provided evidence that was profoundly disturbing at that time. One of the devastating conclusions was that on average only one bomber within three got within five miles of the target; and, in poor conditions, that could fall to one in fifteen.

The Singleton Report was released on 20 May 42 and reviewed the policy and practices surrounding the bombing campaign and to estimate the probable results that could be obtained over the succeeding 6, 12 and 18 months. One of the major themes within that report and the subsequent responses within the Air Ministry embraced the continuing and projected difficulties with navigation and target acquisition.[95] Director of Signals commented that GEE was never intended to be a Blind Bombing device. DB Ops noted that the Germans had exploited GEE equipment from RAF bomber aircraft that had crashed in Germany and that an attack on Essen in early Jun 42 had revealed enemy countermeasures against the system. Within the course of his inquiry, Mr Justice Singleton met with two experienced officers who had used GEE in night bombing raids over Germany. Those officers reported that, with a specially trained crew, it would be possible to establish a position within 4 mls longitudinally and 2 mls laterally from the target. Singleton concluded that until better accuracy was achived in target acquisition, it would be better to plan for larger targets that could be found more readily. Bombing results immediately prior to the report being issued were not encouraging except in almost perfect weather conditions; and those conditions arose on only a few days in any month. In effect, bombing accuracy had not notably improved since the earlier Butt Report. Singleton noted that the Whitehall Targets Committee was not in sufficiently close liaison with Bomber Command; and that the final decisions on target selection must rest with the CinC.

Moving forward into mid-1943, there was intense analysis of targets and bombing in the context of the enemy long-range rocket installations in Northern France, from which the V-1 or V-2 weapons would be launched. This is discussed in more detail later in this chapter. The target analysis had focussed in part on concrete structures that were 100 yd by 100 yd square; and other concrete platforms that were 95ft in diameter.[96] The analysis had determined that direct hits or very near misses would be necessary with large penetration bombs. The key point was that the probable bombing accuracy was taken as a CEP of 1000 yds by day and 1500 yds by night. It should be noted that these targets were at short range for the available navigation aids located within the UK, of which *Oboe* was the most likely candidate.

Moving further forward into the preparatory phase for the OVERLORD landings, during the spring of 1944, there was another round of intense argument

---

95. Air 8/1015, The Singleton Report and Air Ministry comments.
96. AIR 20/8199.

about the strategic bombing target selections. This has been discussed in detail earlier in this chapter. In the context of that argument, DB Ops (Bufton) quoted a Mean Radial Error – which means the same as CEP – of 640 yds for bombing accuracy, including an allowance for errors in TI markers. This claim was also predicated on the much shorter range of those French transportation targets from the UK-based navigation aids than were other strategic targets in Germany.

The analysis of Bomber Command's bombing accuracy was generally evaluated by the Command Operational Research Section. A number of reports were published during 1943–45 which dealt with the various target marking and bombing techniques that were used. However, the Operational Research Section (ORS) Report No. 250 embraced many of those separate reports and provided post-war statistical comparisons.[97] The majority of the analyses refered to *Oboe* and Low Level Visual ground-marking, mostly at night but some during the day from the autumn of 1944 onwards, with subsequent bomb fall accuracies. The evidence for bomb impact points was derived from PR imagery and from forward plotting of bomb-release point photography. The analyses included targets in Germany and in occupied territories, noting the difference in enemy air defence resources and their effect on bombing accuracy. The data summary provided the following averages:

		Low Level Visual Marking	*Oboe Marking at Night*	*Oboe Marking by Day*
Overall Systematic Error		235 yd	750 yd	355 yd
Standard Errors about	Line	330 yd	585 yd	440 yd.
Mean Point of Impact	Range	395 yd	725 yd	545 yd
	Radial	515 yd	930 yd	700 yd

The Overall Systematic Error represents the average displacement from the intended Aiming Point. The Standard Radial Error represents the average bomb fall dispersion around the Overall Systematic Error and may be regarded as the CEP, but centred on the Overall Systematic Error and not the intended aiming point. The notable difference between Oboe marking by night and by day almost certainly includes some visual input during daylight; as a 'radio navigation aid' Oboe would be substantially unaffected by the time of day.

The Low Level Visual marking was mostly conducted by No. 5 Group and it was clear that this technique was most successful, both in occupied territories and in Germany. This demonstrates the absolutely key point that Visual Target acquisition and marking was the most reliable bombing technique; but the statistical results DO NOT SHOW the proportion of raids when that technique was applicable. The great majority of Bomber Command night raids did not have that benefit.

---

97. Air 14/4541: BC/S.27320/ORS, Operational Research Section Report No. 250 dated 23 Oct 45.

The greater proportion of raids on German targets were conducted from altitudes between 15,000 and 19,000ft. When raids were conducted from lower altitudes, the bombing accuracy improved. The Overall Systematic Error from an average attack altitude of 8,000ft using Low Level Visual target marking was shown to be 135 yd.

This brief summary of Bomber Command's typical bombing accuracies at different phases of the war must not be interpreted as meaning that 'precise' bombing was never achieved. This is discussed later in this chapter, but the general prerequisite for 'precision' was good visibility of the target(s).

The 8th USAAF Experiences

This section summarises a wide range of the 8th USAAF experience, under three separate headings:

- Bombing techniques.
- Bombing results.
- Spillage onto German Cities.

BOMBING TECHNIQUES

By way of comparison between Bomber Command and the 8th USAAF, the American claim that a bomb could be aimed with the Norden Bombsight and 'landed in a pickle barrel' as shown from field trials in the USA, turned out to be so much nonsense in the European combat environment. The trials over California's Muroc Lake from an altitude of 20,000ft did demonstrate that a 100ft circular target on the ground could be hit; and this gave rise to a completely false misapprehension concerning high-altitude bombing.[98] A vital ingredient of that bombsight technique was visual target identification during a steady bombing run into the point of bomb release. This was usually denied over German targets either by cloud, poor visibility, smoke decoys on the ground or the distraction of air-to-air combat and flak.

The USAAF bombing technique was for a Lead Aircraft to act as the bomb-aimer and for the combat group, flying in formation with the Lead Aircraft, to synchronise their bomb release. The bomb impacts largely mirrored the dispersal of the bomber formation and any positional errors in the Lead Aircraft were copied to all other aircraft in that group. To be quite specific, even with the smallest formation of a six-aircraft B-17 bomb group, there would be a cross-track displacement of over 200ft and an along-track displacement of over 300ft between those separate aircraft. It was soon recognised that the Lead Bombardier had to take account of that bomber formation dispersal and use an aiming point that was further along track past the intended target. There was very high pressure for the bombers to remain in accurate formation and that could not always be achieved because of air-to-air combat and bomber losses during the bomb run.

The first H2S radar-guided mission by the 8th USAAF was flown by a force of 244 bombers on 27 Sep 43 against Emden; the second such mission, also against Emden, was flown by 339 bombers on 2 Oct 43. There were 14 other H2S or H2X

---

98. Bib. A34, Ch. 2, pp. 22–23.

radar-guided bombing raids by the 8th USAAF before the end of Dec 43. The Bombing Accuracy Sub-Section produced the Operations Analysis report on those missions. Colonel Scott prepared it with assistance by Major Darwin. The source of information on the bomb impact point data from those missions was photographic reconnaissance by the PRU. The results were disappointing. Three of the four leading wings of the twelve wings in both missions that bombed achieved a CEP of half to one mile. The fourth wing had a CEP of two to three miles. Only one of the leading combat wings caused damage to the target. The official USAAF History of this period corroborates the evaluation; the bomb patterns made by radar-guided bomber forces in that time period were too scattered to effect more than accidental damage to any particular industrial plant or installation of importance. The results over the following months through to the end of the year progressively made it clear that H2S/H2X was not a method for precision bombing. There were those in the USAAF who believed that a frankly stated programme of area bombardment should be added to the bombing offensive plan, at least for the winter of 1943/44.[99]

Although radar bombing by the 8th improved during Jan-Mar 44, it clearly was not 'precision' bombing. It was a different kind of 'area bombing'.[100]

> The outcome had been better described as 'area bombing of a precision target'.

BOMBING RESULTS

In a wider context, in that period Oct 43 to Mar 44, only 55–60 per cent of the visual attacks made by the 8th were against targets with pre-assigned aiming points. The weather was the dominating factor; it was often impossible to bomb either the assigned primary or secondary target because of the lack of target visibility. Instead, the bombers would visually attack other 'targets of opportunity'. In this same time period, it was also recognised that the accuracy of bombing decreased as the number of bomb groups increased. Separate Bomb Groups interfered with each other on the bomb run; smoke and debris obstructed the target for the following Groups. Bombing accuracy could be recovered if the groups were separated in time but that increased their vulnerability to flak and fighters.

As to the bomber losses during that period, the 8th USAAF ORS found that the major causes were:

- Single bombers becoming a 'straggler' and therefore deprived of the group collective defence.
- Engine damage from enemy gunfire; flak over the target was severe but enemy fighters could strike at any point during the mission, especially against 'stragglers'.

---

99. Bib. A25, Vol. 1 'Europe: Torch to Pointblank', pp. 720–721.
100. Bib. A21 'Operations Analysis in the US Eighth Air Force in World War 2', p. 111.

- Fuel shortage caused by many separate factors; lost time during the initial forming up of the raid, navigation errors, excessive fuel consumption when trying to maintain formation, etc.

By the middle of 1944 flak became the dominant threat. There was intense debate about methods that may reduce that threat.[101] The inescapable problem was that operational tactics to minimise the flak threat over the target area had a direct and adverse impact on bombing accuracy.

For the third quarter of 1944, Bib. A21 shows how bad weather effected the Allied strategic bombing operations into Germany. Because of the greater accuracy that was available from visual bombing as compared with radar-guided bombing, there was a strong preference to persist with visual methods even in poor weather and that caused a high proportion of 'mission failures' – nearly one third of all raids. During that period there was intense study and trials to determine and measure the factors that affected the accuracy of H2S/H2X bombing. Much of that work was concentrated into what became known as 'The Oxford Experiment in H2X Bombing'.[102] The conclusions of that trial were:

> The experiment emphasizes however that the chance of hitting a pre-assigned industrial target with any reasonable force within a built-up area of a city is extremely slight. The results obtained during the trial showed a CEP of 5630ft [i.e., more than one mile] using Oxford City centre as the pre-assigned aiming point and a CEP of 3370ft using the Morris Motor Works as the aiming point. Those results were obtained over 320 trial bombing runs. The same three bomb crews used the same two targets, the same IP and there was no combat distraction. The trial concluded that combat conditions would degrade the trial results considerably; and made the comparison, as with the Norden bombsight, that the inherent capability of that equipment was defeated by combat and weather conditions.

The USAAF came into the war with the policy and intention to conduct 'precision bombing'. That did not happen in practice over Germany. The RAF and US bomber forces had broadly similar equipments, but it must be noted that the UK did not release Oboe to the USAAF for use during daylight bombing.[103] The 8th USAAF did use Gee-H, Micro-H and H2S/H2X. The extent of their radar-guided bombing is indicated by the fact that during the last four months of 1944, 58 per cent of all bombing by the 8th was done with aid of H2X. To be specific, as an instrument for 'precision bombing' through 10/10 cloud cover, H2X was ineffective. It was, however, a reasonable instrument for area bombing of large targets.[104] It did not matter whether that was in daylight or at night. Typical examples of bombing by the 8th are as follows:[105]

---

101. History of the Battle Damage Sub-section, 8th USAAF ORS, Dec 43 – May 45, p. 30.
102. Bib. A25, Ch. 8 'Bombing Accuracy' pp. 214–220.
103. Bib. A21: Ch. 7, Radar Bombing, p. 174.
104. Bib. A13: Ch. 11, pp. 292–293.
105. Bib. A13: Ch. 11, pp. 199–201.

- On 9 Oct 43 the 8th bombed the Fw190 factory at Marienburg in *ideal bombing* conditions. 60 per cent of the bombs fell within 1000ft of the aiming point. General Eaker called that 'a classic example of precision bombing'.
- In another attack, by B-24s of the 389th Bomb Group on the V-1 site at Belloy-sur-Somme, 90 per cent of the bombs fell within 2000ft of the aiming point but only 5 per cent fell within 1000ft. The small NO-BALL target was not hit.
- In a third attack, on 12 Dec 44 the 448th Bomb Group attacked Aschaffenburg. The attack was led by a 93rd Bomb Group lead aircraft using Gee-H for navigation. No bombs fell in the target area.

During the last quarter of 1944, the 8th USAAF began to use the Micro-H radar bombing system. One ground transmitting station had been set up at Namur, Belgium, and another at Verdun, France. The range of the system was limited to about 180 miles for a bomber at 25,000ft. The system was used almost solely by the 3rd Air Division of the 8th, to the exclusion of Gee-H. In November 1944, seven missions were flown using the Micro-H radar bombing system. One hundred and seventeen squadrons, each of 12–13 aircraft were dispatched: 86 squadrons attacked their assigned targets using Micro-H; the remainder attacked either the primary or secondary targets using H2X or visual methods. The results were reported as follows, showing the percentages of bombs that fell within specified distances of the assigned aiming point:

Bombing Method	½ mile	1 mile	2 miles	3 miles
Pure Micro-H	25%	45%	75%	95%
Micro-H and Visual	15%	50%	100%	100%
All types	20%	45%	85%	95%

The general analysis of the 8th USAAF bombing accuracy *under good to medium visual conditions* yielded the following averages of bomb impact points in relation to the aiming point:

Year	1943	1944	1945
%age within 1000ft	18%	35%	44%
%age within 2000ft	38%	63%	72%

There are very many factors hidden within that extremely broad overview. This book does not need to enter into those details; they are extremely well presented in Bib. A21. There are however a few points that do merit attention:

- As the strategic bombing progressed through 1944, the 8th USAAF daylight bombing attacks progressively rose to higher altitudes. In the first quarter of 1944 only 37 per cent of the bombing in good visibility was done above

21,000ft. In the second quarter 50 per cent was done above 21,000ft. That rose to 75 per cent in the third quarter and in the fourth quarter 97 per cent was done from above 21,000ft. The bombers had been driven to higher altitudes by the heavy air defences at German industrial targets.
- The increased size of bombing forces led to a reduction in accuracy, as noted on p. 130.

The compensating improvement in bomber survivability was more valuable and the broad strategy was to mount a lesser number of large attacks, in favourable weather, rather than larger numbers of small attacks.

Visual bombing under conditions of *poor visibility* showed that enemy smoke screens caused slightly over 25 per cent of that problem. Four to five times the bombing force was needed to put a given weight of bombs on targets protected by smoke screens. No effective countermeasure was devised; the lesser accuracy of radar guided bombing did not solve this problem.

In comparison, the results obtained when *using non-visual techniques in total overcast* were 'near failures or worse'. Under those conditions, the 8th USAAF delivered just 40 per cent of all bombs dropped within 3 miles of the target and 58 per cent within 5 miles; only 0.2 per cent landed within 1000ft of the target.

So why did the Whitehall warriors expect Bomber Command, operating at night, to be capable of delivering 'precision bombing', notwithstanding that the USAAFs could not do that even in daylight unless there were 'ideal bombing conditions'? The USAAFs continued to describe their attacks as 'precision' because that was their policy, it was good for the American aircrew morale and it was good for American public relations.

> Harris, from RAF Bomber Command, did not pretend to deliver 'precision bombing' and he then paid the political and personal price for that honesty.

Spillage onto German Cities

It was never the avowed policy of the USAAFs to bomb German cities. There was a very clear statement by General Eaker to General Spaatz, on 1 January 1945, advising against sending heavy bombers to attack transportation targets in small German towns:[106]

There would be many civilian casualties and the German people might be convinced the Americans were barbarians, just as the Nazi propaganda charged. You (Spaatz) and Bob Lovatt are right and we should never allow the history of this war to convict us of throwing the strategic bomber at the man in the street.

However, the 8th was responsible for a large part of the devastation of those cities.[107] In the stress of combat there were many times when the 8th did not know

---

106. Bib. A25, Vol. 3, 'Europe from Argument to V-E Day, Jan 44 to May 45', p. 733.
107. Bib. A21, Ch. 11, 'The Last Big Report on Bombing Accuracy', p. 297.

with certainty what had been bombed. The 'Combat Chronology' entry for 7 Oct 44 states:

Over 1,300 heavy bombers in 4 forces bombed five synthetic oil plants, an armament, a tank and an aero engine works; plus 16 identified and 19 other unidentified targets in the area.

In January 1945, the 8th completed heavy bomber missions on 20 days. On every one of those days, marshalling yards and transportation targets were bombed; on 6 days, *'city areas' were bombed.*[108]

In February 1945, the assigned targets included Berlin and Dresden, the latter with the intention of 'causing confusion in civilian evacuation from the East as the Russian army closed in on those and other cities'. On 3 February, nearly 1000 B-17s flew to Berlin, with the assigned targets as the marshalling yards and the government district. The weather conditions allowed visual bombing and the accuracy was good, even though the bombs were dropped from 24,000–27,000ft. Severe damage was inflicted on the assigned marshalling yards and railway stations throughout Berlin, together with many German government targets. *Civilian casualties were exceedingly high, the number of fatalities reaching perhaps 25,000.* Swedish newspapers were full of lurid details about that attack on Berlin. There was serious recrimination from Washington DC. In reply, General Spaatz reported that:[109]

The Americans were not bombing cities indiscriminately but attacking transportation facilities inside cities on operations which the Russians had requested and seemed to appreciate.

Then came the Allied strategic bombing Operation THUNDERCLAP, which included Dresden. The consequences inspired press reports of 'deliberate terror bombing' as a 'ruthless expedient' to hasten victory. It was noted in the US records that 'Bomber Command was merely continuing the policy of area bombing, to reduce German war production by attacking workers in their homes rather than bombing their factories'. The reader is refered back to Footnote No. 61 in Chap 3 showing a War Cabinet position to this effect in Apr 42. In the UK the Prime Minister later wrote that infamous personal Note dated 28 Mar 45 in which he castigated 'terror bombing'. In the US General George Marshal tried to reconcile the conflict between newspaper reports of terror bombing and official statements calling it precision bombardment.[110] The Operations Analysis Section of the 8th USAAF was required to prepare a memorandum showing the bombing accuracy of the 8th on those raids against Berlin and Dresden. One of the authors of that memorandum was Dr Griffith Baley Price, who had completed his

---

108. 'The Army Air Forces in WW2, Combat Chronology 1941–45' – see January 1945, 8th AF.
109. Bib. A25, Vol. 3, 'Europe from Argument to V-E Day, Jan 44 to May 45', p. 726.
110. 'The Simon and Schuster Encyclopaedia of World War 2', edited by Parrish and Marshall, p. 163.

doctorate at Harvard in 1932. He reported for duty with the 8th at Pinetree on Thanksgiving Day, 1943. In a post-war memoir he concluded that:

> If the US public knew the facts about our blind bombing in Europe, perhaps the outcry over the indiscriminate destruction caused by the atomic bomb would not have arisen.[111]

The basic reason for bombing German cities was 'spillage'. The assigned aiming points were almost invariably military or industrial targets, but many of these were within or on the edge of cities. For the reasons of lack of bombing accuracy, as discussed above, it was inevitable that many of the bombs fell on non-military or non-industrial points and inadvertently constituted an attack on German cities. No blame is attached to this; it was part of the war. But it should be noted that there was conspicuous evasion of the truth by some senior political and military personnel. Perhaps a most cogent outcome was within the US Air Forces Training Manual No. 67 'How to Improve Formation Bombing', which was first published on 2 April 1945.[112] In the Introduction was the statement:

> It is intended to present here a simple statement of the inter-relation of pattern size and aiming error and how they affect the percentage of bombs dropped by a formation which actually strike the target. If the commanding officers of bombardment units understand the relationships between pattern size and aiming error, they will find them of material assistance in evaluating the performance of their commands and taking the necessary steps to improve their bombing accuracy.

Precision Bombing

So what was the term 'precision' intended to mean at the time? The context in which 'precision' was *reasonably* applied at the time was generally in relation to large targets such as major industrial plants, railway marshalling yards, dockyards, etc, whose size may well have extended more than one mile in either or both the along-track or across-track dimension as seen from the bombing approach path. The pre-flight briefing to the bomber crews would have identified specific aiming points within such large area targets; for example, particular buildings or workshops, major track junctions, engine maintenance sheds, harbour 'choke points', etc. In these cases, most bombs that fell within the overall target 'area' would have had some other useful collateral effect. Perhaps coincidentally, this was consistent with the pre-war expectations of the IIC – see p. 59.

Navigation aids such as GEE and *Oboe* had no possible means of identifying such aiming points or targets. *Oboe* was better than GEE but both had increasing range errors with distance from the ground stations. The on-board radars such as H2S and H2X, the US version, would hardly ever have provided an image that was capable of identifying even a large specific building within a complex of

---

111. 'Gremlin Hunting in the Eighth Air Force, European Theatre of Operations, 1943–45', pp. 96–97.
112. Held at the Simpson Historical Research Center, Maxwell AFB, Alabama.

buildings. Indeed, as an instrument for 'precision' bombing through 10/10th cloud cover or on 'dark nights', H2S and H2X were ineffective; they were, however, reasonable instruments for 'area bombing' of large targets. These radars generally provided images that helped with terminal navigation on the bombing run or the visual location of a suitable Datum Point. It was in fact quite common for the bombers to have to use a Datum Point to fix their position and then fly a dead-reckoning course to the target when that target was otherwise invisible to the eye. Whenever the PFF was present on a raid, the marker flares provided the key aiming point. At an airspeed of 200kt the bomber would move about 330ft along track in one second, subject to the prevailing wind speed and direction. The wind at the altitude of the bomber could be quite different at other altitudes through the bomb ballistic path after release – see Table on p. 125; this is an indication of the scale of errors that aggregate into the CEP.

When the term 'precision' was used in the context of small targets, such as a particular factory in a general industrial or housing area, the same preconditions apply to the identification of that 'small target' by the bombers – but the probability of hitting that target is increasingly diminished as its size reduces. Likewise, the probability of causing collateral damage to non-target structures increased. There is a most revealing report that demonstrates this situation with remarkable clarity.[113] The context was the high level political and military concern about the German V-2 Long Range Rocket programme and the heavy reinforced facilities being built in the Pas-de-Calais area. Specific target items included the circular concrete bases, such as those at Wissant, some 10 miles south-east of Calais, which were of 95ft diameter; the target dimension was increased by 30ft to allow for very near misses. Another specific target item was a launch area 100 yards by 100 yards square at Watten, 16 miles south east of Calais. These sites were seen to be aligned for attacks on London.

The reference report discusses the nature of the targets. To achieve any appreciable damage effect it was judged necessary to disturb the foundations by direct hits or very near misses with large penetration bombs. The weapons then available were the 4,000lb MC bomb used by the RAF and the 2,000lb MC bomb used by the USAAF. The much more effective bomb that was anticipated but not then available was the 12,000lb TALLBOY and the argument was that the development of that bomb must proceed with the highest priority. The absolutely key point with regard to 'precision bombing' was the assessment of the probability of hitting those targets, as shown on the following page.

The report goes on to show that the expected average bomb impact point error by day would have been 1000 yds; and by night would have been 1,500 yd, using the available radio navigation aids and Target Illuminating flares.[114] It should be noted that these targets were at the shortest possible range from UK and would

---

113. Air 20/8199: 'Attack on BODYLINE Installation in Northern France', EJS/HEC 10 Aug 43 (MOST SECRET).

114. Authors Note: The archive reference in Air 20/8199 has an interesting handwritten pencil note that the American Heavies average error was 25% of bombs within a 1000ft radius. The subsequent analyses show that this was 'optimistic' – see the previous section on p. 80.

		Bomb Impact Point Average Error		
		500 yd	1000 yd	1500 yd
Target Site	Dimensions	Number of Bombs to secure One Hit		
Watten	100 yds x 100 yds	100	400	900
Wissant	125ft diameter	734	2,933	6,625

have had the benefit of the smallest errors in radio navigation, as is discussed in the preceeding sections. When these aggregate navigation and bombing errors generate CEPs that are well in excess of the intended target size, the use of a term such as 'precision' was as *uninformed* at that time in WW2 as it would be today in the 21st century.

However, it would be quite wrong to suppose that 'precision' was not and could not be achieved at all. The Main Force operating at night was seriously handicapped. But other operations had different prospects. During the autumn of 1943, the AOC 2 Group had plans for the use of his Mosquitoes to make 'precision' attacks in daylight.[115] One of the most successful of those low-level daylight Mosquito attacks was Operation JERICHO on 18 Feb 44 against the German prison at Amiens, specifically to breach the prison walls and allow Resistance fighters to escape from the Gestapo. Those attacks would have catered for a larger range of possible targets when the Mosquito was adapted to carry the 4,000lb 'cookie'. The MEW subsequently compiled an 11-page memorandum with no less than 102 specific targets for daylight Mosquito attack, all within 600 miles of Mildenhall.[116] That memorandum was MOST SECRET and sent to Air Cdre Bufton, DB (Ops).

What would have been 'precision bombing' for Main Force heavy bombers was for the CEP of the bombs to fall within the intended target area or aiming point as a matter of predictable and reliable operational process. That simply did not happen, either for Bomber Command or the USAAF; it does not always happen today either. Weapon delivery today uses GPS as a navigation, target location and weapon-homing aid and usually achieves less than 10 metres error.

The term 'precision' was used and abused by many individuals and committees in positions of authority during the combined bombing offensive. It can reflect no credit on those individuals and committees; there was no excuse; they should have known better than to argue about 'precision bombing' when the operational capability of the bomber forces – RAF and USAAF – was unable to satisfy such tasking.

115. Air 40/1815: MEW to DB (Ops), dated 9 Oct 43.
116. Ibid.: 'Targets for Precise Attack in Daylight' dated 26 Oct 43.

> Without such an understanding, the concurrent and ongoing criticisms of the results of those bombing operations were and are intellectually barren; and very regrettably the same criticism applies to many post-war historical assessments and arguments about the bombing offensive.
>
> The debate has moved to the morality of target selection regardless of the ability to locate or bomb the intended target.

There is an illuminating statement within a note to the CAS from DB (Ops) (Bufton); the note related to the War Cabinet meeting on 5 Apr 44, attended by both officers, which discussed at great length the bombing policy in preparation for D-Day. The War Cabinet was divided between Transportation targets in direct support of the Allied invasion landings and subsequent breakouts into France, or POINTBLANK strategic targets in Germany. One of the political issues was the likely number of French civilian casualties. In the note DB (Ops) (Bufton) quoted a Mean Radial Error – which means the same as CEP – of 640 yds for bombing accuracy, including an allowance for errors in TI markers.[117] By that time in the war, various navigation aids were in regular operational use and the French targets were comparatively close. Yet it must be seen that even in Apr 44 the bombing accuracy was a long way from 'precision' and both CAS and DB (Ops) knew that perfectly well.

Towards the end of the war the specialist Bomber Command squadrons using the heavy TALLBOY and GRAND SLAM bombs usually achieved the best accuracy. But those attacks were often conducted with visual target identification. Such conditions were rarely available over Germany to the main bomber forces, operating either by day or by night, above cloud and against a very capable enemy air defence system. The sequence of attacks by 617 and 9 Sqns against *Tirpitz* using TALLBOY is instructive:

- The first such attack on 15 Sep 44, operating from the Russian airfield at Yagodnik, was not seen to be effective and no hits were claimed. The ship was partially obscured by a dense smokescreen and only 15 TALLBOYs were dropped from altitudes between 11,350 and 17,500ft. It was subsequently determined that the ship had been crippled, largely by shock wave damage, and was not available for sea-going operations. She was subsequently moved on 15 Oct 44 to Tromsö.[118]
- A second attack was made with TALLBOYs on 29 Oct 44, but cloud cover denied visual target acquisition. The bombs were dropped on the estimated position of the battleship and there were no hits.

---

117. Air 20/5307: This Minute followed from a War Cabinet Mtg on 5 Apr 44 in which French casualties during pre-Normandy bombing raids were discussed. An important issue was the smaller CEP of 550 yd put forward by Zuckerman, who had advocated that value in consultation with Bomber Command. In the event, the bombing of French transportation targets by Bomber Command was more accurate than the CinC Harris had expected.
118. Bib. A31, Ch. 6, pp. 147–150.

- The image on Plate 2 shows the fall of 12,000lb TALLBOY bombs from a force of 29 Lancaster bombers that attacked *Tirpitz* at Tromso between 09.41 and 09.49 on 12 Nov 44.[119] Only 16 bombs were dropped, from an altitude of 14,000ft. There was no enemy fighter defence for the ship at that time. The target was acquired visually; it was emitting heavy smoke immediately prior to and during the attack but the stern section was visible to the bombers. The dispersion of the bomb impact points is important. The ship was nearly 1300ft long; four of the bombs fell outside the area of the chart, at least 1500ft from the ship; there were two direct hits. The scale of the chart is shown in the lower left hand section; it represents 200ft. The CEP of the bombs on this raid was about 350ft. The raid was a complete success and the two direct hits were 'precise' but it was quite exceptional and flown by RAF bomber squadrons that could very reasonably have been described as 'The Best of The Best'.

Three TALLBOY raids were necessary to secure the final eclipse of *Tirpitz*. Over 60 of those bombs were dropped from altitudes between 11,000 and 18,000ft and there were 2 direct hits. About half of the bombs were dropped on an estimated target location and about half against a target that was partly visible through smokescreens. At all times the ship was stationary. The bombing altitudes were lower than was usual against targets in Germany and occupied territories to improve bombing accuracy.

> It has always been a disappointing fallacy to claim or expect that 'precision' bombing was routinely available either to Bomber Command or to the USAAF during WW2.
> It may well have been expedient to have made such a claim but it was inconsistent with the truth in the real world.

Summary

The facts were and remain that bomb aiming at the time was a very imperfect science. By the end of the war, typical bomber crews in either Air Force under medium to good visual conditions had a 40–50 per cent probability of delivering a bomb, released at an altitude of 20,000ft, within 1,000ft of the intended bomb impact point.

Under non-visual conditions, typical bomber crews in the 8th USAAF using radar-guided bombing techniques would do very well to achieve a CEP of even one mile from the intended bomb impact point. When using H2X radar bombing through 10/10th cloud cover, the evidence shows just 40 per cent of bombs landing within three miles of the intended bomb impact point.[120]

---

119. Air 24/299 RAF Operations Record Book, Bomber Command, November 1944.
120. Bib. A21 'Operations Analysis in the US Eighth Air Force in World War 2', Ch. 11, p. 292.

None of the above sections on bombing techniques and results can or should be taken as any sort of criticism of the bomber crews.

Their bravery and perseverance in the face of daunting obstacles has too frequently been dismissed but it is only too well deserving of national recognition even now.

This author salutes those crews for the results that they did obtain, usually with equipment that was inadequate for the task.

Postscript

During the Falklands Campaign in 1982, RAF Vulcan bombers attacked the runway at Stanley. Two sticks of 21 x 1000lb bombs were dropped from an altitude of 10,000ft in clear visibility, using NBS navigation and bomb-aiming with a ground speed of 320kt. The Argentine air defences had not engaged the bombers during the bomb run. The runway was hit by two of these bombs and it was certainly put out of full operational use. Hercules transport aircraft could operate after the attack but fast-jets did not. The runway was considerably larger than was *Tirpitz*.

The key point is that this BLACK BUCK operation was 38 years after 1944 and the bombing accuracy remained imperfect. During WW2 most of the strategic bombing was done from an altitude of 20,000ft in poor visibility or at night and against a very active enemy air defence system. Those WW2 bomber aircrews were expected to deliver 'precision' bombing by many people in power who had no informed idea about the real operational challenges and limitations. They continue to be castigated by some post-war authors and historians who had no better understanding of that situation despite the availability of the archive records and the facts.

If the argument that persists today focuses on the morality of the strategic bombing offensive, then it is outside the scope of this book.

CHAPTER FIVE

Signals Intelligence within the Service Ministries

'For also Knowledge itself is Power.'

Francis Bacon, 1597

In time of war the ultimate object of all Signals Intelligence (Sigint) work was and remains to produce Intelligence – intelligence that is useful strategically, tactically, politically or economically to the prosecution of the war. Thus, for instance, the conduct of the Battle of the Atlantic may bear clear and close relation to the British reading of the Atlantic U-boat ENIGMA message traffic and also to the German reading of the British and subsequently Allied naval ciphers.

This chapter will look at the difficulties that existed at the start of the war concerning the functions of Signals Intercept, Cryptanalysis and Intelligence production. It will then provide an overview of the relationships that existed between GC & CS and the separate Service Ministries in London.

Signals Intercept, Cryptanalysis and Intelligence

There were particular problems that existed before the start of the war with regard to the practice of signals traffic interception and the related tasks of decoding and intelligence production. This has been briefly described in Chapter 7 of Bib. B28. There were other problems that related to the structure and resources of the three Service Y-organisations that conducted the signal traffic interception; and their need for rapid expansion and personnel training during the periods of general mobilisation and early stages of the war.

From the start and through a great deal of the war there was unresolved controversy about the function of Signals Intercept, otherwise known as Y-material, and the directly related task of Cryptanalysis. Signals intercept activity resided primarily with each of the single Services and the Foreign Office; and Cryptanalysis resided with GC & CS. The essence of the fundamental controversy, as described in Bib. B28 and elsewhere, revolved around misconceptions of the separate tasks and the 'ownership' of the signals products that were being generated. This became even more fractious when using the terms 'cryptography' and 'intelligence'. The nature of this controversy was uncompromising. There was no agreement even between the single Services. The Air Ministry stated that:

Cryptographers are not Intelligence Officers, but only exist to provide the material from which Intelligence is produced; and it is as well to keep the intelligence side as far divorced from the cryptographic side as possible.[1]

The Deputy Head of GC&CS expressed the view that such attitudes were mistaken and that:

It is quite obvious that cryptographers will always know more of interception than the interceptors can possibly know of cryptography.[2]

A statement by Gp Capt. Blandy, then Deputy Director of Signals (Y), in relation to the parochial attitudes of the single Services in general with regard to signals intelligence at the start of the war, was that:

The trouble is that people don't realise that the whole point of wireless is that there are no wires.[3]

His point was that signals and radio propagation obey the rules of physics. In the past, telephones were connected by copper wire and the signals followed the route of that wire via the appropriate switchboards. That was a physical constraint, subject only to wire-tapping and wire cutting. But with 'wireless' transmission, a signal transmitted between any two or more parties could be intercepted by any other parties who had a suitable radio or intercept receiver, irrespective of where they were located. The physical constraint resided with the rules of signal propagation through the atmosphere.

In the early stages of the war, the Army Y-Service intercepted a great deal of the German Air Force ENIGMA traffic that was of particular value to the RAF. There was at that time much less German Army ENIGMA traffic to intercept and it may be noted that the Army was not immediately aware of the origin of the traffic. But after some initial ENIGMA traffic had begun to be read early in 1940, it was suggested by Mr Josh Cooper, Head of the Air Section at Bletchley Park, that the Air Ministry should take a hand in intercepting that high-grade traffic. The reply from Gp Capt. Blandy was:

My Y-services exist to produce Intelligence, not to provide stuff for people at Bletchley to fool around with.[4]

Bletchley Park was not absolved from this controversy at all. GC&CS had always taken too little interest in the 'wireless traffic' by which it lived and in Traffic

---

1. HW 43/1, Ch. VI, 'Y' Versus 'Cryptography', p. 184.
2. HW 43/1, Ch. VI, 'Y' Versus 'Cryptography', p. 185.
3. HW 3/83, Commentary by Mr Josh Cooper, Head of AI 4f, the Air Section at Bletchley Park.
4. HW 3/83 Post-War Notes by Josh Cooper, Head of AI 4(f), p. 27.

Analysis (T/A) as a separate source of valuable intelligence. GC&CS was too reluctant, perhaps hiding behind the shield of security, to release any feedback to the intercept stations and their traffic analysts. Consequently, there was much wasted time and effort on false trails and absurd conjectures. The Air Section was a notable exception to this controversy and had close interaction with RAF Cheadle and RAF Kingsdown.

There was another fundamental and continuing source of conflict within the overall provision and planning of signals intelligence intercept resources, i.e. within the separate Y-Services of the military and foreign office departments. This problem was very much of pre-war and parochial origin. The provision of the single-service Y-resources was based upon the organisation of the separate military Services that they were intended to support; thus, one B-type for Corps, one A-type for Army, etc. The proper basis should have been to scale them on the enemy's organisation and the use that he made of his signals communications assets.[5] This would have required assessment of the enemy's communication assets but no attempt was ever made to derive such assessments:

If signals intelligence dances to the enemy's tune – and the saying is true, then it is provident to guess the enemy's programme before the band starts playing.[6]

Had such assessments been conducted, however roughly, the inadequacy of resourcing the British Y-Services would have become ridiculously obvious even to the most unimaginative and hide-bound Ministries. It may at least have formed the basis for a sensible expansion programme as the war developed. It was comparatively easy to increase the number of signals intercept receivers at any site, but it was very difficult to find trained operators to use them. Too much emphasis cannot be laid on the need for trained Y-operators. They are the first step in the signals intelligence ladder and their training generally took at least 6 months before reaching a basic level of competence. The shortage of trained and experienced Y-operators was a limiting factor for at least the first two years of the war.[7]

Another problem with GC&CS staffing was the conundrum of Service regulations and their application to Sigint staff appointments. For example: (1) no RAF commission could be granted to a fit man under the age of 35 given that his employment would not be on active service; (2) A man who was unfit for active service could be commissioned for Sigint work, but he would not be allowed into a war zone.

Coupled with this, the need for rapid personnel expansion of GC&CS – and also the separate Y-Services – during the initial mobilisation phase and the early wartime phase created a substantial dilution of the existing experienced staffs with unskilled personnel. The channel for recruitment that served very well for GC&CS was direct contact with the Universities and secondary schools. This channel had yielded 60 high-grade people and more as the war progressed.

---

5. HW 50/50: Memorandum by Nigel de Grey, 17 August 1949.

6. Ibid., p. 15.

7. Ibid. p. 12.

However, there was friction with the Treasury after mid-1940 relating to the numbers of such people; and there were diminishing numbers of suitable candidates as men and women joined the armed services and the research establishments.

There was never any clear understanding about the staffing of the individual Service sections at GC&CS. Everything tended to be done as a short-term solution of an immediate problem, coupled with the fact that there were very few regular service personnel; the great majority were war entry people. By an informal agreement, the separate services provided large blocks of the rapidly growing staff at GC&CS, e.g.

- The Women's Royal Naval Service worked the Bombes,
- The Army provided the Traffic Analysis staff for SIXTA (Hut 6, Traffic Analysis),
- The RAF and the Women's Auxiliary Air Force supplied much of the staff for the Air Section,
- The Women's Auxiliary Air Force worked the Communications facilities.

As a matter of record, Josh Cooper from the Air Section described the scale of ENIGMA decryption in Aug 42 as follows:

> The cryptanalysts in Hut 6 were reaping the full fruits of research in discriminant systems, key repeats, re-encryptments and stereotyped cribs. Fifty different ENIGMA keys were recognised everyday in the Control Room; 480 keys were broken in a single month releasing 40,000 message parts for decrypting and thus overwhelming the personnel and machines of the Decoding Room. The amount of ENIGMA intelligence that could be produced seemed to be limited only by the availability of intercept operators, personnel at GC&CS and Bombes. There was still no sign of any enemy action that would impose the least check on this flow of information.[8]

It must never be thought that GC&CS was able to decrypt every ENIGMA message that was intercepted; and it must never be thought that every ENIGMA message was in fact intercepted. Nothing could be further from the truth. One of the debts owed by the cryptographers was to the Traffic Analysis (T/A) work, which had often been disregarded by Hut 6 for various reasons: Faults in organisation; excessive safeguards on security; and Hut 6's own narrow outlook. The stultifying effect of security was widely attested and was recorded by the Hut 6 Historian in the words:

> We shall never know what was lost in the supposed interests of security.

The division into watertight security compartments within GC&CS and the outstations became simply unworkable and broke down finally through internal combustion rather than any official change of policy. The attitudes of some of the best-known members of GC&CS staff were often at the root of problems. As late

---

8. Bib. B1, Vol. 2, p. 627.

as Jun 41, Gordon Welchman was uncompromisingly hostile to Hut 6 T/A – well known as SIXTA. Stuart Milner-Barry, who was later to succeed Welchman, thought that Traffic Analysis was a 'fad'. But it was slowly realised and accepted that:

> *The only way of sorting messages without discriminants was by reference to the networks on which they passed. T/A records and T/A advice thus became essential to the efficient sorting of ENIGMA and a special department was formed within Hut 6 to study key discriminants in terms of the W/T picture and frame sorting instructions accordingly. This department was in fact a T/A party engaged on the special task of interpreting T/A information for an essential cryptographic purpose.*

As the volume of high-level traffic increased, especially after the scale of strategic bombing progressively wrecked internal landline communications in Germany and forced the enemy to use ENIGMA and FISH for much more signals traffic, there was a complementary increase in the pressure within GC&CS. The use of the Bombe machines was absolutely crucial to any hope of keeping pace with the incoming high-level traffic; but there was always the need for human translation, interpretation and the generation of ULTRA output messages to the appropriate addressees.

Relationships between GC&CS and Ministries
The relationships between GC&CS and the three Service Ministries differed significantly. The following sub-sections briefly describe examples of the individual arrangements within each of the three Services.[9]

Admiralty
Through until the end of 1940, the Naval Section at GC&CS had despatched to the OIC in Whitehall a translation of every decrypted text. This reassured the OIC that it retained the responsibility for appreciating the intelligence. But the Naval staffs at GC&CS were studying the material for a different purpose and in a different manner, to help with the work on decryption. They became more expert in interpreting the linguistic nuances and the specialised terminology; and then more expert in analysing the implicit information about the German Navy organisation and tactics. The OIC acknowledged that these skills were complementary to their own operational experience and that there was much to be gained not only by engaging with GC&CS about the evaluation of the Sigint but also by seeking their suggestions. This convergence between the OIC and GC&CS Naval Section was marked at the end of 1940 by the return to GC&CS of responsibility for Traffic Analysis, with relations becoming increasingly closer and mutually beneficial. The key sections within GC&CS were Hut 4 and Hut 8, with support from Hut 3 where ULTRA items of Naval interest were identified by the RN Advisers.

---

9. Bib. B1, Vol. 2, Appendix 2.

The Battle of the Atlantic

In war, so many factors besides good intelligence impinge on the conduct of operations that it is difficult to single out any single battle or period in which ULTRA was of decisive importance by itself. Yet there is one instance where one can say that this Special Intelligence played a decisive role in countering the enemy capabilities. By the first half of 1941, as more and more submarines were being produced, the German U-boat force was having a shattering impact on the maritime trade routes on which the survival of Great Britain depended. The curve of sinking of British, Allied, and neutral shipping was climbing upwards ominously.[10]

The German U-boats were controlled closely from shore and a massive amount of ENIGMA wireless signalling went back and forth to coordinate the movement of the evolving wolf pack organisation and tactics. Through the early spring of 1941, Bletchley had little success in solving the German navy's codes. However, on 12 March 1941, Bletchley received an ENIGMA key list that had been snatched from the German armed trawler *Krebs* during a commando raid in the Lofotens. In mid-May 1941, Bletchley also received a copy of the Kriegsmarine weather-reporting document that had been captured by the Royal Navy from a German weather ship, *München*, with considerable material detailing the settings for the German naval codes. This was supplemented by a second copy of that document from the *U-110* submarine, together with an ENIGMA machine and the accompanying material.[11] Thus, Bletchley was able to start breaking into the U-boat traffic during April and May, although this early work was of little operational value because of the time needed for the decryption process. However, as this was increasingly being read more quickly at Bletchley, the Admiralty gained invaluable information ranging from the number of U-boats available to tactical dispositions and patrol lines.

The first table opposite contains British Merchant Navy losses at sea within the North Atlantic, the North Sea and UK coastal waters to U-boats and aircraft through the six months ending on 31 May 1941. This excludes other British Merchant Navy ship losses to surface raiders, mines and E-Boats; losses to fishing ships; and ships lost in harbour to German bombing, etc.[12] During the first three months of 1941, there were extensive losses to North Atlantic convoys caused by the heavy surface ships *Admiral Scheer*, *Scharnhost*, *Gneisenau* and *Admiral Hipper*. The table does not contain neutral ship losses and does not address ships that were damaged but reached a safe harbour.

---

9. Bib. B1, Vol. 2, Appendix 2.
10. 'The War at Sea, Vol. 1', Captain Roskill, p. 616.
11. Bib. B29, See the 'Afterword' by Ralph Erskine, p. 267–268.
12. Author's Note: This information is taken from the daily Official Ship Casualty List of all Merchant Navy ships lost to enemy action during WW2 and recorded by the Registrar General. See BT 347/1 to BT347/7 for the years 1939–1945. During the first three months of 1941, the enemy also made extensive use of heavy surface ships such as *Scheer*, *Scharnhorst*, *Gneisenau* and *Hipper* to attack North Atlantic convoys. ENIGMA was unable to provide any useful naval information in that period about the operations of those surface warships.

British Merchant Navy Shipping Losses December 1940–May 1941

Month	Losses to U-boats		Losses to Aircraft	
	Number	Tonnage	Number	Tonnage
December 1940	25	163,316	3	6,104
January 1941	15	105,091	12	46,882
February 1941	32	173,685	15	51,096
March 1941	28	174,317	17	68,662
April 1941	30	188,607	15	40,754
May 1941	41	233,944	9	37, 444
Total	171	1,038,960	71	250,942

Once GC&CS had a full two months' experience inside the German U-boat traffic, they were able to continue breaking the German U-boat message traffic for the next five months. The impact that this dominant ULTRA intelligence, supported by other detection systems, had on the Battle of the Atlantic was almost immediate, as is indicated within the following table:

British Merchant Navy Shipping Losses June–November 1941

Month	Losses to U-boats		Losses to Aircraft	
	Number	Tonnage	Number	Tonnage
June 1941	35	201,772	16	39,228
July 1941	17	71,850	5	5,378
August 1941	16	60,575	4	13,851
September 1941	36	151,161	8	21,730
October 1941	19	101,094	5	12,848
November 1941	10	55,148	4	6,607
Total	133	643,600	42	99,642

However, it would be incorrect to suppose that the use of ENIGMA was the sole cause of these monthly reductions in Atlantic shipping losses, noting that there was a progressive increase in the size of the U-boat fleet. There were other important factors at work:

- By late spring 1941 the Western Approaches and other UK coastal waters had become increasingly hostile to U-boat operations, both because of an increased number of Royal Navy surface escorts and RAF air patrols primarily by Coastal Command. This forced the U-boats to operate further out into the Atlantic with the attendant problems of longer transit times and endurance limitations on station.

- The performance of Naval convoy escorts, their tactics and detection systems were improving.
- From June 1941 onwards some U-boats were deployed away from the Atlantic, coincident with the start of the German attack on Russia. Admiral Doenitz had recorded his irritation that Hitler had insisted on many U-boats being transferred to the Arctic and to the Mediterranean. Certainly there were heavy losses on the Arctic convoys during 1942, but Doenitz had argued that those U-boats would be more successful in Atlantic waters where there was even greater convoy traffic.
- There was an imperative to take no actions on the western side of the Atlantic that would provoke the USA into a declaration of war, notwithstanding that the US Navy was increasingly providing Atlantic convoy escorts from August 1941 onwards.

Most of the losses caused by aircraft attack related to the GAF use of the long-range reconnaissance bomber aircraft Focke-Wulf 200 Kondor (See Plate 3), typically operated by KG.40 from French airfields such as Bordeaux, along the coast of the Bay of Biscay. The Kondor had an endurance of 12–14 hours with a patrol range in excess of 2000 miles and could carry a 3000lb payload of bombs or mines. These aircraft operated individually to provide tactical information on convoys, their composition and their routes; they also attacked convoys and at such times it was likely that they would operate with two or more aircraft together. Their early tactics were low to medium level bombings and, by the end of 1940, KG.40 had sunk over 108,000 tons of shipping. The RAF Y-Service at Cheadle provided valuable information on KG.40 and kept a close 'ear' on its activities until the enemy evacuated the airfield at Bordeaux after the D-Day landings; a brief overview of this activity is provided within Appendix B. Some use of Sigint information was made when Bomber Command raided the Bordeaux base on 22 Nov 40 and brought about a reduction in KG.40's operations, for three weeks.[13] The recorded minutes discuss the use of Y-information to assess the probable timings of the return of these aircraft to base and recommended that bombing attacks be mounted at dusk. However a later minute, dated 23 Dec 40, noted that with the limited operational resources available to Bomber Command, such operations could not be undertaken. That minute was written by Gp Capt. Baker, who later became Director Bomber Operations (DB (Ops)).

The activities of KG.40 continued to be a serious problem, not only with bombing but also particularly with reconnaissance. There is further evidence of a Kondor operating from Bordeaux, attacking a convoy 95 miles north-west of Cape Wrath and then landing at Stavanger in Norway.[14]

The pattern of patrols was seen to be along a semi-circle from Bordeaux to Norway and, as a result, it was decided in London to revise the routeing of convoys south of Iceland. The Prime Minister became directly involved with the Directive entitled 'The Battle of the Atlantic', issued on 6 Mar 41.[15] It was read to Parliament in a Secret Session on 25 Jun 41: at Paragraph 1 it said:

---

13. Air 40/2321, DDI 3 Minutes, 16 Dec 1940.
14. Air 40/2322, DDI 3 Minutes, 20 February 1941.
15. Bib. B30, Vol. III, pp. 107–109.

We must take the offensive against the U-boat and the Focke-Wulf wherever we can and whenever we can. The U-boat at sea must be hunted, the U-boat in the building yard or in the dock must be bombed. The Focke-Wulf and other bombers employed against our shipping must be attacked in the air and in their nests.

Very soon afterwards, the Prime Minister wrote to the First Lord of the Admiralty and the Secretary of State for Air to say that:

The German use of aircraft to guide the U-boats onto the convoys was largely responsible for the heavy shipping losses. No effort should be spared to destroy the Focke-Wulfs.

He had directed that methods should be found to disturb the radio communications between the aircraft and the U-boat Controller at Brest; and certainly that those aircraft radio communications should be D/F'ed. This is perhaps indicative of the overall awareness and grasp that the Prime Minister had on so many details.

Coincident with the US entry into the war in Europe, following the Japanese attack on Pearl Harbor in Dec 41, the German Navy modified its use of the ENIGMA machines and began to use a fourth rotor. The introduction of four-rotor encryption and the separate issue of a new version of the Kriegsmarine weather-reporting document in Jan 42 largely defeated Bletchley's efforts on German naval decryption throughout 1942. But that did not mean that there was no CX/MSS material on enemy naval plans. Z/MSS 6 was a summary of CX/MSS material that reported on enemy intentions against convoys on the Gibraltar run, the intention was to operate a force of Fw-200s, Ju86s and torpedo-carrying He111s in conjunction with U-boats, similar to the effort that had been used against the Arctic convoys.[16] Further details are provided within Appendix B.

Allied shipping losses on Atlantic routes soared through 1942. This was not reversed until the end of 1942, following the incredibly brave action by three members of the crew of HMS *Petard* on 30 October 1942, when they boarded the submarine *U-559* as she was sinking. They recovered a copy of the latest weather-reporting document that provided Bletchley with the 'cribs' into the U-boat message traffic. Two of the RN crew were drowned when the submarine sank; one survived. All were awarded the George Cross for bravery.

The Battle of the Atlantic continued unabated. During the Spring of 1943 the Kondors were known to have been equipped with precision bombsights for high-level attacks.[17] The preliminary directive for 'The Bomber Offensive from the United Kingdom' as approved by the Combined Chiefs of Staff, at the 65th Meeting on 21 Jan 43, placed German submarine construction yards as first priority in the target list, but also with direct interest in the operating bases on the Biscay coast.[18] There is an illuminating letter signed by VCAS, then Air Vice

---

16. HW 14/43: Z/MSS 6 dated 17 Jul 42. This report was based on CX/MSS material.
17. Air 20/1172, 'GAF Activity Bay of Biscay Area' dated 18 Jun 43 from AI 3b.
18. Air 14/1220, E61B.

Marshal Medhurst, to the effect that the War Cabinet had agreed that those French ports were to be destroyed.[19] The letter explicitly used the words,

The towns as well as the ports should be razed to the ground, thus denying to the Germans any facilities whatsoever in those areas.

That direction from the War Cabinet implicitly called for 'area bombing' against the submarine bases, which were in French coastal cities. A subsequent signal from the Air Ministry to Bomber Command on 14 Feb 43 stated that attacks would be confined to Lorient; the received copy of that signal at Bomber Command has the handwritten note by the CinC: 'Gp Capt. Ops – *Action*'.

The Admiralty and some senior ministers were calling for the bombers to provide escorts for convoys. But some basic operational factors were not well appreciated. If a convoy was 4 hours flying time from say Cornwall, then how long would a bomber aircraft have over the convoy before it had to return to base for fuel. How many bombers would therefore be needed to provide continuous cover during the daylight hours for that one convoy; what about convoys outside of that radius? Doing the simple arithmetic, it is not difficult to see that those bombers would have spent a great deal of time in transit over water with little or no operational benefit.

Meanwhile, the continuing success of the German xB-Dienst, the Kriegsmarine codebreaking section, appeared to escape the attention of the Admiralty:

It may be important to read the enemy's signals; it is no less important to prevent him reading your signals.[20]

The Allied navies could not use cipher machines to encrypt all their various signals traffic until November 1943. The reason stemmed in no small part from inadequate resources and from the inability of the RN and the US Navy to find common ground on the cipher machines to be used.[21] Until mid-1943, the xB-Dienst read most of the daily Allied signals giving the disposition of U-boats and were consequently able to appreciate the evasion routes for the convoys. It was not until early 1944, when new Allied cipher equipment became fully operational, that the xB-Dienst was unable to exploit the Allied naval message traffic apart from direction finding and location data.

It should not pass without comment that one particular aspect of U-boat ENIGMA traffic that secured great attention and success was that associated with the 'supply U-boats', otherwise known as the '*Milch-Kühen*'. It was appreciated that the loss of these submarines would have a disproportionate impact on the overall fleet of 'attack' U-boats. There was serious discussion between the RN and the US Navy about the strategy and tactics that should be employed; much surrounded the imperative not to compromise the ENIGMA source. The most

19. The Harris Archives, H16: MOST SECRET: VCAS to CinC Bomber Command dated 12 Jan 43.
20. Bib. B29, German naval codebreaking, p. 273.
21. Ibid. p. 273.

successful actions were taken by the US Navy escort carrier (CVE) task groups in the Atlantic. They used ULTRA data to track down and engage U-boats and their supply boats.[22] As a consequence, many U-boats were unable to re-fuel and re-arm at sea and had to return to port; and the loss of the French Atlantic ports after D-Day very seriously compromised that logistics requirement. The success of these CVE operations came close to compromising the ENIGMA source and there were serious UK concerns about the operational usage of that material by the US Navy. Bib. B29, on page 280, also shows that a very worrying message was sent from the Abwehr (the German Intelligence Service) in mid-Aug 43 that reported:

> *For some months German Naval ciphers giving orders to operational U-boats have been successfully broken. All orders are read currently.*

The source was said to be a Swiss-American in the US Navy Department; his existence or identity remain a mystery. A leading German expert on the Battle of the Atlantic has noted:

> *I am sure that without the work of many unknown experts at Bletchley Park, the turning point of the Battle of the Atlantic would have come not in mid-1943, but months – perhaps many months – later. In that case, the Allied invasion of Normandy would not have been possible in June 1944 and there would have ensued a chain of events very different from what we have experienced.*[23]

In the later stages of the war from mid-1994 onwards, the value of Sigint was again demonstrated when the new U-boats, Types XXI and XXIII, were being brought into service. The OIC in Whitehall was able to determine the German industrial production plans for these new U-boats, together with the operational intentions of Admiral Doenitz for all U-boats in the home waters of the Baltic Sea, the North Sea and the English Channel. The coincident breaching of the Dortmund-Ems and the Mittelland canals by Bomber Command in November 1944 severely handicapped the transportation of prefabricated sections of U-boats to the assembly yards. That was exacerbated by the equally successful mining operations in the eastern Baltic, again by Bomber Command, which seriously impacted on the U-boat working-up programmes. And the final air attacks, often by Mosquitoes and Typhoons, took place when the operational U-boats were making the hazardous sea passage in comparatively shallow water from Kiel out into the North Sea. The general contribution of Sigint to those air operations was of vital importance, not least in terms of D/F accuracy and rapid reporting.

One final incident should serve to underline the high price of German carelessness where signals security was concerned. *Bismarck* and *Prinz Eugen* had broken out into the Atlantic in May 41 on a raiding expedition. After sinking the

---

22. Bib. B29, The American Contribution, p. 280.
23. Jurgen Rohwer, 'Ultra and the Battle of the Atlantic: the German View', included within 'Changing Interpretations and New Sources in Naval History' edited by Robert Love, jr. (New York, 1980).

battle cruiser HMS *Hood*, they managed to slip away from shadowing British cruisers. The pursuing British admiral decided at 1800 hours on May 25 that the *Bismarck* was making for Brest. Within an hour, the Admiralty had confirmation of that opinion through a Luftwaffe, not Kriegsmarine, intercept. Luftwaffe authorities had radioed their Chief of Staff, then visiting Athens during the German invasion of Crete, that *Bismarck* was heading for Brest.[24] The reason for that message was that the Chief of Staff's son was on board *Bismarck*.

The War Office

The Military Section at GC & CS was originally directly subordinate to MI 8. It had a purely cryptanalysis function and Traffic Analysis was conducted elsewhere, only joining to GC & CS in 1942. It had no intelligence commitment and the military decrypts from GC & CS passed through MI 8 to the War Office, as did the separate products of Traffic Analysis.

Military Intelligence had received a good deal of information from the GAF ENIGMA decrypts during the German offensives into Western Europe, but from June 1940 that traffic had little value for the War Office. The War Office Y-Service had been taking ENIGMA traffic from the GAF, initially under the assumption that this was German Army traffic. GC & CS had had no more success with German Army signals traffic than it had with the Navy. In the case of the German Army, their medium and low-grade codes were not broken during 1940. For what were perfectly justifiable reasons, the War Office decided to move its Traffic Analysis work to Bletchley at the end of 1940. But the Director of GC & CS opposed this, on the grounds that GC & CS should be a 'cryptographic centre'. It was particularly inconsistent because at the same time the Naval Section was assuming responsibility for Traffic Analysis on behalf of the Admiralty. There were other factors, including the grave shortage of working space that was then available at Bletchley; and the covert worry that GC & CS could become subordinated to military control.

The Air Ministry

The Air Section at GC & CS was initially responsible for medium and low-grade W/T cryptanalysis work, a responsibility that was shared with the main RAF Y-Station at Cheadle. This became a most productive arrangement and produced a large volume of Sigint material. Radio Telephony (R/T) had been conducted as a separate activity within the RAF Y-Service and the Air Section had no access to these results until the autumn of 1940, when Air Intelligence AI 4 realised that Kingsdown and the Home Defence Units (HDUs) were unable to solve some of the R/T codewords and map grid references. The HDUs were the individual RAF signals intercept stations mostly located around the south-east coast of England.

But the Air Section was for nearly three years prohibited from having any separate contact with operational users of intelligence; the entire Sigint product had to be sent to the Air Ministry. This was a security rule rigidly applied initially by the Deputy Director of Signals (Y) and then carried into Air Intelligence AI 4

---

24. Bib. B29, Ch. 5, pp. 84–85.

and maintained until late in 1942. Even then there was considerable reluctance to allow any contact, especially to Bomber Command.

By a decision taken in December 1940, the Air Section was also debarred from any control of or access to GAF ENIGMA work. This restriction was a direct consequence of a rigid application of ENIGMA security rules by the management of GC&CS. That rule also remained in force for a long time.

The early success during the spring of 1940 by GC&CS in breaking the GAF ENIGMA Yellow key demonstrated that neither GC&CS nor the Whitehall departments were equipped to handle those decrypts efficiently. The textual content of the traffic eluded the GC&CS staff's ability to make intelligent interpretation; and the Air Section was excluded from this high-grade subject.

Air Intelligence, with its responsibility for co-coordinating intelligence from all sources and with its internal concerns to control the interpretation and assessment of that intelligence, frowned on the efforts of the GC&CS Air Section to fuse together the separate sources of Sigint. Other problems arose as a consequence of the attachment to GC&CS of RAF officers, to advise on the interpretation of ENIGMA decrypts and the selection of such messages for onwards transmission to the Air Intelligence staff in London. The Air Section at GC&CS became a sub-section of Air Ministry Intelligence DDI 4, when that branch became responsible for Air Sigint in April 1941.

A most pointed overview of the relationship between Air Intelligence in London and the Air Section at GC&CS was written by Joshua (Josh) Cooper, who had been appointed as Head of the Air Section in 1936 and remained in that appointment for most of war. He was a most respected senior member of GC& CS and held Deputy Director status from 1944. In a personal report that he wrote in 1944, for the Director of GC&CS, the opening words were:

On looking back over the various difficulties experienced by Air Section during the German War in its relations with Air Ministry, I find it a little hard to separate out difficulties due to personalities from those inherent in the set-up itself. Five men – Allen, Blandy, Cadell, Fitch and Daubney – had ruled over Air Ministry Sigint in the relative period and only one of these was really satisfactory to work with. But after all, a set-up which only works when one exceptional man is in charge cannot be regarded as wholly satisfactory.[25]

When Huts 6 and 3 were formed as independent sections at Bletchley, they lay right across the accepted and planned pre-war and early wartime organisation. Hut 3 reported relevant ULTRA direct to the Admiralty – in liaison with Hut 4 – and to Military Intelligence and to specific sections within Air Intelligence, bypassing MI 8 and DDI 4. The judgement on 'relevance' rested with the separate Service Advisors within Hut 3. The details of the Air Intelligence organisation and its evolution within the Air Ministry are shown in Chapter 6.

Hut 3 had direct ULTRA communication with Military and Air Commands overseas, through the Special Liaison Units (SLUs); but not to Bomber, Fighter and

---

25. HW 3/83: Attached to a hand-written covering note to Frank Birch, dated 11 Jun 48, was a typed report. That report was written in 1944 and intended only for the eyes of the then Director of GC&CS, Sir Edward Travis, KCMG.

Coastal Commands within UK, except for the informal 'leak' to Coastal Command via the Naval Section. Hut 3 was in effect providing a function similar to that which NID provided for the Admiralty, except that it was debarred from reporting lower grade Sigint source material otherwise used by the Military Section and the Air Section. GC&CS had unknowingly created a most complicated internal structure that violated the official chains of reporting for Sigint, driven partly by the security regulations for the handling and dissemination of ULTRA material. At that time, DDI 4 within Air Intelligence failed to organise and bring coherence across the various Air Intelligence Sigint elements that had been created.

The history of the relations between GC&CS and Air Intelligence shows ongoing difficulties that essentially result from this bad organisation. There were improvements from 1942 onwards, but at all times the channels set up and the entrenched interests had to be respected and this resulted in 'tinkering operations' which added to, as much as they reduced, the overall complications. The outcome was at least some reduction in the gross waste of intelligence that had been occurring primarily during the first three years of the war but which continued in varying extents throughout the war. This waste of Air Intelligence material arose from several factors:

- The severance of contact between the various forms of Sigint, e.g. High, Medium and Low-grade decrypts; R/T and T/A.
- The tendency outside of GC&CS to accept 'facts' and ignore 'implications' in the reported Sigint.
- Lack of knowledge within GC&CS in presentation of the reported Sigint products, to highlight the operational content in a concise fashion.
- Lack of personal contacts between GC&CS and the operational users.
- Lack of skilled Sigint interpretation by the recipients, both within the Air Ministry and the Commands.

In the reverse direction, a long battle was waged to obtain 'feed-back' of tactical information from the Services, regarding position of own troops, local intelligence, commanders' intentions, etc. These difficulties varied enormously, but corresponded roughly to the problems of acquiring the original enemy signals traffic and to the value that it could deliver to the Allied commanders in the field.

Associated with this information exchange problem was the challenge of multi-national Allied Commands and the inherent exchange and liaison with intelligence material.

For the first three years of Bomber Command's war over the continent, ULTRA could provide little useful intelligence. On the other hand, throughout 1942 and 1943, ULTRA information provided valuable insights into what the Germans and Italians were doing in the Mediterranean and North Africa.[26] Allied naval and air

---

26. HW 14/43: A valuable insight into the extent of that ENIGMA material is provided in the MOST SECRET message from Bletchley Park (Nigel de Grey) to 'C', sent as 1701/20/7/42+++. It describes the situation in the North African battle, with special attention to Tobruk. Reference is made to about two dozen CX/MSS intercepts that identify in detail the intentions and situation for the German/Italian forces and their

commanders were provided with detailed, specific knowledge of the movement of Axis convoys from the Italian mainland to the North African shores. By Mar 43, Anglo-American air forces operating in the Mediterranean had virtually shut down seaborne convoys to the Tunisian bridgehead. Allied army commanders were provided with comparable details of Axis army movements and intentions. Allied information was so good, in fact, that the German air corps located in Tunisia reported to its higher headquarters (in a message ironically intercepted and decoded):

the enemy activity today in the air and on the sea must in [the] view of Fliegerkorps Tunis, lead to the conclusion that the course envisaged for convoy D and C was betrayed to the enemy. At 0845 hours a comparatively strong four-engine aircraft formation was north of Bizerte. Also a warship formation consisting of light cruisers and destroyers lay north of Bizerte, although no enemy warships had been sighted in the sea area for weeks.

All the evidence pointed to the need for clear agreement between the Allied nations that there had to be complete liaison; that there had to be a single intelligence controller within a given theatre; and that the greater the level of integration, then the greater the harmony and efficiency of the combined intelligence products.

---

dependence on shipping transport. What was particularly noted by de Grey, from the enemy reports within ENIGMA, was that the Allied air and naval attacks were doing little harm in comparison with the vastness of the target opportunities (e.g. CX/MSS/1211/T21). The evidence was clearly showing that those opportunities would be lost by about 25–26 July, when the enemy would have restocked. Those enemy messages reported that Tobruk was inadequately defended, particularly against torpedo bomber attack (CX/MSS/1199/13).

CHAPTER SIX

Air Ministry Intelligence

'In general, every student must hold in suspicion whatever most captures and holds his understanding; to keep the understanding clear and balanced.'

Francis Bacon

Introduction

This chapter will provide an overview of the organisation of the Air Intelligence directorate throughout the war. It will then provide a description of those Air Intelligence functions that had:

- Particular association with the provision of Sigint, intelligence appreciations, target selection and targeting material for Bomber Command and subsequently also for the USAAFs.
- Direct and indirect association with the Air Ministry Directives that set down the targets and their relative priorities for the strategic bombing operations.

Sigint was only one part of the overall function and responsibility of Air Intelligence within the Air Ministry. There were many other important activities and there is no intention whatsoever to discount those other activities by not addressing their functions and achievements in this book, other than where those activities had direct association with Sigint within the context of the bombing offensives. That association was usually as a user of the Air Sigint products.

To illustrate the relative size of the Air Intelligence directorate and the various deputy directorates, their personnel strengths at different periods during the war are summarised at Appendix C. These strengths would generally have reflected the 'established' strength of the separate deputy directorates. In this context, the word 'established' has very significant importance because it identifies exactly how many personnel, with their different military ranks, were authorised in the different deputy directorates. There would have been prior discussion, argument and compromise in the process of setting these 'establishments', not least with the Finance branch regarding the cost and the overall budget that was allowed by the Treasury. Even in wartime, the finance and budget had to be taken into account.

The key point, which is drawn from these personnel strengths, is that Air Sigint had but small numbers of personnel; this is seen from Appendix C which contains details of the established strength of the Air Intelligence Directorate as the war progressed. It may be that these small numbers reflected the generally accepted status and perceived value of Sigint at that period in time. There was no previous experience in the overall task of appreciating, managing and disseminating Sigint products, in the context of an air war where events happened relatively quickly. That experience was to be gained on a day-to-day basis, under the pressure of concurrent combat operations; usually by personnel who had little military training or experience or knowledge of the operational intelligence requirements of the Air Commanders in the field. In the light of the variable but generally very high volume of signals traffic and derived reports, primarily from GC&CS and the RAF Y-Service, it may be that there was unknowingly inadequate staffing to adequately cater for the actual task, as it evolved throughout the war. This is amplified later in this book at pp. 201–203 within a section that examines the responsibility for Air Sigint.

A related and equally important factor would have been the availability of suitable personnel. There were many other wartime appointments and requirements, far beyond the Air Ministry, for men and women who may have had the potential to become good intelligence officers. Comparison is made here between the different approaches taken towards recruitment by Air Intelligence and Bletchley Park. The Air Ministry did not appear to have the contacts with the universities, as had been developed by Cdr Denniston, the Director of GC&CS. The Services' attitude, not unique to the Air Ministry, was that men of military age should not go to 'civilian posts'. A key example of this may be the recruitment of Mr A W Bonsall, by Bletchley Park. He joined the Air Section on New Year's Day 1940 as a civilian assistant from Cambridge University.[1] Mr Bonsall became one of key members of the Air Section for the remainder of the war; and subsequently Director of GCHQ from 1973 to 1978. Other key members of the Air Section were also recruited from Cambridge as 'computor clerks', following the agreement that Denniston secured with Gp Capt. Blandy that he could recruit directly for the Air Section rather than via the Air Ministry.[2]

Organisation Changes during the War
At the start of WW2 the Directorate was housed in the Air Ministry Building, King Charles Street, Whitehall. The exception was AI 1(b), which then dealt with target information and was located at Iver in Buckinghamshire. In Aug 41, the majority of the intelligence sections relocated to the new Air Ministry building in Westminster. The internal organisation went through major changes which are summarised in the following sub-sections. The purpose is to provide the reader with an idea of the tortuous path of Signals Intelligence within the Air Intelligence Directorate. The sub-sections are:

- From Pre-War to the end of 1940
- From January 1941 to August 1943
- From September 1943 to the End of the War.

---

1. HW 3/83, Personal Notes on GC&CS 1925–1939, by Josh Cooper (undated), p. 30.
2. The term 'computor clerk' was an echo of the War Office cover-name 'signal computor' used for cryptanalysts.

From Pre-war to the End of 1940

Prior to the outbreak of war, the Directorate of Intelligence was small and consisted of a director, three deputy directors [DDI 1–3], one assistant director and a Map Branch. There was no technical intelligence section. DDI 1 was then responsible for the receipt and dissemination of Air Intelligence, including Signals and Wireless intelligence which was initially handled by the Deputy Director of Signals (Y) in the Air Ministry Signals Directorate. There was one squadron leader and one flight lieutenant responsible for signals intelligence in DDI 1. Even less attention was paid to photographic intelligence, which was served by a single squadron leader. The harsh lessons of combat were to expose these shortcomings. A statement that resonates clearly was by Josh Cooper, Head of the Air Section at Bletchley:

We had not the least idea of the scale of the problem that was to confront us.[3]

The total staff of Air Intelligence in Sep 39 was about 40 officers, of whom about half were re-employed retired officers. Many of these were retired Army officers and that may have reflected the fact that the RAF was still a relatively 'new' Service. It was intended that this small staff would be supplemented in war from the RAF Staff College, but at the outbreak of war it rapidly became apparent that those regular officers at Staff College were being appointed to other duties.[4]

In order to supplement the officer personnel of the Directorate from sources other than currently serving regular officers, steps were taken to earmark a number of civilians for appointments in the Directorate when war started. These civilians undertook to join the RAF in case of war and formed a Civil (Staff Duties) Reserve, which was entirely an Intelligence organisation. But it was soon realised that the number of such civilians was insufficient. It had not been possible in pre-war 'peace time' to obtain people with the necessary experience and knowledge. It therefore became necessary to seek and recruit additional civilians, who received just a one-week training course.

Intelligence officers were also required at Commands, Groups and stations; after selection and recruiting, they also were required to attend the Directorate for a one-week familiarisation visit. There is only so much that can be contained within a one-week course; aggravated by the fact that the scope of the course did not and could not have covered anywhere near enough of the as yet unknown and unforeseen requirements.

The first year of the war saw rapid expansion in the number of personnel in Air Intelligence, growing from 40 to about 230. One new section that was created in May 1940 was AI 1(w), with the purpose of providing a group of Duty Officers for 24-hour coverage of Air Intelligence. Until that time, the night duty officer was provided from a roster from all sections. It became apparent as the war developed, just prior to the German invasion of France, that there was a need for a permanently staffed central office to deal with the receipt, assessment and distribution of urgent signals and messages. Later, AI 1(w) was re-titled as AI 3(a)(1) and maintained an unbroken watch until the end of hostilities in May 1945.

---

3. HW 3/83, Personal Notes on GC & CS 1925–1939, by Josh Cooper (undated).
4. Air 40/1493 Air Intelligence Handbook, Part III, Ch. 9.

By November 1940, the pre-war geographical basis of the internal Air Intelligence organisation had become meaningless in the light of the German occupation of most of Europe. The first major internal revision since the start of the war created an organisation as shown below.[5] The complete organisation is shown at Appendix D:

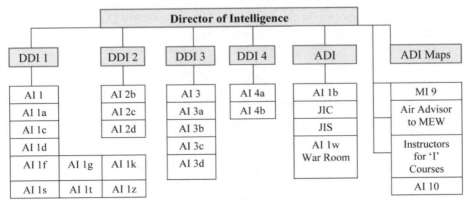

Air Intelligence Organisation – Late 1940

There were then four Deputy Directorates and one Assistant Director, each headed by a Group Captain and having the following broad responsibilities:

- DDI 1: Receipt, Record and Dissemination of Intelligence matters.
- DDI 2: Neutral unthreatened countries.
- DDI 3: Germany and occupied countries. Within DDI 3, there was a slow but progressive move towards section specialisation on a functional basis: AI3 (b) dealt with order of battle and organisation; AI3(c) dealt with aircraft production, air raid damage and attacks on transportation; and AI3 (d) dealt with airfields.
- DDI 4: (Newly created): Italy and the Balkans, and Middle East countries likely to be involved in the Italian war.
- ADI: Production of the Air Ministry Weekly Bulletin; Air staffing in the War Room and the JIC/JIS.

The Director was Air Cdre Boyle. AI 1c was Wg Cdr F W Winterbotham, then responsible for Liaison Duties and what would subsequently become the Special Liaison Units (SLUs), which were attached to many of the overseas Commands and provided the signals connections to Bletchley Park for the ULTRA reports; this is described later in this chapter. He later became Gp Capt. and, long after the war ended, author of 'The Ultra Secret' (Bib. B27).[6]

---

5. Air 40/1493, Air Intelligence Handbook (draft), Organisation of Intelligence.
6. Author's Note: Another member of the Intelligence staff at that time was Dennis Wheatley, the subject of an exchange of minutes between D of I (O) and Vice-Chief of Air Staff in July 1941 concerning the Weekly Air Intelligence Summary. Dennis subsequently wrote a series of well-known books such as *The Satanist*.

From January 1941 to August 1943

By April 1941, the original Intelligence Directorate had grown substantially and was upgraded to Air Board level with the appointment of an Assistant Chief of Air Staff (Intelligence) – ACAS (I) – at Air Vice Marshal rank and three new Directorates each at Air Commodore rank. These new Directorates of Intelligence were Security, Operations and Allied Air Cooperation and Foreign Liaison (DAFL). This organisation is shown below, down to Deputy Director (DD) level. A complete structure is shown at Appendix E:

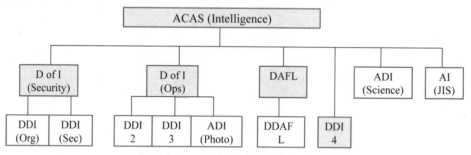

Air Intelligence Organisation – 22 July 1942

A further element of this expansion was the complete revision of the functions of DDI 4. The previous territorial functions of DDI 4 were re-allocated to DDI 2 and DDI 3, consistent with their increasingly functional specialisations.

The significance of Sigint had become increasingly apparent to some minds and in consequence the Deputy Directorate of Signals Y (Gp Capt. Blandy), responsible for the study of enemy wireless traffic, their codes, ciphers and call signs and the production of intelligence from decodes, was transferred from the Signals Directorate into Air Intelligence and re-designated as the new DDI 4, reporting directly to ACAS (I). The previous AI 1e was re-designated as AI 4, subordinate to DDI 4.

The functions of the new DDI 4 are shown below, as they prevailed in Dec 41. The functions of DDI 4 are examined in more detail later in this book, at pages 201 *et seq.*

Internal Organisation of DDI 4 at December 1941

AI4 (a)	Ground and Air Enemy RDF inventions; new Radio Aids; all unknown forms of transmission other than signals communications.	2 Sqn Ldrs; 2 Flt Lts. 1 Sect Off; 1 LACW.
AI4 (b)	All German Air radio traffic; control and allocation of tasks at the RAF Y stations, to secure maximum intelligence information. The Section worked on a 24-hour watch basis.	1 Wg Cdr; 1 Sqn Ldr. 2 Flt Lts; 2 Fg Offs; 2 Sect Offs.
AI4(c)	Analysis of GAF W/T traffic to determine enemy Order of Battle, Serviceability, casualties, location	1 Sqn Ldr; 1 Fg Off; 1 Flt Off; 4 Sect Offs.

of Units, movements & the general structure of GAF Operations. Compilation of enemy Call sign indexes.	Plotting Room: 1 Flt Sgt; 3 Sgts; 3 Cpls; 9 ACWs.
AI4 (d) Research into special lines of signals traffic. German Signals and Y Organisation.	1 Flt Lt; 1 Sect Off. Watchkeepers: 1 Flt Lt; 3 Fg Offs
AI4 (e) Organisation and Personnel matters: Home and. Overseas Y activities.	
AI4 (f) GC&CS Air Section, located at Bletchley Park.	

From September 1943 to the End of the War

There were further changes as the war continued. The major change, in the autumn of 1943, was the creation of a new Directorate of Intelligence (Research) [D of I (R)], which absorbed the previous DDI 4 and DD1 2 and became responsible for Air Sigint in a more coordinated manner. The high-level organisation within the whole Air Intelligence department is shown in the table below; with the complete structure shown at Appendix F.

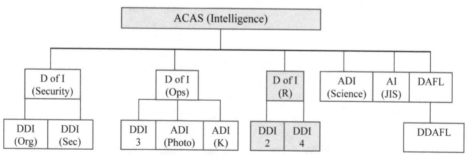

Air Intelligence Organisation – April 1944

Coincident with the creation of D of I (R) was a substantial re-organisation of the Directorate of Intelligence (Operations) [D of I (Ops)]. DDI 2 moved to D of I (R); prisoner of war interrogation was elevated to an Assistant Directorate, ADI (K); and the functions within DDI 3 were revised significantly and are shown in comparative fashion in following table:

Comparison of Functions within DDI 3.

Functions of DDI 3 before and after September 1943	
January 1941–August 1943	*September 1943 to End of War*
AI 3a Distribution of Teleprinted Intelligence; FO telegrams; Selection, précis & allocation of General Int to ACAS (I), DDI 3 & other Int sections; Political &	AI 3a (1) Distribution of Information; Liaison with other Service Depts & RAF Commands; Preparation of Daily Int Summaries.

	Strategic Int; General assistance to AI (JIS)	AI 3a (2)	Editing the Weekly Int Summary; Political & Strategic Int; Preparation of Appreciations & Collation of information from Specialist Sections; Preparation of Daily Summaries of General Int; General assistance to AI (JIS); Liaison with other Govt Depts & the BBC.
AI 3b	Air Forces of Germany, Italy, France, Spain, Portugal, Bulgaria, Romania, Hungary; General Int on Ireland, Iceland, Greenland and Spitzbergen; Current Enemy Air Ops; Forecast of Future Intentions & Scales of Attack.	AI 3b	Order of Battle of German & Satellite Air Forces; Liaison with RAF & USAAF Command Int Sections, the Admiralty & the War Office; Estimates of Future Scales of Attack & Forecasts of German Air Intentions.
AI 3c	Target Int; Enemy air craft losses; Assessment of Air Raid damage; Fuel Int.	AI 3c (1)	Production of Target Material for use by RAF and USAAF; Liaison with MEW.
		AI 3c (2)	Results of Bombing, Sea-mining & Attacks on Shipping by RAF & USAAF in European Theatre.
AI 3d	Middle-East & Far East national air forces, including Russia & Japan.	AI 3d	Japanese Air Force Order of Battle; Scales of attack & Forecast of Intentions.
AI 3e	GAF Intelligence; POW Interrogation; Research & Recording of Past Campaigns & Operations.	AI 3e	Organisation of GAF (other than Order of Battle); GAF Transport & Training; Personnel & POW Interrogation; Research & Recording of Past Campaigns & Operations.
		AI 3f	Organisation & Operations of Air Forces of Russia and neutral countries.
AI 3 (USA)	USA & South American air forces	AI 3 (USA)	USA & Latin American Air Forces Orders of Battle & Organisation; Liaison with USAAF in UK, the US Embassy & the RAF Delegation in Washington (RAFDEL).

It is these new and revised functions within D of I (R) and DDI 3, and the previous DDI 4 back to the spring of 1941, that have much relevance to the examination of the operational intelligence and Sigint support that was provided to the Bomber Offensives. To illustrate the relative size of the Air Intelligence Directorate throughout the war and the specific size of that section, latterly DDI 4, which was directly responsible for Sigint, the personnel strengths at specific dates during the war are shown in Appendix C. An overview of these personnel strengths is shown in the table below:

Overview of the Personnel Strength of Air Intelligence.

Date	Feb 40	May 41	May 42	Nov 42	Mar 43	Nov 43	Oct 44	Jan 45
Overall Strength of Air Intelligence	54	271	251	291	365	408	459	412
DDI 3	18	29	64	73	95	103	116	112
Sigint & Y staff (DDI 4 from Dec 41)	3*	5*	17	22	29	26	20	26

Note: (1) These figures are derived from the Air Force Lists for the particular dates and do not include NCOs, airmen and civilian grades below clerical officer.
(2) *The Sigint and Y staff totals for Feb 40 and May 41 are unclear; the work was done by one section within DDI 1; see Appendix C.

At the end of the war in Europe there were over 700 members of staff of all ranks and grades within Air Intelligence; but significantly, only ten of these were regular officers, all in the rank of Gp Capt. or above.

Specific Functions and Sections
The following sections provide a description of those Air Intelligence functions that had:

- Particular association with the provision of Sigint and intelligence appreciations for Bomber Command during the Bombing Offensives.
- Direct and indirect association with the Air Ministry Directives behind the bombing offensive, target selection and targeting material such as photographic reconnaissance.

These functions are shown in the Air Intelligence Organisation charts at Appendices D, E and F, where it may be noticed that the responsible Section changed from time to time as the whole Directorate evolved. The following functions are described:

Special Liaison Duties; with direct access to ACAS (I)	AI 1c
Photographic reconnaissance and interpretation.	ADI (Photo)
Aircraft industries; Production estimates; liaison with MEW and MAP.	AI 2
Preparation of Appreciations & Collation of information from Specialist sections. Liaison with Government offices, Service departments and RAF Commands.	AI 3a
Order of Battle for the Air Forces of Germany & the Satellites, except Finland.	AI 3b

Production of Target material for RAF & USAAF, including liaison with MEW.	AI 3c
Organisation of GAF other than Order of Battle; GAF Transportation & Training.	AI 3e
Liaison with USAAF in UK; the US Embassy; RAF Delegation in Washington.	AI 3 (USA)
Signals Intelligence Policy. Enemy radar & navigation aids. Signals Traffic and Call Sign section. Station 'X' (GC&CS), Bletchley Park	DDI 4
Enemy Scientific Research.	ADI Sc
Joint Intelligence Staff (Air)	AI (JIS)

Special Liaison Duties

Function and Development

The main function of the Signals Section (3S) at Bletchley Park was to ensure that ULTRA from Hut 3 was delivered promptly and accurately to ULTRA recipients in London.[7] Initially this was done by typed messages and hand-carried to Broadway for distribution to the Admiralty, the War Office and the Air Ministry. It was soon realised that this was not fast enough and a Hut 3 – Broadway teleprinter circuit was installed, with Broadway re-teleprinting to the ministries. Those teleprinters had the utmost security. The arrangements for dissemination between Bletchley Park and Broadway for ULTRA and non-ULTRA messages demanded the highest security and speed and used a combination of enciphered signal, secure teleprinter to London, or hand-carried bag to London.

A very important lesson during the Battle of France was that ordinary military signals channels failed to deliver a satisfactory service for the passage of high-grade information from GC&CS to the Field HQs. Special Signals (and Cipher) Units (SSUs) were created to provide and maintain direct contact between Field Commanders and GC&CS.[8] A key element of the task of AI 1(c) became the operation of the Special Liaison Units (SLUs), subsequently under the command of Group Captain F W Winterbotham and in the closest co-operation with the Signals Section at Bletchley Park; see Appendices D, E and F.

The first overseas deployment was by 'SSU No. 1' when it was despatched to Cairo in Apr 41. It was to be a completely self-contained unit with its own cipher and signalling personnel, its own equipment and its own transport.[9] Its function was to receive ULTRA information in cipher direct from Hut 3 at Bletchley Park, to decipher that traffic and to pass it to a strictly limited group of specially

---

7. Bib. B8, Ch. 8.
8. Bib. B8, Ch. 9.
9. HW 14/40; Letter from Air Commodore Lywood to ACAS (I) AVM Medhurst about an urgent need to install a high-speed secure signals system at Bletchley for priority ULTRA traffic to Suez Road. This letter dated 13 Jun 42 was less than three weeks before the first Battle of El Alamien, in July 1942, when the 8th Army under the command of General Auchinleck held General Rommel's advance on Alexandria.

authorised recipients. Responsibility for the complete security of the ULTRA material rested with the officer commanding the unit, which was ultimately under the control of 'C' the Head of MI6 in London. The unit at Cairo was the first operational SSU and was the forerunner of an organisation that grew to over 40 similar units across Europe and the Middle East, in addition to those that formed in India and the Far East. Not only did the units handle incoming cipher traffic but they provided the means of contact back to Hut 3 with questions or other requests for clarification.

As the organisation grew, it was decided to split the functions of an SSU into two inter-connected functions; the signalling and transport functions became the Special Communications Unit (SCU) and the responsibility for ciphers, security and liaison became the Special Liaison Unit (SLU). The SLUs were made responsible to Section IIB of the SIS. The title for the units changed from SSU to SLU to eliminate the miss-conception that it was a 'secret service unit'. Group Captain Winterbotham of Section II (B) was appointed Officer Commanding of all SLUs. There were changes from time to time in the detailed functions and one example was the 'Coordination of Selection and Transmission of Special Material to Commands Abroad'.[10] That instruction clarified the distinction between 'Special' and 'MSS' which had previously been ambiguous. The term 'Special' would continue to be used by GC & CS to cover any material from cryptographic sources and, when that material was sent abroad, it would also carry the prefix ULTRA. The sources included German ENIGMA; Spanish and Italian machine ciphers; Japanese machine ciphers and High Grade diplomatic book ciphers. When ULTRA messages were sent to Naval commanders at sea, the messages were to be burnt after reading. The utmost care was to be taken in briefing pilots for operations based on ULTRA material; they were to have only such information as may have been obtained from other sources – this was implicitly aimed at anti-shipping operations in the Mediterranean. It remained clear that GC & CS had no direct connectivity with home Air Commands at that time.

The Officers Commanding the SLUs had an overriding duty to protect the security of the material even after it left his control; and the discharge of that responsibility sometimes became delicate when senior officers engaged in potential breaches of security. A most stringent rule was that no outgoing signals message that had any possible relation to ULTRA could be passed across normal service signals channels. The Admiralty already had arrangements for the transmission of such material to commanders at sea using one-time security pads. The following signal sent in Oct 43 from London to the Allied Commander in the Mediterranean set out the principles:[11]

---

10. HW 14/37: Draft Changes dated 19 May 42 for the War Office (Brigadier Vale), Admiralty (Capt Haines, DNI) and the Air Ministry (Air Cdre Blackford, D of I(S)), copy to Bletchley Park (Nigel de Grey). Formal Instructions issued from Gp Capt. Winterbotham to Field Commanders via Hut 3 on 17 Jul 42 as R2000/17/7/42 AS/BB++++ (See HW 14/43).
11. HW 3/165, 'Ch. X: The Story of the SLUs' p. 6.

*The OC SLU is subordinate and responsible to AI 1(c) in London, representing 'C'
and the Directors of Intelligence, for all administration and operations of his Unit.
This includes:*

- *Dissemination and control of the use of ULTRA in accordance with the
  regulations.*
- *Maintaining direct relations with and interpreting the requirements of all three
  services.*
- *Investigating and regulating in conjunction with the respective Service authorities
  security matters arising out of ULTRA which are able to be dealt with locally.*

There were particular problems that arose with US Field Commands in the
European theatre because of the attachment of a US Military Intelligence Service
(MIS) officer who was primarily responsible for handling ULTRA information.
These US officers were given training and then attached to US Field Intelligence
staffs with the sole duty of handling ULTRA information and briefing the
authorised recipients.

New SCUs were created during Jan–May 44 in preparation for OVERLORD, to
receive ULTRA directly from Hut 3 at Bletchley Park via Broadcast or secure
landlines:[12]

Month	Location	To serve	Signal Address Code
January	Norfolk House	SHAEF Planning (COSSAC)	NH
	Bushey Park	USSTAF	ST
	St Paul's School	21 Army Group	AG
March	Stanmore	AEAF	KF
	Uxbridge	Tactical Air Force	TA
	Bryanston Square	1st US Army Group	FU
April	Portsmouth	2nd BR Army HQ	ON
May	Wycombe Abbey	8th USAAF	DL

By D-Day there were additional SCUs at Portsmouth and other UK locations to
serve additional Allied HQs, not least the Forward SHAEF from where the
invasion was controlled. After D-Day a number of SCUs were established in the
Forward Area as the Allied troops gained a secure foothold in France and
progressively rolled back the enemy forces from the occupied territories through
the second half of 1944 and then into Germany. Before D-Day, the secure
teleprinter network also included:

Bentley Priory	ADGB (Fighter Command)	AD
Wycombe Abbey	Bomber Command, via Wycombe Abbey (Pinetree)	MI

---

12. HW 50/32, Army/Air Sigint for the Western Front.

It should be noted that the existence of those connections to the two Home Air Command HQs did NOT change the previous dissemination restrictions for ULTRA traffic. There was still no relaxation of the protocol that those Commands received high-grade Sigint intelligence only from the Air Ministry.

It is illustrative that Fighter and Bomber Commands were the last to be given that direct connection from Hut 3 for ULTRA; and in the case of Bomber Command, it was then via the 8th USAAF HQ at Pinetree.

> If it had been determined that the volume of ULTRA traffic for Bomber Command had not previously justified setting up an SCU, how was it determined that the need existed for the 8th USAAF?

The very principle of 'Linked Routeing' should have been applied – see Chapter 9 – on the clear grounds that the two commands were jointly engaged in the same theatre of operations and that they should therefore receive the same ULTRA material. This breach of the protocol can only have happened as a result of an executive decision well above the level of Hut 3 at Bletchley Park; we can only speculate that Air Intelligence in Whitehall was involved.

Current Archive Records

The availability of archived records for ULTRA traffic is a very mixed bag; some material is readily available within TNA but a great deal of material has been destroyed. No small part of that destruction arose at the end of WW2 at the express direction of the Prime Minister, to minimise the extent to which other nations may over time have become aware of the enormous amount of diplomatic, military and commercial intercept that had been conducted and which may have continued to be conducted.

For the purposes of military intercept related to the work done by Hut 6 and Hut 3 at Bletchley Park, a very useful precis of the decrypted ULTRA material is available within Appendix 1 of Bib. B34. The details are as follows:

ENIGMA decodes from Hut 6 were bound into 'brown books' by Hut 3 staff.	Destroyed
Verbatim translations of these decodes were sent to London, with comments on the texts by the Military or Air Advisers in Hut 3.	Only a small part of these decodes remains. The absence of much of that material makes it very difficult to form an accurate and complete impression of the overall value of ULTRA to the Directors of Service Intelligence. The Naval material is best preserved.
ULTRA signals sent to Field Commanders from Hut 3.	Most of these signals are available at TNA. There is no explanation of the abbreviations that show which Commanders got which

	signals. A few of these signals have been withheld from TNA archives.
ULTRA intelligence appreciations and forecasts.	These were prepared for and sent to the War Office and the Air Ministry. None is available within TNA.
The Card Indexes for Military and Air data within Hut 3.	These cards were the essence of Hut 3's work and would contribute most striking visual and intellectual testimony to its operations. None is available and all have probably been destroyed.
Internal Hut 3 memoranda; instructions on the preparation and despatch of ULTRA to commanders; the integration of the US Military advisers.	None of this material is available at TNA. ** The absence of instructions for the despatch of ULTRA to Commanders has great significance with regard to the Home Air Commands.**

Note: The research for this book cannot confirm all of this detail but only a few discrepancies have been noted. In particular, there was a Hut 3 memorandum within Q2007 Historical Notes dated 24 Nov 43 that referred to ULTRA for the Home Air Commands. No further details have been located.

Photographic Reconnaissance

Background
Aerial photographic reconnaissance (PR) had been recognised as a major intelligence collection tool during the First World War, but it had been regarded as a tactical tool that was valuable only to actual or imminent military movements. No further developments had taken place until 1935 when the RAF had become involved in intelligence collection prior to the Italian–Abyssinian troubles. At that time, the Director of Military Operations and Intelligence drew attention to Air Target Intelligence as 'an outstanding example of a case in which intelligence is received from multiple sources, necessitating careful and elaborate collation before it can be put to effective use'.[13] This led in due course to the establishment in Jun 36 of an Air Targets Sub-Committee, under the chairmanship of the Foreign Countries Intelligence chairman and with members from each of the three Services. One key point is that this constituted the beginning of inter-departmental collaboration in the interpretation of intelligence in the economic field.

The covert activities of the pre-war SIS Flight, alias the Aeronautical Research and Sales Corporation, must not be overlooked. Partly in conjunction with the French Deuxième Bureau and the IIC, from 1936 onwards an increasing amount of covert aerial photography was done. Wg Cdr Winterbotham met with Mr Sidney

---

13. CAB 54/3, DCOS 3 of 22 July 1935.

Cotton in Nov 38 and a most beneficial arrangement was created.[14] Two Lockheed XII aircraft were ordered through British Airways Ltd, one for the SIS Flight (registered as G-AFKR) and the other for the French. Early 'operations' covered much of the western area of Germany and the border countries. The PR so gained subsequently had great value when plans were being discussed in 1939 for an 'Attack on Rail and Road Transportation in western Germany'.[15] The SIS Flight made many photographic records not only of continental Europe but also the Middle East and Red Sea areas, not always with any prior approval or authority. That PR found its way subsequently into the Central Interpretation Unit (CIU) when it was formed at RAF Medmenham during the Spring of 1941. The 'Aeronautical Research and Sales Corporation' found it necessary to form an arrangement with the Aircraft Operating Company and an associated company Aerofilms, which had a sophisticated photogrammetric mapping machine (known as Wild A5) made in Switzerland.[16] Eventually that combination of companies metamorphosed into what became the Photographic Development Unit at Wembley, as it was named on 17 Jan 40.

The Air Ministry prolonged the development of aerial photography by an almost doctrinal opposition to specialisation in such matters.[17] Photography continued to be regarded as one of the many functions of the all-round flying man so that, although cameras were installed in aircraft and aircrews were trained to take photographs, no plans were evolved for specialised reconnaissance aircraft. In 1937 Bomber Command was insisting that such aircraft would be essential in the event of war. Evidence of the complete lack of any policy regarding the means by which photography could be obtained in time of war may be found within the 'Annual Report on the Present State of Bomber Command and its Readiness for War' as submitted to the Air Ministry in Mar 39 by CinC Bomber Command, Sir Edgar Ludlow-Hewitt.[18] The CinC roundly deplored that grievous absence of policy, pointing out that the success of the bombing offensive would depend on the accuracy and completeness of the information obtained by photographs and other reconnaissance; and that the Command must be fully equipped and trained in that respect. From the terms of the related archives it is clear that the CinC despaired of convincing the Air Ministry of the necessity of providing fast reconnaissance aircraft.[19] It was written at the time that one of the leading factors in the Air Ministry policy failure with regard to PR was the dislike of specialisation in any form. That did not rest only with PR.

When the war started the general function of coordinating aerial photography rested with AI 1(b) but the machinery for handling photographs had to be brought to an advanced state of development by Bomber Command

---

14. Bib. B33, Ch. 5 'Sidney Cotton's Air Force' contains an excellent description of this arrangement.
15. Air 41/6, Photographic Reconnaissance, Vol. 1, p. 38.
16. Bib. B33, Ch. 5, p. 93.
17. Bib. B1, Vol. 1, Ch. 1, Organisation of British Intelligence, p. 27.
18. BC S/50693/1A.
19. Air 41/6, Photographic Reconnaissance, Vol. 1, p. 56.

itself. The initial work had been done by Sqn Ldr Riddell who devised the organisation and procedure for running photographic interpretation within Bomber Command; that same process was subsequently used by the CIU at RAF Medmenham. The focus of that initial work within Bomber Command in 1939 was concerned primarily with the targets and the assessment of attacks; the focus within AI 1(b) was of a wider strategic interest. The situation even after 12 months of war was described by the then DCAS Air Marshal Peck when he declared:

> Our pre-war policy had been to organise a number of squadrons and a large number of cameras, but for the most part the squadrons which we had organised were unable to penetrate to their targets.[20]

In May 44, then as a Gp Capt., Peter Riddell became the Senior Air Staff Officer with No. 106 (PR) Group when it was formed to coordinate and control all RAF and USAAF strategic PR activities.

Photographic Interpretation
The Photographic Development Unit was re-named as the Central Interpretation Unit on 7 Jan 41 and progressively relocated to RAF Medmenham, the move being completed on 23 May 41.

The CIU then provided what was probably the world's most efficient photographic interpretation and analysis service and the USAAFs collaborated fully with this unit, even though the 8th USAAF also developed an associate unit at Pinetree. The product of these two units was a most prolific source of air intelligence, comparable only with the Sigint sources. After the war ended in 1945, the Air Ministry concluded that it had failed to appreciate (in the mid-1930s) the potential intelligence value of photography for other than tactical purposes.

There is further detail about the RAF and USAAF elements of PR at p. 243 and p. 250.

Aircraft Production and Airfield Intelligence
The responsibilities of AI 2 that related to the Bomber Offensives were the collection and maintenance of intelligence on German aircraft production and the associated industries, in liaison with MEW and Ministry of Aircraft Production (MAP); and also on their airfields.

The Purpose
The purpose of enemy aircraft production intelligence was twofold:[21]

- To assess enemy aircraft output and future strength, to gain an indication of the size of friendly forces that would be required to oppose that strength,
- To provide details of the industrial targets that should be attacked to weaken those enemy air forces and thereby to contribute to the acquisition of air supremacy.

---

20. Ibid. Vol. 1, Pt. I, p. 62.
21. Air 40/1493, Air Intelligence Handbook, Draft, 1945.

The purpose of airfield intelligence was to evaluate and correlate all-source intelligence on existing and potential new enemy airfields, to support GAF order-of-battle and readiness estimates; and also to support planning and target selection for RAF and Allied air operations.

The dependence of modern armies (WW2 timescale, but completely relevant to this day) on the industries that support them represented a weakness which, properly exploited, would bring defeat to even the most powerful of military forces. At the start of WW2 neither Germany nor the UK had appreciated the potential scale of strategic bombing; and there was evidence that Germany had then believed that that form of attack could not seriously affect her industries. For example, a German Abwehr agent was sent into the UK to try to put the de Havilland aircraft factory at Hatfield out of action. This may have been one cause for the failure of the Luftwaffe to seriously attack British aircraft industries prior to or during the Battle of Britain; and may also have led to the concentration of German aircraft production into large complexes, from which rapid dispersal had to be undertaken when they were seriously attacked by the Allied bomber forces as the war progressed.

MEW was responsible for the overall study of enemy industries and, although MEW usually accepted Air Ministry estimates of aircraft production, they remained the authority on subjects such as production capacity, industrial manpower, supplies of raw materials and the overall industrial picture. The MAP provided information on UK aircraft production programmes and problems, which enabled comparisons to be made and probable German achievements to be put into perspective; much of this work was done jointly with MEW. It should be appreciated that the activities of AI 2 were intentionally confined to the estimation of actual aircraft production and the preparation of target programmes for attacking the enemy aircraft industry.

Aircraft Production Intelligence in Peacetime

Aircraft production capacity and technology should have been a topic for continuous data collection and analysis in the pre-war period, particularly during the middle-to-late 1930s, as the Nazi Party was gathering its strength. It is a matter of recorded history that this was not conducted rigorously by the government of the period, notwithstanding the very visible arguments and protests of Mr Churchill during his 'time in the wilderness' as a backbench MP.[2] This has been partly covered within Chapter 3, under the section addressing the Industrial Intelligence Committee. The achievements of that Committee were admirable in determining many courses of action for industrial intelligence collection and collation, but minimal funding by the Government handicapped progress.

The activities of RAF Air Attachés, foreign office staffs, industrial representatives, etc, were all valuable; but that activity needed to be cohesive and the data needed to be collected together and collated. But most important, the intelligence so derived and the consequent appreciations needed to be accepted and understood by the government. There is little evidence that the government of the time was open to that information and its implications.[23]

---

22. Bib. B30, Vol. I, Ch. VII, IX and XIII.
23. Ibid. Ch. XIII, pp. 204–210.

Aircraft Production Intelligence in Wartime
The sources of information change from peace to war and this was precisely what happened after war started. The typical sources of information were as follows.

a. Intelligence on the German exploitation of the French and other European nation's aircraft industries. This was based largely on agent's reports that maintained a high standard of integrity. In Germany itself, the quality of such reports was unreliable with regard to output production but was often valuable with regard to airframe, engine and separate component factory locations.
b. Photographic intelligence as a means of confirming the existence of suspected factories; for providing target material for bombing attack; and as a means of making assessments of bomb damage and subsequent enemy repair actions. Vulnerabilities of this source were the weather and the limitations of photographic interpretation.
c. Wireless telegraphy interception was a valuable source of aircraft production information, not least because of the enemy radio call sign numbering system. This was not complete data because not all types of German aircraft were fitted with W/T communication systems; those types that had W/T were generally multi-engine.
d. The examination of crashed enemy aircraft was a continuous source of information, not only by the collation of airframe and engine type and part numbers; but also by the exploitation of on-board equipment, any documents and the associated technologies. This source suffered from two problems: an inadequate appreciation of the value of that data in the early years of the war and a shortage of experienced inspection officers as the war progressed.
e. Allied air attachés based in neutral countries were often able to collect information from indirect contacts with German industrialists; in that context, just as much during WW2 as today in the 21st century, the attachés needed to be well briefed on what information was already known and what new information may be available.
f. At the highest grade of Sigint material, ULTRA provided vital evidence in many different ways:

- CX/MSS/T108/47 dated 28 Feb 44: Reference to most severe bottleneck in propellers for Me 109 and Fw 190 aircraft.
- CX/MSS/T205/35 dated 4 Jun 44: Delivery of S/E fighter aircraft from the repair industry suffering from shortage of wings.
- Japanese Ambassador in meeting with Speer 11 Aug 44: The production of fighter aircraft in underground plants was making remarkable progress (COM. 020076); in a later message, Speer had said the proportion of aluminium production for aircraft construction had risen from 50 per cent to between 70 and 80 per cent (COM. 020078).

g. In the final phases of the war, PoW information became increasingly valuable and eventually helped with target information for the bombing offensive.

A very clear point was made within the post-war Air Intelligence Handbook, as drafted through 1945, that experience had shown the critical importance of having an efficient registry and recording system for incoming intelligence information. Two particular points were made, neither of which have any exclusive application to AI 2 but which have broad application across all intelligence sections:

- The majority of incoming material needs to be seen by the Head of Section, either in toto or in summary; and any such material that has application to other sections is made available to them promptly.
- The system of recording depends absolutely on the experience of the staff with regard to the application of specific information and the location of collated information. Under the wartime conditions, when information could be required at very short notice, it was quite unsatisfactory to be dependent on a 'general purpose' registry support service that had multiple 'masters'.

Driven by the shortfall of information, it was often necessary to share the process of aircraft production assessment with the Order of Battle assessments made within AI 3, with whom joint assessments were frequently made. The methods varied with the type of information that was available. From time to time, the SIS organisation was able to provide official German figures for airframe or component production rates; such specific data may well have come from ENIGMA material, which became more plentiful as the war progressed into the 1944–45 period. But more generally, production assessments were based on aircraft works numbers and manufacturing dates; this was also closely associated with component source and works number data. The most satisfactory method was seen to be to maintain a running graph(s) onto which all available data could be plotted. One vulnerability that was subsequently recognised was that this method was essentially historical and could offer little guidance where there were major changes in manufacturing priority and output rates, as indeed did occur from time to time when Speer was Reichsminister for War Production.

Dissemination of Aircraft Production Intelligence
AI 2 issued a variety of reports to a variety of users; broadly, these were:

- Monthly Reports that provided a schedule of estimated aircraft production output for the previous month, with a summary of any new intelligence that could affect target selection or future operational plans. These reports had a wide distribution both within and outside Air Intelligence.
- Periodical Special Reports on particular topics, providing additional details to those provided in the regular monthly reports.
- Inputs to the 'Jockey' committee; this committee was formed in Jun 43 when the German Fighter Aircraft industry became the top priority for strategic bombing attack. The committee sat weekly from June 1943 to April 1945. A series of schedules were prepared of targets to be included within the strategic and tactical bombing attacks; it was the function of the committee to assess the status of each target, to add targets where appropriate and to recommend priorities.

The 'Jockey' committee issued a weekly signal to the air commands concerned showing targets suspended on account of damage already inflicted; targets that merited further attack as damage repairs were effected; and new targets. A separate priority list was also issued dealing with targets for the strategic bombers, together with recommendations for the towns that were associated with the enemy aircraft industry as candidates for area bombardment. The findings of the 'Jockey' committee provided a basis for strategic target selection (see Chapter 8). The informal nature of the committee proceedings allowed for representatives from the bomber commands to discuss available intelligence and to understand how the conclusions were formed. Much of this work was an ongoing daily activity, so that vital intelligence should not be held until the next meeting. The activities of the 'Jockey' committee may be seen as an example of good liaison and information exchange between intelligence staff and operational commands. An example of the nature of 'Jockey' committee reports is illustrated at Appendix H, which covers proposed attacks on German jet aircraft production facilities. AI 2a acted as Secretary to that committee.

Airfield Intelligence

The building of new airfields and the development and/or repair of existing airfields, including emergency and satellite strips, was closely watched. Information was available from a wide variety of sources of which the most valuable were generally photographic reconnaissance and, to an increasing extent as the war progressed, ULTRA. The value of ULTRA was that it disclosed many examples of new runways and emergency strips, which then allowed the targeting of photographic sorties.[24] The combination of these two separate sources was very productive, augmented by the various agent and prisoner-of-war sources.

Airfield intelligence was from time to time able to provide evidence of the enemy's intentions and any major changes in strategy so far as air operations were concerned. Examples of this are;

- During the winter of 1940/41 there was an extensive airfield construction programme in North West France. A large number of airfields with long runways and facilities for night bombers pointed to a major increase in the night offensive aginst the UK. There was nothing hurried about this programme and in fact there was a substantial re-deployment of GAF aircraft to support the invasion of Russia. That airfield construction continued in slow time and suggested at the time that Germany may return to the attack on the UK after the Russian campaign had been completed.
- Things did not go well on the Eastern Front and the associated airfield construction programme showed that a major supply line was being created to the southern end of that front.[25]
- In Sardinia in 1943, the enemy's general failure to maintain and repair his airfields suggested that he would withdraw from the island.

While airfield development was being studied in the summer of 1944, it became apparent that a number of unusually long runways with good approach paths

---

24. Air 40/2680: AI 2 (b) Report dated 15 November 1945.
25. Air 40/2680: 'Russian Airfield Development by GAF', by DI 2(b) dated 9 October 1943.

were being constructed. These were associated with the planned entry into service of the German jet aircraft.[26] The credibility of that information allowed AI 2(b) to state with confidence that these aircraft could only be operated from specific airfields. That information was used to target bombing attacks, particularly just before the Allied crossing of the Rhine in March 1945.

Consequent upon the increase in ULTRA evidence during the final 12–18 months of the war, it was possible to maintain a daily Airfield Intelligence report that gave the serviceability state of most of the enemy airfields on the Western Front, with damage reports and estimated recovery times. This also recorded the number and type of aircraft at each airfield. ULTRA was providing a great deal of information on such things as hangars, dispersal areas, fuel stocks and ammunition; and also the deployment state of radio controlled bombs and aircraft torpedoes.

The operational value of that information was rather more useful for tactical air operations than strategic bombing, except where the strategic bombing was used in direct support of the Allied armies. An example of this may be seen in the reference message sent from the US Liaison Officer with AI 2(b) to Colonel Douglass at the USSTAF HQ (Rear).[27] In another Loose Minute, there was reported evidence that the hasty preparation of usable airstrips on damaged airfields did not always restore an operational capability; the evidence related to the number of enemy aircraft which were damaged on landing owing to the rough surfaces of some of these airstrips.[28]

Post-War Comments

There was a very frank self-appraisal of the work within AI 2 relating to enemy aircraft production assessment, as it was seen soon after the war ended.[29] It recorded that the estimates of aircraft production for certain types, particularly S/E fighters, became increasingly unreliable from mid-1943.[30] The reasons for those errors were recorded as follows:

- A marked improvement in security introduced by the Germans in relation to airframe works numbering. The earlier AI 2 practice of assuming that the numbering system was sequential had led to unjustified confidence in its validity. This led to equally unjustified confidence in the production assessments, but without any critical and correcting review.
- There were a number of different intelligence sections each interested in and recording W/T call signs; airframe works numbers, etc, for their own purposes. This duplication of effort should have been recognised by Air Intelligence and centralised; and, as a consequence, manpower should have become available for those sections to concentrate more closely on their primary tasks. However, it would in fact have been futile for individual

26. Air 40/2680: Top Secret ULTRA Minute from AI 2(b) dated 19 December 1944.
27. Air 40/2680: Top Secret ULTRA message dated 20 January 1945.
28. Air 40/2680: Top Secret ULTRA Minute from AI 2(b) dated 13 January 1945.
29. Air 40/1493: Draft Air Intelligence Handbook, Part IV – by AI 2a, 29 Aug 45.
30. Bib. B1, Vol. 2, Ch. 25, pp. 516–517.

sections within Air Intelligence to attempt this work without the complete MSS and Y-material data that was available only at Bletchley Park.[31]

There had been a conspicuous failure to appreciate the massive increase in German S/E fighter aircraft production from late 1943 through much of 1944. It has been shown, not least from the post-war Bombing Surveys (see Chapter 9) that peak production occurred in mid-1944. Critics of the strategic bombing offensive have often cited the growth of German fighter production in 1944 as evidence of the offensive's failure; but such criticisms completely fail to appreciate the growth that would have happened if it had not been for the achievements of the bombing offensive. The target of 80,000-plus aircraft in the German production plans for 1945 gives an indication of the direction in which Field Marshal Milch and his staffs were aiming. It may be noted that the supply of pilots and fuel for so many aircraft would have been a significant challenge.

There should have been a separation within AI 2 between the enemy aircraft production assessment work and the target selection work for bombing raids. These two aspects of the work were functionally different. It was seen, after the war ended, that a better arrangement would have been for aircraft production assessment within AI 2 and order of battle assessment within AI 3 to have been merged and a closer liaison to have then been formed with MEW and MAP. This had indeed been intended from the start, but in practice it did not flourish; one reason was the operational urgency attached to target selection and the acquisition of adequate targeting material. This latter task was subsequently seen to have become the most important function for AI 2. Even this task suffered diversions, for example when the German V-1 and V-2 weapons were deployed and the Aircraft Production section was then required to concentrate on those weapons at the expense of their work on the Aircraft industry. Such was the price of experienced manpower shortages – again no change from current 21st-century problems!

There is a surprising statement within the Draft Air Intelligence Handbook (as at Aug 45) that, at the time of the most intense strategic bombing attacks on the German aircraft industry, much time was devoted by AI 2 to assessing the effects of those raids in terms of lost production. Those assessments were subsequently seen to have been wholly inaccurate; and the cause was seen to have been the quality of information that was available at that time. But during that same period – late 43 through much of 1944 – there was an increasing amount of high-grade ULTRA intelligence derived from the German economic and industrial systems.

The curious thing is that additional ULTRA aircraft industrial intelligence would have been sent from Bletchley Park to MEW in that same period. It is noted

---

31. HW 50/58 'Access to and Use of ENIGMA': The complex task of fusing the MSS (ENIGMA) material and the lower grade Y-material to achieve a proper entry into the call-sign allocation and analysis work had only been achieved as a matter of routine at Bletchley Park by the spring of 1944. The identification of enemy fighter units was vital, since this was the only way of discovering the airfields from which the fighters were operating and which therefore had massive operational significance to Order of Battle during Operation OVERLORD.

that there had been previous serious disagreement, during 1940–41, between Air Intelligence and MEW about enemy aircraft production capacity and quantities (see p. 26). That disagreement had reached the desk of the Prime Minister. We may speculate that there was perhaps some covert legacy conflict between Air Intelligence and MEW that could have led to information being withheld from AI 2 and could that have contributed to these wholly inaccurate assessments of enemy aircraft production.

> The final word from AI 2a, in the draft Air Intelligence Handbook, was that any future assessment of enemy aircraft production could not function unless it was given:
>
> *'access to all forms of raw intelligence, however Secret'.*

Intelligence Appreciations and Summaries

The work of AI 3(a) included the editing of the Air Ministry Weekly Intelligence Summary; this had previously been a responsibility of AI 1(b) – see Appendix D. There was a wide range of subjects covered within this Summary, from time to time addressing topics as diverse as enemy politics and economy, population morale, enemy propaganda, Allied and enemy operations and their effects, and the enemy war production. The Summary was produced at a SECRET security classification and could not therefore contain any high-grade intelligence material, but there were many times when there was reference to 'special sources' that can now be recognised as having a high-grade Sigint origin. There was selective use of photographic reconnaissance material together with general appreciations of raid damage.

A small selection of extracts from these Weekly Summaries is available at Appendix I, where there are topics of some relevance to this book; the point is to show one example of SECRET level intelligence dissemination that was used by the Air Intelligence branch. It was very much for general interest, especially at Commands and stations where it would be held in the Intelligence Libraries. It would have had little value for bomber raid planning and target selection because it was necessarily circumspect and had no operational time-scale, but it did provide some commentary on bomb damage that may not otherwise have been available to bomber aircrews.

For further discussion, please see the Sections on Air Sigint and on the Joint Intelligence Staff later in this chapter.

Order of Battle and Dispositions

In the study of the German Air Force and the satellite air forces, four main tasks were assigned to AI 3(b) across all theatres of the war:

- Order of Battle and Dispositions: to assess the enemy air strength in all theatres and in all sectors by aircraft type and unit.
- Operations: to assess the enemy scale of effort daily across all theatres and campaigns.

- Wastage and Input: to estimate losses and rates of loss in comparison with the availability of new and repaired aircraft, in conjunction with AI 2.
- On the basis of the information from the first three functions, to assess trends in enemy air policy and potential.

In operational activity, it was seen that one of the main sources of information regarding GAF dispositions and strength was the intercept and collation of wireless and radio traffic, i.e. the Sigint provided via the Y-Services. This was as a rule far more accurate, up-to-date and reliable than reports from ground sources. On the other hand, it also became clear that the study of enemy operational activity without a secure base in 'order of battle' data became liable to wide fluctuations and substantial margins of error. In this context, the work on order of battle and 'wastage and input' provided a cross-check on each other. For these various reasons, the nature of the work within AI 3(b) was more centralised than in most of the other sections within DDI 3. The agreed figures within the weekly 'Disposition of the German Air Force' represented a consensus view within AI 3(b).

The following sub-sections will outline the methods of work, the development of the Fighting Value of the GAF and the value of ULTRA within the work undertaken by AI 3(b).

Methods of Work
AI 3(b) was not a source of intelligence; it was the section to which all relevant items of information were required to flow. Given the receipt of a piece of new information, it was necessary to determine the authenticity of the data; and this led to a series of questions and searches that sought to establish any corroborative evidence. For example: what type of aircraft or unit was involved; what operation or movement was being undertaken and for what purpose; what would be the effects of that operation or movement; how would it change the strength or scale of attack that may be planned at the new location or the location from where the aircraft had moved? Such corroborative searches would often involve outside departments or other armed forces, e.g. the Admiralty, MEW, GC & CS, home or overseas commands, our Allies, etc. In such a fashion, the intelligence product from AI 3(b) progressively became more soundly based.

There was however an area where the claims of AI 3(b) were not supported by the facts. This area specifically related to the claim that enemy fighter reaction to daylight and night bombing raids could be assessed with reasonable accuracy 'on the basis of order of battle information'; and that the bomber commands were therefore able to route their forces to the best advantage away from the heaviest concentration of enemy defensive forces.[32] This is at best an incomplete statement and could indeed be invalid. The claim makes no reference to the availability of Sigint that initially allowed the earlier development of GAF order of battle and organisation; and which subsequently revealed the style of night-fighter command, control and tactics. The former information on order of battle was progressively assembled and reported in the SALU Reports from GC & CS.[33] These daily reports

---

32. BP Archives, The Work of AI 3(b), Air Intelligence Handbook, Part IV, p. 7.
33. See Bib. B28, Ch. 8, p. 58/59.

were sent to Air Intelligence from January 1941 but they were neither used nor forwarded to operational commands until some two years after their initial production. In January 1942, the Air Section challenged the Air Intelligence assessments of GAF fighter strength as being too low; and this contention was borne out by the scale of fighter resistance to the early daylight bomber raids into Germany. The latter information on command, control and tactics was assembled at GC&CS by the Air Section and reported in the various daily BMP reports, from June 1942.[34]

There were periods of time when Air Intelligence actively suppressed these reports and effectively denied their availability to Bomber Command.

The claim by AI 3(b) may in fact be an example of the internal politics within Air Intelligence, regarding their relationships with outside intelligence producers that effectively obstructed the timely delivery of best available intelligence to Bomber Command.

The Fighting Value of the GAF

One of the most important regular products of AI 3(b) was the monthly report 'The Fighting Value of the GAF'. This report, issued as a SECRET document, used a variety of Sigint sources including carefully concealed ULTRA material. That use of ULTRA could either be as covert collateral for a lower-grade Sigint source or as a basis for an otherwise unsupported estimate – as is shown in the following paragraph. The report generally had the following sections:

- Present Distribution of Forces.
- Present Value of the Fighter Force.
- Fighting Value of the Bomber Force.
- Aircraft Production by Type.
- New Equipment.
- Effects of Bombing Attacks on GAF Targets.

As an example of this series of monthly reports, with particular relevance to the Combined Bombing Offensive, the issue dated 1 Mar 44 discussed the heavy enemy fighter losses incurred against the USAAF daylight raids with escort fighter protection.[35] In seeking to maintain the combat strength of the GAF Air Defence fighter forces, it was necessary for Germany to bring in fighter units from other theatres of war to protect the Reich.[36] Allied attacks on airfields in Holland and West Germany had led to a re-distribution of the enemy fighter forces within Western Europe, resulting in an estimated increase in strength within north-west Germany of 15 per cent as compared with Feb 44. As a result, the fighter defences for Occupied France, Belgium and Holland had been reduced to 185 S/E and 250

---

34. Ibid., Ch. 2, p. 22/23 and Ch. 8, p. 63/66.
35. Air 20/1172, 'Fighting Value of the GAF', 1st March 1944.
36. Hut 3 Highlight Reports: CX/MSS/T349/42 ULTRA report.

T/E fighters. In spite of those increases within the Reich, the GAF was unable to prevent heavy bombing in Germany by the escorted day bombers and the night bombers during moonless nights.

An earlier report also discussed the extent to which the Eastern and Mediterranean Fronts were being weakened by the withdrawal of GAF fighters to the Reich; this had significantly diminished the level of support for the German Field Armies on those Fronts during the summer and autumn of 1943.[37] This was a major factor in the reverses that the Germans had suffered in Russia and Southern Italy.

That same report discussed the use of enemy T/E night-fighters against the daylight attacks by the USAAF, which had been noted from March 1943 during the heavy raids on Wilhelmshaven and Bremen. Since that time the T/E night-fighters, with greater range and endurance than the S/E fighters, had been regularly used against the daylight raids. But the consequence was that the combat losses of highly-trained night-flying crews could ill be spared; even as early as April 1943, the GAF issued instructions that night-fighter crews with 20 or more night victories were no longer to fly on daylight operations.

During the summer of 1943 the GAF began to use 21cm Rocket Mortars on S/E fighters in the Mediterranean theatre. This was an ordinary infantry weapon that could be readily fitted to combat aircraft and quickly proved its value in dispersing heavy day-bomber formations. The S/E fighters could carry two of these weapons; but the T/E fighters (Me 110 and Me 410) could carry four. These T/E fighters became operational within north-west Germany during the summer of 1943. The USAAF P-51 Mustang and the P-47 Thunderbolt became very effective against them, so much so that the enemy T/E fighters needed S/E fighter escort themselves; which detracted from the primary purpose of those S/E fighters, which was to attack the bomber formations. The tactical response by the GAF was interesting in that they took advantage of the range limits of the USAAF escort fighters. The GAF stopped using their T/E fighters with rocket mortars against the heavy bombers until after the US escort fighters had had to withdraw in order to reach their home airfields.[38]

The operational impact of the redeployment of fighter forces from distant battlefronts back into Germany in order to defend the homeland against the Allied strategic bomber offensives had many implications:

- By the end of 1943 approximately two-thirds of GAF fighters were concentrated within Germany and Western Europe.
- The GAF fighter strength in Russia and the Mediterranean had become so weakened that adequate support for the German Armies on those fronts had become impossible.
- The Russian Army was consequently permitted to become better equipped with air support, which had been a contributory factor in the German failure on that front.

37. Air 20/1172, 'The Evolution of German Fighter Defences in 1943' dated 27 Nov 43.
38. Hut 3 Highlight Reports: CX/MSS/T97/97, 18 Feb 44: Description of tactics adopted by GAF aircraft armed with mortars.

- In the Mediterranean, the lack of adequate German fighter strength had allowed the Allies to acquire air supremacy over Sicily and Southern Italy.

It is difficult to overrate the magnitude of the contribution to Allied successes in army operations during late 1943 and into 1944 that stemmed from the concentration of GAF fighter forces into Germany, to defend against the strategic bomber operations from the UK. This had set the scene where Germany had become focussed on defensive fighter operations in preference to maintaining the offensive and ground support operations that had been so well demonstrated with the previous Blitzkrieg tactics. That defensive attitude had in turn become subjected to increasing pressure as the Allied strategic bombing was increased from both the UK and the Mediterranean bases.

'The Fighting Value of the GAF' was a convenient means of disseminating information on new enemy aircraft and equipment. The advent of the German jet- powered aircraft Me 262, He 280 and the Ar 234 were all described in various issues, as was the rocket-powered Me 163. The He 280 was in fact passed over in favour of the Me 262; and the Ar 234 entered GAF service as a reconnaissance bomber. The early experimental or prototype phases of new heavy bombers, the He 274 and the Ju 390, were also described. For example, the Ju 390 was reported as having six BMW-801 engines, a bomb load of 22,000lb and a cruising range of 4000 miles. The text can be seen to rely in part on the availability of ULTRA material, with frequent use of words such as 'it is possible that', 'it is said that', 'it is reported to be', etc.

By no means least, these reports also carried broad details of bombing attacks on GAF-related industrial production, assembly or maintenance facilities. The evidence for these details was generally from PR sources or from photography taken by the bombers at the time of attack.

Bomber Command and the USAAFs received copies of these regular reports.

The Use of ULTRA within AI 3(b)

At the end of the war, AI 3(b) produced a short summary report that showed the value and the risks of using the available ULTRA material.[39] With that high-grade material, AI 3(b) had been able to build up a picture of the strength, deployment, efficiency and the working methods of the German Air Force which could be presented with confidence; and against which the enemy reactions to Allied air operations and plans could be judged and explained. Without that high-grade material, no confident picture could have been presented; and assessments and appreciations would have been subject to the variances of day-to-day operations.

It was in the mass of detail from ULTRA concerning operational units, their airfields, strengths, aircrews, operations and failures that represented the greatest value. On occasions, it provided advance knowledge of German intentions. But that knowledge was of questionable value unless it was accompanied by the knowledge to assess the enemy's ability to deliver those intentions. That knowledge was derived from the study of the detail within ULTRA, detail that was sometimes of little or no immediate significance.

---

39. Bletchley Park Archives, Top Secret U report from AI 3(b) to D of I (R) dated 9 Oct 1945.

This does not in any way detract from the value of other sources of intelligence. There were occasions when ULTRA was providing little or no value on whole theatres of war. In the earlier years, during 1941 and 1942, any ULTRA relating to the Western Front was looked on as an event of great note. On these occasions, the fundamental value of lower-grade Y-intelligence and photographic reconnaissance was outstanding. For long periods of time, the Y-intelligence provided a much better picture of the German bomber, reconnaissance and T/E fighter forces than ULTRA ever did. But even here, the assessment and appreciation of the other intelligence material was more reliable as a result of the background knowledge provided by ULTRA. The criticisms that were raised about the ULTRA material, in this immediately post-war report, were related very much more to the application of the material rather than to the content.

> The user staffs tended to rely too heavily on ULTRA and, as a consequence, to neglect other sources. It was this excessive reliance on ULTRA that presented the key vulnerability. Excessive reliance can and did lead to flawed assessment arising not least from incomplete signals intercept.

Not all messages were intercepted; some enemy operational orders were cancelled but those cancellations may not be heard. The great strength of the lower-grade Y intercepts was the aggregate complementary signals traffic, often from lesser units but usually much more timely in the context of ongoing operations. However, within the Air Ministry, timeliness was a great problem because of the separation from the actual field intercept process. This inevitably created time delays in the transfer of material; personnel were not always available to form immediate 'appreciations'; and the signals communication resources suffered from traffic capacity problems.[40] The Air Ministry was better able to assess longer-term 'strategic' matters rather than the immediate 'tactical' situations.

Target Intelligence
The Air Intelligence section that had primary responsibility for economic and industrial Target Intelligence was AI 3(c), heavily supported by the CIU at RAF Medmenham and the photographic reconnaissance units in conjunction with ADI (Photo) within the Air Intelligence Directorate.

The subject of economic and industrial Target Intelligence was of vital importance to the bombing offensives. One of the various sources of that intelligence was Sigint and, as the war advanced through 1943 and into 1944, the contribution of the high-grade ULTRA material became ever more important. But it should be noted that excessive reliance on any one source of intelligence was and remains inherently dangerous; and there were times during WW2 when that risk became a crisis, for example the failure to appreciate the overall intelligence indicators prior to the Ardennes Offensive in Dec 44. The attention of the reader is drawn to the section below entitled 'Signals Intelligence and Organisation'

---

40. Author's Note: WW2 had no monopoly of this problem; it is alive today.

(see pages 206–208) containing further details about Target Intelligence and Sigint dissemination.

Throughout the war there were various Target Committees that assessed and recommended economic and industrial target selection and priority. The authority rested either with the Chiefs of Staff, operating through the Air Ministry as their agent; or the Supreme HQs, operating through the Deputy Supreme Commander. In some cases, the War Cabinet in Whitehall and the US President exercised an ultimate authority. The executive decisions were encapsulated within the various Bombing Directives that were issued to Bomber Command and, from the summer of 1942, to the USAAFs.

CinC Bomber Command and the Commanding General of the 8th USAAF had a great deal of discretion in selecting particular targets. The day-to-day decisions rested with the Commanders of these bomber forces, influenced by the host of tactical operational issues. Target selection made at Bomber Command HQ was based partly on the best intelligence immediately on hand. That was not necessarily as good as the intelligence otherwise available in Whitehall – or even at the 8th USAAF – because of the policy and constraints that limited the dissemination of the high-grade ULTRA material. Appendix A contains some details from the MEW for bombing targets in 1942; it may be noted at Item 2 of the Appendix the implicit reference to what was otherwise described as 'area bombing' of urban areas.

The MEW was the major UK source of economic and industrial strategic target intelligence, as defined in the functional charter that has been described in Chapter 3. But that MEW Charter covered only part of the overall objective of the bombing offensives. The wider objectives also covered the full range of military targets within the context of tactical support to the field armies and the maritime war.

The following sub-sections provide an overview of the work conducted by AI 3(c):

- The use of ULTRA within AI 3(c).
- German Aircraft Production.
- The German Oil Industry.
- Transportation.

The Use of ULTRA within AI 3(c)
The extent to which ULTRA contributed to the search for economic and industrial Target Intelligence was heavily constrained by the restrictions that were placed on the dissemination of that material. For several years those restrictions presented a very serious limitation on the operational use of ULTRA. The most notable exceptions in those early years were the Battle of the Atlantic and the desert war in North Africa – these have been described in Chapter 5. In both of those cases the enemy use of ENIGMA was a feature of their necessary reliance on radio for communications over long distances; and that radio traffic was liable to extensive signals intercept. That did not apply anywhere near as extensively in the search for economic and industrial target intelligence related to the strategic bombing offensive of Germany, until bombing had extensively damaged the internal landline communications in Germany. The German authorities then had to use encrypted radio communications – ENIGMA.

An example of the way that ULTRA was used in the context of economic and industrial target intelligence is seen in the Note to the Vice Chief of Air Staff (VCAS) referring to the 322nd Meeting of the COS on 30 Dec 43.[41] That Note was related to the high proportion of German torpedoes being supplied from the Italian factory at Fiume in Italy. There was a large amount of Allied shipping at risk from U-boat attack in the Mediterranean and the covert reference to ULTRA in that Note was that 'We have also heard from most secret sources that the Germans have recently allocated heavy AA guns for the factory's defence'. Very soon afterwards, on 8 Jan 44, that factory was designated for attack by the MAAF.[42]

On a quite different topic, there was major concern about the German 'death camp' at Birkenau in Upper Silesia with very high-level political correspondence in Whitehall through the middle of 1944. One item was from D of I (O) to Gp Capt. Winterbotham in AI 1(c) specifically requesting that every effort be made to find any related ULTRA material'.[43] Part of the reason was the need for precise location of the camp before any long-range and most dangerous PR sortie could be flown, noting that this was not a vital military operation.

There is a Loose Minute from DCAS to CAS on the subject of 'precision bombing' of a uranium plant in Oranienburg, near Berlin.[44] There was reason to believe that the plant was associated with weapons development.[45] At that time, Oct 44, it seemed quite clear that both CAS and DCAS believed that only the Americans could undertake a precision attack on the target. The attack would have had to be in daylight with good visibility; given those conditions, that would have created a very hazardous long-range operation over heavily defended enemy territory.[46] RAF Lancasters were making daylight raids into Germany at that time with fighter escort, but a good number of those RAF daylight operations late in 1944 were conducted above cloud and relied on non-visual target acquisition that could not have supported a 'precision' attack. At that time, the degree of air superiority against the German day fighter defences had shifted the balance of risk in favour of the survivability of the UK and US bomber forces.

There was a profound observation by GC&CS on the quality of the Sigint appreciation conducted within the Air Ministry, even as late as the Spring of 1944 prior to D-Day. The point of the observation was that inadequate skills were available to assemble a 'Sigint Appreciation' because the staffs did not have the specialised experience to assess the lower grade materials, which required interpretation; these lower grade materials were often regarded as 'unreliable' but their very nature meant that they were usually more current.[47]

---

41. Air 20/3232, Loose Minute from DCAS Bottomley to VCAS.
42. Air 20/323; IMMEDIATE MOST SECRET Air Ministry cypher AX.259 dated 8 Jan 44.
43. Air 20/3232; TOP SECRET D of I (O) /420/44 to AI1(c) dated 13 Aug 44.
44. Air 20/3232; TOP SECRET & PERSONAL: DCAS to CAS dated 16 Oct 44.
45. AIR 20/3232; TOP SECRET, Loose Minute from ADI(Sc) RV Jones to CAS, 13 Oct 44.
46. FO 935/115 and 116: Bomber Command flew daylight operations into Germany from late in 1944 with fighter escort, but the majority of their operations were by night.
47. HW 3/99, Hut 3 History, p. 78, Footnote (1).

The German Aircraft Industry

The paper titled 'The Attack on the German Air Force' is regarded as a valuable example of the nature and scope of work done by AI 3(c).[48] By that time in the war, April 43, Germany had control of almost all of the industrial capacity in Western Europe and that Paper covered aircraft and aero engine production in all of those occupied territories. The object of the Paper was to consider the possibilities of making a concerted attack on the GAF and to ascertain what targets should be selected for the various striking forces that were available. There was a comprehensive analysis of the aggregate enemy aircraft and components production industry, identifying the main aircraft assembly and aero engine plants as well as subsidiary component factories. The specific aircraft assembly and engine plants had their individual Target Designation Codes and there was map and photographic data to form a basis for target and aiming point definitions. A great deal of the data for the Paper would have been generated in liaison with MEW. It provided tabulated data that designated the range from the median UK home airfields to different target sub-sets for Bomber Command and the 8th USAAF to launch raids. (see page 3 Plate section)

Looking at the various aircraft types, an example of the detail that was provided related to the Focke-Wulf Fighter Aircraft Assembly Plant at Neuenland, about 2½ miles due South of the centre of Bremen. That Plant was the main producer of Fw 190 fighters and had the Target Designator Code GY-4772. The complete factory complex covered an area of about 770 by 730 yards, adjacent to the Bremen Airfield, as shown in the image above. It will be noted that the date of this AI 3c paper was 9 Apr 43. It will be shown later – see Chapter 8 – that the 8th USAAF attacked this plant on 17 Apr 43. The subsequent detailed analysis of that raid and the damage assessment was that the Fw 190 production had been relocated to Marienburg several months earlier. Such were the gaps and risks associated with industrial intelligence within the MEW and Air Intelligence at that point in the war.

In the Bremen area there were four other subsidiary factories, as follows:

Target No.	Works	Production	Distance from Main Target
GY-4777	Weserflugzeugbau	Bomber (Ju 87) Assembly	5¾ miles NW
GY-4773	Focke-Wulf	Major Components for Fw 190	Hastedt – 3¾ miles E
GY-4805	Focke-Wulf	Components for Fw 190	Hemelingen – 3¼ miles E
GY-4779	Weserflugzeugbau	Components for Ju 87	Delmenhorst – 6¾ miles E

Another example of the data within the Paper related to aero engines. In looking at the engines for twin-engine fighters, there were two dominant types: Daimler-

---

48. Air 40/253: 'Attack on the German Air Force', AI 3(c), 9 Apr 43.

Benz (DB) 605 engines for Me 110 and Me 210; and BMW 801 engines for Do 217 aircraft. The factories that were producing those engine types were identified and tabulated in the following manner:

Range in Miles from Base	Number of Works within Range		Percentage of Production within Range
	DB 605	BMW 801	
350–400	1	Nil	5%
400–450	2	2	37%
450–500	3	3	53%
500–550	5	3	90%
550–600	5	5	100%

Similar details were provided within the AI 3(c) paper for all other known German aircraft and aero-engine factories together with the associated component factories. The style of presentation of details within the paper remains impressive. With consideration to typical ranges of night and day bomber operations, there was tabulated information on prospective targets. For example, given a 450-mile range, only one third of the total enemy fighter aircraft main assembly plants lay within that range. That specific range was at the time a limiting factor for the 8th USAAF. The paper brings out the great importance of an extra 100 miles, because at a range of 550 miles about 90 per cent of the enemy fighter aircraft engine production and assembly plants would have been included. Ten specific towns had been identified within the 450 miles as tactically suitable targets for attack by high-level daylight bombing by the 8th USAAF and night raids by Bomber Command. Those targets were:

Town	Most Important GAF Target	Other Targets
Bremen	Assembly plant for Fw 190s.	Four aircraft component works and one U-boat yard.
Brunswick	Assembly plant for Me 110s; Manufacturing plant for DB 605 engines.	Two aircraft component works; one repair depot; and one research laboratory.
Kassel	Assembly plant for Fw 190s; Manufacturing plant for DB 605 engines	Two aircraft component works.
Hamburg	Manufacturing plant for BMW 801 engines	Five aircraft component works; aircraft propeller works; aero piston works. Four U-boat yards.

Town	Most Important GAF Target	Other Targets
Schweinfurt	Ball bearing works	Main centre for production, not only for aircraft but also for MT and AFVs.
Hanover	Aero tyre works	Main centre for aero tyre production; also for MT tyres.
Stuttgart	Bosch Ignition, Electrical Equipment and Fuel Injection Pump works	Four aero engine component works; Ignition equipment not just for aero engines but also for MT and AFVs.
Gotha	Assembly plant for Me 110s	
Eisenbach	Manufacturing plant for BMW 801 engines	
Oschersleben	Assembly plant for Fw 190s	

Attached to the paper were maps and illustrations sufficient for target planning, dealing with these ten selected towns within the 450-mile radius and showing the relationship of the targets themselves within the towns. The level of detail that was provided would have been sufficient for target planning.

With regard to all the various targets dealt with, it had to be understood that the position was not static and that outputs of the many factories, the airfields used and the repair facilities varied considerably from time to time, not least as a result of earlier bomb damage, and that therefore the picture presented in the Paper was a snapshot. In that context, emphasis was laid on the progressive bomb damage intelligence obtained from the analysis of PR material after raids had been made and, later, during repair and recovery work. It should also be noted that valuable intelligence on bomb damage, repair and recovery work was being derived from ULTRA material; and that this high-grade material would also reveal the future intentions with regard to abandoning factories or relocating the manufacturing process to another site. Typical of such material are:

- CX/MSS/T131/7 dated 22 Mar 44: Berlin orders that salvage of crashed fighter aircraft take priority over all other salvage work. Same order repeated in T228/92 dated 24–28 Jun 44; and similar order in T343/57 dated 20 Sep 44.
- CX/MSS/ T157/97 dated 18 Apr 44: Heinkel works hit in raid on Rostock on 11 April; heavy damage in centre of town.

Bomb Damage Assessment

There is no doubt that bomb damage assessment was a difficult and skilled task. There were three major sources of information that contributed to damage assessment work:

- Primarily PR taken after the raids by PRU aircraft and, as the war developed, photography taken by the bombers during the raids,
- Agent, PoW and other human sources of information.

- ULTRA and other Sigint, which had increasing value over the last two to three years of the war.

The assessment and appreciation of the damage effects was a complex study undertaken by many different agencies; the most important were the CIU, MEW, AI 3(c) and the separate bomber commands – RAF and USAAF. A fundamental factor in the assessment process was that PR may reveal the visible effects of the damage and the CIU would derive as much information as possible from the photography; and for particular targets there would be periodic PR to reveal the progress of repair work. But PR could not reveal information that the camera could not see and it was in this context that ULTRA and other Sigint sources were able to reveal enemy assessments of the damage effects and their anticipated repair plans, or in some cases their abandonment of particular facilities.

Bomb damage assessment skill and expertise grew significantly through the war, but it must be noted that this skill really did not exist in the early years and was an ongoing area of argument and disagreement. Not least in this area was the effectiveness of the bombing in those early years, when there was a great deal of emotion, protection and politics relating to the bombing campaign and the future of Bomber Command. This has been described previously, within Chapters 3 and 4.

Early Appreciations of the Bombing Offensive

There was ongoing failure within Air Intelligence to recognise the bombing achievements of Bomber Command. An example is seen in the lack of up-to-date appreciations of what had been accomplished in particular spheres of the campaign. A case in point was the achievements of the bombing raids on U-boat construction yards and component factories between Apr 42 and Mar 43. The Admiralty had been pressing again for re-direction of the bombing offensive, towards the operation of anti-submarine patrols and raids on the submarine bases in the French Atlantic ports. Air Intelligence had been unable to respond in a timely manner with a cohesive statement of what had already been achieved by Bomber Command in support of the Battle of the Atlantic. CinC Bomber Command had provided a comprehensive damage appreciation that had been prepared by his Command Intelligence staff; a brief summary of that Appreciation is at Appendix J.[49] The argument by the CinC was that Air Intelligence in London should maintain this information using material from all sources, not all of which were available at Bomber Command. But in fact, Air Intelligence seemed only to offer generalities with little or no hard evidence. An associated point was that such an appreciation could not be made by MEW, because of the need to understand and incorporate the operational factors as well as the political background.

The first internal response by Air Commodore Inglis, ACAS (I), to CAS on this submission from Bomber Command agreed that Air Intelligence should produce such appreciations.[50] But he noted that the Directives to Bomber Command had

---

49. Air 8/883, ATH/DO/4 dated 30 Mar 43, from CinC Bomber Command to CAS.
50. Air 8/833, Minute from ACAS (I) to CAS, dated 8 Apr 43.

been so broad that it was difficult to associate an individual raid to a specific element of the Directive; and that many industrial plants had been destroyed fortuitously when the object of the raid had been to destroy the centre of the city. In the minute to CAS, Inglis said that:

> Within the last 12 months the only definite fact we can record with regard to the effect of bombing on the enemy aircraft industry was that Heinkel at Rostock lost production over a period of three to four weeks. Yet, without doubt, our bombing of industrial cities must have seriously dislocated production of all types of armament.

An MEW letter at that time recorded that they were 'much impressed with the speed with which the Germans were able to repair damaged industrial buildings' and the Heinkel Works had been no exception.[51] It was not known what effect the bombing was having on the general war production programme, because there was no knowledge of the enemy war production 'targets'. If the 'reliable' information was used as the sole basis for assessments, they would have fallen far short of the dislocation actually achieved. But to go beyond that 'reliable' data would have entered into 'guess-work' and could therefore have been discredited.

A further response by ACAS (I), dated 21 Apr 43, is equally illuminating.[52] To record and produce at monthly intervals the operational statistics of Bomber Command's activities required a War Room staff of two officers and four WAAF other ranks. To maintain the sort of records that CinC Bomber Command had advocated would have required the addition of a similar staff to the Raid Assessment Section, which at that time consisted of just three officers. Such a staff would also have needed a broad knowledge of the German war industry, which was not easily available. ACAS (I) went on to note that in the first big raid on Cologne, over 250 factories were destroyed or damaged; but in only some 50 of those factories did either Air Intelligence or MEW have knowledge of what was being manufactured. Indeed, in the reply to CinC Bomber Command by CAS there is acknowledgement of a lack of accurate information on the factory activity and bomb damage impact of Bomber Command's operations.[53] All confirmed damage was said to be recorded by the MEW, with whom Air Intelligence had close liaison. The final comment from ACAS (I) on this topic was that:

> So long as the present bombing directive stands, we shall have to confine our appreciations to the following subjects: Morale,[54] Delays to U-boat sailings, Transportation, Raid damage to German dwellings.

Transportation was then being attacked and MEW had been asked to undertake Raid Damage assessment.

---

51. Air 40/1814: MEW to Ministry of Home Security, dated 20 Jun 42.
52. Air 8/833, Minute from ACAS (I) to CAS, dated 21 Apr 43.
53. Air 8/833, unreferenced DO letter dated 27 April 1943.
54. Bib. A20, p. 34: One of the consequences of the first few air raids on London during WW1 was the impression that the psychological effects of bombing far outweighed the damage that may be caused. The general view was that the effect of air attack upon morale was immensely greater than the material results. This was later to be seen as mistaken.

The brief reply from CinC Bomber Command, dated 29 Apr 43, included as a final word:

> *Surely someone in Whitehall should keep an up-to-date record of damage ... and that this would have been particularly appropriate to submarine building and transportation.*
>
> *I should have thought this would have been the first duty of intelligence staffs in Air Intelligence and the MEW concerned with the Bomber Campaign.*

MEW Damage Reports

As time went on, the MEW produced a Weekly Damage Report, starting from the autumn of 1943. These reports became increasingly comprehensive and the final issues during 1945 carried a great deal of detail.[55] The content of those reports generally conformed to the following layout, at least from the preparation period before OVERLORD:

- Bombing Operations and Targets Attacked, typically Transport, Fuels and Military sites. This section of the report was brief and provided a summary of operations.
- The Effects of Previous Raids, typically oil plants, aircraft and aero-engines, steelworks, chemicals, rubber, public utilities and area attacks. This was the major section of the report and provided a valuable amount of damage assessment information based primarily on PR evidence. The appreciation appeared to have been derived from industrial intelligence records of manufacturing products, capacity and previous attacks. There is no apparent correlation with Sigint evidence.[56]

Within the section dealing with area attacks there was usually a fair assessment of the extent of damage to industrial and economic targets. For example:

- Against the town of Hanau from raids on 12 and 13 Dec 44, the report stated that transport targets suffered severely. Hanau is the junction for the main lines to Frankfurt from Berlin and Munich. Severe damage had been done to the goods depot, a large transshipment shed, the loco depot and the repair shops. Nearly a fortnight after the attacks, although the through lines were running, no large-scale clearance or reconstruction had begun. The sidings were still wholly out of use and a considerable amount of damaged rolling stock remained.
- A later report, No. 73 for the week ending 9 Feb 45, covered a Bomber Command attack on the Dortmund-Ems canal. This was the fifth attack on this section of the canal. It had been previously successfully breached and heavily damaged on 1 Jan 45. Repairs and reconstruction were, as with previous

---

55. FO 935/114, /115 and /116 Economic Advisory Branch, Damage Assessment Unit: Weekly Damage Reports for Apr 44 – Apr 45.
56. Bib. B35: HW 11/9 Appendix L – Bomb Damage Descriptions in ENIGMA.

attacks, pushed ahead with great speed. By the time of this latest attack, reconstruction of the damaged walls of the western aqueduct was far advanced although no traffic had been resumed. The eastern channel has been abandoned.

- A third example covers Bomber Command and MAAF attacks against Brüx in Czechoslovakia on 16/17 Jan 45. The target was the Bergius hydrogenation plant that had an estimated annual output of 700,000 tons. PR evidence showed very extensive damage across all of the plant, which was estimated to be out of action for 2 months. Among the more important items were both the old and the new power houses with their switch and transformer houses; both compressor houses; five injector houses; all parts of the coal preparation plant; the liquid oxygen plant; two fractionating columns and two low temperature carbonising plants. Damage was also visible in both labour camps and among storage tanks, pipelines and unidentified buildings.

It is illuminating to consider the distribution list for these reports. They went to many addresses within Whitehall, e.g. AI 3(c) and DB (Ops) in the Air Ministry; the Mediterranean theatre, for example the MAAF Targets Analysis Section; SHAEF (even including Public Relations?) and most of the Army Groups; to the Resident Ministers in Cairo and Algiers; etc.; to a total number of 50–65 copies.

> But not to Bomber Command or to the 8th USAAF, the bomber forces that actually did the bombing!! Why?

Is this yet another example of isolating and subordinating Bomber Command from routine information and assessments? MEW was not best known for disseminating information to Bomber Command. The extent of the damage assessment and other information, which usually covered 10–15 pages, would surely have been valuable to Bomber Command when compiling target priorities and aiming points for subsequent raids within the scope of the prevailing Target Directives.

Enemy Transportation System

Overview
The German transportation system encompassed three major ingredients: the Reichsbahn railway service, the inland waterways and roads. Air transport was a very small resource and almost exclusively used for military purposes.

The Reichsbahn was a very well regarded service, but it should be noted that it had serious problems through the late 1930s. One major factor had arisen as a consequence of the implementation of Hitler's 1936 Four Year Plan speech. That speech framed massive objectives for the German military and industrial resources. One of the re-armament tasks required what were in fact unachievable outputs from the steel industry. Late in 1936 there were dangerously low stocks of iron ore and there was a drastic cut in domestic supplies of steel; in that sense, domestic meant anything that was not military. By 1938 the Reichsbahn was unable to obtain even half of the steel that it required to maintain the then current rail infrastructure and rolling stock. By the last days in September 1938, as the Munich crisis reached its climax, the Reichsbahn was under very serious pressure. It had suffered almost a decade of systematic neglect. That led to a form of rail freight rationing in which priority went to the Wehrmacht and then to perishable foods, coal and high-priority export orders. The Reichsbahn did its best to compensate by making ever more efficient use of the resources, but from 1938 onwards the gap between the freight capacity of the system and the increasing volume of traffic widened inexorably.

The German economy, like all its European counterparts, was overwhelmingly dependent on coal. Ninety per cent of Germany's energy needs were derived from coal and, in addition, coal derivatives such as gas and various chemicals were vital materials in many forms of production. Coal was the only basic raw material with which Germany was richly endowed. But the coal had to be transported to the places of use and the freight demand upon the railway was massive. On a typical day, at least one third of all rail freight consisted of coal and its derivatives.[57]

In Jan 40, Goering described the transport system as *the* problem of the German war economy.

It was generally recognised in the Air Ministry at the start of the war that the efficiency of the German war effort depended very largely on transport; and that the dislocation of their ground transport would be an effective way of reducing their capability. The RAF attacks on enemy transport services had begun when the Low Countries were invaded in 1940, with the direct object of these attacks being to prevent supplies and troops reaching the battle areas. After the collapse of France, attacks on transportation were continued as part of the general air war, i.e. to contribute to the general breakdown of railway working and consequently of economic activity and the German war effort. Later, when the Allied forces were preparing for and during the re-occupation of Italy and France, air attacks on transportation were mounted in direct tactical support of the Allied armies. From the autumn of 1944 to the end of the war, air attacks on transportation had:

- The strategic effect of causing the collapse of the enemy war economy,
- The tactical effect of providing direct support to the Western armies during their occupation of the German homeland.

Air Intelligence Effort
However in the early days of the war, owing to lack of staff, Air Intelligence focussed almost entirely on enemy air operations and order of battle. Primarily the War Office conducted the analysis of enemy railway and other ground transportation requirements and capabilities. It was not until Aug 40 that it was

---

57. Bib. A23 'The Wages of Destruction', Ch. 10, p. 343.

possible to begin any Air Intelligence study of the German transportation system insofar as it supported enemy Air activities. That initial study was conducted by one officer from AI 3(b), the section that then dealt with all matters relating to Germany within the original 'territorial' division of functions within Air Intelligence.

In Nov 40 this work was transferred to AI 3(c) and continued as such until Aug 41. At that time, AI 3 (e) was created with the task of conducting what was initially regarded as longer-term research.[58] The primary fields for research fell under three main headings: German Air Transport; Training; and General Organisation. This progressively opened up new fields for study and over the following years the scope of the section became considerably wider. Natural extensions of the work included the study and assessment of the German Air Transport capacity to support paratroop operations; another was to assess the production rate of military transport aircraft. Other extensions of the work that became very important were the study of the enemy railway system and the organisation of the V-Weapon programmes. The latter developed from the primary task of General Organisation within the German Air Force. A key constituent of all of that research was the need for an effective synthesis and indexing system for the incoming raw intelligence; this was never appreciated by those responsible for the supply of clerical staff within the Air Ministry.

The build up of intelligence on the enemy railway system began with the assembly of pre-war data on basic targets such as marshalling yards, railway centres, key junctions, locomotive repair shops, bridges and tunnels, cuttings and embankments, etc. This data had been compiled by the (British) Railway Research Service, with the intention of providing a basis for liaison and co-operation between the various national railway services across Europe. This formed a valuable basis of information on the Reichsbahn but as a rule it required additional data before it would be possible to select and identify a target with sufficient detail for air attack. For example, what could the raid planner use as an aiming point in a given target area? For this purpose, it was necessary to obtain good up-to-date air photography; to examine material held in libraries such as the British Museum; and to obtain agent reports through the Secret Service.

There was at first very little information available within Air Intelligence on the various operational questions that arose, for example:

• How much train space is required to move a given Air Force unit?
• How much train space is required to supply a given unit when conducting sustained operations?
• How is such transport organised?

Answers to such questions were necessary in order to appreciate how fast the Germans could build up a striking force in an existing theatre of operations; how they could sustain those operations; and what was the vulnerability of the transport system to air attack?

---

58. Air 40/2635, The Air Intelligence Handbook, Pt IV, The Work of AI 3(e).

Careful intelligence appreciation of the damage inflicted by a raid was required within AI 3(e) for several reasons. A heavy raid on a marshalling yard and locomotive servicing works may prevent movement within and through the yard and also reduce the available locomotive effort. If the attack was to cause immediate interference with military traffic, then the effectiveness of the attack must become known quickly as well assessing how long the interruption to service would last. If the attack was intended to deny use of the railway for other reasons, then knowledge of how long it would take to repair the damage was more valuable. Such knowledge was then used to assess repair times after other attacks and to determine when further raids should be planned.

The Contribution of ULTRA Material

Photographic reconnaissance was the best source of damage effects on railways for the first few years of the war. But from the end of 1943, ULTRA evidence became increasingly available to reveal actual German reports both on damage effects and on repair time-scales. This ENIGMA traffic was forced into use by the progressive destruction of landline telephone and teleprinter services used by the German political, economic and military authorities; it was one of the benefits of the strategic bombing offensive.

The nature of this evidence may be seen in the Hut 3 Highlight reports within the Bletchley Park Archives. These Highlight reports were distributed only to named individuals within Bletchley Park for the express reason of keeping the various Sections informed on the broad content of the overall ULTRA material.[59] The Highlights do not provide a full transcript of the original signals traffic. A few examples are shown in the following table; the original Bletchley Park archives contain thousands of such ULTRA messages:

Examples of Hut 3 ULTRA Highlight Reports on Railways

Report No.	ULTRA CX/MSS	Date	Topic
842	T353/16	30 Oct 43	Bomb damage to railway bridge over R. Moselle will interrupt traffic between Trier and Coblenz for a long time.
8119	T27/46	9 Dec 43	Kesselring's Chief QM acknowledges orders from Keitel on Fuel economy, but emphasizes difficulties caused by Allied bombing of railways and consequent need to move motorized formations by road.

59. These CX/MSS Highlight Reports are stored in the Bletchley Park Archives, in multiple separate storage boxes. The history is that the boxes were offered to the PRO by the GCHQ Archives many years ago; were then declined and forwarded back to Bletchley where they remain in excellent condition. They cover Highlights of every CX/MSS report issued from Hut 3.

Report No.	ULTRA CX/MSS	Date	Topic
8192	T34/90	17 Dec 43	B-17 Fortress raid on Innsbruck 15 Dec: moderately heavy damage to rail traffic; considerable damage to residential area; several hundred casualties, including 100 killed.
9738	T176/10	6 May 44	Keitel requires Commanders in the West to make good damage to railways caused by air attacks. At present, only inadequate repairs being done.
9755	T178/86	9 May 44	Main effort of Allied air activity on 7 May against railway lines and waterways along the Seine; confirmed view that Allied invasion is planned for area of Le Havre-Cherbourg.
60	T196/68	26 May 44	CinC West requests release of about 125 POWs for work on locomotive repairs, because situation increasingly serious after heavy air attacks.
73	T197/13	27 May 44	CinC West report 23 May: Damage to railway installations includes interruption to line near Brussels for 8 days and damage to 115 locomotives.
123	T199/99	30 May 44	Heavy damage to Wagon and Tank works at Lyon – in CinC West's report on Allied raids on 24 and 25 May.
619	T218/93	17 Jun 44	Railway area – Caen: only night traffic to run in this area.
716	T222/44	21 Jun 44	Flak ammo train completely destroyed by aircraft fire south of Poitiers.
790	T225/111	25 Jun 44	Considerable railway damage at Saintes in raid 24 Jun.
804	T226/118	25 Jun 44	Heavy damage at Beauvais railway stn in raid 24 Jun.
904	T231/62	30 Jun 44	CinC West Appreciation, 19–25 Jun: Allied air attacks to block railway transport to the battle area very large in scale and having corresponding effect; supplies to the battle are suffering badly.

This ULTRA material was properly disseminated from Hut 3 to the designated external recipients in Whitehall within separate reporting channels, usually in a complete transcript and where appropriate with amplification by GC&CS advisors; as but a typical example, a report dated 22 Feb 45 from the Japanese Naval Attache in Berlin said that 'the bomb damage is disorganising fuel supply and distribution on the lines of communication'[60] It is specifically noted that RAF Bomber Command was not in receipt of this ULTRA evidence. Bomber Command

---

60. HW 13/181: ULTRA/ZIP/S/R/ 953.

may at best have received an 'appreciation' of the material from Air Intelligence in some subsequent written form but that would have had no operational value as to planning the next night's targets.

An outstanding example of the availability and use of the ULTRA material relating to the German transportation services was the Paper prepared by AI 3(e) at the specific direction of the DCAS Air Marshal Bottomley in Feb 45, who wished to know what information was available from Special Intelligence sources.[61] The original Paper identified 87 separate CX/MSS ULTRA messages that contained specific transportation problems arising from air attack. The description of those problems covers damage effects, consequent movement failures and repair time-scales where possible. The impressive quantity of ULTRA evidence within that Paper made a compelling case for air attacks on the enemy transportation services; and it was so used by DCAS and General Spaatz in planning the strategic bombing operations from the beginning of Mar 45. A summary of the paper is provided at Appendix K. The most critical aspect of that evidence was that it revealed:

'Previously disregarded intercepts establishing the existence of coal shortages, lack of power and substantial falls in industrial output – which indicated that the whole German industrial system had started to break down by September 1944 as a result of the paralysis of the railway system, mainly due to the impossibility of moving coal and other supplies from factory to factory.'[62]

Intelligence Reports from MEW

There are complementary reports from the Enemy Branch (MEW) that support the levels of damage to the German railway system through the autumn of 1944.[63] The weekly Intelligence Note produced for the week ending 29 Sep 44 has the following text:

An analysis of available evidence indicates that the series of heavy Allied air attacks on important railway centres throughout Western Germany in recent weeks, coupled with the widespread fighter-bomber and machine gun attacks on transport facilities of all kinds, and with the completely disturbed political, economic and traffic conditions in the area (in particular the evacuation movements, the transport of workers for fortification purposes and military traffic) has completely disrupted normal railway working through the area west of the Rhine and had direct repercussions over a much wider area; it is unlikely there is now much economic traffic at all in the area west of the Rhine.

61. HW 11/9, Appendix N, 'Extracts from Decrypts giving Effects of Air Attacks on German Transportation', dated 20 Feb 45. This Paper is directly related to the claim by Prof Zuckerman that a substantial quantity of ULTRA material on the enemy transportation problems had been ignored by DB (Ops) and the MEW: see p. 213 below.
62. Bib. A20: Ch. 7, p. 147.
63. FO 935/143 Weekly Notes of Economic Intelligence, from the Enemy Branch (MEW & FO).

In the next weekly Intelligence Note for the week ending 6 Oct 44 from the Enemy Branch (MEW) there is the following text:

On the night of 23/24 Sep 44 twin channels of the embanked section of the Dortmund-Ems canal (Glane by-pass) near Ladbergen were successfully attacked by Bomber Command. 12,000lb bombs breached the banks of each and both have been drained of water. This very successful attack has at one stroke completely disrupted through water communications between the Ruhr and Rhineland on the one hand and the industrial areas of Central and Eastern Germany and the North Sea ports on the other. Coming as it did at a time when all forms of German transport are struggling to meet military and priority economic demands in the very difficult circumstances caused by the Allied advance to the frontier, the increasing scale of air attack in Western Germany and the oil shortage, not to mention the peak season for harvest transport, this attack must have very far-reaching effects in both military and economic fields. The photographs taken ten days after the attack showed no signs of repair work being undertaken.

And in the next Intelligence Note for the week ending 13 Oct 44:

Photographic reconnaissance shows considerable damage to railway facilities at Hamm and Osnabrück as a result of air raids which took place between mid-September and the beginning of October. These are the two principal railway centres situated respectively on the two main rail routes running north-east from the Ruhr industrial area. As these routes are the only direct alternatives to the Dortmund-Ems canal, there will have been as yet no possibility of diverting traffic – held up by the attack on the canal – onto the railway. In view of the considerable time likely to be required for repairs to the canal, the damage will have far-reaching effects particularly if attacks on railways in north west Germany are continued.

Bomber Command's recent successful attack on the Dortmund-Ems canal should bring about a further serious reduction in German iron and steel production. As long as the canal and rail outlets remain unusable, the German rate of production is likely to fall to something of the order of 4 million tons of pig-iron and 8 million tons of steel per annum compared with our previous estimate of 9 million tons of pig-iron and 14 million tons of steel before these successful air attacks.

For the week ending 6 Jan 45, there was a most significant commentary on the critical shortages of coal and transportation from the Ruhr during the previous October and November.[64] The reports were that coal output fell to 33% of normal levels and that transport difficulties interfered so seriously as to stop production in many factories, even as far away as Berlin. Sixteen coal mines in Essen were out of production in November because of bomb damage. Owing to the lack of transport, large stocks of coal had been accumulated at other pitheads but could not be delivered to the industrial users. In the frontal areas, the transport situation was reported to be chaotic.

---

64. FO 935/143: Notes of Economic intelligence. 6 Jan 45.

Liaison with the USAAF

Liaison between the Air Ministry and other Allied Air Forces varied considerably; the closest being with the US Air Forces. The branch that had primary responsibility for liaison with those other non-Commonwealth Allied Air Forces was the Directorate of Allied Air Co-Operation & Foreign Liaison (DAFL). However, this is not to diminish the separate liaison and co-operation with the Commonwealth Air Forces who contributed heavily to RAF and Allied air operations.

Because of the dominant liaison with the US Air Forces, the AI 3(USA) branch was created with the express responsibility for intelligence liaison when the US entered the war in Europe. It also become a clearing house for a variety of other subjects such as operations and organisation; in practice, about 50 per cent of AI 3 (USA)'s work was involved with other Air Ministry internal departments outside of intelligence.

General Information Exchange

Supply to British Units of Information from the USA. Information on the organisation, actual and projected strength and equipment of the US Air Forces was in day-to-day demand by British formations. In most cases the format of the US information was not readily understandable to most British formations and particularly to government departments; those departments significantly included the Prime Minister's Office, the War Cabinet, the Admiralty, the General Staff and GC & CS. It then fell to AI 3(USA) to break down that information and supply details in a format similar to that used by the RAF.

AI 3(USA) also distributed to British units a variety of regular USAAF-originated air operations reports, air intelligence reports and routine statistical summaries. One of the outcomes of this effort was that AI 3(USA) was usually able to promptly answer many of the questions that would otherwise have been seen by the USAAF HQs as duplicated and unco-ordinated.

Distribution of British Documents to the USA. The supply of British intelligence to the US Air Forces was dealt with by DAFL until Apr 42; thereafter it was done by AI 3(USA), who also provided liaison with the US Embassy in London. The supply of air intelligence information to the US fell into two categories: information for the US Air Forces in Europe; and information to Washington DC. In Apr 42 a US major was attached to ACAS (I) to act as the intelligence liaison with the US Air Forces in Europe.

The RAF Delegation in Washington DC. The RAF Delegation in Washington DC was seen by Air Intelligence in London as the correct channel for distributing information within the US. However, many of the US agencies within the US conducted their own liaison with the Air Ministry in London, usually through the various military attachés and their own London-based staffs. This amounted to a substantial and largely duplicated work load for AI 3(USA), not least in protecting as far as possible the other Air Ministry departments and many British air-related research, operations and intelligence sections from multiple and time-wasting requests.

Intelligence Exchange
The Intelligence work covered the following areas:

Operational Aspects of the GAF. This was the responsibility of AI 3(b) and liaison with the US Air Forces was generally straightforward. There were initial problems that arose from the fact that the USAAFs had no 'air intelligence' infrastructure, a consequence of their 'Army' subordination. In the early days in 1942 the US opinions on the GAF tended to fluctuate substantially and gave rise to incredible exaggerations; but the various USAAF operational HQs and the US Air Attaché made frequent visits to (RAF) Air Intelligence to discuss problems and to acquire information on the enemy tactics and procedures.

Particularly for the 8th USAAF, liaison with (RAF) Air Intelligence became very close. There were frequent meetings to discuss operational matters such as routeing the bombers in their attacks on German targets and the tactics of the enemy day fighter and air defence system. This contact became so extensive that the majority of the USAAF A.2 Sections spent periods of time with AI 3(b) and developed very good working relationships, a practice that lasted throughout the war in Europe.[65]

The extensive in-office working intelligence relationships with the USAAFs appear to be absolutely correct and proper. No such familiarity was accorded to the home air commands; perhaps it was not requested by either party or perhaps it was not policy. The records show very clearly that air intelligence as supplied from the Air Ministry to those home air commands was in the form of 'appreciations' and 'routine reports and summaries'. The nature of that material had little or no tactical value and may well have reinforced operational perceptions that Air Intelligence had little to offer. The thing that seemed to be so sadly lacking was that 'personal' working involvement as was developed with the USAAFs; it may be that the USAAF staffs were grateful 'customers' whereas the home air commands may have been 'critical'. Going further, the Air Ministry went to great lengths to isolate the home air commands from the very real tactical intelligence that was being developed at GC&CS, notably by the Air Section.

Organisation of the GAF. This was the responsibility of AI 3(e), who created a close relationship with various USAAF staffs in the European theatre. Target information was passed to the 8th, 9th and 15th USAAFs and copies of papers produced by AI 3(e) were sent to all the large US Commands.[66] A USAAF officer was attached to AI 3(e) from Apr 44 onwards; this officer became Secretary of the POL Depot Working Committee under the CTSC. Perhaps interestingly, towards the end of the war, the USAAF liaison officer was provided with complete lists

---

65. Author's Note: It is apparent from these records that the relationship between Air Intelligence and the USAAFs was substantially different to that with Bomber Command.

66. Author's Note: Again it most be noted that the nature and depth of support to the USAAFs was significantly different to that provided to Bomber Command, i.e. target information being supplied direct to the operational USAAF command. That would seem to have a degree of urgency quite distinct from the passage of such information through one or other of the 'target committees'.

of all German Generals and General Staff officers in the rank of Colonel and above who may be candidates for interview by the USSBS. In the case of the more senior officers, there were biographies and photographs.

German Aircraft Production. This was the responsibility of AI 2(a). The reference material has an illuminating statement:[67]

> *Since the Production Section was closely connected with the selection of targets for the USAAF, as well as for the RAF, a close liaison was built up with the US Intelligence organisation.*

The USAAF officer who was attached to AI 2(a) functioned as Deputy to the Head of Section; his presence greatly facilitated liaison on all day-to-day operational matters with the USAAFs in Europe. There was no such amplification of any liaison with Bomber Command.

German Airfields. This was the responsibility of AI 2(b). Again, there were USAAF officers attached to the section to provide liaison with their operational HQs; and the section provided training for other USAAF officers prior to their taking up appointments on the Intelligence staffs of the Field Commands. The advantages of these attachments were profoundly beneficial to both the RAF and the USAAFs. Continuity of objectives and working methods was achieved; and day-to-day operational matters were readily addressed with the 8th USAAF.[68]

There was an inter-change of staff and material between AI 2 and the US counterpart, the Air Movements Branch, relating to enemy airfields and their infrastructure. This started during the winter or 1942/43 and led to a steady improvement in the quality of intelligence and a reciprocal agreement relating to geographical areas. AI 2(b) took responsibility for enemy airfields in Europe and as far East as India; the US Movement Branch took responsibility for enemy airfields in the Far East and the Pacific. The US provided AI 2(b) with the technical facilities for rapid reproduction of airfield maps and plans; and Operational Air Maps covering most of the world.

Air Signals Intelligence and Organisation

This section provides an overview of the DDI 4 Deputy Directorate within Air Intelligence that had primary responsibility for the collection, assessment and distribution of Air Sigint. In particular, DDI 4 was responsible for the RAF Y-Service and its many facets, including the relationships with the Army and the Navy; and the overseas air commands and theatres that were supported by the RAF Y-Service at different periods through the war. DDI 4 was also responsible for the Air Section (AI 4f) at Bletchley Park. A summary of those responsibilities is at Appendix L.

---

67. Air 40/1493, Air Intelligence Handbook, Pt. III, Ch. 5, para. 4.
68. Author's Note: The author served as an RAF Intelligence exchange officer with the USAF, during the Cold War, and can substantiate the value of that Exchange Programme which had developed from mutual experiences during WW2.

DDI 4's Responsibilities

As Head of the RAF Signals Intelligence Service, DDI4 had always considered it was his privilege to decide what distribution should be given to Air Sigint reports. But it will be seen that this was far from straightforward as the scope and quantity of reports from Bletchley Park and the Air Section progressively expanded. Not least were the arguments and the rigid attitudes that persisted prior to and after the official approval of the Air Section as a fully-fledged Intelligence Producing Centre in Aug 42.[69] At that point there was a watershed in status and orientation of the Air Section, with primary responsibility for timeliness in reporting to operational users of the intelligence. This is elaborated on below at p. 206 and also within Chapter 8 of Bib. B28, which discusses Bletchley Park and the supply of operational Sigint for the Bombing Offensive.

DDI 4 always was a small element of the overall Air Intelligence Directorate. Appendix C shows the Establishment of Officer and Civil Service equivalent grades within Air Intelligence at several stages through the war. DDI 4 was never more than about 7–8 per cent of the Directorate and sometimes less than 5 per cent. But the overall portfolio of work was really very extensive; this is indicated within Appendix L. The manpower effort that was available to provide direct support to the Home Air Commands was completely inadequate. The Liaison Records for Fighter, Bomber, Coastal Commands and 100 Group under Folders Q. 1222, 1223, 1224 and 1227 within Appendix L are quite trivial in the wider context of the scope of work.

In retrospect it may be seen that the control, collection, collating and reporting of Air Sigint was far too widely scattered and cut into too many small pieces for either a simple system to work effectively or for the most effective results to be obtained. The original theory was that the responsibility for Air Sigint collection and reporting stopped when an item had been dispatched to the correct user authority. Conceivably this may have been appropriate for one single line of Sigint traffic but it could never deal with the complexities of the numerous codes and ciphers of the GAF organisation; and the associated security compartments of the separate levels of high, medium and low-grade material. No Ministry or Command Intelligence ever developed an adequate knowledge of those complexities to enable the miscellaneous mass of information from Sigint to be sorted out and fitted into the puzzle.[70] But the original 'theory' died hard and was clung to by many different offices. This can be seen either as territorial or as a failure to acknowledge the scale of the problem, but the consequence was a consistent failure to make the best use of the available Air Sigint material. The outstanding exception was the cohesive collation, assessment and reporting process that evolved from the Air Section at Bletchley, often in the face of official obstruction from the Air Ministry.

It may be argued that to disseminate Air Sigint in an acceptable timely operational form and comply with the many rules of security then in force would have been an act demanding ingenuity of a very high order. The security barriers prevented free and full use being made of all sources of Air Sigint in any cohesive form. It is recorded that in the latter stages of the war the Air Section (AI 4f) alone

---

69. HW 3/99, Ch. VI, p. 28–29.
70. HW 3/99, Hut 3 History, p. 72.

was issuing Sigint product in eighty-six different forms of report. Should any doubt remain in the mind of the reader of this book about the complex structure that had been created for the Air Sigint dissemination process, then he or she is invited to consider the straightforward lines pursued by Naval Sigint dissemination. It is fair to note that Naval Sigint had fewer authorities and covered a much smaller subject area, but the *organisational structure* was capable of supporting additional subject matter merely by increasing the strength of the Signal Section.

It appears from the available recorded evidence that DDI 4 took an administrative control of Air Sigint and the RAF Y-Service rather than a proactive operational control. In many ways that is not surprising when considering the broad span of the portfolio that was covered by the Deputy Directorate and the small staff. It may well be asked how they managed so much with so little.

Apart from the provision of services and equipment, DDI 4 played no significant role in the development of Air Sigint at Bletchley Park. Even at RAF Cheadle and RAF Kingsdown the development of processes needed to exploit the GAF tactical signals traffic was done on the initiative of the staff on the spot. As far as the German Air Section at Bletchley Park was concerned, contacts with DDI 4 were mostly limited to receiving lists of Intelligence requirements which were irrelevant to the material that was being worked. DDI 4 failed to realise that the nature of Air Sigint was radically different from what had been foreseen before the war and that new methods had to be developed and new possibilities had emerged to meet the needs of the Air Commands. This led DDI 4 to insist on the out-of-date definitions of the division of responsibilities, in particular that GC&CS should not interpret the intelligence significance of the material that was being worked. That responsibility for 'Appreciation' was most jealously guarded by DDI 4 even though they had no ability to perform that work.

This created the situation where the main focus for the application of the German Air Section intelligence product was for the overseas Air Commands and that it was the USAAF which had the fullest benefit and value. The DDI 3 sections within Air Intelligence in London were responsive to that Sigint product from the German Air Section at Bletchley Park but the use that they made of it was primarily to add it to their general intelligence picture; whereas the overseas Air Commands and the USAAFs used that Sigint in the planning and conduct of their air operations.

[These Notes are taken from Sir Arthur Bonsall's unique contribution to the research for this book. See Acknowledgements on p. 11.]

Internal
The specific responsibilities of the DDI 4 sub-sections varied from time to time as the overall organisation evolved during the war. However, as a snapshot at an important period prior to D-Day, the following table shows the main responsibilities of the various personnel and sub-sections, together with the officer staffs:[71]

---

71. HW 50/25, Air Ministry Dossiers, Q1191 dated 6 Apr 44.

Internal Organisation of DDI 4 at April 1944

DDI 4 Gp Capt. Daubney.
Responsible for all matters of Signals Intelligence policy, VHF and RDF investigation, operational direction of all Sigint and Y-Units.

AI 4 Wg Cdr Card (Signals).
Deputy Head of Branch. General supervision of the internal workings of the Branch. Provision of equipment and personnel for Sigint duties; communication and technical aspects of the RAF Y-Service.
Wg Cdr Davies (Intelligence).
Deputy Head of the Branch; acts for DDI 4 in his absence. General supervision of all intelligence produced and distributed by the branch. Responsible for organisation at RAF Sigint Units and arranging dissemination of operational Sigint to the RAF and USAAF Commands.

AI 4a Study of enemy radar devices, navigational aids and associated radio transmissions of a non-traffic character.
Enemy night-fighter control system and ground radar organisation.
Analysis of German Y-Stations and flight reports on enemy signals investigation.
Air investigations by 192 Sqn (within 100 group). Preparation of investigation programmes for ground radars and mobile vans.
Liaison with the Operational Research Sections and with the US Air HQs.
Preparation of periodic returns and reports.
Circulation of daily reports on changes in enemy radar dispositions and tactics.
Staff: 2 Sqn Ldr; 1 Flt Lt; 1 Fg Off; 1 Acting Sect Off.

AI 4b French, Spanish, Italian and Japanese air forces.
W/T and R/T Police watches; identification of interference with Y reception.
Enemy communications equipment and W/T daily traffic activity reports.
Enemy recognition signals, captured documents and maps.
Day Fighter R/T traffic analysis and reporting.
Liaison with USAAF bomber commands: Bomber VHF R/T; GAF day fighter Order of Battle and patrol summaries.
Night fighter R/T traffic; R/T reaction to Bomber Command RCM.
Enemy radio beacons and broadcast stations.
Staff: 1 Sqn Ldr; 5 Flt Lt; 1 Flt Off; 2 Fg Off

AI 4c Analysis of GAF W/T traffic with the purpose of determining enemy Order of Battle, serviceability's and casualties.
Movements and the general nature of GAF operations.
Investigation of enemy training, transport and civil aircraft.
Indexing enemy air call signs; identification of enemy aircraft into operational and non-operational units.
Staff: 1 Flt Lt; 1 Sect Off; 1 Acting Sect Off.

AI 4d GAF Signals Organisation and Y-Service.
Staff: 1 WAAF Sgt

AI 4f The Air Section at Bletchley Park (GC & CS).

The primary Air Sigint out-stations in UK were RAF Cheadle, Kingsdown and Chicksands within the RAF Y-Service; each being supported by out-stations which provided intercept and D/F. Kingsdown's out-stations were called Home Defence Units (HDUs) and were located on the coast. A large number of RAF Y-stations overseas were established at various times during the war in relation to the prevailing military situations in the different theatres of operation. There was 24-hour watchkeeping within AI 4b and AI 4d.

It will be seen that DDI 4 was indeed a numerically small branch within Air Intelligence.

Responsibilities to Other Air Intelligence Sections

There are many other detailed aspects that merit attention.[72]

The medium and low-grade Air Sigint in so far as it concerned GAF signals communications was reported to DDI 4 from the RAF Y-Service. Some of that traffic was passed on at AI 4's discretion to the other appropriate intelligence sections within Air Intelligence. Those intelligence sections have been discussed earlier in this chapter and were:

- AI 2a, covering enemy aircraft industries and production,
- AI 2c, covering 'Air Technical Intelligence'
- AI 3b, covering the strength and order of battle of enemy air operational units,
- AI 3c (separated from AI 3b in Aug 41) covering enemy air non-operational units and GAF organisation in general,
- ADI (Sci) covering scientific intelligence (discussed later in this chapter) – the line between AI 2c and ADI (Sci) was hazy.

The high-grade Sigint from GC & CS was reported into specific sections within Air Intelligence, including DDI 4 and AI 4c, directly from Hut 3 – see Appendix M. DDI 4 had no control or responsibility for that reporting. ADI (Sci) was also served with relevant intelligence from all Sigint sources by the Technical Research Party in Hut 3 at Bletchley Park.

It should also be noted that in the autumn of 1943 there was further re-organisation within Air Intelligence when the Directorate of Intelligence (Research) [D of I (R)] was created – see Appendix F below. This new directorate absorbed the previous DDI 2 from Director of Intelligence (Operations) [D of I (O)]; and DDI 4, which had previously reported directly to ACAS (I). The task of the new directorate was:

Responsibility for the investigation and dissemination of information on enemy technical development in relation to aeronautical matters; for industrial intelligence so far as enemy aeronautical industries were concerned and for all signals intelligence.

However, DDI 3 remained part of D of I (O) even though the two larger Air Sigint-absorbing sections, i.e. AI3b and AI 3e, were heavily engaged on intelligence research.

---

72. Bib. B2, Vol. 2, pp 546–548.

There was a further anomaly that had arisen early in 1942, soon after the US had entered the war. At that time a new section was created within DDI 3 and styled as AI 3(USA). This section came to include a number of US personnel who were integrated into various sub-sections and tasks. The task of AI 3(USA) was:

> *Dealing with a close ally and being ready to exchange full and accurate information with the USAAF on matters regarding each air force; and thus acting as a Clearing House for information and intelligence transfer between the two air forces.*

As a result of these organisational actions within Air Intelligence as a whole, it is clear that DDI 4 was in no position to control the handling and management of Air Sigint in general either within the Air Intelligence directorate or externally, especially with regard to the USAAF. That ethos remained as a material legacy and was liable to obstruct rather than facilitate the task. It may well be argued that the co-ordination and exploitation of Air Sigint within the Air Intelligence directorate was seriously muddled. That was certainly not helped by the very restricted dissemination of ULTRA and the very small size of the DDI 4 deputy directorate. It was certainly exacerbated by the general lack of real appreciation and understanding of the value of Air Sigint by the chains of command both within and outside of Air Intelligence. The words of Josh Cooper ring loud:

> *On looking back over the various difficulties experienced by Air Section during the German War in its relations with Air Ministry, I find it a little hard to separate out difficulties due to personalities from those inherent in the set-up itself. Five men – Allen, Blandy, Cadell, Fitch and Daubney – had ruled over Air Ministry Sigint in the relative period and only one of these was really satisfactory to work with. But after all, a set-up which only works when one exceptional man is in charge cannot be regarded as wholly satisfactory.*

Air Sigint Appreciation

The responsibility for the combined appreciation of Air Sigint, PR, Agent Reports and other sources that related to the bomber offensive and to the effects of that offensive was spread widely within Whitehall. Different branches within Air Intelligence, Bomber Operations within the Air Ministry and the departments of MEW all had contribution to that responsibility and it is difficult to see if anyone had overall responsibility. There were various positions adopted by different contributors who had particular purposes to pursue or positions to defend. The combined appreciation of that aggregate intelligence material was of massive importance to the Combined Bombing Offensive but there is no evidence that it was routinely made available to Bomber Command from Air Intelligence and DDI 4. Perhaps the Appreciations that were prepared at Bletchley Park by the Air Advisors in Hut 3 could have got to Bomber Command via Air Intelligence/AI 4 (Wg Cdr Davies) who had responsibility for dissemination of operational Sigint to the RAF and USAAF bomber commands. No records have been located to answer this speculation.

The bureaucratic nature of the Ministry was incapable of responding to tactical Sigint reporting and arguably should never have been involved in that domain. The speed of aircraft operations imposed a special condition of speed on tactical

Sigint reporting, whether that was to support an air-to-air intercept by Allied fighters or the avoidance of enemy fighters by the Allied bomber forces. The worst consequence was that DDI 4 positively obstructed two-way communication between the Bletchley Park Air Section and the Home Air Commands for such a long time, indeed through to early 1944 and sometimes later.[73]

Dissemination of Air Sigint by the Air Ministry

The task of dissemination of the high-grade messages, together with the security instructions that prevailed at various times, was a continuous challenge. Summaries of relevant high-grade messages were sent to Bomber, Fighter and Coastal Commands, addressed to the Senior Intelligence Officers. It is far from clear how often they were generated, beyond the assumption that they may have been infrequent in the early phases of the war but would have become increasingly frequent as the war developed; after D-Day, it is possible that they may have become regular daily summaries. The ENIGMA signals traffic was not the only high-grade source and the more prominent element of those summaries would have been the Appreciations that were generated by the Air Advisors in Hut 3 at Bletchley Park. Those summaries were to be destroyed by the home air command addressees within 24 hours of receipt and form no part of any identified and available archives today. It is impossible to determine what was reported and how it was used within those Command HQs, recognising that within Bomber Command the CIO was the only authorised recipient.

But a great deal of Air Sigint lent itself to progressive analyses over a longer period of time and typical of such work was aircraft call sign analysis; order of battle development; and individual unit identification, subordination, location and redeployment. The responsibilities for that work lay with AI 2 and AI 3; and DDI 4 would have been responsible for providing those other sections with the air Sigint material.

Concurrent with this handling and dissemination of high-grade messages was a daily RAF Wireless Intelligence Service summary that was distributed to Bomber, Fighter and Coastal Commands.[74] This daily summary contained brief details of W/T intercepts, including the radio frequency used, the time and content of the message.

The handling of CX/MSS messages was under further discussion in June 1941, between D of I (O) and VCAS.[75] The concern at that time arose initially from an error in the use of telephones to pass intelligence data, but the Loose Minute went on to record that CX/MSS messages were passed to field commanders in the Middle East by members of C's staff [C was the Head of MI6, Sir Stewart Menzies]; the Air Ministry had no control over those transactions. Indeed, the primary medium for passing CX/MSS traffic to overseas air commanders was the Signals Section of Hut 3 at Bletchley.

The responsibility for Air Sigint reporting within the Air Intelligence directorate was discussed on 7 Apr 44 at a meeting chaired by D of I (R) and

73. Bib. B28, Ch. 8.
74. Air 20/2766 – W/T Intelligence Summary No. 376, 15 Sept 40.
75. Air 14/2766, Loose Minute to VCAS dated 17 Jun 41.

attended by DDI 4, AI 4f and the commanding officers from Cheadle and Kingsdown.[76] The reporting of operational air Sigint was divided into three functions and the responsibilities were agreed as follows:

- Immediate message-to-message reporting – by RAF Cheadle and Kingsdown.
- Quick or Short-term narratives – also by RAF Cheadle and Kingsdown.
- Final appreciations and periodical research reports – by AI 4f.

It will be noted that DDI 4 and AI 4 did not figure on that list of reporting responsibilities. The digest of the Day Fighter activity that would remain as a Kingsdown responsibility and the reporting of the main GAF code system 'Orchestral' which would be done by AI 4f.

It had become apparent in May 44 that AI 4f had added names to the distribution lists of certain Air Sigint reports without reference to the Ministry.[77] DDI 4 reminded AI 4f that centralised control of all reports that were issued on RAF Sigint was essential and that clear instructions were to be issued to that effect within AI 4f. There was a qualification that the time had been reached, in May 44, when the distribution lists in general had become due for overhaul noting that Direct distribution was obviously desirable in many cases to cut down the time delay.

Further correspondence in Jun 44 reveals that AI 4f was responsible for the production of intelligence of Air interest from the following sources.[78]

- Sigint,
- Non-Sigint sources, where those sources provided a more complete evaluation,
- CX/MSS, but subject to the arrangements made with Hut 3 and approved by GC&CS.

AI 4f would then be free to make reporting arrangements, direct to RAF and USAAF commands, within the framework of the policy and security conditions laid down by the Director General of GC&CS. In this respect, it was the duty of AI 4f to keep DDI 4 informed of any changes to those arrangements. The distribution arrangements at that time for some specific reports are detailed within Appendix M. An important qualification was that prior approval by both GC&CS and D of I (R) was required for any extension of ULTRA to any RAF or USAAF authority who had not previously received ULTRA material. In this context the Weekly Notes for ACAS (I) after Operation OVERLORD in Jun 44, prepared by AI 3e and at the Top Secret ULTRA security classification, were distributed to Bomber Command explicitly for Air Commodore Paynter, the CIO.[79]

The evidence uncovered during the research for this book justifies the claim that the Air Intelligence staffs in Whitehall and the wider Air Staff were

---

76. HW 3/118, Minutes of Meeting held in the Air Ministry, on 7 Apr 44.
77. HW 3/118, Loose Minute to AI4f from DDI4, dated 23 May 1944.
78. HW 3/118, AI4f responsibilities and reporting actions, dated 6 Jun 44.
79. Air 40/2685, Weekly Notes for ACAS (I), 6 Jul–28 Aug 1944.

knowingly or unknowingly delinquent in their management of Air Sigint appreciations and dissemination. There was a clear distinction between the supply of Air Sigint to the home Air Commands and the overseas Air Commands. There was an equally clear distinction between the supply of Air Sigint to the USAAFs and to Bomber Command. That distinction was most apparent in – but not confined to – the direct supply of ULTRA material from Hut 3 to the overseas Air Commands and to the USAAFs, whereas the home Air Commands never did have that service. The single exception is with Coastal Command, arising from the essential operational integration with the Admiralty; and that exception arose from actions originally taken between Bletchley Park and Coastal Command that finally became 'formalised' several years later.[80]

This research has exposed a critical impression that the Air Staff persisted with the policy of trying to control Bomber Command – in a similar way to Fighter Command during 1940/41. The operations of these two commands were in many respects 'on the door step of the Air Ministry and Whitehall' whereas the overseas commands were 'out of sight'. It will be shown later, at Chapters 10 and 11, that there were personal and political factors that dominated the Whitehall scene. These factors were very largely predicated on pre-war policies that failed to move with the realities of air warfare as these evolved during WW2. The entrenched policies that were formed from the First World War had continued through the 1930s and fixed the mindset of the most senior air marshals and politicians in Whitehall.

Scientific Intelligence

Policy
The staff complement of ADI (Sci) was always very small. It had started with just three members, headed by Dr RV Jones, who had been transferred into Air Intelligence from the MAP in the Spring of 1941; this was at the express request of CAS in the light of the 'Beam War' successes and has been described in Bib. B15. It is however illuminating to reflect on the views that were held in some other departments about scientific intelligence. The Admiralty had taken the view that such work would be best conducted from within the British research establishments; but the counter-argument was that those experts may well see things differently than their German counterparts. Scientific and weapon development can stem from many diverse origins and there is always the risk of the 'Not invented here' syndrome; indeed, that risk will always be present. It was to be seen that the establishment of the ADI (Sci) branch was one of the best decisions made by the Air Ministry during the war.

80. HW 14/84, MOST SECRET GC&CS Internal Memos dated 3 Aug 43 and 9 Aug 43 between Cdr Frank Birch in the Naval Section and Mr Josh Cooper in the Air Section. Information had always been passed from the Naval Section to Coastal Command by 'secrophone', a process which was concurred by the Admiralty but unknown by Air Intelligence.

There was much to be said for having a small organisation; there were never more than 11 members of staff. Recruitment into the Branch was deliberately very slow and depended on suitable people becoming available. The view was expressed in a memorandum to ACAS (I) on 20 Nov 42 that:[81]

> *It has been part of our policy to keep the staff to its smallest possible limits consistent with safety because the larger the field any one man can cover, the more chance there is of those fortunate correlations which only occur when one brain and one memory can connect two or more remotely gathered facts.*
>
> *Moreover, a large staff generally requires so much administration that its Head has little chance of real work himself and he cannot therefore speak with that certainty which arises only from intimate contact with the facts.*

If ever there were prophetic words, these must rate at the very top of any list. One is left to wonder why that policy did not apply across Air Intelligence as a whole, which grew from 40 to over 700 members of staff between 1939 and 1945?

There were to be many important topics for the small branch to investigate and resolve, which topics have been so excellently described by Dr Jones himself in Bib. B15. However, for the purposes of this book, attention will be focussed on a sample that had most impact on the bomber offensive:

- German Radar.
- German Nightfighters.
- Identification Friend or Foe (IFF).

A preliminary note on the working methods of the Branch will set the scene.

Working Methods

Perhaps the fundamental ingredient of the working practice within ADI (Sci) was the principle that one could never have too many sources of intelligence, regardless of how strong any single source may appear. At any time, one or more sources may fail to deliver information. The scientific intelligence officer needed to be skilled in, or at least understand, the individual methods of all available source material. Thus ULTRA was a most valuable source, but there was always a drive to identify and pursue collateral sources even if they were of lesser immediate value. At some time or another each source proved to have special value. The intention and the effect was to place scientific intelligence in a central collating position for all sources of intelligence and to maintain the closest contact with all of those sources. By having an overview of all sources it was possible to detect and suggest possible improvements to any individual source, in the light of a fuller appreciation of the aggregate intelligence picture. This practice worked very well with GC&CS and with the CIU, whose individual contributions to scientific intelligence were exceptional. It is noted particularly that ADI (Sci) had a very close interface with ULTRA products from Hut 3 and this generated a mutual benefit. However, the key factor may well have been the acceptance of

---

81. Bletchley Park Archives: ASI Interim Report dated 25 Sep 45.

ADI (Sci) staff within SIS, which allowed a 'collating function' within the heart of that most important 'collecting agency'. The strength of this practice cannot be overstated and it remains just as valid today as it was during WW2.

At the central collating position, the separate pieces of intelligence were fitted into a coherent picture. Where there were gaps, the collection agencies could be briefed on specific areas of search. But another equally important aspect of the process was that no single collection source should send material directly to operational users; the problem to be avoided was the prospect that a single source could present an incomplete or incorrect impression. There were of course exceptions to this on specific occasions, such as operational urgency, but only with the prior approval of the scientific intelligence staff. By no means least, any final product would acknowledge the contribution from all appropriate collection sources.

This working practice was quite different from the general Whitehall trend of creating committees to solve problems. Not withstanding the calibre and talents of committee members, the key distinction was that the 'central collating' function within ADI (Sci) gave direct responsibility to individual members of the team; as distinct from the collective responsibility often assumed by committees and their members. The records show that different Whitehall committees could have overlapping responsibilities and this gave rise to conflicts of opinion and different decisions on the same issues.

A very specific point was made within the ADI (Sci) Interim Report that committees had their proper functions, but they usually do not include solving intelligence problems.[82]

Another aspect was the relationship of experts in the analysis of intelligence problems with other experts in various research and development fields. Each has its own strength but they are very rarely the same and their separate skills and responsibilities must be recognised if the best results are to be obtained. This is very relevant to countermeasure programmes, where the scientific intelligence officer would have closer appreciation of the enemy's methods and possible weaknesses; but the countermeasure officer would have better appreciation of technical possibilities and engineering practicalities. The best outcome was when the two sets of skills were merged into an operationally effective solution.

The final but by no means least important element of the scientific intelligence process was the reporting and presentation of results to those staffs with responsibility for operations and research. There should be the strength of character to make staffs clearly aware of the results of investigations, even when they may be unpalatable, and equally to advise where there may be no conclusive evidence. Many commanders would value some advice early, rather than a complete story too late.

The success of scientific intelligence as delivered from ADI (Sci) was partly due to the approval of 'C' in allowing their presence inside SIS; and the agreement of

---

82. Ibid.

ACAS (I) to one of his sections spending much of the time outside of his offices. The final comment in the ADI (Sci) interim report was that:

> *While there will arise techniques of Intelligence beyond our present knowledge, the nature of future weapons may render them easy to conceal and difficult to counter. Yet, though the fortunes of Intelligence may fluctuate and its methods change, its principles will remain the same; and if during the past war our work has helped to clarify these principles, this may well prove its most permanent contribution.*

Specific Topics

GERMAN RADAR

For the first three years of the war, the most important enemy application of scientific developments lay in radio-navigation and radar. The existence of and approximate performance of German radar had been deduced by the summer of 1940. The OSLO report from Nov 39 had provided important clues but had been rejected by some influential groups in Whitehall.

Disbelief was only dispelled after the analysis of some low-level oblique photography. The image on Plate 4 was taken during a PR sortie flown on 22 Feb 41 by Flying Officer Manifould and shows two *Freya* radars at a site near Auderville. This information was connected with an ULTRA report from Jul 40 that had identified a *Freya Gerät* in the same area as this photography; earlier high-level photography had been unsuccessful.

The TRE had intercepted radar transmissions in Sep 40 from a location in the Gris Nez area. The pieces of the jigsaw were assembled and it revealed persuasive evidence of German radar deployments, which confounded the doubters in Whitehall.

GERMAN NIGHTFIGHTERS

The confirmation of radars being used by the German air defence system had major impact on the night operations of Bomber Command. Air Vice Marshal Medhurst, then ACAS (I), required ADI (Sci) to assume responsibility for compiling the intelligence picture of the enemy capability. It soon became obvious that there was another type of radar that was being used for Flak control; this radar became known as the *Würzburg*. The progressive identification of the various elements within the German night fighter defence system and the methods of operation was an amalgamation of information from multiple sources:

- Photographic reconnaissance,
- Sigint, using high-grade ULTRA, the lower-grade W/T and R/T traffic; particularly with the assiduous assembly and appreciation of that material by the Air Section at GC & CS,
- Radar transmission intercepts from land and air platforms, the latter from 192 Squadron that conducted air intercept operations.[83]

---

83. Author's Note: 192 Squadron became part of No. 100 (Bomber Support) Group at the end of 1943. After WW2 ended, 192 Sqn was re-numbered to 51 Sqn. No. 51 Sqn remains in operation to this day with Nimrod-R aircraft on active service in the Gulf area and Afghanistan.

- Documentation from crashed or captured aircraft.
- Informers and agents.

The overall product of the analyses revealed the structure and methods of use of the Kammhuber Line, the German Ground-Controlled Intercept system and the various complementary night-fighting and control techniques that were instituted in response to the many and varied RCM jamming equipments that were used by Bomber Command and No. 100 (Bomber Support) Group as the war developed. This has been extensively described in Bib. B28 and other reference publications.

No small part of the German air defence system was their equivalent of the RAF Y-Service. It conducted very successful intercept, identification and tracking operations against the combined bombing offensive and was able to exploit many innocent or careless transmissions from RAF and USAAF bombers. It thereby provided early warning of raids even as they forming over East Anglia and elsewhere. Just one example of those transmissions, which perhaps innocently compromised many operations, was the use of the British H2S or the American H2X radar navigation aid. It was a long time before it was accepted that this radar aid was being gratefully used by the Germans to detect and track incoming bombers. Given eventual acknowledgement of that tracking by the enemy, orders were issued by the Deputy CinC at HQBC that the radar was not to be used until the aircraft were within 50 miles of German-held territory; Allied bomber losses were thereby reduced.[84] Soon afterwards, a further order was issued giving very high attention to the breach of that order dated 13 Oct 44 and laying direct responsibility on the guilty crews for the loss of their colleagues.[85] But it is noted that even as late as 20 Mar 45, there continued to be breaches of signals security by some bomber aircrews regarding H2S transmissions.[86]

THE IFF MENACE

The Identification Friend-or-Foe (IFF) equipment was the cause of much controversy in the context of the bomber raids. Some bomber crews believed that IFF served in some way as a countermeasure to enemy searchlight and flak control. Not withstanding the arguments of ADI (Sci), Bomber Command insisted at a meeting on 26 Sep 41 that the captains of the bomber aircraft must have the option to use IFF in that manner. But it was untrue to imagine that IFF caused any degradation of those enemy air defence systems; it did in fact demonstrate no more than that the enemy was making a positive identification of the aircraft using IFF.

At the second meeting of the RCM Committee on 10 Jul 43, the Air Ministry was asked to approve the discontinuation of IFF on outbound flights.[87] At the 3rd meeting on 24 Jul 43, the Air Ministry stated that it needed to consult with the 8th USAAF with regard to daylight sorties and with the Admiralty with regard

---

84. BC/TS. 32130/Air/Ops dated 13 Oct 44; from D/CinC to all Groups, with copies for all Units.

85. BC/TS. 32130/Air/Ops dated 7 Dec 44; from D/CinC to all Groups.

86. Air 14/745, E8A: 'Radio Silence – Use of H2S', Loose minute to D/CinC from Chief Signals Officer, Bomber Command dated 20 Mar 45.

87. Air 20/8509, E9A: Minutes of the 2nd RCM Committee.

to any overflight of convoys. This practice became vitally important after the first use of WINDOW on 24/25 Jul 43, when the enemy radar systems were seriously disabled.[88] Thereafter, the erroneous practice of using IFF as a 'counter' to searchlight and flak became a most serious compromise of the entire bomber streams and may have partly contributed to the losses that were sustained through the winter of 1943/44.

The work of scientific intelligence in support of Bomber Command, closely combined with the Sigint and PR sources, had been more difficult and less spectacular, had extended over a wider field and had lasted longer than any other investigation. When independent Allied officers examined the German night-fighter system at the end of the war during the POST MORTEM surveys, they said that:[89]

> We heard of no equipment in operational use whose existence had not been revealed by our intelligence. Our scientific and signals intelligence had clearly fulfilled its role admirably.

Joint Intelligence Staff (Air) and AI (JIS)

Function and Organisation

From the outset of the war and even beforehand it was recognised that the activities of the three Fighting Services must be closely co-ordinated. This was controlled at the highest level by the COS organisation. Subordinate to the COS were various staffs and sub-committees, one of which was the Joint Intelligence Sub-Committee (JIC). The JIC was itself supported by a full-time staff – the Joint Intelligence Staff (JIS) – which comprised members from each of the three single Services, the Foreign Office, MEW, etc.[90] The RAF contribution was known as JIS (Air). The JIS worked adjacent to the War Cabinet Office and was responsible for providing the JIC with draft Appreciations of enemy intentions and capabilities. It worked closely with the Joint Planning Staff and was constantly informed of operational events and requirements; and likewise the Joint Planning Staff was provided with the available intelligence advice.

In addition to the JIS, there was the Intelligence Section (Operations) – IS (O) – that was set up as a channel for factual intelligence of all kinds as required by the Joint Planning Staff, both within the War Cabinet and in operational Commands. The IS (O) acted as a Central Clearing House for such factual information on an inter-service basis before it reached the Joint Planning Staffs. In other words, the function of the IS (O) on the purely factual side of intelligence was closely analogous to the JIS in the realm of intelligence appreciations.

The bulk of the Intelligence appreciations were called for by the COS or the Directors of Plans; exceptionally, by the War Cabinet or the Defence Minister.

88. Air 14/1764: POST MORTM, GAF Night Fighter System, para. 14.
89. HW 14/84, CX/MSS/3003/T20 dated 28 Jul 43, from the Chief Signals officer of GAF Night-Fighter 2JD. This ULTRA report has an immediate appraisal of WINDOW and sets out appropriate responses for the German Air Defence system.
90. Bletchley Park Archive Data: draft Air Intelligence Handbook, Part III, Ch. 12 dated 20 Jul 45.

After the US entered the war, an American COS organisation was set up in Washington DC along the lines of the British COS Committee with a similar JIC and JIS. There was a Combined Anglo-American JIC organisation that met periodically in Washington. There was no similar organisation for the Russians, but there was a British Staff Mission in Moscow.

Within the Air Intelligence Directorate, there was a specific section that dealt on a staff level with the JIC. That section was AI (JIS) and it can be seen within the organisational charts at Appendices D, E and F. The establishment of AI (JIS) was one Wg Cdr, one Sqn Ldr and a clerk. The Air structure is represented in the following diagram:

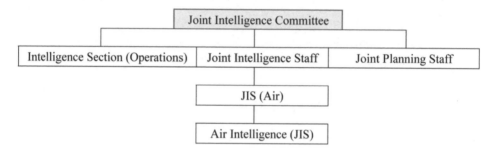

The Use of ULTRA by the JIS
There have, however, been some broad criticisms of the use of ULTRA by the JIS. It was reported that there was a tendency to forget that ULTRA, like other forms of intelligence, was never complete.[91] The JIS was too ready to deduce a great deal from very little; and conversely were prepared to argue against a case on the grounds that 'It is not in ULTRA; therefore it cannot be!' This did have the effect from time to time of constraining JIS forecasts of enemy strategy. In this context, it was reported that Hitler's unpredictable intuition and the measure of his ignorance were always the jokers, of which the JIC were reluctant to take cognisance. An interesting pencil subscript to the archive report of 29 Oct 45 (see Footnote 89) reads:

> The JIS members were not and could not be experts in any subject. They were representatives of the departments in their ministries.
>
> They produced appreciations for this purpose; valuable, but their existence as an inter-service body masked the need for inter-service working at the Intelligence Research level.

It seems axiomatic that it is impossible to have too many sources and that it is unwise to build an intelligence system around any one source, no matter how powerful that source may be.[92] But the power of ULTRA was seductive to some readers and some assessments were consequently compromised. The causes of

---

91. AI/JIS 29 Oct 45, to D of I (R) (within Bletchley Park Archives).
92. ASI Interim Report, dated 25 Sep 45 (within Bletchley Park Archives).

various intelligence appreciation failures regarding ULTRA were subsequently described by the JIS to be as follows:

- Not enough effort was given to assessing related low-grade material,
- Too much emphasis was given to ULTRA evidence,
- Too much reliance was placed on the absence of ULTRA,
- Misleading appreciations were formed within JIS and JIC following receipt of an order (German) but not any subsequent counter-orders.
- Some ULTRA messages were originated with the purpose of impressing the higher (German) authorities and contained inaccurate or incomplete information; and some of Hitler's orders towards the end of the war were incapable of execution.

Overall, ULTRA intelligence – and particularly ULTRA air intelligence – gave a depth of understanding and a record of reliability to the JIC that was most unlikely to have been available without 'the golden goose'. If the JIS sometimes overworked the goose, then this was a fault of the JIS and not of the ULTRA material. That is not a criticism of individuals per se, but of the intelligence organisation. It is perhaps an inevitable consequence of the huge expansion of the organisation within a short period of time, together with staffing by members who had little or no experience in the business of intelligence fusion and appreciation. It illuminates the criticisms of some intelligence products that were raised by operational users.

CHAPTER SEVEN

Operational Intelligence at HQ Bomber Command

'Give us the tools and we will finish the job.'

Sir Winston Churchill

Introduction

This chapter provides an insight into the organisation and conduct of the Command Intelligence Section, with particular regard to:

- Target Intelligence and Damage Assessment,
- Directive Targets,
- Enemy Air Defence Intelligence including: Enemy Fighter and Air Defence tactics; and Bomber Support operations,
- High Grade Intelligence,
- Photographic Intelligence,
- Operational Planning.

It was in Dec 40 that the various sub-sections identified as Int. 1, Int. 2 and Int. 3 were formed within Bomber Command HQ.[1] Their functions are shown at Appendix G. There will be indication of the linkages with the Air Intelligence staffs in London and other departments, including the MEW.

Target Intelligence and Damage Assessment

The development of Target Intelligence and Damage Assessment closely mirrored the development of the strategy and tactics of the Command, within the overall context of the Allied strategy and the operational capabilities of the bomber aircraft and the bombing techniques as these evolved.[2] This can be divided into five periods through the war, each having its own separate characteristics:

---

1. Air 14/1225: (BC/S.32395/1) Bomber Command Headquarters Intelligence, Int. 3 dated 1 Jan 44.
2. Air 20/10189 and Air 20/10190.

- Pre-Incendiary raid period, from Sep 39 to Mar 42.
- The development of Fire Attack and of Navigation Aids, from Apr 42 to Mar 43.
- Strategic bombing of Germany, from Apr 43 to Mar 44.
- Pre D-Day attacks on targets in France and the Low Countries, from Mar to Jun 44.
- Post D-Day tactical attacks in support of the Invasion; and the final strategic bombing of Germany, to May 45.

Pre-Incendiary Period

From the outbreak of war to Dec 40, target intelligence consisted solely of dossiers that covered the most important industrial targets. The information content was sparse and there was almost no Photographic Reconnaissance (PR) of a scale suitable for adequate damage assessment; there were then no alternative means of checking on the results of bombing raids. During this early period there was almost no high-grade Sigint to provide any form of damage assessment. When the enormous scale of bombing errors was appreciated, the next step was to attack larger targets. By that time, there was experience within the UK of bomb damage from the Luftwaffe raids; and the Air Ministry made the decision to attack German towns and cities. Bomber Command then selected aiming points and approach routes, which were distributed to the Groups and stations for reference during subsequent raid planning. During this period, it was the task of the Target Intelligence Officer to advise the CinC on the relative importance of different towns and the principal industries within the area in which the CinC judged the weather to be suitable for an attack.

Attacks on towns and cities were then the primary mode of operation and photographs were beginning to be more useful, but the damage levels were depressingly low. It had become evident that the type of blast bomb being used was not appropriate for destroying buildings; and the experience in London and other UK cities showed the value of incendiaries. There was at that time almost no intelligence on the structure of German buildings and one of the necessary steps was to have a study done by RE8, a branch within the Ministry of Home Security. The first experimental incendiary raid was made against Lübeck on the night of 28/29 Mar 42, chosen because of the tightly packed half-timbered buildings; it was a commercial seaport of some significance and it was an easy target to locate. To help offset the damage this raid had done to German civilian morale, Hitler launched a series of retaliatory 'Baedeker' raids starting with Exeter on 23 Apr 42.

The Development of Fire Attack

Bomber Command became committed to an incendiary battle against German industrial and built-up areas and the required bombing techniques, tactics and navigation were developed. The function of target intelligence expanded appreciably; and damage assessment began to play an increasingly important part of target selection.

However, there was very little detailed knowledge held at Bomber Command HQ about the German war industries. The first task was to acquire that information and valuable help was provided by the Air Intelligence Target

Section, AI 3c(1) Wg Cdr Verity, throughout the remainder of the conflict – see Chapter 6, Target Intelligence and Appendix E. A large number of MEW, CIU and AI (K) reports were assembled, filed and cross-referenced on an 'Industrial Card Index' for immediate access. A dossier was prepared for every town, containing all available information on the industries, structure and activities. When it was necessary, Int. 1 was responsible for requesting a PR sortie to be flown for damage assessment purposes.

Int. 1 attended the morning conferences with the CinC and was expected to produce a photograph and a brief description of any target that the CinC may consider. If that target(s) was/were selected, then the Aiming Point mosaic was presented and a short statement was given on the principal industries and on the structure and distribution of the main built-up areas. There were several methods devised to improve the presentation of target information, both to speed-up the delivery of material within the conference and to accommodate the vagaries of forecast weather and the available general target areas. Successful attacks with high concentration of bombing were usually only possible in good moonlight conditions; but these conditions also favoured the GAF air defence system.

This period saw the start of the '1000-bomber raids', the first being against Cologne with enormous damage being caused. It is noted that the make-up of such large raids required the involvement of the Operational Training Units and that presented security problems with the distribution of target information and their interpretation of that material, not least with aiming points. During this period there was the beginning of the 'Briefing Notes', for all bomber crews for the raid in question. These Notes gave the reasons for attacking the selected target(s) and their strategic importance.

This period also saw the beginning of Fighter Command sweeps over northern France, accompanied by light bombers from No. 2 Group, Bomber Command, who were detailed to attack industrial and transportation targets. These were practically the only daylight bombing operations conducted at that time – they were known as 'Circus Operations'. They were co-ordinated through the Air Ministry Target Committee under the chairmanship of DB (Ops). Bomber Command (Int. 1) was a member of that committee which met every two weeks. The committee issued Target Directives to Bomber Command for the strategic raids on German targets; and the raids in France, that also included operations against the U-boat bases on the Atlantic coast. Through 1942, the bomb damage to the enemy targets began to increase and it became necessary to keep track of existing damage when planning repeat raids.

> It became very apparent that target selection could not be divorced from damage assessment.

This was addressed when Gp Capt. Paynter became CIO and the staff and responsibilities of Int. 1 were increased, as follows:

Int. 1A and 1B   Target selection; Target intelligence; Enemy transportation systems;
Photo Recce requirements;
Marine intelligence and ship recognition.

Int. 1C and 1D   Bomb damage assessment and analysis; Methods of estimating damage;
Damage appreciations; Effects on labour and enemy morale;
Enemy damage effects on UK targets.

A major problem that complicated the situation was that there was no single section within the Air Ministry that covered Target Intelligence and Selection – and Damage Assessment:

- MEW, AI 3c and Bomber Operations handled target intelligence and selection.
- Damage assessment was handled by AI 3c(2) and the distribution of target material was handled separately by AI 3c(1) from a different building.

The target intelligence section at Bomber Command had to become very much more self-sufficient than would otherwise have been necessary, particularly with regard to target information records. Just as an example, there were so many different standards of Air maps, Military grid maps, separate European national maps, etc, all with their own characteristics and a common lack of standardisation.

This period came to an end as the techniques of using the new navigation aids began to be better understood – see Chapter 4 – and, as a result, raids were increasingly effective on darker nights.

Strategic Bombing
This period saw a steady increase in the weight of bombing and an enormous increase in the relative effectiveness. The destruction in the 9 months from Mar to Dec 43 was about 10 times that achieved in the first 42 months of the war. Damage assessment became ever more important both as an element of strategic target selection and the identification of the need for repeat attacks. This was increasingly coordinated with the 8th USAAF. The methods that were used were analysed and compared and there was continual exchange of ideas and information. There was also close co-operation with the Photographic Production section of the CIU. The analysis method that was finally adopted opened up wide fields of intelligence research on the effectiveness of attacks on large areas with multiple types of target. One of the benefits was that the previous simple assessment of industrial damage by the summation of 'area damage' became meaningless. It became feasible to assess industrial damage more effectively. The associated photographic imaging and the Kodatrace techniques proved immensely valuable, especially as target selection became a more urgent operational requirement in response to changing priorities and battlefront time-scales. 'Kodatrace' was a commercial transparent film which served to record bomb damage and to overlay other photographic images.

One of the documentation products was the famous 'Blue Book'. This was produced in a very limited quantity for a special distribution list. That list included HM The King, the Prime Minister, President Roosevelt, the CAS and Deputy Supreme Commander. Each book was hand-produced because no practical method of 'mass production' was found. But at a more immediate operational level, routine reports on bombing raids were generated. These were known as 'Immediate Assessment of Results'. They were produced within 48 hours of the receipt of PR.

During the spring of 1943, the first edition of the 'Bombers Baedaker' was issued by MEW. In spite of some shortcomings, this proved a helpful document. It provided an Industrial guide to Germany which listed all the major factories in or adjacent to each town and allotted to each factory a 'Key Point Rating' (KPR), which corresponded to the assessed importance of that factory to the overall German war machine. It enabled the total 'Key Point Rating' of each town to be compiled and thereby to place towns in a relative priority by industrial value. However, there was a serious drawback from the point of view of planning bomber raids; there was no standardisation of distance associated with the inclusion of any factory within any town.

The date of the first issue of the MEW 'Baedaker' provides a vivid illustration of how poorly informed were the Whitehall departments, certainly through the first 3 years of the war.

The reader might be justified in reaching very negative conclusions on what this says about the Whitehall understandings of the German war economy and industry.

The procedure at the morning conference – see the Section below for more detail – always closed with a briefing on the available effects of the previous days operations. The CinC required information on industrial damage. Clearly, the intelligence staff at Bomber Command HQ was not well equipped to provide that information quickly and reliably, except from early-morning photographic reconnaissance and night photography of bombing.

It was in this area that high-grade Sigint played an increasing hand, but the timeliness of ULTRA material relating to German damage reports was very variable and rarely was available quickly.

This was part of the intelligence information that did not reach Bomber Command.

During this middle period of the war, nominally from the start of 1943 to the end of March 1944, the selection of target(s) by Bomber Command was influenced by four factors:

- Specific industries within the Combined Bombing Offensive target priority lists,
- The aggregate KPR of the associated town (s),
- The extent of previous air raid damage and German recovery actions,
- Weather forecasts and enemy air defence resources.

The overall strategic damage effects to German targets were progressively becoming serious and widespread. Many other attacks were mounted against industrial targets in France and, at the request of the Admiralty, against the Atlantic coast U-boat bases. In order to assemble all of the available information in an attempt to show what Bomber Command was achieving, the Intelligence Branch produced two reports.

- 'Progress of the RAF Bomber Command Offensive against Germany.'
- 'Progress of the RAF Bomber Command against German Industry.'

Pre-D-Day Operations
The objectives and the arguments within Whitehall and the Chiefs of Staff about the scale and intentions of the pre D-Day bombing offensive are described in Chapter 4. It will be recalled that the aggregate bombing Directives for that period included strategic targets in Germany; and also tactical targets in France and the Low Countries to prepare for the Allied landings in Normandy. The change in bombing policy for this period had a considerable effect on the working of Target Intelligence at Bomber Command, with the emphasis moving back towards target selection rather than damage assessment. One unintended consequence of this diversity of targets was the ability to make maximum use of the prevailing weather and state of the moon. For example, with good moonlight conditions that provided good visibility, transportation targets were attacked in France; that avoided the intense enemy air defences within Germany, where targets were attacked on the darker nights. There was very clear direction from the War Cabinet and CAS that transportation targets in occupied territories were to be attacked only when there was good visibility and a high probability of accurate bombing, to minimise the possibility of civilian casualties.[3]

The target planning for railway marshalling yards required good PR coverage to identify key aiming points and bomber approach routes. The Operational Research Section at Bomber Command calculated the probable weight of attack to achieve the required damage; this reflected the various factors that have been discussed in Chapter 4. A 'Marshalling Yard Blue Book' was created using Kodatrace overlays to show the various yards and their facilities; aiming points and bombing runs; bomb plots and damage. As successive PR material came available, these overlays were updated to show the enemy progress with repairs and to provide a basis for planning repeat attacks.

---

3. Air 20/5307; Minute from CAS to DCAS dated 27 Apr 44, with the direction that orders were to be passed to Bomber Command. That was done by telephone to the CinC at 15.00 hrs on 27 Apr 44.

The order of priority for the transportation target attacks was liable to change and it was therefore necessary to develop a recording and planning system that accommodated these changes with the necessary urgency, to achieve the required operational time-scales. In response both to tactical requirements and weather, these changes often happened on a daily basis – and post D-Day, would happen several times a day.

The tactical operations of the heavy bomber forces also engaged enemy coastal batteries and radar stations. These attacks had to be planned in such a manner as to avoid giving the enemy an indication of the selected sites for the landings. Int. 1 maintained a careful record of these attacks for the Air Staff, to allow the planning of an even distribution of attacks; this was also co-ordinated with the 8th USAAF and the AEAF Target Section.

In the immediate run-up to D-Day, there was a complicated schedule of attacks covering D-3 to D-1 and the night before the landings. These night attacks were focused on coastal batteries and important road and railway junctions behind the beach landing areas. To maintain security, no information was released to Groups and stations about the targets for the night before D-day until that afternoon.

Post-D-Day and Final Strategic Bombing
Within this period there were three distinct phases for Bomber Command. Each of these three phases had distinctly different challenges for Bomber Command intelligence:

- From Jun to Oct 44, under the command of the Deputy Supreme Commander, primarily against tactical bombing targets to support the Allied armies advancing from Normandy but also with a significant amount of strategic bombing against Directive Targets.
- From Oct 44 to Mar 45, under the command of the CAS, primarily against strategic bombing targets but on-call for direct support to the Allied Armies, especially during the Ardennes Offensive at the turn of the year.
- From Apr 45, the bombing targets were primarily tactical in close support of the Allied armies in the final stages of the conflict.

These three phases are briefly described as follows:

A. *From Jun to Oct 44*, the tactical bombing targets for all the Allied air forces were selected at the daily conference held at AEAF HQ. This started at 11.00 hrs and sometimes went on past 15.00 hrs. The Bomber Command representative (AVM Oxland) telephoned the final list of targets, their relative priorities and the objectives, to Int. 1 at Bomber Command. It was not uncommon for raids to take off within 6 hours of that telephone call. The pressure of planning and intelligence work was intense, to get the Groups, stations and aircrews briefed and ready in such a short period. Co-ordination was maintained with the 8th USAAF to avoid overlap or interference with raid plans. An example of the multiple aspects of that work involved the selection of en-route tracks and altitudes, aiming points, bombing approach runs, times and the number of bombers for each target. The bombers had to prepared, fuelled and bombed-up with the required choice of bombs. Another of the detailed aspects of planning related to the range to target(s) and the availability of the various navigation aids; and not least, to the accuracy of final navigation and the bombing runs. In some cases, the Master Bomber had to rely on photographs to locate and mark the intended target. It was not uncommon for Group HQs to send an aircraft to RAF Halton, close to Bomber Command HQ, to collect copies of photographs for those night's operations. The availability of suitable maps continued to be a major problem. And by no means least was the planning for the associated RCM bomber support operations by 100 Group. Techniques were developed within the Intelligence Branch at Bomber Command to support those requirements.[4]

It was also essential to maintain far more complete records than had previously been necessary. Three different sets of records were created and maintained:

- The Daily Attack Book – a running record of all raids by Bomber Command and their results.
- Target Attack Cards – a record of any raid by any Allied air force against any target within the operational radius of Bomber Command aircraft. It was frequently necessary to know when or if any raids had previously been made on a given target.
- Air Ministry Summary of Operations – this War Room summary was issued monthly, with the result that it did not offer a complete and up-to-date picture of Allied raids. It was simply a method of filing all the monthly War Room records and needed amendment on a day-to-day basis.

Many of the attacks made in close support of the armies were against defended enemy positions close to the Line of Troops. Navigation and target identification had to be correct to avoid the ever-present risk of 'friendly fire', especially as ground movements were often unpredictable. Allied artillery did engage Allied bombers; Allied bombers did drop bombs on Allied troops. Sadly, that was and still remains part of the cost of close air support operations. One of the planning actions to minimise this risk used the 'probable bomb-fall ellipse'.[5] This pattern of probable bomb-fall had become recognised and could be set over the intended target on a map to indicate the likely bomb impact area. That would immediately show the optimum aiming point and the bomber approach path to secure the intended result. Some targets would require multiple aiming points; and it was then necessary to consider the wind direction to avoid later aiming points being obscured by smoke and debris from preceding bomb-falls.

Notwithstanding these primary commitments, Bomber Command maintained strategic attacks on German targets. Those targets included the synthetic oil plants in the Ruhr, which then saw the first full-scale daylight raids by Bomber Command since the start of the war. Those raids were escorted by Allied fighters, as were the USAAF daylight raids. By Jul 44, damage assessment of oil targets had become streamlined. Oil experts had been added to the CIU at Medmenham and they reported daily to DB (Ops) and the Intelligence staffs at the Air Ministry and the USSAFE. Thus, within 24 hours of an aerial reconnaissance of an oil target, the

---

4. Air 20/10189, Section 5, 'The Final Stages'.
5. See Ch. 3 above, 'Circular Error Probable' and Air 14/1210, p. 44.

status was established and forwarded to those authorities.[6] This footnote reference had the intention of providing the bomber commands with the latest situation on oil facilities within a 24-hour period rather than the previous 7–12 day period. This information was complemented by Sigint sources. It is noted that no complementary effort was put in place for any other target sets. That reflected the exclusive focus on oil targets within some quarters in Whitehall.

B. *The middle phase, from Oct 44 to Mar 45,* covered the final strategic bombing attacks on Germany. The CSTC was formed at the start of October. It met weekly and was attended by Bomber Command Operations and Target Intelligence sections. The weekly signal from the CSTC contained the selected strategic Target Sets and their priority. Separate target lists were issued from the SHAEF in support of the Allied armies; these targets had an over-riding priority. The lists both from the CSTC and SHAEF were liable to change as new intelligence became available – see the 'The Afternoon Conferences' below for an example of these changes. One of the responsibilities of Bomber Command Int. 1 was to keep all these target lists up-to-date with ongoing operations and their results; and to use discretion as events overtook the official target lists and their priorities. This necessitated a complete change in the presentation of target intelligence material at the daily Bomber Command planning conferences. The questions that had to be considered were:

1. What Directive targets were currently available?
2. Where were those targets located?
3. What types of targets were they: Oil, Transportation, Aircraft factory, U-boat yards, etc.
4. What were the current priorities for the target sets; and any specific target within a set?
5. Which targets were within or outside the range of the available navigation aids?
6. What were their locations with respect to Allied troops and the current Strategic Bomb line?
7. What did those targets look like from the air: how large, were they in built-up areas, etc
8. When did Bomber Command or any other Allied AF last attack a given target.
9. If the latest results had been photographed, what was their present condition?
10. If no PR had been conducted, what other information was available on the target?

*** This final question left open the availability of Sigint material ***

These questions led to a further set of records and presentation material, for the conferences and for operational intelligence records.[7] By way of example of the

---

6. Air 8/1018, Addendum dated 27 Jul 44 to Memo for CAS, dated 24 Jul 44, from Lt Col W L Forster. It is noted that Lt Col Forster had been recalled from Washington explicitly to coordinate the activities of that oil assessment work.
7. Air 20/10189, Section 1, Ch. 5 'The Final Stages', pp. 47–48 and Section II, Appendix A.

Bletchley Park Mansion. (*Bletchley Park Trust*)

Lancaster dropping a 4,000lb Cookie and 30lb incendiaries. (*IWM CL 001404*)

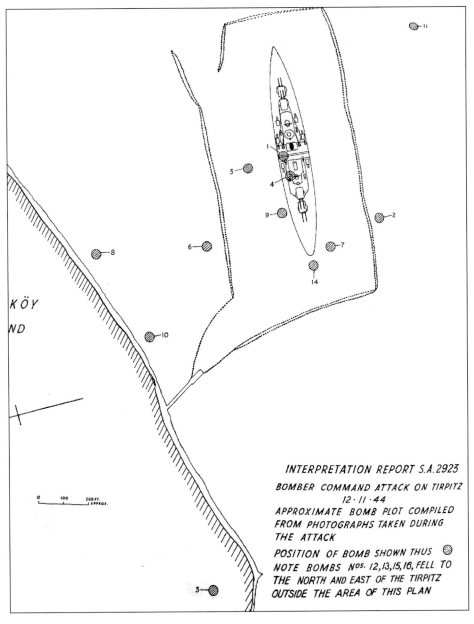

No. 5 Group raid on *Tirpitz*, 12 November 1944. (*TNA Air 24/299*)

Focke-Wulf
200 *Kondor*.

Focke-Wulf aircraft factory at Bremen. (*TNA Air 40/253*)

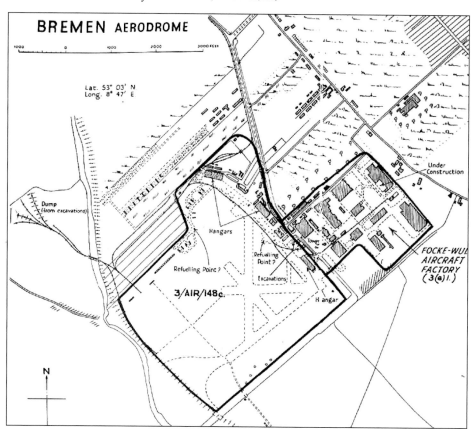

PR image radar site at Auderville, taken on 22 February 1941.

Plan of V-2 launch site in Normandy. (*TNA Air 40/2887*)

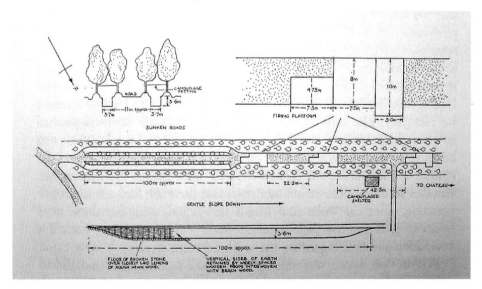

4.

Würzburg, ground control radar.

Schweinfurt ball bearing factory map, issued October 1943.

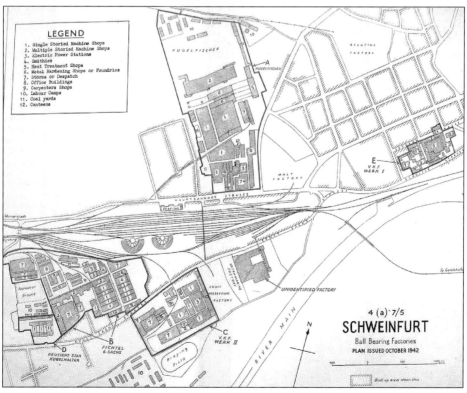

WAR DEPARTMENT
BUREAU OF PUBLIC RELATIONS
PRESS BRANCH
TEL.—RE 6700, BRS. 3425 AND 4860

FUTURE RELEASE

FOR RELEASE BY PRESS AND RADIO

After

4 p. m., Eastern Standard Time
TUESDAY, OCTOBER 30, 1945

For Use in Morning Newspapers Appearing on the Streets After the Above Time

US War Department press release, 30 October 1945. (*TNA Air 48/194*)

88mm anti-aircraft Flak gun in field deployment.

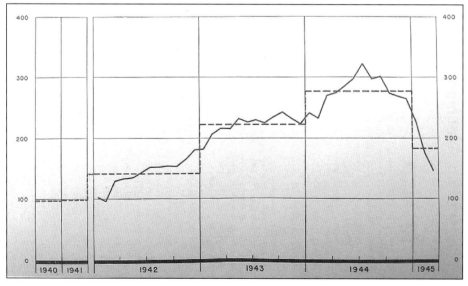

Total German Armament Production, 1940–45. (*TNA Air 48/194*)

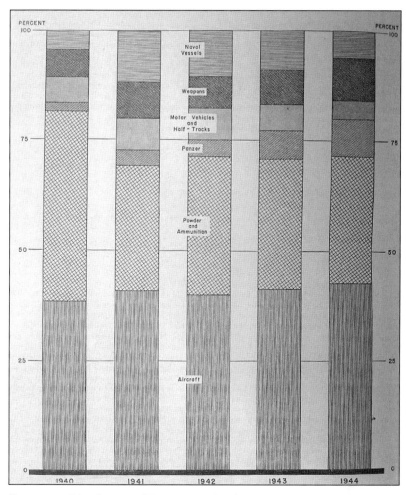

Percentage Distribution of Armaments Production. (*TNA Air 48/194*)

RAF Lancaster and 22,000lb Tallboy. (*IWM CH 015375*)

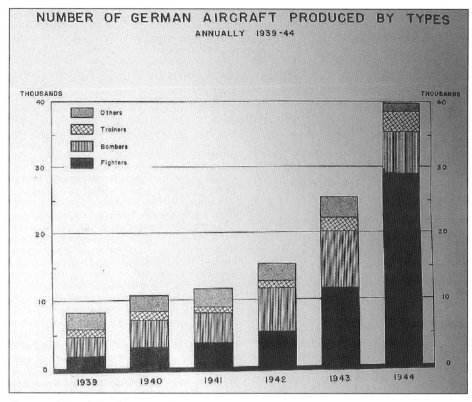

German Aircraft Production, 1939–1944. (*TNA Air 48/194*)

A schematic plan of an underground lubricating oil plant at Porta, Westphalia. (*TNA Air 8/1019*)

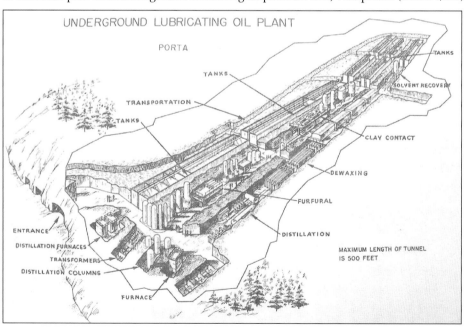

continuing extent of bombing operations against a range of strategic targets, widespread chaos became the order of the day for German factories, supply routes, dockyards and operational ports. The German Controller of Submarines stated in a post-war interrogation that:

> By the end of 1944 conditions in the U-boat industry were chaotic everywhere. Components and main assemblies for pre-fabricated boats could not be moved. Lack of electrical motors and batteries caused severe bottlenecks; the Accumulateron Fabrik plant at Hanover was the only battery producer still functioning and main electric motors were practically unobtainable. The destruction of floating cranes brought assembly of the more powerful 1,600 ton Type XXI boats almost to a complete stop even when the sections did manage to reach the assembly yards. Canal transportation came to a complete halt in early 1945 after the RAF attacks on the Dortmund-Ems canal.[8]

C. *The final phase, from 1 Apr 45*, began when the Allied armies crossed the Rhine at the end of Mar 45 and began spreading across Germany. Strategic bombing rapidly diminished and the main effort went towards close support of the troops on the ground. Effectively, overall control returned to SHAEF who issued a daily signal listing targets for the next 24 hours. Those signals rarely arrived in time for the afternoon bombing conferences at Bomber Command HQ – largely due to delays in securing clearance and approval from the Russian 'allies' for the targets to support the Eastern Front. The targets were largely transportation centres and yards, airfields and a few special targets such as Berchtesgaden. The last operations were food supply drops over Holland; and the evacuation of PoWs.

V-Weapons and Operation CROSSBOW

Operation CROSSBOW was the codename for Allied operations against the German long-range weapons programme. On 15 Nov 43 the original codename BODYLINE was replaced by CROSSBOW.

There had been an immense amount of UK intelligence effort devoted to the German V-Weapon programmes, with information from many separate sources. The first slender evidence went back to the Oslo Report in 1939 where there was mention of 'rocket powered radio-controlled gliders'. Then there was a report in Dec 42 from a Danish chemical engineer who described the firing of rockets; the first successful firing of a prototype V-2 was on 3 Oct 42. Later, there was a conversation between two German generals who had been captured after El Alamein and talked between themselves about things that would go up 15kms into the stratosphere. The focus fell upon the site at Peenemünde with the subsequent PR and the excellent photographic interpretation by Constance Babington-Smith.

Bomber Command attacked the site on the night of 17/18 Aug 43 under the codename HYDRA with 596 heavy bombers. A precondition was that it should be a clear moonlit night, but there were patches of stratocumulus cloud that caused uncertain visibility. The operation plan was to attack from a lower height

---

8. Bib. A31, Ch. 11, p. 242.

than was usual to improve the bombing accuracy. The Master Bomber was Gp Capt. Searby from 83 Squadron, part of the PFF. Some of the PFF marker flares fell to the south of the main site and about one third of the first wave of 227 bombers were led astray; their bombs falling on Camp Trassenheide and there were many casualties among the foreign labourers. The third wave of bombers was also led astray and many of their bombs fell 2000–3000 yards beyond the Experimental Station. Bomber Command lost 40 aircraft, mostly to German fighters in the final phase of the raid. It was variously estimated that the V-Weapons programme was delayed by several months.

On 22 Aug 43 a small unmanned aircraft crashed into a field on Bornholm Island in the Baltic. It had the identification number V83 and photographs were taken by a Danish Naval officer Lt Cdr Christiansen. He was arrested and tortured by the Gestapo; was rescued and subsequently awarded the Distinguished Service Cross. Those photographs found their way to British intelligence via the Chief of Danish Naval Intelligence and it was realised that the unmanned aircraft was a prototype V-1, otherwise known as FZG-76 (FZG = Flak Zielgerät = anti-aircraft aiming apparatus). Then there were reports of unidentified sites being built near the Channel coast, all facing towards London. PR images showed that they were ski-shaped structures 250ft long – thereafter they were known as ski-sites.

But all was not well in the UK intelligence world and there were many opposing and dissenting views; and a number of apparently pointless and conflicting committees. The Prime Minister had remarked on the possible otioseness of these committees. Even the JIC was undistinguished in this galaxy of committees. The UK Chiefs of Staff suggested to the Prime Minister on 15 Apr 44 that 'a single investigator should be appointed to call on such scientific and intelligence advice as was necessary' and they had proposed Duncan Sandys, who was the Joint Parliamentary Secretary to the Ministry of Supply. Perhaps the Chiefs had overlooked the fact that there was an ADI (Sci) within the Air Intelligence Directorate? But it should be noted that Sandys had been involved with the Cabinet's Defence Committee on the subject of the V-Weapons from at least the end of Jun 43. When the evolving evidence on the FZG-76 was better understood, Sandys took the view that unmanned aircraft should remain a subject for the Air Ministry but he chose to retain responsibility for assessments of the V-2 weapon.

Driven in part by the Allied success with OVERLORD, Hitler opened his offensive with the V-1 flying bombs on the night of 12/13 Jun 44. The Prime Minister called a CROSSBOW War Cabinet committee meeting on 19 Jun 44 to report on the V-1 and V-2 programmes and the related Allied countermeasures; and appointed Sandys as the Chairman. A very good description of the intelligence history of the V-Weapons is within Bib. B15, Chapters 38, 44 and 45, by Prof R V Jones who was a key member of that committee.

The impact of the substantial effort by the heavy bombers against the V-1 sites was mixed. Starting from Dec 43 and through the spring of 1944 they were very successful, the network of ski-sites was in ruins and the large storage sites had been damaged.[9] However, in the second phase, from Jul to Sep 44, the enemy had

---

9. Bib. A25, Vol. 3, p. 525.

devised 'modified launch sites' that were simple to construct and repair; or replace with new sites at a different location. Those sites were difficult targets, well camouflaged, small with generally good anti-aircraft artillery defences. During Jul–Aug 44, the 8th USAAF made 164 attacks against a total of 67 CROSSBOW targets.[10] The bomb aiming was mostly visual but with about 40 per cent using G-H. An attack by B-24s of the 389th Bomb Group on the V-1 site at Belloy-sur-Somme resulted in 90 per cent of the bombs falling within 2000ft of the aiming point but only 5 per cent fell within 1000ft; the small target itself was not hit. There was significant success by 617 Squadron with the TALLBOY bombs against the large V-1 storage site at St Leu d'Esserent just north of Paris, on 4 and 7 Jul 44.

Generals Spaatz and Arnold believed that the heavy bomber was not the correct means of attacking those launch sites, but that those bombers would be better used against strategic targets. Eisenhower's orders to give those sites a high priority during Jul–Aug 44 was very much a public relations decision driven by the intensity of the V-1 attacks on London and the south-east of England.

The efforts by Fighter Command and the UK anti-aircraft gun defences were more effective against the V-1s as they flew across southern England, helped by the use of the SCR584 gun-laying radar and predictor with proximity-fused shells. The Official History 'The Defence of the United Kingdom' shows that 8617 V-1s were launched against England and that 2340 fell within the London Defence Region.

The USAAF senior staffs were not satisfied with the conduct of the CROSSBOW committee. General McDonald, Director of Intelligence at USSTAF HQ, was exasperated by the persistent 'inadequate dissemination of intelligence' by Whitehall staffs and 'time lag over damage assessment', which resulted in unnecessary duplication of attack and waste of bombing effort.[11]

McDonald might well have been experiencing the same sort of problem that Harris at Bomber Command suffered continuously with the Whitehall staffs.

McDonald wrote to ACAS (I), Director of Intelligence in the Air Ministry, on 15 Jul 44 to state that:

Nothing less than a joint and balanced Anglo-American CROSSBOW committee formed exclusively from representatives of the (RAF) Air Staff and USSTAF would answer the requirement.

A revised CROSSBOW committee on the lines suggested by McDonald held its first meeting on 21 Jul 44 and produced a revision to the V-1 target priorities. It was quickly appreciated that 'heavy' bombing of the modified V-1 sites was not effective and would never prevent the launch of V-1s from unidentified tactical

---

10. Bib. A21, Ch. 11, pp. 277–278.
11. Bib. A29, Ch. 4, p. 222.

sites, which were better targets for the Allied fighter-bombers from the AEAF based in France.

In several respects that was also the situation with the V-2 weapons, first used against England on 8 Sep 44. The major V-2 factories were at Peenemünde, the Zeppelin Works at Freidrichshafen and the Rax Works at Wiener Neustadt; each of these three factories was to have produced 300 rockets per month. They were all bombed several times. The Germans then concentrated the production in a large underground factory at Nordhausen, which from Aug 44 onwards was producing 600 rockets per month. That factory made use of foreign labourers from a local concentration camp known as 'Dora'. It was subsequently realised that some of the intelligence reports came from Polish workers at that camp. There were in addition large reinforced underground assembly and launch facilities, such as La Coupelle (Wizernes); but there were also many small well concealed launch sites, as shown in Plate 4, and transportable launch facilities.

ADI (Sci) suspected that the V-2s might have had some form of radio control. Part of the evidence came from the V-2 rocket (W. Nr. 4089) that had crashed near Gräsdals Gärd in Sweden on 13 Jun 44. The wreckage had then been flown to England in the bomb-bay of a Mosquito and examined at Farnborough. There was a complex radio control system in that rocket, but it was not appreciated at the time that the radio system was associated with a different test programme for the *Wasserfall* anti-aircraft missile.[12] There was also some evidence for a radio beam control of the rocket during the early stages of flight. Many sorties were flown by 192 Squadron of 100 Group to conduct airborne search for these radio signals; and many other sorties were flown by 214 and 223 Squadrons to perform jamming of the radio signals that were suspected to be used by V-2s on their way to London. Those airborne search and jamming sorties were part of the BIG BEN operations intended to detect and counter the V-2 threat. It was not until the end of the war that it was known that these operations were unnecessary; the V-2 was a ballistic weapon and used internal gyroscopes and accelerometers for control and guidance.

German records at the end of Apr 45 revealed that they had then successfully launched 1,115 V-2 rockets against London, of which 501 fell within the London Civil Defence Region. Antwerp suffered more than London; 1610 V-2s and 8696 V-1s were launched at that city.

Prof. Jones within Bib. B15 at Chapter 45, p. 439–443, has amplified the USAAF sentiments about the Whitehall committees in detail. He had minuted the CAS on 26 Jul 44 to complain about the 'continuous sniping that was coming from Duncan Sandys and his array of experts.' Three days later, Jones drafted a Note to ACAS (I) AVM Inglis offering his resignation, which included the warning that:

> *Our sources will be miss-handled; collation will be wild and incomplete; and presentations will be political […] unless officers can be found who will defend the traditions of intelligence to the last.*

---

12. Bib. A30, Ch. 3, pp. 61–62.

That draft note was never delivered; Prof. Jones was too deeply troubled by the 'mess that might result if (he) ceased to watch the rocket.' Events that then transpired were astonishing. The wreckage of the V-2 from Sweden had been examined at Farnborough. The Poles had over many months been collecting pieces of V-2 rockets after they had fallen back to earth. Those pieces had been loaded into an aircraft that made a night landing in Poland for delivery to England, eventually arriving at Hendon on 28 Jul 44. Prof. Jones then compiled a most accurate and comprehensive report on the V-2 rocket programme, which was delivered on 26 Aug 44. It described a rocket that was between 12 and 13 tons at launch with a one ton warhead that would be ready for use by the middle of Sep 44, but could be used in small numbers almost immediately.

CAS withdrew that report as a result of objections from Sandys, who considered that it was unjustified and unfair to his 'experts'. The consensus within that body of experts was for a rocket that was in excess of 20 tons with a warhead in excess of 5 tons; the estimated damage effects of such a weapon had already caused the War Cabinet to consider the need to evacuate people from London. The technical credibility of those 'experts' included one who had not thought about gyroscopes to control the stability of the rocket; and another who exclaimed that the PR images of the V-2 rockets were really only 'inflated barrage balloons'. But there were others who were well recognised in their disciplines: John Cockcroft, Robert Watson-Watt, Edward Appleton. However, none of them had ever made a rocket that flew at all. A USAAF officer who was assigned to (RAF) Air Intelligence had been invited to examine the opposing arguments and found that what emerged was a solid intelligence argument for a one ton warhead. He commented on the 'the academic and bureaucratic structure and their capacity for bloodless tribal warfare.'

There was a very politically embarrassing outcome in that Sandys held a press conference on 7 Sep 44 to announce that the Battle of London was over. The papers the following morning showed Sandys making that proclamation. That same evening the first V-2 rockets fell on London. The sad failure of Operation MARKET GARDEN at Arnhem then resulted in a vital V-2 launching area around the Hook of Holland and within 200 miles of London remaining in German hands until the spring of 1945. German records showed that by Apr 45 they had successfully launched 1,190 V-2s against London from that area.

It is illuminating to consider the impact that the strategic bombing offensive had on the development of the German V-Weapon programmes. This may be regarded to have started with the raids on Peenemünde. There are many arguments about the delays that were introduced into the programmes by Bomber Command and the 8th USAAF. But it is clear that without that bombing, the V-1 and the V-2 programmes would have reached operational readiness many months earlier. Indeed, both of those weapons could well have been used by Hitler against the Allied landings in Normandy.

As a matter of subsequent history, Werner von Braun who had been the inspiration for the V-2 rocket project went on to become one of the key figures in the US space exploration programme and the Saturn launch vehicles for the Apollo moon landings.

Directive Targets

CinC Bomber Command found it necessary to write formally to the SofS for Air, Sir Archibald Sinclair, to report the progress made by the Command within the scope of the Combined Bombing Offensive, as at mid-January 1944.[13] With the exceptions that were forced by short nights, moonlight and other weather factors, all Command operations since the adoption of Operation POINTBLANK had been against targets within that Directive. The point of the letter was to attempt to dispel the view held in some Air Staff directorates that Bomber Command had not performed its full share of POINTBLANK operations.

Soon afterwards, the CIO at Bomber Command wrote to Director of Intelligence (Operations) about the availability of intelligence information.[14] The specific point was that DB (Ops) was receiving information from Air Intelligence in the course of making target selections. This had become apparent from various Target Directives. At Bomber Command, Sir Arthur Harris expected his CIO to know why each target was on the Directive and what the reason was for its selection. That information did not reach Bomber Command. The reply from London was rather ambiguous, referring to 'moonlight targets' and noting that the full assessment of those targets would not be the sort of information that D of I (O) would wish to put before the CinC – perhaps they were relatively unimportant? Be that as it may, there would seem to be no reason why the CIO should not have been informed. The reader may question whether this was but another example of the Air Ministry not knowing how Bomber Command went about its business?

CSTC Target Lists

The reader is referred back to Chapter 4. There was exasperation at Bomber Command about the content and presentation of the Directive target lists. There were several major areas of concern as described below.

The Target lists were copied directly to multiple action addressees, but with no indication of individual responsibilities.[15] This was a concern both with Bomber Command and the 8th USAAF: Who was to attack which targets? Some targets would reasonably have been candidates for both day and night raids, but no account was taken within the Directive target lists of the tactical suitability of any specific target for one or the other bomber forces. The operational problems for Bomber Command were quite different to those of the 8th USAAF. The winter weather made things more complicated because of the long time delays that were often incurred before bomb damage effects could be assessed from PR sorties. This was a serious factor when considering the need for repeat attacks, without wasting operational effort in over-bombing. But during 1943 and increasingly from Jan 44, ULTRA material was providing valuable and timely information on the German's own assessments of damage and repair times. Appendix K has a few selected examples of this ULTRA material, relating to Allied attacks on the German transportation system from 1 Oct 44 onwards. There is no record of this

---

13. Air 20/4764. BC/MS. 29961/CinC dated 21 Jan 44.
14. BC/S. 24990/Int dated 2 Apr 44: from CIO Bomber Command to D of I (O).
15. Air 14/1206, Minute 34 dated 28 Oct 44, from Int.1 to CIO.

material being made available to Bomber Command for use within operational target selection and raid planning.

A CSTC target list dated 27 Nov 44 contained 25 towns that had been selected for their transportation or economic importance – readers may wish to refer back to Chapter 6 and the section on 'Target Intelligence'. By 23 Jan 45 most of those towns had been attacked, with the result that the original list had been reduced to 9 large towns, all in Eastern or South-eastern Germany. On a number of occasions the CSTC had been requested to update and increase the number of towns; but the committee refused to do that and maintained that the

Command could attack any town they liked and that there was no need to amend the original list'.[16]

The view was taken at Bomber Command that that amounted to the CSTC escaping its responsibilities; and that it was wrong to leave Bomber Command to make a choice when the CSTC had available the best information to prepare a priority list of targets. The Air Ministry had clearly identified the availability of such 'best information' within the Directive dated 19 Jan 45, issued by DCAS, which included the statement:

A list of industrial area targets calculated to make the best contribution to our strategic aims has already been issued to you. This may be amended from time to time.

Bomber Command's concern was intensified by the fact that the Baedaker and the KPR data were hopelessly out of date and both failed to take account of the current situation. One of the functions of the CSTC should have been to put the lists of targets within the separate target sets in priority order and to discard those targets which had no further significance. The CSTC target list should also have taken into account a number of operational as well as economic and industrial factors, as follows:

- Targets must be well spaced geographically to allow for the variations in weather.
- Damage already done may have created fire-breaks that would diminish the value of the target.
- The selection of any candidate target town must take account of navigational coverage from *Oboe* or G-H; or the suitability of the target for H2S navigation.
- The structural characteristics of the targets and their suitability either for fire or explosive attack.

DB (Ops) acknowledged this in his reply to the CIO.[17] In that reply, Bufton expressed himself in full agreement with the concern at Bomber Command and raised the matter with MEW. There was an underlying feeling in the Air Ministry

16. Air 14/1206, Minute 38 dated 23 Jan 45, from Int.1 to CIO.
17. Air Ministry CMS.606/DB (Ops)/DO dated 29 Jan 45; from Air Cdre Bufton to Air Cdre Paynter.

that Bomber Command could have sent more senior representatives to the CSTC meetings, but that begged the question that they could be spared from their operational duties. Bomber Command was usually represented at the weekly CSTC meetings by officers from the Operations and the Target Sections. As in many cases, face-to-face discussions may have been beneficial outside of the meetings during the analysis and assessment stages of CSTC work, but it should be noted that the strategic targets and bombing were 'thrashed out in detail and opinions were expressed with complete freedom and sometimes with considerable heat'.[18]

The facts were that the Target Section at Bomber Command was directly responsible for keeping the CSTC Directive Target Priority Lists as up-to-date as possible on a day-to-day basis in the light of intelligence and other information that was available at Bomber Command HQ.[19] But it should be noted that Bomber Command did not receive the ULTRA information on bomb targets and damage effects. For operations against targets that were identified by SHAEF in direct support for the Allied Armies, the target lists could change several times a day in concert with actual operations on the ground. Clearly some of those SHAEF targets were attacked by the Tactical Air Forces, but Bomber Command and the 8th USAAF became involved when heavy weapons were required.

Almost coincident with that exchange, there was a most illuminating paper on 'German Troop Movements from the Western Front to the East' issued from AI 3(e).[20] This paper explicitly used ULTRA material and within the text there was a very clear statement about access to ULTRA information; within the CSTC Transportation Sub-committee that access was restricted to AI 3(e), the Foreign Office and MEW, the US EOU and the Railway Research Service. The details in the paper included knowledge from ULTRA about the movement of the 6th SS Panzer Army from south west of Cologne to a new area near Berlin. That movement would have involved 250–300 complete train loads of personnel and equipment. The movements were planned between the dates 25 Jan to 5 Feb 45. The general destination area was bounded by Berlin, Cottbus, Leipzig, Magdeburg – and Dresden. The success of the Russian campaign and the possibility of an early Allied victory had relegated the war on the Western Front to a secondary place from the German point of view. The direct suggestion within that AI 3 paper was that the first priority bombing targets should be those that were most calculated to help the Russian Armies in the East. A comprehensive list of railway targets was provided, to dislocate the movement by the 6th SS Panzer Army. The list contained selected major railway centres as far to the east as possible because the movement was already in progress, for attack by the heavy bombers. The final provision was that if those attacks could not be made before 5 Feb, then the CSTC Transportation Sub-committee would adjust the next Target Priority List.

The records show that a revised list of target towns was issued by the CSTC on 8 Feb 45.[21] In events that were to become of the very highest political perception

---

18. Air 14/1210, Section II, Appendix A, p. 2.
19. Air 14/1210, p. 46.
20. Air 20/4819, AI 3(e) dated 30 Jan 45, TOP SECRET ULTRA, to DB Ops.
21. SECRET Cypher Message MSW207 dated 8 Feb 45; from the CSTC to Bomber Command, USSTAF and SHAEF.

and sensitivity, the 1st and 2nd priority towns were Berlin and Dresden, followed by Chemnitz and Leipzig as 3rd and 4th priority. The MEW appreciation of Dresden at that time was:

Population of 640,000; had now become an important town in relation to the Russian offensive; the industry comprised 39 plants, of which three were Priority 1 and nine were Priority 2.[22]

That was but four days before the Bomber Command and 8th USAAF raids on Dresden, which subsequently had such a major impact on the whole Allied political and public perceptions – and on post-war historians and publications.

It should not be forgotten that those targets were selected by the Allied authorities in Whitehall on the basis of ULTRA intelligence and issued to Bomber Command and the USAAF.

That ULTRA intelligence was not released to Bomber Command.

Enemy Air Defence Intelligence

Within the Intelligence Branch at HQ Bomber Command, the section that dealt with all matters relating to the enemy's Air Force and their defences was Intelligence 3; see Appendix G for a brief summary of the scope of work. A complete description of their work is available within the 'Composition and Duties of Intelligence 3, HQ Bomber Command – 1939–45'.[23] It was the responsibility of Int. 3 to inform the Air Staff on all matters relating to the enemy air defence for operational planning purposes; the Command Signals staff for the use of RCM; and all Groups and stations principally guidance and information to aircrew. After any operations by the Command, Int. 3 was responsible for consolidating all information and reports that related to the planning and those operations and the enemy's reactions. This was provided within the 'Interception Tactics Report' for all day and night operations. The key external agencies that routinely provided information to Int. 3 were:

- Air Intelligence AI 3b: Movements, Order of Battle, Losses and Aircraft Production data.
- Air Intelligence AI 2b: Enemy airfield data including maps and targeting information.
- Air Intelligence AI 2g and ADI(K): German Aircraft and Equipment.
- Air Intelligence AI 4b: GAF Fighter reactions to bomber raids, including interception tactics. These reaction signals and reports were eventually provided directly from AI 4f (the Air Section at Bletchley Park, together with the RAF Y-stations at Cheadle and Kingsdown, later from Canterbury.

---

22. Air 14/1206, Enclosure 82A 'Target Priorities for Area Attacks', Appendix B.
23. Air 14/1207: Historical Summary, Section 7.

- No. 100 Group: Immediate summaries of RCM and Intuder operations in support of the bomber raids.
- Air Intelligence ADI Sci: Air Scientific Intelligance data on German radar and signals systems.
- MI 15 and the CIU: Searchlight, Flak and Barrage Balloon data.
- Bomber Crew Reports: The post-flight de-briefs from the bomber crews after the raids.

All this information had to be assessed and recorded in order to provide Intelligence briefings at the Command morning and afternoon conferences, together with immediate access for operational planning purposes.

The following sub-section describe some aspects of Int. 3's day-to-day tasks.

Tactical Sigint Support

The Historical Summary of Int. 3's work recorded that the tactical Signals Intelligence provided more value to bomber operations than did any other single source of intelligence.

The primary source of that information was the Air Section at Bletchley Park in the closest co-ordination with the RAF Y-Service. As that operational relationship with Bomber Command and 100 Group evolved, the timeliness of Sigint reporting became most impressive. The Y-Stations and sites were fully active from the time before the bomber and bomber support aircraft left their airfields until they had returned from their missions over enemy territory. During those periods, signals intercept operators kept a constant watch on enemy air defence and night fighter R/T and W/T channels. Any intercepted message that was classed as Priority had to be reported by telephone to Bomber Command and 100 Group HQs within one minute of being intercepted. The organisation for that level of immediate operational support is described in Chapter 8 of Bib. B28.

An overview of the secure telephone and teleprinter network that was created is shown in the following diagram. It is noted that the closely integrated network within Bletchley Park included access to Hut 3 where relevant ULTRA material was available to help clarify or resolve any details within the medium and low-grade real-time tactical Sigint, within the immediate context of operations in progress over enemy territory. It should be noted that it was usually impractical to use that immediate intelligence to divert the very large bomber streams as they were en-route to their targets, but it was often possible to revise RCM operations and – towards the end of the war – to provide tactical advice to the Mosquito intruders as they were operating over Germany.

A very similar service was provided for the 8th USAAF during daylight operations, as is noted in Chapter 8 below. That daylight service was of course available to Bomber Command when it resumed daylight bombing missions with escort fighter support from the autumn of 1944 onwards.

The Night Hook-Up was of major importance since 100 Group made immediate operational use of this information.[24] Amplification of the Night Hook-Up was recorded in the Order from OC Kingsdown to all subordinate

---

24. Air 40/2229, Kingsdown to all HDUs, dated 14 May 1944.

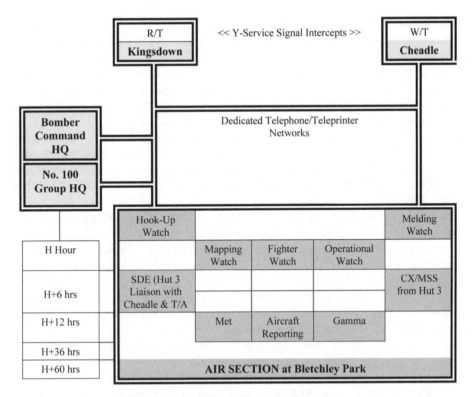

Schematic Representation of the Hook-Up Service

Notes:
H Raid Plans: Start time of the Raid(s).
H+6 hrs: Early report by telephone to No. 100 Group HQ.
H+12 hrs: Preliminary report and Map by D/R to Bomber Command HQ.
H+36 hrs: Sigint feedback to Kingsdown and Cheadle.
H+60 hrs: Final report to BMP/N.
SDE = Smith, Davies and Evans – the originators of this liaison process.

HDUs, dated 28th May 1944. This emphasised the operational use made by 100 Group of the Y-Service traffic during night raids. In order to help 100 Group inflict maximum damage on the enemy night fighting system, the hook-up gave as clear a picture as possible of the movements of German fighters and particularly the times and places of their take-off and landings. Whenever a German fighter movement was given, a statement of Allied bomber positions was required in order to show the German movement in relation to those bomber positions. Supplementary details that were to be passed included movements and positions of enemy formations or single aircraft and plots on British aircraft, using the GAF Fighter Grid system. These were to be regarded as Priority messages and passed immediately. Other traffic that was to be passed included references to Beacons, bomb target identification reports, flares, combat claims, etc., and indications that the control of enemy aircraft was being transferred between different German authorities.

As the bomber operations routinely penetrated more deeply into enemy territory, the ability of the HDUs to intercept enemy VHF R/T communications decreased as a direct consequence of radio signal propagation characteristics. To minimise this Sigint loss by the HDUs within south-east England, arrangements were made to deploy Signals Units forward behind the battle fronts as the Allied armies advanced eastwards into occupied territory and eventually into Germany. At the time those arrangements caused a great deal of political and military concern because many of the best Sigint operators were female and the culture of the time did not approve of their deployment close to enemy troops. The arrangements that were agreed involved the assurances of the Supreme Commander about their safety and the satisfaction of Director WAAF about their accommodation.

Another most valuable tactical service was the airborne intercept of enemy air defence and fighter control communications from Allied aircraft either close to or over enemy territory. Mr Bonsall put the initial concept forward from the Air Section at Bletchley Park in May 43. That was quickly followed by a meeting within the Air Ministry on 17 Jun 43 at which it was agreed to conduct a trial using a 192 Squadron Halifax, if possible in co-ordination with 8th USAAF operations.[25] That co-ordination was set up with Col Putnam, commanding the USAAF base at Thurleigh, for a briefing with American bomber crews. The concept moved forward and there was correspondence between ACAS (I) AVM Inglis and General Eaker following a request for operational USAAF aircraft to carry the Sigint intercept and recording equipment. Eaker agreed that on 13 Oct 43.[26] See Chapter 8 and Appendix L, Q1261. The purpose was to provide operational information to the 8th USAAF bomber and fighter division formation commanders about the disposition of enemy fighters as the missions progressed.[27]

There was difficulty in obtaining suitable recording equipment for aircraft use and that element of the concept did not become operational until Mar 44. Soon afterwards there was a letter from 100 Group to Air Intelligence DDI 4 reporting on the large volume of German fighter VHF R/T traffic that was being heard by 192 Squadron aircraft operating in support of Bomber Command raids and stressing the urgency of obtaining and installing additional suitable equipment.[28] Another difficulty was the availability and training of suitable airborne operators: the working environment was hostile, the required skill level was high and the operational pressure was intense.

Enemy Fighter and Air

Some of the most valuable tactical information that became available to Bomber Command, and the 8th USAAF, was the knowledge of enemy night and day fighter tactics. That information came from the Sigint material that was intercepted by the RAF Y-Service and exploited by the Air Section at Bletchley

---

25. Air 40/2717; AI 4f dated 17 Jun 43.
26. HQ 8th USAAF, APO 633: dated 13 Oct 43.
27. HQ 8th USAAF, APO 634: 413.44 dated 15 Mar 44.
28. 100Gp/S.301/3/3/Int dated 6 May 44: from AOC 100 Group to DDI 4.

Park. The great value of that material was the timeliness of its availability and the quality of the information, together with a security classification that allowed its immediate application to live operations. Very closely associated with that Sigint was the RCM support and the Night Intruders that were operated by No. 100 Group. This is described in detail within Bib. B18, B28 and others.

By Oct 42, the mechanics of preparing the daily BMP reports were sufficiently well established to allow them to be tailored to particular user requirements. Following visits by the Air Section to HQBC, the ORS became one of the most important recipients. The need for details of night-fighter patrols and pursuits resulted in changes to the BMP format, with additional details such as overall times, average height, direction of pursuit and vectors, and any significant remarks within the R/T; and a map was added showing the specific location of patrols operating against a given raid.[29] There is a MOST SECRET note dated 13 Apr 43 stating that DDI 4 (Gp Capt. Fitch) had requested the distribution of the ZIP/BMP reports to HQBC, for the ORS Section, and to the 8th US Fighter Command within the 8th USAAF.[30]

Another series of reports was started – PEARL/ZIP/DISTAC/N – to provide a daily resume of the main points of tactical interest in the daily BMP/N reports for senior staffs at Bomber Command.[31] The abbreviation DISTAC came from 'Distilled Tactics'. This series of reports was discontinued in Jan 44 but the content was then provided within the daily summaries of the night activities BMP/N.

But it was perceived by the Air Section at GC & CS that the BMP/N was lacking in some quality that would make the full weight of the intelligence felt and appreciated by the raid planners at Bomber Command.[32] The Bomber Command Intelligence Officer, Gp Capt. Paynter, visited Bletchley on 24 Jan 44.[33] He was very interested in the DISTAC/N reports and took copies of the last six issues. His specific requests were that HQBC received:

- The night BMP/N as at present (not abbreviated).
- DISTAC/N reports for every major raid.
- TAC reports, reviewing the trend of events and comparing raids within a series.

He was also very keen on direct co-operation between the BMP authors and the Command Intelligence staff and suggested a routine contact between the two parties, as the reports were being written. The importance of timeliness was critical to the bomber raid planning process. In that same visit, he emphasised the need to include 100 Group in the overall process.

Eventually, it was agreed that the Head of the Planning Staff from Bomber Command would also visit the Air Section. He was able to indicate just what

29. HW 3/105, p. 61.
30. HW 14/73.
31. HW 3/105, p. 69.
32. HW 14/93: Letter dated 2 Dec 43 from Gp Capt. Daubney, DDI 4, to Josh Cooper, Head of the Air Section at Bletchley Park. This letter covered a very complimentary letter from the AOC 11 Group, Fighter Command, about the BMP Reports.
33. HW 14/96 dated 24 Jan 44.

information could be used and he insisted that any conclusions or lessons that the report authors could extract should be stated unequivocally, even if they were highly critical. Nothing could have proved more instructive and encouraging to the BMP staff.[34] The understanding of the way that raid planning was conducted was of major value to subsequent BMP report writing. The moral of that is:

> 'That contact between the actual producers of Signal Intelligence and those whose business it is to make use of the information is of prime importance.'

The point was well marked by subsequent events during the heavy bomber raiding that grew in intensity prior to the invasion of Normandy. The BMP reports thereafter were looked upon with great favour at Bomber Command. In Mar 44, the Bomber Command Intelligence staff asked if the daily BMP/N reports from Bletchley on the preceding night's raids could be delivered more quickly. This had long been a wish of the Air Section and, immediately after the request, a despatch rider delivered the maps of that night's raids and night-fighter movements to HQBC for the daily briefing to the CinC, Sir Arthur Harris. Soon afterwards, again at the request of the Bomber Command Intelligence staff, the maps were attached to narrative on the main points of interest on the night's raids and formed the 'Preliminary Version (PV)' of the daily BMP. This proved so valuable that the practice continued throughout the remainder of the war.[35] In response to this, Bomber Command began to supply the Air Section with copies of the 'Immediate Assessment of Results' which were produced after each nights operations.[36]

100 Group Bomber Support RCM and Night Intruders

The air battle over Germany had by 1943–44 become so intense and complex that it must be doubted whether the bomber or night-fighter aircraft from the earlier phases of the war would have stood the slightest chance of executing a successful mission. The air superiority that was eventually achieved by the bomber force, from the later months in 1944 until the end of the war, had – in view of the immense effort by the GAF to destroy the bombers – only been achieved by a comparable effort and an even greater degree of skill by the Allied forces, the research establishments and the industrial support.[37] But the most important organisational RCM decision had been to establish a specialist RAF unit to become responsible for the operational development, application and co-ordination of all RCM programmes, from the air and from the ground. Bomber Command initially suggested the role for what became No. 100 Group in June 1943; it was approved by the Air Ministry on 29 September and became operational in December 1943. No. 100 Group subsumed No. 80 Wing.

---

34. HW 3/99, History of Hut 3, Ch. VI, p. 46.
35. HW 3/109, p. 50.
36. HW 14/101, BC/S.30329/Int dated 2 Apr 44 from Air Cdre Paynter to Josh Cooper.
37. Air 14/1394.

An extremely brief overview of 100 Group operations is as follows:

- Throughout June 1944, MANDREL screens were flown on a number of nights subject to the tactical limitation that there should be no jamming in the Channel due to interference with Allied Army and Naval communications and radars, post D-Day.
- During August, 192 Sqn set up the continuous 24hr watch for V-Weapons; and on the 16/17th there were was a great success by the Spoof Force during main force raids on Kiel and Stettin. During September, the advance of the Allied Armies further into Europe saw new developments in the MANDREL/ WINDOW spoof techniques, taking advantage of the withdrawal by the enemy from most of his forward early warning sites.
- In October, 100 Group realised the need to secure better co-ordination with the Main Force that was then using low-level approach tactics under radio silence. The Group began the issue of the Daily Intentions Orders to all Bomber groups, consistent with the main force operational planning for the night's raids; an example is on the next page. For the first time, the other Groups became fully aware of the protection and support that 100 Group was providing; and one perhaps unexpected outcome was that some Groups claimed that others were being 'better treated'.
- During the major raids into the Ruhr during November, the enemy adopted the practice of keeping his night-fighters in that area regardless of spoof operations and therefore the 100 Group Special WINDOW Force was used to invest the whole area with vast quantities of WINDOW. Throughout the year the Fortresses of 214 Sqn and, later, the Liberators of 223 Sqn, had been providing their radar and communications jamming support from within the Main Force bomber streams. By December, they were of even better value by being fully equipped with CARPET jammers against the enemy *Würzburg* radars and PIPERACK against the SN2 AI radars. It was also during December that 192 Sqn Mosquitoes provided inbound Y-recordings of enemy R/T traffic, then provided PIPERACK jamming of SN2 until well after the main force attack had finished, to protect any 'stragglers' on their return to UK airfields.
- A great regret in January 1945 was the loss of the support from the 36th Sqn of the 8th USAAF. The Squadron had been providing MANDREL support for Bomber Command night operations, but was more urgently required to support the USAAF daylight raids. However, in Feb 45, the 492nd Bombardment Group began operations with the WINDOW Force: their role was to provide heavy bombing attacks in conjunction with the WINDOW screens. As the depth of main force raids into Germany was increasing, the effectiveness of the WINDOW screen diminished and more use was made of multiple spoof raids with MANDREL jamming and WINDOW. On one night, not having heard a Recall message, one B-17 Fortress from 214 Sqn completed the planned sortie alone and was plotted by the enemy as a force of 20–30 aircraft.
- In March, 199 Sqn completed conversion to Halifax III; the Group might have completely converted to Halifax 'heavy aircraft' had it not been for the difficulty of fitting JOSTLE into British aircraft. The JOSTLE equipment weighed 600lb and required 8KW of prime power. In the course of Spoof operations in March,

the 100 Group heavy aircraft dropped over 200 tons of WINDOW; this was dropped by hand at the rate of one bundle every two seconds by operators in full flying kit under oxygen conditions and in extreme cold.

A typical Daily Intentions Order from 100 Group HQ is summarised below:[38]

- To screen the approach of Nos. 1 and 6 Groups: A MANDREL screen at 15,000ft will be disposed between 17.50 hrs when the first bomber is at 0330E and will continue until 19.40 hrs when the last bomber is approaching liberated air. The MANDREL screen will move forward when the last bomber of the second main force has passed through it. This is to create confusion in plotting and jamming of ground and airborne radars.
- To present the enemy defences with a diversion: A WINDOW force at 20,000ft will break off from the first main force at 0530E and proceed on the same track to 0710E when it will return as far as the Front Line on the reciprocal track WINDOWing heavily the whole time.
- Fighter Bombers will break out from the WINDOW force and attack Shark airfield.
- To jam HF and VHF communications and enemy SN2 AI with Nos. 1 and 6 Groups, using JOSTLE and PIPERACK.
- To jam *Würzburg* radars throughout the Target area and the Spoof Target area thus rendering ineffective that part of the Early Warning system, GCI of night-fighters, searchlight conning and Flak gun laying.
- To harass enemy night-fighters by patrolling assembly areas on the way to the real and spoof targets; by covering the real and spoof target areas during the bombing attacks; intercepting the enemy night-fighters when recovering to their landing airfields; and covering the activities of No. 3 Group by fighter support.

Bomber Command was continually improving its tactics, including the use of 'spoof raids' and multiple routes, and taking advantage of the operational reporting services provided from Bletchley Park and the support of 100 Group. An appreciation of the cordial and successful co-operation between 100 Group and the Air Section at Bletchley Park was expressed by the AOC Air Vice Marshal Addison.[39] The operation of multiple routes and 'spoof' raids, with the complementary use of jamming screens, caused considerable dispersion of and confusion to the enemy night-fighter force, leading to reduced overall combat effectiveness. Generalleutnant Schmid, Commander of the GAF Air Defence System, reported after the war:

> *The task of forming a picture of the emerging air situation, during a bomber raid using supporting RCM, was one of the most exciting and difficult functions of command.*

---

38. Air 14/2971, 29 Dec 44, Time of Release: 1210A.
39. HW 14/110: HQ 100 Group, EBA/DO/3 dated 26 Aug 44 from AOC 100 Gp to Josh Cooper, Air Section, Bletchley.

At the end of the war, the Bomber Command Signals staff declared their professional opinion that the use of RCM and Bomber Support operations had saved at least 1000 bomber aircraft and their crews.[40] In addition, those techniques and operations placed a very substantial strain on the enemy's radio research and production organisation. Another unseen dividend was the impact on the morale of the enemy night fighter crews and the ground operating staffs, as the performance and effectiveness of their equipments and control communications were so seriously degraded.

Application of Intelligence Material

Whatever may have been the nature, scope and value of the various intelligence information that was actually available, it was and remains absolutely correct to note that any such information has no value if it is not read and understood by all those people who need that information. This is equally true for the highest-ranking commanders and decision makers as it is for the most junior aircrews. Their vulnerabilities may be quite different: the former may make poor decisions; the latter may lose their lives.

There was more than a suspicion that a great deal of intelligence information was not seen by many people who should have seen that information, at all levels of rank and responsibility. Some of that comes down to the problem of time, pressure and even knowledge that such information is there to be seen. As an example of the awareness and concern about this problem there was an exchange of internal Minutes between the HQBC Senior Air Staff Officer, CIO and other staffs about the use of the information at squadron and aircrew levels. It was clearly recognised that aircrews were not making use of the Intelligence Libraries as much as they should have been.[41] There were various reasons for that:

- Aircrews were often fatigued after night operations and the mental effort was not there.
- Station Intelligence Libraries were not always open and manned by a Duty Intelligence Officer to help aircrews find material that was important.
- The number of copies of some information was inadequate for the number of readers.

The problem was not new and it never went away. Fresh reminders were sent to Squadron Commanders and Station Intelligence Officers to be conscientious about this problem and to ensure that opportunities were not lost on days when no flying was possible. In practical terms, the best that could be done was to be as conscientious as possible and to make sure that the existence of important information was made clear. As an aside, there was a situation at Bomber Command HQ early in the 1970s when the persistence of that problem again became visible.[42] It is a constant problem and requires constant vigilance.

---

40. 'War in the Ether – RCM in Bomber Command', by Signals Branch, Headquarters Bomber Command, Oct 45.
41. Air 14/457, Minute No. 18, from CIO to SASO dated 1 Jan 43.
42. Author's Note: The problem was demonstrated again in the early 1970s. The topic then was intelligence about the Soviet surface-to-air missile system SA-5. It was found that

High-Grade Intelligence

The dissemination of reports from ADI (Sc) to the Operational Research Section (ORS) at Bomber Command was subject to a ruling from CAS. When the ORS was established, CAS had ruled that material coming from 'Most Secret Sources' – otherwise ENIGMA – was not to be released to the Section; they were only to see such information in a 'digested' form. This ruling was specifically quoted in a letter from ACAS (I) to CinC Bomber Command, covering a copy of an ADI (Sci) report on the enemy RDF systems.[43] The letter was addressed personally to CinC Bomber Command. The Acting-CinC at the time was AOC 3 Group, Air Vice Marshal Baldwin. Approval had been obtained from the then Deputy Chief of Air Staff on the grounds of operational importance to extend access to that specific report for the Head of ORS, with the proviso that the report was for his personal use only – it was not even to be seen by the CinC. The problem with material that had been 'digested' was not only that the origin of the material was disguised but also its scientific or technical detail could be lost or confused. That could be very misleading; it is curious that such a ruling was in force but it was consistent with the denial of such high-grade material to Bomber Command.

The report in question was ADI (Sci) Report No.13, dated 10 Jan 42: 'D/T (Enemy RDF – *Freya* and *Würzburg*)'.[44] That was a subject of very great importance to Bomber Command. Not only did the report describe the RDF system, but it also explained the application to the Flak guns. It included discussion of the potential vulnerabilities of the enemy RDF system, namely low altitude approach and saturation with multiple targets. At that time, Bomber Command had not been permitted to use RCM against the RDF system; that approval was not forthcoming until 6 Oct 42.[45] The only countermeasure to the enemy RDF system would have been tactical, i.e. route, altitude and concentration. The independent sources of intelligence that were brought together within this report included Sigint, particularly the research into the German night-fighter R/T by GC&CS and the RAF Y-Service; photographic reconnaissance; and also some of the earlier material from the Oslo Report that had been received in September 1939.

The 'History of the SLUs'[46] specifically identifies the installation of a high-grade teleprinter service for Bomber Command before D-Day, albeit co-located with the 8th USAAF HQ service at Wycombe Abbey (Pinetree).[47] These high-grade teleprinter lines had the discrete address identifications of MI and DL respectively, with the Bomber Command service routed through RAF Stanmore, which had the address identification of AD. In addition, the 8th USAAF at Pinetree had a direct courier service for high-grade hard-copy material from

---

the DI Report on the latest intelligence was held in the Command Library. Hardly anyone knew that it was there and a librarian was reported to have said that it had never been accessed.

43. Air 14/3557, ACAS(I)/39A/42 dated 20 Jan 42.
44. Air 20/1629, ADI (Sci) Report No. 13, dated 10 Jan 42.
45. Bib. A28, p. 19 – RCM in Bomber Command.
46. HW 3/165, *History of the SLUs*, pp. 33–34.
47. Author's Note: Pinetree, previously Wycombe Abbey School for Girls, had been requisitioned as the HQ for the 8th USAAF early in 1942.

GC & CS (Hut 3) from 28 May 1944, which was later extended to include material for Bomber Command – but not until 15 Oct 44. Bomber Command had then to collect their material from Pinetree. This reflects a covert subordination of Bomber Command in some attitudes that prevailed within the Air Ministry. However, the archives are not mutually consistent. There is separate archive evidence that the secure communications services from Hut 3 as at D-Day did NOT cater for Bomber Command.[48] Examination of the secure Typex and W/T links, through the sites at Leighton Buzzard, Birdlip, London, Windy Ridge and the Admiralty, clearly shows all the line connections for the various operational command HQs at D-Day, including:

- USSAFE, with line address code ST.
- 8th USAAF, with line address code ZU.
- 15th USAAF, with line address code JY.

There is no mention whatsoever of Bomber Command.[49] No archive data has been located to resolve this conflict of evidence. All that can be said is that having a secure high-grade teleprinter service in place does not offer any evidence of what may have been sent on that service. There is no evidence to show that the Hut 3 Advisors were directed to use such a service for Bomber Command. This was noted by Bennett in Bib. B11 at page 163 but no explanation has been identified.

Photographic Reconnaissance

There is no intention whatsoever to diminish in any way the very high value of PR and photographic interpretation by not giving weight and space to that source of intelligence within this book. But this book is focused on the extent to which Bomber Command received Intelligence support, and that primarily surrounds the provision and use of Sigint and ULTRA.

In comparison the provision and use of PR and photographic interpretation within Bomber Command had far less controversy. That is not to suggest that all was perfect, indeed the pre-war attitude of the Air Ministry was unbelievably blinkered (see Chapter 6). There was at times during 1941/42 a great deal of controversy about the provision and retention of a subordinate PR unit within Bomber Command to provide PR for bomb damage assessment work. The outcome was the progressive development of the PRUs and ultimately 106 (PR) Group under the direct control of Air Intelligence ADI (Photo); and the development of the CIU, later named as the Allied CIU, at RAF Medmenham. The Senior Air Staff Officer at 106 (PR) Group was Gp Capt. Riddell who had developed the procedures for generating and handling PR within Bomber Command HQ in the immediate pre-war period and until Jun 40, when he joined the embryo Photographic Interpretation Unit.

The development and magnificent performance of the overall PR and photographic interpretation effort are acknowledged without reservation.

---

48. HW 50/32, 'Army and Air Sigint for the Western Front'.
49. Bib. B1, Vol. 3–2, Appendix 6, p. 782.

Readers are referred to Bib. B33 for an excellent historical record aptly titled *The Eyes of the RAF*.

The extent of the co-operation between PR and Sigint during WW2 was deep and wide with many examples where one source guided the other towards the aggregate assembly of 'best intelligence' – otherwise known now as data fusion. The initial photography of the early German radar at Bruneval in Dec 41 and the associated Sigint evidence; the progressive photography and interpretation of the V-Weapons development site at Peenemünde combined with the ULTRA material; the PR detection of *Bismarck* before she left Norway in May 41 on that fateful short operation with the various ULTRA intercepts as she proceeded; these all form discrete examples of that combination of PR, interpretation and Sigint. The two separate sources formed equally valuable and indispensable elements of the overall intelligence jigsaw.

Planning Conferences

For the majority of the war Bomber Command operated only at night and the Planning Conference was held in the morning before that night's bomber operations. Later in the war, given the successes after OVERLORD, Bomber Command recommenced daylight operations when they had escort fighter support available for the mission.

The Morning Conference

The pattern of the Morning Planning Conferences became standardised, as follows:

1. At 09.15 hrs the CinC and the Air Staff reviewed the operations during the previous 24 hours. The chart showing routes and targets, the enemy responses, their strength and tactics were discussed. Much of that information on the enemy responses came from Sigint and, as the war progressed, that information became available more quickly and in greater detail. The BMP/N reports from the Bletchley Park Air Section became the primary source of that immediate tactical information from night operations.[50] Similar tactical information from the daylight raids was included within the daily BMP/D reports for the 8th USAAF.

2. The Photographic Intelligence staff presented the PR results from previous operations, much of which would have been more than 24 hours earlier but some would have been from immediate early morning PR taken as daylight was breaking over the key targets, given suitable weather. That PR information included a Night Plot, an H2S plot, strike photographs and preliminary damage assessments. The CinC always required information on any industrial targets that had been attacked. This involved the clear distinction between photographic intelligence and damage assessment, where the latter fell within the scope of Int. 1 and demanded the collation and fusion of multiple sources of information. Some of that information would be from previous records of each factory's output and importance; from earlier damage that may have been inflicted; and some would be from the very latest information, not least from ULTRA and other Sigint sources.

---

50. See Bib. B28, p. 63–66.

3. Having then reviewed the aircraft readiness situation and the weather forecast, the CinC would consider the attack options for the coming night. Int. 1 was responsible for preparing target information, to include the relative importance of the target options together with details of previous attacks and damage already inflicted, with information about any repairs that may have been made. There was a very real need for Bomber Command to have that latest information to allow informed decisions on target selection for that coming night. In this immediate operational context, a target priority list that may have been generated in Whitehall a week or more beforehand was simply not an adequate basis for decisions. The target list may well have had revisions but it did not contain clarifications as to relative priority between comparable targets.

4. It was important to make those decisions early in the day, because of the immense amount of planning and preparation that had to be done. Not only did that involve the Main Bomber Force and the PFF but also the Bomber Support RCM operations, by 100 Group under the command of AVM Addison and his staff at Bylaugh Hall in Norfolk from Jan 44; and the Sigint support from the Air Section at Bletchley Park and the RAF Y-Service. There is more than the suspicion that many people in Whitehall who were associated with Target Selection would have had no real appreciation of the extent of the task involved between a committee decision to attack a target somewhere in Germany and then laying on that attack in operational practice against an enemy who had a very capable air defence system.

The Air Staff Conference started at 10.00 hrs. Int. 1 was responsible for the provision of aiming point and approach path data. The Enemy Defence Officer advised on routes to be taken to and from the target(s), with information on enemy fighter deployments, tactics, flak and searchlight defences.

By no means least, the raid planning preparation needed to accommodate the RCM Bomber Support operations that were planned and provided by No. 100 Group. Target selections, detailed map co-ordinates and attack timings had to be provided to the Pathfinder Force for planning the target marking scheme for the individual targets and for the setting up of appropriate *Oboe* or GH ground navigation aids. The same detail was required for 5 Group, who used special low-level target marking by Mosquitoes for some operations.

The 8th USAAF had to be informed at the earliest opportunity of Bomber Command targets for that night to minimise the chance of unnecessary duplication by daylight raids the next day.

Briefing Notes had to be prepared for Groups and stations, so that the bomber aircrew should all have a full description of the target(s), their importance and as much detail as possible on the target location(s) using map and photographic material.

It will be appreciated that the target information that needed to be available at the morning conferences went far beyond a list of priorities for various target sets, as issued from London or the SHAEF. There was a host of details on many operational factors that had influence on the selection of target(s) for the coming nights. Making those decisions was only at the start of a long chain of consequential actions from the Command HQ down to Groups, stations, squadrons and individual bomber crews. The captain, navigator and bomb aimer of every aircraft had to know what and where the target(s) were and when they were to be attacked; each aircraft's ground crew had to make the aircraft serviceable for that operation and loaded with the appropriate bombs. The time between the target selection decision at Bomber Command and the required take-off time from squadron dispersals was often no more than 6–8 hours and sometimes less.

The obstruction, delays and withholding of any intelligence or target information that was available within Whitehall and that may have influenced the operational decisions on target selection was unforgivable. The decisions may have been and often were criticised by Whitehall staffs after the operations had been flown, but the lives of the bomber crews were at stake during the operations.

The Afternoon Conference

The Afternoon Planning Conferences determined the targets for daylight operations on the following day. A preliminary conference was held by the Deputy CinC, Air Marshal Saundby, and attended by senior air staff officers and the Intelligence and Targets staff.

One of the inputs to this conference was the latest state of Target Priority Lists, especially any changes that had arisen through the morning. As an example, the following changes had arisen during the morning of 21 Mar 45:[51]

Army Support	3 new targets requested by SHAEF	Bochult, Dulmen and Dorsten: Priorities for existing targets to be moved down.
Oil	To be reinstated	Zeist – PR from the day before had shown repair work from the Bomber Command attacks on 16/17 Jan 45.
	To be suspended	Misburg – PR from the day before and seen to be inactive after recent attacks on 15/16 Mar.
	In consequence:	Priorities for all other oil targets adjusted.
Transportation	To be suspended	Arnsberg Viaduct – PR from the day before had shown the viaduct was destroyed by Bomber Command on 19 Mar. (See image on p. 182 below)
	In consequence:	Priorities for other Transportation targets adjusted; this was during the Transportation Plan (see Isolation of the Ruhr at pp. 210–211 below).
Area Targets	To be suspended	Mannheim – Had been severely devastated on 1 Mar.
	In consequence:	Priorities for other area targets adjusted.

---

51. Air 14/1210, Review of Work of Int. 1 at HQBC, Appendix B, pp. 14–15.

The weather forecast was suitable for daylight attacks on the Army Support targets just north of the Ruhr. The importance of these targets lay not in their size, they were very small, but in the concentration of enemy troops and supplies. All of these targets required only moderate bombing forces. The Deputy CinC decided that the Bremen Bridge would be attacked; this was one of the interdiction bridges described in the Transportation Plan on pp. 213–214 below. This was a target type that called for the special type of attack that 5 Group practised. There was the capacity to attack another of those bridges in the same operation and the choice was Niemburg, which had been attacked but not completely destroyed on 20 Mar. If the weather at the time of the attack the next day was unsuitable, the Vlotho Bridge was designated as the alternative target.

A limiting factor on the number of these tactical targets that could be attacked was the number of available target marking aircraft. To make the best use of the remaining marker aircraft, Deputy CinC selected an 'area target'. The majority of 'area targets' on the Priority Target list were too deep into Germany for a daylight penetration with only marginal escort fighter support, so the choice was Hildesheim. That town contained a large factory that made jet engine castings (see p. 186) and the raid was set on for aircraft from 1 and 6 Groups with Pathfinder marking. CinC approved the plan for the next day and the essential preparations were similar to those for the night operations that had been described above.

The scope, pressure and urgency of the daily Planning Conferences cannot be underestimated. Bomber Command and the 8th USAAF became massive machines and were capable of enormous effect, but the planning, direction and control of that effect was an equally massive responsibility.

Subjected to frequent criticism and attack from the shifting sands and intrigues of Whitehall policy; denied intelligence that would have provided clarification of some of the most critical and contentious issues; the CinC Sir Arthur Harris and his Command deserved far better recognition of their enormous contribution to the Allied victory than has been the case.

CHAPTER EIGHT

Signals Intelligence within the 8th US Army Air Force in the UK

'When you have eliminated all alternatives, whatever remains must be the truth.'

Arthur Conan Doyle, 1890

Arrangements for the 8th USAAF

Within this section there is a broad survey of the progressive setting up of the organisation to handle intelligence within the fledging 8th; the initial forays into target intelligence and the primary target selection; the creation of the Combined Operational Planning Committee (COPC) and then a summary of the development of strategic operations from the issue of Operation POINTBLANK.

The 8th USAAF operated directly within the scope of the Combined Bombing Offensive and initially responded to the joint Directives that were issued by the RAF through the Deputy Chief of Air Staff, Air Marshal Bottomley.[1]

The US Strategic Air Force (USSTAF) was formed in Jan 44 under the command of General Spaatz to co-ordinate the strategic bombing operations of all USAAFs in Europe. The 8th was the principal Army Air Force from the perspective of strategic bombing operations from the UK, in co-ordination with the 15th in the Mediterranean theatre. In Mar 44, the command of the Offensive switched to the Deputy Supreme Commander (Air Chief Marshal Tedder) in preparation for the D-Day landings.

During the whole period of strategic bombing operations by the 8th USAAF the principle target identification and selection material was provided within the joint intelligence arrangements with the RAF, the MEW, the target committees and the CIU.

---

1. Air 8/1078, MOST SECRET CYPHER TELEGRAM OZ 296, dated 1 Feb 43.

The reader is invited to refer back to Chapter 4 for additional detail on the build-up of the 8th in UK.

Activation in February 1942

When the 8th USAAF was created at Pinetree in Feb 42 as a bomber command under General Eaker, the initial arrangement for intelligence liaison between the 8th and RAF Bomber Command was agreed between the two commands.[2] The establishment of a single Intelligence Staff was mutually accepted as being impracticable and it was decided to operate with two independent intelligence sections but with the closest co-ordination. It was not accidental that the two HQs were within a few miles of each other. The build-up of the 8th began to expand through the summer of 1942 as the first Bomb Groups and then the first Fighter Groups arrived in UK.

The 8th USAAF was in receipt of the Bomber Command Weekly Digest. There was a letter from Sir Arthur Harris to General Longfellow, who had just become the Commanding General of the 8th Bomber Command, which declared that the Digest was being upgraded to contain 'Most Secret' political and economic source material on the results of bombing raids on Germany and Italy.[3] In that new form, the grade of secrecy was higher and the circulation was restricted to Generals Longfellow and Spaatz. The letter stipulated that the Digest was to be burnt after it had been read. It should be appreciated that the Weekly Digest did not contain ULTRA material because Bomber Command was not in receipt of such material; it would however have contained digested or 'sanitised' information that may have been partly derived from ULTRA and other TOP SECRET material before delivery to Bomber Command from Whitehall.

The 8th USAAF initially received the same basic intelligence distribution within UK, as did Bomber Command. There was an Intelligence Liaison Officer from each bomber command at the other HQs, plus an RAF Liaison officer with each USAAF Bomb Group as the 8th gradually expanded. The state of the USAAF intelligence was reflected in the absence of any intelligence appointment below the level of command HQs. During the period until the end of 1942 General Eaker as Commanding General of the 8th Bomber Command requested fifty intelligence officers 'as soon as possible'.

As US intelligence personnel arrived in UK, some took appointments either within the Air Ministry or Bomber Command. In a reciprocal arrangement RAF officers took appointments within the 8th Air Force HQ, Bomber and Fighter Commands. So effectively did this arrangement flourish that several sections within Air Intelligence in Whitehall, particularly associated with Order of Battle, operational, tactical and technical intelligence, were virtually 'Anglo/American'. There was no attempt within the 8th to build-up any equivalent to the RAF Y-Service; the 8th received Sigint from the RAF and GC&CS.

One area in which British experience was inadequate lay in the business of maps. The daylight operations by the USAAF required detailed maps not only of

---

2. The Harris Archives, H100: Letter from Gen Eaker to CinC Bomber Command, dated 6 Apr 42.
3. The Harris Archives, H100, ATH/DO/3OC dated 27 Dec 42.

the targets but also the routes. The US prepared special maps that showed a perspective of the initial landfall as the bomber approached the enemy coastline and also the target area for use by the aircraft navigator. These perspective maps became known as Geerlings Maps, named after the originator.[4] It was of course imperative that the weather conditions would permit visual navigation and target identification. Sadly these conditions were often not present.

The exception to the full integration of UK/US intelligence arose with ULTRA. In the spring of 1943 a party of officers from the US Military Intelligence Service and the US Signal Security Agency visited Bletchley Park. For the first time, US Military Intelligence became aware of the dimensions of the British success against high-level German ENIGMA communications. Although such intelligence had been provided to Eisenhower during the invasion of North Africa, US Army Intelligence had not been fully aware of its origins. Now the British agreed to share this intelligence with the US Army on an unrestricted basis, in exchange for reciprocal access to American communications intelligence on the Japanese. Soon after, in May 1943, US Military Air and Ground Advisors became embedded into Hut 3 at Bletchley Park; from which point the distribution of relevant ULTRA material began to flow directly to the 8th USAAF. By the end of the war, there were 25–30 officers within the 8th HQ who were cleared to receive ULTRA.[5] That access was not available to Bomber Command.

Photographic Intelligence
One of the major intelligence contributions of the USAAF in Britain was its PR capability, which was an organic element of the US air forces but mostly assigned to the joint PR units. This had the effect of a retaining the option of a direct chain of command between the USAAF bomber forces and their PR units; unlike that of the RAF PR units which were placed under centralised control from 1941 – see Chapter 2: 'Changes during 1941 and 1942'.

Until Mar 43 the 8th depended on the RAF for photographic interpretation via the CIU at RAF Medmenham. US staffs had joined the CIU earlier in 1942 and as at Mar 43 there were 30 USAAF, 30 US Army and 11 US Navy personnel working at Medmenham. Whereas some USAAF PR aircraft had arrived in UK from Sep 42, they were quickly taken into operational use within TORCH in the Mediterranean. One unit that remained in UK was the 13th PR Sqn that operated from Mount Farm in Oxfordshire and was equipped with Lockheed F-4s and F-5s, the photographic versions of the P-38 Lightning. The 14th PR Sqn equipped with Spitfires arrived in Jun 43 and the two squadrons formed the 7th Photo Recon Group. That group became the nucleus of the large USAAF photographic

---

4. Bib. A29, Ch. 3, p. 135. The images were published in 1944 by the USAAF for public knowledge within a booklet titled 'Target: Germany', available at a cost of One Shilling and Sixpence. That booklet was an official story of the 8th USAAF Bomber Command's first year over Europe. There were 119 pages in that booklet. The reader may note a complete difference between the US and the UK so far as the availability of public information was concerned.

5. SRH-023, 'Reports by US Army ULTRA Representatives with Army Field Commands in Europe, 1945', p. 26.

organisation that subsequently developed in UK. In Jun 43, the 7th Photo Recon Group joined the RAF No. 106 (PR) Wing, which then controlled the operations of all strategic air PR units in the UK except those allocated to the Tactical Air Force.

Relations between the RAF and USAAF PR units had always been very harmonious until Jan 44 when General Doolittle, having just taken command of the 8th, made it known that he wanted independent control of the USAAF PR units. That had been available prior to Jul 43 even though it was very rarely exercised. This led to some difficult negotiations and the outcome in May 44 was to form No. 106 (PR) Group, which replaced No. 106 (PR) Wing, to co-ordinate all joint air strategic PR operations. No. 106 Group had very strong US representation. At the same time, the CIU at RAF Medmenham was renamed the Allied CIU and the Joint PR Committee was set up to ensure that duties were equitably apportioned between the UK and US staffs.

The CIU provided what was probably the world's most efficient photographic interpretation and analysis service and the USAAFs collaborated fully with this unit. The 8th USAAF developed an associated interpretation and analysis unit at Pinetree. The product of these two units was the most prolific source of air intelligence, comparable only with the Sigint sources. The development of PR and photographic interpretation during WW2 is extremely well described in Bib. B33.

Arrangements for Target Intelligence

The different strategies of day and night bombing had a direct impact on the target intelligence that was required. The 8th USAAF strategy was 'precision bombing' and this demanded precise target information. For example, a directive to attack an oil plant was quite insufficient; which specific structures within that oil plant were to be hit? It became apparent that the target information compiled by the MEW and RAF Air Intelligence tended to address the enemy's economic and industrial capabilities from a perspective that was devoid of adequate technical detail.[6] The 8th had need for information that pinpointed the specific critical structures and their vulnerabilities. It was at this time and for that reason that the Enemy Objectives Unit (EOU) was formed within the US Embassy in London, which began to work directly with the Target Section of the 8th USAAF. The EOU was expected to fill the gap between the intention to conduct precision bombing and the absence of precise data. A key output from the EOU was the Aiming Point reports, based on the full range of existing information that was available from UK and US sources. Those reports provided much of the detail that subsequently went into the individual target folders together with precise aiming point information for bomb release, bomb types and fuses. In the conduct of that work the EOU was given complete access to (RAF) Air Intelligence material. In that context, there is a direct statement about the 'reluctant Air Ministry Intelligence' support.[7] There is no explanation for that reluctance: it may have been that the required detailed data was not actually available; or that Air Intelligence did not want to disclose such data?

---

6. US OSS War Diary, Vol. 4: and Bib. A4, Vol. 1.

Just as important as precise target information was subsequent bomb damage assessment. In this aspect of the work the Target Section of the 8th worked closely with RE.8, the British Research & Experimental Dept set up in 1940 to study and examine German industrial plant construction and vulnerability. Damage assessment was fundamental to the intention to conduct precision bombing because it influenced decisions on which targets to attack, at what intervals and with what forces. This sounded very good but in practice the entire process was fraught with difficulty and uncertainty. It depended on intelligence that often was not available. It involved assumptions about the relative importance of individual targets within a broad target category. The physical damage to targets that may have been revealed from PR did not always align with the actual effects on factory productivity. In this respect, attention is drawn to the 'determined efforts to avoid exaggeration' that were being made by MEW and RE.8.[8] Notwithstanding that claim within one of the official war history records, it should be noted that bomb damage assessment was a very difficult and contentious skill. The efforts and adaptability of the German industrial machine usually defeated the Allied assessments.

The early raids by the 8th through the late summer and autumn of 1942 were against U-boat support facilities on the Atlantic coast of France. The target intelligence was then very heavily based on existing British information. The reinforced concrete U-boat pens were properly regarded as invulnerable, certainly to the bombs that were then available; but the assessment was made that the 'soft' infrastructure at those bases was a viable target. An MEW report on 21 Jul 42 had assessed the factories that produced U-boat components; that report was also discouraging, estimating that the vital items were protected or that they had redundancy. At that same time, DB (Ops) in the Air Ministry concluded that even if successful any attacks on the U-boat construction facilities would take nine months to have any effect on the Battle of the Atlantic, because of the number of U-boats already undergoing sea trials. By the end of Nov 42 the 8th had flown only ten missions against Atlantic coast U-boat bases. The intelligence assessments were mixed; the Admiralty reported itself well satisfied, in a report dated 20 Nov 42, but the 8th was far less satisfied. The German concentration of air defences around those bases had caused heavy losses and by the end of 1942 the 8th was suffering an 8 per cent loss rate per mission. The comparatively minor damage that had been inflicted on the bases led to the conclusion that the bombing effectiveness was 'quite disproportionate to the (aircraft) losses that were being sustained'.[9] The reader may note that the proclaimed intention of the 8th to conduct 'precision bombing' had not then been realised under the combat and weather conditions in Europe. It never would be except under exceptional visual bombing conditions with no hostile enemy air defences and smoke screens operating in the target area – see Chapter 4.

---

7. Bib. A29, Ch. 3, p. 138.
8. Bib. B1, Ch. 25, pp. 515.
9. Air Intelligence Report dated 7 Jan 43.

General Arnold, Commanding General of the USAAF in Washington, required that a comprehensive analysis be conducted of the anti-submarine operations. The USAAF conclusion was that it would be impossible to destroy the U-boat threat within the next 12 months regardless of the method of air operations.[10] However, the report argued that the operation of 50 bombing sorties per week against each of the five major U-boat operating bases on the Atlantic coast would secure a material decrease in the operating efficiency of those bases. This led to a major controversy within the USAAF about the value of anti-submarine operations. It will be noted that CinC Bomber Command was hardly ever convinced about the operational benefits of attacking those bases with the resources that he then had available. But those bases did become part of the first priority for air attack following the Casablanca Conference at the end of Jan 43, at which conference General Eaker had argued persuasively in support of 'precision bombing'. The final German records at the end of the war revealed that the air attacks on U-boat bases and construction yards had no significant effect on the overall U-boat offensive until much later in the war.[11] The most valuable effect was in fact derived from the decryption of German U-boat ENIGMA messages and the operational application of that information by the Admiralty within the Battle of the Atlantic– see Chapter 5.

The impact of the U-boat crisis was however critical to the survival of UK and did therefore justify the highest priority for any strategic offensive response. There was however no Allied consensus on the impact of the bombing attacks. There was no adequate appreciation at that time of the inherent difficulties involved in assessing bomb damage and the effect that the damage had on the capability of the targets. By no means least, the value of intelligence, even when it was complete, could not compensate for the lack of an adequate bombing capability. Certainly at that time, late in 1942 and early in 1943, the 8th had totally inadequate resources largely because of the bomber diversions to Operation TORCH in the Mediterranean and the US pressure to build-up capability in the Pacific.

It must be noted that the 8th USAAF in Europe at that time was still a fledging command and did not attract much support or sympathy from the US Army and Navy at the higher levels of command. Given the level of that US opposition to the strategic air offensive in Europe it is conceivable that better air intelligence could have resulted in less extensive USAAF bombing operations.[12] What did happen was that a new US Air War Plans Division report (AWPD-42) late in 1942 accepted that:

An air offensive would be a prelude to an ultimate ground assault that would come after the enemy had been sufficiently weakened through air bombardment.

Very soon afterwards in Dec 42 General Arnold created the US Advisory Committee on Bombardment, subsequently called the Committee of Operations

---

10. Bib. A29, Ch. 3, p. 144.
11. Bib. B1, Vol. 2, pp. 754–756.
12. Bib. A29, Ch. 3, p. 149.

Analysts (COA).[13] The task was to provide Arnold with an estimate on when the strategic bombing offensive was likely to have reached a point where a successful land invasion of Europe could be launched. COA sub-committees with their own expert advisors were formed for each of the perceived major target sets. Those committees included a range of members who brought operations research and economic analysis skills to the table. Such a membership may have been seen to improve the visibility within the higher political authorities in Washington such as the Secretary for War and ultimately the President. There were reservations and conflicts between COA and some military commanders, who feared that the committee would interfere with operational judgements. An analogy could well be made to the politics in Whitehall and the influence of the MEW. The COA report was delivered in Mar 43.[14] Of greatest concern was that COA had relegated enemy transportation services and electric power from the top group of priority targets. Post-war analyses have shown that both these target sets were critical: the COA judgements were predicated on the assessed redundancy that was available within both target sets and that neither offered a set of target objectives that was within the scope of any foreseen strategic bombing capability. Those analyses also show good comparison with the thinking within the MEW in Whitehall, except – significantly – that COA had stated that if the land invasion of Europe was to be delayed until 1944 then a general attack on enemy transportation could offer real opportunities to achieve a state of collapse within the Axis economy. The official British History commented on the COA proceedings with the observation that:[15]

> *Much of the economic planning always depended on assumptions that could not verified in the circumstances of the time.*

The major event that had then shaped the course of strategic bombing operations was the Casablanca Conference at the end of Jan 43 between Churchill and Roosevelt and their chiefs of staff. There was no Russian involvement. That conference set the ground for the Combined Bombing Offensive and subsequently the issue of Operation POINTBLANK on 14 May 43.

Development of Strategic Operations

POINTBLANK
There was a conflict of aspirations between the strategic bomber forces. CinC Bomber Command had believed that strategic bombing could win the war; the USAAF had accepted that strategic bombing would be a prelude to victory. Perhaps no great significance should be attached to such a difference, in that the means to achieve either objective would have followed substantially the same path. The incorporation of U-boat construction yards in the priority list within

13. Bib. A21, Ch. 1, pp. 9–12.
14. Report of the COA with Respect to Economic Targets within the Western Axis, dated 8 Mar 43.
15. Bib. A4, Vol. 2, p. 220.

AWPD-42 as issued late in 1942 was rather more a reflection of broad strategic considerations than intelligence analyses; and a recognition that AWPD-42 would not have secured endorsement by the US Joint Chiefs without those construction yards being included. The top priority for strategic bombing in the mind of the USAAF was the German industrial war machine through the various priority targets. The great arguments that came later, especially through most of 1944, about the relative priority of different target sets were not predicated on either one or the other of those separate aspirations by the bomber commanders.

At Casablanca, the intelligence assessment held by General Arnold had been that no increase in the strength of the GAF fighter force was to be expected. Only four months later, the Joint Chiefs were noting that the GAF fighter force was increasing by over 100 aircraft per month and the projection was that the force might have 3000 fighters by the spring of 1944. Even by the middle of 1943 the 8th was suffering heavy loss rates on its daylight raids and the bombs were not hitting the targets.

The major obstacle was the GAF air defence system that had been so seriously underestimated by the USAAF. During 1942–43 the intelligence assessments of the enemy fighter force were far from accurate. This was still a subject of serious and continuing argument within Whitehall and reflected the internal conflicts between MEW and Air Intelligence about the relative weight of the various sources of information and the application of Sigint, including the lower grade tactical traffic and the high grade ENIGMA traffic. This was not helped by the exaggerated claims for enemy fighter losses from USAAF bombers. The US claim for enemy fighters shot down during the 14 Oct 43 raid on Schweinfurt was 186; the actual fighter losses were 38.[16] There was a raid against the Focke-Wulf plant at Bremen on 17 Apr 43 that exposed these intelligence gaps and risks – the reader is invited to refer back to Target Intelligence in Chapter 6. The prior intelligence assessment was that the Bremen plant was producing 80 Fw.190s per month. The 8th lost 15 bombers during that raid. The initial damage assessment was that half of the factory had been destroyed or damaged. Subsequent closer analysis revealed that the primary Fw.190 production facility had actually been relocated to Marienburg several months before the raid.[17] The GAF fighter force became the highest priority target set as far as the 8th was concerned.

Soon afterwards in Jun 43 the Allies established the Jockey Committee within the Air Ministry to monitor the enemy aircraft industry and to recommend targets within the scope of POINTBLANK; see Chapter 6 above and Appendix H. It should not be forgotten that there was then a substantial gap between the bomber target aspirations and the operational capability to engage those targets, especially those that were deeper into Germany. Such targets presented far higher risks; the 8th was then engaged primarily with targets in occupied Europe and coastal targets. Intelligence was exposing the fact that Germany was relocating the majority of its aircraft production programme, particularly fighters, to the east. In Aug 43 it was assessed that only 12 per cent of enemy fighter aircraft

---

16. Bib. B1, Ch. 25, p. 520.
17. 'Air Spy' by C Babington-Smith, pp. 184–185; and 'The Mighty Eighth War Diary' by Roger Freeman, p. 54.

production was within 500 miles of London; but that did also show that 80 per cent of aircraft production was within 400 miles of Allied bases in the Mediterranean theatre. There had been significant changes thoughout 1943, as may be seen in a comparison of earlier data in Chapter 6. The assessments of German fighter aircraft orders of battle then showed that 60 per cent was deployed across the Western Front, 22 per cent on the Russian Front and only 18 per cent on the Mediterranean Front. An interesting piece of advice even as late as Dec 44 from General Anderson, Deputy Chief of Operations at USSTAF, to General Doolitle, then commanding the 8th, was that the Jockey reports were not Directives but that

> They were intended to provide the bomber commanders with information on which to base their decisions.[18]

Going back to the autumn of 1943, the 8th and the 15th jointly began to engage fighter aircraft production factories in southern Germany with bombers from the 8th then going on to land in North Africa. One of the intelligence contributions to those raids was the AI 3c monthly reports of the 'Fighting Capability of the GAF' – see Chapter 6.

Coincident with those raids on the aircraft factories was the start of attacks on the ball-bearing factories at Schweinfurt. The COA report from Mar 43 had placed ball bearings immediately below fighter aircraft production in the priority list for strategic attacks. This coincided with the view from within Whitehall and was consistent with the priority list from POINTBLANK. The intelligence held by the US at that time was that Schweinfurt produced 42 per cent of the total German production output and that the six factories were easily identifiable and in a relatively vulnerable area.[19] The image on Plate 5 is taken from an AI 3c report dated Apr 43.

The raid on 17 Aug 43 was flown by 376 B-17s against Schweinfurt and Regensburg; the latter thought to be producing 200 Me 109s per month. The 8th suffered heavy losses on that raid; 60 B-17s were shot down and a further 24 were so badly damaged that they never flew again. Sixty of the B-17s that continued on to North Africa after the raid on Regensburg had to be left behind in North Africa for repair.[20] On 14 Oct the 8th again attacked Schweinfurt; this time with 291 B-17s of which 60 bombers were shot down and 138 returned to bases in UK with battle damage. That point was regarded as the time when the 8th lost any sense of superiority in air combat over Germany.[21]

The outcome of these raids did not have a material impact on ball-bearing production. The initial bomb damage analysis was optimistic, partly based on strike photographs that showed at least 100 bombs falling in the main factory complex and collateral damage to the adjacent railway marshalling yard. The UK

---

18. Bib. A29, Ch. 4, p. 194.
19. Bib. A29, Ch. 4, p. 201.
20. Bib. A13, Ch. 14, p. 256.
21. Bib. A25, Vol. 2, 'TORCH to POINTBLANK' p. 705.

JIC report was more cautious and concluded that ball-bearing production at Schweinfurt would fall by 15–20 per cent over the following six months. The Allied intelligence had made no provision for stocks on hand across Germany or the level of imports from Sweden and from Switzerland. The damage to the vital machine tools was confined to about 10 per cent of those machines. Adverse weather and other operational factors prevented any repeat attacks and the Germans successfully dispersed ball-bearing production and would suffer no further serious shortages until the very end of the war.

As ever, the quality and quantity of intelligence was variable. Poor weather not only handicapped the bombers, it also handicapped the PR missions. Despite the best efforts of photographic interpreters, there was a tendency to over-estimate the effects of the damage on the targets' productive capacity; this was an area where experience and skills were in short supply. At that period in the war, ULTRA information about industrial outputs, damage and repairs was infrequent. The 8th and 15th AAFs, and later the USSTAF, depended on British intelligence and were therefore exposed to the same disagreements within Whitehall as was Bomber Command. Those disagreements were compounded by similar problems within Washington and the US intelligence committees, e.g. COA and the EOU.

Much of that intelligence analysis and assessment was breaking quite new ground and it is not surprising that many of the participants were very much 'learning on the job', but that does not explain or justify cases of laying aside intelligence material because it did not fit a predetermined opinion or policy. The job of intelligence and assessment staffs is to provide the best analysis of the available material. It may well then be appropriate to take an operational decision that conflicts with the available intelligence. That could be a professional judgement by a commander and it is a fine line; hindsight as ever is a vicious critic.[22]

The claims of 'precision bombing' were not delivering the expected results. It is regrettable that so many of the wartime and post-war records maintain the illusion that 'precision bombing' was a routine operational feature when the evidence so clearly defeats that mythology.

Even the Official History of British Intelligence in the Second World War falls into this trap when writing about the 'steady increase in the 8th USAAF precision bombing during 1943' – Bib. B1, Vol. 2, Chapter 25, p. 519.

The Operations Analysis of the 8th in WW2 provides a factual record that is quite different – see Bib. A21 and Chapter 3 above.

---

22. Author's Note: The political controversy about Weapons of Mass Destruction after Gulf War 2 may be viewed as an example where there may have been some manipulation of intelligence evidence to fit a political decision.

A powerful source of information came from the German Ministry of Aircraft Production and provided details of the plans and intentions for enemy fighter aircraft production. The planned increase in production rate was reported to be from 500 aircraft per month in Jan 43 to 2000 per month by late 1944 and to 3000 per month by Apr 45.[23] There would necessarily have been most careful assessment of the reliability and validity of such a report. Reliance on a single source is a dangerous course of action but it set a benchmark against which other sources could be compared. The most serious challenges for the Allied intelligence assessors late in 1943 related to the industrial capacity to deliver that production quantity and to take accurate account of bomb damage effects on the aggregate fighter aircraft production output. The data subsequently gathered during the post-war Bomb Surveys was able to show that enemy fighter aircraft production rates by mid-1944 had exceeded that plan – see the section on German Aircraft Production in Chapter 10. The insuperable problems that the Germans did not solve were safeguarding that industrial output from bombing attacks on aircraft parks and the astonishing loss rate associated with delivery to operational units by inexperienced pilots. That loss rate may be contrasted with the outstanding service provided by the Air Transport Auxiliary pilots, many of them women, who successfully delivered huge numbers of aircraft of all types and in all weathers within the UK.

Operation ARGUMENT was issued on 23 Nov 43 to provide a joint US/UK attack on aircraft assembly and component factories, which included one ball-bearing factory and one rubber production plant. The operation could not be put into effect until the middle of Feb 44 because of poor weather but in that intervening period the 8th had received long-range P-51 escort fighters. It became known as 'Big Week' between 19–26 Feb 44 with daily attacks by the 8th with up to 600 heavy bombers and several hundred escort fighters. The 15th supported the operation from its Mediterranean bases and Bomber Command mounted five night raids on associated cities. The USAAFs lost 226 bombers and 28 fighters with about 2300 crew members killed, seriously injured or missing in action. The initial intelligence assessment was that operation ARGUMENT had substantially reduced the fighting value of the GAF in Western Europe and Germany. The GAF was claimed to have lost about 300 fighters in combat but just as seriously it lost up to 50 per cent of the replacement aircraft on the ground.

The recognition was that this presented an opportunity to plan missions that actively sought to engage with the GAF fighters in daylight combat, taking advantage of the increasing number of long-range escort fighters – the Little Friends – that were becoming available. However, as time went by, incoming intelligence was changing the initial damage assessments of the effects of Operation ARGUMENT. What became apparent was that whereas a high proportion of the factory buildings had suffered visible damage, the vital machine tools inside had not been appreciably damaged and they were being salvaged. The true consequence of the Operation had been to expedite the dispersal of the enemy fighter aircraft production facilities, which had been

---

23. Special Intel Rpt No. 65, HQ MAAF, 'Air Attack on German Single-Engined Fighter Production', 26 Dec 43.

started in the previous autumn as part of the major industrial plan generated under Speer's direction. But the USSTAF had committed to the intention to actively seek out and engage the enemy fighters during the strategic bombing operations. During the spring of 1944, ULTRA evidence revealed the extent to which the GAF was redeploying fighter units to defend the Reich against these attacks – as described in Chapters 2 and 6.

The spring of 1944 was marked by the intensity of the debates about the use of the strategic bombers to support the preparation for OVERLORD and the subsequent support to Allied armies after the landings, as had originally been planned within POINTBLANK. This has been discussed in some depth earlier in the book, at Chapters 2, 4 and 7. There is no need here to review those discussions. Perhaps the most important fact is that Eisenhower chose to support the Transportation Plan because it promised direct support to the Normandy landings, whereas the Oil Plan offered longer term and more strategic support. In making what was acknowledged as one of the most important decisions of the war, he was undoubtedly focussing on the imperative need to secure and hold a successful landing in Normandy. Failure of that operation would have had a catastrophic impact on the future for the war in Europe. The oil plants could be dealt with later as events unfolded.

Combined Operational Planning Committee

Following the release of the POINTBLANK Directive on 14 May 43 there was a meeting held at HQ Fighter Command to consider the formation of a 'Joint' Operational Planning Committee. The Fighter Command location reflected the provision of Escort fighters for USAAF daylight raids and also the operational display facilities via the Radio Direction Finding service. The senior air staff present were AOCinC Fighter Command, Air Marshal Leigh-Mallory; the Commanding General 8th USAAF, General Eaker; and ACAS (Ops), Air Vice Marshal Bottomley. Given the strategic decisions and priorities from the target selection process there was the need to make detailed plans for the various raids. The Minutes of that meeting show that ACAS (Ops) was actioned to draft a Directive and to initiate the establishment of the Committee for the RAF.[24]

The organisation and administration of the Committee was detailed in the subsequent instruction issued by the Chairman, Air Cdre Sharp.[25] That instruction included the internal organisation of two Operational Planning Syndicates, the Intelligence Section and Administration. The Intelligence Section was charged with:

- Collection and co-ordination of current enemy intelligence, particularly as it concerned the enemy air defensive effort.
- Posting of all Flak and Fighter maps.
- Analysis of each bomber operation with conclusions and recommendations for future operations.

---

24. Air 14/802: FC/S.32974/SASO dated 15 May 43.
25. Air 14/802: COPC/ S.1001/Air dated 11 Jul 43.

By constant liaison with the Operational Planning Syndicates, the Intelligence Section was to make available the latest data on enemy fighter strength, disposition, reactions, tactics, flak and morale; and to forecast enemy fighter reaction with the view to selecting routes, timings, diversions and fighter escort for the bombing operations. On completion of any operation, the designated Intelligence Officer was to collect and collate the RDF and Y-Service information on that operation and report on:

- The effectiveness of the plan noting any alterations and their effects,
- Whether the enemy reaction was consistent with the intelligence brief,
- What effects the enemy reaction had on the success or failure of the operation.
- What lessons may have been learned from the conduct of the operation.[26]

The COPC became principally concerned with USAAF daylight operations as was seen within the Minutes of the Commanders Conference held at COPC, Pinetree, on 31 Jul 43.[27] The RAF Bomber Command representative was AOC 2 Group, Air Vice Marshal Embry; being the only force operating at night, Bomber Command formulated its own tactical methods.

USAAF theories at that time about the vulnerability of the German economy to precision bombing proved somewhat unrealistic. While bomber attacks did inflict heavy damage on the German aircraft industry, the industry was in no sense destroyed. Likewise, the attacks on ball-bearing plants failed to have a decisive impact. True, damage to Schweinfurt caused the Germans some difficulties, but the battering that the 8th took in the Aug and Oct 43 attacks was such that, despite intelligence information that the Germans would be back in business quickly, the 8th would not repeat the mission. In 1944, however, the nature of the USAAF bombing capabilities and target selection changed, reflecting the long-range escort fighter support to make deep penetration raids possible.

Formation of the USSTAF

The USSTAF HQ – otherwise known as WIDEWING – was formed at Bushey Park in West London on 5 Jan 44 with General Spaatz in command. The functions of the Operational Intelligence Division (OID) of the HQs are shown below, being an amalgam of the organisation as it developed from the start of 1944 through to the end of the war in Europe.[28] The key sections of the OID were initially:

- German Air Force Intelligence.
- Combat Intelligence.
- Technical Intelligence.
- Photographic Intelligence.
- The War Room.

---

26. Air 42/15, E.18A.
27. Air 14/802, COPC/S. 1003/3/Air dated 1 Aug 43.
28. Bib. A12; Appendices 4 and 5, which describe the organisation and function of the USSTAF Op Intel Division of the Directorate of Intelligence between Jan 44 and May 45. This Division handled the Sigint and ULTRA material.

The work is described on the basis of two periods: from the inception of the USSTAF in Jan 44 through to the establishment of the Advanced HQ on the Continent in Aug 44; and from that time through the internal re-organisation at the start of Jan 45 and on to the end of the war.

Inception and Development

Initially the Operational Intelligence organisation was a Section; it became a Division early in 1945. Most of the elements of the Section at that initial point were assumed from and duplicated those already in place and functioning within the 8th USAAF HQ at Pinetree, i.e.: The War Room, Enemy Order of battle, Enemy airfields, Y-intelligence, PoW intelligence, Photographic intelligence and other reports and publications. Shortly after the activation of the 8th USAAF, well before the USSTAF was created, a Daily Operations/Intelligence Summary was prepared and disseminated. This was believed to be the only American Air Intelligence publication that was published without break from the beginning of US air operations in the European Theatre until the end of that conflict.

A major change that was instituted by General McDonald, the USSTAF Director of Intelligence, related to the daily briefings. Within the 8th AAF HQ those briefings had been conducted at a SECRET level, with comparatively few restrictions on personnel allowed to attend. But within the USSTAF HQ, the level of those daily briefings went to a TOP SECRET level with only the Commanding General Spaatz and his senior staff officers present. Those Operational Intelligence briefings were a blend of 'all source' material to keep the Commanding General and his senior staff fully and adequately informed on matters that predicated their operational decisions. An abbreviated version of that briefing was provided to subordinate commands including the 8th. There were other special appreciations and reports, usually involving high-grade intelligence, that were passed to the 8th whenever they were generated; as well as the free exchange of information and analysis by secure telephone and personal conference.

General Spaatz and General McDonald agreed that there was nothing to be gained by duplicating the processes of the (RAF) Air Intelligence Directorate in Whitehall with regard to intelligence on the GAF. There was a further merging and co-operation between the Intelligence staffs of the RAF and the USAAF, which resulted in the start of the 'Exchange process' with certain staff members being seconded to functional appointments within the other Air Force as distinct from liaison appointments.[29] This also resulted in a sharing of substantially all of the 'raw intelligence material'.

In the case of the ULTRA product from Bletchley Park this was available directly via the US Liaison Officers in Hut 3 who selected and forwarded that high-grade material directly to the USSTAF HQ and to the 8th and 15th Air Forces. There had been a continuing increase in high-grade Sigint from before the start of 1944 that coincided with Germany's growing conviction that 1944 would bring the opening of the Second Front. There were many important ENIGMA decrypts during the first five months of 1944 that provided detailed evidence of the German assessments of

---

29. Author's Note: The author of this book served as an Exchange Officer within the USAF Intelligence Division at Wright-Patterson AFB during part of the Cold War period.

Allied intentions. The following examples of ULTRA material can be seen within a wider context by reference to pp. 50–52, pp. 194–195 and Appendix K:

- On 12 May 44, 935 B-24s attacked synthetic oil plants in Germany. Almost immediately, the commander of the 8th received confirmation from ULTRA that these strikes had threatened Germany's strategic position. On 16 May, the US Air Advisors in Hut 3 at Bletchley Park forwarded to the 8th an intercept cancelling a general staff order that Luftflotten 1 and 6 were to surrender five heavy and four light or medium flak batteries each to Luftflotte 3, which was defending France. Those flak batteries were to move instead to protect the hydrogenation plant at Troglitz, an important German synthetic oil plant. In addition, four heavy flak batteries from Oschersleben, four from Wiener Neustadt, and two from Leipzig-Erla, where they were defending aircraft factories, were ordered to move to defend other synthetic oil plants.[30]
- On 7 Jun, the US Air Advisors in Hut 3 at Bletchley Park provided the following ULTRA report, originally issued from the GAF High Command on 5 Jun:[31]

As a result of renewed interferences with production of aircraft fuel by Allied actions, most essential requirements for training and carrying out production plans can scarcely be covered by quantities of aircraft fuel available. Baker four allocations only possible to air officers for bombers, fighters and ground attack, and director general of supply. No other quota holders can be considered in June. To assure defence of Reich and to prevent gradual collapse of German Air Force in Russia, it has been necessary to break into OKW strategic reserves. All units to arrange operations so as to manage at least until the beginning of July with present stocks or small allocation that may be possible. Date of arrival and quantities of July quota still undecided. Only very small quantities available for adjustments, provided Allied situation remains unchanged. In no circumstances can greater allocations be made. Attention again drawn to existing orders for most extreme economy measures and strict supervision of consumption, especially for transport and planning flights.

The previous attacks on oil, combined with the raids by the 15th USAAF in Italy against Ploesti, had reduced German fuel production by 50 percent. The bombing of Ploesti on 15 Jul was reported to have destroyed six oil reservoirs and damaged three others. The total loss was 27,000 tons of oil, 4500 tons of crude and 1000 tons of paraffin.[32]

The CinC at Bomber Command did not receive those ULTRA messages.

The USSTAF HQ needed to have all operational intelligence available immediately on a 24-hour-a-day basis to respond to the requirements of their General Staff and there was consequently an independent internal analysis and appreciation capability.

---

30. Hut 3 Archives: CX/MSS/T185/106, 16 May 44.
31. Hut 3 Archives: CX/MSS/T207/69, 7 Jun 44. The reference in the text to 'Baker Four' allocattions was a fuel-rationing code used by the Germans.
32. Hut 3 Archives: CX/MSS/T252/95, 22 Jul 44. Further details reported in CX/MSS/T260/13, 29 Jul 44.

> It should be noted that the USSTAF did not intervene or obstruct the flows of intelligence into the 8th USAAF that had existed prior to the creation of USSTAF in Jan 44.
>
> In that respect there was a profound difference to the dependence of Bomber Command on the Air Intelligence directorate for intelligence dissemination.

Much of the incoming intelligence at WIDEWING arrived in relatively unprocessed form and Operational Intelligence had the task of fusing this into the daily briefings; in the preparation of appreciations; the maintenance of cohesive records and the dissemination to other commands. In those tasks, the co-ordinated working with RAF Air Intelligence and the connection with other UK Government departments in Whitehall was a major benefit to USSTAF HQ.

Tactical Air Intelligence
In the period from mid-1943 to early-1945 the support work by the Air Section at Bletchley Park and the RAF Y-Service, not only in UK but also when deployed close to the forward areas of the land battle following OVERLORD, became of very great importance to the 8th. The 'Hook-Up' service supported the 8th during daylight operations in much the same way as it supported Bomber Command during night operations. Further detail about this service is provided in Chapter 7.

This section will look at tactical air intelligence as it applied (a) to strategic air operations and (b) to tactical air operations.

STRATEGIC AIR OPERATIONS
One of the most important aspects of the USSTAF Operational Intelligence work on the GAF was assessing its reactions to the USAAF missions over Germany and estimating its probable response to future missions. The principal sources of that knowledge came from the RAF Y-Service and the Bletchley Park Air Section, not least via the real-time day 'Hook-Up' service that connected the USAAF HQs into the same system that operated at night for Bomber Command – see Chapter 7; and from the daily BMP/D Reports on the Day Operations of the 8th against targets in Germany and enemy occupied territory.[33] That tactical information included enemy instructions from the ground controllers, reports from the German air raid warning and plotting system and R/T traffic from the enemy fighters during their combat operations.

Of increasing significance and value were the operational airborne R/T intercepts of the German fighter and ground control traffic made from the US Bomber Forces during their missions.[34] The Air Section at Bletchley Park initially

---

33. Author's Note: This has been described in Bib. B28, Ch. 8; and the BMP/D Reports are held in the HW 13 series of folders at TNA, Kew.
34. Air 40/2717 (Q.1261 – see Appendix M below): The particular aspect of this folder is that the first enclosure is a three-page handwritten draft by Mr Bonsall (later Sir Arthur Bonsall, Director GCHQ) at the Bletchley Park Air Section that was the starting point

conceived this valuable source of tactical intelligence. It complemented the ground based intercept sites and solved the problem of VHF radio line of sight propagation obstruction. The immediate operational benefit from these R/T intercepts was the tactical data that provided the Bomber Forces and the Escort Fighter formations with rapid awareness of the enemy fighter reactions[35] for example, the scrambling of enemy fighter units from their airfields, the instructions as to their heading and altitude, combat R/T traffic between the fighters themselves and the recovery orders to either their home airfield or a dispersal airfield.

There was a report from the 15th USAAF that identified the work of Sgt. Hauschildt who had flown with the 97th Bomb Group early in Feb 44 and who had warned of impending fighter attacks. That report clearly indicated that airborne R/T intercept of enemy fighter communications had already been successful over several months.[36] In a subsequent briefing convened by Col. Young, A-2 at HQ 15th USAAF on 18 Mar 44, Sgt Hauschildt explained how he was able to inform his Formation Leader when enemy fighters were airborne and the direction of their approach. That provided the opportunity for the Formation to close up and prepare for action, which diminished the risk of surprise attack. General Born, A-3 at the HQ 15th, confirmed that Operations were very impressed with the immediate tactical value of that airborne R/T interception. Flt Lt Simmonds from No. 276 Wing also attended that briefing. He advised on the need for careful security to be maintained and for the intercept operators to have a 'cover story' to use in the event of their being interrogated.

The 8th bombers carried a certain number of German-speaking operators to maintain logs of the intercepted R/T traffic. Those logs were subsequently transferred most urgently to the Air Section at Bletchley Park after the bombers landed and the crews were debriefed, for melding in with the collateral Sigint that they had acquired from the RAF Y-Service. The value of that collated information was seen within one of the reports from the Air Section on 28 Apr 44, which spoke of:

> *The further light that had become available on the extent to which inter-Jafue reinforcement had become the pivot of the German defensive policy. For instance during the raid on targets in the east on 9 Apr Jafue-2 was reinforced by singles from Jafue-3 which penetrated to the Baltic. In turn Jafue-2 reinforced Jafue-3 on 13 Apr and shared in the opposition encountered in the target area in southern Germany.*[37]

The volume of airborne intercept evidence that was being collected was substantial and added great value to that otherwise being collected by ground-based sites. In particular, the exceptional quality of work done by Top Sgt Felix Spoerri was highlighted because of the considerable skill that he demonstrated

---

of the programme for these airborne intercepts and recordings of the enemy fighter R/T traffic.

35. Air 40/2717: 'Report on Airborne Interception of Enemy R/T Traffic' HQAAF dated 1 Nov 44 (TOP SECRET).

36. Air 40/2717: HQ 15th USAAF, 676.351/2–211 dated 22 Feb 44.

37. Air 40/2717: AI 4f message dated 28 Apr 44.

in following radio frequency changes when they were announced over the enemy R/T.[38]

However, Operational Intelligence at the USSTAF HQ made its own independent study of the enemy reactions to the USAAF missions, to include a detailed scrutiny of the combat reports from the returning bomber aircrews. After each raid, secure telephone discussions were held between the Bletchley Park Air Section and the Director of Intelligence at USSTAF HQ, in which all available ULTRA and Y R/T evidence was examined and an interpretation agreed upon. A Special Reaction report was prepared on each major mission for General Spaatz. Those reports were also forwarded to the 8th and 15th AAFs.

TACTICAL AIR OPERATIONS

During the preparations for and direct air support after OVERLORD, the 9th USAAF was heavily involved in attacks on the French and Belgian transportation networks. The 9th was also deeply involved with PR collection and analysis to meet the immediate demands of the land battle. It has been argued that PR was the primary source of tactical intelligence on those transportation networks, with ULTRA providing the valuable insight into the German appreciations of the transport situation.[39]

The HQ AEAF concluded that the enemy would be unable to maintain a heavy ground counter-attack in the face of Allied air superiority and his probable heavy casualties.[40] But that was not agreed by US intelligence that believed that Germany would do everything possible to prevent the Allies securing a foothold. What is clear here is that the US commands were in receipt of ULTRA information that revealed German intentions for redeployment of GAF assets to allow a strong defence against any Allied landings.[41] What is also clear is that all the GAF ENIGMA decrypts that were available to Hut 3 at Bletchley were carefully card-indexed and copies of the reports sent immediately by teleprinter to Air Intelligence in Whitehall, who prepared the intelligence summaries. Neither those card indexes nor the summaries remain in the archives.[42] Bennett could find no explanation for this and commented on the difficulties that had been created for factual historical analyses; he would

38. Author's Note: There was one quite different and equally exceptional situation concerning an operator with the 351st Bomb Group whose log sheets were found to be spurious (See Air 40/2717, AI 4 to 8th USAAF HQ, Signals Communications, dated 24 Feb 45). He was found to have been entering false data since starting operations in Oct 44. His procedure was to make extracts from previous log sheets and GAF Fighter Patrol Diaries to which he had full access and, by changing the grid references to suit the mission on which he was operating, to make a convincing series of logs. The fact that the GAF was generating spoof traffic to mislead Allied intelligence increased his chances of escaping detection – but it was identified and that says a great deal for the scrutiny and validation of the whole volume of Sigint intercept messages.
39. Bib. B1, Vol. 3, Pt.2, pp. 113–114.
40. HQ AEAF, 'Overall Plan for Operation NEPTUNE', Annex I 'Intelligence', dated 15 Apr 44.
41. Bib. B1, Vol. 3, Pt.2, pp. 103–104.
42. Bib. B22, Ch. 2, pp. 56–62.

have known about those ENIGMA decrypts and the card indexing, having been in Hut 3 at the time.[43]

An example of the card indexing is as follows:[44]

Original GAF ENIGMA decrypt: 'Request allocation of 10 Jumo 004 to Flensburg. Entire stocks lost as result of air attack. JG7, Major Fuchs.' Six points emerge:

Point	Card Index Action
Location of JG7 at Flensburg	JG7 card
Location at Flensburg of JG 7	Flensburg card
Fact that Major Fuchs belongs to JG7	Major Fuchs card
Fact that JG7 possesses a Major Fuchs	JG7 card
Fact that Flensburg had a heavy attack	Allied attacks
Existence of **Jumo 004** jet engines if not known. or if not previously connected with JG7.	Jumo 004 and/or JG7 cards[45]

In fact the GAF's response to OVERLORD was weaker than had been expected by the US. The fusion of the medium and low-grade tactical Sigint with relevant ULTRA had allowed the Allied intelligence staffs to make effective and timely use of the information to support tactical air operations during and after the landings. Throughout Jun 44, the AEAF HQ was able to read many GAF messages about air movements and operations; there is no suggestion that this was complete information but it was very useful. ULTRA again provided the insight into GAF intentions and the lower-grade Sigint intercepts provided the immediate tactical information. It should not be forgotten that there was an immense amount of work that took place between the original intercept of any ENIGMA message and the subsequent production of an ULTRA decrypt. The fact that ULTRA was used successfully in the fast-moving tactical context of post-OVERLORD operations reflects the very highest credit on all of the Sigint staffs involved:

- From the field-level Sigint intercept operator who initially transcribed the five-digit encrypted ENIGMA text and sent that via the secure communications routes to Bletchley Park,

43. Author's Note: It is likely that the card indexes were destroyed during the immediate post-war period, when so many of the records and the decryption machines such as Colossus and Bombes were destroyed at the explicit direction of the Prime Minister. By this time in 2008 there are very few card indexes that remain in the Bletchley Park archives, having escaped the 'holocaust'. But the Air Intelligence summaries should have been retained in the Air Ministry records.
44. Bib. B8, Ch. 5, p. 38.
45. Author's Note: The **Jumo 004** was the world's first turbojet engine in production and operational use. Some 8000 units were manufactured by Junkers in Germany during late World War 2 and powered the Me 262 and Ar 234 aircraft.

- To the decryption, translation and interpretation staffs within Bletchley Park, who were handling thousands of ENIGMA messages daily on a non-stop 24 hour/day process – see Bib. B8 and B31,
- And the subsequent transmission across the secure communications routes to the operational staffs in the battlefield via the SCUs – see Chapter 6.

An interesting aspect of this period was the extent to which the separate levels of Sigint were fused in the process of analyses and then used in direct support of tactical planning. It would appear that the US did that more effectively than did the UK.[46] The principle of collocated Air and Army equivalent HQs contributed significantly to the effective application of air intelligence to the land battle. Whether that completely solved the distribution challenges that arose with ULTRA may never be answered. For example, an ULTRA message that related to an enemy ground movement or action would have been sent to an Allied Army Special Security Officer via one of the SCUs; but the fact that some of those messages were also relevant to air operations may have escaped the routing protocols.

There were several times when the UK Sigint security services became worried about the possible compromise of ENIGMA within the US Sigint handling and reporting processes.

Within weeks of securing the landings Eisenhower had given General Spaatz at USSTAF almost a free hand in using the 8th and 15th bomber forces, notwithstanding the priority associated with V-1 and V-2 weapon sites and facilities – see Chapter 7 above in the section about CROSSBOW. Whereas Spaatz had attacked the transportation targets prior to OVERLORD, he soon went back to the fighter aircraft industry and oil targets in Germany. The US intelligence and target selection agencies were strongly focussed on oil as *the* priority target when OVERLORD became secure. They believed that the Tactical Air Forces could handle the battle across France and into the other occupied territories. It is however worth noting a much later American summary that between 1 May 44 and 31 Mar 45 the 8th and 15th AAFs and Bomber Command delivered 555 separate attacks on oil plants and related depots and fuel dumps. The 8th made 222 oil-related attacks but that constituted only 13 per cent of the total bomb tonnage dropped in that 11-month period. The great arguments, especially in Whitehall, about the direction and relative priority for the strategic targets sets have been described in preceding chapters.

When the specific subject of the transportation targets came back into the heat of debate in Nov 44, the USSTAF intelligence staff vehemently opposed the Supreme HQs and Tedder. The US air staffs were worried that any relaxation on oil would lead to an increase in the GAF fighter reactions to the daylight raids and particularly to an increase in the number of the new German jet fighter aircraft. The Me 262 had first been seen by the 8th in combat on 1 Nov 44. The response by Spaatz had been to give the Me 262 production facilities a priority second only to oil, but it was then realised that the enemy Me 262 production dispersal and underground facilities were negating that response by the USSTAF.

---

46. Bib. A29, Ch. 4, pp. 233–235.

In Dec 44 the assessments of Me 262 production and availability were showing cause for concern, with the projection that production numbers could climb to 250 aircraft per month from Apr 45. What was neither known nor appreciated was that those projections failed to take account of the very serious logistics problems within the German jet aircraft industry and the availability of trained and experienced fighter pilots. The Me 262 was not an aircraft that could be successfully operated in combat by a pilot straight out of training.

Then came the shocks of the Ardennes offensive and the dawn strike by the German air force against Allied bases in Holland and Belgium on 1 Jan 45. The Allies lost about 150 aircraft destroyed and 100 damaged in that dawn strike. The intelligence services seem to have been caught off-guard. There were Sigint messages that had provided prior clues to both actions but it would seem that the Allies were not listening. The same had been true with MARKET GARDEN in Sep 44 but General Montgomery may not have wanted know about German forces in the Arnhem area. There was then a great deal at stake apart from current intelligence; perhaps one of those situations where the commander on the ground takes a decision based on his judgement – or his personal aspirations *vis-à-vis* other Army commanders.

Relocation to France

On 30 Aug 44 the USSTAF Advanced HQ was established in France, firstly at Granville and later at St Germain and then at Rheims as the battlefront moved to the East. When General Spaatz moved across to his Advanced HQ, he was able to work more closely with the Supreme HQ. It is noted that his command was very much a part of the US Army, as distinct from Bomber Command being part of an independent Air Force.[47] There was an imperative to supply Spaatz with current Operational Intelligence at that Advanced HQ to keep him fully informed on the enemy air and strategic target situation. A highly mobile Signals Unit and a Mobile Operational Intelligence Unit were obtained and adequately equipped with communications, display facilities and immediate records.

At the time of the move to Granville it was thought that the Main HQ would move from Bushey Park and many of the staff did initially relocate. But that was a transient situation and a proportion of those staff returned to Bushey after a brief stay in France. WIDEWING at Bushey Park remained the Main HQ until 1 Dec 44 when it did finally relocate to St Germain. This created a somewhat difficult problem. The entire structure of the USSTAF Intelligence organisation had been predicated on co-operation with the Air Ministry and other British agencies and departments, most of which were in the London area. There was

---

47. Air 20/5307; There were several observations within the Air Ministry that General Spaatz had become too responsive to the US Army and less integrated into the Combined Bombing Offensive, e.g. Enclosure 1/248, from DCAS to CAS dated 24 Dec 44, at p. 2 stating that: 'It may be considered that General Spaatz by his location alongside the Army is being unduly influenced if not by the immediate needs of the battle then at least by the emphasis which the Army place on enemy transportation.' That concern within the Air Ministry was most probably driven by the weight of the UK oil lobby.

therefore a need to retain a USAAFE Rear HQ in London, including a substantial part of the Directorate of Intelligence. That necessarily included portions of Operational Intelligence, such as the Enemy Air Reaction Section and most of the Target Section.

Early in Jan 45 on the direction of General McDonald there was an overall study of the functions and organisation of the Directorate of Intelligence. One of the purposes was to centralise the responsibilities into a limited number of Divisions which each had related functions. It was at that time that the Operational Intelligence Section moved to Division status. It then incorporated the previous Target, Current Intelligence, Photographic Intelligence and Flak Intelligence Sections; each becoming Branches and dealing with operational aspects of the USSTAF responsibilities. The Target Branch was jointly under the Operational Intelligence Division and the Special Intelligence Division at the Air Ministry, under Colonel Douglass. The original Target Section and then the Target Branch worked with the various strategic target committees within Whitehall. One element of that work related to transportation targets and increasingly close co-operation with the Armies. Although it was no natural function of USSTAF to select ground co-operation targets, this was seen to be of assistance to the Commanding General in the latter phases of the war from Jan 45 onwards.

Following the reorganisation early in Jan 45 the daily briefings were expanded to include considerable target intelligence, with the specific intention of keeping the Main HQ staff fully informed on the status of the principal target sets and the condition of targets of special importance.

Operational Intelligence was frequently required to prepare or participate in the preparation of special reports and appreciations bearing on the operational application of the strategic air forces. These reports and appreciations were often at the highest security levels. During the critical months of Jan–Mar 45 the situation required constant appreciation of the enemy capabilities, Allied air operations and target policies. One of those areas concerned the introduction of the enemy jet fighters and their impact on 8th and 15th AAFs strategic missions. Another area was the need to review the effectiveness and basic concepts of strategic air operations within the war situation as it was then developing. Some of that work was done in conjunction with the CSTC in Whitehall. When the plan to 'Isolate the Ruhr' was evolved, the Operational Intelligence Division prepared an analysis and estimate of the USSTAF support for the bridge interdiction element of the programme. Similar work was done in the context of Operation CLARION against German transportation targets; and separate studies were done for operations against POL, ammunition and ordnance targets.

At all times the Directorate of Intelligence needed to maintain the closest liaison with the G-2 and A-2 divisions of SHAEF. From Sep 44 General McDonald or his deputy and representatives from Operational Intelligence attended the daily briefings at SHAEF HQ. The Weekly Air Commanders Meetings at SHAEF HQ were of great operational importance, at which all of the US and UK air commanders discussed the previous week's operations and the plans for the coming week.

The Value of Signals Intelligence to the Combined Bombing Offensive

'Better lose a Battle than lose a Source.'

Sir Winston Churchill

The full contribution of Signals Intelligence to the winning of WW2 is still emerging slowly, over sixty years after that conflict ended. Throughout the war the intelligence services of the Allied powers (particularly the British) intercepted, broke and read significant portions of the Axis political, economic and military top-secret message traffic. Within the political traffic, the Japanese-German message exchanges were particularly valuable. That special intelligence, under the general code name ULTRA, played a significant role in the effort to defeat the Axis and achieve an Allied victory.

The British and their American allies evolved a carefully segregated dissemination system that limited the flow of ULTRA to selected political leaders and military commanders. That dissemination process lay outside normal intelligence channels. For example, the intelligence officers of the 8th USAAF would not be aware of the existence of ULTRA and would therefore not know the duties of the ULTRA Special Liaison Officers. Those liaison officers, in turn, would forward ULTRA intelligence only to the commander and his most senior staff.

That direct service did not exist for Bomber Command. Within the GC & CS archives there is a powerful observation about the restricted access to and use of ULTRA material, as determined by the Air Ministry. Once the principle of fusing the high-grade ULTRA and the medium/low grade Y sources had been developed within the Air Section, during 1943, it had become obvious that the intelligence reports should be based on this combination of source material. But the problem was that the Air Ministry did not allow the home air commands to see ULTRA. There is a hand-written note in the margin:[1]

The principle was established (in 1943) that ULTRA and low-grade material should be fused within the Air Section reports. Bomber Command not entitled to see ULTRA; so the reports could not be distributed to the only authority who really needed them.

The topics covered within this chapter relate principally to the period from spring 1944 onwards:

- The Linked Routing Protocol.
- Tactical Intelligence.
- Strategic Target Selection.
- Bomb Damage Assessment.
- Isolation of the Ruhr.
- Failure to use ULTRA.

The Linked Routing Protocol

Within GC&CS at Bletchley Park, Hut 3 was responsible for translation and annotation of the high-grade ENIGMA signals and reporting the results to Ministries and to overseas commanders in the field. Intelligence was first handled in the Central Watch Room, where the Watch and the Naval, Military and Air Advisers worked around the clock. The separate Naval, Military and Air Sections formed the Current Intelligence Sections; they supported their separate Advisers and co-ordinated liaison with the ministries and commands. But in the case of the Air Advisers this meant the overseas air commands, not the home air commands that were supposed to be served via the Air Ministry.

The basis of the service provided by Hut 3 to Ministries and overseas commands was factual reporting of the translated German signals with notes as were necessary. This involved three main activities: textual, traffic analysis and intelligence. Interpretation of the evidence on textual and traffic analysis problems called for experience and good records, both of which were the exclusive preserve of Hut 3 so far as the ENIGMA material was concerned.[2] The direct intelligence service from Hut 3 to overseas commands was predicated on two considerations: that the available ULTRA material was unambiguous and that the urgency and content of the message had 'direct and immediate value' for the command, as distinct from 'interest'. The Head of Hut 3 arbitrated on any dissemination issues.

In the spring of 1943, a party of American officers from the US Military Intelligence Service and from the Signal Security Agency visited GC&CS at Bletchley Park. For the first time, US Military Intelligence became aware of the dimensions of the British success against high-level ENIGMA communications. The British agreed to share this intelligence with the US Army on an unrestricted basis, in exchange for reciprocal access to American Sigint on the Japanese. Soon afterwards, in May 1943, US Army air and land advisors became embedded into

---

1. HW 50/58 'Access to and Use of ENIGMA'. These handwritten notes were attributed to Mr Bonsall, a senior member of the GC&CS Air Section; later Sir Arthur Bonsall, KCMG, CBE, Director of GCHQ between 1973 and 1978.

Hut 3 at Bletchley Park; from which point the distribution of relevant ULTRA material began to flow directly to the US commands and notably to the 8th USAAF.

Bomber Command remained isolated from that direct distribution of relevant ULTRA. Hut 3 and the Air Advisers at Bletchley were not instructed to add Bomber Command to the distribution, which continued to go to the Air Ministry. It is not at all clear what the Air Ministry then did with onwards dissemination. The only officer at Bomber Command HQ who is known to have had the security clearance for ULTRA was Air Cdre Paynter, the CIO. There is a major distinction between having that security clearance and being in routine receipt of such information. Having the clearance allowed the CIO to attend meetings in Whitehall where that information was under discussion; it did not mean that he was on any of the distribution lists for ULTRA products. Later in 1943, in the preparations for D-Day, that direct intelligence service supported the Supreme Commander and his various staffs within the UK.

However, there was a long-standing crucial aspect of dissemination that applied when two or more commands were co-ordinating their actions. That was the principle of 'linked routing' which was allowed to override the principle of 'direct and immediate value'.[3] Within the scope of the Combined Bombing Offensive there could not be the slightest doubt that Bomber Command and the 8th USAAF were jointly involved. Why was the principle of 'linked routing' not applied? The fact that the USAAF benefited from the ULTRA material is not open to question.[4] The Official History of the Army Air Forces in Europe during WW2 concluded that:

The 8th USAAF was probably more indebted to the British for Intelligence support than for support in any other field or function.[5]

---

2. HW 14/84, Organisational Changes in Hut 3 dated 9 Aug 43. The Introduction to this internal directive within GC&CS emphasises the absolute imperative for coordination not only between successive Duty Watches in Hut 3 but also between Hut 3 and other sections within GC&CS. There is not a shred of doubt that this coordination was crucial to the continuity of ULTRA appreciation and the timely onward reporting to the external authorities; and that it could be done successfully and effectively only within Hut 3. The single weakness was the constraint imposed by the established numbers of experienced staff that were available within Hut 3 and the impact of that problem that varied with the incoming ULTRA traffic flow from Hut 6 and the external operational pressures at the various external authorities. Air Intelligence in London had a quite different attitude. They maintained that the appreciation of 'operational' ULTRA material, its correlation with Y and subsequent dissemination could only be done by DDI 4 – see HW 14/84, AM File No. 820/AI 4 dated 4 Aug 43. That attitude failed to recognise the depth of knowledge and coordination that could only have been done within GC&CS.

3. HW 3/119: Hut 3, General Policy & Organisation, p. 12; and HW 3/126, Hut 3 Directives, that show the distribution of ULTRA reports to the USSTAF, SHAEF, AEAF, TAF and 8th USAAF – but NOT to Bomber Command.

4. Bib. A12.

5. Bib. A25.

At the end of WW2, the Assistant Chief of Staff (Intelligence) for the US Strategic AF (Brig Gen McDonald) said:

The British contribution (to Air Intelligence) remained predominant throughout the war, although the American participation gradually expanded both in extent and significance.

A very important part of that support was the receipt of high-grade ULTRA material from GC&CS at Bletchley. Given the very nature of the joint strategic bombing operations, it is impossible to understand why the USAAF should have had that high-grade intelligence support but that Bomber Command did not. The failure to provide Bomber Command with a direct service for ULTRA material represented a clear breach of the Linked Routing Protocol. This reflected a systematic subordination of Bomber Command within the attitudes that prevailed within the Air Ministry and Whitehall in general.

Tactical Intelligence

Sigint provided a massive amount of information to the overall scope of tactical intelligence in support of the Combined Bombing Offensive. The greater majority of this was at low and medium-grade and consequently not subject to the same strict rules on dissemination that applied to the high-grade ULTRA material. However, the rules that were constructed and operated by Air Intelligence in Whitehall for that medium and lower grade material were still remarkably rigid with the consequence that some most valuable operational information was either completely withheld from Bomber Command or was subject to delay. Any delay in operational intelligence may well mean that the information reduces in value or may even become valueless; it is known as 'perishable'.

There is a letter dated 30 Apr 42 from DB (Ops), then Air Cdre Baker, to CinC Bomber Command referring to the daylight raid on Augsburg. That letter, written on the instruction of CAS, was to tell the CinC that if he had any other special targets and would like to have up-to-the-minute information, then the latest intelligence would be made available without prejudice to security.

> The security classification of the letter from DB (Ops) implied that high-grade intelligence material was available within the Air Ministry but that it was not normally released to Bomber Command.

The research into the German low grade tactical codes and their R/T traffic – notably by the Air Section at GC&CS and at RAF Cheadle – had a great deal to offer to the improvement of operational intelligence. It was Sigint that led the way into an understanding of the enemy night-fighter threat and the ground organisation within the Kammhuber Line. The bulk of that Sigint was low-grade W/T and R/T with very little direct ENIGMA support. The Air Section at GC&CS was accomplishing this analysis with very close support from the RAF Y-Service stations at Cheadle, Kingsdown and their subordinate HDUs. But the Air Ministry held firmly to the belief that only the Air Intelligence staff in London could judge what would be useful to the home air commands. This begged the premise that Air Intelligence had enough effort and understanding of the Sigint material to make reasonable appreciations. There was a direct exchange between GC & CS and overseas air commands and the mutual benefits were clear; the only difference was that Air Intelligence was not involved. The improvements would have taken place much more quickly for the home air commands had Air Intelligence not continued to obstruct direct exchange of information. The Deputy Directorate was DDI 4, the size of was far too small to make such appreciations from the aggregate volume of Signals Intelligence.

That direct exchange did take place much more quickly between GC & CS and the 8th USAAF. Air Intelligence could not obstruct that process and there is substantial evidence that the 8th had far greater benefit than did Bomber Command. The fusion of high, medium and low-grade Sigint sources by the Air Section at GC & CS became increasingly routine through 1943 and thereafter.

By Jul 43 the Air Operational Watch, set up in the Air Section, joined in the 'same-day' reporting of tactical Sigint to Coastal and Fighter Commands. The Air Section requested approval to set-up a similar service to Bomber Command and this was agreed with the Command Intelligence Officer, then Gp Capt. Paynter. It is indicative of the overall lack of awareness within Air Intelligence in Whitehall that, by Nov 43, the service from the Air Operational Watch to the Home Air Commands was used by Hut 3 for sending occasional urgent messages to the Bomber Command Intelligence Officer. That route did not provide an ULTRA connection but it did cater for other Sigint material and voice dialogue. The 'proper' route from Hut 3 was to AI 4 in Air Intelligence; from AI 4 to AI 3(a)1 and finally to Bomber Command, see Appendix F. Not only was that route impossibly slow but also the Duty Officers in those two sections were completely unable to answer any questions because they had no familiarity with the original Sigint.[6] This is but another example of the obstruction that Air Intelligence created in the supply of operational Sigint to Bomber Command. The Air Operational Watch was to remain in existence until the end of the war. It provided great value during the preparations for OVERLORD in 1944 and the continuing strategic bomber offensive, with particular regard to the GAF fighter defences and tactics.

ULTRA intercepts revealed a clear picture of German efforts and successes in attempting to repair damage that the Allied air campaign was causing to the railway system of northern France. A mid-May staff appreciation signed by Field Marshal von Rundstedt, CinC West, warned that the Allies were aiming at the systematic destruction of the railway system and that the attacks had already hampered supply and troop movements. ULTRA intelligence made clear to Allied tactical air commanders how effective the attacks on the bridge network throughout the invasion area were and the difficulties that German motorised and mechanised units were having in moving forward even at night.

ULTRA also gave Western intelligence a glimpse of the location and strength of German fighter units, as well as the effectiveness of attacks carried out by Allied tactical aircraft on German air bases. An ULTRA message at the end of Mar 44 indicated the severity of GAF fighter aircraft shortages and provided details

---

6. HW 3/99, The History of Hut 3, Ch. VI, p. 40.

of the importance of aircraft salvage, both for return and repairs – and for the recovery of components. Furthermore, those intercepts indicated when the Germans had completed repairs on damaged fields or whether they had decided to abandon operations permanently at particular locations. Armed with this information, the Allies pursued an intensive, well-orchestrated campaign that destroyed the Germans' airfield base structure near the English Channel and invasion beaches. These attacks forced the Germans to abandon efforts to prepare airfields close to the Channel and instead to select airfields far to the southeast, thereby disrupting German plans to reinforce Luftflotte 3 in response to the cross-Channel invasion. When the Germans did begin a post-invasion build-up of Luftflotte 3, the Allied destruction of forward operating bases forced it to select new and inadequately prepared sites for reinforcements arriving from the Reich. ULTRA intercepts proceeded to pick up information on many of the movements, which indicated airfields and arrival times for the reinforcing aircraft.

A substantial contribution of ULTRA to the Allied success was its use in conjunction with air-to-ground attacks. An example of the detail and timeliness of some ULTRA intercepts was seen on June 9 and 10 that revealed to Allied intelligence the exact location of General Leo Geyr von Schweppenburg's Panzer Group West HQ. Obligingly, the Germans left their vehicles and radio equipment in the open. The subsequent air attack not only destroyed most of Panzer Group West's communications equipment but also killed seventeen officers, including the chief of staff. The strike effectively eliminated the HQ and robbed the enemy of the only army organisation they had in the West that was capable of handling large numbers of mobile divisions.

ULTRA was able to indicate to Allied air commanders on the continent the effectiveness of their tactics and the extent of the difficulties that faced the GAF. It was the basis for informed intelligence to support the planning and direction of tactical air operations.

A summary of the value of ULTRA to 2nd TAF within the AEAF during OVERLORD was provided to GC&CS by DDI 3.[7] The summary does provide considerable detail and insight into the use of that high-grade Sigint, but it is surprising that this was four months after the war ended and started with an apology for the delay in completion. One very specific comment by DDI 3 was that the Light Bomber Group within 2nd TAF did not receive any ULTRA and that no advantage would have been served by such dissemination; the fighter and fighter-bomber groups did however receive ULTRA. There is no explanation or justification for that denial of ULTRA to the bomber group but it is consistent with the apparent wartime policy within Air Intelligence in Whitehall. There is however an illuminating statement on p. 6 of that DDI 3 report, to the effect that senior officers should only see selected messages. However, on pp. 7–8 there is the statement that the volume of Sigint provided from GC&CS would need to be constantly reviewed in the light of the prevailing and emerging status of any campaign. If the campaign was likely to last for some months then the AOCinC must be informed on the enemy's future plans and intentions. Further, that a closer personal liaison with GC&CS would have been advantageous and that

---

7. HW 3/175, 'Use of ULTRA by 2nd TAF' dated 4 Sep 45.

additional officer establishments should have been created at GC&CS to carry out such liaison. That responsibility was wholly at the discretion of Air Intelligence and could have been accomplished at any time during the war through DDI 4 and the Air Section at Bletchley Park. Later, on p. 10 of the DDI 3 report was the recommendation that all RAF Intelligence Officers who used ULTRA should spend time at GC&CS to gain a full understanding of possibilities that existed. Noting that this was written after the war had ended, there is a striking similarity with the function and conduct of the Naval OIC and the appointment in 1940 of a Captain, RN, based in the OIC in Whitehall but making frequent visits to Bletchley. The outcome was totally successful and the Admiralty and GC&CS remained in close contact and agreement through the remainder of the war – see Chapter 2 above. How sad that Air Intelligence did not see that need until after the war ended.

Strategic Target Selection

The Ministry of Economic Warfare was designated as the major UK source of economic and industrial strategic target intelligence, as defined in the functional charter described in Chapter 2 above. But that MEW Charter covered only part of the overall objective of the strategic bombing offensives, which also covered the full range of military targets within the context of both strategic operations and tactical support to the field armies and the maritime war. A most crucial internal conflict within Whitehall during the last quarter of 1943 concerned the US/UK planning for OVERLORD and the associated use and control of the heavy bomber forces. The heavy bombers were the sole means of attacking the German homeland within the context of the Casablanca agreement and Operation POINTBLANK. The planned assignment to directly support OVERLORD did have adverse consequences for operations against strategic economic and industrial targets in Germany but that decision had been taken at Casablanca at the very highest level in the light of the relative priorities.

The research conducted in the course of preparation of this book has shown that some departments within Whitehall and Washington were influenced by parochial and personal attitudes that interfered with the selection of strategic targets and the planning and implementation of the bombing offensives. The root of that problem lay in the political and military inability to find common agreement between the strategic value of industrial targets and the tactical value of military and transportation targets, where both target sets were so closely inter-dependent.

It should be noted that the history of WW2 has many examples of transportation failures that crippled major military and industrial campaigns:

- The German North African desert war and the invasion of Russia both failed because of inherent transportation problems, the latter of course under the pressures caused by the Russian winter.
- The Battle of Stalingrad revealed the immense transportation task that confronted both the Germans and the Russians.
- The Allied invasion of Italy prospered because the Italian transportation system was devastated by strategic and tactical bombing attacks, notably under the command of Allied military leaders and not Whitehall committees.

- The dispersal of the German war industries, not least the Oil industry, became critically dependent on internal transportation to serve the delivery of raw materials and then distribution between different factories and the end users at the battle Fronts. That transportation system ultimately failed.
- For the UK, the Battle of the Atlantic was all about transportation for the support and resupply of the UK Home Base. Had that battle been lost, UK would not have survived.

However, the research behind this book reveals that many of the power brokers in Whitehall had closed minds to transportation as a strategic target. They all thought that they knew how to run a strategic bombing campaign but none of them had ever done that. They may well have been dazzled by the visibility and stature of the multiple oil committees. The oil lobby was widespread within and beyond those committees and had ready access to the top decision makers. It was only because of the insistence of the Deputy Supreme Commander ACM Tedder in the run-up to OVERLORD that the strategic bombing engaged and crippled the Belgian and French railways as a prelude to that invasion; and again in the Isolation of the Ruhr. He called transportation the 'common denominator' and he had field experience of that in North Africa and Italy.

The great intelligence challenges for the bombing offensive remained the same as they had been from the start of the war: strategic target selection and bomb damage assessment. The damage to enemy strategic targets in the 9 months from Mar to Dec 43 was about ten times that achieved in the first 42 months of the war. Damage assessment became ever more important both as an element of strategic target selection and the identification of the need for repeat attacks.

What had been possible for the strategic bombers in France in good weather and at short range, during the Spring of 1944 before the D-Day invasions, did not carry into Germany in bad weather and at longer range during the autumn and winter in the face of a determined enemy air defence capability. That was the key fact that was not appreciated by so many of the Whitehall and Air Staff critics of the bombing offensive – and by many of the post-war historians. It is very debatable whether or not the MEW, the oil barons and the panacea target lobbies were correct in their strategic target selections. Harris was not the only commander who doubted the accuracy of some of those selections by the MEW and later by the CSTC.

There were very serious clashes of opinion throughout 1943, 1944 and into 1945 between Whitehall, the Air Ministry, the USSTAF, the Target Committees and eventually with the Supreme Headquarters, about the strategic targets for the bomber forces. The key aspect of the strategic bombing offensive in the Final Phase was the continuous disagreement between Whitehall, Washington and the Supreme Headquarters on the continent as to whether oil or transportation targets should have higher priority.

Isolation of the Ruhr

This specific strategic operation is taken as an example of the use of the heavy bombers in direct support of both industrial and military objectives. The following description has three major sections:

- Background.
- Transportation Attacks.
- Typical ULTRA Evidence.

Background

The Ruhr included the densely built-up and heavily industrialised area not only of the Ruhr Valley but also of the upper valley immediately to the south. It was some 40 miles from east to west and 25 miles from north to south, a total area of about 1000 square miles.

This area was the 'power house' of the German war industry and was more heavily and continuously bombed than any other similar sized area during WW2. German documents that became available early in Mar 45 provided the basis for the following comparisons of average reductions in daily productive output of the key heavy engineering and raw material facilities:[8]

	Coal Tons/Day	Coke Tons/Day	Pig Iron Tons/Month	Steel Tons/month
1943/44	77,128	26,973	502,350	624,342
1945	40,115	11,715	151,548	161,552
Percentage Reduction	48%	57%	70%	74%

The loss of Upper Silesia as the Russians advanced early in 1945 re-emphasised the importance of the Ruhr to the remaining German war effort. From that time, the armament industry, the railways and public utilities such as gas and electricity became almost entirely dependent on the raw material output from the Ruhr.

Transportation Attacks – Early 1945

After the collapse of the Ardennes Offensive, the strategic bomber forces resumed their heavy attacks on the transport system and the oil plants. It was agreed at the highest level of Allied command that the Tactical Air Forces would extend the scope of their operations against transportation to the east of the Rhine, in co-ordination with the strategic bomber forces. The Transportation Sub-committee of the CSTC met at SHAEF HQ at the request of the Deputy Supreme Commander on 10 Feb 45 to consider how the Tactical Air Forces could be co-ordinated with the strategic attacks on transportation.[9] The major elements of the subsequent combined operations by the strategic and Tactical Air Forces were as follows:

- The Bridge Interdiction Scheme (Bremen – Coblenz). In conjunction with the strategic plan to disrupt railways in West Germany that approached the Ruhr,

---

8. Air 14/1426; BC/S.30329 dated 24 Mar 45.
9. Air 20/3377; Review of Operations by CSTC Working Committee (Communications), Part IV, Ref Z611, 17 Jul 45.

by attacks on major rail centres, the Tactical Air Force was used to attack bridges between Bremen and Coblenz. The plan was to sever the Rhineland, Westphalia and the Ruhr from the rest of Germany (18 Feb 45).

- The New Target Priority List, known as 'The Isolation of the Ruhr'. The Transportation Plan now concentrated only on the northern sectors of the western front and the Ruhr, to prevent the reinforcement and supply of forces fighting on the front and to prohibit the Ruhr from contributing to the general German war effort. This concentration of attack in a small area greatly increased the effectiveness (28 Feb 45).

- Operation CLARION. This operation was carried out on 22 and 23 Feb, by the 8th USAAF and Tactical Air Forces. The targets were some 90 lightly defended minor railway centres in an area bounded by Hamburg, Brandenburg, Halle and Kassel. Part of the operation was to determine whether the 8th could operate in small groups at low altitudes. The operation was criticised as too diffused and in an area that was not appropriate to the primary object of the Isolation of the Ruhr.

- Provision of Additional Weather and Filler Targets in Southern Germany. The 8th USAAF requested an extended list of targets to include rail centres in southern Germany. Some of the original rail targets in the northern sector were by then within range of artillery fire (7 Mar 45).

- Importance of the Bielefeld Viaduct. On 22 Feb Bomber Command destroyed three arches on the northernmost of the twin viaducts, on the main line between Hanover-Minden-Hamm. The enemy had nearly built a temporary single-track loop line to compensate for the loss of one viaduct. It was therefore decided to attack the nearest railway centres on either side of the break.

- Support for the Rhine Crossings. The military situation had developed rapidly and favourably for the Allies and by 11 Mar the armies had closed to the western bank of the Rhine continuously from Coblenz to Wesel. The previous capture of the Remagen bridge had provided a foothold on the eastern bank. These army advances were contributing to the strategic plan to isolate the Ruhr. By that time the successes that had been achieved and the prospect of improving weather allowed the inclusion of targets along the fringes of the Ruhr that would also facilitate the tactical needs of the 21st Army Group, commanded by Field Marshal Montgomery.[10]

- Revision to the Transportation Plan. There had been three notable successes in the second half of March: Bomber Command used the TALLBOY and GRAND SLAM bombs to completely breach the twin viaducts at Bielefeld on 14 Mar; the Arnsberg viaduct was destroyed using those very heavy bombs on 19 Mar (see the image on p. 182); and the Vlotho bridge had been made temporarily impassable. This completely cut out the three main rail centres to the east of the Ruhr. There were consequent revisions to the target priorities to focus the heavy bombing on to four bridges that served lines through Rheine, Munster and Osnabruck in direct support for the 21st Army Group advance across the

---

10. Bib. A28; p. 433. Churchill's decision to promote Montgomery on 1 Sep 44 was seen as a sop to the 21st Army Group Commander. It infuriated Patton and Bradley, which became an irreparable split during the Ardennes offensive.

Rhine near Wesel. Given the destruction of the Arnsberg viaduct on 19 Mar, those four bridges were at the top of the major interdiction target list. Because of the fluidity of the ground operations, it was agreed that transport targets were to be kept under review as the battle progressed (21 Mar 45).

- The Frankfurt (Main) – Hanover Line. This line was seen from PR to be in regular use for the movement of troops and supplies. SHAEF took the view that this was not of immediate tactical concern but delegated tactical attacks on the line and its infrastructure to the 9th Air Force.

- The Isolation becomes a Fact. By 24 Mar, the day before the Allies crossed the Rhine at Wesel, the Isolation of the Ruhr had been accomplished. One or more spans of 14 out of the 16 bridges that formed the original line of interdiction had been brought down and the remaining two had been neutralised by the US 3rd Army's advance from the Remagen bridgehead. Twenty out of 25 railway centres and marshalling yards that handled virtually all the traffic in the area had been so heavily damaged as to prevent either through traffic or marshalling. Only two locomotives out of 193 that were observed by PR were in steam; earlier PR had shown 82 locomotives in steam out of a total of 251. It was estimated that the potential rail and waterway services between the Ruhr and the rest of Germany had been reduced by at least 75 per cent.

The complete interdiction of the Ruhr was obtained by increasing attacks on transportation until only an insignificant proportion of bulk economic traffic was able to move eastwards out of the area. By the same process, military traffic across the area was acutely dislocated. The enemy did indeed expend a tremendous repair effort on the damaged services but this was nullified by regular 'policing' and reattacks by fighter and fighter-bombers.

Typical ULTRA Evidence
As with so many of individual situations, the ULTRA evidence came from multiple decrypted sources: political, economic, military, police, etc. The following examples are intended only to represent a cross-section of the many different ULTRA reports that were generated by Bletchley Park in relation to the isolation of the Ruhr; the tense reflects the original messages:

- French Foreign Ministry, 21 Feb 45: The transport crisis that was already particularly acute has lately become still worse as a result of recent military developments. The Reichsbahn is no longer in a position to control the traffic as its services are dislocated. Innumerable wagons remain stranded and this is having very serious repercussions on the work of many factories. Those that have been evacuated cannot be set up again in the withdrawal areas. Others are short of coal.

- CX/MSS/T478/4 dated 27 Feb 45: Fuel situation has meant that use of railways as supply route is necessary, resulting in delay and damage to equipment from Allied air attacks.

- CX/MSS/T479/40 dated 28 Feb 45, CinC Southwest, Army Group C, Day report: The enemy's air offensive has been continuous for some days especially against traffic routes into the Reich. Attacks on these transport routes must be interpreted as a sign of an impending large-scale attack.

- CX/MSS/T476/13 dated 1 Mar 45: The transport situation has deteriorated. Scarcely any trains are now running through from Westphalia since the railway lines are extensively destroyed. In addition, there is an increasing lack of wagons.
- CX/MSS/T486/85 dated 12 Mar 45: Night fighters to operate only in defence of the Reich as from 12/13 Mar; no longer to operate against returning Bomber Command aircraft over England.
- CX/MSS/T492/76 dated 17 Mar 45: Preparations for destruction of 500 bridges in the Ruhr under consideration by Army Group H. Contrast with agreement by Speer and Model on 9 Mar that railway bridges in the Ruhr should not be destroyed but rendered unusable.
- CX/MSS/T497/48 dated 22 Mar 45: Report by 1st Army that all movement according to plan made impossible by Allied mastery of the air, by bomb damage and lack of fuel.
- CX/MSS/T506/81 dated 30 Mar 45: Army Group B reports that situation has become critical because of state of troops, shortage of fuel and ammunition and impossibility of moving men and supplies by rail: 'The Army Group has not at its disposal sufficient to influence decisively the enemy's further intentions'.
- CX/MSS/T507/5 dated 1 Apr 45: General Student to Kesselring on plans for counter-attack against flank of 21st Army Group (British) advance: (1) Insufficient ammunition and fuel; (2) Intend to block supply road to Rheine, Zero Hour 1900/2/4, about 10 mls SE of Rheine; (3) Attack on Haltern to be carried out when ammunition, fuel and more troops have been brought up.

This small selection of abbreviated ULTRA material provides an indication of the scale and nature of the information that was available. There is no implicit statement about the extent to which it was used and by whom, but it is clear that the messages were sent forward from Bletchley Park to designated recipients within SHAEF, the Field Commanders and the normal recipients within Whitehall.

Failure to Use Special Intelligence

Within the deeply serious arguments about the relative merits of different strategic target sets, the availability and use of ULTRA was a mixed blessing. Not surprisingly this became most contentious after D-Day when the increasing volume of ULTRA material provided various depths of insight into German economic, industrial and military affairs. There is no shadow of doubt that this depth of insight was unprecedented and of immense value to the Allies – for economic, political and military staffs. However, it was not without its problems and this has been discussed above in Chapter 6 where there is commentary on some of the use and misuse of the ULTRA material within the Joint Intelligence Staff. That use and misuse may well have been based on attributing too much value to a single source; or on an overwhelming volume of material; but there is no suggestion or available evidence that it was manipulated to suit particular purposes by the JIS.

That explanation or excuse cannot be used in the specific case of the meetings and arguments about the relative values of the Oil and Transportation target sets, particularly through 1944 and into 1945. The extent of that contention has been briefly summarised in Chapter 2, which sets the scene as the war developed, and in Chapter 9, which summarises the actual effects of the bombing offensive. There is evidence that shows not just an abuse of ULTRA material but also a political attempt to subvert the facts to suit a particular position. The internal Whitehall argument was strongly in favour of oil as the primary strategic target. This could be traced back to pre-war days when the Industrial Intelligence Committee had direct access to the Foreign Office and the Cabinet; and this continued with the Hankey and Hartley committees during the early years of the war. Transportation did not have a supporting lobby in Whitehall; this was reflected even into the autumn of 1944 after the CSTC had been created in Sep 44. There was immediately an Oil sub-committee; but a Communications (actually Transportation) Working Group was not formed within the CSTC until later in 1944 as a direct result of pressure from the military chiefs of staff.

At the time of the Ardennes Offensive late in Dec 44 and into Jan 45 the CSTC concluded that air attacks on rail movements had never stopped troop deployment into the Ardennes and that industrial traffic had not been substantially reduced. But the Supreme Headquarters remained steadfast in its belief that the bombing attacks on the marshalling yards and the canals were proving disastrous for the German economy; and by the end of Jan 45 was concluding that these attacks may have caused more far-reaching dislocation of war production than previously realised.

In Feb 45, DCAS (Air Marshal Bottomley) ordered a complete review of ULTRA material relating to transportation targets and this revealed that the CSTC had systematically suppressed ULTRA data both on the Reichsbahn and on the German economy that had underlined the extent of the enemy's difficulties.[11] One relevant message, unused by Whitehall departments since its decryption in Oct 44, indicated that by that date and due to transportation destruction and bottlenecks,

from 30–50% of all factories in West Germany were at standstill.[12]

Other previously disregarded ULTRA reports had established the existence of coal shortages, lack of electric power and substantial falls in war production output. In the light of that staggering revelation of the suppression of high-grade intelligence, target selection for the strategic bombing was revised in an effort to isolate the Ruhr by further attacks on the marshalling yards, bridges and viaducts around the area; by the end of March, German industrial activity had effectively ceased. The inescapable conclusion remains that during the late autumn and early winter of 1944, the Whitehall target selection staffs and the CSTC denied information to the strategic bombing forces so that they reduced their attacks on enemy transportation services and may consequently have extended the war by several months. The wider consequences for the timing of the eventual collapse of German military capability and the subsequent location of the Iron Curtain across the Eastern Front cannot be measured. Another vast consequence that could have become absolutely fundamental to post-war Europe was the possibility that the first atom bomb could have been used against Berlin in order to force a German unconditional surrender.

---

11. Bib. A29, Ch. 8, pp. 412/413.
12. 'Collapse of the German War Economy' by Alfred Mierzejewski, p. 167.

CHAPTER TEN

Post-War Bombing Surveys and Other Reports

'War is nothing but a continuation of politics with the admixture of other means.'

Clausewitz, 'On War' 1832–4

Introduction

It is important to have an appreciation of the real impact that the Allied Bombing Offensives had on the German war economy and military capability. The post-war Bombing Surveys by the US and the UK authorities recorded that impact. There is ongoing argument about the conduct and objectivity of those surveys. This chapter summarises the outcome of the surveys and the disagreements.

At the end of the war in Europe, the UK was acutely impoverished, badly damaged and deeply in debt financially to our US ally, partly because of the cost of the wartime Lend-Lease programme which began in 1941. Large quantities of goods were in Britain or in transit when Washington suddenly and unexpectedly terminated Lend-Lease immediately after VJ-Day at the end of Aug 45. The UK needed to retain some of this equipment in the immediate post war period. As a result the Anglo–American Loan came about. Lend-lease items retained were sold to the UK at an initial value of £1,075 million. Payment was to be stretched out over 50 years at 2 per cent interest. The interest rate that was charged may have reflected a post-war US aversion to helping a foreign socialist government, as Great Britain had then become. The wartime closeness between Prime Minister Churchill and President Roosevelt did not travel to the post-war relationship between Attlee and Trueman. The final payment of £42.5 million was made on 29 December 2006. Both world wars in the 20th century were good business for the US, protected from homeland attack by the Pacific and Atlantic oceans.

The post-war Marshal Plan (officially known as the European Recovery Program) was subsequently created by the US to provide a platform for rebuilding the nations within Europe and to act as a foundation for opposing Soviet expansion westwards. The UK was a major benefactor from that Plan.

Before the end of the war in Europe, the US Congress had authorised a complete survey of the effects of the Bombing Offensive, to be effective before there was any appreciable recovery by Germany. That work started before May 1944, with initial interviews and interrogations of senior German personnel. The survey was extensively documented and was promptly released to the American public.[1]

Within UK, one of the consequences of the immediate post-war poverty may have been a negative attitude towards a British survey of the effectiveness of the RAF strategic bombing offensive. There was a great deal of delay and debate before a relatively small-scale survey was authorised. It is difficult to determine the true rationale for that vacillation. The cost was primarily driven by the salary of the survey team. An interesting point was made from the Economic Advisory Branch of the MEW; having declared a great interest in the bombing survey and having earmarked suitable staff, the letter went on to explain that staff would only be available for a few weeks before the MEW was closed down.[2] But there is a suspicion that in some quarters there was profound resistance to any survey of the bombing offensive and its consequences, because it would have revealed the true extent of the effectiveness of that strategic offensive against the overall war economy of the enemy. No evidence has been found to directly support this suspicion, but it is unlikely that such evidence would exist in official files. What has been found from the archives is a staggering level of inter-departmental bureaucracy and obstruction. The reader is referred to Appendix N for a summary of the various political points of view. There were powerful interests within Whitehall that had persistently pressed for particular targets to have priority. They would not have welcomed any independent evidence that challenged their judgements.

Whitehall had tried to initiate a joint Survey with the US, but this failed to find agreement. The US feared that such a Joint Survey would become trapped in the swamp of bureaucracy that flourished within the Whitehall corridors; and events were to show the validity of that fear.

A UK survey was eventually approved and was conducted from the end of Jun 45 to the middle of Sep 46. The findings are now in the public domain, albeit after over 50 years. The image on Plate 6 shows that the US Survey Report was completed and released at the end of Oct 45.

> These surveys did not just assess the effects of the bombing offensive; they also – perhaps more importantly – assessed the Allied objectives and the policies.

The following two sections provide an overview of the main findings of the surveys, where they are most relevant to this current book:

- The US Strategic Bombing Survey (USSBS).
- The British Bombing Survey Unit: 'The Strategic Air War against Germany, 1939–1945'.

---

1. Air 48/194 'The Effects of Strategic Bombing on the German War Economy'.
2. Air 20/5366, Letter from MEW/EAB to British Bombing Research Mission dated 17 May 1945.

The final reports issued by the USSBS and the BBSU are available within The National Archives (Bib. A17 and A24 respectively).

The third section in this chapter contains information provided by senior German military and civilian officials who were well placed to judge the effects of the Allied air attacks.

The US Strategic Bombing Survey

Introduction
In reviewing the effects of the Bombing Offensive on the German war economy, three main considerations were necessary:

- The massive increase in the weight of bombing that was delivered as the war progressed. When the RAF began bombing in 1940, the average monthly weight of bombs was 1,100 tons. When the USAAF began bombing from August 1942, the net monthly average had increased to 6,000 tons. That more than doubled during 1943 to 26,000 tons. During 1944 the monthly average became 131,000 and finally in 1945 it reached 170,000 tons.
- There were significant improvements in operational techniques. These included major advances in Allied aircraft navigation – so important at night and also in daytime with poor weather; bomb aiming devices and accuracy; and weapon design. In 1940 the heaviest bomb used by the RAF was one ton; in 1944/45, it was ten tons. The advent and operational use of escort fighters, night intruders and coordinated RCM support, provided the heavy bombers with much-needed protection against the German air defence system. And by no means least, the operational use of Sigint provided invaluable insight into German air defence tactics and intentions.
- Throughout the bombing offensive the choice of primary targets was mostly driven by strategic objectives, largely determined by committees mostly in London. That choice was itself subject to operational and feasibility judgements by the Air Commanders. However, in the months preceding and following D-Day in Jun 44, the bombing offensive was subordinated to the Supreme Commander, General Eisenhower. It was then partly directed against tactical targets in support of the Allied landings in Normandy and the drive eastwards towards Germany. Paradoxically, it was during this phase that some of the greatest strategic successes were achieved.

Various Committees, mostly in Whitehall but also in America, heavily dominated the choice of strategic targets and their relative priorities. The work of those committees was guided by a number of factors, of which Intelligence was but one. The as yet unanswered question is whether those committees made the best use of available intelligence.

An outstanding feature of the German war economy was the surprisingly low level of production of armaments in the first three years of the war.

The accepted rationale was that the German High Command did not plan and was not prepared for a long war; the policy of Blitzkrieg was dominant and Hitler did not expect to fight a war of attrition with an Allied opponent. The underestimation of Russia's strength was another major miscalculation. The defeat before Moscow and the entry of the US into the war in December 1941 forced the German leadership to face the prospect of a prolonged series of offensives on three fronts. From Feb 42, the German war economy moved progressively onto a quite new footing, following the appointment of Albert Speer as Reichsminister. He set about replacing the then existing industrial control structures with a new organisation, manned by key people with production and technical skills. They were charged with increasing war production by a combination of design simplicity, standardisation, reducing the diversity of armament manufacturing programmes and improved production processes. The effect was a threefold increase in armament production over the following 30 months. In battle tanks, the increase was nearly six-fold. The USSBS questioned if even that represented the full utilisation of the German war industry potential. The turning point in that general increase in productivity came in the autumn of 1944, in the face of the massive onslaught by the Combined Bombing Offensive. It will remain an open question whether, if Germany had prepared for and started the war with that level of armament production and a comparable depth of reserve stocks, the outcome would have been different.

As it was, the basic resources of the German war economy fell into three distinct elements:

- *The available capital equipment and machinery.* Whereas the strategic bombing offensive was aimed in part at the destruction of equipment and machinery used to support the armament industry, the German economy had a general excess of capacity. At the start of the war, much of the German machine tool capacity was of a universal nature and was therefore easy to convert into armament production. But the key point was that most of that potential capacity was effectively lost by working only single-shifts, except in a very few cases such as aircraft engines. By comparison, the British and US industries were generally using their capital equipment on a 24-hour, seven day a week basis.
- *The industrial labour force and the appropriate skills.* With the progress of the war, both Britain and the US increased their mobilisation of manpower but Germany did not. One of the MEW's interesting comparisons was that in Britain the proportion of women in full- or part-time work increased by 45 per cent during the war, but the proportion in Germany was practically unchanged.[3] However, this may well be another topic where the MEW information was incomplete. On 31 May 39, according to the Reich Statistical Office, the German workforce consisted of 24.5 million working men and 14.6 million working women. In fact

---

3. Air 22/77, Weekly Air Ministry Intelligence Summaries, No. 176, dated 16 Jan 43. In describing the labour problems as they were seen at the end of 1942, an article by the MEW spoke of the limits that applied to married women taking full-time employment. It did not qualify what those limits were.

one third of all married women in Germany were economically active and more than one half of all women between the ages of 15 and 60 were in work. But by far the largest sector of women's work was in agriculture, which increased as men were drafted into the Armed Forces. By maintaining the food supply, German women provided an indispensable service to the German war effort.[4] Another factor was the high level of manpower in the German public administration system; some 3.5 million workers were employed. Speer tried to reduce this number, but was unsuccessful.

- *Raw materials.* Germany's dependence on imported raw materials was always regarded as the main weakness of her war economy. One very important contingency, starting from 1936, was the development of synthetic production facilities for rubber, oil, textiles and fats. The annual production rate of synthetic oil was increased from 1.6 million tons in 1938 to 6 million tons by early 1944; and in the same period, annual production of synthetic rubber increased from 5000 tons to 117,000 tons. But she still started the war with substantial dependence on foreign supplies of many vital raw materials. That was however alleviated to a very large extent by the early occupation of much of Europe: to the south into Italy, west into the low countries, Belgium and France; and to the east into Poland, Czechoslovakia, Romania, etc., with those various national raw material resources and stocks then falling under German control.

Armaments

Overview

Armaments production was not a dominant part of Germany's gross national product (GNP), nor was it a major user of labour, prime power or transportation services; but armaments were a dominant user of products such as steel, copper and aluminium. In the years 1940–42, armaments production was only about 10 per cent of the GNP; this may be seen as a reflection of the Blitzkrieg policy, with no expectation of a sustained war of attrition. By 1943, armaments rose to about 35 per cent of GNP and continued to increase until the middle of 1944 at which time the effects of the Combined Bombing Offensive progressively starved the industry of raw material and transportation. The two charts on Plates 6 and 7 show:

- The changes throughout the war in gross German armament production annually during 1940–45, as originally published in the USSBS Report.[5]
- The percentage distribution between different sectors of the armament production annually during 1940–44, also originally published in the USSBS Report.[6]

The expansion of the armaments industry relative to other sectors of the economy was to some extent achieved by converting surplus capacity, notably in the

---

4. Bib. A23 *The Wages of Destruction*, Ch. 10, p. 258–259.
5. Air 48/194, Effects of Strategic Bombing on the German War Economy, Ch. VIII, p. 140, Exhibit D-1.

machinery industry. It is valuable to record the history of the armaments industry from the middle 1930s, following on from the deprivations after the First World War. By 1936 Hitler had largely eliminated unemployment and was able to progress with his main task of rebuilding the armament industry and securing an adequate raw material base within the Reich. The inherent problems were that the industry was fragmented and that the High Command had placed too much faith in the policy of sharp incisive attacks in overwhelming force – the Blitzkrieg. This worked very well initially, when the supply lines were short within Europe; but it failed in the North African offensive and it collapsed terminally during the Russian offensive.

The problems of fragmentation were addressed and solved by Speer and his colleagues from the beginning of 1942. He had selected the best men for the job, in their respective fields of armament; they were each to extend the most efficient production processes over the whole field, to simplify product design and to put as many industries as possible on a rationalised mass production basis. But even Speer was unable to cope with the terminal transportation problem in the last 12 months of the war.

The Stalingrad disaster, Allied victories in Africa and the mounting intensity of bombing attacks on the German homeland by Bomber Command, after the appointment of Sir Arthur Harris as CinC – coincidentally at the same time as Speer was appointed as Reichsminister – put Germany onto the defensive as 1942 came to a close.

The earlier Allied bombing strategy had been as follows:

- The first systematic bombing raids against German armament production were against submarine construction yards and support bases, initially by the RAF alone during the early phases of the Battle of the Atlantic in 1940–41 and subsequently forming a main target for the 8th USAAF during the first six months of 1943. The effects of these raids were minimal; the actual production of submarines was up to the expected level throughout the period.
- The next major target was the aircraft industry, with key attention to fighter production. Those raids began by the middle of 1943 and they caused a 13 per cent loss in production in the six months to Dec 43; but part of that loss arose from the German dispersal plan for the aircraft industry, itself of course a direct consequence of the bombing offensive. The reader is invited to see the following Section for further details. The attacks against ball bearings had no appreciable effect on production, notwithstanding the high visibility that this target was given in Whitehall.[7]

Armoured Vehicles

The main weight of the bombing offensive came during 1944 and saw panzers and motor vehicles added to the list of key targets – see pages 41 and 44. Of the three types of armoured vehicles used by the Germans, i.e. panzers, half-tracks

6. Ibid. p. 144, Exhibit D-3.
7. Air 48/194, Ch. VIII, German Armament Production, p. 146.

and wheeled, it was usually only the panzers that were used in direct combat. These came as tanks, assault guns and self-propelled guns. The heaviest panzers were the Tiger I and the Tiger II, 54 and 68 tons respectively. The military significance of panzer production was far greater than its small 8 per cent share of the overall armaments production.

Panzer and assault gun production had both increased rapidly from the start of 1943, not least as a consequence of the losses that were sustained on the eastern front and particularly around Stalingrad. The losses there were catastrophic: 500 in Nov 1942, 200 in December, 700 in January and 2,200 in February 1943 when the German forces finally surrendered. Indeed, so seriously was the situation then seen by Hitler that he issued a decree on 22 Jan 43 that demanded that:

All necessary measures are to be taken immediately to increase panzer production – even if by those measures other important branches of the armament industry are adversely affected for a time.[8]

Specifically, that directive authorised Speer to provide panzer production facilities and their component suppliers with technicians, raw materials, machinery and electric power even if that meant drawing upon the capacities and resources of other war production industries; and workers in the panzer production facilities were excluded from being drafted into the armed forces. To put this into perspective, even if that directive had been fully implemented, Germany would still have remained seriously behind the Allied production of armoured vehicles. The comparative production figures for 1943, as provided by the Germans, showed an Allied total of 68,000 vehicles against a total of only 12,000 German. It should be noted however, that the Panther and Tiger heavy tanks were of very high quality and well respected by the Allied armies.

The panzer production had suffered from area bombing raids. The Bomber Command attack on Friedrichshafen on the night of 27/28 Apr 44 was reported by German officials to have been the most damaging single attack ever delivered on panzer production: the ZF gearbox plant was beyond repair and the Maybach plant was destroyed except for the motor assembly building. Several of the Bomber Command raids on Berlin had damaged the Daimler-Benz and Alkett plants. Yet there was little impact on the overall output of finished tanks. The net production loss over the period from October 1943 to June 1944 was some 700–800 tanks and assault guns; the actual output in the same period was approximately 14,000 panzers of all types; losses were 5 per cent of total production.

By comparison, in the five months after D-Day 10,000 panzer vehicles were destroyed or abandoned in retreats largely across France and the Eastern Front. From August to October 1944, the panzer production industry suffered heavy attack as a primary target set. All of the assembly plants and the several of the engine factories were successfully bombed. The resultant damage was severe but there was appreciable recovery during Nov and December 1944 when bad

8. Ibid. p. 168.

weather initially reduced the scale of the strategic bombing attacks and higher priority was given by the Allies to oil and transportation targets; and that was followed by the Ardennes Offensive which claimed a significant proportion of the strategic bombing effort. Attacks on panzer production were not resumed until February 1945 and they unquestionably caused a further loss in production, but by that time the increasing disruption to the transportation system was reducing the normal flow of raw materials and components.[9] The USSBS found that it was impossible to segregate these different factors.

The impact of panzer production losses on military operations was debatable because of the coincident losses in enemy stocks of gasoline and diesel, which impaired their mobility, and ammunition that defeated their battlefield utility. On certain fronts and at certain times, the German commanders had fewer tanks and guns than were desired – as evidenced in some cases by the delivery of these items directly from assembly factories to front line units. No definite correlation could be established between panzer production losses due to bombing and the reduction in the combat effectiveness of the German armies.

Motor Vehicles

In a quite different context, motor transport was at most a supplement to the highly developed German railway system. The German armies relied on motor vehicles and half-tracks only for short haul movements and in the battle areas. Half-tracks were used as general-purpose vehicles for hauling guns, other heavy equipment and as personnel carriers. The industrial and consumer sectors of the economy could virtually manage without motor transport so long as they could rely on the railway. Trucks were the most important single item in the motor vehicle production programme, amounting to about two thirds of all vehicles produced.

It is interesting to note that at the outbreak of the war, passenger car production was cut by 75 per cent; some of that capacity was diverted to military use but the majority was apparently allowed to remain idle. That negligent attitude continued through the first easy victories and lasted several months into the Russian offensive. During that period the German armies took only 60 per cent of the trucks that were produced, for their battle losses had been small and large numbers of enemy vehicles had been captured. The entire western offensive in May and June 1940 had cost the German armies only 5185 trucks – about three weeks production. By the beginning of 1941, the stock of trucks was in excess of 150,000. The motor vehicle plants in France, Belgium and Holland were used to augment home production.

> There was no apparent need to expand the home production rates; just as there was seen to be no apparent need to fully exploit the Reich's industrial potential in other spheres.

---

9. Air 20/3218, SHAEF Report DSC/TS.100 dated 7 Feb 45. Army intelligence review of strategic bombing, by General Strong, ACoS, G2. The review concluded that the attacks on transport would have a far more widespread effect on armament production than attacks on tank assembly plants.

That changed with the first winter of the Russian offensive. Truck production was increased during 1942 to a total of 81,276 units, compared with 62,400 during 1941; but that increase resulted wholly from non-German factories; domestic production actually fell. There was a failure to plan for the time when it would no longer be possible to requisition vehicles. That failure became critical after Stalingrad; in January 1943 the Germans lost over 50,000 trucks. There certainly were increases in domestic production through 1943, with the output of trucks reaching nearly 110,000, but the rate began to fall again towards the end of the year. There was also the increasing impact of strategic bombing although through 1943 the raids were of relatively low intensity. The Renault plant was heavily damaged; attacks on ball bearings threatened but never caused a problem with the motor transport industry. Production of trucks appeared to have been more seriously handicapped by the policy of dispersal of industry to avoid air attack. The conclusion of the USSBS analysis of motor transport production was that strategic bombing cost Germany one-third of a year's production of motor vehicles and one-sixth of a year's production of half-tracks.[10] Most of these losses occurred in the final months of the war when there was a massive requirement for motor transport to provide some compensation for the disruption of rail transport. Whether the critical shortage of motor transport hindered military movements more than the acute shortage of petrol was unclear; there were certainly instances in the battle zones where motor vehicles and tanks were without fuel.

Weapons and Ammunition

Artillery production was never a specific target for bombing attack; area raids and occasional precision attacks interfered with output but never to a significant extent. The same was true for ammunition. The major problem for the ammunition industry as the war proceeded was the shortage of raw materials, a most important item being nitrogen. The drastic interruption of nitrogen production, a by-product from the synthetic oil processes, led to a 33 per cent cut in aggregate explosives output by the start of 1945.

The USSBS analysis of the effects of bombing on the ammunition industry focussed on two main factors: production losses from the bombing as compared with what may otherwise have been possible; and the output of anti-aircraft ammunition to combat the bombing offensive. Hitler was probably the chief exponent of the importance of anti-aircraft artillery defence. His theory was that there could never be enough fighters to prevent bombers from reaching their targets, but at the target areas they could either be destroyed by artillery or would have their bomb aiming distracted. There is a consistent theme about German war production that is echoed when ammunition was considered; the low levels of production in the early years coupled with the low levels of consumption. The entire offensive against France in 1940 consumed only about one seventh of the ammunition consumed during just July 1944. German stocks were at their highest throughout the war at the start of the Russian offensive in the middle of 1941. Hitler had ordered a general cutback on munitions production in Sep 1941,

---

10. Bib. A16: Ch. VIII – Motor Vehicles and Half-Tracks, p. 178.

probably on the grounds that the Russian offensive was expected to close quickly. The German authorities subsequently claimed that decision as a major factor in the low rate of munitions production later in the war, but it may be noted that munitions production was a reasonably stable element of the aggregate war production – readers are referred to Plate 7.

Through 1942 and probably 1943 the bombing of Germany had negligible effect on the munitions industry. Whereas there was a moderate increase in productivity during 1943 to Sep 1944, the striking feature is the change in proportions of the finished products with anti-aircraft ammunition showing a 73 per cent increase. This was almost certainly a reflection of Hitler's faith in anti-aircraft artillery and perhaps his diminishing trust in Goering and the GAF as the war proceeded. An argument was made that the anti-aircraft defences had been made so strong as to diminish the risk of serious bomb damage to the economy. But if that was valid then the bombing offensive could not have been seen as worthless; the result was the large share of war production resources and personnel that were devoted to air defence.

The particular weapon that was widely deployed was the 88-mm gun, of which 5,618 were produced in 1944 alone. Had those guns and their crews been available to the field armies, then the land battles would certainly have been fiercer and the Allied losses of tanks and troops would have been much higher.

Yet another fact in this mosaic is that the supply of 88 mm ammunition towards the end of 1944 had diminished not in total stocks but in immediately available rounds in readiness at gun emplacements; and there was an order to limit the usage of that ammunition. After a visit to the Ruhr in Nov 1944, Speer had reported that anti-aircraft ammunition was so short that only one-third to one-half of the amount required was actually fired; that was another reflection of the widespread transportation crisis. Yet another twist was that the production of 88-mm ammunition remained steady into 1945, even as the aggregate ammunition production went into steep decline.

It should not be overlooked that another very important item in the ammunition industry was the production and supply of torpedoes for the German Navy. There was never any deficiency in that supply; even in 1944 the consumption of torpedoes was 12,363 against a stock holding of 18,771 at the end of the year, equivalent to about 18-months' supply at an equivalent rate of use. Likewise, the supply of bombs to the GAF was always sufficient at the prevailing rates.

The Allied bombing offensive was credited directly with about a 14 per cent net production loss of ammunition throughout 1944.[11] However, the aggregate production loss through 1944 also included losses attributed to the lack of powder, explosives and shell cases; and all of these ingredient requirements suffered from the aggregate and progressive reduction in transportation of the raw material and the finished products. The supply of powder and explosives was seriously affected by the cut in nitrogen output from the synthetic oil industry. The consequent shortage of ammunition to the German armies through 1944 was assessed to be about 22 per cent. The repercussion on the German

---

11. Bib. A16: Ch. VIII, Weapons and Ammunition, p. 190.

armies fighting effectiveness was another of the decisive effects of the Combined Bombing Offensive.

The Aircraft Industry

A key target for strategic bombing was the aircraft industry. Raids during 1943 caused an estimated 13 per cent loss of aircraft production; but part of this was due to the dispersal of manufacturing facilities as protection against further raids. In the context of aircraft production it was specifically noticed that the Allied bombing did substantial damage to the factory buildings, but often had far less impact on the machine tools that were used for production. In the aircraft engine industry for example, only about 5 per cent of the machine tools were destroyed. This was a much smaller impact than Allied Intelligence had assumed and often led to the resumption of productivity long before further raids were planned. One aspect of the finished products was a reduction in quality as compared to that typically found at the start of the war, but there was little evidence as to any material effect on combat performance.

For the first four months of 1944, the bombing raids had major impact on the aircraft industry. This was key to the Allied planning for D-Day and the perceived military need to secure Allied air superiority for the landings and the breakout from the beachheads. It was estimated that these raids alone caused production losses of 15–20 per cent.[12] According to Messerschmitt, the Feb 44 attacks on his factories caused a 50 per cent loss in production for one month. The losses at the eastern plants of Focke-Wulf were about 20 per cent for two months. The peak production was in July 1944 when nearly 4300 aircraft were delivered to the GAF. The reason was that the energetic rationalisation and standardisation measures that had been set in train under Speer's leadership were yielding major dividends. It is a tremendous tribute to the energy and efficiency of the aircraft industry that it continued to make significant increases in output notwithstanding the weight of bombing attacks, as is reflected on Plate 8.

The dispersal of the aircraft industry to reduce its vulnerability to air attack inevitably had an adverse effect on production rates, initially because of the disruption that was involved and latterly as a consequence of the dependence on transport over and above that previously required in more centralised production. The rapidly increasing disorganisation of the transportation system seriously compromised the advantages of improved survivability. At the end of the war, there were about one million square metres of underground workspace, although there never was a complete aircraft assembly line. There were however complete V-2 underground assembly plants, for example at Nordhausen from early 1944.

The raids on the aircraft industry continued through the summer of 1944, but the centre of gravity moved from aircraft construction to engine production. This element of the industry was more difficult to disperse and had a lack of excess capacity. Finished aircraft production in December 1944 was only 60 per cent of what it had been in July and the aggregate loss through those six months, from direct and indirect bomb damage, was about 25 per cent.

---

12. Bib. A16: Ch. I, Overall Effects of the Air Offensive, p. 12.

One particular element of the aircraft programme was the entry into operational use of the Me 262 jet-engine fighter. This design had been flown experimentally in 1941 but was then rejected by the High Command perhaps because it was seen to be too complex or more likely because at that time there was seen to be no need. At that time, the priority was on bomber aircraft production. But the intensity of the Allied bombing offensive from late 1943 forced the need for better fighters. Not only did the Me 262 have superior speed, it did not use high-octane aircraft fuel and that was a major bonus at that time. Production was started in Mar 44, largely in dispersed or underground factories. Several senior GAF officers testified that a large proportion of the production had to be returned for rectification or modification, and that consequently there were relatively few in combat. The point here is that reliability was compromised, not the operational performance.

From late 1943 and through much of 1944, there was profoundly critical argument within Whitehall about the apparent ineffectiveness of Bomber Command, being judged by the continuing increase in the strength of the GAF. It was quite clearly unappreciated in Whitehall that the German production capacity was outstripping the increasing bomb damage. Without that damage, the GAF Order of Battle would have increased even more sharply and the effectiveness of the enemy Fighter forces would have reached even higher levels. The losses of Allied bombers and aircrews might then have become unaffordable?

From the point of view of operational effectiveness, the data on aircraft production can be misleading. For the period Jan–Sep 44, there were major discrepancies between numbers of aircraft completed and related increases in front line strength. There were several related factors:[13]

- Losses of aircraft on the ground increased substantially after the middle of 1944. In one case there were 1000 aircraft parked at factories, ready for despatch but only 92 survived bombing raids.
- High percentages of operational aircraft on the ground were lost from battle damage and shortages of spares. Wastage rates on the Western Front were said to be about 600 aircraft per month.
- In other cases, some 20 per cent of aircraft delivery flights failed to reach their destination because of the deterioration in fighter pilot training since 1943.
- The progressive increase in quantity and quality of Allied aircraft.

During this same period there was argument within the German war production programme about the relative value of fighter aircraft and their fuel requirements, that in effect there was an unbalanced programme. Speer was accused of focussing exclusively on the number of completed aircraft without regard to the directly associated factors of pilot training and fuel. It was not until the end of 1944 that Speer accepted the inconsistency of disproportion between fighter aircraft production and their aggregate fuel consumption.

During the early years, as shown on Plate 8, not all of the aircraft production potential capacity was used. There was an exaggerated opinion within the

---

13. Air 48/194, 'Production Decline and Military Defeat', p. 159.

German High Command of their effective air strength. The early conquests in the west and the capitulation of France were so rapid that they cost Germany only six weeks' aircraft production. After the occupation of France, with the general feeling that the war was ending, production had continued to increase but slowly with no obvious preparations for the assault on Russia. The failure to build-up operational strength and reserves was largely a consequence of the attitude of Goering and the General Staff, after the initial rapid victories during 1940–41 both in the west and the east, leading then to the report that:

> Germany is entering the final struggle with so overwhelming a superiority of armament capacity that the result can no longer be in doubt.[14]

The perception in the German High Command was that the Russian offensive would be swift and that victory would be achieved in about three months. History was to show otherwise.

The Allied economic and political pressure to attack the ball-bearing industry did secure a significant loss in production through the second quarter of 1944, amounting to some 60 per cent. However, the Germans had substantial stocks; there were continuing import options from occupied and neutral countries; an energetic dispersal of production had been implemented; and by intelligent redesign, they had minimised the need for high quality anti-friction bearings and the demand for ball bearings. The impact of ball-bearing losses on overall war production of finished armaments was negligible.

As to the German aircraft production programme and its remarkable achievements, it was the consistent and often intense pressure of bombing and air combat that enabled the Allies eventually to gain air superiority in the sky over Europe. That must be counted as one of the most decisive Allied victories of WW2 by any of the separate Allied forces.

The Steel Industry

A variety of evidence indicated that the bombing offensive on the Ruhr was chiefly responsible for the steady decline in crude steel production from 1.2 million tons in Aug 44 to 0.3 million tons in Dec 44. This decline resulted principally from damage to auxiliary facilities such as power and gas supplies, transport services within the plants and the general area; rather than from direct damage to steel production installations such as blast furnaces and rolling mills. Saturation bombing of an entire steel plant area resulted in substantial production losses. There was little evidence that precision attacks on steel plants would have been more effective in reducing the output.[15]

Broadly speaking, steel mills themselves were not attractive targets for precision air attack with the weapons that were available to the Bombing Offensive, except perhaps for the Grand Slam and Tallboy British bombs that Dr Barnes Wallis had designed. The machinery and equipment used in steel production was massive and built to withstand great strains. A direct hit by a typical 1000lb WW2 bomb on such a point target was not much more formidable than the normal hazards of

---

14. 'Die Deutsche Rüstungsüberlegenheit', *Der Deutsche Volkswirt*, 28 February 1941.
15. Air 48/194 'The Effects of Strategic Bombing on the German War Economy' p. 108.

daily operations. The structural design of a blast furnace is similar to that of an air-raid shelter. Most German steel plants were found to be well supplied with the facilities to make quick repair to ordinary bomb damage.

The extraordinary effects of GRAND SLAM and TALLBOY were different; the bombs weighed 22,000lb and 12,000lb respectively and were carried only by modified RAF Lancasters. They were used against key targets: capital ships; reinforced pens for U-boats; major viaducts, tunnels and canals; reinforced V-1 and V-2 launch sites; and major industrial sites, etc. The image on Plate 7 was taken during an operation by 617 Squadron on 19 Mar 45 against the Arnsberg Viaduct; it shows the point of release of the bomb.

Experience from the 1943–45 bombing raids showed conclusively that the steel industries lines of transportation were the most vulnerable. Effective bomb damage was found to be present on vital elevated and underground service piping and power lines. The bombing had important effects on the inter- and intra-plant railways; and there was widespread evidence that the bombing constantly interfered with the receipt of raw materials and the distribution of finished products.

> The records show with clarity that the drastic reduction in steel supply during the latter months of 1944 and the early part of 1945 came about, not by direct damage to the main production facilities, but principally by disruption to the vital utilities such as transport, gas, water and electric power. Of these, transportation was the crucial factor.[16]

Even in mid-44 at the peak of production demands, the steel supply was on the whole sufficient. The decline in steel output resulting from the bombing offensive later in 1944 came too late to have a decisive effect upon the output of munitions in Germany. By the time that steel shortages could have delayed armaments production, those plants were themselves reduced by bombing and, in addition, losses of territory and disruption of transportation services had considerably reduced Germany's capacity to sustain output of all types.

Oil Targets
One of the more perceptive commentaries on the Allied strategic bombing offensive and the difficulties involved in securing decisive results against oil plants, made special note that:

> The oil plants could only be successfully attacked under visual conditions.[17]

One of the reasons behind that statement was the explicit need to hit either key points within any specific oil plant, which could often extend to over one square

---

16. Ibid. p. 109.
17. Air 8/1019, COS Committee Report , AO (46) 1, 8 Mar 46, Appendix 20.

mile or more, or to locate and hit the smaller dispersed above-ground sites that were being built as a consequence of the dispersal programme. Visual aiming conditions were particularly important for the successful outcome of any attack and these conditions were not commonly present, not least as a consequence of smoke screens. The three important oil plants at Leuna, Ludwigshafen and Troglitz-Zeitz represented 22.4 per cent of German synthetic oil production capacity. These three plants covered a total area of three and one half square miles. The daylight attacks on these plants by the 8th USAAF had the following effects:

- 146,000 HE bombs were dropped. This represented 38.3 per cent of all bombs dropped by the 8th on hydrogenation plants and may therefore be regarded as representative of the overall effect.
- In round numbers, out of every 100 bombs dropped, 87 missed the targets completely; a further 8 landed inside the target areas but within open spaces and had no effect; and 2 failed to explode. Only 3 bombs out of every 100 that were dropped did any important damage.

In a more general context, the aggregate effect on German oil production can be seen in the following Table that shows percentages of production against the reported normal capacity of the oil plants:[18]

Month	Percentage of Oil Capacity	Percentage of Aviation Fuel Capacity
Aug 44	46	65
Sep 44	48	30
Oct 44	43	37
Nov 44	60	65
Dec 44	59	56
Jan 45	51	33
Feb 45	40	5

The impact was far and away most acute on aviation fuel and this eventually rendered the GAF incapable of an adequate defence of the Reich and of the German armies in the field. It handicapped the Wehrmacht for lack of motor fuel and diesel oil. However, there is an illuminating observation in the USSBS Report when describing the characteristically frugal use of diesel fuel by the German armies, as compared with the far more profligate consumption by Allied armies. In the case of the massive engagement at Stalingrad, it appeared that the more pressing reason for oil shortages by the Armies was transportation across such large distances.[19]

---

18. Speer Papers, Vol. 7, FD 2690/45: Material dealing with German fuel production in 1944/45.
19. Air 8/1019, USSBS Report on the Effects of Strategic Bombing on the German War Economy, p. 77.

As a by-product, the strategic bombing offensive caused a drastic reduction in the output of a number of chemicals including nitrogen, methanol and synthetic rubber because of the inter-relations between the synthetic oil and chemical industries. The impact on the enemy war economy caused by the urgent attempts at reconstruction, dispersal and underground constructions under the Geilenberg programme are all consequences of the offensive against oil.

The physical vulnerability of oil production lay first of all in the fact that in early 1944 18 hydrogenation plants accounted for 35 per cent of German supply of all oil products and 90 per cent of her aviation fuel. These plants were known to Allied intelligence services and most were within range of the heavy bombers from UK airfields. On the other hand, the crude oil refineries represented a much less vulnerable group of targets. There were three reasons for that:

- There was a larger number of refineries than synthetic plants,
- The total refinery capacity of Axis Europe was in excess of the crude oil supply until late in 1944,
- the nature of crude refineries was less vulnerable to bombing attack.

The recovery of oil production after bombing attack was far greater than had been expected and on average the plants were back in production within six weeks and sometimes within a few days. The bombing effort to keep the enemy oil production under any form of control was therefore several times greater than had been expected by the Allied oil committees. The great unresolved question was the timing of bombing attacks as a priority target set as the war progressed, against the available bomber force and the vulnerability of that force. There were profoundly deep and serious arguments that have been described throughout this book but one factor that is very specific to oil target selection is the extent to which the Fischer-Tropsch plants and crude refineries should have been attacked.[20] The Fischer-Tropsch plants produced no aviation gasoline and accounted for only 5 per cent of the gross German oil supply. However, they received 20 per cent of the bomb tonnage dropped on oil targets. Between Jun and Sep 44 every major Fischer-Tropsch plant had been bombed at least twice. The crude oil refineries produced 25 per cent of the gross German oil supply but less than 1 per cent of the aviation gasoline; and they were less vulnerable to bombing attack than were the hydrogenation plants.

The question of target selection again arose with regard to the major plant at Ploesti. The 15th USAAF dropped 10,000 tons of bombs on that plant and a few thousand tons on the transportation facilities in Romania. The net effect was to deny Germany about 700,000 tons of semi-finished and finished oil products. It is apparent that the most critical impact arose from the transportation attacks.

It is a great tribute to the German capacity to improvise and economise that the very large cuts that were imposed on civilian liquid fuel consumption did not itself disrupt the economy. That consumption was ruthlessly stripped to support the aggregate Army and Navy needs.

---

20. Ibid., pp. 82–83.

The strategic bombing offensive against oil production targets in Germany and Romania during the last year of the war accomplished the purpose by the sheer weight of effort, but the post-war USSBS found that the detailed oil target selection process and the identification of critical aiming points was inadequate. Whatever improvements may have been possible, even if the intelligence and other knowledge had been available, they would have to be set against the ability of the bomber forces to deliver the necessary precision. That would almost certainly have been an unachievable objective.

Transportation

This summary is largely taken from the USSBS Report 'The Effects of Strategic Bombing on German Transportation'.[21] The following sub-sections address:

- Background.
- Post-OVERLORD.
- The Final Stage.
- Economic Effects of Air Attacks on Transportation.

A potentially illuminating policy paper on German transportation was produced immediately after the war by Maj Gen Napier, Chief of the SHAEF G-4 Division (Movements and Transportation).[22] The purpose of that paper was to set up a procedure whereby any documentary and other evidence which came to hand on German transportation subjects should be safeguarded. No recognised channel had previously existed for the collation and distribution of intelligence on transportation subjects. Such material was ultimately to be passed to the Central Intelligence Section. This perhaps indicates that throughout the war, transportation as an intelligence topic and as a bombing target was subordinated in the mind of Allied policy makers and planners. No such documentation and recording process has been identified for the German transportation system within UK intelligence records.

Background

Prior to the war Germany had a most complex and well-maintained railway system. There was in general an over-capacity of permanent way and an excess of engineering and maintenance facilities. There was also a strong inland waterway system connecting the great rivers of North Germany, the Ruhr and Berlin; this waterway system provided over 25 per cent of the aggregate freight transportation capacity and was well adapted to the movement of heavy cargoes into and out from the Ruhr. Conversely, road transport provided less than 5 per cent of that aggregate capacity.

The invasion of Poland in late 1939 brought about not only a large increase in traffic but also an increase in freight wagon turn-around time. This was very significantly compounded by the assault on Russia in 1941. Thereafter, the available railway systems – including those in occupied countries – were under

---

21. Bib. A16, Air 48/175, January 1947.
22. Air 20/4819: SHAEF/3021/3/2/Mov dated 21 May 45.

some consistent strain because of the military demands and the relocation and dispersal of so much German industry. It was determined by the USSBS from post-war German records that the detailed plans for dispersal of industry were often made without sufficient regard to the then available transportation services. It was found necessary to build new yards at critical points such as Munich; and to construct bypass lines for vulnerable viaducts and bridges.

Early in 1943 there was a drive to spread out both routine traffic and also the typical autumn peak demands for heavy freight such as coal and coke. The working shifts at large industrial complexes were staggered to reduce the peak demands for commuting. These contingencies satisfied the normal levels of demand.

The size and complexity of the German railway system made it a very difficult target, particularly in the light of the operational capabilities and limitations of the Allied strategic bomber forces. There were many times during the bombing offensive when the primary target could not be reached and an alternative target was attacked; elements of the railway system were frequently bombed as a secondary target by those specific raids. Prior to the spring of 1944, Bomber Command had dropped practically all of the bombing that may have affected the railway system during 1941–43 either in area raids or in the early stages of the Combined Bombing Offensive. In the last nine months of 1943, in the 94 attacks on 29 industrial centres, the rail facilities suffered a considerable amount of damage. There had been no dedicated pattern to the bombing of German transportation targets until Mar 44 when, as a preliminary to D-Day, there was a concerted effort against the French and Belgian railways and the German railways leading west into Belgium and France. By late May, just before the attacks on the Seine bridges, overall rail traffic was down to 55 per cent of that in Jan 44. Destruction of those bridges reduced traffic levels to 30 per cent by 6 Jun and thereafter the level of railway utilisation declined to 10 per cent. By mid-June the system in western France had virtually ceased to operate. In Jul 44, the Germans could operate only 9 per cent of the traffic volume compared with Mar 44.[23]

The impact on the railway system was a major contribution to the overall success of the Normandy landings and to the ultimate success of the Allies in WW2. Destruction of the transportation system forced the German infantry to fight without adequate artillery support; it was difficult to move motorised and mechanised units past broken bridges at night; day movement was virtually impossible.

No significant effects on the German transportation system could be found from the operations of Coastal Command against coastal shipping, which never provided more than 3 per cent of the capacity of the aggregate rail freight. In fact, Coastal Command was credited with sinking 273 vessels and seriously damaging a further 747. That cumulative damage was evenly distributed between enemy merchant shipping and naval vessels. Most of those attacks were fairly evenly distributed along the entire western coastline of Europe, with concentration on specific occasions against tactical areas such as the Dutch coast in late 1942 and early 1943, which succeeded in closing the port of Rotterdam.

---

23. Air 37/1261, Bombing Analysis Unit Report No. 1 dated 4 Nov 44 and Report No. 8 dated 6 Dec 44.

Post-OVERLORD

As the Allied armies advanced to the east through France and into Belgium, so the combined bombing offensive became increasingly targeted on the German transportation and oil industries. The effects of the heavy attacks on transportation from Sep 1944 were felt at once and were clearly apparent in the traffic and operating statistics of the Reichsbahn, which were examined by the USSBS. Building up in the Saar area, then the Cologne plain and shortly after into the entire territory from the Ruhr to the Swiss border, the attacks of September and October produced most serious disruption in the Reichsbahn operations over the whole of western Germany.

At that same time, successful attacks were mounted on the waterways. On 24 Sep 44, the Dortmund-Ems and Mittelland canals were closed, preventing through traffic between the Ruhr and points on the north coast and central Germany. By 14 Oct, the Rhine was blocked at Cologne. The effect on the Dortmund-Ems canal was very serious; from Oct 44 to Mar 45, traffic on the canal averaged only 12 per cent of the normal monthly capacity and water movement of coal to the south was stopped.

Serious effects on the enemy's industrial output developed quickly and resulted in large measure from the decline in rail traffic marshalling capacity, with accumulations of trains being set aside short of their destination. The backlog of delayed trains reached 1700 in the second week of Nov. Extensive cutting of track aggravated the problem; on one day in December, the two Rhine lines were cut in 21 places. The bad weather at that time came partly to the rescue of the Reichsbahn, which was able to recover slightly as bombing attacks were prevented. But this was only temporary and in the second half of December the backlog reached 2000.[24] At that level, some 100,000 wagons were out of effective use with their loads inaccessible.

The production of hard coal in the Ruhr fell from 10.5 million tons in Aug 44 to less than 5 million in Feb 45. But in that same period, coal stocks at the collieries in the Ruhr actually increased from 400,000 tons to over 2 million tons; and coke from 600,000 tons to over 3 million tons. That was a direct consequence of the transportation problem, notwithstanding the fact that complete trainloads of coal or coke were given priority whenever any rail movement was possible.

The industrial consequence was most severe. Certain components were always in relatively short supply and depended on regular transportation to avoid interruptions in the overall production and assembly cycle. From the end of October the Reichsbahn was frequently unable to satisfy those requirements. It became impossible to track the movement of individual wagons with important components or finished armaments. Assembly manufacturers who depended on such components suffered badly, with a serious impact on virtually all munitions

---

24. Author's Note: The reader's attention is drawn to some numerical differences between the USSBS and the BBSU reports. In this same period, the BBSU Report (Ar 10/3866, Ch. 22, p. 130; Bib. B28, Ch. 11, p. 100) has somewhat lower numbers of train backlogs. The difference may rest between average backlogs within the BBSU and peak backlogs within the USSBS. An independent and well respected record of the Reichsbahn is available at Bib. A22, with a brief summary at Appendix O.

and other finished end-products from the middle of Nov. The direct consequence of the breakdown in transportation was regarded by the USSBS as the single largest factor in the final collapse of the German war economy.

It was noted that the military traffic continued to have top priority and was the largest proportion of the declining traffic volume, closely followed by coal and coke freight. To the extent that lines were open and running, they were increasingly used for the immediate tactical needs of the German army. But by the end of Dec 44, even those top priority movements were subjected to serious delays and often prevented military units reaching their required destinations in anything like the required operational timescales.

The Final Stage

By the turn of the year the situation had become desperate. There was a massive bombing effort against railways from Jan 45 onwards. The first plan had been prepared by the Communications (Transportation) Working Group within the CSTC and the aims were:

- Intense attacks on the railways north and east of the Ruhr, with priority to the viaducts at Bielefeld and Paderborn.
- Continued denial of rail services in areas west of the middle Rhine.
- Ultimate denial of services in the area bounded by the Rhine on the west and 9° east, from Cologne to Stuttgart.

The details of the successes against these targets are available in Bib. A16. The viaducts at Bielefeld, Altenbeken and Arnsberg were destroyed.[25] At the same time, the 15th USAAF attacked transportation targets in southern Germany and Austria; and the 12th USAAF attacked the Brenner Pass that served transportation to and from Italy, as the Germans with forced to withdraw into Germany. The cumulative damage to all these targets and the outstanding success against others enabled the Target Committee to drop some rail centres and introduce additional targets. One of the specific operational plans was CLARION. Another, and perhaps of great significance, was the series of attacks in the East to assist the Russians. This included Dresden, raided on 12–14 Feb 45.

In the latter part of February there was a further plan, that time to 'Isolate the Ruhr'. The intention was to paralyse all railway movement between the Ruhr and surrounding areas to stop all movement of supplies, particularly war materials and coal. The elements of the plan were to:

- Cut a vital bridge or viaduct on every track in a wide arc from Bremen in the north to Coblenz in the south.
- Subject every yard, line and centre of any importance to heavy and consistent attack.
- Attack any rail traffic on the lines with fighters and fighter-bombers; this forced large-scale use of night traffic that had serious consequences for overall efficiency.

---

25. Author's Note: Readers are referred to the image on Plate 7.

By 24 March, when the Rhine was crossed near Wesel, the Ruhr was practically isolated from the rest of Germany. Sixteen of the 18 major bridges or viaducts had been put out of use; some 20 of the 25 major railway centres had been heavily damaged; and a large proportion of minor yards, centres and junctions had been seriously disrupted.

With the Ruhr isolated and the Allied armies moving rapidly east, the transportation system remained the highest priority target and the decision was to attack the Halle-Leipzig-Chemnitz zone because of the presence of the armament factories which were still in enemy hands; and it was also a nodal point on the way to the enemy 'National Redoubt'. Heavy attacks were made but, by the middle of April, the Chiefs of Staff determined that the remaining tasks for the combined bomber forces should be decided by the Supreme Commander in response to day-to-day situations on the ground as the armies continued to occupy German territory.

The weight of attack in the early months of 1945 prevented any recovery of transportation services and forced them into further decline. The lateness of the effective attacks on transportation prevented the full impact from becoming apparent to the front line German troops, who were in many cases unaware that their war production and resupply chain had broken completely.

That did not stop the very admirable efforts of the Reichsbahn officials and the German people in their race to attempt repairs to the railways. There seemed always to be a plentiful supply of 'pick and shovel' labour, much of which was from foreign workers and some prisoners of war. But there was an absence of adequate mechanical equipment and, not least, replacement rail track and points, etc., because of the combined problems of diminished steel production and a lack of transportation to the repair sites. It must have been very disheartening to watch repairs being undone by successive attacks.

Economic Effects of Air Attacks on Transportation

The USSBS reasonably decided, in the light of the complexity of the task and the budget for the Survey, to address the specific operation of major and discernible causes that acted as limiting factors on broad groups of industries. It was felt that this would allow judgements on possible 'overbombing', defined as attacking industries that had already been immobilised by transportation or raw material shortages. It was also dependent on the availability and content of record keeping by candidate industries; the dispersal or destruction of records was a common problem. In the final stages of the war, record keeping often stopped in the face of chaos; in many cases this arose because the postal system had collapsed and high-level summaries were difficult, even impossible to assemble. The following analyses address Coal and Steel.

COAL

The most important and widely used raw material was coal. Throughout the war the coal supply was tight both as regards production and transportation. The expansion of the war industries led to an increase in demand with which the transport services could cope only under stress. It represented 39 per cent of the aggregate railway freight and had the highest economic priority, so it was not affected by the elimination of marginal traffic. The effect of coal transportation failures was the best single index for the impact of transportation disruption on overall production. The criteria for 'proof' of a coal transportation problem were agreed as the presence of declining:

- Production, but at the same time rising stocks of raw material at the point of production.
- Deliveries (receipts) and vanishing stocks of raw material at the point of utilisation.
- Output of the end industrial product.

These criteria were markedly present in many cases; they reveal that transport bottlenecks were of very considerable importance and in many cases were disastrous.

The following sequence began with the start of the pre D-Day attacks, in March through to Sep 44. These attacks on the Ruhr transportation system had an immediate and appreciable effect, even though the reduction in rail wagon capacity fell by not more than 10 per cent. The railway repair effort was equal to the damage. Production losses were avoided by using stocks, which in normal times would be capable of supporting 15 days' to 3 months' production, depending on the process. The first contingency measure taken by the German authorities was to suspend the usual movements of coal for restocking winter supplies.[26]

The second phase was the three months from Oct to Dec 44. Under the intensity of the bombing the transportation losses became cumulative. Each attack aggravated the situation; the repair resources could not keep up with the rate of damage. Coal consumption and stocks diminished simultaneously. In some case, production was maintained at the expense of exhausting stocks.

The third phase, starting in Jan 45, 'reaped the whirlwind', as Sir Arthur Harris had projected when Bomber Command was fighting alone. Coal movements fell to small fractions of the required levels. Commercial deliveries were made only to the armament industry; in some cases, small stocks at local levels being taken from less urgent productions such as cement factories and given to ammunition factories. This phase marked the point when the cumulative damage created such uncertainty, risk and confusion that the administrative processes broke down. Speer later characterised these three phases:

Transport crisis; Transport emergency; Transport catastrophe.[27]

The USSBS considered whether, in the light of the total failure of transportation in the Ruhr, such an approach could not have provoked a complete collapse of the overall German war effort. The interdiction of three or four coal regions was probably operationally feasible. It would certainly have reduced, or even avoided, the 'over-bombing' of many other elements of the overall target sets. But

---

26. Author's Note: This of course was seen later to be a factor in the coal crisis as the 1944/45 winter approached and transportation became so much worse. See Appendix Q.
27. Air 48/175; USSBS Survey 'Effects of Strategic Bombing on German Transport', Ch. VII, p. 80.

the creation of the all-important administrative chaos in those regions would have depended heavily on hitting the coal and transportation targets in an unpredictable but sustained manner.

In its final conclusions, on transportation and coal, the USSBS found that the Reichsbahn had been an excellent system with a well-balanced traffic flow. The users of the rail services had for years enjoyed those services without appreciating the possible vulnerabilities. For example, the decisions on dispersal and relocation of production plants had taken little or no account of the associated transportation implications.

STEEL

The German steel industry extended across the country, but the Ruhr was the dominant region. There were two types of steel producing areas: those based on coal to which iron ore was transported, and those based on iron ore to which coal was transported. It was those latter areas that depended on coal transport that suffered, but it was equally clear that 'long-haul' iron ore movement was not a cause of production disruption. Officials from the Ministry level down to working levels made continuous reference to coal transportation problems either of a 'long-haul' type into and out from the region; or of a 'short-haul' type within regions and often within industrial plants themselves. The fact is that coal is of much greater importance by weight in steel-making raw materials. A general observation from the German officials who were interviewed was that the steel production installations sustained little damage.

Overall Effects of the Bombing Offensive

Prior to mid-1943 the bombing offensive had little appreciable effect on Germany's armament production or on the national output in general. The area attacks by the RAF did considerable damage to buildings and caused local delays in production by the need to divert labour to repair damage and clear debris. But considering the scale and nature of the German war economy at that time, it is not possible to conclude that the early bombing had caused any sustained impact The effects of the raids became more obvious from mid-1943 onwards due to the increasing weight and accuracy of the RAF raids and the growing operational strength of the combined bomber forces.

The oil and nitrogen plants, the German transportation system and the steel production in the Ruhr were subjected to heavy attack from early 1944. In addition, there were continuing heavy raids on the aircraft, motor vehicle and tank production industries. The attack on oil was concentrated on the synthetic plants, which were producing 90 per cent of her aviation fuel and 30 per cent of the road vehicle fuel. Combined production, from hydrogenation and the Fischer-Tropsch process, fell sharply as a result of the bombing raids prior to and after D-Day. The attacks on the synthetic oil plants also cost Germany a considerable part of her synthetic nitrogen, methanol and rubber. The nitrogen and methanol reductions had a direct impact on ammunition production, which suffered a 20 per cent loss in the final six months of 1944. This had unintentional adverse impact on the German logistics for the Ardennes offensive at the end of 1944.

The analysis of the Allied bombing effort against German aircraft production was related to the effort against the oil production industry. The conclusion was drawn that from late 1943, the operations of the GAF were inflexibly limited by the shortage of aviation fuel. The USSBS recorded that the bombing effort against the aircraft industry became disproportionate, because from the spring of 1944 the enemy air operations were increasingly restricted by fuel shortages. The success of the attacks on aviation fuel production had then rendered superfluous any further attacks on aircraft production.[28]

The heavy attacks over the last three months of 1944 on the steel industry in the Ruhr reduced its output by 80 per cent. Even though steel production continued to fall even lower from Jan 45 onwards, this was not itself a cause of the decline in finished armament production. The sustained attacks on transportation, beginning in Sep 44, were the single most important factor in the ultimate collapse of the German war economy.

Between Aug and Dec 44, freight wagon loadings fell by 50 per cent. The consequences were found to have first affected goods that had often been shipped in partial trainloads. These goods were finished and semi-finished manufactured items, components and perishables; many of them in transit between dispersed sections of the war production system. But the over-whelming effects were in coal transportation, which normally constituted 40 per cent of the rail traffic. Coal shipments by rail and waterways fell from 7.4 million tons in Aug 44 to 2.7 million tons in Dec 44. By Mar 45 they were scarcely sufficient even for the railways. The operation of Germany's raw material industries, her manufacturing industries and her power supply were all dependent on coal and coke. By Jan 45 the stocks were becoming exhausted and collapse was inevitable.

By the third quarter of 1944, the effects of the bombing had absorbed a substantial proportion of the war industry labour force. This amounted to an estimated 4.5 million workers, nearly 20 per cent of the available manpower. Of that number, some 2.5 million workers were involved with clearance, reconstruction and dispersal projects; 1 million were engaged in replacing civil and domestic goods lost through raids; and 1 million were producing and manning anti-aircraft weapons.

From Dec 44 onwards, all sectors of the war economy were in rapid decline. This collapse was due to the effects of the bombing offensive in combination with other factors. But statistical figures fail to show the full extent of the deterioration. Coke production had fallen to 38 per cent of normal; the supply of electricity and gas fell similarly. Railway wagon loadings in March were only 15 per cent of previous normal monthly levels. Albert Speer reported that:

The German economy is heading for an inevitable collapse within 4–6 weeks.

The British Bombing Survey Unit Report

The British Bombing Survey Unit (BBSU) eventually secured approval in Jun 45, albeit with the expectation that it would subsequently be subsumed into the British Bombing Research Mission, for which approval was even then still

---

28. Author's Note: It will be seen that a dominant consequence was the severe reduction in pilot training, with the inability of the GAF to take advantage of the production of fighter aircraft through 1944.

pending.[29] There was already a (British) Bombing Analysis Unit and that was expected to be well qualified to help the BBSU. The USSBS was already well advanced with its work; it was a much larger organisation and employed about 900 members of staff, including specialists in all fields of industry.

The BBSU was to carry out a factual investigation of the bombing offensive with the following specific Terms of Reference:

- To determine the effect on the fighting capacity of the enemy.
- The comparative efficiency of the various bombing techniques and weapons.
- The nature and success of the enemy operational air defence system.
- The accuracy of Allied bombing assessments made prior to any field investigation.

The BBSU Final Report was an appraisal of the objectives and policies within the UK and US and the subsequent economic and strategic results of the bombing offensive against Germany. For the collection of primary data the BBSU divided into nine separate Panels, each responsible for its own sub-report. In the study of German oil supplies, the BBSU joined forces with the Technical Sub-Committee on Axis Oil within the Joint Intelligence Committee, and the Oil Sub-Committee of the Combined Strategic Targets Committee. This perhaps portrays the maze of committees that were created within the Whitehall infrastructure and which remained in situ after demobilisation of the armed forces.

There are several pertinent factors about the conduct of the Survey:

- The bulk of the information about the Allied bombing was derived from contemporary German records; some assistance from senior German military and industrial staffs; and also a great deal from the USSBS that had far greater resources than the BBSU.
- It did not attempt to give an account of the fight for air supremacy, which was a determining factor in the planning and conduct of the bombing operations.
- It did not overlap with the post-war despatches of the CinCs; the Bomber Command Despatch by Sir Arthur Harris was withheld from public dissemination.[30]

The following sub-sections of this book provide an overview of specific sub-sections of the BBSU Final Report:

- The Results of the Area Offensives
- The Results of the Offensive against Oil.
- The Results of the Offensive against Transportation.

The Results of the Area Offensives
There were multiple independent factors that collectively forced the need for night bombing and the policy of area offensives. These were as follows:

---

29. Air 20/3180, Notes of a Meeting in the Air Ministry, dated 31 May 1945.
30. Bib. B28.

- The inability of the British bomber aircraft to adequately defend themselves against fighter attack, which caused unaffordable losses in daylight.
- The inability of those bomber aircraft to locate and attack point targets in bad visibility or at night, largely because of inadequate navigation equipments. It has been shown that this inability was shared with the USAAF strategic bomber forces in their daylight operations when visual target location was not available.
- Part of the Combined Bombing Offensive directive as agreed at Casablanca in January 1943 by Churchill and Roosevelt was to 'undermine the morale of the German people to the point where their capacity for armed resistance is fatally weakened.' The attacks on built-up areas associated with the war industries were consistent with this directive.
- The dispersal of enemy war production facilities as a consequence of the bombing raids made it impossible to identify or attack very small elements of production that were scattered throughout otherwise built-up areas.

The area attacks affected German war production in two ways:

- They caused losses due to actual damage to industrial plant and the destruction of products; to the interruption of utility services such as power, water, gas and telephones; and to labour shortages due to absenteeism when homes were damaged or destroyed.
- They also caused diversion of effort to the replacement of essential plant and services; and also to the provision of basic resources for the population.

Both the BBSU and the USSBS found it impossible to quantify the specific effects on war production of any single city raid from mid-1944 onwards, but a common factor was the breakdown of transportation services.[31] However, the evidence obtained by these two Survey teams was unambiguous in showing that from mid-1944 there was a levelling or reduction in actual finished quantities of armaments, tanks and other tracked vehicles and aircraft. Having considered as many measurable factors as possible within the categories of direct production and indirect production loss, the surveys reached the following conclusions about the effects of area bombing on aggregate production within the Reich:

Year	Bomb Tonnage Dropped	Annual Reich Production Lost
1942	37,826	2.5 %
1943	143,578	9.0 %
1944	254,666	17.0 %
1945 (Jan–Apr)	97,443	6.5 %

Within these figures, war production had the highest priority and suffered less than than other parts of the aggregate German economy.

31. Air 48/26: 'A Brief Study of the Effects of Area Bombing', USSBS Report No. 8, 26 Oct 1945.

It must also be noted that the aggregate production was increasing year on year until the autumn of 1944. (See Plate 8)

The BBSU conducted a unique analysis of the effects of area bombing by comparing the productivity of a group of 14 cities that were practically free from air attack with a second group of 21 cities that were heavily bombed, within a 15 calendar month period from Apr 43 to Jul 44. The 14 'control' cities were well distributed geographically in western and central Germany. The 21 'bombed' cities were a representative sample of all bombed cities. The analysis process is detailed but, for the purposes of this book, only the results are relevant.[32] Over the period that was studied, the total productivity was rising in all 35 cities. But the aggregate productivity increase in the bombed cities was some 14 per cent less than that in the other cities. This disguises some interesting factors; in the bombed cities, the proportion of war production was maintained at a reasonably steady rate against that in the unbombed cities, by diverting effort from other 'non-essential' production.

The conclusion that was drawn from the analysis was that the area attacks could not have been responsible for more than a very small part of the actual fall in overall war productivity that occurred by the early spring of 1945. However, they caused an increasing toll in casualties, housing destruction and domestic supplies; and this became an increasingly difficult problem for the German political and economic systems during 1944. For example, from data obtained by the USSBS, a very large proportion of building and construction labour and materials was being used to maintain and repair factory space that was damaged by area bombing; and also to construct new buildings for the expansion and dispersal of vulnerable elements of the war industry. This work had priority over domestic needs and there was consequently a profound deterioration in housing standards during the last two years of the war. This had a depressing effect on the morale of the population and their motivation.

Another significant effect of the area attacks was the considerable diversion of GAF fighter aircraft to the defence of the German homeland, which aircraft would otherwise have been available to support the Armies in the field. In addition, as Hitler lost confidence in Goering and the GAF, he gave increasing personal attention to anti-aircraft artillery that was perceived by some members of the German High Command as a more effective counter to the bombing raids. In fact, the proportion of overall weapons production that was allocated to air defence rose to 25–30 per cent during 1943–44, as was some 15–20 per cent of all ammunition. The flak defences used over 850,000 personnel during 1944–45, excluding German Army flak forces. In those later stages of the war, the flak personnel for home defence included a proportion of elderly men, boys and women who would not have been otherwise combat capable. The USSBS calculated that the artillery strength of the German armies could have been almost doubled if so many guns had not been used for home defence against the bombing offensive – which of course included all raids and not just area attacks. In this context, the most significant example was the German 88-mm anti-tank gun, widely used in anti-aircraft emplacements.

---

32. Air 10/3866, Ch. 16, 'The Extent to which Area Attacks lowered War Production'.

The Results of the Offensive against Oil Plants

At the end of Jan 44, the British Chiefs of Staff took the view that there was no need to make oil the first priority in the tasks for the strategic air forces. In the first week of March, the USSTAF urgently pressed for oil to be lifted to first priority above transportation targets. This was then supported by the RAF Intelligence Dept and the Director of Bombing (Operations). One of the unintended consequences of that pressure was that the attack on oil became regarded as an alternative to the attack on transportation, rather than complementary.

In retrospect, it can be seen that the strong pressure that was brought to bear by the advocates of the 'oil plan' came from the assumption that both the US and the RAF heavy bombers were capable of precision bombing. Whatever the appearance on paper of the enemy's oil system and its attraction as a target whose destruction would force a breakdown in the enemy's war effort, it should have been obvious to the Intelligence and Planning departments that such a target set was an unachievable task for those bomber forces. There is however no doubt that the efforts of the combined bomber forces against the oil targets in the months before D-Day were very successful. This was continued after D-Day until the first half of Sep, while the bomber forces were under the command of the Deputy Supreme Commander. By that time, the accepted appreciation was that German oil production had fallen to about 25 per cent of the pre-attack level, i.e. from Feb 44.

It was recognised that such a reduction could only be sustained if there were continuous attacks to undo the high priority repairs that were being made. It was now that the weather became adverse and the ability to maintain follow-up attacks was seriously handicapped.[33] In fact, the oil outputs from synthetic plants in Sep, October, Nov and December 1944 were 12 per cent, 20 per cent, 35 per cent and 30 per cent respectively of the pre-attack level.

Military Effects

From the military point of view, the effects of oil and fuel shortages must be considered in the light of the German attitudes and expectations. Army programmes of mechanisation fell far short of those that prevailed in either the British or US armies. The GAF could not have sustained large bomber fleets; indeed, they were not regarded as a primary element of the GAF. The one area where shortages of aviation fuel had most impact was GAF pilot training, from which there were serious consequences from Jun 43 when only 60–70 per cent of the required quantity of fuel was supplied. That fuel allocation continued at the same monthly level until mid-1944. This is a significant point; the production of

---

33. Air 8/1019: COS Paper A.O. (46) 1, dated 8 Mar 46: 'Oil as a Factor in the German War Effort, 1933-1945', Section XII 'The Concluding Phases of the Offensive' p. 64, Footnote (5) : In the last three months of 1944 Bomber Command carried out 38 attacks on oil targets (20 by day and 18 by night). There were (only) 7 other nights and 3 other days when weather conditions might possibly have permitted attacks but other strategic targets were taken. In the case of the 8th USAAF, oil targets were persistently attacked in October. But bad weather on 37 days in the last three months of that year resulted either in no operations being flown or scheduled attacks being abandoned. Attacks could only be mounted when there was less than 5/10ths cloud cover.

fighter aircraft through 1944 outstripped the capacity of the GAF to bring them into operation through the lack of trained pilots. Those additional fighters, including the new Me 262 jet fighters, would not have altered the eventual outcome but would certainly have caused higher losses to Allied bombers and their aircrews and may well have extended the war.

This point has very considerable significance. If the war in Europe had extended by even a further 90 days, then it would have become possible for the US to have dropped the first Atom Bomb on Berlin using USAAF B-29 bombers from a base in the UK. Had that happened, there is not a shadow of doubt that strategic bombing would then have concluded military operations in the European theatre. The subsequent political implications for the post-war occupation of Germany and Eastern Europe are outside the scope of this book.

But Germany was prepared to pit her military skills against the Allies in spite of the oil handicap – a fact which was given little weight in Allied intelligence or planning, which worked on the basis of comparison with Allied oil and fuel consumptions which were much higher. There was in fact substantial ENIGMA evidence to reveal just what the German army fuel consumptions were expected to be. That evidence came from multiple CX/MSS reports that identified 'consumption units'. Those units were expressed in cubic metres of fuel and were fixed at Army HQ level, based on an estimated consumption for one day at full operational activity.[34] It is worth emphasising that however parsimonious the fuel situation may have been at the fronts, it seemed acceptable to the enemy commanders and the troops who had never been accustomed to much better. In this context, the fuel shortages which had such impact in the North African offensive were a result of transportation problems over long supply lines, exacerbated by the British attacks on shipping from Italy.[35] There was no shortage of oil or fuel at the refineries and depots. General Kramer, the Commander of the Afrika Korps under General Rommel, vividly described that situation in the following words:

Alamein was lost before it was fought. We had not the petrol. Vast stocks of petrol and material were lying around in Italy and the Italians were supposed to bring them over, but they could not do it.[36]

Later, in the defence of Italy, General Kesselring had referred to the shortage of fuel as follows:

34. HW 14/56, CX/MSS/S/27 dated 23 Oct 42; CX/MSS/945/T12 dated 2 May 42 from Chief Quartermaster of Panzer Army; and many other CX/MSS references.
35. Author's Note: The operational use of ULTRA material had much to do with the success of these attacks. See Bib. B11: 'Behind the Battle', Ch. 3, pp. 81, 99, 102.
36. Air 10/3866, Ch. 25, p. 144.

I managed to save enough to carry out necessary movements, although the situation was tense.[37]

It was difficult to see that any General in the Allied armies would have taken such a view.

Thus, by curtailing consumption and stimulating production both from natural and synthetic sources, the oil position for the German military was broadly acceptable until after D-Day. The Germans were defeated in France before oil or fuel shortages presented serious problems at the front; the problems at the front related to the attacks on the transportation system between Western Germany and the forward battle areas. Notwithstanding the losses to stocks as the Allies reoccupied France and Belgium, Germany was able to mount the Ardennes Offensive in Dec 44. The failure of that offensive as it ground to halt lay partly in the shortages of oil and fuel at the front, arising from the decline in refinery production and the critical inability to transport supplies from depots to the operational units at the front.

Conversely, the operation of the U-boats was not adversely affected by the oil and fuel situation until Mar 45, but by then the outcome of the war was settled.

Industrial Effects

The German oil plants had initially been provided with little protection against air attack. The gravity of the situation, immediately after the 1944 spring offensive, was emphasised in a personal letter from Speer to Hitler, dated 30 June 1944.[38] In that letter, Speer insisted on the necessity of taking every possible step to protect synthetic plants and refineries. That was accepted and one element of the response was the Geilenberg Plan to disperse and reconstruct the synthetic oil industry; Hitler gave this Plan priority over all other industrial activities. The Plan called for a major decision regarding either the repair of damaged plants or the dispersal of new plants, including underground installations. In the light of multiple factors, such as the probable length of the war and the estimated requirements of the German armed forces, it was initially decided to continue with repairs to damaged plants. It was here that the Plan failed, because of the ability of the Allied bomber forces to time the oil attacks reasonably quickly after the completion of repair programmes.[39] By Sep 44, it was decided by Geilenberg that it would be necessary to adopt a dispersal and underground policy for new plants, which were then expected to come into production in Feb 45. The failure of this revised plan was due to the fact that it was set in hand too late; the German industrial machine was suffering badly and the dominant issues were the lack of transportation and skilled labour to implement the Geilenberg Plan.

There was a great deal of interdependence between different industries that relied upon derivatives of the synthetic oil plants. Attacks on these plants had serious consequences for the ammunition, fertiliser and rubber industries. For example:

---

37. Ibid., Ch. 26, p. 150.
38. Ibid., Ch. 26, p. 148.
39. Author's Note: One key factor here was the increasing availability of ULTRA evidence to show what was planned and what progress was being made with repairs to the oil refineries and depots.

- The ammunition industry was widely dispersed and had ample capacity, but was relatively weak in the supply of raw materials – notably nitric acid and toluene. The attacks on oil fortuitously deprived the ammunition industry of much of the essential raw materials. One decision by the Germans was to divert nitrogen supplies from fertiliser production to munitions, but this was progressively handicapped by transportation shortages.
- The effect on the reduction in fertilisers had a significant impact on the 1944 harvest, which was some 22 per cent less than expected.
- The five synthetic nitrogen plants also made the process gas required for the production of 20 per cent of the synthetic oil.
- It was established that hydrogen from the Leuna plant was used in the manufacture of half of the rubber products.

The USSBS authorities were highly critical of the 'Allied military intelligence' for the failure to appreciate that the synthetic oil plants were the keystone to many of the chemical industries. This dependence was seldom noted in the minutes of either the Oil Sub-Committee or the main CSTC meetings. The real point however is that the German chemical industry could have been a more fruitful target for strategic bombing.

However, it should not be forgotten that the German industrial machine was primarily powered by coal and derivatives such as coke and gas. Those raw materials were delivered to the point of use by rail or waterways and thus had a critical dependence on mass transportation. The generation of electricity was heavily dependent on coal-fired power stations.

The Results of the Offensive against Transportation

Transportation in various ways had been bombed throughout the war by Bomber Command and then by the Combined Bombing Offensive from the middle of 1943. However, until after D-Day, the overall transportation target set was massive following the German occupation of most of Europe. That changed with the preparations for D-Day when attacks were focussed against the French and Belgian railway systems that served the eastern routes from Germany and the northern routes towards the Channel; combined with other attacks on the German railway that served routes towards the west. The German waterways were also high on the list of specific targets in the CSTC Transportation Plan that was produced in Oct 44. The three main targets being the Dortmund-Ems Canal; the Minden Aqueduct; and the ship-lift at the junction of the Mittelland Canal and the Elbe.

The extent to which the essential war industries in the west became paralysed was illustrated in a German report dated Jan 45, which stated that the deliveries of coal and coke had fallen to less than one tenth of normal supplies.[40] Moreover, deliveries into and products despatched from the region had fallen to 5 per cent of the August 1944 level, which was itself well below normal. But not even this fraction of products was reaching the intended destinations because rail conditions and general information communications were so disrupted that consignments could not be traced.

---

40. From the Ludwigshafen-Mannheim administrative region of the Ministry of Armaments.

Another important by-product of the attacks on transportation was the impact on the building industry, which was enormously important to maintain the war production and to implement the dispersal plans. Building materials were an early casualty of the transportation crisis. With each new raid on a rail centre, the need for repairs increased and the prospect of making those repairs diminished.

The catastrophic fall in wagon allocations, the equally disastrous increase in turn-around times, the congestion of rolling stock arising from the destruction of marshalling centres, the blocking of through routes and the elimination of regulating equipment and telecommunications had, from the last quarter of 1944, brought Germany into a crisis from which there was no escape. By Mar 45, the wagon supply in the Reichsbahn had fallen to one eighth of the level for the previous July. The Russian advances from the east only compounded that crisis.

> The remarkable fact as seen by the British and the US surveys was that all these effects of the attacks on transportation and their by-products were given so little attention within Whitehall.

The Intelligence and Planning staffs, the CSTC and the MEW in Whitehall, seemed to have little appreciation of the magnitude of the impact that was taking place on the ground.[41]

The BBSU concluded that in the light of the railway data that had become available for their study, it was difficult to avoid the fact that even the one-day all-out bombing effort against transportation under Operation CLARION was akin to 'shutting the door after the horse had bolted'. By the time CLARION was approved and implemented, on 22 Feb 45, the aggregate damage to transportation within the Ruhr was so advanced that the movement of coal from the Ruhr had fallen to one third of normal levels. There were grave doubts within the German High Command that the Reichsbahn could satisfy even the minimal requirements of the Army.

Another feature of the target selection for air attack, after the handover of command back to the CAS and USSTAF, was the priority allocated to ordnance depots. The CSTC had determined that ordnance and ammunition factories should have priority above transportation. Even as late as 4 Apr 45, the CSTC was arguing against transportation and debating an 'ordnance plan'. Before this was settled, a small party of observers was despatched from Whitehall to investigate the effects on the ground following the Allied armies advances into Germany. Those CSTC observers saw large numbers of depots, full of equipment and supplies that had

---

41. Author's Note: There is a very powerful statement in the RAF Historical Society Proceedings No. 9, dated 1991 (Bib. A15). The subject of those Proceedings was a seminar on 29 Oct 1990 entitled 'RAF/USAF Co-operation'. One of the Speakers was Lord Zuckerman who said: 'We also know that the CSTC was sitting on ULTRA intercepts which told the true story from October 1944; they had 20,000 intercepts a week which they did not have any interest in or the staff to deal with. It is now known that had we gone on hitting at those nodal centres in a concerted way, the Air Forces would have played a greater part in ending the war than in fact they did.'

been impossible to move to the front where they were badly needed because of the lack of transport. One of the reports sent back to the CSTC said:

> The effects of the bombing on transportation were everywhere directly and indirectly visible. I ascribe the failure to remove valuable equipment from the depots to the front chiefly to the disorganised state of transportation.

The Major Cause of the Transportation Crisis

The evidence was clear that in its main essentials the process of the transportation breakdown in Germany was precisely the same as that which had taken place earlier in Italy, in France and in Belgium. The destruction of rail centres was the key, as emphasised in the independent evidence provided by Dr Passauer and in the testimony of the higher Reichsbahn officials who had been questioned after the war. For example, Dr Ganzenmuller, the Deputy Director General of the Reichsbahn, stated that the capacity of the rail yards in the last few months of 1944 had fallen to 40 per cent of the normal traffic and freight; and to about 20 per cent in the spring of 1945. In addition, the inability of adjacent yards to accept diverted traffic, particularly mixed traffic, only compounded the overall crisis. The more detailed evidence that was recorded by the USSBS had the same conclusion.

Separate attacks had in many cases destroyed or damaged bridges and viaducts; and the Tactical Air Force had largely denied train movement in good visibility. The weakness of the attacks against bridges was that there were often alternative routes; and the destruction of all bridges across major rivers would have had a serious effect on the Allied advance. Hitler had instructed that such major bridges were to be blown up as the German Army retreated; well known examples are the canal bridge at Eindhoven during Operation MARKET GARDEN and the bridge at Remagen on 7 Mar 44 – the latter badly damaged by the Germans but still usable.[42] But it was the chaos introduced at nodal points in the Reichsbahn system that caused the overwhelming paralysis.

The enemy was in no doubt about this point. Indeed, in a pamphlet issued by the Chief of GAF Operations, the recommendations for air attacks on the Russian railway system were strikingly similar to plans later executed by the Allied air forces. Before the D-Day landings, General Von Rundstedt expressed the fear that rail paralysis would settle the battle in the west. Almost without exception, the senior officials running the German war economy regarded the disruption of transportation as the decisive factor in the outcome of the war. The BBSU and USSBS reached the same conclusion: that the collapse of the German transportation system that began from August 1944 was the fundamental reason for the collapse of the German war machine.

Many historians have and continue to challenge this conclusion; they argue that oil was the decisive factor. But oil did not drive the German war industry; it drove the German military machine and that depended critically on oil being delivered to the many points of military need: on the battlefields, at the airfields and at the U-boat pens. Those deliveries rested on the Transportation system and primarily on the Reichsbahn that was itself critically dependent on coal. Alfred Mierzejewski,

---

42. Bib. B30, *The Second World War*, Ch. XXIV – Crossing the Rhine, p. 357.

who draws on sources that include Nazi Party membership records and Reichsbahn internal memoranda, offers probably the only complete and independent survey of the Reichsbahn under Hitler's regime from post- World War One through to 1945.[43] His conclusion was that the collapse of the Reichsbahn and the consequent collapse of the German war industry began in earnest during October 1944 and accelerated over the following months; and that the primary raw material was coal. A brief summary is at Appendix O, 'The End of the Third Reich'.

The author observes that the complete factual picture contains the basic ingredients of coal, oil and transportation. To some extent their relative importance may be academic but neither coal nor oil had any value in the wrong place; and transportation was the sole solution to that problem.

> One fact is indisputable: the collective damage was done predominantly by the Bombing Offensive.

A compelling word on this subject can perhaps be taken from Albert Speer, Reichsminister for War Production. In Nov 44 he reported that if the decline in railway traffic continued it would result in:

a production catastrophe of decisive significance.[44]

And history was to show that his forecast was absolutely correct.

Reports by German Military and Civilian Officials
The following extracts are from interviews and reports by German officials who were well placed to observe and comment on the effects of the Allied air attacks.[45] These extracts are grouped within military and civilian staffs. There is then an overview of records and reports that concern Albert Speer, Reichsminister for War Production.

Military Reports

FIELD MARSHAL VON RUNDSTEDT
Former CinC Western Front, who said that four factors were decisive in his country's defeat:

- The tremendous Allied air superiority that paralysed movement of land forces.
- Lack of fuel for tanks and the 'few planes we still had', after the loss of the Romanian oilfields.
- Systematic destruction by the Allied air forces of rail and road transportation.
- Destruction of industrial centres and the loss of Silesia, which prevented the production of arms and ammunition.

---

43. Bib. A22, Ch. 3E, 'The End of the Third Reich, 1944–1945', pp. 158–161.
44. Bib. B30 'The Second World War', Ch. XIII - The Liberation of Western Europe, p. 179.
45. Air 40/1558 'German Assessments of Allied Bombing – 1945'.

FIELD MARSHAL KESSELRING
His view was that there were three reasons for Germany's defeat:

- Allied strategic bombing behind German lines.
- Attacks by low-flying Allied fighter aircraft.
- Terror raids against the German civilian population – he said that with regret, having been an Air Force commander.

HAUPTMANN ZIMMERMAN, CHIEF AIR WARDEN, PORT OF BREMEN
He reported that the U-boat war was severely handicapped through consistent bombing of the Bremen Assembly plants and the U-boat pens. There were only 6 instead of 12 U-boats launched from the plants owing to bomb damage and supply difficulties. According to one of the construction engineers at the Assembly plant, the bombing of U-boat works at Bremen, Hamburg and Kiel had denied Admiral Doenitz's plan to throw a 'ring of steel around the British Isles'.

Civilian Reports

PROFESSOR HOUDREMONT
Controller of the Krupps Works at Essen, which employed 50,000 men.

It was not so much the complete destruction of the plant itself that stopped or reduced output, but the paralysing effect of bombing raids on the supply systems that caused most damage to war production. I would classify the effect of the air raids as follows:

- *Bomb hits destroying installations, workshops, machines and buildings.*
- *Bombs hitting power mains, water pipes, railway bridges and canal barges, thereby cutting off supplies of power and raw materials.*
- *Loss of production hours through alerts which were very much longer that the actual raids and meant a complete standstill for several hours whilst all personnel were marshalled into shelters to keep our casualty figures very low. As a consequence of the raids, using skilled personnel for a considerable time, sometimes weeks, clearing up debris and repairing roads, buildings, roofs, etc.*
- *The necessity of transferring important parts of the plant to central and eastern Germany out of bombing range.*

DR PAUL MAULIG
Managing Director of the Steel Syndicate at Düsseldorf.
Dr Maulig stated that the German steel production had been reduced through Allied bombing from 20 million tons per year to practically nil at the beginning of 1945. According to his evidence it was mainly damage to railway and canal transportation that was responsible for the reduction in output, whereas direct hits on furnaces were only responsible for 20 per cent reduction in output. He said:

In the end we could not continue to repair railways because we needed steel for the rails and we could not produce steel because the railways did not carry the ore and coal to the furnaces.

DR ING GERHARDT VIRTZ
Mannesmann Reechrenwerke, Rath nr Düsseldorf.

His opinion was that the incidental damage stopped production, although many installations were actually destroyed. It became apparent that the rail interdiction offensive as well as the bombing of the Dortmund-Ems Canal had as much a paralysing effect on war production in the Ruhr area as did direct hits on factories.

DR KARL EUGEN SPANIER
Chief Technical Director, Ruhr-Chemie Plant, Sterkrade-Oberhausen.

One of the first and best equipped synthetic oil plants in Germany, which had produced 5000 tons of petrol from coal every month. From June to Nov 1944 the air raid damage had completely put the plant out of action; and in Jan 45 the management abandoned any hope of repairs. The huge factory became a hollow shell.

Albert Speer

The post-war interviews with Albert Speer were perhaps most illuminating in that he had had overall responsibility for war production since Feb 42. The available records are copious and there is no reason to attempt any overall summary within this book, but there is cause to provide a few highlights of his official letters written as the war progressed because of his most senior position in the German economy.[46] These letters had considerable detail on specific production outputs, which were available to and used by the post-war BBSU and USSBS surveys. The examples below relate to his wartime correspondence with Hitler; these letters were not available until after the war:

- 30 Jun 1944: A very serious problem at that time was the production and distribution of aviation fuel. In April the Luftwaffe used 165,000 tons and 175,000 tons were produced. But the production for June was only 53,000 tons.
- 20 Jul 44: Speer urged a redistribution of civilian manpower. He compared the numbers working in the war production programmes with those being used to maintain a standard of living and particularly to those working in the 'administration'. In broad terms, there were 5 million workers in the war production industries and 1.5 million in mining and iron raw materials. But there were over 3 million in 'administrative' work and 1.5 million in domestic work. Speer complained that this was disproportionate and amounted to a gigantic 'organisation' that he said was characteristic of over-rating the value of such work, with the habit of sub-dividing each facility into as many independent units as possible. That was not only a waste of manpower but also a waste of materials that were held in separate stocks for the separate armed forces. He went on to detail the gradual simplification of armament and war production and the consequential unbelievable increases in productivity. [*This resonates very clearly with his later letter dated 6 Dec 44 that is summarised below.*] But he did not spare the German armed forces from his criticisms: the Navy

---

46. Air 20/5769 'Attacks on Hydrogenation Plants – Speer Reports', 1944–45.

had more admirals than in the Great War but now has no Fleet, mainly U-boats and small ships; the Army organisation suffered from over-elaboration in the command chain; and the Luftflotte structure is incompatible with the number of aircraft and the fighting units. He did say that England had a similar 'tradition bound' problem but that the US did not. Speer directly wrote in this letter to Hitler that:

> We can only win this war if we carry out a simplification of organisation of Army units and their affiliate organisations and thus achieve the most stringent control of man-power. The Supreme Command of the Army does not have the power to carry out such measures.

- 29 Jul 44: The attacks on the hydrogenation works and refineries during the month of July again proved disastrous. In almost every case the enemy succeeded, shortly after work had been resumed, in destroying them so effectively that instead of the expected increase in production there was a decrease.[47] The letter goes on to stress the difficulties of keeping the GAF supplied with aircraft; the delivery of combat-ready aircraft fell by 50 per cent from the 1st June to the 27th July. The day before, Speer had written:

> Is it not more to the point to protect the synthetic oil plants for the moment so well with fighters that a part production at least will be possible, instead of the usual method where one knows with certainty that the air force at home as well as the Front will be ineffectual owing to a lack of petrol.

- 30 Aug 44: The last air attacks have again hit the most important chemical works heavily. Thereby the three hydrogenation works at Leuna, Brüx and Politz have been brought to a complete standstill for some weeks. As the Home Defence against air attacks promises no appreciably greater results in September as against August, chemical production in September must now be considerably lowered. Nevertheless no effort will speared to restore the chemical works so that past production, at least, can be made possible in a short time.
- 3 Oct 44: Speer criticises an order from Hitler that, by 14 Oct 44, 60,000 men would become due for call-up. He said that he could not be responsible for production if that order was implemented and that there would be a curtailment of supplies for the fighting forces. Simultaneously, 30,000 railway workers were to be called-up despite the Minister for Transport having pointed out that this will compromise the transport of munitions. Speer urged Hitler to reconsider the order. Goebbels commented to Hitler about the letter from Speer and recommended that the call-ups be deferred until replacement workers had been trained; he made an interesting additional comment:

> For the first time, the intelligent classes will be affected by the war.

---

47. Hut 3 ULTRA Highlight Reports; CX/MSS/T266/34 reported the damage to Leuna on 28 July 44.

- 5 Oct 44: The insufficient production of fuel from hydrogenation plants continues to have serious effects on the chemical industry, so essential for gunpowder and explosives where we predict the most severe problems. The employment of all fighter forces at our disposal for the protection of war production in the Ruhr has become even more vitally important since the transport situation has deteriorated so considerably. Whereas in Sep 1943 we could transport 19,900 wagons of coal daily in the Ruhr area, this fell off during the last few days to about 8,000 wagons each day. This means that after 8–12 weeks the raw material stocks within the steel and other industries will be exhausted, even though there are likely to be increasing coal dumps at the pits. Speer made a very clear recommendation to Hitler:

> *Mein Führer, There is therefore for the next month only one problem: to raise the GAF fighter force to such a height as is possible and then concentrate this fighter force for the protection of the armaments industries and the transportation system.*[48]

- 6 Dec 44: There was great concern about the mobilisation of men for the German Army and the consequential loss of skilled employees within the armament and war production industries. The policy that had been in place since Feb 42 was that skilled operators had been graded UNABKOEMMLICH (indispensable) but, notwithstanding this policy, 687,000 such workers had been drafted; in the last four months alone, 254,000 had been lost to the key industries. The immediate and drastic effects are that vital programmes such as the mineral oil industry repair and dispersal plans, the steel and coal industries and aircraft production are compromised unless these workers can be effectively screened from call-up. Coincident with this, the continuous alterations in munitions production that are being ordered by Hitler are causing very considerable delays, not least when experienced workers are being drafted. The common denominator that was exacerbating all these separate production processes was the increasing lack of adequate and reliable transportation.

There were was an interesting letter to Bormann dated 16 Sep 44. Speer was writing about the hydrogenation plants and their repair work, and in that context he referred to the construction of underground facilities particularly for aviation fuel. But he was well aware that as a consequence of the bad weather, the strategic bombing would be significantly diminished and that the GAF would need less fuel. He went on to observe that the production of fighters was ever increasing and that, with a resumption of aviation fuel production as repairs were unimpeded by air attacks, then the GAF would be able to mount stronger air defences.

The best summary might be from Alfred Mierzejewski when he argued that:[49]

> *Oil was not in fact as basic to German industry as was coal; coal distribution was utterly dependent on the railways; and it was the assault on the railway marshalling yards in particular that brought Germany to her knees.*
>
> *The real 'panacea' for strategic air power would have been the rail/coal nexus, a potentially war-winning target.*

---

48. Air 20/5769, Translation Reference FD 3353/45, Speer to Hitler, dated 5 Oct 44.
49. Bib. A19, Within the Ch. headed: 'The Allied Air Offensive', by Malcolm Smith, p. 79.

CHAPTER ELEVEN

The Final Analysis

'Among the calamities of war may be numbered the falsehoods which interest dictates and credulity encourages.'

Samuel Johnson, 11 Nov 1758

Introduction

This chapter will bring together the arguments and conclusions from the main body of the book. The two crucial issues were identified in Chapter 1 as:

1. Did Bomber Command receive the best Intelligence support?
2. How was Intelligence used to support the planning, control and implementation of the strategic bombing offensives against Germany?

Many other factors have arisen as the archive and documentary evidence has been identified and analysed. These factors have to some extent revolved around the personalities and politics within Whitehall that related to the planning and direction of the bombing offensives. There was a general lack of awareness and understanding of the economic and industrial structure of Germany, which obstructed the identication of strategic targets and their relative priorities. There was also a general lack of awareness and understanding of the operational realities that dominated the implementation of those bombing offensives.

That lack of awareness and understanding should not be misconstrued or taken out of context. The concept of strategic bombing against the war economy of an enemy was quite novel. The scale of that concept, following the rapid occupation of most of the European continent by the German armies, was massive; no-one had previously contemplated a strategic air offensive against an entire continent. The preoccupation of British political thinking and foreign policy through the 1930s had been to avoid another major conflict. Appeasement was the focus of much of the national foreign policy. Notwithstanding the work done through the 1930s by the Industrial Intelligence Centre, the Ministry of Economic Warfare was not created until the war started on 3 Sep 39.

Within the Air Ministry, the doctrinal belief in strategic bombing as a means of successfully waging war was in part predicated on the misery of trench warfare from the First World War. There was a widespread belief that 'the bomber would get through to the targets'. The perceived freedom of the air to overfly and attack the enemy was correctly identified as a major element of future warfare, but many of the essential pre-requisites had not been recognised. At the start of the war and for several years thereafter, Bomber Command was incapable of delivering the strategic bombing concept known as the Trenchard Doctrine. The courage of the aircrew was the only factor that was available. The undeniable fact stands out with crystal clarity that strategic bombing against an enemy war economy that spanned an entire continent was then an untested method of successfully waging war.

Within the scope of other factors there are significant topics that demand further attention but are beyond the reasonable scope of this book. These topics have in some cases been addressed in separate books, of which the most relevant are identified in the bibliography. They include topics such as the ethical and humanitarian arguments for bombing 'civilian' targets as distinct from 'military' targets; the specification and development of aircraft and technologies to support strategic bombing operations, navigation and target location; and most importantly, the National and Allied policies for conducting the war and determining the various strategic bombing objectives. In this context it is noted that 'War is nothing but a continuation of politics with the admixture of other means', from Clausewitz. It is therefore not surprising that the military readiness of the UK to enter into war with Germany was as poorly prepared as were the politics. There are yet further topics that are peripheral to the analysis and use of Intelligence but which point to suspicions that are identified in the Afterword to this book.

By no means least there has been a sustained flow of assorted literature, some written soon after the war ended and then through the intervening 60 years into the 21st century, which has developed and amplified various criticisms of the bombing offensives. In some cases, that literature makes judgements from the standpoint of post-war peacetime conditions and therefore can have no validity within the context of the overriding national emergency and conflict during 1939–1945. That does not in any way diminish the value of ethical or other arguments about the conduct of war, but that must be balanced against the need for national survival against the Axis threat in a Total War situation. The world has not been in a Total War situation since 1945. But there have been fundamental shifts in political, public and media sensitivities that have brought disrepute to some decisions and outcomes that took place in a far different environment. The contribution of Intelligence to the planning and conduct of those WW2 bombing offensives has been conspicuously absent from the majority of that literature. The aim of this book has been to address this deficiency.

The sections in this chapter address and summarise the following topics:

- The changing British political thinking; how did that impact on the bombing offensives and the production of the post-war bombing survey report.
- The lack of knowledge about the actual capabilities and effectiveness of the available bomber forces and their installed equipment.
- The process of evaluation and selection of the strategic economic and industrial targets.

- The emergence of power groups of people – political and military – who were dedicated to specific target sets and courses of action on the basis of inadequate factual grounds.
- The mishandling and inadequate dissemination of Intelligence material within Whitehall and the Air Ministry.

Evidence has been taken from the available official records at The National Archives; from the Harris Archives at the RAF Museum and the Bletchley Park Archives; and complemented by the bibliography, which embraces the official records and many additional archival factual sources.

Finally, there is an overview of the contribution of the Bomber Offensive to the outcome of the war.

Changing British Political Thinking

Towards the End of the War

In the latter few months of the war there was an increasing change in the thinking of the Prime Minister Mr Churchill about the effects of the bombing offensive. He wrote:[1]

I felt that the time had come to reconsider our policy of bombing industrial areas. Victory was close and we had to think ahead. If we came into control of a entirely ruined land there would be a great shortage of accommodation for ourselves and the Allies; we must see to it that our attacks do not do more harm to ourselves than they do to the enemy's immediate war effort.

In judging the contribution of strategic air power to victory it should be remembered that this was the first war in which it had been used to anything like the extent of the Combined Bombing Offensive. Lessons had to be learned from hard-won experience. The reserves of production capacity within the German industry had been seriously under-estimated prior to and for several years after the start of the war. Likewise, the great resources that Germany acquired from her occupation of many European states were also seriously under-estimated. The German people withstood a level of property damage and personal grief that went far beyond what had initially been thought possible by the British government.

The extent of the overall damage was reflected in correspondence between several of the Allied Commanders during the last months of conflict. A most relevant letter was from the Supreme Commander to Sir Arthur Harris.[2] The letter was written immediately after a visit by General Eisenhower into occupied Germany, the text of which includes:

As the Allied Armies advance into the former industrialised area of the Rhineland, they are everywhere confronted with striking evidence of the effectiveness of the

---

1. Bib. B30, *The Second World War*, Vol. VI, p. 471.
2. The Harris Archives, H55: From The Office of the Supreme Commander to Harris, dated 6 Mar 45.

bombing offensive carried on for four years by Bomber Command. The effect on the war economy of Germany has obviously been tremendous; a fact that the advancing troops are quick to appreciate and which unfailingly reminds them of the heroic work of their comrades in Bomber Command and in the USAAFs. I should like all your units to know that the sacrifices they have made are today facilitating success on all Fronts.

Much of the reporting by the Allied Press during those last few months of the war, as the Allied Armies were pressing further into Germany, paid tribute to the 'effects of the Allied artillery bombardments and the Tactical Air Force attacks'.[3] Examples of this were from Cologne and Düsseldorf, two of the many major cities of the Ruhr and the Upper Rhineland that were reduced to ruin by the Strategic Bombing over the previous three years. There was hardly any Press mention of the effects of the strategic bombing offensive and the vast destruction of the industrial capability, with the attendant benefits to the advancing Allied armies. What the Allied Press was able to see and report was the progress of the armies and the Tactical Air Force. Press reporting then, as now, can be a very tunnel-vision exercise; often with little regard to the prior circumstances that may have created the effects that are displayed immediately before the reporters' eyes. As Churchill said at that time:

At long last, our great bombing offensive was reaping its reward.

But the political leaders and some of the senior military commanders may not all have wanted to know what had been achieved. It may be that some at least were uncomfortable with what the strategic bombing had accomplished and may have regretted their personal association with the acrimony, decisions and the Directives. There was a sense of bitterness in the Note from Churchill to the Secretary of State for Air:

Why is it necessary to fly aircraft in such great numbers over London during the night? Has this any war value at all? It is a great nuisance. (Personal Minute M353/5 dated 18 Apr 45).

The answer from SofS Air was very simple:

The bombers were going to Pilsen in Czechoslovakia – about the limit of their range. They were routed over London as it was the shortest cut to the target and left the biggest margin of safety.

History shows that there was in Whitehall a very strong lobby that was anxious to distance itself from the facts and to suppress any recognition of the achievements of the Allied bomber crews and their commanders – and the

---

3. The Harris Archives, H55, ATH/DO/29N dated 1 March 1945, from Harris to Eisenhower.

ultimate price that many had paid for that overwhelming contribution to the Allied victory. The Air Council appears to have been part of that lobby.[4]

By the end of the war in Europe there was a General Election in the offing in UK; the preparation for the Potsdam Conference of the three Allied leaders was in hand; the full horrors of the Russian occupation of Eastern Europe and Poland were already beginning to unfold; as were the realities of the concentration camps. Churchill was profoundly anxious about the future for Europe and set out his deeper worries to President Truman with his first vision of 'The Iron Curtain' in his telegram of 12 May 45. He ended that telegram with the most prophetic statement:

The issue of a settlement with Russia before our strength has gone seems to me to dwarf all others.

Subsequent Historical Analyses

Much of the time in Jun 45 was devoted to party politics within the UK. For Churchill this was physically and mentally exhausting after the five and a half years of unbroken effort and stress. Throughout that pre-election period he felt that much that had been fought for was slipping away and that the hopes of an early and lasting peace were receding.[5] In that context, even the Pacific War had lesser urgency than the immediate post-war relationship with Russia. Churchill and Eden were replaced during the Potsdam Conference late in Jul 45 by Attlee and Bevin. President Truman had only recently come into office after the sad demise of President Roosevelt. Stalin had the advantage of continuity and arguably had the greater force of character and personality, albeit not handicapped by the need to speak the truth. The cost of those personality and associated priority changes among the western Allied leaders was paid by post-war citizens in Eastern Europe as the Iron Curtain descended and was to remain in place until the Berlin Wall was demolished in Nov 89. The final act in the drama of the Berlin Wall, for so long a most visible symbol of the Iron Curtain, was played out at the Brandenburg Gate when it reopened to East–West traffic.

There was extensive assembly and dis-assembly of the available information within Whitehall regarding the achievements and conduct of the strategic bombing offensives. In some cases this arose because of a lack of understanding in some Whitehall departments; in other cases, because of entrenched positions taken by some authorities and other parties; and in yet further cases, because of some personalities and their ambitions.

In a great many instances, the progressive release of wartime records into the current public domain has revealed material that was not available to the public when most of the Official Records were compiled. This is not to say that the authors of those records were unaware of such retained material but, even given that they were aware, they could not have used that material in documents that were intended to be for public readership at those earlier times. Even at the present time in 2009, there is still WW2 archival material that has not been

---

4. Air 2/9726: Minute from CAS to Secretary of State, dated 13 October 1947.
5. Bib. B30, Vol. 6, p. 528.

released either because it continues to have application in current activities or because the effort to conduct pre-release surveys has not become available. The Freedom of Information legislation has not overtaken that problem.

There is also the unexplained loss or destruction of many WW2 historical records. The storage and maintenance of such records has a cost equation and the government authorities have sometimes been cavalier with disposing of these records on cost grounds. A notable example concerned a set of records that related to some aspects of the OVERLORD operation. They dealt with manpower and casualties and had been held in the Cabinet Office Historical Section, from where they were reportedly moved in 1968 to the Ministry of Defence records. There were 164 boxes of such records. None can now be located.[6] It has been separately stated by the MoD library that a great deal of historical material was confined within a basement and subject to Health and Safety control because of asbestos contamination; if that was the case, then disposal may have become a convenient option.[7]

It is illustrative to remember that the 'Despatch on War Operations' at Bib. A1, written by CinC Bomber Command at the end of the war, was withheld from general publication by the Air Ministry. The British public was therefore denied an official report from Bomber Command until that Despatch was eventually released into the public domain in 1995, some 50 years after the war had ended. The absence of any official Air Ministry record sustained the flavour of post-war politics and left the field open to a multitude of uninformed publications, speculation and the spread of misinformation that collectively did no credit to the actual achievements of Bomber Command and its contribution to the final victory. The subsequent books by Sir Arthur Harris and Trevor Roper did not provide the general public with an official source of information. No such denial was applied to the various Army and Navy commands and offensives.

There have been extensive and prolonged academic and military analyses of the strategic bombing offensives and their impact on the outcome of WW2. If there is a single denominator in all those analyses, it is that there has been no common agreement on the actual impact of the strategic bombing offensives on the outcome of the war.

The Strategic Air Offensive against Germany, 1939–1945 by Sir Charles Webster and Dr. Noble Frankland, at Bib. A4, is the major Official History of the RAF bombing offensives but this was not published by Her Majesty's Stationery Office until 1961. There is a personal letter written by Sir Arthur Harris to Denis Richards, the author of the well-regarded and authoritative book *The Hardest Victory* (Bib. A9). An extract from that letter, written on 16 Apr 77 when Harris was recovering from a severe case of pneumonia, is as follows:[8]

---

6. Bib. A28, Ch. 15, p. 255, Footnote 1.
7. Authors Note: Telecon with MoD Library, mid-2007.
8. Richards Archives: held privately when this book was in preparation but subsequently transferred to the RAF Museum, Hendon, in conjunction with the RAF Historical Society and the author.

Use my letter as you wish. Webster seems to have little regard for facts, if truth, vide that damn silly official History of which he personally told me he knew nothing of the business but had agreed to take it on only if Frankland would co-author. F's typical junior officer's 'I know better' views were already available in the thesis he wrote for his Doctorate, i.e. Webster sold his thumbmark for a mess of pottage.

If that letter should be seen as an unjustified criticism of Webster and Frankland by Harris, then it would be reasonable to reflect on the official Air Ministry decision to withhold his 'Despatch on War Operations'. The collective criticisms and rejection within the Air Ministry and Whitehall of that Despatch were dishonourable. There may well be truth in the argument that the criticisms of the Despatch by the Air Ministry and Whitehall reflect guilt or liability in the mind of those critics and there would be little wonder that Harris may have felt bitterness about the authors of Bib. A4. That possibility should be considered in the light of the unending struggle by Webster and Frankland to secure official release of their work. Noble Frankland makes a very clear and very damaging comment in the preface to his subsequent book *History of War*:[9]

Sir Charles Webster and I had to fight a severe and prolonged offensive to secure the publication of our history on our own terms as opposed to those of officialdom. The battle was to defeat a concerted attempt to emasculate our history so that it would fit the convenience of the mandarins in the 1950s and early 1960s.

Those mandarins in Whitehall included senior members of the government establishment and air marshals who had direct involvement with the strategic bombing offensives and the surrounding politics. There were personal reputations at stake. The truth was an uncomfortable companion. Here was yet another example of Whitehall's determination to conceal the facts relating to the strategic bombing offensives.

Hardly any of the post-war and subsequent analyses have given consideration to the content and use of the signals intelligence that was available at the time. This obviously excludes the Official Histories of Intelligence and Sigint at Bib. B1, B2 and B3; but not Bib. A4. But even those Official Histories of Intelligence are open to the criticism that they have given attention to the production of signals intelligence and its availability within Whitehall and the Service Ministries, but far less attention to the availability and application of that intelligence by the Air Commanders. In the particular case of Bomber Command, there has been very little comment within those Official Histories on the signals intelligence that was made available from the Air Ministry. The absence of such comment raises the question of what was actually available, either at the time or to the historians after the war ended. This book has attempted to address that question.

It is appropriate to give recognition and comment to the publication in 1998 of the BBSU Report, with the Introduction and Preface written by the Head of the RAF Historical Branch.[10] It is emphasised that this release was some 53 years after

---

9. History of War, by Noble Frankland; preface; first published in 1998.
10. Bib. A24, Published in 1998. 'The Overall Report in Retrospect', p. xxiiv.

the end of the war. The relevance of the Introduction and Preface is in the description of the bureaucratic jungle that existed within the Whitehall structure, at the time in 1944-45, when the proposition to form the BBSU was in circulation. That bureaucratic situation was predicated on the competing interests within Whitehall and Washington with regard not only to the formulation of the strategic bombing policy, but also to the investigation of the results of that policy. Over six months were lost between May and December 1944 before the UK proposition was even put before the Prime Minister. He had a very adverse attitude when the proposition was eventually put before him and he then refused approval. One of his key objections was based on the perceived cost; as the war continued, the UK economy sank into increasing problems but across the Atlantic the US business economy was buoyant. Part of that was formed from the Lease-Lend agreement. Across the Atlantic, President Roosevelt had approved without hesitation the initiation and funding of the USSBS three months earlier. In Whitehall, the arguments, obfuscation and frustration about the nearly stillborn embryo BBSU continued unabated even until after the war in Europe had concluded. Eventually it fell to the CAS to grasp the nettle and authorise the creation of the BBSU.

One of the consequences of that delay of well over 12 months, from May 1944, was that the key players most closely associated with the BBSU came to be seen by some later historians as less than 'independent'. The Chief of Air Staff at the time was Sir Arthur Tedder, who had previously been Deputy Supreme Commander; the Scientific Adviser was Professor Solly Zuckerman; and the Head of the BBSU was Air Cdre Pelly. These three powerful players had been strongly supportive of bombing attacks against the enemy transportation services from well before D-Day. It should be noted that the Whitehall oil lobby declined to support the BBSU but did prepare a separate Final Report from the Chiefs Of Staff Technical Sub-Committee on Oil, Report AO (46) 1 dated 8 Mar 46, thereby demonstrating even after the war had ended that there was no mutual reconciliation between members of the CSTC. A summary of that report is at Appendix P.

The caution that is advanced within the 1998 release of the BBSU Report is that the three key players may have had a vested interest in shaping the Report in favour of the Allied strategic and tactical bombing attacks on the enemy Transportation System. The truth of such a situation may be impossible to resolve with the passage of time, but there is surely another yet more major concern:

> Why was it impossible within the Whitehall corridors of power to find any agreement on the creation and objectives of the BBSU?

These questions may well be far more challenging than the caution advanced in the 1998 release of the BBSU Report about the three key players. To question their motives without questioning the motives of the Whitehall bureaucracy calls for reappraisal. The very fact that they were so closely involved with the strategic bombing operations, as a major part of the overall Allied land and air operations before and after D-Day through to the end of the conflict in Europe, indicates that they were fully aware of the context of the strategic bombing offensive. They would have been far better informed than some of the Whitehall bureaucracy, who had a more limited perspective and who had political positions to defend. Further detail on the tortured progress of the BBSU through the Whitehall machinery is provided at Appendix N.

Whatever may be the truth of that situation, there are powerful factors in the 1998 release of the BBSU Report that resonate strongly with this book. In no particular order:

- The long-accepted view that the US strategic air forces' bombing in Europe was more 'precise' than that of Bomber Command has been shown to be false. This has been examined in detail within Chapter 4. The criticism and underestimation of the aggregate effects of 'area bombing' remains a serious shortcoming and has sadly been influential in the work of many subsequent historians.
- The depth of argument and the lack of consensus between the various Departments, Allied Commanders and Target Committees about the merit of different target sets and their value as strategic or tactical targets. This may well continue for as long as people have any interest in WW2, even without trying to change the facts or to rewrite history.
- The strength of feeling of those staffs within Whitehall who favoured oil as the primary target, noting the in-built bias of the CSTC towards oil; and the self-serving persistence of those feelings within the CSTC and the US EOU even after the Ardennes Offensive.
- The continuous problems for Bomber Command and also the USAAFs arising from their inadequate equipment, i.e. navigation, target identification, bomb aiming and the bombs themselves. The equipment may often have been the best available at the time, but it was inadequate to satisfy the political and military Directives. If there was fault, then the fault lay with the originators of the bombing policy in setting Directives that could not be discharged with the resources that were available. This is also strongly reflected in Chapter 4.
- The German policy of industrial dispersal as a defence against the bomber offensive had the unintended consequence of becoming increasingly dependent on transportation.

There are other topics in the 1998 release that have been clarified:

- The assessments of the German war economy and industrial productivity through the war. The early dependence on the policy of Blitzkrieg had placed no intention to support an extended war of attrition.
- Associated with this, from 1942 onwards there was increasing diversion of military resources from the battlefronts to defend the Reich against the increasing Allied bombing attacks. The 1998 release asks why this would have been necessary. That diversion was predominately fighter defence and anti-aircraft guns. The justification was that the German war industry was increasingly vulnerable to the weight of the strategic bombing offensive.
- The impact of German manpower effort that was lost as a consequence of the air raid warnings and subsequent bomb damage, presenting itself as the absence of many workers from their place of work.[11]

---

11. Bib. A24, 'The Overall Report in Retrospect' , p. xxxi.

- The RAF development of the large bombs by Barnes Wallis to secure the penetration of some of the hardened targets. Those large bombs were not developed just to compensate for inaccurate guidance systems but because the conventional HC/MC bombs were incapable of penetrating those targets.

There is one further intriguing item in the 1998 release of the BBSU Report – Hitler may not have intended to go to war in 1939 because the German industrial machine was still preparing for a future conflict that may have commenced in 1942 at the earliest.[12] It is a matter of history that the British Government declared war on Germany. That may have been a very major miscalculation by Hitler, who may well have been confident that the UK would not act on its political undertaking to support Poland. After all, the pro-appeasement policy of the Chamberlain government and other governments earlier in the 1930s would hardly have justified any German expectation of a declaration of war on behalf of a third party.

However, where there may be justified criticisms of the BBSU Report within the 1998 release, it should be remembered that the BBSU was itself born under most contentious circumstances and was seriously deprived of resources and support from other Whitehall departments. Those departments had had major involvement with the formulation of policy and target selection for the bombing offensive. In many areas of detail, the BBSU was able to take advantage of the far greater resources and support that were available from the USSBS, which had much better strength on the ground in Germany as the conflict was ending and consequently much quicker access to German personnel and industrial records.

Finally, it is noted that the interim USSBS Report was placed into the public domain at the end of October 1945. The BBSU Report was not released into the public domain until 1998. This speaks volumes about the unrecorded story of the BBSU and the surrounding bureaucratic controversy.

There was a very interesting observation by the Director of Intelligence (Ops) to the ACAS on 6 Oct 41 about the then bombing policy which was under review by CAS with regard to operations over the winter months of 1941 and into 1942. The essence of the discussion came down to dispersal or concentration of bombing effort. Much would depend on the weather and the prospect of successful target location and identification by the bomber force. But the point raised by the Director of Intelligence (Ops) relating to bombing policy was very clear:[13]

> *Today, there are too many people with a finger in the pie; too many persons and departments whose opinion must be consulted. Consequently, there is no clearly defined plan.*
>
> *There is no consensus of opinion or real concentration of effort, but merely compromise and confusion. We try to please everybody and we end up by pleasing nobody – not even ourselves.*

---

12. Ibid., p. xxx.
13. Air 20/2766, Loose Minute from D of I (O) to ACAS, dated 6 Oct 41.

A remark that was unwittingly to remain true not only as the war progressed but also in subsequent post-war analyses and histories.

Lack of Knowledge about Bomber Capabilities

'We enjoy the comfort of opinion without the discomfort of thought.'

John F Kennedy

The strategic bombing capability and the delivered performance of the RAF and USAAF bomber commands were in fact similar and one element that was generally absent was 'precision' bombing, notwithstanding that RAF Bomber Command usually operated at night and the USAAFs operated by day. The operational conditions over German targets and the available navigation and bombing aids denied anything like 'precision' bombing in all but good visual conditions and uninterrupted by enemy air defence reactions. The best that was achieved from 1943 onwards was by the specialist squadrons, such as 617 Sqn using the heavy UPKEEP, TALLBOY and GRAND SLAM bombs under visual bombing conditions. This is not to say that the typical British or American bomber crews were incapable of hitting 'precision targets'; far from it, as is so well shown in Bib. A9 between pp. 268–269 with photographic images of 'precision' bombing. But it was very much a matter of statistical chance. The dominant and incontrovertible fact is that the vast majority of strategic bombing by both British and American forces could in no way have been properly described as 'precision'.

The most credible explanation may rest with the pre-war acceptance of the Trenchard Doctrine by the Air Council within the Air Ministry. The Air Council had placed great store on the claim that strategic bombing would change the nature of warfare. It certainly did do that, but the implication was that strategic bombing would be 'precise'. This claim was discredited by the Butt Report and the later Singleton Report. The very real risk in the first years of WW2 was that Bomber Command could be dismantled. Even so, the concept of selective bombing died hard and the Air Ministry persisted in the search for a target which was at once vital to Germany and limited enough for the RAF.[14]

There was intense competition between the three Services for resources, the claim to deliver 'precision bombing' was part of the RAF's argument. Some very senior Air Force officers held firmly to the view that 'precision bombing' was a routine matter. There was no professional excuse for persisting with claims that were operationally untenable; but there may have been personal and political grounds within the hothouse of Whitehall intrigues and jealousies.

The facts were and remain that bomb aiming at the time was a very imperfect science. The speed of technical developments was so great that it is no exaggeration to have said that air strategy and tactics had changed as much in two years as naval strategy and tactics had changed in two hundred years. By the end of the war, typical bomber crews in either Air Force under medium to good

---

14. Air 41/57, Ch. 3, p. 46.

visual conditions had a 40–50 per cent probability of delivering a bomb, released at an altitude of 20,000ft, within 1000ft of the intended bomb impact point. Under non-visual conditions, as were usually the case because of haze, smoke or decoys, typical bomber crews in the 8th USAAF using radar-guided bombing techniques would do very well to achieve a CEP of even one mile from the intended bomb impact point. The USAAF statistical evidence shows just 40 per cent of bombs landing within three miles of the intended bomb impact point (see p. 133).

A very basic difference between the British and American bomber commanders as the war progressed was that the CinC Bomber Command spoke of 'area bombing' and the USAAF commanders spoke of 'precision bombing'. Area bombing came to be regarded as ineffective. That USAAF claim was first presented by General Eaker at the Casablanca Conference in Jan 43 and it was reflected throughout the Combined Bombing Offensive. Such a claim sold well within the external context of news media and encouragement of the general public within the US, where there was ambivalence to the competing needs of the European and the Pacific Fronts. What sold well within the British news media was knowledge that Bomber Command was delivering damage to the enemy that reflected the damage that was being done by the Luftwaffe, not only to British cities and civilians but also to cities and civilians on the European continent. The reality and personal grief of that threat never confronted the American public.

Evaluation and Selection of Targets

At the time of the Munich Crisis in 1938, when the German rearmament programme was well advanced, there was a view in London that the British armaments industry was more flexible and more fertile than was the German industry. This perhaps illustrates how profoundly naive was the wishful thinking of some departments within Whitehall; it is therefore no surprise that their appreciations of the German armaments industry capacity and production were so wrong. The complexity of these subjects meant that MEW needed reliable methods for economic and industrial assessments and forecasting, and a great store of accurate information. As it was, the methods did not exist and the information was not forthcoming. Despite the noble efforts of Sir Desmond Morton within the Industrial Intelligence Centre during the 1930s to deliver the organisation for economic and industrial intelligence that he had foreseen, the bottom line of the problem was that the wartime MEW lacked both suitable staff and adequate funding to undertake the immense amount of work to collect, collate and interpret the information. Perhaps no criticism should be aimed at individuals; the real criticism must rest with the government for such a lack of foresight. The problem was exacerbated after the war started because information then became much harder to collect.

The major theme that went through British estimates of German economic and industrial strength in the early and middle stages of the war was one of underestimating the reserve capacity that was available in the aggregate war production capacity of the enemy. This largely disguised the impact of the strategic bombing offensive and in turn led to incorrect assessments of the performance of RAF Bomber Command, the 8th and the 15th USAAF. German war productivity did not peak until the middle of 1944, at the point where the strategic bombing offensive was in fact taking serious toll of the enemy's aggregate war production.

The Chiefs of Staff in conjunction with the War Cabinet laid down the general strategic objectives of the Allied bombing policy. The most important single Directive was from the Casablanca Conference in Jan 43, where Churchill and Roosevelt met with their Combined Chiefs of Staff to discuss and plan the future objectives and conduct of the war. Stalin did not attend that Conference. One of the outcomes of the Conference was the Directive to the British and US Air Commanders to initiate a Combined Bombing Offensive against Germany from airfields within the United Kingdom. The Directive stated that:

> *Your Primary Objective will be the progressive destruction and dislocation of the German military, industrial and economic system, and the undermining of the morale of the German people to a point where their capacity for armed resistance is fatally weakened.*

The planned implementation of that Directive was contained in Operation POINTBLANK as issued from the TRIDENT Conference in Washington, DC, in May 1943.

On the specific subject of 'morale' the reader is invited to consider the following points. The Government had long considered itself morally freed from its initial commitment to bomb only military targets; this was a consequence of the Blitzkrieg attacks and the bombing of cities in the UK. Indeed, this was encapsulated into much earlier Bombing Directives from 9 Jul 41 onwards with the then official statement that Bomber Command should apply its main effort towards 'dislocating the German transportation system ... and destroying the morale of the civic population as a whole and of the industrial workers in particular'.[15] Critics have subsequently taken the view that 'destroying morale' was a euphemism for 'killing'. The intention was to make it difficult or impossible for industrial workers who were essential to the German war machine to remain at their places of work. The inclusion of 'morale' within the POINTBLANK Directive gave rise to arguments and questions about the 'morality' of strategic bombing. History shows that the MEW and the Political Intelligence department within Whitehall had long been competing with each other to expose the weakness of German morale and their recommendations were supported by the public and private individuals alike. There was a strong conviction in the UK that German morale was a potential source of weakness. This had become a decisive influence on the War Cabinet direction of strategic bombing and was central to the 'Trenchard Doctrine'.[16] Events were to show that the Germans were a brave, patriotic and disciplined people. They had an additional spur to continue working despite the bomb damage because the Gestapo would regard them unfavourably if they did not. Harris was later to observe 'The Germans do not have the luxury of morale'.[17]

---

15. Bib. A4: Vol. 4, pp. 135–140.
16. Air 41/57, Ch 3, pp. 48–50; by Dr Frankland, April 1951.
17. Bib.A9: h 8, pp. 85–86.

A persistent and unresolved question throughout the bombing offensive, even from 1940 but increasingly strident during 1944, was whether Oil or Transportation represented the most effective economic and industrial target set for the strategic bombing operations. The point here is that Oil had strong champions within the Whitehall 'committee culture' from pre-war days. These champions had the ear of the War Cabinet and therefore were able to exert considerable influence. This was to continue throughout the war and may well have contributed to the dominance of oil as a 'Whitehall target' throughout the bombing offensive. Those corridors of influence and power were closed to all but the residents.

In the final analyses of the post-war bombing surveys by the UK and the US teams, and also the commentaries from senior German officials, a common theme was that oil was not the most critical element from the German point of view. The most critical element that affected the German military forces and the complete war production supply chain was the shortage of transportation; and the consequent inability to supply coal and raw materials into the war industries and to deliver finished products to the military users. That aggregate product included oil and fuel as one of the 'finished products'. This historical evidence was of course unavailable during the war but it challenges the wartime judgement of the oil champions in Whitehall and Washington. The archives show that there was much evidence of the widespread chaos resulting from the attacks on transportation.

There were of course major military target sets that gained first priority from time to time, notably the U-boat bases and their industrial support facilities during peaks in the Battle of the Atlantic; the GAF fighter production industries; and of course the tactical support for the Allied armies in preparation for, during and after the Normandy landings. The policy and agreement between the UK and US at Casablanca in Jan 43 was that command of the combined bombing offensive, in preparation for that land invasion, would be assigned to the Supreme Commander in order to secure the best advantage for the OVERLORD landings. That assignment of the strategic bombing offensive, particularly the attacks on transportation in France, Belgium and West Germany, was seen in many influential quarters in Whitehall and Washington – and initially by Sir Arthur Harris – as a wasteful diversion from strategic bombing attacks on Germany. This arose in no small part through the maze of staffs and committees that were directly and indirectly concerned with the formulation of the strategic bombing policy, plans and targets.

There were again from time to time various so-called 'panacea' targets that purported to offer a quick solution but which in fact never delivered their promise. For example, the post-war bombing survey reports are very clear that ball-bearings never were a critical issue for Germany. Stocks were high enough and imports remained sufficient until the German equipment design changes had reduced the need for ball-bearings to levels that could be sustained by internal production. From examination of the records and personalities in the ball-bearing industry, the user industries and the testimony of war production officials, there is no evidence that the destruction of the ball-bearing industry would ever have had a critical effect on essential war production. This is fully documented by

Speer in interviews after the war ended.[18] It is difficult to see other than that the MEW was wrong with regard to this 'panacea' target.

In comparison with Army and Navy operations, there were fundamental differences so far as strategic bombing was concerned. For example:

- When Montgomery and Tedder undertook the battle against Rommel in the North African desert, the conflict was between military forces. Both of these British commanders had access to ULTRA material that was extremely valuable in exploiting the vulnerability both of German radio communications and their transportation services across long ranges. Churchill's decision to appoint Montgomery before the Battle of El Alamein was made on military grounds. Churchill had personal experience of military operations and command.
- When the Admiralty undertook the Battle of the Atlantic against the German U-boats, the conflict was also between military forces. The unarmed merchant shipping and the civilian crews were the target of the German attacks and the enemy objective was to strangle the UK economy; this was a part of Total War. The Admiralty had a major advantage for some periods in having the ULTRA material that provided such valuable data on the U-boat operations; but it should not be forgotten that the enemy was also reading many Allied Navy codes. The whole purpose of the British and Allied convoy system was 'transportation'. There is a very powerful record within the MEW papers that compares Allied conveyors with the German railway in terms of vital national assets.[19]

The political forces within Whitehall were not directly involved with the detailed conduct of those Army or Navy operations, other than in the allocation of resources. Those operations did not impact on the capacity of the industrial war machine of Germany; the naval blockade of Germany had no impact on supply routes by rail or road. The German Army and Navy depended on the product of the industrial war machine, but that production capability was completely outside the reach of the British and Allied armies and navies until the very end of the war in Europe as the Allied armies penetrated deeply into the German Homeland.

The strategic bombing offensive was a completely new style of conflict. There had been sporadic bursts of aerial bombing against civilian targets in the UK even back into World War 1 not least with zeppelins, but World War 2 witnessed the British, Commonwealth and US air forces directly engaging the industrial war machine of the enemy as part of the Total War. In that context, the civilian workers and their sustenance were just as much a target set as were armaments, aircraft production, oil, transportation, U-boat bases and all the other elements of the overall strategic target portfolio. This was reflected within the Directive from the Casablanca Conference that specifically identified the morale of the German people as part of the overall objective.

---

18. Bib. A4, Appendix 37, p. 389.
19. Air 40/1814: MEW Tn. 1c dated 1 Dec 42.

It may of course be argued that the Germans initiated Total War with their Blitzkrieg attacks on European cities with their civilian populations and the Blitz against UK cities.[20] At that time the UK stood alone against the Nazi military machine; Commonwealth assistance was totally dependent on the merchant navies for transportation; and the US was not then engaged. History shows very clearly that the Western Allies in the shape of Bomber Command and subsequently the 8th and 15th USAAFs progressively became able to deliver a heavier weight of munitions than did the Luftwaffe and that the effects were increasingly critical upon the German war economy and industry. To that end, the Casablanca and POINTBLANK Directives were accomplished. These bombing Directives were from the very highest level of Allied Command, namely the Allied Political leaders.

The MEW expressed its views on the importance of the many economic targets and on the bombing policy that should be pursued, at the various Target Committees and in continuous and informal contact with the Air Ministry. That coordination between the Air Ministry and MEW can be widely seen not least within the various Whitehall and Ministry target committees, their working groups and the stream of Bombing Directives. But there was virtually no direct contact between the MEW and Bomber Command. There is however an MEW paper, dated 2 Feb 42, that had the following statements:[21]

The sole merit of night bombing is that it enables large, slow and unescorted bombers to take the offensive in spite of fighter opposition and ground defences which would decimate them in daylight. It is obvious that the only targets that can be attacked effectively at night are areas, however great or small, and whatever they contain, into which it is possible to drop enough bombs to do effective damage. It is much less obvious what those targets may be.

But the better that MEW can understand the capabilities and limitations of the night bomber forces, then the less likely is it to waste time on examining impracticable projects or to exasperate the Air Ministry and Bomber Command by proposing them.

The danger is not so much that proper coordination will not be achieved between MEW and Bomber Command...but that it will be rendered impracticable and ineffective by subsequent amendments at a higher Political or Service level.

Given that very reasonable appreciation which most accurately described the capabilities of the then bomber forces, it is difficult to see how there could have

---

20. Author's Note: The Official Records show that my home city of Portsmouth was subjected to 67 German air raids between 11 Jul 40 and the end of May 44. The material damage was severe and widespread; there was not one part of the city that did not show scars and in some places complete devastation. Such were the results of nearly four years of bombing, much of it ostensibly aimed at what the enemy called the 'military installations' but which actually included purely residential suburbs and non-military areas. [These details taken from *The Smitten City: Story of Portsmouth under Blitz 1940–44'*, prepared and published by the *The Evening News*, Portsmouth at a price of 2 shillings and 6 pence].

21. Air 40/1814, 'Night Bombing as an Instrument of Economic Warfare', from MEW to the Secretary of State (Air).

been ongoing arguments and Directives to engage in 'precision bombing'. As it was, the call for 'precision bombing' had started well before 1942 and continued until the end of the war in May 45. The term 'precision' was used and abused by many individuals and committees in positions of authority during the bombing offensives. It can reflect no credit on those individuals and committees; there was no excuse; they should have known better than to plan on the basis of 'precision bombing' when the operational capability of the bomber forces – RAF and USAAF – was unable to satisfy such tasking.

Power Groups

Within the overall context of the Whitehall planning and targeting of the Bombing Offensive there were several influential power groups, each with their own ambitions and objectives but not all mutually compatible. The common denominators of those power groups included their political visibility and their access to the highest levels of decision-making; combined with an incomplete perception of the overall complexities of the strategic bombing task. Probably the most significant common denominator was that none of the power groups had responsibility for the operational conduct of the strategic bombing offensive.

The projection of specific views without the counter-balance of alternative options and the full range of facts was (and remains) a dangerous consequence of the power groups and their lobby members who populated the many Whitehall committees. The Whitehall plethora of committees and sub-committees, of advisory bodies and technical experts, aggravated rather than smoothed the path of decision making and complicated rather than clarified the definition of bombing policy. The effect was to create pre-dispositions in the minds of some senior political and military decision makers, who often chose to rely on the advice of one or other of those various committees and experts. There was much room for persuasive argument without the burden of fact.

The RAF and the USAAF had a single Supreme Commander for just six months from Mar to Sep 44. Even throughout that period prior to and after the OVERLORD landings there were multiple shifting sands of political and policy argument within both Whitehall and Washington. The difference in that period was that the Supreme Commander and his Deputy had one driving objective to secure a foothold in France from which to advance into the occupied territories. It was their responsibility to use the strategic bombers to best serve that objective. If there was spare capacity then the other strategic targets could be and were attacked.

During that period of six months or more, the proportion of Bomber Command's effort that was applied to strategic targets in Germany fell to only 30 per cent. Those targets may well have required precision attack – but Harris knew and understood that this was not possible with the bombing capability at his disposal.

> What became possible in France in good weather and at short range, during the Spring of 1944 before the D-Day invasions, did not carry into Germany in bad weather and at longer range in the face of a determined enemy air defence capability.

That was the key fact that was not appreciated by so many of the Whitehall and Air Ministry critics of the bombing offensive – and by many of the post-war historians. The MEW was not always correct in its strategic target selection. Harris was not the only commander who doubted the accuracy of some of those selections both by the MEW and later by the CSTC.

So who or what were these Power Groups? This section identifies and comments on the three significant Groups:

• Ministry of Economic Warfare,
• The Oil Lobby,
• The Directorate of Bombing Operations within the Air Ministry.

The research behind this book has been focussed primarily on the collection and use of Intelligence to support the strategic bombing offensives. That research progressively identified questions and suspicions about the use, abuse and misuse of Intelligence within these Groups. The following sub-sections provide a brief summary as part of the overall context of Intelligence and strategic bombing.

Ministry of Economic Warfare

The Government agreed before the war that the conduct of economic warfare should be in the hands of a single independent Ministry. The MEW was accordingly established on 3 Sep 39 with a Charter that covered a major part of the overall objective of the strategic bombing offensives. The wider objective outside of the MEW Charter also included military targets in the context of support to the field armies and the maritime war.

The extent of the pre-war German rearmament programme had been profoundly ignored by some departments of the Government that adhered to a policy of moderation, half-hearted measures and keeping things quiet. The IIC was a single beacon of light in that period. At the time of the Munich Crisis in 1938, when the German rearmament programme was well advanced, there was a view in Whitehall that the British armaments industry was more flexible and more fertile than the German industry. The MEW estimates from the start of the war failed to move closer to reality because they continued to suffer from a more serious limitation. MEW did not understand the nature and capability of the German economy as a platform for her war industry. Parallels may be made with a similar lack of understanding by the Chamberlain government both before and after the Munich Agreement. The MEW did not have an auspicious beginning and this may have set a tone that continued for most of the war. The relationships between MEW and the three Service Ministries were at best uneasy. This was most damaging for the Air Ministry and strategic bombing. The Admiralty and the War Office did not attack the German war economy and industry. It was a popular misconception that blockading Germany would by itself win the war just by stopping the flow of oil and essential war materials. The attempted naval blockade had been unsuccessful, primarily because of land routes into Germany through Russia, Italy and Vichy France.

By the spring of 1940 there was a serious lack of credible information on the outputs and reserve capacity of the German war industry. Whitehall continued to believe that the enemy economy was stretched from the outset. That was a false assumption based on an invalid appreciation of the German rearmament programme from 1936 onwards. During the first year of war, the MEW was persisting with optimistic estimates that Germany was rapidly coming to an oil supply crisis and that she would have to sue for peace very quickly. This persistence was based on the opinions of the early oil committees. MEW underestimated the part which any lack of raw materials and other difficulties might play in disrupting the German war effort. The position was complicated by the activities of numbers of influential but inexpert and self-appointed advisers who wished to exploit their own pet theories on the basis of what they had heard in their clubs and so forth.[22]

The major theme that went through MEW estimates of German economic and industrial strength in the early and middle stages of the war was one of underestimating the reserve capacity that was available in the aggregate war production machine.[23] The basic raw material for economic intelligence and analyses was 'a variety of conflicting reports and statistics'. For example, the first 1000-bomber raid at the end of May 42 destroyed or damaged over 250 factories; but in only some 50 of those factories did either Air Intelligence or MEW have knowledge of what was being manufactured.[24] Indeed, in the reply to CinC Bomber Command by CAS there is acknowledgement of a lack of accurate information on the factory activity and bomb damage impact of Bomber Command's operations. This has been reflected by Bennett when he recorded that the MEW was not equipped to judge either the weak points in the German economy or the effectiveness of the bombing raids; and this was to restrict the value of its advice throughout the war.[25] During the period Nov 40 to May 41, Harris was DCAS. He then saw the MEW criticisms of Bomber Command's achievements and noted the absence of any appreciation of the operational factors that mitigated against successful attacks particularly on small targets.[26] The MEW was to become an arch enemy of Harris long before he became CinC Bomber Command.

Germany had instituted trade agreements with the many occupied countries and the aggregate effect was that the inwards flow of goods and commodities across land routes and transportation began to exceed the German internal and military consumption. This largely disguised the impact of the bombing offensive and in turn led to critical and incorrect assessments of the performance of both RAF Bomber Command and the 8th USAAF. The period of greatest German war productivity was not actually reached until the middle of 1944, at the point where the bombing offensive was in fact having serious toll of the enemy's aggregate war production.

One major aspect with regard to the Bombing Offensive concerned the operational strength and production rates of enemy fighter aircraft. MEW usually

22. AIR 14/1814: An internal MEW document dated 17 Jul 42, providing a short summary of Bombing Processes.
23. Bib. B30, Vol. 6, Ch. 32, p. 471.
24. The Harris Archives, H42: DO letter from CAS to CinC Bomber Command, 27 April 1943.
25. Bib. B11, Ch. 4, p. 142.
26. Bib. A8, Ch. 6, p. 111.

accepted Air Ministry estimates of aircraft production output, but it remained the authority on subjects such as production capacity, industrial manpower, supplies of raw materials and the overall industrial picture. The truth of enemy fighter production did not begin to emerge until Air Sigint intelligence was appreciated and accepted within Whitehall.

The responsibility for the combined appreciation of Air Sigint, photographic reconnaissance, agent reports and other sources that related to the bomber offensive and to the effects of that offensive was spread widely within Whitehall. Different branches within Air Intelligence, Bomber Operations within the Air Ministry and the departments of MEW all had contribution to that responsibility and it is difficult to see if anyone had overall responsibility. The combined appreciation of that aggregate intelligence material was of massive importance to the Combined Bombing Offensive but there is no evidence that it was cohesively or routinely made available to Bomber Command.

There are many instances where the importance of transportation was identified and emphasised by members of MEW through to and including the Minister in the early months of the war and that recognition was clearly conveyed to the War Cabinet and the Air Ministry. It is apparent from later years that the earlier recognition of the value of transportation targets had become submerged under the weight of the powerful oil lobby within Whitehall. There are credible claims that MEW had disregarded ULTRA evidence during the autumn and winter of 1944/45 that established the existence of coal shortages, lack of electric power and substantial falls in industrial output.[27] That evidence had shown the whole German industrial system starting to break down by Sep 44 as a result of paralysis of the Reichsbahn and the consequent inability to move raw materials and products into and between factories and users. The extent to which the essential war industries in the west of Germany became paralysed was illustrated in a later German report dated Jan 45, which stated that the deliveries of coal and coke had fallen to less than one tenth of normal supplies. But not even this fraction of products was reaching the intended destinations because rail conditions and general information communications were so disrupted that consignments could not be traced.

Much of the original ULTRA evidence appears to be no longer available, having been destroyed either at the end of the war or as a result of subsequent archive cost savings. The remarkable fact as seen by the BBSU and the USSBS was that all these effects of the attacks on transportation and their by-products were given so little attention within Whitehall. The MEW and the CSTC seemed to have had little appreciation of the magnitude of the real impact that was taking place on the ground.

The Oil Lobby
The Oil Lobby had a major impact on the conduct of the strategic bombing offensives and upon the political relationship between the MEW and Bomber

---

27. HW 11/9, Appendix N, 'Extracts from Decrypts giving Effects of the Air Attacks on German Transportation' dated 20 Feb 1945; Bib. A20, Ch. 7, p. 147; RAF Historical Society Proceedings, No. 9, p. 66.

Command. Both the Hankey and Lloyd committees placed much weight on oil as a single immediate weakness of the entire German economy. This was to play an important part in giving oil targets primary place in the British bombing directive of Jan 41. These oil committees had the ear of the War Cabinet and therefore were able to exert considerable influence. This was to continue throughout the war as oil committees flourished and sustained the dominance of oil as a 'Whitehall target' for the duration of the strategic bombing offensives.

However, the enemy oil stocks were replenished and reinforced from acquisitions in occupied territories. By Oct 40 Germany had responded to Romanian requests and had sent initial military missions to help, which opened the door to Romanian oil resources. By Mar 41 the German oil situation was seen to be comparatively strong. The major bombing offensive by Bomber Command against synthetic oil plants in Germany had then been abandoned. The MEW Intelligence Weekly subsequently recorded that the bulk of Romanian oil stocks, some 600,000 tons, had indeed been relocated to Germany during the period Jul-Sep 41 as a safety precaution; and paid notable tribute to the tremendous feat of transportation so involved.

In Apr 42 the Prime Minister approved the formation of a new Technical Sub-Committee on Axis Oil. This became known as the Hartley Committee, which subsumed the work of the Hankey and Lloyd committees.

It is strange that there was so little appreciation of the greater dependence on coal and transportation and the most vital impact that these two ingredients had on the whole German war economy and war industry. Oil required transportation to the point of operational use in just the same way as any other military consumable. That is not to argue that the German military had a lesser need for oil products; indeed, the military had a very real and pressing need for oil products. But the military had equally pressing needs for all of the other outputs from the German war industry. As was so clearly stated by a German General late in 1944:

A tank without ammunition is no more use than a tank without fuel.

The point was well made by the Deputy Supreme Commander, Tedder, when he defined transportation as the 'common denominator' of the enemy war machine.

The German oil industry was the primary focus of effort in the development of intelligence to support target selection for the strategic bombing offensive during the second half of 1944. Sigint provided testimony that was positive and unambiguous about the crucial state of the enemy's fuel supply. On 7 Jul 44, the Air Ministry and the USSAFE set up another new working committee – the Anglo-American Oil Targets Committee. This committee was to supervise the oil offensive more scientifically and to reach quicker decisions on target priority for attack and reattack.

Very soon afterwards, the CTSC was formed to study specific target sets and to recommend priorities – but not to make policy! Noble Frankland gave a post-war impression of the CSTC, as follows:[28]

---

28. Air 41/57, Ch. 9, p. 146; by Dr Frankland, April 1951.

An international committee which is not executive can at best produce a compromise and at worst can degenerate into a propaganda platform. Most of the members were convinced advocates of the Oil Plan. The committee was jealous of protocol. When the Transport Plan threatened to extend into the strategic sphere, it was seen by the CSTC as a threat to the Oil Plan and the Deputy Supreme Commander Tedder was seen to be exceeding his authority.

A key element of the strategic bombing offensive in the Final Phase was the continuous disagreement between Whitehall and the Supreme Headquarters as to whether oil or transportation targets should have highest priority. But in the final analyses of the post-war bombing surveys by the UK and the US teams (see Chapter 10) a common theme was that oil was not the most critical element from the German point of view. The more critical element that affected the entire enemy war industry and supply chains was the progressive shortage of transportation.

The Whitehall bureaucratic and political classes were not accustomed to being challenged from outside their circles. The Army and Navy commanders conducted their operations outside of those circles and suffered no appreciable interference in their decision making and command functions. However, the MEW was part of the Whitehall class and regarded itself as in charge of strategic bombing target selection, but did not recognise or understand the operational issues. It was those operational issues that weighed critically on the daily decisions by the British and American Air Commanders on target selection for the next strategic bombing operations; their military judgement and timeliness was absolutely crucial.. Those operational issues were not and could never have been a committee function, but the committees should have made themselves fully aware in order that they reached operationally achieveable decisions.

Sir Arthur Harris had the final responsibility for UK strategic bombing operations including target selection on a night-by-night basis for 41 consecutive months. His immense task deserved the full support of the Whitehall bureaucracy but very sadly he frequently had nothing short of obstruction for no better reason than that he challenged its decisions, on grounds where it had neither responsibility nor understanding.

Directorate of Bomber Operations
The primary function and remit of Bomber Operations within the Air Ministry was to provide CAS with the necessary professional advice with regard to the bombing offensives. One absolutely key aspect of that advice would have been the best available knowledge of the effectiveness of those bombing offensives. By no means least, that also required a complete understanding of the operational and technical requirements of Bomber Command and the representation of those requirements within the Whitehall departments, not least the Ministry of Aircraft Production and the variety of specialist suppliers of equipments. Specific issues within that broad portfolio included not only bomber aircraft production, but many very important specific topics such as navigation and bomb aiming equipments; the supply of 0.5in guns for use by the bombers against enemy fighters; and the provision of improved incendiary bombs and their release mechanisms. As late as Jan 45, Harris wrote to VCAS to complain again about

'the procrastination and incredible technical incompetence' that continued to surround that latter topic.[29] These were topics where the Directorate of Bomber Operations should have been at the forefront in representing the needs of the Command within Whitehall and in the face of competing Army and Navy requirements. The evidence suggests that effort was not applied anywhere near as vigorously as was the personal ambition of the Director of Bomber Operations, after the change in 1942 from Baker to Bufton.

The accomplishments of the Bomber Operations staff in general are not in question. The outstanding and unresolved issue is the personal and professional incompatibility between Harris and Bufton. That incompatibility was expressed many times in the written records and subsequently by many other authors, but perhaps a most telling statement was that written by Harris to Portal on 14 Apr 44:

I have personally considerable regard for his ability and honesty of purpose, but in practice he has been a thorn in our side and the personification of all that is un-understanding and unhelpful in our relations with the Air Staff.

If Bufton could rid himself of his idée fixe that he could have the fun of running the bomber offensive his way while the CinC took the responsibility, it should be possible to put relations on a proper footing.[30]

The written reply from Portal to Harris on 16 Apr 44 contained the following actions that Bufton should undertake:

- He should keep in touch with the Command's needs, thought and practice, through contacts at different staff and command levels.
- He should use his knowledge to help the Command both in the Air Ministry and elsewhere.
- He should advise Portal in relation to his own higher responsibilities for the bomber offensive.

Harris replied with the statement that Bufton could not discharge those actions unless he collaborated closely with the Command Headquarters and avoided pressing his own theories on its organisation, operations and requirements without prior consultation on their merits. After this exchange of correspondence the relations eased for a while, but Bufton never visited Harris and the tensions returned soon after D-Day.

Harris was deeply suspicious of the prognostications of the MEW and believed – quite correctly – that Bomber Operations was too willing to adopt MEW target decisions without adequately representing the actual operational factors. There is little evidence to show that the Directorate of Bomber Operations was well enough informed to make those representations. An exchange of written correspondence with Bomber Command would never have been sufficient. Much has been made elsewhere of Bufton's earlier experience as a bomber pilot before he was appointed as Deputy Director Bomber Operations, but that was in 1940–41

---

29. Harris Archives, H15 dated 17 Jan 45; and Bib. A1, Appendix C, Section III, pp. 95–95.
30. Bib. A8, Ch. 13, pp. 267–268 and The Harris Archives, H83, E28.

and by 1943–44 the situation over Germany had changed substantially. Bomber Operations staff would have had to make frequent visits to the Command HQ to participate in and understand the entire working process. Such visits would have had some consequential benefit for both parties. If Portal's written assurances to Harris had been conveyed to Bufton as an order and then properly implemented and checked, the problem may have diminished. The fault here rests with Portal in not securing the compliance of Bufton to the intention that he had expressed in writing to Harris.

By the same token it is recognised that Bomber Command staff did attend some of the target committee meetings in Whitehall, but that is not the same as being integrated with the analysis of the details at a working level outside of those meetings and forming recommendations for the meetings to consider. In comparison, the USAAF was far more closely involved through the presence of the Exchange Officers within key branches of the Air Ministry – and of course the US staff at Bletchley Park who had the responsibility to select and provide high-grade intelligence directly to the US Commanders. The presence of those US Exchange Officers was entirely commendable and there can be no doubt that it helped substantially with Anglo-American air coordination. There is however another side to the story that will not have been written in any of the records and official archives. The presence of those USAAF Exchange Officers may well have led to quite unintended consequences, as follows:

- Their primary purpose was to represent the USAAF and to benefit from the experience within the Air Ministry. In that primary sense, those officers would have represented the policies and the claimed capabilities of the USAAF. There was no comparable representation by or for Bomber Command.
- The USAAF consistently claimed to be delivering 'precision bombing'. The facts about 'precision bombing' were almost completely unknown at the time to most of the various authorities, but within Whitehall there was a ready acceptance of any such claim regardless of the facts. That may well have sharpened the political distinction between Bomber Command's operations and those of the USAAF, in the minds of the largely uninformed Whitehall committees.
- The USAAF came to the table in 1942 with a conspicuous absence of air intelligence and target information data. The Air Ministry provided the USAAF with a massive amount of that information, be it correct or not, and the USAAF was sincerely grateful. That gratitude expanded as the war progressed. The Sigint information from Bletchley Park was particularly well received. A consequence of that dependency was a willingness to accept much of the assessment and appreciation work from Air Intelligence and Bomber Operations. That is no more than a human inter-personal relationship. But that would have formed another distinction between Bomber Command and the USAAF. In the mind of the Air Ministry, the USAAF may have been seen as more amenable than was Bomber Command - that then had thirty months of battle experience and was definitely not amenable to uninformed committee direction.

Even after the war ended, Bufton lost no opportunity to attack Harris when he wrote a lengthy 10-page critique on the formal Bomber Command Despatch on

War Operations that was produced under the signature of Harris.[31] That critique was largely devoted to defending the positions that had been adopted by Bomber Operations within the Air Ministry rather than constructively commenting on the Despatch. One general comment on 9 stands out as deeply contentious:

> The air war over Europe was won almost wholly by the American Strategic Bomber (including fighter) Forces; Bomber Command's contribution being small and incidental, being mainly to city attacks.

It is of course well known that the Despatch was not issued into the public domain until 1995. The internal correspondence during 1945-47 within the Air Ministry that collectively criticised and rejected the Despatch was generally self-serving and dishonourable.[32] Within the few favourable comments at that time were those from Air Vice Marshal Cochrane and Air Vice Marshal Baker, who had been respectively AOC 5 Group and a former Director of Bomber Operations; and also from Group Captain Sheen, who had become Deputy Director of Bomber Operations:

> Cochrane: 'I feel that the Despatch provides a very fair summing up of the situation and […] I should have thought it entirely suited for publication.'[33]

> Baker: 'However unpalatable some of the Marshal's (Harris) opinions may be, they deserve a niche in history, if only as providing the generations to come with an opportunity of avoiding the mistakes we made and of seeing that they do not weaken the structure which he was at such pains to build.'[34]

> Sheen: 'In general I found it to be a valuable document which, with its appendices, gives a clear and detailed picture of Bomber Command operations in the period under review.'[35]

Bufton's critique however formed the basis of a subsequent Air Staff Note on the Despatch, which was not circulated outside of the Air Minstry.[36] This Loose Minute recognised that ex-members of Bomber Command and others found the absence of a Bomber Command Despatch conspicuous amongst the many Army Despatches which had then been published. The Air Staff Note contained 8 pages and closely reflected the critique from Bufton.[37] It is surprising that over 15 months elapsed between Bufton's critique and the Air Staff Note being issued.

---

31. Air 2/9726: DO letter from Bufton to Air Cdre McEvoy, Director Staff Duties, Air Minstry,dated 10 December 1946.
32. Air 2/9726: Air Ministry and the Harris Despatch; multiple letters.
33. Ibid. CinC/DO/752 dated 5 September 1946, from HQ Transport Command.
34. Ibid. DO letter dated 10 September 1946 from Baker, then DG Personnel, to Air Cdre McEvoy, DSD, Air Ministry.
35. Air 20/5302, Loose Minute from DDBOps to ACAS(Op) dated 12 August 1946.
36. Air 2/9726, Loose Minute from Air Cdre McEvoy to VCAS, dated 22 April 1947.
37. Air Ministry (DST), C.28933, dated March 1948.

The official Air Ministry position was expressed by the CAS to the Secretary of State.[38] This 4-page Minute made several comments that illuminated the Air Council thinking, that Despatches were 'something of an anachronism' notwithstanding the statement in Parliament in August 1945 about the publication of Despatches of general interest. The Air Council held the view that Air Despatches should somehow 'balance' those published by the other Services. The Bomber Command Despatch was not required to balance any other individual despatch, even though the USAAF had published three reports on strategic bombing operations. A key reason advanced for not proceeding with the Bomber Command Despatch was that 'it contained strongly expressed criticisms of the Air Ministry.' Another reason was that the story of Bomber Command throughout the war was a single story and that to focus on the last three years would have been wrong. The Air Council held the view that it could not justify the extra work to prepare despatches that covered the periods of previous commanders in chief.

It will always remain an indelible stain on the record of the Air Ministry that no formal recognition of the achievements of Bomber Command was put before the British public immediately after the war when the need for that visibility was paramount.

Another unresolved issue regarding the relationship between Harris and Bufton is the position of the CAS Sir Charles Portal. There can be no doubt that he should have been fully aware of that unsatisfactory situation and the immense amount of valuable time that was lost in the acrimonious exchanges. It is surprising that he did nothing to effectively resolve the issue. His letter to Harris on 16 Apr 44 set out a basis for resolution but it was not actioned by Bufton. There is no evidence to adequately explain why Portal allowed the matter to remain as a major impediment to relationships between Bomber Command and the Air Ministry. But there is no doubt that any resolution of the issue was ultimately a responsibility and in the end a failure of Portal.

Handling of Signals Intelligence

The predominance of Sigint as a source of intelligence concerning not all but most subjects directly connected with political activities and military operations had not been foreseen prior to or even during much of the war. Ill-conceived notions and an ingrained attitude of mind often hampered the collation and the working-up of Sigint information. This was compounded to a very large extent by the official attitudes that impaired and often obstructed the development of new lines of intelligence investigation, on the basis of privilege and prejudice concerning 'who may do what'.[39] It was not until the beginning of 1942 that the Service Intelligence staffs in London had started to recognise and acknowledge that it was at Bletchley alone that the German high, medium and low-grade signals traffic were - and only there could be - studied together with each other. That recognition was even further impeded within some other non-military Whitehall

---

38. Ibid. Minute from CAS to Secretary of State, dated 13 October 1947.
39. Bib. B2, The Official History of British Sigint, Vol. 2, Ch. XVII. The author of this History was Frank Birch, a long established and very well respected member of the signals intelligence service before, during and after the War.

departments. The Admiralty was in the forefront of that recognition within the context of the Battle of the Atlantic.

The archives reveal with no shadow of doubt that the progressive collection, collation and appreciation of medium and low-grade air-related Sigint made massive strides during the first four years of the war. The primary agent for that improvement was the Air Section at Bletchley Park.

However, those same archives reveal that there was consistent obstruction and delay from the Air Ministry and Air Intelligence with regard to the dissemination of that information to the operational air commanders within the UK.

Some of those obstructions were overcome during the Battle of Britain, with notable reference to the RAF Y-Service and Fighter Command; but that did not include the direct release of relevant ULTRA material. Even those lessons were not carried forward. So far as Bomber Command was concerned, the first regular operationally useful Sigint product that reached the Command was the daily BMP report on night operations. Those BMP reports started the day after the first 1000-bomber raid on Cologne on the night of 31 May / 1 Jun 1942. Even thereafter there was persistent obstruction and prevarication within Air Intelligence about the creation of direct two-way contact between the Air Section and Bomber Command.[40] That did not really happen until the middle of 1943 and did not achieve full and immediate two-way information flow until the end of that year. Only then was the Air Section in a position to fully appreciate the operational needs of Bomber Command and consequently shape the BMP into a form that best suited those needs. The CIO at HQBC had expressed that recognition in his letter to the Air Section, dated 28 Mar 44. No such guidance had ever been forthcoming from Air Intelligence in London. The Air Section at Bletchley Park laboured under a chain of command that went directly to DDI 4 in Air Intelligence. There is indisputable evidence that two-way contact with Bomber Command could and should have been in place much earlier. The clear conclusion is that Bomber operations would have benefited from that information. Bomber losses would have been reduced and the effectiveness of the strategic bombing would have increased.

The BMP daily reports and other irregular reports on specific air subjects did slowly evolve into 'all-source' Sigint products, with the careful insertion of 'sanitised' information from ULTRA. The initiative for that rested squarely with the Air Section and was cautiously developed in the light of the irrefutable and obvious correlations that they were able to see between the various grades of air-related Sigint information. The Air Section was very much pushing the boundaries of its approved authority, which for so long prohibited the generation of any 'appreciation' of aggregate Sigint as distinct from the production of basic uncorrelated ingredients from separate Sigint items. Those correlations were never successfully made elsewhere, notwithstanding the formal remit of Air

---

40. Bib. B28, Ch. 8.

Intelligence in Whitehall to be the sole source of such 'appreciations'.[41] Nigel de Grey at Bletchley Park had formed the view that the Home Commands should be put on exactly the same basis as overseas commands and that they should all receive ULTRA direct from Hut 3 (see HW 14/69 AZ/228 dated 3 Mar 43).

> It is illuminating to note the quite different relationship that existed between the Air Section and the 8th USAAF. That relationship actively flourished with an open and direct two-way connection (see Chapter 8).

The single and most obvious distinction was that no such connection was allowed to exist with Bomber Command until the end of 1943 and even then was largely constrained to medium and low-grade Sigint material.

Following the Allied intelligence failure to correctly appreciate the Sigint evidence prior to the German offensive in the Ardennes late in 1944, there was a searching inquiry within Whitehall instituted by the Prime Minister. Part of that inquiry involved an analysis of the appreciation issued from Air Intelligence on 6 Dec 44.[42] Within the conclusion of that Air Sunset report was the statement:

> *Increased emphasis over the past fortnight on defence of the Reich suggests that whatever intentions the GAF may have had [...] for the original plan for the 'Lightning Blow' [...] may with some certainty be said to have lapsed [...] and that the GAF is clearly thrown back on the defensive.*

After the event GC & CS described that appreciation as 'a disaster' and pointed to the risks of relying too much on the high-grade Sigint.[43] It was dangerous to assume that even such high-grade material was ever complete, for 'it was not always possible to decrypt everything'. The Director of Military Intelligence subsequently stressed the neglect of other sources and the lack of general inquisitiveness. The ACAS (I) agreed that:[44]

> *Tactical reconnaissance, active patrolling, interrogation of prisoners of war and the like must in spite of ULTRA still remain the sure guide to enemy intentions for commanders in the field.*

This book has no remit to review the whole subject of Sigint evidence prior to the Ardennes Offensive. There is an excellent summary with Bib. B1, Chapter 52. Just to indicate to the reader the enormous range of high-grade material that was subsequently seen to have provided clues:

---

41. HW 14/74: The records of a meeting chaired by ACAS(I) on 23 Apr 43 regarding the dissemination of ULTRA to overseas Air Commanders clearly show that he continued with the policy that the Air Ministry should remain responsible for 'appreciations' of ULTRA from Hut 3 and/or other sources as was considered necessary.
42. Air Sunset 260 dated 6 Dec 44.
43. Bib. B1, Vol. 3-2, Ch. 52, p. 429.
44. Ibid.

- The U-boat commander advised his forces that their weather reports had contributed decisively to determining the start time of the great offensive in the West.
- GC&CS did NOT issue a decrypt dated 1 Dec 44 that disclosed that a course for Nazi leaders scheduled for the period 3–16 Dec had been cancelled because of an 'impending special operation'.

This does no more than demonstrate the imperative for cohesive handling and appreciation of all sources; and the shortcomings of separated departments. The concept of 'Joint' was still imperfect. The final summary stated that there was a tendency to place too much value on ULTRA and therefore to neglect all the other sources that were available; and that had been the greatest weakness in our Intelligence organisation.

The very restricted distribution of ULTRA material was always a serious problem. The preservation of the security of ULTRA was absolutely imperative and it remains amazing that the enemy, notwithstanding some suspicions, acknowledged no compromise of ENIGMA signals traffic. One consequence of the paranoid interpretation of that security was the denial of some most valuable information to some senior commanders. The Air Ministry maintained the belief that only the Air Intelligence directorate could judge what intelligence would be useful to the home air commands.[45] The question must be posed whether the Air Ministry and the Air Intelligence staffs really understood what would be useful to the home air commands and particularly to Bomber Command, which was waging a strategic economic and industrial bombing offensive the like of which had never previously been conducted.

The bombing Directives issued from the Air Ministry had usually been economical with their interpretation of the Allied COS intentions within Operation POINTBLANK. Director of Bombing (Ops) sustained unrelenting pressure for an increase in the bombing of oil targets and at the end of Sep 44 had claimed that:

Unimpeachable evidence is received daily of the very great effect which the resulting oil shortage is having upon the enemy's ability to conduct military operations.

That unimpeachable information was without question from ULTRA material.[46] Given the strength of the MEW and Air Ministry appreciations of that material, why was it not made available to Harris at Bomber Command? That failure of dissemination was culpable. The USSTAF received that ULTRA material and so did the 8th USAAF. That was a clear breach of the principle of 'Linked Routing'.

The point here is absolutely central to the extended strategic bombing policy arguments between the Air Ministry and Bomber Command. So many of the formal papers that were circulated on limited distribution within Whitehall contained information that Harris never saw.[47] We will therefore never know if

---

45. Ibid. p. 237.
46. Air 8/1018, 16 Oct 44, para. 1 and 4.
47. Air 8/1018, Examples of Strictly Limited Distribution TOP SECRET material: War Cabinet JIC Sub-Committee Reports on the Oil Position in Axis Europe: JIC (44) 247

those papers at TOP SECRET classification would have helped to clear the controversy, not least between Harris and Portal with regard to bombing policy and target priorities. Portal must have known that Harris had profound suspicions about Intelligence, based on his earlier experiences. Portal really should have taken effective action to address those suspicions and ensure that his senior Commander was fully briefed on the available intelligence evidence. He had referred to 'the irrefutable evidence of Sigint' in his correspondence at the end of 1944 with Harris. The aggregate weight of Sigint evidence may have been compelling, but Portal was unable or unwilling to personally demonstrate the case to Harris. In his letter to Harris dated 8 Jan 45, Portal had enclosed a dossier that included some ULTRA material; the archive records do not reveal what that material was.[48] It is important to note that in his reply to Portal, Harris recorded that he had not seen those items before – see H84, ATH/DO/4 dated 18 Jan 45 – which were returned to Portal under the cover of that same letter. That does not just mean that Harris should have routinely seen just the Intelligence appreciations, compiled by MEW and the Air Ministry; he should also have seen the original ULTRA material on which those appreciations were based. That ULTRA material was directly derived from information that the enemy had generated; it had no Whitehall flavour that Harris could or should have suspected.

> We will never know how much damage was done by the non-disclosure of that ULTRA material to the Air Commander who had most need for that information.

In the end there is an unavoidable fact that continues to have resonance into the 21st century. Within the context of Western democracy and the associated high-level chains of command leading from prime ministers and presidents, as it was then and as it remains today, no military offensive will have ultimate success if the prevailing political leadership and will is lost. The planning and conduct of a military operation – be that large or small – has a certain momentum. The political will and implicit approval may shift without warning on the basis of a change of personality or expediency. The shadow of that doom chases every current and planned operation. It may happen in an instant as a consequence of a decision taken or not taken many miles away from the combat theatre.

General Aspects of the Strategic Air War

It is conceivable that Germany could have snatched victory on more than one occasion during the war, but she was potentially beaten from the moment that the series of Blitzkriegs came to an end in 1941.

The UK progressively developed a strategic bomber force whose powers of destruction at the end of the war in Europe were unequalled. The US developed

---

(C) Final dated 12 Jun 44; JIC (44) 218 (O) (Final) dated 27 May 44; JIC (44) 320 (O) (Final) dated 24 Jul 44; JIC (44) 403 (O) (Final) dated 18 Sep 44.

48. The Harris Archives, H84 dated 8 Jan 45: Portal to Harris, p. 5.

a complementary bomber and escort fighter force that was eventually capable of operating at will in daylight across all of Germany. Germany had progressively been forced into the development of an air defence system and a defensive fighter force that in the end was unable to protect the industrial war machine.

Although it is clear that the paralysis of her Transportation system and the destruction of her synthetic oil plants were major factors in Germany's defeat, these factors cannot be taken alone to imply either that strategic bombing won the war or alternatively that Germany would not have been defeated if there had been no strategic bomber offensive.[49] Those who have seen the oil and the transportation plans as contradictory have ignored the fact that the oil offensive robbed Germany of her road and air mobility and the associated military operations; just as the transportation offensive robbed her of the railway mobility. It was the latter mobility that proved most important because Wehrmacht troops, armoured units, the bulk of their logistic support and the shipment of bulk supplies such as food, coal, oil fuels and ammunition all depended on the railways and the inland waterways.

Economic paralysis was an inescapable consequence of the destruction of the Transportation infrastructure. The Allied landings into France and the progressive reoccupation of the German occupied territories across Western Europe would still have been bitterly opposed by Germany, but the output of the enemy war industries would have been inexorably reduced from the start of 1944 if the Allies had given more attention to transportation targets.[50] This point had been acknowledged even as early as 1941 when it was reported that:

Transport might indeed prove to be one of the weakest links in the German economic chain.[51]

The compelling fact is that the strategic bombing offensive made Operation OVERLORD and the subsequent advances into Germany possible and ultimately paved the way for an Allied victory.

The cost of building and running RAF Bomber Command was no more than 7 per cent of the British national war effort.[52] The proportion accounted for by the British Army was eight times as much. The effort that was devoted to the Army was seen to have far less risk than that allocated to the strategic bombing offensive. In this context, the bombing offensive was substantially unsupported by recognised facts and the decisions were swayed more frequently by argument and speculation than by a cold appreciation of the realities. The strategic air war may yet have failed because of these limitations in direction, intelligence and planning. When the political and personal cross-currents within Whitehall that obscured the presentation of intelligence and the elaboration of policy and plans during the war were surveyed after the war, there was clearly seen to have been room for considerable improvement. The lack of precision in the Bombing

---

49. Bib. B1, Ch. 29, p. 168.
50. Ibid., p. 169.
51. Air 41/57, Ch. 3, p. 47, Footnote (1) – JP(41)444, p. 19.
52. Bib. A14, Part 2, Ch. 7, p. 34.

Directives made them an adequate cloak for a variety of conflicting interpretations and decisions. Sir Arthur Harris had written:

> *The natural result was a multiplicity of Directives embodying one change of plan after another and so cautiously worded at the end with so many provisos and such wide conditions that the authors were in effect guarded against any and every outcome of the orders issued.*[53]

There was also a serious criticism addressed to the Intelligence that became available to the air forces. The BBSU reported that Intelligence weaknesses were due to the methods that were used by Political, Military and Intelligence staffs in appreciating that information. Appreciations were often coloured by pre-conceived ideas or by wishful thinking. The most important shortcoming of those appreciations was related to the German economic and war production capacity and the associated selection of strategic bombing targets. However accurate those intelligence appreciations may or may not have been with regard to specific targets, they were basically responsible – either by commission or omission – for the Allied failure to recognise the over-riding strength and potential reserves of the German war production capacity. The BBSU reported that the gravity of that error was so fundamental as to be impossible to understand.[54] That report went on to say that:

> *But unless a way could be found to secure the best available staffs to undertake such appreciations, then the UK would never avoid the situation where rhetoric and debating skills remain a more dominant factor than analysis and judgement in reaching future strategic air policy and plans. It is therefore essential to remember that the determination of operational policies is vastly more complicated than any after-the-event historical analyses can represent.*

It was most apparent that if war was to recur at some later time, then the promise that was implicit within air power must be better directed. But there was no assumption that air power would hold any overwhelming advantage in all situations. The dominant issues would remain as:

- The acquisition and appreciation of intelligence to determine and locate the key targets,
- The accuracy of finding and attacking those targets,
- The appropriate selection of munitions to achieve the required effect on the targets,
- The availability of air superiority at the time when the targets are attacked.

Contribution of the Bomber Offensive to the War

The initial attacks on the enemy's oil supplies and transportation systems in 1940–41 were as much a failure as the offensives in 1944–45 against the same targets sets were outstanding successes. The early bombing attacks on German

---

53. Harris, 'Bomber Offensive', p. 215.
54. Air 10/3866, Ch. 29, p. 170.

industrial cities reveal themselves as inconclusive in so far as the enemy war production was concerned, notwithstanding the powerful emotional boost that they provided to the British people as retaliation against the German bombing attacks on British cities.

The ultimate breakdown of the German war industry was mainly a result of the dislocation of her transportation system; combined with the significant reduction in the availability and distribution of liquid fuel and chemicals from the oil plants. But it was concluded that any analysis of the effects of strategic bombing against either one of those target sets in isolation would have been unreal. For example, the damage that was done to the transportation system prior to D-Day was a major contribution to the successful landings in Normandy and the subsequent breakout across France towards Germany; but the parallel attacks on oil handicapped the German land and air mobility in response to those Allied land advances. By no means least, one consequence of those land advances was the progressive reduction in the German early warning system of radar and signals intercept stations located in France. Coincident with this reduction in early warning, the Allied deployment of air navigation systems and Y-stations further forward towards the Line of Battle provided deeper radar and signals coverage into German territory for the benefit of the combined bomber forces.

From German records, it was concluded that the attacks on oil through the autumn of 1944 – which had such high visibility and political pressure within Whitehall - would have been largely buffered by the execution of the Geilenberg programme of repairs and dispersal.[55] This programme was however itself defeated by the industrial chaos that resulted from the bomb damage to the transportation services. That damage was often a consequence of 'area damage' as distinct from 'precision' attacks, by both of the major bomber commands. There was a further report written after the war by the Technical Sub-Committee on Axis Oil: this report is briefly summarised in Appendix P but has an interesting and perhaps surprising final statement, at page 86 in the original report:

> It can therefore be concluded that the German national economy was so attuned to operate on a minimum of oil that the eventual depriving of such quantities as were allocated for non-military use did not directly contribute to Germany's final collapse. Thus the results of the bombing offensive against oil were almost exclusively military in their effects upon German resistance.

The serious disruption of the steel industry in the Ruhr through the winter of 1944 and spring of 1945 came about largely as a result of the area damage to such vital utility services as water, electric power and gas; and to the transport of basic raw materials. The more intense and widely distributed the damage to the transportation system, the more wholesale and dispersed was its effect on the enemy war industry and military activity.

The attacks on the aircraft industry largely failed to decrease production output through 1943 and until mid-1944. The enemy's ability not only to sustain but also increase production in the face of these attacks was a direct consequence of the

---

55. Air 10/3866, Ch. 28, p. 162.

massive organisational improvements inspired by Speer and his principal colleagues. Indeed, if it had not been for the scale of bombing attacks and their actual effectiveness, then the operational strength of German fighter aircraft would have been dramatically higher with consequential increases in losses of Allied bombers. A pressing problem for the GAF from the middle of 1943 was the shortage of aircrew training capacity and aviation fuel.

There is a powerful comment about the unpredictable impact of the weather across Germany, noting the operational limitations of the navigation and bomb aiming systems that were available to the RAF and the USAAF bombers. They were often unable to deliver precision attacks on specific targets at specific times. The weight of attacks on some targets was in fact excessive but understood to be taking best advantage of the fleeting opportunities. One important reason for such apparent over-bombing was the lack of good intelligence about bomb damage assessment and the sometimes contradictory appreciations of the intelligence that was available.

The major conclusions of the BBSU may be seen as follows:

- In a highly integrated industrial economy such as Germany had, with great reserves of capacity, the effects of damage to or destruction of point target systems such as airframe assembly plants could be readily neutralised if the main economic structure of the country remained healthy. That general health depended on the labour supply, capital equipment and raw materials; together with the transportation and prime power supplies to weld them together. The bombing offensive hardly affected the first two of these factors; the key vulnerability of the third factor was the capacity of the transportation system to move raw materials to the place of work. The overall enemy war effort would have been equally threatened if it had been possible to deny the availability of prime power supplies; but this was correctly assessed to be operationally difficult or even impossible. It was therefore assessed that the transportation system with its all-pervasive sphere of influence represented the single most valuable target system.
- Until it was crippled, German skill and reserve industrial capacity was able either to make good damage to almost any point target system or to identify and implement an alternative design and production route. But once the dislocation of the transportation system had precipitated a widespread industrial collapse, the attacks on specific point targets were bound to be increasingly fruitful. In that context, it was seen to be highly significant that one of the main lessons drawn by the USSBS in their study of the Pacific War was that the attack on transportation would have been far more effective in destroying Japan's economic structure than was the elimination of individual cities and factories.

It is instructive to recognise that the Russians, still our allies until after the end of WW2, regarded the strategic bombing offensive as 'The Second Front'. The western armies and navies had nothing to offer. This had compelling and potentially overwhelming political weight. There was no other means of delivering a 'Second Front' during those absolutely critical years of 1941–43, when the Russians were holding back the German invasion. Had that invasion been successful, or had Stalin sued for peace with Hitler before the outcome of Stalingrad was clear, how would the conduct of WW2 then progressed. The strategic bombing offensive may be seen through many points of view, but this is one of the most critical and yet one of the most unrecognised.

Equally critical yet unrecognised is the impact of the strategic bombing offensive on the defeat of the German war economy. This was a unique and previously untested offensive. Without the sustained strategic bombing offensive against the German war industry, the war in Europe may well have lasted longer. The German war economy would probably have delivered the means to sustain the land armies and the air forces on both Fronts. In that event, the first Atom bomb might well have been used over Berlin rather than over Hiroshima.

Looking into the multiple aggregate achievements of the strategic bombing offensive, the following key elements are also indisputable:

- The delays to the new Type XXI ocean-going and XXIII home waters U-boat programmes which would have otherwise have entered into the Battle of the Atlantic and the Channel early in 1944, with potentially significant impact on Atlantic convoys that were delivering the build-up of resources for Operation OVERLORD.
- The delays in the V-1 programme which could otherwise have caused havoc among the assembling troops, ships and landing craft along the south coast of England during the spring of 1944.
- The massive reduction in the scale of the V-2 programme which if unhindered would have caused devastation in London and south east England.
- The crippling of the railway network between west Germany and the Channel coast which obstructed the free movement of German Army reinforcements to repel the Allied Normandy landings.
- The Allied air superiority for the Normandy landings and the subsequent advance into the occupied territories.
- The diversion of one million German servicemen, reserves and their weapons engaged on the air defence of the Reich which would otherwise have been available for the land forces on the Western and Eastern Fronts.

A very fair summary was provided within a signal from the CAS to CinC Bomber Command, in which Sir Charles Portal stated:[56]

The progress of the Allied Armies across Germany brings to light every day how fatally the German war machine has been weakened by the devastating blows of the Strategic Bomber Forces against industrial and military targets.

Bomber Command was the pioneer of the Strategic Bomber Offensive and all formations and units are deserving of the highest praise for the part they have taken with our American allies in bringing it to a successful conclusion.

56. Air 20/3246: Air Ministry Telegram IMMEDIATE A.34 16 Apr 45, released at 161549B.
57. Bib. B30, Vol. .5, Ch. 29, p. 469

After the war the Prime Minister wrote of the British and American bomber aircrews that:

> *They never flinched or failed. It is to their devotion that in no small measure we owe our victory. Let us salute them.*[57]

The strategic bombing offensive began with small operations by Bomber Command in 1939 and became a massive combined UK/US offensive from the autumn of 1942 until the end of the war in Europe. It made an invaluable contribution to the successful outcome of the war. But those achievements, the personal effort of so many people and the heavy price of operational aircrew losses were sacrificed by the devastating impact of the loss of political support for that strategic bombing offensive in the final phase through the spring of 1945.

Political sensitivities in the UK and the US had then recoiled from the human cost of that bombing offensive within the prevailing Total War situation. That Total War situation was precipitated by Hitler with the Blitzkrieg offensives but was sustained by British and US political decisions made in the face of the Axis threat to Western and World democracy. It must never be forgotten that the fundamental and most honourable political decision by the British Prime Minister Mr Chamberlain was to declare war on 3 Sep 1939 against Germany in response to her attack on Poland.

Afterword

The Introduction to the final chapter mentioned several topics that demand further attention but are beyond the reasonable scope of a book devoted to Signals Intelligence and its use. These topics have in some cases been addressed in separate books, of which the most relevant are identified in the bibliography. They include topics such as the ethical and humanitarian arguments for bombing 'civilian' targets as distinct from 'military' targets; the specification and development of aircraft and technologies to support strategic bombing operations, navigation and target location; and most importantly, the National and Allied policies for conducting the war and determining the various objectives.

In the opinion of this author, based on his extensive reading of the archives and bibliography, there was a power group within the Air Ministry and Whitehall that had the covert purpose to remove Sir Arthur Harris from his position as CinC of Bomber Command. During the early phases of the war, Sir Arthur Harris held two appointments where the various failings of Intelligence and the MEW estimates would have been very visible to him. From Sep 1939 to Nov 1940, he was Air Officer Commanding No. 5 Group within Bomber Command; and, perhaps more importantly, from Nov 40 to May 41 he was Deputy Chief of Air Staff. The memory of those early intelligence and estimation failures and their operational consequences, largely predicated on the inadequacies of the then Air Intelligence capability and the infant MEW economic intelligence, may have remained with Harris as the war developed.

It would seem from the aggregate archival and bibliographical material that there were those within Government and the Air Ministry who resented the close relationship between Churchill and Harris that arose in part as a result of the proximity between their residences at Chequers and Springfield respectively. That personal relationship was mutually beneficial for several years through 1942–44 but it diminished towards the end of 1944. It clearly cut across the conventional lines of command; it may have placed Portal in an awkward position and was noted by other members of the Air Ministry. Bufton observed after the war that 'it gave Harris some backing for his private war of city bashing'.[1] Such a comment clearly ignored the War Cabinet and official bombing directives that required 'area bombing'. However, that comment from Bufton also disclosed his failure both to appreciate the full facts surrounding the strategic bombing offensive and his own animosity towards Harris.

---

1. Bib. A26, Ch. 9, p. 384.

There were others who harboured a deep resentment against Harris, who commanded such admiration and respect among his officers, airmen and airwomen.[2] He had inevitably tangled with some of the War Cabinet and Labour Party's leading members – not least with Attlee who became Prime Minister in 1945. Long after the war in 1960 when Attlee had publicly criticised the strategic bombing offensive, the response from Harris was to observe only that the bombing offensive objectives had been decided by the War Cabinet of which Attlee had been a leading member.

After the results of the combined Bomber Command and 8th USAAF raids on Dresden during 12–14 Feb 45 had become common knowledge there was rapid covering action by many of the senior politicians and some military commanders on both sides of the Atlantic to escape public association with the formal Directive to mount the attack. Fingers of blame were immediately pointed at Harris but strangely not at the USAAF Commanders who authorised the associated daylight raids. It should be remembered that Dresden was second on the Whitehall list of priority city targets for attack at that point in time. Churchill himself later wrote that infamous Note dated 28 Mar 45 in which he spoke of 'bombing simply for the sake of increasing the terror' and made direct reference to the Foreign Secretary Mr Eden who had the view that there should be 'more precise concentration upon military targets'. That Note was withdrawn and replaced on 1 Apr 45 with a second Note that called for 'a review of the so-called area bombing of German cities'. That policy itself also had the approval of the War Cabinet.

Within the various levels of Whitehall 'committee management' of the strategic bombing offensive there were several departments and individuals who rejected combined bombing target plans other than those prepared by themselves. The Director of Bomber Operations, the MEW and the CSTC were at the forefront from the UK side; the USSTAF and the Enemy Objectives Unit from the US side; and the Supreme HQ staff that also had their ideas. Each thought their own plan was best and challenged or dismissed others. There was a strong vein of self-interest present in the Allied hierarchy. Churchill himself earlier in the war had condemned the RAF Air Staff for their 'jealousies and cliquism'.

The appointment as CinC Bomber Command was a prize that several might have aspired to: the analogy of Caesar and the Senate may be drawn to Sir Arthur Harris and the Air Ministry – and within the Ides of March (1944?). It may be considered that the overt and covert criticisms of Harris were in part an attempt to create a situation where he would have resigned or would have been relieved of command. The fact that neither Churchill, who had previously relieved from command both General Wavell in Jun 41 and General Auchinleck in Aug 42, nor Portal took that step is an indication that they both saw no better officer than Sir Arthur Harris for the massive task at Bomber Command.

In themselves these topics are peripheral to the analysis of Intelligence and therefore fall outside the scope of the core research behind this book. But they may have relevance to the use, abuse and misuse of Intelligence by various departments and individuals within Whitehall. This being so, this author currently proposes to address these topics in continuing research leading perhaps to a future book.

John Stubbington

2. The reader's attention is drawn to Appendix R, which offers a comparison with the scandal related to the sacking of Sir Hugh Dowding from Fighter Command after the successful outcome of the Battle of Britain.

Bombing Targets for 1942 – MEW

The attached details are from Air 40/1814, a revised list for Wg Cdr Morley, Bomber Operations 1, from the MEW, dated 7 Oct 42.

Area Targets

On economic grounds there are no targets to compare with the Ruhr for this type of attack, since it was without parallel as a heavy industry centre and is of absolutely vital importance to the German war effort despite efforts to develop alternative capacity elsewhere. This whole area also has a continuous urban development.

Priority	1	2	3	4	5	6	7
Target	Essen	Duisburg	Bochum	Dortmund	Düsseldorf	Köln	Wuppertal

Specific and Semi-Specific Targets

1. Industrial Targets (Specific targets).

- Electric Power targets, in the Ruhr–Rhineland areas.
- Synthetic Rubber Plants.
- Special Components for Aircraft, Armaments and Engineering.
- Oil Targets.
- Alumina Plants.
- Alkali Plants.

2. Cities and Towns (Semi-Specific targets).

Within the approximate radius of effective bombing there are 15 cities with a population of 250,000 and over; and 25 cities with a population of 100,000 and over. A large proportion of both classes form part of the conglomeration of the Ruhr–Rhineland. They contain a high percentage of industry of great importance to the enemy's war effort. Particular importance is attached to those cities and towns where a high proportion of the population is engaged in some specialist activity, since it is assessed that in such cases that there is some certainty that heavy damage will affect either the industrial plants or the supporting urban areas.

A preliminary classification of the comparative importance of the 15 large cities of western and central Germany is as follows:

Priority	1	2	3	4	5
Target	Stuttgart, Hanover	Duisburg, Essen, Gelsenkirchen, Bochum, Dortmund, Düsseldorf	Frankfurt, Mannheim-Ludwigshaven	Köln-Mülheim, Magdeburg, Wuppertal	Hamburg, Bremen

The low priority accorded to Hamburg and Bremen derives from the fact that, apart from shipbuilding, the majority of their manufacturing had depended on imports from overseas in peacetime.

Of the 25 smaller cities and towns, a number may be eliminated as of minor economic importance. A preliminary grading of the remainder is as follows:

Priority	1	2	3
Target	Kassel, Kiel	Brunswick, Krefeld, Remscheid, Oberhausen, Hagen, Wilhelmshaven	Rostock, Karlsruhe, Aachen, Solingen, Saarbrücken, Lübeck

Analysis of Priority Targets

Of the industrial targets of first economic priority, it is suggested that electric power targets are not suitable for night attack. The synthetic rubber plant at Schkopau has attracted higher value since the successful attack on Hüls. Some of the 'special components' targets are likely to be severely affected by attacks on the towns where they are situated, apart from any damage to the factories themselves. The Bosch (electrical accessories and injection pumps) and VDM (propeller) factories at Stuttgart and Frankfurt would not be affected in the same way owing to the much larger size of the city. The Philips works at Eindhoven is in occupied territory and special consideration must be given to minimise civilian casualties and collateral damage; a daylight attack would be more suitable.

The economic value of attacking the synthetic oil plants is greatly reduced until or unless successful attacks can be made on the Romanian oil fields at Ploesti. It would be tactically difficult, even impossible, to inflict decisive losses on the

German oil supply through attacks on these synthetic oil plants alone; they therefore should have at least temporarily a low priority.

Damage to the alumina plants would need to be inflicted by a direct attack; their activity would probably not be affected by an area attack. The effects of attacks on the three German plants would probably take some time to 'work through' to alumium plants unless complementary attacks were mounted on the large plants in southern France and Italy, which are out of range.

Examples of RAF Y-Service Sigint against KG 40/ Fw 200 Operations

References: Brit Int., Vol. 1, Ch. 10, p. 330; Air 40/2322, p. 6; HW 14/43 Z/MSS 6 dd 17 Jul 42.

RAF Y-Service Records

RAF Y-Service records have the following selected Sigint details for KG = Kampfgeschwader:

- IKG 40 Based at Trondheim; Attacks Russian convoys and operates armed recce to Iceland:
  - Search band 5/6000 and 8/10,000 kc/s.
  - Sends spoof, e.g. IAR N8 LW = Time & No. of groups; does not give QSL to spoof.
  - Aircraft use 3-symbol c/s; Ground Station uses 4-symbol with last letter low in alphabet.
- IIKG 40 Based at Bordeaux; Covered Western Approaches and shipping:
  - Search band 5/6000 k/cs and 7/9000 k/cs.
  - Sends Vs half hourly on both bands but c/s are different on both bands, e.g. Vs on 8610 = KRC; Vs on 5330 = MLD.
  - Aircraft often use the last symbol of c/s as a contact, e.g. LRC, using C as contact letter.
- V KG 40 Based at Lorient: Attacks aircraft hunting for submarines, etc:
  - Also known as ZKG 40, Z being short for *Zerstorer* (Destroyer);
  - Sends Vs half-hourly; Ground Station uses aircraft c/s.
  - 3-symbol c/s for aircraft.

Z/MSS 6

Refer back to Chapter 5, 'Battle of the Atlantic'. This specific summary report dated 17 Jul 42 contained a great deal of supporting evidence, mostly from

CX/MSS sources. The convoy operations against targets off the French, Spanish and Portuguese coasts had declined substantially during the first five months of 1942. This was related in part to the increase in co-coordinated operations against Arctic convoys and U-boat attacks on shipping off the American east coast. The first reinforcement of Fliegerfuhrer Atlantik (Flf. Atk) was in May 42 when two Gruppen of Ju 88s were withdrawn from operations against Malta and transferred to Brittany. From early Jun 42 a series of evening or night attacks were made against coastal convoys along the Channel west of the Isle of Wight. This may have been a reprisal for the first '1000-bomber raid' on Cologne on the night of 30/31 May. However, during Apr–Jun 42 there had been growing evidence of an intended resumption of co-ordinated operations against Gibraltar convoys. Part of that evidence came from agents in Gibraltar who were known to be reporting convoy sailing times.

SALU Reports
The following extracts from GC&CS 'SALU' reports were partly based on CX/MSS material (ULTRA). Extensive records of the SALU reports are in The National Archives, in the HW 3-series.

1. *CX/MSS/SALU West No. 810, dated 27 May 43.*
Summary of GAF Offensive Bomber, Recce and Coastal Operations: 16–22 May 43.
Luftflotte 3 – Fliegerfuhrer Atlantik; III KG 40 and II KG 40 (Bordeaux and Cognac)

After a period of 10 days during which there were only 2 sorties with weak forces, a dawn sortie was made on 17 May during which SS *Arundel Castle* was sighted, but not attacked, at 48.08N, 16.45W. The following day 4 aircraft operated during the afternoon and landed around midnight, probably carrying out an armed recce against *Arundel Castle*. Six aircraft carried out an uneventful recce on the 19th and the following day there were no operations.

Reports of concentrations of British shipping were probably responsible for a recce carried out on the 21st by 6 aircraft. The approximate area covered was a triangle with the apex being the north-westerly point of Spain and the base line 38N/17W to 36.45N/14.30W. The aircraft took off so that this southernmost line was reached by 17.00 hrs. No shipping was reported.

The only attack by Fw 200s during the week occurred on the 22nd when two aircraft of the 7th Staffel alone operated. The attack was made at about 17.30 hrs 15 miles WSW of Cape St Vincent on the SS *Alpers* which had been towed out of Lisbon and was on the way to join Convoy SL129. The ship was abandoned in a sinking condition shortly afterwards.

2. *CX/MSS/SALU West No. 812, dated 9 Jun 43.*
Summary of GAF Offensive Bomber, Recce and Coastal Operations: 30 May–5 Jun 43.

a. Luftflotte 3 – Fliegerfuhrer Atlantik; III KG 40 and 2 KG 40 (Bordeaux and Cognac).

Operations were resumed after a lapse of 4 days on 30 May with 6 aircraft of the K Staffel. At 10.17 HMS *Trent* escorting convoy KX10 reported being attacked by one aircraft at 37.36N/9.17W; no damage resulted. At 11.00 two Fw 200s attacked a small convoy of 3 ships and 2 escorts; the SS *Llancarvon* was sunk.

Five or six aircraft operated again on the 1 Jun, 4 from the 'A' Staffel. The homeward- bound Convoy MKF15 was located at 20.30; the sighting aircraft stating that conditions were unfavourable for an attack. On 2 Jun no effort was apparently made to re-locate MKF15, which reported being sighted by a Ju 88 at 08.00 that day. Two Fw 200s were active during the day but their task and area of operation are unknown.

b. Luftflotte 5 – Fliegerfuhrer Northwest; 1/F 120 (Stavanger).

The identified activities of this unit were a night flight off the East Scottish coast; a day recce over the Orkneys on the 30 May; and a message from one aircraft on 5 Jun to the effect that 'task was not carried out owing to weather'.

3. *CX/MSS/SALU West No. 837 dated 1 Dec 43.*
Summary of GAF Offensive Bomber, Recce and Coastal Operations: 21/27 Nov 43.
Luftflotte 3 – Fliegerfuhrer Atlantik; III KG 40 and 2 KG 40 – Atlantic Recce.

There were four convoy operations during the week, and the first two attacks by He 177 Greif aircraft.

1. The first attack was on Convoy MKS30/SL139 on 21 Nov. This convoy had been shadowed from 14 to 19 Nov and had been the target of an abortive U-boat attack between 18 to 20 Nov. The attack followed the usual pattern: a recce force over the target area by first light; a relief shadower; and finally the attack. The main point is that the relief shadower failed to carry out the mission and as a result only half the attacking force found the target.

   The initial recce force was five Fw 200s and one Ju 290 Seeadler; on the morning of 20 Nov, two Fw 200s had failed to locate the convoy and a Ju 290 that was to act as shadower in the evening was shot down. The attack developed in two phases, first by 3 aircraft, almost certainly He 177s but reported by the convoy as Fw 200s. The main attack took place 60–90 minutes later; 8 aircraft were counted. Another ship, not with the convoy, was shadowed by the relief Ju 290 and attacked by a single He 177. Apparently 27 He 177s were part of the operation and about 20 or more were heard on W/T.

   Ju 88s of 15/KG 40 were airborne from Bordeaux during the period of the outward flight of the He 177s, either to escort or provide protective sweeps. At the same time, Ju 88s, probably from Lorient, were held at readiness to scramble against any British attempt to intercept the returning He 177s.

   Two escort ships were attacked and missed; two merchant ships damaged, of which one was abandoned; and one escort ship was attacked by two Hs 293s, both of which were shot down. The Hs 293 was an air-launched anti-ship guided missile. There is no reliable evidence that any of the German aircraft were lost.

2. The second attack took place on 26 Nov against a convoy off the North African coast. The convoy reported about 30 aircraft; 22 unit markings and about 12 factory markings were heard. Glider bombs were launched exclusively at the escort ships but scored no hits. Torpedoes were launched against the merchant ships and several ships were sunk. The convoy claimed 4 He 177s, 2 Fw 200s and 2 unidentified destroyed. During landing, the aircraft were warned of a crash on the runway at Cognac. The W/T traffic offered little evidence to confirm or deny the claimed aircraft losses. The W/T callsign procedure and a reference to aircraft markings suggest that the aircraft were from II/KG 40.

3. Recce was conducted against two other convoys for the benefit of U-boats. A southbound convoy, KMS33 was the target between 22 and 24 Nov; the convoy was not attacked because the reported position from the aircraft was 2 degrees North of the actual convoy position. The U-boat command issued two statements that the convoy was presumed to have passed further to the west.

4. On 26 Nov recce for the next northbound convoy began. MKS31 was sighted by a Ju 290 and on 27 Nov by Fw 200s in the morning; and then by a BV 222 Wiking that sighted the convoy in the evening and sent beacon signals on which the U-boats took bearings. By means of these beacon signals, the U-boat command plotted the position and course of the convoy for the benefit of the U-boats.

4. *CX/MSS/SALU West No. 838 dated 9 Dec 43.*
Summary of GAF Offensive Bomber, Recce and Coastal Operations: 28 Nov–4 Dec 43.

a. Luftflotte 3 – Fliegerfuhrer Atlantik; Atlantic Recce.

Recce for the northbound convoy MKS31 was broken off after sightings on 26–27 Nov, the convoy having evaded the U-boats by taking a course closer to the Spanish coast than usual.

The next series of recce operations lasted from 29 Nov to 1 Dec against the southbound convoy KMS34. Fw 200s and Ju 290s took part; the main convoy was never sighted except possibly by one Fw 200, which was shot down by a carrier-borne Martlet before it had sent a sighting report. This recce was abandoned after 1 Dec.

On 4 Dec a new series of recce operations began against a slow-moving westbound convoy on the North Atlantic route to America. Advantage was taken of the long range of these recce aircraft, but the convoy was not sighted having been routed well to the north.

b. Luftflotte 5 – Fliegerfuhrer Northwest and Lofoten.

The usual coastal patrols, escorts and patrols against blockade-runners were carried out.[1] On 2 and 3 Dec the two commands reacted to the Russian convoys

---

1. Author's Note: In this context, the term 'blockade runner' relates to German shipping seeking to evade the Royal Navy blockade of ports used by the enemy; the air recce was for the direct benefit of those ships.

to the extent of 8 BV 138 flying boats, 6 Fw 200s and 3 He 115s. There were no significant sightings reported by W/T.

5. *CX/MSS/SALU West No. 841 dated 29 Dec 43.*
Summary of GAF Offensive Bomber, Recce and Coastal Operations: 19–25 Dec 43.

a. Luftflotte 3 – Fliegerfuhrer Atlantik; Atlantic Recce.

A new series of convoy recces began on 19 Dec against the southbound convoy KMS36 and the northbound MKS33. Operations on 19 Dec were cancelled; and on 20–21 Dec produced no sightings.

It is not clear at exactly what point convoy recce ceased and recce for blockade runners began all the units of Flf. Atlantik began to work on a set of common fixed frequencies from 18 Dec. This very considerable simplification of W/T procedure may have been for the convenience of the German Navy shore listening stations or the blockade-runners who listened to the air recce channels. Air recce continued to be co-ordinated with U-boat patrol lines, but after 21 Dec there was no further mention of air recce in connection with U-boats.

b. Luftflotte 5 – Fliegerfuhrer Northwest and Lofoten.

Recce for the Russian convoys, the presence of which was first established by the German Y-Service, was to have been started on 19 Dec but was delayed until 22 Dec by the adverse weather. From that date, Fw 200s of I/KG 40, BV 138s of 2/F 130 from Trondheim and BV 138s of F 130 from Tromsö carried out daily recces against the convoy and the Battle Group, also detected by the Y-Service as approaching from the southwest. The convoy was sighted and the results of this operation are too well known to need further comment.[2]

---

2. Author's Note: The Battle of North Cape. These air recce operations by 1/KG 40 and 2/ 130, and the Sigint operations by the German Y-Service, were in direct support of the German Navy Operation OSTFRONT, to intercept the Allied Arctic convoy JW55B bound for Russia. The convoy consisted of 19 cargo ships supported by eight destroyers and a minesweeper. Five of the destroyers were from the RN and three from the RCN. On 23 Dec, the German battle cruiser *Scharnhorst* left Alta Fjord with five destroyers to intercept the convoy. Also in the area was convoy RA55A returning to the UK from Russia, escorted by eight destroyers and a minesweeper. The Royal Navy had two Battle Groups in the area: Force 1 (commanded by Rear Admiral Burnett) comprised three RN cruisers, one of which was HMS *Belfast* – much later to be restored and placed on permanent display to the public on the Thames. Force 2 (commanded by Admiral Sir Bruce Fraser) consisted of the battleship HMS *Duke of York*, the cruiser HMS *Jamaica* and five destroyers. The ensuing naval action, The Battle of North Cape, led to the sinking on 26 Dec of *Scharnhorst* and the loss of all but 36 of her crew of 1,968.

Established Officer Strength of the Air Intelligence Directorate

	Air Cdre	Gp Capt	Wg Cdr	Sqn Ldr	Flt Lt	Fg Off	Plt Off	CO	Total
Feb 1940									
D of I: Major Boyle									1
DDI 1		1		2	3	6		1	13
Retired Officers									7
DDI 2		1	1	3	1	1		1	8
Retired Officers									3
DDI 3		1	2	2	1	6	1	1	14
Retired Officers									4
DDI 4		1							1
Map Branch									3
Total									**54**
May 1941									
D of I (Sec) *	1								1
DDI (Org) **		2	3	8	3	36	88	3	143
D of I (Ops)	1								1
DDI 1			2	2		6	15		25
DDI 2		1		2	3	4	8	1	19
DDI 3			1	2	2	10	12	2	29
DDI 4			1	5		1	10		17
DD AAC/FL	1 ***		2		6	6	11		26
ADI Maps									7
ADI Photo			1			1	1		3
Total									**271**

* See Table in main text; DDI (Sec) not yet formed
** Note the very large numbers of new junior officers
*** Air Cdre Boyle, ex Major Boyle D of I in Feb 40

	Air Cdre	Gp Capt	Wg Cdr	Sqn Ldr	Flt Lt	Fg Off	Plt Off	CO	Total
May 1942									
D of I (Sec) *		4	2	7	14	27	16	4	74
D of I (Ops)		1							1
DDI 1				1	3	9	1		14
DDI 2			1	1	6	18	12	1	39
DDI 3			1	4	8	29	19	3	64
DDI 4		1	1		1	5	9		17
DD AAC/FL	1		3	4	6	8	9		31
ADI Photo		1	1	1		2	3		8
ADI Science									3
Total									**251**

* D of I (Sec) covers DDI (Org) and DDI (Sec)

	Air Cdre	Gp Capt	Wg Cdr	Sqn Ldr	Flt Lt	Fg Off	Plt Off	CO	Total
November 1942									
D of I (Sec)		1							1
DDI (Org)		1	1	2	10	24	13	4	55
DDI (Sec)		1	1	3	12	6	10	1	34
D of I (Ops)		1		2	5	7	2		17
DDI 2		1	1	1	11	12	16	1	43
DDI 3			2	4	16	25	25	1	73
ADI Photo		1		2		3	2		8
DD AAC/FL		1	4	4	11	5	9		34
DDI 4		1	1		4	4	12		22
ADI Science									4
Total									**291**

	Air Cdre	Gp Capt	Wg Cdr	Sqn Ldr	Flt Lt	Fg Off	Plt Off	CO	Total
March 1943									
DDI (Org)		2	6	8	33	18	19	5	91
D of I (Sec)		2	3	8	9	9	4	1	36
D of I (Ops)		1	2	4	12	7			26
DDI 2		1	3	8	26	8	6	1	53
DDI 3		1	8	18	29	21	16	2	95
DD AAC/FL		1	5	10	13	5	1		35
DDI 4		1	3	4	7	7	7		29
Totals									**365**

	Air Cdre	Gp Capt	Wg Cdr	Sqn Ldr	Flt Lt	Fg Off	Plt Off	CO	Total
November 1943									
ACAS (I) staff			2	2		1			5
D of I (Sec)	1								1
DDI (Org)		3	4	9	38	20	9	6	89
DDI (Sec)		3	2	9	14	6	2	1	37
D of I (Ops)	1		1	1	4				7
DDI 2		1	4	12	24	13	5	1	60

	Air Cdre	Gp Capt	Wg Cdr	Sqn Ldr	Flt Lt	Fg Off	Plt Off	CO	Total
DDI 3		1	8	16	39	29	8	2	103
ADI Photo		1		3	4	1	3		12
ADI (K)			1	6	15		1		23
DD AAC/FL	1	1	4	11	19	3	0	0	39
DDI 4		1	2	2	7	11	3		26
ADI Science									6
Totals									**408**
October 1944									
ACAS (I) staff	1			2	2				5
D of I (Sec)	1	2	4	10	20	7	4	1	52
DDI (Org)		4	6	16	45	25	15	5	116
D of I (Ops)	1		1	1	4		1		8
DDI 3		1	8	17	45	32	14	1	116
ADI Photo		1		3	4	2			10
ADI (K)			1	7	17	1	1		27
D of I (R)		1							1
DDI 2		1	5	13	23	15	8		65
DDI 4		1	3	4	8	3	1		20
DD AAC/FL	1	1	3	13	19	2			39
Totals									**459**
January 1945									
ACAS (I) staff				2	2				4
D of I (Sec)	1								1
DDI (Org)		4	4	18	43	17	17	5	108
DDI (Sec)		2	3	10	20	8	2		45
D of I (Ops)	1		1	1	4		1		8
DDI 3		1	7	17	47	26	14		112
ADI Photo				3	4	3			10
ADI (K)				1	7	18	2		28
D of I (R)	1								1
DDI 2		1	5	9	26	12	7		59
DDI 4		1	3	4	9	7	2		26
DD AAC/FL *									
ADI Science									10
Totals									**412**

* DD AAC/FL not listed within ACAS (I) in the Jan 45 Air Force List

Notes
1. Sqn Ldr includes Squadron Leader and Squadron Officer (WRAF).
2. Flt Lt includes Flight Lieutenant and Flight Officer (WRAF).
3. Fg Off includes Flying Officer and Section Officer (WRAF).
4. Plt Off includes Pilot Officer and Assistant Section Officer (WRAF).
5. CO includes Higher Clerical Officer and Clerical Officer.
6. AAC/FL is (Directorate of) Allied Air Co-Operation and Foreign Liaison.

Air Intelligence Organisation – 14 January 1941

Directorate of Intelligence

DDI 1

AI 1
Receipt, record & Dissemination of Int. matters. Admin of Clerical staff for D of I unit. Air Attaches.

AI 1 (a)
Int. personnel & censorship; Int. Establishment.
D of I Unit Admin.
Printing of Int. Handbooks & Weekly Int. Summaries.
Receipt & distribution of S & C publications within D of I.

AI 1 (c)
Liaison duties

AI 1 (d)
Liaison duties

AI 1 (f)
Foreign liaison

AI 1 (k)
Interrogation of PoWs.

AI 1 (t)
Translation section

DDI 2

AI 2 (b)
Air Int. of Russia, Sweden, Finland, Iran, Afghanistan & NW Frontier.

AI 2 (c)
Air Int. of Japan & China, French Indo-China, Thailand, Netherlands East Indies, Macao & Timor.

AI 2 (d)
Air Int. of the Americas.

AI 1 (g)
Technical Int. liaison with MAP.

AI 1 (s)
Internal security.

AI 1 (z)
Postal & Telegraphic censorship.

DDI 3

AI 3
Co-ordination of Work.
Liaison with Admiralty & War Office.
Appreciations & Summaries.

AI 3 (a)
Combined Int. Committee.
Anti-invasion, politics & strategic Int.
Eire & N Ireland.
Enemy propaganda.
Airborne troops & gliders.
GAF Personalities & German press.

AI 3 (b)
GAF Order of Battle. Technical liaison with AI 1 (g).
Order of Battle of French, Spanish, Portuguese, Romanian, Swiss & Hungarian Air Forces.
PoW reports. Investigation of captured maps.
Targets in UK. Collation of W/T call signs.

AI 3 (c)
Aircraft industries.
Assessment of Air Raid damage & issue of summaries.
GAF aircraft strength, production & general info.
Recording claims of enemy losses.
Targets on land; Transportation; Recording of shipping losses.

AI 3 (d)
Recording, studying & distribution of info concerning aerodromes in Germany, Norway, Denmark, Holland, France, Spain, Portugal, Switzerland.

ADI

AI 1 (b)
Air Ministry Weekly Bulletin

AI 1 (w)
Intelligence War Room

Inter-Services Topographical Section

Joint Intelligence Sub-Committee member

DDI 4

AI 4 (a)
Air Int. of Italy, Greece, Yugoslavia, Bulgaria.
Italian Order of Battle.

AI 4 (b)
Air Int. of Turkey, Syria, Egypt, Sudan, Arabian Peninsula, Palestine & Iraq.

ADI Maps

Liaison with Geographical section, General Staff, War Office. Preparation of maps & sketches. Map & Chart Library.

Miscellaneous

Air Advisor to MEW.

MI 9

AI 9
Target maps

AI 10
Interdepartmental liaison.

Instructors for Intelligence Courses.

Air Intelligence Organisation – July 1942

Assistant Chief of Air Staff (Intelligence) [Sheet 1 of 2 >>]

Director of Intelligence (Security)

Director of Intelligence (Operations) (cont on Sheet 2)

DDI (Org)

AI. 1
Air attaches, RAF Missions, Printing & Distribution of Int. Handbooks, Summaries & Papers. Censor stamps, Control of Clerical Staff.

AI. 1(a)
ACAS (I) Admin & Establishments

AI. 1(a)(P/W)
Liaison with MI 9, Allied POW intelligence

** AI. 1(c)
Liaison Duties.
Has direct access to ACAS (I)

AI. 1(p)
RAF & WAAF Int. personnel Selection Boards. Home & Overseas Language study.

AI. 1(T)
Translation section

Air Warfare Analysis section

Intelligence School

DDI (Security)

AI. S.1
Security Advice & Coordinator

AI. S.1(a)
Individual security records, Loss of S&C documents

AI. S.1(b)
Security questions in connection with:
(a) Aviation other than RAF,
(b) Civilian companies,
(c) Official Air Mails,
(d) Issue of Official docs outside RAF

AI. S.1(c)
Co-ord of Home & Overseas security

AI. S.1(d)
Policy regarding prevention of Sabotage. Security measures at Protected places & Prohibited areas.
Security of Photographs, Commercial drawings & Publications sent overseas.
Censorship policy.
Closing of Roads.
Passports & Exit Permits

AI. S.2
Security Education Policy & Preparation of material.

AI. S.3
Policy regarding release of Technical information, State of Security records, Security R.T.I Committee

AI. S.(7)
Liaison Duties
(Has direct access to D of I (S))

AI. S.4
Operational security & inter-Service Security Board. Liaison Duties.

AI. S.8
Postal & Telegraphic censorship & Port Liaison.

DDI 2

AI. 2(a)
Aircraft industries

AI. 2(b)
Aerodromes

AI. 2(c)
Liaison with MEW and MAP.

AI. 2(g)
Armaments, Chemical warfare, Navigation equipment, Oxygen apparatus, Salvage, Life Saving gear. Signals & Electrical equipment, radio-nav aids. Heating & De-Icing. Parachute Troop equipment. Production of CD 131.

DDI 3

AI. 3(a)
Distribution of Teleprinter Int. & FO telegrams.
Selection, précis & allocation of General Int. to ACAS(I), DDI 3 & Int. sections.
Political & Strategic Int.
Gen assistance to AI (JIS)

AI. 3(b)
Air Forces of Germany, Italy, France, Spain, Portugal, Bulgaria, Rumania, Hungary.
General Int. on Ireland, Spitzbergen, Iceland, Greenland.
Liaison with RAF N Ireland, AA Dublin.
Current Enemy Air Ops.
Forecast of Future Intentions & Scales of Attack

AI. 3(c)
Target Intelligence.
Enemy aircraft losses.
Assessment of Air Raid damage.
Fuel intelligence.

AI. 3(d)
Middle East Air Forces.
Russian, Finnish, Swedish, Japanese, Chinese, Thailand, Netherlands, East Indies & French-Indochina Air Forces.

AI. 3(e)
GAF Intelligence.
PoW intelligence.
Research & Recording of Past Campaigns & Operations.

AI. 3 (USA)
USA & South American Air Forces

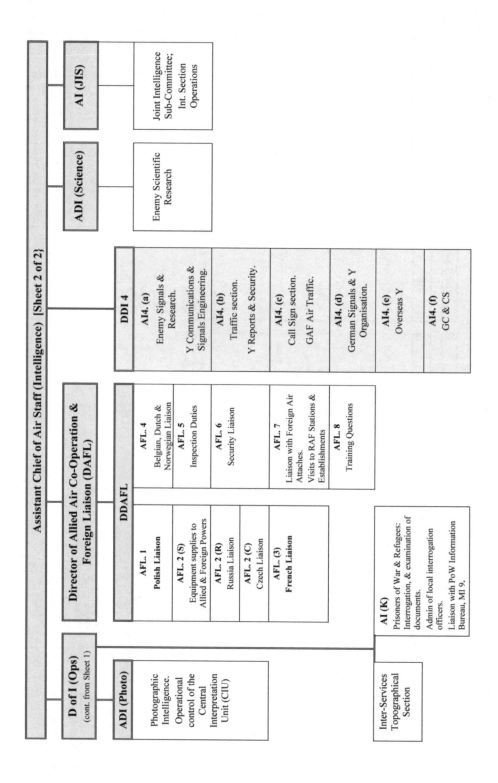

Assistant Chief of Air Staff (Intelligence) [Sheet 2 of 2]

D of I (Ops)
(cont. from Sheet 1)

ADI (Photo)

Photographic Intelligence. Operational control of the Central Interpretation Unit (CIU)

Inter-Services Topographical Section

AI (K)

Prisoners of War & Refugees: Interrogation, & examination of documents.
Admin of local interrogation officers.
Liaison with PoW Information Bureau, MI 9.

Director of Allied Air Co-Operation & Foreign Liaison (DAFL)

DDAFL

AFL. 1
Polish Liaison

AFL. 2 (S)
Equipment supplies to Allied & Foreign Powers

AFL. 2 (R)
Russia Liaison

AFL. 2 (C)
Czech Liaison

AFL. (3)
French Liaison

AFL. 4
Belgian, Dutch & Norwegian Liaison

AFL. 5
Inspection Duties

AFL. 6
Security Liaison

AFL. 7
Liaison with Foreign Air Attaches.
Visits to RAF Stations & Establishments

AFL. 8
Training Questions

DDI 4

AI4. (a)
Enemy Signals & Research.
Y Communications & Signals Engineering.

AI4. (b)
Traffic section.
Y Reports & Security.

AI4. (c)
Call Sign section.
GAF Air Traffic.

AI4. (d)
German Signals & Y Organisation.

AI4. (e)
Overseas Y

AI4. (f)
GC & CS

ADI (Science)

Enemy Scientific Research

AI (JIS)

Joint Intelligence Sub-Committee;
Int. Section Operations

Air Intelligence Organisation – April 1944

Assistant Chief of Air Staff (Intelligence) [Sheet 1 of 2]

Director of Intelligence (Security)

Director of Intelligence (Operations) (cont on Sheet 2)

DDI (Org)	DDI (Security)		DDI 3	
AI. 1 * Air attaches, RAF Missions, Printing & Distribution of Int. Handbooks, Summaries & Papers.	**AI. S.1** Security Advice, Coordination, Organisation & Liaison. Representation at the Security Executive	**AI. S.2** Security Education Policy & Preparation of material.	**AI. 3(a) 1** Distribution of Information. Liaison with Government offices, Service departments and RAF Commands. Preparation of Daily Summaries.	**AI 3(d)** Order of Battle of the Japanese air forces; estimates of their scales of attack & forecasts of future intentions. All other int & research on JAF regarding past campaigns & operations.
AI. 1(a) ACAS(I) Admin & Establishments	**AI. S.1(a)** Security relating to individuals. Individual security records, Loss of S&C documents	**AI. S.3** Policy regarding release of Technical information, State of Security Records, Security R.T.I Committee.	**AI. 3(a) 2** Editing of A.M.W.I.S. Politics & Strategic Int. Preparation of Appreciations & Collation of information from Specialist sections. Preparation of Daily Summaries of general Int. General assistance to and liaison with other Govt Depts & the BBC.	**AI 3(e)** Organisation of GAF other than Order of Battle. GAF Transportation & Trg. PoW intelligence. Research & Recording of Past Campaigns & Operations.
AI. 1(a)(P/W) Liaison with MI 9	**AI. S.1(b)** Security questions in connection with: (a) Aviation other than RAF, (b) Official Air Mails, (c) Classification of documents.	**AI. S.4** Operational security & inter-Services Security Board liaison Duties.		
AI. 1(c) Liaison Duties.	**AI. S.1(c)** Co-ord of Home & Overseas security. Allocation of Privacy equipment. Correct transmission of Categorised documents.	**AI. S.(7)** Liaison Duties	**AI. 3(b)** Order of Battle for the Air Forces of Germany & her Satellites, except Finland. Liaison with RAF & USAAF Command Int. Sections, Admiralty & the War Office. Estimates of Future German Intentions & Scales of Attack.	**AI 3 (f)** Organisation & Ops of the Air Forces of Russia, Finland, Sweden, Spain, Portugal, Switzerland, China, Turkey, Iraq, Iran, Afghanistan & Egypt.
AI. 1(T) Translation section	**AI. S.1(d)** Policy regarding prevention of Sabotage. Security measures at Protected places & Prohibited areas. Carriage of cameras in & photography from aircraft.	**AI. S.8** Postal & Telegraphic censorship & Port Liaison. Unit censorship policy; censorship stamps.	**AI. 3(c) 1** Production of Target material for RAF & the USAAF. Liaison with MEW.	**AI 3 (USA)** USA & Latin American Air Forces Order of Battle & Organisation. Liaison with USAAF in UK, American Embassy & RAF Delegation in Washington.
AI. 1(p) RAF & WAAF Int. personnel Selection Boards. Home & Overseas Language study. Leakage of information. Passes, Permits & Identity docs. Security questions regarding PoWs. Policy on employment of Aliens.			**AI. 3(c) 2** Results of bombing, Sea-mining & Attacks on Shipping by RAF & USAAF, in the European Theatre.	
* Administered by DAFL				

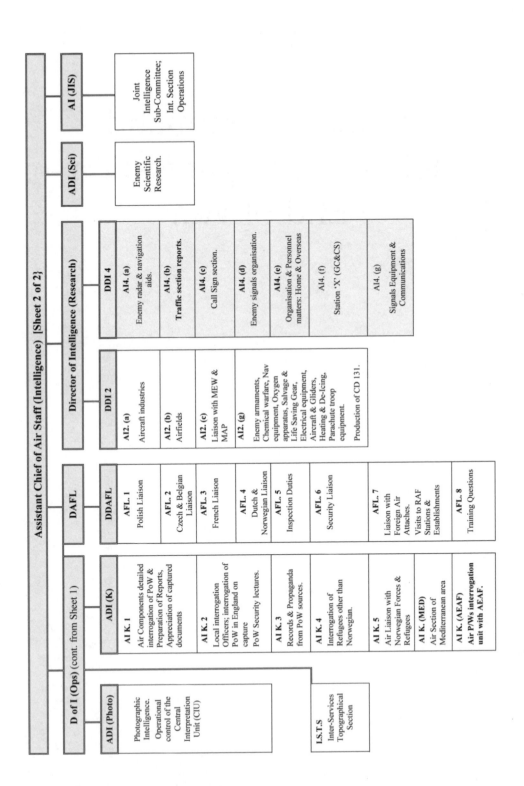

Assistant Chief of Air Staff (Intelligence) [Sheet 2 of 2]

D of I (Ops) (cont. from Sheet 1)

ADI (Photo)

Photographic Intelligence. Operational control of the Central Interpretation Unit (CIU)

I.S.T.S
Inter-Services Topographical Section

ADI (K)

AI K. 1 — Air Components detailed interrogation of PoW & Preparation of Reports, Appreciation of captured documents

AI K. 2 — Local interrogation Officers; interrogation of PoW in England on capture. PoW Security lectures.

AI K. 3 — Records & Propaganda from PoW sources.

AI K. 4 — Interrogation of Refugees other than Norwegian.

AI K. 5 — Air Liaison with Norwegian Forces & Refugees

AI K. (MED) — Air Section of Mediterranean area

AI K. (AEAF) — **Air P/Ws interrogation unit with AEAF.**

DAFL

DDAFL

AFL. 1 — Polish Liaison

AFL. 2 — Czech & Belgian Liaison

AFL. 3 — French Liaison

AFL. 4 — Dutch & Norwegian Liaison

AFL. 5 — Inspection Duties

AFL. 6 — Security Liaison

AFL. 7 — Liaison with Foreign Air Attaches. Visits to RAF Stations & Establishments

AFL. 8 — Training Questions

Director of Intelligence (Research)

DDI 2

AI2. (a) — Aircraft industries

AI2. (b) — Airfields

AI2. (c) — Liaison with MEW & MAP

AI2. (g) — Enemy armaments, Chemical warfare, Nav equipment, Oxygen apparatus, Salvage & Life Saving Gear, Electrical equipment, Aircraft & Gliders, Heating & De-Icing, Parachute troop equipment. Production of CD 131.

DDI 4

AI4. (a) — Enemy radar & navigation aids.

AI4. (b) — **Traffic section reports.**

AI4. (c) — Call Sign section.

AI4. (d) — Enemy signals organisation.

AI4. (e) — Organisation & Personnel matters: Home & Overseas

AI4. (f) — Station 'X' (GC&CS)

AI4. (g) — Signals Equipment & Communications

ADI (Sci)

Enemy Scientific Research.

AI (JIS)

Joint Intelligence Sub-Committee; Int. Section Operations

Bomber Command Intelligence Organisation – End of War

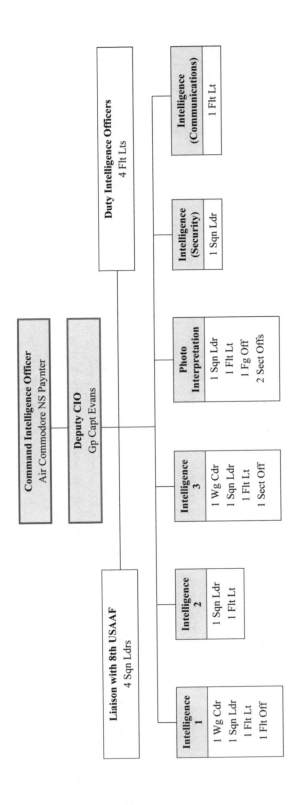

Allocation of Duties within Bomber Command Intelligence Staff.

Intelligence 1	Intelligence 2	Intelligence 3	Photo Int	Intelligence (Sec)	Duty Int. Officers
• Study of possible targets • Industrial intelligence • German towns • Valuation of targets • Raid damage in enemy territory • Enemy transportation system • Briefing Notes • Recce requirements • Co-ord of Damage reports • Effects of damage • Damage diagrams • Preliminary damage plots • Immediate Damage Assessment reports	• Target maps and material • Enemy decoys and camouflage • Landmarks • Liaison with Target Int. in London • Aids to Escape for British PoWs • Provision of Int. Publications to Groups and Stations • Provision of S&C Documents • Personnel & Staffing	• Enemy defences. • GAF Order of Battle • Enemy & Allied Airfields • Enemy aircraft equipment & performance • Flak, Searchlights & Balloons • Enemy Radar • Enemy Observer Corps • Enemy aircraft losses • Own Bomber losses • Enemy air tactics • Enemy Army	• Plotting night photos • Issue of Plot & Report on all Night Photos from each Operation • Day photos with bombing • Liaison with CIU on all PRU matters • Provision of photographic information to all Groups & Stations • Maintenance of Photo Library • Maintenance of Plotting Maps • Damage assessment from PRU sorties • Marking up of all Ops Room Mosaics on Damage effects	• Keep CinC advised on State of Security within the Command • Special Security measures • Test & Trial of secret equipment • Maintain watch for security leakages • Censorship • Security education • Direct link with D of I (Sec) in Air Intelligence	• Write BC Int. Narrative & Reports • Deal with Top Secret mail during the night • Deal with incoming and outgoing Int. questions • Maintain liaison with BC Ops and Groups for all operations • Maintain contact with all PRU recce & damage assessment sorties • Maintain liaison with RAF Kingsdown on current operations

Jockey Committee Report

Reference: Air 20/3218, 'Jockey/1/45: Bombing Attack to contain German Jet Aircraft', 26 Jan 45.

Background

The subject report sets out recommendations by the Jockey Committee for a bombing attack to contain the German Jet Aircraft threat. The report was issued at TOP SECRET classification and drew upon MSS intelligence material. There was no direct reference to ULTRA material. The report distribution included Bomber Command (Air Cdre Paynter and Air Cdre Constantine) and the 8th USAAF. It is typical of Jockey Committee reports and is included here for illustrative purpose.

Present Position

The enemy was making urgent preparations to regain air supremacy over Germany by creating a large force of jet-engine fighter and reconnaissance aircraft. By the end of 1944 some 700 Me 262s and about 100 Ar 234s had been produced. Those aircraft were expected to enter service in increasing numbers and to reduce the effectiveness of the Allied long-range escort fighter screen. It was therefore recommended that some (accurate) visual bombing effort be used to contain that new fighter threat, or it would be necessary to forego deep penetration raids from mid-1945.

Problem of Bombing Attack

(A) *Airframes:* A substantial proportion of these airframes are produced underground. Sub-components are produced in small dispersed factories. There is no firm knowledge of the sub-component manufacture locations. At least one large underground jet aircraft assembly factory is in preparation. It would seem that the possibility of systematic bombing would be costly in effort and may be ineffective.

(B) *Jet Engines:* Three jet power plants are planned for production: the Ju.004, the BMW.003 and the Heinkel/Hirth unit. The Junkers engine is most advanced, but it is suspected that there is no great reserve of these engines. This target set was well dispersed, with one major underground component and assembly area – at Niedersachswerfen. An attack on this target was expected to have valuable results:

- It would impact on the Me 262, Ar 234 and single engine jet fighters.
- The engine was required to support jet aircraft already in operational use.

Jet Engine Castings

Four companies had been identified as suppliers of jet engine castings. They were: VDM Heddernheim, VDM Hildesheim, Honsel and Metalgussgesellschaft. There was virtually complete intelligence on this target set. Most of the work was being done above ground and the factories had not been dispersed; the work was associated with all of the jet engine types. The disadvantages were that only a portion of the factories would be devoted to jet engine castings and the process was reasonably robust. Any attack would therefore have to achieve widespread destruction.

The production of the high-speed and temperature turbine blades would have been an attractive target set. Three factories had been identified as possible sites but there were no target identification details.

Proposed Programme

(A) An immediate attack on the jet engine production through the metal casting industry and the main Junkers factories.
(B) Intensive intelligence work be done on jet aircraft development in general, airframe assembly and flight training locations.
(C) An emergency bombing programme be defined to form the basis for a massive attack at short notice. That attack must achieve widespread success; the enemy has previously survived bombing attacks because they were of inadequate weight. A method of attack on underground facilities should be developed.

Air Ministry Weekly Intelligence Summaries

Reference: Air 22/77; this reference is within the Air 22/69–83 series, which covers Summaries from September 1939 to October 1945.

Introduction

This Appendix contains a small cross-section of articles that have relevance to the subject of this book. The point is to show one example of the SECRET level dissemination that was used by the Air Intelligence branch. It was very much for general interest, especially at Commands and stations where it would be held in the Intelligence Libraries. It would have had little value for bomber raid planning and target selection because it was necessarily circumspect and delayed in time.

Selected Articles

One article described the effects of the bombing raids on the German iron and steel plants in the Ruhr. It makes note of the difficulties in causing any long-term damage to these plants. The key points occupy only a small part of the overall built-up works area; they are resistant to anything but a direct hit by a heavy bomb; fire is unlikely to cause more than local damage except to coal dumps; and stocks of raw material, finished and semi-finished products are proof against most kinds of damage except for scattering and bending.[1] In a later article which referred to raids in Jun/July 1942, it was noted that as a result of bomb damage to steel plants in the Ruhr, the Germans had increased production at two large steel works in Eastern France. This was stated in the Summary to demonstrate the readiness to divert raw material to more or less idle plants rather than maintain partial production in plants that had been damaged.[2]

---

1. Author's Note: These remarks align very closely with the post-war surveys of iron and steel production in Germany both by the UK and US Bombing Survey Teams (see Ch. 9).
2. Author's Note: This also demonstrates the reserve production capacity that was available within the Occupied countries, but which was not adequately reflected in MEW assessments of war production (see Ch. 2 (MEW) and Ch. 9).

An article on raid damage to communications emphasised the importance of waterway and railway transport systems. In that article there was reference to 'an intelligence source' that gave specific details of effects after raids at Düsseldorf, Mannheim and Saarbrücken. A further separate comment quoted another intelligence source that stated that the raid on Saarbrücken on the night of 29/30 July 1942 had dramatic consequences because the Reichsbahndirektion Building was housing a number of important officials from Berlin and that many of them were killed. That could obviously not have been determined from photography and may demonstrate an example of high-grade material being carefully woven into a SECRET-level product?

The Summary dated 28 Nov 42 contained a large article that described the general effects in 'Germany on the Eve of the Fourth Year of the War'. This discussed the impact on the population so far as food, clothing, housing, heating and transport were concerned. There is however a fundamental error in that article, which was highlighted in the post-war bombing survey reports; the statement was that: 'The German people were over-worked even before the war, in the period of re-armament; but they are still more overworked now.' It may be accepted that they had a great deal more domestic work to cater for bomb damage repairs – but so much of industry was still on single-shift working. That conclusion may well have been consistent with a political view in Whitehall that was rather more 'wishful thinking' than hard fact. It was 'internal propaganda' and may well have had merit in raising the morale of readers of the Bulletin.

In that Summary issued on 16 Jan 43 there was an article 'The German Economic Situation –1', which had been written by the MEW. That article identified two steadily increasing threats: the shortage of raw materials and the shortage of labour; it went on to address the labour situation. It stated that 'The first six-months of 1942 were dominated by the manpower crisis consequent upon the heavy demands of the armed forces'. The second half of the year had shown the results of measures to overcome that problem; in June 1942, there were 2.5 million foreign workers employed; there were also upwards of 1.5 million working prisoners of war of various nationalities. But there was a high turnover of that labour source and a consequent reduction in the level of skill in some industries. That was partly addressed by the Sauckel Decree of 13 Jun 42 that put an end to male labour mobility in specified war industries; the initial decree was replaced after three months or so by a further issue which covered women and juveniles as well as men. Labour priorities were laid down by the Decree issued on 22 Aug 42 that established the following priorities:

- The war industries of Germany,
- German civil and military occupation authorities,
- Agricultural requirements in occupied countries,
- Industries working in the German interest,
- Industries working for their national interests.

Results of Allied Air Attacks
The Summary No. 181 dated 20 Feb 43 contained a reasonably extensive outline of bombing attacks and their results. There were some details of raids in Italy,

Denmark, France; and more extensive reports of raids in Germany. Industrial damage was described on a steel works in Duisburg. Again there is reference to a 'source' that provided a considerable amount of detailed information – far more than could be derived from photography. One comment was that the greatest cause of lost production was excessive dilution of labour, from Sep 1942 onwards. There had been an influx of over 700 workers but production had declined in quantity and quality; a major problem was language. A very specific point was that many Duisburg firms would have worked three 8-hour shifts had the skilled labour been available, but they were compelled to operate on two 10-hour shifts.[3]

---

3. Author's Note: This comment about shift-working must be cross-referred to the post-war bombing surveys and their findings about single shift working – see Ch. 9, p. 63.

Bomber Command and the U-boat Campaign: April 1942–March 1943

Reference:
1. Air 8/833, ATH/DO/4 dated 30 March 1943, CinC Bomber Command to CAS.
2. Air 41/3507, 'The Contribution of Bomber Command to the Submarine Campaign', 8 Jul 42 (This reference provides substantial detail in the 12 months to Apr 1942).

Introduction

The CinC Bomber Command wrote to CAS on 30 Mar 43 to present the evidence of his Command's contribution to the U-boat campaign. In that letter he said:

It seems to me that there is at present a considerable gap in our (Air Ministry) Intelligence records of the progress of the offensive which ought to be filled.

A case in point is the results of our attacks on the U-boat building yards and component factories. A paper on this was obviously required to meet the latest Admiralty proposals for misusing the Bomber Forces, and is the kind of thing which I feel that Air Intelligence are supposed always to have available for production at a moments notice.

My own experience is that they tend to offer us only generalities that have little or no evidential value on matters of this kind.

This is not a job that can be done by MEW. To be of any real use, the facts must be assembled and the appreciations prepared by someone who knows the operational possibilities and also the political background in this country.

There is an internal note on that letter from CAS to his ACAS (I) dated 31 Mar 43 that says:

What do you say to this? I am inclined to agree that it is our job and I often feel the need for a construction of this kind. Initialled by CP, 31/3 (CP was Charles Portal, CAS).

The response from ACAS (I) is covered in the main text, at p. 113.

The Contribution of Bomber Command to the Anti-Submarine Campaign
(Original Report issued by Int. 1, Bomber Command HQ, 29 Mar 43).

During the period 1st April 1941 to March 1942 Bomber Command flew some 12,000 separate sorties against enemy harbours, shipbuilding yards, docks and submarine bases.

During the period 1st April 1942 to 28 March 1943 Bomber Command flew some 26,143 sorties against the following targets:

Towns in Germany with U-boat building yards	8,590 sorties
Other towns containing U-boat component factories	12,311 sorties
Towns in Italy containing U-boat yards or component factories	2,165 sorties
U-boat bases on the West coast of France	2,999 sorties
Other targets relating to Submarine warfare	78 sorties

In addition, 12,385 mines were laid of which 3,400 were directed primarily against U-boats.

It had been estimated that on 1 March 1943 there were 202 U-boats building and a further 68 fitting out. That work was carried out at 18 separate yards in 12 different towns. The most notable damage has been:

- Almost total destruction at Nordseewerk at Emden.
- Delays of 10–12 months in U-boat construction at Wilhelmshaven.
- Delays of 3–4 months in the U-boat construction at Kriegsmarine, Kiel.
- Delays have also been caused at Bremer haven, Hamburg, Lübeck and Flensberg.

The Admiralty had estimated that these attacks had caused delays in the completion of about 40 U-boats.

Naval Intelligence Dept Report 01730/43 dated 15 Mar 43 contained a list of 109 factories in Enemy, Enemy-occupied and Neutral countries manufacturing components for U-boats. Of those 109 factories, only 47 are located in towns that have not been attacked; 2 are in neutral countries and 35 are either out of range or located in small towns that are difficult to locate at night. The remaining 68 factories are located in 21 towns, all of which have been attacked since 1 Mar 43. The types of components produced in those factories were:

- Torpedoes, components and equipment.
- U-boat Diesel engines.
- U-boat Electric motors.
- Accumulators.
- Air compressors.
- Miscellaneous items and fittings.

Submarine Bases on the West Coast of France

Lorient: The shipbuilding workshops, naval slips, accumulator shops, torpedo store, welding shop, foundry and ships stores were among the more important dockside buildings destroyed or severely damaged. Electricity, gas and water supplies had been cut off.

St Nazaire: Serious damage to workshops at both shipbuilding yards, the power station, stores, railway tracks and rolling stock. Photographic reconnaissance reports were not available for the latest raids.

In spite of the extensive devastation at both ports, there had been very little evidence of its effects on U-boat operations. The pens had been hit several times but the bombs had not penetrated the structures. Until a weapon was produced that would penetrate the reinforced concrete pens, the damage was likely to slow down U-boat turn-arounds but not do long-lasting damage.[1]

NB. Bomber Command noted that more effective damage would have been achieved by attacking the German towns where U-boat assembly and component production were done.

Other Targets in Occupied Territories related to U-boat Warfare

On 27 Feb 43 a very successful attack was made on the Naval Storage Depot at Rennes. Heavy explosions occurred probably from ammunition stores. The depot was the main distribution point for naval stores to the west coast of France.

On 29 Jan 43 the Morlaix viaduct was attacked and this cut the only direct route to Brest.

General attacks on the transportation system had caused delays in the output of building yards and component factories.

Effect of Sea Mining

From 1 May 42, prior to which the records are unreliable, 137 ships were known to have been sunk and 89 damaged by mines. Since 1 Apr 42 it was known that mines off the west coast of France had sunk 4 U-boats; and mines in the Baltic damaged 3. The actual total of such losses was unknown.[2]

---

1. Author's Note: The TALL BOY and GRAND SLAM bombs were not available at that time.
2. Author's Note: At that time, 31 Mar 43, Bomber Command had very little access to ULTRA evidence.

Conclusions

The information in the report was based on Central Interpretation Unit (Photographic Reconnaissance) reports; Air Ministry Damage Assessment Reports and Admiralty statements. A great deal of the evidence was derived from photographic reconnaissance, which can only tell part of the overall story.

Appendices

- Schedule of Sorties dispatched: 1 April 1942 – 29 March 1943.
- Schedule of U-boat Building Yards and Reported Damage.
- Schedule of Damage to U-boat Component Factories.

[The Appendices are not summarised in this extract but are fully available in Air 8/833.]

Extracts from Decrypts giving Effects of Air Attacks on German Transportation

Source: PRO HW 11/9, Appendix N.

Introductory Note

AI 3(e) compiled these extracts at the request of DCAS who, with General Spaatz, needed to make decisions on the use of the strategic bomber force from 1 Mar 45. They wished to know what information was available from Special Intelligence sources.

The content of this Appendix is a brief overview of the nature of the various evidence within the full paper by AI 3(e).

Diplomatic Messages

A telegram from the Turkish Minister in Stockholm on 15 Feb 45 recorded that all recent arrivals from Germany had stated that it was impossible to travel by train south of Berlin. The transport of refugees from the East and continuous air raids were causing great dislocation in the Reichsbahn. The Ruhr and the Saar areas and the transport routes had been smashed by incessant bombing, with the result that there was an acute shortage of coal throughout the country.[1] Although there were accumulations of coal in places were it was produced, the inability to transport them was having an adverse effect on war supplies.

Decrypts of Air and Military Signals after 1 Oct 44

The original Paper dated 20 Feb 45 contains 87 separate CX/MSS ULTRA messages that each identify specific transportation problems arising from air attack. The descriptions of those problems generally cover damage effects,

---

1. BJ 141347, available 15 Feb 45.

consequent movement failures and repair timescales where possible. The following short list is a sample of that Special Intelligence:

- The Fuehrer had ordered on 5 Oct 44 that special dispersal and camouflage measures were to be taken in the west and south-west because of the increasing air attacks on railways and roads.[2]
- From Railway Station HQ II/173 on 9 Oct 44: both exit tracks from Rushkirchen in the direction of Cologne and Bonn destroyed by a direct hit from a super heavy bomb.[3]
- Speer reported on 20 Oct 44 that on account of destruction of traffic installations and lack of power, thirty to fifty per cent of all works in West Germany were at a standstill.[4]
- On 30 Oct 44, the transfer of GAF Gruppe III/JG 26 from Grossrecken to Plantluenne was impossible, since tracks in the vicinity were for the most part destroyed by bombing.[5]
- From GAF Gardelegen to JG 11 Wunstorf on 31 Oct 44: no track available for two weeks, please send new orders. It was a question of fetching technical equipment.[6]
- Dated 26 Nov 44: Day attack on large railway viaduct near Altenbeken – both tracks and bridge destroyed.[7]
- Report on raid at Hamm on 29 Nov 44: railway was principle target. Considerable damage and destruction on all sectors; two bridges destroyed.[8]
- Luftgau VII on 18 Dec 44 ordered that in view of the continuously rising scale of attacks on traffic installations in the areas of Rosenheim, Innsbruck, Salzburg and Ulm, railway anti-aircraft units were to be brought up in order to prevent further severe damage to the South German rail network.[9]
- Attack on Cologne-Nippes railway station on 21–22 Dec 44: permanent way and entire superstructure destroyed. Repairs will take 5 days; single track working in 48 hours.[10]
- The Chairman of the Armaments Commission and the Wehrkreis Commissioner XIIB reported on 29 Dec 44 that enemy fighter-bombers had destroyed traffic installations on an extensive scale and brought laborious repair work to nothing within a few hours. Telephone facilities hardly existed at all and it was impossible to re-route trains.[11]

2. CX/MSS/(Series 2)/329/T55.
3. CX/MSS/(Series 2)/334/T31.
4. CX/MSS/(Series 2)/347/T46.
5. CX/MSS/(Series 2)/353/T130.
6. CX/MSS/(Series 2)/355/T30(2).
7. CX/MSS/(Series 2)/384, para. C2.
8. CX/MSS/(Series 2)/385/T53.
9. CX/MSS/(Series 2)/402/T82.
10. CX/MSS/(Series 2)/413/T17.
11. CX/MSS/(Series 2)/416/T34.

- Report from the Director General of Transport (West) on 28 Dec 44: clearance of traffic in Monsheim, Landau, Neustadt and Gruenstadt impeded badly owing to many tracks being out of action.[12]
- On 28 Dec 44; attack on the Cologne/Grenberg marshalling yard, all traffic blocked. Resumption within about 14 days.[13]
- Bridge situation report from CinC West on 31 Dec 44: Remagen – bridge damaged by bombing and probably closed for several weeks; Koblenz – ship and road bridge open only for pedestrians; Bingen – railway bridge undamaged but the feeder tracks on the right bank of the Rhine were hit and no traffic is possible.[14]
- Report from Wehrkreis XII on 29 Jan 45: Koblenz – 500 HE bombs around the main station; the through highway to Buppard and Hunreuckhohen Strasse blocked; railway tracks from Ehrenbreitstein–Niederlahnstein, Koblenz–Mainz, Koblenz–Niederlahnstein blocked. Camp – railway track Camp–Kestert damaged. Kaiserslautern – 20 HE bombs on railway installations; railway repair works, goods station and locomotive sheds hit.
- Heidelberg – 8 HE bombs on armed forces transport train; railway tracks and loaded vehicles damaged. Kichein/Heidelberg – 5 HE bombs on armed forces transport train.[15]

There are many other similar CX/MSS reports within the source Paper.

Similar Examples relating to Oil and Other Targets
The following examples are taken from TNA HW 11/8, as amplified within Bib. B28, Appendix E:

- CX/MSS/260/T13: Attack on Ploesti Oil Refineries, 15 Jul 44.
- CX/MSS/323: Area Attack on Karlsruhe, 29 Sep 44.
- CX/MSS/466: Attack on Synthetic Oil Plant, Schelven, 17 Feb 45.

---

12. CX/MSS/(Series 2)/416/T91.
13. CX/MSS/(Series 2)/417/T3(2).
14. CX/MSS/(Series 2)/419/T89.
15. CX/MSS/(Series 2)/ 450/T23.

Overview of DDI 4 Activity

Introduction

The primary purpose of the Appendix is to indicate the scope of the portfolio that was the responsibility of DDI 4, formerly AI 4 and DDSY in the earlier years, as the overall scale and organisation of Air Intelligence expanded from 1939 onwards. The material for this Appendix has been mainly derived from the Air 40/2888–2890 series, which provide a brief chronological index to AI 4 paper and war records between 1939 and 1945.

The dominant subject within the DDI 4 portfolio was the RAF Y-Service and its many facets, including the relationships with the Army and the Navy; and the many overseas commands and theatres that were supported by the RAF Y-Service at different periods through the war.

DDI 4 was a small element of the overall Air Intelligence Directorate. Appendix B above shows the Establishment of Officer and Civil Service equivalent grades within Air Intelligence at several stages through the war. It is immediately obvious that DDI 4 was never more than about 7–8 per cent of the Directorate and sometimes less than 5 per cent. The manpower effort that was therefore available to provide direct support to the Home Air Commands was tiny, as may be seen from the Liaison Records for Fighter, Bomber, Coastal Commands and 100 Group under Q. 1222, 1223, 1224 and 1227 below. This should be seen as indicative and not as an absolute proportion.

Detailed War Records

Within the following Table, the Q references in the left hand column relate to folders that contained papers and records under the relevant subject heading. Where there is no 4-digit number in the left hand column, the immediately preceding number in the row(s) above will apply. Many of these 'Q-Folders' no longer exist. Q-Folder numbers outside the numerical range 1152 – 1353 do not relate to activities by the DDI 4 deputy directorate.

Q Refs	Date	Subject
1159	6 Jun 41	Mtg to discuss staffs: Appointment of 'Senior Computor' at Cheadle: Mapplebeck suggested.
	6 Apr 44	AI4f to DDI4: Functions of the Operational Watch.
1162	16 Feb 43	Formation of No. 1 SSU (372 WU) in 26 Gp at Chicksands.
1168	—	Depot Policy
1169	—	Depot Establishment
1170	—	Chicksands Policy
1171	—	Chicksands Establishment
1174	—	Chicksands Weekly Bulletin
1175	—	Kingsdown Policy
1176	14 Feb 43	Need for electric heating; in operational huts coal dust detrimental to the equipment.
1177	—	Kingsdown Establishment
1183	22 Mar 44	Kingsdown Broadcast to start on 8 Apr 44.
	6 Apr 44	Kingsdown callsign to be 5PL
	14 Jan 45	Moyes to AI4b: Brief narrative reports to be given within the Broadcast on German night fighter reactions to Bomber Command operations.
1189	7 Dec 42	Evidence of overlapping between duties of ADI (Sc) and DDI4
1191	5 Jun 41	DDSY Branch in course of transfer to ACAS (I), to become DDI4.
	12 Nov 42	Proposed new establishment of DDI4
1193	21 Nov 41	ACAS (I) agrees to increase strength of 192 Sqn to 8 plus 4 Wellingtons.
	25 May 43	Request for increased establishment owing to extra air investigation of enemy jamming of British navigation equipments over enemy territory by 192 Sqn.
1197	2 Oct 44	AEAF to DDI4: Agree to institution of 'Y' Broadcast on the continent.
	11 Nov 44	Air Staff Instruction No. 33: Formation of Forward Detachment (364 WU) of RAF Canterbury in Western Europe.
	11 Dec 44	DofI (R) to VCAS: Problem of accommodation of WAAF Y-Service personnel in Forward Area; suitable RAF personnel not available.
1200	24 Nov 44	From Scott-Farnie: Policy and Org of Air Sigint, Western Europe.
1201	14 Apr 44	AEAF to DDI4: Request for list of raids at the end of the Kingsdown Digest to include Commands carrying out each operation.
1204	22 Feb 44	Scott-Farnie to DDI4: Report of GAF reaction to Allied Day and Night raids.

Q Refs	Date	Subject
	4 Mar 44	AEAF to AI4: Details of Exercise FRANK; test to accustom operators to possibility of enemy issuing false orders during air operations.
1226	5 Jun 41	Blandy to ACAS (I): Difficulty in supplying Y-detachments for work overseas.
1220	13 Nov 39	Ashbridge to Blandy: resume of BBC interception work carried out at Tatsfield during Oct-Nov 39.

Liaison with Fighter Command

1222	10 Sep 40	Evidence that Fighter Command R/T traffic is being intercepted and used by the enemy; R/T should be reduced to a minimum.
	5 Nov 40	Note from Cooper at GC&CS about the information being gained by German Y Service from British inter-squadron comms.
	7 Nov 44	Fighter Command now agreed to use codes for inter-squadron comms.
	10 Feb 41	DDSY: If Fighter Command wants extension of Kingsdown 'Hook-Up' to No. 11 Group, so that Y-Section could tie up with messages from Cheadle and RDF plots, they must arrange it themselves.
	3 Aug 42	Budge to Cadell: re shooting down of an aircraft from the GAF Unit III/F.122 on information received from Cheadle via Kingsdown.
	8 Aug 42	List of enemy aircraft shot down on Y-Service information.
	20 Oct 42	Requests for raid reports to be made to AI4, not to GC& CS/AI4f (The Air Section).[1]
	11 Dec 42	AOCinC Fighter Command to USofS: Request that information being passed to Groups also be passed to Duty Officer at Fighter Command HQ.
	30 Dec 42	ACAS (I) to AOCinC Fighter Command: not practicable, suggest Fighter Command get information from own Groups.
	5 Oct 43	Possibility of exploiting knowledge that enemy fighters orbit visual beacons in large numbers until their Ground Controller can direct them to the true bomber targets.

Liaison with Bomber Command

1223	7 Mar 40	Mtg to discuss a Committee to safeguard W/T security in Bomber Command.

---

1. Author's Note: An example of the Air Ministry Intelligence Dept not allowing direct contact between GC&CS and air commands in the UK.

Q Refs	Date	Subject
	28 Sep 40	Mtg to consider whether Bomber Command should set up their own organisation to study enemy M/F Beacons, instead of this work being done at Cheadle. Decision to continue as before at Cheadle but to have a direct line from Cheadle Beacon Control to Bomber HQs.
	20 Jul 42	HQ 2 Gp to DDI4: request that information on enemy fighters be passed as 'red hot' to No. 2 Gp, Mosquito Bombers, instead of via Bomber HQ.
	25 Jul 42	Bomber HQ to Cadell: Agreed to treat 2 Gp as Fighter Command if comms arranged.
	26 Dec 42	Cadell to Paynter, CIO at Bomber HQ: No. 5 Gp request for BMP reports rather than Bomber Command operations summary.

Liaison with Coastal Command

Q Refs	Date	Subject
1266a	1 Oct 39	DDSY to Cheadle: Coastal Command to receive beacon messages; not Fighter Command.
1224	19 Feb 40	CIO Coastal HQ to Blandy: Instructions on functions of Y-section at Coastal HQ.
	21 Mar 40	CIO Coastal HQ to Blandy: memo on ZENIT meteorological flights. (ZENIT covered GAF naval recce into the Atlantic against Allied convoys).
	29 Mar 40	Josh Cooper at GC&CS to DDSY: Would like more cooperation with Coastal Command about meteorological reports and the ZENIT operations
	14 Feb 41	Mtg to discuss Y cooperation in relation to signals intercept of GAF Fw 200 naval recce operations (ZENIT) from Bordeaux.
	2 Dec 43	Budge to all HDUs: Proposal to extend R/T warnings to PRU aircraft.
1218	8 Apr 41	Blandy does not agree with GC&CS that it is unnecessary for Naval Stns to take Air intercepts. Would be of value if Naval stns could D/F the H/F R/T fighter patrol info.
	12 Sep 41	Mtg to discuss possibility of obtaining full information for Coastal HQ ORS.
	19 Sep 41	Blandy to Haines: AM will decide how information is passed to Coastal Command.[2]
	18 Feb 42	AI4b: Kingsdown will pass R/T intelligence to Coastal Command.

---

2. Author's Note: On what basis would the Air Ministry make that judgement? The operationally vital element of time would be lost and the value of such information would be compromised.

Q Refs	Date	Subject
	4 Jan 44	Mtg to discuss training programme for WRNS and Naval ratings in GAF procedures.
	3 May 44	DDI4 to Kingsdown: Functions of Naval Watch at Kingsdown.

100 Group Policy

1227	11 Dec 43	AOC 100 Gp to ACAS (I): Formation and role of 100 (Special Duties) Group.
	6 May 44	AOC 100 Gp to USofS: Request for 100 Gp to have enemy beacon, frequency and call sign information.
	9 May 44	DDI4 to AOC 100 Gp: 100 Gp to have Kingsdown Weekly Summary.
	19 May 44	DDI4 to AOC 100 Gp: re letter dated 6 May; requests advice on how 100 Gp would use that information. Possible consequence could be that Bomber Command would forfeit intelligence on enemy fighter movements.
	29 Jun 44	Memo on Bomber Support Intruder sorties; impact on enemy aircrew morale.
	22 Jan 45	From B Ops 2a: Request that 100 Gp condense their Operational Reports.
1228	3 Jan 41	Blandy to DofS: Suspicion that U-boats have some form of RDF.

Liaison with No. 80 Wing

1229	18 Dec 40	Lywood to DDSY: Not satisfied with cooperation between Cheadle and 80 Wing on countermeasures.[3] Blandy to Cheadle: Enclosed two reports from 80 Wing showing the importance of passing information to 80 Wing and the results obtained.[4]

Combined Operations

1232	19 Aug 42	Summary of wireless activity by GAF bomber units during operations in response to the Allied attack on Dieppe (Supplement to BMP No. 72)
	23 Oct 42	Memo from Cadell: Request advice on information likely to be required from immediate Y intelligence during Combined Ops and any future landings on the French coast.

---

3. Author's Note: The co-operation that is refered to here concerns the 'Beam Wars' against German bombing of UK targets.

4. Author's Note: This is a most illuminating set of correspondence that demonstrates that there was, at that time and in that context, an appreciation of the vital importance of timeliness in passing operational signals intelligence. It would seem that this appreciation was lost as personalities changed in Air Intelligence.

Q Refs	Date	Subject

Y Watch on RN Ships

1233 — Collection of Reports relating to Y activity on board ship during a wide range of operations, from Dec 44 to May 45.

Wireless Telegraphy Board

1234 — 24 Jun 41 — Mtg to discuss support from the BBC; construction of 3 high-power broadcasting stations to provide connection with overseas activities.

15 Aug 41 — Mtg to discuss possible use of the Trans-Atlantic telephone cable.

7 May 42 — Need for uniformity with US on common W/T procedures. Inter-ship use of VHF channels in the 100–125 Mc/s band.

Composite Group-Army/Air Support – Y Policy

1236 — 16 Jul 43 — AOC Fighter Command to USofS: Statement of requirements in the TAF for Y-Facilities, RCM, a 'J Watch' and Jamming measures.

Sept 43 — Report on the formation and operation of a Y-unit embodied into the TAF.

Air Interception Committee (AIC) [See also Q1261 below]

1236 — 4 Dec 44 — Appreciation of airborne countermeasures against enemy air-launched flying bombs against targets in UK.

1 Feb 45 — AIC report on the use of Wellington aircraft equipped with Mk III or Mk IV ASV to provide information to coastal shipping for interception of enemy surface craft at night.

6 Feb 45 — Memo on use of fighter aircraft under control from an airborne radar station.[5]

27 Apr 45 — Mtg to examine: Reports of Air Interception operations; Countermeasures against air-launched flying bombs; Fighter Direction ships; Use of Wellingtons equipped with ASV (see AIC Report at 1 Feb 45 above).

21 Jun 45 — Note by ACNS (W) on the inter-service airborne early warning sub-committee.

ORC Committee on Enemy Night Fighter Defence e

1238 — 4 Oct 42 — Report on enemy NF defence system, with an estimate of efficiency and tendencies.

Dec 42 — Memo from MI 14e: Bombing heights in relation to Flak.

Jul 42 — Tactical countermeasures to combat enemy anti-aircraft searchlights and guns.

---

5. Author's Note: A very early example of an Airborne Warning and Control station.

Q Refs	Date	Subject
	8 Jul 43	Mtg to consider effect of concentration of bomber forces on loss rate during bright nights.
	9 Sep 43	Mtg to consider tactical countermeasures against enemy NF and AA defences.
	23 Jun 44	Report on Aids to the bomber offensive during the winter of 1944/45.
	14 Mar 45	List of the RCM being used and their effectiveness. Operational Research Sections – Middle East; Mediterranean Allied AF; TAF; AEAF; Home air commands; USAAF; ADGB; India.

Polish Co-operation

1250	28 May 43	Proposal from Polish Air Force to form a small Polish Wireless Intelligence Section within the RAF Y Service.
	22 Jul 43	DDI4 to Kingsdown: Key Polish personnel attached to Kingsdown for instruction.
	1 Sep 43	DDI4 to AFL 1: Polish airmen leaving Kingsdown for Gorleston.

Russian Co-operation

| 1251 | | A great deal of correspondence between Oct 42–Jul 43, covering activities with the UK Y-Committee and possible co-operation with Russian forces. The general impression suggests that any co-operation was one-sided and indeed on 3 Mar 43 a Russian spokesman said that they desired no Y co-operation. |

American Liaison

| 1252 | | Collection of correspondence during 1944 that covers: various joint investigations, exchange of equipments, training at Sutton Valence, exchange visit reports, etc; and the list of US Publications that had been circulated form AI3 (USA). Within that co-operation framework, US personnel were attached to Cheadle, Bletchley Park and Weymouth. |

Liaison with US Commands

1253	27 Sep 43	8th USAAF to AM: Request for transmission of Radio Intercept intelligence to 8th Air Support HQ from Kingsdown.
	12 Jan 44	Budge (at Kingsdown) to DDI4: decision to separate hook-ups related to Marauder and Fortress operations.
	20 Jan 44	8th Fighter Command: suggestions for improvements in Y service as result of mtg at AM.
1254	Nov 43	Training of Intelligence Officers for Air Force radio squadrons; start in Dec 43.

Q Refs	Date	Subject

| | 5 Feb 44 | DDI4 to HQ 9th AF: arrangements being made for R/T personnel to be trained at Sutton Valence. |

Wireless Deception (Spoofing)

1257	12 Aug 41	Mtg to examine:

Extension of present scale of spoof programmes.

Co-ordination with 'Q' sites.

Concealment of approaching 'Circus' operations.

Desirability of instituting R/T spoof in Bomber Command operations.

| | 15 May 42 | Memo on spoofing operations on Bomber Command since Aug 1941. |
| | 7 Sep 42 | Mtg to examine: |

Deception activities in Bomber Command,

Scale of future deception,

What changes to the present Signals Security staff are required in Bomber Command.

Signals Security Policy

1258	16 Nov 44	Blandy appointed Inspector of RAF Y Service
1260	22 Apr 42	DDI4 to Cheadle: W/T watch on RAF comms to be used to examine specific problems.
	28 Jul 42	DofS to all Commands: In near future Y service will start scheme for analysis of RAF R/T and W/T traffic.
	3 May 44	DofS to DDI4: re monitoring of W/T channels used by Commands.
	17 Jun 44	HQBC to USofS: Cannot agree to transfer of whole or any part of the Bomber Command monitoring organisation to Cheadle.

Reply from DofS on 4 Jul 44 that all other commands agree with centralisation of monitoring service; will HQBC reconsider?

Further note from HQBC to say that no change to present arrangements are required.

Finally, from DofS to AOC 26 Gp, on 24 Oct 44 to create a centralised monitoring unit within 26 Gp.

Airborne Interception of R/T [See also Q1236 above]

1261	31 May 43	Memo by Bonsall, Air Section at Bletchley Park: Case for intercepting German fighter R/T by means of airborne intercept stations.
	17 Jun 43	Mtg to discuss test of airborne interception by a Halifax of 192 Sqn.
	21 Jun 43	Report on airborne search for German VHF R/T, over Dutch and Frisian areas.

Q Refs	Date	Subject
	2 Oct 43	ACAS (I) to 8th USAAF: Request from COPC for extension in range of the present cover of enemy R/T by the Y-service.
	13 Oct 43	8th USAAF to ACAS(I): Agree to request; receiving equipment to be installed into operational aircraft of the 8th USAAF.
	15 Mar 44	8th USAAF to USofS: request for commanders leading missions to receive intelligence from the Y service re disposition and intentions of enemy fighter formations.
	6 May 44	AOC 100 Gp to USofS: airborne interception of R/T satisfactory; therefore propose to use aircraft on routine flights to amplify the int picture built up by ground stations within UK.

BIG BEN Intercept Reports

1264	11 Feb 45	Report by Ackermann on 382 WU results from radio intercept of V-Rockets.
	13 Jun 45	ACAS (I) Memo on German long-range weapon intelligence.

BIG BEN Equipment

1265		Multiple reports and correspondence from 13 Jul 44 to 1 Nov 44. The effort covered the type of receiving equipment that should be used; the formation of an Operations Room at Canterbury to control countermeasures against the V-rockets; the prospect of 192 Sqn providing continuous 24-hour cover of airborne intercept; the provision of land-lines to provide dedicated telephone communications for RCM operations, etc.

Y-Service and Home Defence Units Equipment and Work Services

1266–1276		Contain multiple correspondence, instructions and progress reports relating to the provision, installation and improvement of Y service facilities – buildings, site services, antennas and D/F systems, power supplies, heating, etc.

Communications Policy and Requirements

1277–1280		Contain multiple correspondence, instructions and progress reports relating to the requirements for and the provision of secure telephone/teleprinter services across the entire UK-based RAF Y-Service including data lines into Bletchley.
1277	9 Mar 42	AOC 26 Gp to USofS: Need for standardisation of operational signalling arrangements between Y receiving stations and Y D/F stations.
1279	2 May 41	Note on total RAF landline requirements at Chicksands.
1280	17 Jun 43	DofTels to Post Office Research station: New circuit requirements between Cheadle and its W/T out-stations; use of the Defence Teleprinter Network.

Q Refs	Date	Subject

Overseas Policy

1281	1941–1942	Many items of correspondence and multiple subjects. Much of this would have flowed from the previous DDSY branch, when it was part of the Air Ministry Signals Department prior to the transfer into Air Intelligence as DDI4.
1282	Nov 42– Sep 43	*Reorganisation of Y-Mediterranean* Major topics of concern such as the Policy for RAF Y in the Med area; the creation of a Central Air Intelligence Bureau for the whole of the Med; Air Section comments by Bill Bonsall on the proposed Auchinlek Centre in Malta; the determination of operating sites, creation of personnel establishments, provision of equipment and comms facilities, etc.
1283	Jul 41– Apr 45	*Middle East Policy* RAF Y activities within East Africa, the Levant, Iraq, Persia, Libya
1284/ 1286	Apr 42– Aug 43	*Formation of No. 276 Wing* General idea to form one large station, with out-stations covering the Middle East and the North African desert. Establishments, provision of staff, mobile units, etc.
1287	Sep 41– Apr 45	*Middle East – Returns and Reports* Allocation of receivers; monthly coverage; distribution of field units; plans for mobility and evacuation, if necessary (in third quarter 1942).
1288	Aug 41– Sep 42	*Middle East – Malta*
1289	Sep 41– Oct 43	*Middle East – E Section* Arrangements for detachment from Chicksands to work in the ME from Oct 41. Assessment of likely E traffic during 1943. Procedures for transmission of German E intercept back to UK. Extension of cover to include Black Sea and the Caucasus, etc.
1292	Jul 40– Aug 42	*Combined Bureau – RAF Section* Coverage from Aden, Iraq and Middle East in general. Establishment and staffing for Sigint and D/F tasks. Possibility that Josh Cooper may have been sent to the Combined Bureau from Bletchley Park Air Section; but that was resisted and Prof Boase was sent instead. He returned at the end of 1941 to become Deputy Head of the Air Section at Bletchley; at which time there was another request for Josh Cooper – again denied.
1295	Jan– Sep 43	*Italian Cover* Much activity concerning best use of limited intercept assets, especially for working E traffic.

Q Refs	Date	Subject
1324– 1327	May 43– Jul 45	*Mediterranean Air Command* Reduction in manpower throughout the command; need clarification on future policy for Y (Sep 43). Decision that only mobile units need to be retained. Recommend that No. 276 Wing be disbanded (Oct 43); but in fact No. 276 was re-formed with its Field Units for use in Italy (Nov 43). This Wing subsequently re-located to Malta in Jul 45. Decision by HQ MAAF, Algiers, to form RCM Board for Middle East Theatre (Mar 44). Regular returns and reports through the period on Y operations, across the geographical area extending into SE Europe, the Balkans, southern Germany and Italy.
1296	Aug 43– May 45	*GAF in the Mediterranean* Multiple reports and summaries of GAF signals traffic: this covered Long Range Recce, Convoy escort, German Air Transport, GAF on the Russian Front; reactions to Allied operations and raids; etc.
1329, 1333– 1334, 1336– 1340	Feb 43– mid-45	*380 WU* Located at Algiers but with mobile units along the North African coast. Subsequently, a Signals Wing similar to No. 276 Wing was considered, incorporating Nos. 380, 381 WUs and their Field Units; to be known as 329 Sigs Wing. Establishment and revisions as tasking changes; particularly following the opening up of new enemy comms links (Dec 42). Notes for DDI4: Intelligence production and distribution, information required from Cheadle and Cairo, M/F cover and Fixed Frequencies cover. Enemy night fighters using VHF (Jan 43).
1297– 1300	Apr 41– Jan 45	*351 WU at Gibraltar* Reports on Y activities, lists of frequencies covered, channel tasking, etc. Determination of equipment and transport requirements; training of Y staff, following some unsatisfactory performance; acute shortage of some trades, especially W/T operators. Need for establishment increase (May 42); proposal to use Gibraltar as an out-station from Cheadle (Jan 43). Closure of 351 WU (Jan 45).
1305– 1311	Jul 41– Mar 43	*West Africa – Policy* Formation of 356 WU as a mobile Y-Unit. Operations from Freetown, Bathurst and Kano. Reports on receiving conditions, W/T comms, traffic analyses, general intelligence, etc.
1210	28 Mar 44	AOC 26 Gp: 365 WU to be transferred to 2nd TAF, AEAF, from 30 Mar 44.
1212	27 Sep 44	AM to RAF Cheadle: Commitments for 365 WU
1313–	Oct 41–	*India – Policy*

Q Refs	Date	Subject
1316	Jan 44	Suggestion for formation of a large scale Y organisation in India – equivalent to Bletchley Park? Intention to form Far East Combined Bureau in Ceylon. (Mar 42).; but agreed that the Army would have main centre in Delhi.
		Agreement to set RAF Y in Delhi with out-stations at Rawalpindi and Calcutta. Concern by ACAS(I) at number of personnel envisaged; needs justification for numbers (Mar 42). Decision to form No. 164 Signals Wing in India (May 42). Subsequent need for a Technical Research Section as an addition to the overall establishment (Apr 43). Formation of various WUs in India. Outline of work to be done by 164 Sigs Wg (May 42).
		General concern by DDI4 about state of work in India and the RAF requirements not being understood (Dec 42).
		Problems about American participation in the Joint Sigint Board; related to formation of the South East Asia Command (Dec 43).
1344	Sep 41– Feb 44	*Air Mail Services for Y Material*
		Possibility of using Overseas Canister service for mail to Middle East; some types of Canister had self-destruct features (Sep 41). Weight limits for Airmail services; Rules for carriage of official documents. BOAC still hampered by pre-war rules causing delays and short cargoes (May 42).
1349	Jun 42– Apr 43	*Microgram Service*
		Maximum quantity of correspondence that can be handled per week for incoming and outgoing Y traffic.
		List of countries that are on the Microgram distribution service (Aug 42).
1351– 1353	Feb 42–	*USA Liaison – Y Mission*
		Recommendation for formation of Combined Met Committee. Proposal for combined British, Canadian and US R/T Intelligence Committee.

Distribution of GC & CS Air Sigint Intelligence Reports

Introduction

This Appendix contains two topics:

- The distribution of Hut 3 High-Grade (ULTRA) Intelligence to specific sections within Air Intelligence.
- The distribution of Air Sigint reports from GC&CS direct to Bomber Command and to the USSAAF in the UK.

Hut 3 High-Grade Sigint Reporting to Specific Sections within Air Intelligence

This information was correct as at 4 Nov 44, from HW 50/25:

Section	Section Function		Type of Intelligence
ADI (Sci) Dr Jones	Enemy scientific research	CX/MSS/B AI/MSS CX/MSS/SDE CX/MSS/SER	German radar plots. Appreciations by Air Advisors at Hut 3.
AI 1 c	Liaison Duties	AI/MSS	Appreciations by Air Advisors at Hut 3
AI 2 a AI 2 h	Aircraft industries	CX/MSS CX/MSS/J CX/MSS/SJ	Aircraft markings. Special German radar plots. Secret Weapons (Prof Norman)
AI 3 a (1) and (2)	Distribution , etc. – see Appendix F above	CX/MSS/R CX/MSS/T	Typed reports of Hut 3 material. Teleprinted reports of Hut 3 material

Section	Section Function		Type of Intelligence
AI 3 AL	Assistance to AI (JIS)	MEL/HP BIS/HP CX/MSS/ROB	Appreciations of Allied Order of Battle from Abwehr sources. Russian Order of Battle
AI 3 b	Current enemy Air Ops, forecast of intentions and scales of effort	CX/MSS CX/MSS/J CX/MSS/JS AI/MSS CX/MSS/SDE	Aircraft markings. Special German radar plots. Secret Weapons (Prof Norman). Appreciations by Air Advisors at Hut 3
AI 3 d	MEAFs, Russian, Finnish, Swedish, Jap/Chinese Air Forces etc	CX/MSS/ROB	Russian Order of Battle
AI 3 e	GAF Intelligence, P/W, Research & Recording of past operations	CX/MSS CX/MSS/J CX/MSS/SJ AI/MSS CX/MSS/SDE	Aircraft markings. Special German radar plots. Secret Weapons (Prof Norman). Appreciations by Air Advisors at Hut 3
AI 4 c	Call Sign Section; GAF Air Traffic	AI/MSS	Appreciations by Air Advisors at Hut 3
DDI 3	Head of AI 3 under D of I (O)	AI/MSS BAY/HP CX/MSS/HV CX/MSS/S DT HU Maps	Appreciations by Air Advisors at Hut 3. Int. from Diplomatic & Attaché sources. Ditto. Special reports based on Hut 3 material. Reports on German morale. Hungarian Forces in Russia. Sketch maps of current military situation
DDI 4	Head of AI 4	CX/MSS/R CX/MSS/J CX/MSS/SJ AI/MSS CX/MSS/SDE	Typed reports of Hut 3 material. Special German radar plots. Secret Weapons (Prof Norman). Appreciations by Air Advisors at Hut 3.

Air Sigint Reports direct to RAF and USAAF Bomber Commands

The following list is extracted from Addendum B of the minutes of a meeting in the Air Intelligence directorate.[1] The extracted details show the distribution of particular GC&CS (AI4f) intelligence reports to RAF (Bomber Command) and to the USAAF.

Report	RAF Bomber Command	USSTAF	8th USAAF
ULTRA			
CX/MSS/X/BMP	No	Yes	No
CX/MSS/GAY	No	Yes	No
CX/MSS/OPA	No	AI 3 (USA)	No
CX/MSS/OPD	No	Yes	No
PEARL			
PEARL/ZIP/BMP Pt I	Yes, inc 100 Gp	Yes	Yes
PEARL/ZIP/BMP Pt II	Yes, inc 100 Gp	Yes	Yes
PEARL/ZIP/DISTAC/DAY	No	Yes	Yes
PEARL/ZIP/GAM	No	Yes	No
PEARL/ZIP/LS	Yes, inc 100 Gp	No	No
PEARL/ZIP/TAC/D	Yes, inc 100 Gp	Yes	Yes
PEARL/ZIP/TAC/NIGHT	Yes, inc 100 Gp	AI 3 (USA)	No
ZIP/MET/PROG	Yes	No	No

1. HW 3/118, Addendum B to Minutes of Air Intelligence mtg, 7 Apr 44.

Whitehall and the British Bombing Survey

Reference: Air 20/3180, 20/3181, 20/3182, 20/3415 and Air 10/3866.

Introduction

It is relevant to consider the various views and exchanges within Whitehall in the last nine months of the war, with regard to the possible conduct of a Bombing Survey. The Secretary of State for Air Sinclair put a proposal before the Prime Minister on 14 Dec 44, to which was attached a copy of a note from President Roosevelt to the US Secretary of War.[1] The President had already directed the US War Department to take action to have a group of appropriate specialists selected and appointed to undertake a survey as soon as possible. The US intention was to study not just the visible and physical damage caused by the Combined Bombing Offensive, as conceived and agreed at Casablanca in Jan 43, but also the direct and indirect consequences on industry, transportation and the communities. It was seen to be valuable to gather an indication of the psychological, morale and evacuee problems. The number of people involved with the US Survey rose to at least 900.

The immediate response from Churchill to Sinclair, within a Personal Minute Serial No. M.20/5 dated 3 Jan 45, was that he could not agree with the proposed scale of UK effort and that much would depend upon the circumstances when the war ended. But he agreed that a scheme could be brought before the War Cabinet, given that the staff numbers involved were no more than 20–30 people. This Appendix briefly examines the progress, or lack of it, that the British scheme made within Whitehall.

The War Cabinet

The War Cabinet heard the outline of the proposed scheme to investigate the effects of the bombing offensive and some views are recorded in a brief.[2] One of

---

1. Air 20/3180, White House to War Dept, 9 Sept 44.
2. Ibid. S.4 (C.S.) Cabinet Section, 19 Feb 45.

the first points made in that Brief was from the Parliamentary Secretary of the MEW, who pointed out that 'the results of the investigation would be a most valuable guide for considering the allocation of defence expenditure ... but not too much should be made of that, for fear that we should give the impression ... that we want to justify a claim for more expenditure on the RAF.'[3]

There was great play made on the difficulty of recruiting and training staff, and then getting them out to the continent; but this was directed at the sense of urgency that should attend the task, in order that evidence should not become obliterated and records lost for ever. It was felt that men with the right qualifications would be very difficult to find as the war was drawing to an end. It was further felt that an Advisory Committee should be set up to direct the function and conduct of the study; the 'committee culture' never did subside!.

Later, on 12 Mar 45, the Deputy CAS wrote that care must be taken to avoid a situation where the Treasury gave only grudging support for the proposed study, which could then be subjected to 'fresh obstacles and crippling qualifications.' Other departments were giving thought to investigations for their own purposes, e.g. the War Office, the Ministry of Home Security, etc. Deputy CAS felt that all these should be brought under one organisation. But his major point was that if the study did not secure approval, then the UK would find itself in a position where the only authoritative body which could assess the real value of the bombing offensive by Bomber Command throughout the war would be American. He concluded by saying:

When we have expended so much blood and treasure on these efforts, this seems a queer and indifferent way of writing the History of it for posterity.

Then, within the notes of a War Cabinet Chiefs of Staff Committee meeting on 30 Mar 45 to examine a British Bombing Research Mission, there is the statement that:[4]

We have thus reached a stage where, nearly eight months after it had been approved by the COS, this important project has made no material progress.

Those notes recorded that our land forces were occupying the Ruhr and the Rhineland, areas that had been subjected to the most intensive bombing throughout the war, and we had neither the plans, personnel nor the administrative machinery ready to take advantage of this state of affairs. The Deputy Supreme Commander had stressed the urgency of collecting evidence at the earliest opportunity; he pointed out that if any study was to be of real value then it must be conducted immediately – before the evidence became vitiated. The US Survey was already at an advanced stage with a body of 700 investigators under well-qualified leadership, with a further 200 people in Headquarters and

---

3. Author's Note: This could be seen as indicative of that school of thought within Whitehall that would not have wanted the achievements of Bomber Command to have any visibility. The relationship between MEW and Bomber Command was fragile, particularly at that stage in the war when the very serious argument between CAS and CinC regarding target priorities had only just subsided.
4. COS (45) 224 (0) 30 Mar 45, para. 6.

administrative support in London and on the continent. Roosevelt had also secured the approval of Stalin for the US Survey to operate within the Russian Zone of East Germany.

Further, those notes also recorded that because the American methods of bombing differed from those used by Bomber Command, it was only reasonable to suppose that the US Survey would concentrate on those results for which the USAAFs had been mainly responsible and in which they would be most interested. On the other hand, it would almost certainly ignore or obscure the results of Bomber Command's operations. There would then be a danger that a rather incomplete picture would be given to the world of an offensive in which a large proportion of British resources had been employed throughout the war, initially for some 27 months before the US was even at war.

The Committee agreed that in view of the urgency, the Secretary should place the notes before the Prime Minister immediately. This was done on 4 Apr 45, as COS 506/5 (45), over the signatures of General Brooke, Air Chief Marshal Portal and Admiral Cunningham. The response from the Prime Minister was that he still did not find himself in agreement.[5] He maintained that any study should be limited to '30 experts plus a number of Air groundsmen who will be scattered about Germany during the next few months'.[6]

However, there was a Personal Minute M.320 from the Prime Minister and a Minute from the Chancellor of the Exchequer, dated 7 Apr 45, which set in train the creation of a Planning Committee for an Investigation of the Effects of the Combined Bombing Offensive. The committee contained representatives from the Treasury, Foreign Office, the Service departments and the Offices of the Cabinet, under the chairmanship of Colonel C G Vickers. The committee delivered its report in Sep 45.[7] The conclusions contained the following items:

- Provision should be made for preparing an appreciation of the effects of the strategic bombing offensive against Germany, on lines that we indicate in paragraphs 10–13 of our report.
- The advent of atomic weapons makes it possible to curtail or eliminate some aspects of the enquiry that we should otherwise have recommended.
- Full use should be made of existing machinery and of evidence collected for other purposes, but it is impossible for the task to be carried out efficiently and economically without setting up a certain amount of ad hoc machinery.

---

5. COS (45) 244 (0) 9 Apr 45.
6. Author's Note: The available records show that the major opposition to the British Survey came from the Prime Minister. It is noted that this time period was within two months of the Dresden Raid, following which there was massive recrimination and blame-passing. Mr Churchill had then recently written that infamous personal memo that spoke of 'terror bombing'; that memo may have been written in haste and it was withdrawn and re-written, but it disclosed a political school of thought that was divisive and at serious odds with the military thinking about the bombing campaign and its objectives. Not least, the records show very clearly that one of the political objectives of that campaign had been to provide support to the Russian Army advancing into Germany, which was a dominant reason for bombing Dresden – which Bomber Command had resisted.
7. Air 20/3415, Cabinet Report PBR 14 dated Sep 45.

- The most important part of the task will be appreciating and drawing together agreed conclusions from the evidence available, rather than the collection of new evidence.
- We take note of the existence of the RAF organisation known as the BBSU. The execution of the scheme that we now propose will need an expert staff of about 80 officers for three months.
- Any action that is to be taken on our report should be taken at once, since the resources required are being dispersed and cannot easily be reassembled.

If ever there was a classic case of bureaucratic humbug, this Planning Committee report must take the cake. It took five months to reach conclusions that could have been written in a single day by an informed person. The fact that the evidence was vitiating in real time had no impact on the crucial waste of time in conducting this preliminary planning exercise. The intention to work on the basis of existing evidence leaves wide open the question whether the existing evidence was complete or valid.

If there can be any compensation, an argument with the body of the report makes a good case for the already demonstrated effects of the bombing offensive; namely that the enhanced importance of industrial and urban targets will affect many fields of policy, in particular:

- Strategic planning in anticipation of any future war,
- The balance of the Armed Forces of the Crown,
- The organisation of Civil Defence,
- Protecting from air attack the bases of national life including industry, public utilities, internal transportation, seaports and telecommunications.

The Establishment of the British Bombing Survey Unit
In the face of the political and financial opposition within Whitehall, there was continuing laboured progress towards any executive decision about a British bombing survey team.

The first meeting of any substance was at the Air Ministry on 31 May 1945, to discuss the formation and function of the British Bombing Survey Unit.[8] That meeting was chaired by ACAS (Ops). He noted that notwithstanding the planning and organisational work, for nearly 12 months, there had been no political approval for the Unit to form. The intention at that time was that a British Bombing Research Mission would form at some later date and may then subsume the BBSU. The minutes of the meeting record a number of somewhat disappointing inputs from other Whitehall departments:

- The MEW was to be dissolved in the near future and would have little ability to support the BBSU. The Foreign Office would need to be approached if any representation was required on the BBSU Advisory Committee.[9]

---

8. Air 20/3180, Minutes on Air Ministry Meeting, 31 May 1945.
9. Author's Note: The 'Committee Culture' again; the MEW was at the heart of the CSTC but appeared unwilling to be part of any Survey. Would field information have been inappropriate to any post-war assessment of 'committee' attitudes and decisions

- The Home Office would probably be unable to take a very active part in the survey.

However, the meeting did make the decision to proceed with creation of the BBSU and for the Unit to carry out a factual investigation of the bombing offensive with the following specific Terms of Reference:

- To determine the effect on the fighting capacity of the enemy.
- The comparative efficiency of the various bombing techniques and weapons.
- The nature and success of the enemy operational air defence system.
- The accuracy of Allied bombing assessments made prior to any field investigation.

The Executive Head of the BBSU was Air Commodore Pelly and the Scientific Advisor was Professor Zuckerman.

At the following meeting on 8 June 1945, chaired by AVM Combe, DG Armaments, and with an exclusively Air Force membership, there was an illuminating introduction by Air Cdre Pelly.[10] He explained the short and disappointing history of the Bombing Research Mission, which had then been in existence for seven months but had been unable to make any real progress because of 'political pressures'. The minutes reflect the decision of CAS:

> *CAS had become so exasperated with the political in-fighting within Whitehall that he had decided to proceed with the BBSU as an independent Air Force Unit simply to avoid the political direction and interference.*

The Treasury would not agree to any increase in staff, to allow the BBSU to achieve its tasks. The effort would therefore come from existing Air Force appointments with no prospect of replacement during their attachment to the BBSU. Attachments would be planned not to exceed three months. Familiarisation and training courses for attached staff would be provided from a variety of primarily Air Force sources.

The Bombing Research Mission had been merged with the Bombing Analysis Unit; and administrative and transport facilities were available to allow the BBSU to proceed, with a Field HQ on the continent and the Main HQ in Whitehall.

The organisation of the BBSU is shown in the following diagram:

---

during the conduct of the bombing offensive? Later, in September 1945, there was a Cabinet Paper P.B.R 14 (see Air 20/3415) which set down the Terms and Conditions for an independent enquiry – the Vickers Committee – to find out the effect of the strategic bombing offensive on the fighting capacity of Germany. The political warfare between the various departments and committees beggars belief.

10. Air Ministry, DG Arm, 8 Jun 45 Minutes of Meeting to progress the BBSU.

BRITISH BOMBING SURVEY UNIT
Provisional Organisation

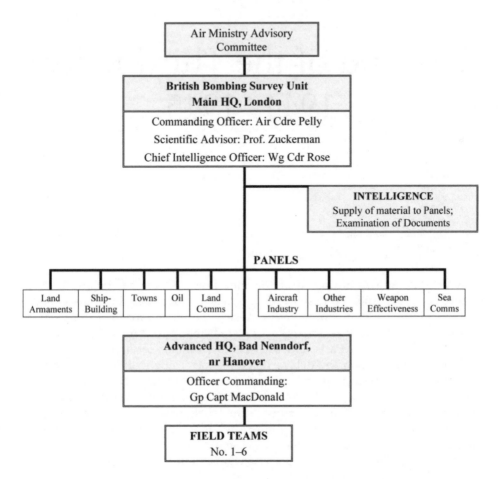

Air Ministry Advisory Committee

British Bombing Survey Unit Main HQ, London

Commanding Officer: Air Cdre Pelly

Scientific Advisor: Prof. Zuckerman

Chief Intelligence Officer: Wg Cdr Rose

INTELLIGENCE
Supply of material to Panels; Examination of Documents

PANELS

| Land Armaments | Ship-Building | Towns | Oil | Land Comms | Aircraft Industry | Other Industries | Weapon Effectiveness | Sea Comms |

Advanced HQ, Bad Nenndorf, nr Hanover

Officer Commanding: Gp Capt MacDonald

FIELD TEAMS
No. 1–6

APPENDIX O

The End of the Third Reich, 1944–1945

This short summary is based on the final sections of Bib. A22: The Most Valuable Asset of the Reich, *Volume 2, 1933–1945, by Alfred Mierzejewski.*

The Allied air attacks during April, May and June 1944 on marshalling yards in France, Belgium and western Germany created havoc on the transportation services for the German armies on the Western Front, and for the Reichsbahn in Germany. Rolling stock and manpower were being moved forward to the main operating divisions in Paris and Brussels to maintain services, but that only added to the congestion and delays. It became increasingly difficult for the main operating divisions in Saarbrucken and Karlsrühe to send trains to the west. Grave problems due to bombing in Germany began at the end of August, when the Allies opened the offensive against the marshalling yards deeper into the west of the country. As that assault continued, the Ruhr industrial region and other industries were becoming seriously dislocated.

At that stage, the Central Transportation Directorate attempted to use coal from Upper Silesia to replace the loss of shipments from the Ruhr; and to use the inland waterways to relieve the pressure on the Reichsbahn. But the capacity of the marshalling yards was dwindling and, in October and November, the major waterways were crippled by air attacks. Through that period the Central Transportation Directorate ruthlessly cut wagon space allocations to any traffic other then coal in the hope of maintaining essential economic activity. A massive repair effort was undertaken to restore the marshalling yards and locomotive sheds, taking advantage of the bad weather that hampered the air attacks; and fortuitously capitalizing on the relief as the strategic attacks were directed to other targets. By Nov 44 well over 100,000 people were struggling to repair and maintain the rail service.

The disruption to rail services in the Ruhr and the difficulty of returning empty wagons back to the region for loading with coal led to a dramatic reduction in coal supplies to the whole German economy. Manufacturing plants and utilities gradually consumed their stocks from the start of September. By the end of Dec 44, supplies had been exhausted and production shrank due to lack of energy.

Finished armament products, especially the badly needed ammunitions, accumulated at the factories forcing many to suspend operations from December and into the first months of 1945. The ultimate effect of the breakdown in the Reichsbahn was the inability to transport weapons and other supplies needed by the troops at the Fronts.

The situation in the East added to the Reichsbahn's difficulties. At one point, the German retreats helped by shortening the supply routes and releasing wagons. But as the retreats continued, the transport demands escalated as the number of refugees increased so rapidly. The Reichsbahn had laid evacuation plans well in advance, but the civilian authorities were reluctant to use them too early and possibly spread panic among the population. The Soviet breakthroughs and advances were unpredictable and those evacuation plans were called on at short notice, often under artillery fire and with thousands of civilians and large quantities of industrial and military goods. In late Jan 45, the National Railway Division at Posen evacuated two million Germans before it was overrun; and at Oppeln, 1.7 million civilians were rushed away from the advancing Red Army. The loss of Upper Silesia removed the major alternative source of coal to the Ruhr, dealing a final decisive blow to the whole German industry and to the Reichsbahn itself.

The disintegration of the Reichsbahn can be traced by examining a few indices of its operational performance. The collapse of traffic and, in turn, the disintegration of the German economy began in earnest during Oct 44. Coal wagon placings in Jan 45 were 56 per cent lower than in Jan 44. By March, they were 89 per cent lower than in Mar 44. The disintegration of marshalling and traffic flow saw a staggering increase in the number of trains held in the backlog. In early May 44, following the air attacks in the west, the backlog was 1600 trains. As the Germans were forced to retreat after D-Day, that backlog declined as the Reichsbahn was able to consolidate its operations. However, it rose steeply when the Allies focused their air attacks on marshalling yards in western Germany from the end of August. By mid-December the backlog had increased to 2000 trains; and to 2800 trains by the end of Feb 45.

The confusion in marshalling and the disruption in flow caused a massive increase in wagon turnaround times. The inability to move wagons in a coordinated and scheduled manner – the hallmark of the Reichsbahn's operating procedures – rebounded on the railway itself when it became unable even to supply coal for the locomotives. That shortage varied between different operating divisions; the outlying divisions at Stuttgart and Munich had less than one day's supply by early Feb 45.

The Reichsbahn made an essential contribution to fighting the war, but it was not consulted when the Nazi government and the Wehrmacht formed their plans in the 1930s for rearmament and an aggressive war. The German economy simply could not function without extensive and efficient rail transportation. Had more resources been given to the Reichsbahn during that period, it may well have survived longer into the war; but it was inevitable that it would eventually succumb to the bombing offensive. In the end the transportation crisis was too strong even for the railway's operational expedients to overcome.

There was profound criticism of the bureaucratic control of the Reichsbahn. One of the most striking criticisms related to operations in the East as the German armies gained huge territories in Russia. The rich resources of raw materials and food that drew Hitler to that region yielded less than was expected; and this was in part a consequence of the attitudes of the rail managers and their labour relations with the local staffs. That reflected the attitudes of the invading German armies and their mistreatment of prisoners of war and non-combatants. Official prejudice was only partially moderated by the behaviour of a minority of the Reichsbahn's German workers who were sympathetic to the plight of the non-German employees. Another major problem was the conservative and prejudiced view that the Reichsbahn officials took on gender issues and the very slow and reluctant incorporation of German women as employees, when many of the men were drafted into the armed forces. In a very real sense, the Reichsbahn reflected the society that it served: obsessed with its internal processes, nationalistic but ultimately unable to manage human issues.

The Oil Factor in German War Effort

Reference: A. Air 8/1019: COS Technical Sub-Committee on Oil, Report AO (46) 1, 8 Mar 46.

Introduction

This Appendix briefly summarises the extensive paper at Reference A above. That report was an account of the German oil economy, from 1932 until the end of the war in Europe, based on all relevant German records that were available including the interrogation of German officials and examination of many bombed targets. The report was generated from Sir Harold Hartley, KCVO, on behalf of the Technical Sub-committee on Axis Oil. This summary of that Report has the following sections:

- Background.
- Position over the First Year of the War.
- The Oil Offensive.
- The Effects of Oil Shortages:
  - On the German Army
  - On the German Air Force
  - On the German Navy
  - On the German War Economy.

Background

An important and instructive commentary in the report related to the development of the German oil production programme, known as the Four Year Plan as announced in 1936. It came at a time when the German commercial interests were unwilling to plunge into the enormous capital costs and uneconomic operation of synthetic oil plants. The development of indigenous oil production under State control was consequently one of the principal objects of the plan. One of the elements of that Plan was continuing large-scale exploration and drilling for crude oil. From 1933, that exploration had located about a dozen new fields within Germany that gave the promise of substantial underground reserves for production in the event of war. That promise was coupled with the prospect of substantial yields from Austrian fields and continuing imports from Romania and Russia., none of which were handicapped by the Blockade that was initiated by Britain at the start of the war.

The responsibility for the Four Year Plan was initially placed with an official named Keppler. He was replaced in 1937 by Krauch, who also found that the large-scale provision of synthetic oil production was fraught with many difficulties. The original ambitious Plan was revised in Jun 1938, under the influence of Goering, and became known as the New Four Year Plan, otherwise known as the Karinhall Plan. This revision was intended to see a final annual production target of nearly 14 million tons of oil products per year by mid-1942.

The target date of mid-1942 coincided with all other ancillary planning in connection with the main plan for oil production, including transportation facilities. German transportation estimates were that 18,000 oil product tank wagons would be needed in the event of war; and that quantity could have been produced by mid-1942 (see Ref. A above, Section I, p. 4). The planned reserve stock storage programme however would not have been completed until Apr 43. However, it became apparent that even the New Four Year Plan would have been impossible to achieve. There were continuous difficulties that hindered the realisation of the projects even before the outbreak of war.

An outstanding fact in all this planning was that the Germans had neither expected nor planned an extended war to start before 1942–43. The pre-war economy lacked sufficient foreign exchange to build up strategic oil reserves to safeguard military supplies, even for a short war. During the first years of the war, no arm of the German forces lacked the fuel that was needed for the offensive operations. The initial concept of the Blitzkrieg did not demand the depth of reserve capacity that became necessary as the war progressed into an extended attrition conflict. The German High Command remained largely unconcerned about oil supplies until the loss of the Romanian fields.

Position over the First Year of War

At the start of the war, the total German stock of fuel oils was just over two million tons. Motor fuel and of aviation fuel were sufficient for only three and five months respectively. There was sufficient Naval diesel oil to maintain active U-boat warfare for at least two years. The calculated war consumption would however have drained German stocks of most oil fuels within a period of eleven months. The clear situation was that Germany had no substantial reserves that would sustain either an extended period of conflict of the loss of national production capacity.

The Head of the Economic Office of the German Supreme Command, General Thomas, is reported to have referred to the:

absolute folly of even contemplating going to war while supplies were so short.[1]

That concern was professionally very sound but Hitler disregarded it. It was soon dispelled by the unexpected speed and economy of the first two campaigns and

---

1. ICF/284 dated 1 Jun 39.

the capture of large quantities of oil in Western Europe. When Italy entered the war, the aggregate oil reserves and refining capacity was quite sufficient for the German war effort at that period. In fact, for the first year of the war Germany operated her war and armament machine on almost exactly the same amount of oil as had been used for the last full year of peace.

During the first year of war, the MEW was persisting with optimistic estimates that Germany was rapidly coming to an oil supply crisis and that she would have to sue for peace very quickly.

The Oil Offensive

The initial list of targets for bombing attack in 1940–41 had the above-ground stocks at refineries and storage depots as first priority, followed by the hydrogenation plants, refineries operating on domestic crude oil and finally the Fischer-Tropsch plants. Sadly, but with hindsight not surprisingly, those early bombing attacks were of no consequence. The bombing techniques and resources at that period were quite inadequate for the task. This is described in detail within Chapter 4. Perhaps the major benefit was the news media reporting and the optimism being put before the general public in Britain. By the spring of 1941 the bombing attacks on oil were suspended.

The next serious offensive against German oil supplies was embraced within the Casablanca Directive in Jan 43. The satisfaction of that Directive so far as oil targets were concerned had to wait for the build-up of the 8th and 15th USAAFs in Britain and the Mediterranean, notwithstanding that Bomber Command maintained vigorous night operations on an increasing scale from the middle of 1942. The bitter arguments within Whitehall about strategic targeting for the bomber offensive are described in Chapters 2, 3, 7 and 11.

It was not possible to begin an all-out attack on oil until the spring of 1944. One specific operation by the 15th USAAF operating from the Mediterranean airfields was against Ploesti in Aug 43. The bomber losses were heavy and the damage to the target was modest. An unfortunate consequence was that the Germans then appreciated that their oil production facilities in Romania were within range for attack and they responded by providing additional defences and protection. The result was that the subsequent attacks in 1944 against Romanian targets were handicapped by those defensive measures.

However, it also reported that in spite of these apprehensions little progress had been made in general with passive air defence measures and the oil plants had little or no protection from either direct bomb hits, blast or splinter effects. Probably the compelling reason for that was the massive cost and effort that would have been entailed; the protection of oil plants is detailed in Appendix 19 of the reference COS paper AO (46) 1.

In post-war interrogations, German officials expressed surprise that the Allies had not conducted systematic attacks on the oil facilities until the spring of 1944. The reasons for that are extensive and complex. They relate to:

- The politics, operational practicality and Intelligence to support strategic target selection.
- The competing priority of different strategic target sets.

- The provision of sufficient heavy bomber and long-range escort fighter assets, with the progressive improvements in navigation and bomb aiming techniques.

The greatest conflict of priority between the various strategic target sets was for oil or transportation. This was never resolved but remained a bitter and entrenched subject, even to this day.

The Russian capture of the Romanian oilfields in Aug 44 exercised a far-reaching and immediate influence on the German oil situation. It not only denied the enemy about 25 per cent of available production but also released the 15th USAAF to attack other synthetic oil plants in Central and Eastern Germany. Those attacks contributed to aggregate oil production in Sep 44 falling to the lowest level in 1944.

The CSTC recognised that German oil production would recover rapidly unless there was consistent re-attack on damaged oil production facilities. The expectation of increasingly adverse weather then created a problem; photographic reconnaissance sorties were seriously handicapped; and it was determined that 'blind bombing' was to be used, despite the consequent need to drop a greatly increased tonnage of bombs to have a chance of achieving comparable results. The major oil targets were mostly at long range from the strategic bomber airfields and the important ground-based radar navigation and bombing aids; for example, at Poelitz and Leuna, both of which were producing significant quantities of fuels. The effectiveness of that long range bombing was destined generally to be poor. That was no reflection on the aircrews; it was an inescapable matter of operational capability and the adverse weather. However, Bomber Command carried out some very successful night attacks against Poelitz and Leuna in the occasional breaks in the bad weather and thereby demonstrated that the great weight of attack by the Lancasters and Halifaxes could be brought to bear against enemy targets across all of Germany.

In the autumn of 1944 Bomber Command conducted 38 attacks on oil targets; 20 by day and 18 by night. The 8th USAAF consistently attacked oil targets through October and November. Those combined night and daylight attacks inflicted decisive damage on oil plants in the Ruhr, which were at shorter range. Some of those plants were crippled for the remainder of the war. For the 8th USAAF, a prerequisite for those daylight operations was not more than 5/10ths cloud cover. Owing to the bad weather, there were 37 days when either no operations were scheduled or planned operations were cancelled. The 15th USAAF operating from Foggia maintained a consistent attack whenever weather conditions over the targets permitted. Those attacks were particularly successful against the Silesian synthetic plants, prior to their capture by the Russians.

When the weather relented a little, in December, the Ardennes Offensive then demanded unplanned high priority bombing support for the Allied armies.

During that autumn, the tremendous repair organisation for the restoration of oil output began to operate with good effect. Geilenberg had been appointed by Hitler in May 44 as special commissioner for the repair and dispersal of the oil plants. To help him achieve that task, he was given powers that in the words of Speer would 'make everyone's hair stand on end'. Those powers gave him unrestricted priority over all other war production measures and he had Hitler's authority to demand assistance from the military as he required. Although skilled technicians were not available in the numbers required, notwithstanding the withdrawal of some technical personnel from the armed forces, there was an abundant supply of unskilled labourers. Many of these were foreign workers. Records do not show the overall numbers but Speer estimated that between 200,000 and 300,000 skilled and unskilled persons were employed.

Geilenberg faced the problem of either repeatedly re-building bomb-damaged oil plants or dispersing the industry, including underground constructions (See Plate 8). That was a momentous judgement to have to make. It demanded knowledge of the likely future conduct of the war, the future fuel requirements of the German armed forces, the possible success of Allied strategic bombing and the effectiveness of German defences. Constructing underground facilities was a task of huge magnitude; the larger hydrogenation plants covered one square mile in area and demanded rapid dispersal of gases. Speer and Geilenberg were originally of the opinion that the industry could not be dispersed and they embarked on a continuous damage repair programme. That was successful during those autumn months of 1944, when the weather was adverse. The partial recovery of production resulted in the output of one-third of a million tons of aviation and motor fuels; which in turn enabled the German armies and air force to continue operating.

In Sep 44, Geilenberg did also start on a dispersal programme, with multiple small sites, that was hoped to start production by Feb 45. That programme was not successful – see Appendix 21 within the COS Technical Sub-committee report. A small but increasing quantity of motor fuel was being produced by these dispersed and concealed sites from Jan 45 onwards, but they were not then capable of producing the higher-grade aviation fuel.

The judgement taken at that time, 24 Jan 45, by the Allied COS committee was that the utmost efforts should be made by the strategic bombing forces to achieve further success against the major enemy oil plants. Very soon afterwards, on 31 Jan 45, that committee revised their decision in favour of strategic attacks on transportation rather than the lesser oil plants. The CSTC conceded that the attack on the transportation system should be comprehensive to effectively deny the distribution of oil products, in coordination with movements by the Allied armies. During Jan and Feb 45 the weather improved and the strategic bomber forces continued to deliver methodical attacks on the enemy's major oil production and storage systems.

The Military Effects of Oil Shortages

Until the start of 1943, the German organisation for distributing the required oil supplies generally worked well and military operations were unimpeded by shortages. Perhaps the key exception arose during phases of the Desert War in North Africa, when fuel supply across the Mediterranean and distribution across the desert handicapped some of Rommel's plans. Part of that problem arose with the intermediate Italian transport services. But as the war moved on, the efficient operation of the German war machine became increasingly handicapped. This was expressed by Keitel in a letter to Speer dated 25 Oct 43:

Owing to the development of the armament programme the discrepancy between (fuel) supply and demand is likely to become more acute during 1944. The especially high increase in the demands of the Luftwaffe is based on the increased aircraft programme for 1944. Even if the armament programme is not fully carried out, a certain fuel surplus is desirable in order to be able to build up a modest reserve to allow for a possible break down in production.[2]

Effect on the German Army

A problem initially arose from reduced driver training that caused increasing problems under battle conditions.[3] This problem initially became apparent during the North African campaign and then in Italy. Field Marshal Kesselring, in a post-war interview with the USSBS (Interview No. 61), said that:

In Africa we had a shortage of fuel and it was decisive. But in Italy I made savings in fuel, even down to the extent that artillery and flak had to be drawn by oxen. A special organisation of supply transport handled all the vehicles, using the best drivers and very careful maintenance; it was a strict rule that every vehicle would have to draw a trailer. I managed to save enough fuel to carry out the necessary movements although the situation was tense.

The D-Day invasion created the largest German fuel demand since the advance into Russia in 1941. An earlier message from Field Marshal von Rundstedt, in command of the Western defences, reported that:

In order to minimise the effect of the anticipated air attacks, fuel dumps were greatly decentralised. It was foreseen that the attack on the railways would cause a diversion to road transport with an attendant increase in fuel requirements.

But that policy intention was poorly implemented. The fuel reserves in anticipation of the invasion were initially only 10,000 tons, primarily located in Bordeaux, Lyons and Paris. The dumps in Bordeaux and Lyons were attacked in August 1943 and the Paris dump was then moved into the Metro tunnels. After D-day, the insufficiency of the fuel reserves became very apparent. The dislocation of the railway system not only impeded re-supply from Germany but forced extra demands on road vehicles. Both rail and road movements were subjected to frequent air attack by Allied tactical fighter bombers and German troops often had to march miles to reach the battle front, arriving in no fit state for combat. By the end of Aug 44, the situation had worsened and was a primary cause of the defeat of the German 7th Army at the Falaise Gap.

During Aug 44, the German Army Group North on the Russian front reported that their position was jeopardised by the lack of fuel; four weeks later, the same

---

2. This is the first in a series of letters from Keitel to Speer that pointed out the paramount difficulties in the supply of fuel; but he contented himself with this correspondence which remained ineffective.

3. COS Technical Sub-Committee on Oil, Report AO (46) 1, 8 Mar 46: p. 73, Footnote 4: 'Driver training for SS Panzer units was badly affected. Drivers were inadequately trained in driving techniques and tactics. Firing from a moving vehicle required thorough training; the shortfall caused poor firing in battle and much waste of ammunition.'

report was made by Army Group South in the Ukraine. The capture of Ploesti by the Russians at the end of Aug 44 was a major loss.

On 7 Nov, Keitel issued a directive to armoured artillery divisions in the south-west that:

> They be equipped in such a way that they could move under their own power, practically without needing any motor fuel in order to avoid the time consuming transportation by railway. This was to be achieved by decreasing the vehicle strength of the divisions, by operating about half the remainder on diesel oil or producer gas; and by arranging for diesel vehicles to tow petrol engine vehicles.

By Dec 44 the supplies of fuel moving by rail from the main depots in Germany to the armies in the field had become a fraction of their requirements. When Hitler briefed his army commanders before the Ardennes Offensive, he is reported to have said that if the offensive did not succeed then the war was lost. However, recorded evidence reveals that less than 30 per cent of the anticipated fuel stocks were available at the start of the offensive. The complications caused by lack of fuel, both before the offensive started and while it was being fought, combined with the extremely adverse weather involving ice, mud and fog, took the punch out of the assault. Certainly that adverse weather minimised Allied air attacks on the German forces, but it caused major problems for ground movement by both Allied and German forces. For example, entire stocks of German bridge-building equipment lay in rear areas and the supply organisation was grossly inadequate. But a most revealing statement in the COS report by the Technical Sub-Committee on Oil (see the reference at the start of this Appendix, at the foot of p. 76 therein) is taken from an account by Speer after the offensive:

> Without any doubt the lack of supplies was due to the transport difficulties caused by air attack.

Von Rundstedt summed up his views after the offensive and enumerated four reasons for its failure:

- The first two were the wrong orders from the higher authority and the inadequate Army forces for the attack.
- The third was the lack of fuel and the failure to deliver the available fuel to units at the front.
- The fourth was the inexperience of drivers due to lack of fuel for training.

From Jan 45 onwards the supply of fuel to the Western Front was reduced to insignificant proportions. Tanks with inadequate fuel constituted a risk, with the main burden of the fighting being carried by infantry troops. On the Eastern Front the situation was no better. Both Jodl and Speer separately confirmed that lack of fuel was substantially responsible for the rapid collapse of the defensive front against the Russian breakout from the bridgehead at Baranova in the third week of Jan 45. There had been 1200 German tanks intended to stem that Russian drive into Upper Silesia but the fuel allocation denied their proper tactical deployment (USSBS Interrogation, 19 May 45.)

At the end of Jan 45, Hitler was planning a counter-offensive in Hungary. His General Staff had argued that a counter-attack in Silesia was a better option, but others had argued that Hungarian oil needed to be safeguarded. Speer had previously declared that Hungary supplied 40 per cent of the German mineral oil production and was therefore of decisive importance, not least because synthetic oil production in Germany was under serious danger because of coal shortages.[4] Hungary had been yielding about four times the quantity of petrol as the oilfields in Zisterdorf, Austria. The planned counter-offensive began on 5 Mar 45, strengthened by the 6th SS Panzer Army, but it was a failure. The lack of fuel was undoubtedly a factor but the dominant issue was the fall of Budapest, that being partly a consequence of the Luftwaffe's inability to re-supply the garrison by air.

Thereafter, the progressive and rapid collapse of the German defences was caused by the denial of railway transportation. The need for road transport and the fuel for its operation increased in proportion to the loss of railway services.

Effect on the German Air Force

The pre-war production capacity and stocks of aviation fuel were barely adequate to sustain the Blitzkrieg campaigns and were nowhere near sufficient for a war of attrition. There had been substantial imports of aviation fuel and this was largely held in the OKW reserve. By Sep 39, that reserve held about 335,000 tons of fuel; about enough for 3 months wartime requirements.

During the campaigns against Poland, western Europe and for the first 12 months of the invasion into Russia, the GAF was able to operate normally and without any restrictions, except for isolated local reasons. But the demands of the Russian and North African campaigns became unsustainable by mid-42 and the consequences began to impact initially on training, followed by reduced bomber and transport operations in the west. There was however no restriction on fighter operations until much later in the war.

It was noted that the GAF tended as a matter of normality to indent for fuel quantities in excess of its real need, perhaps in the expectation that allocated quantities would actually be sufficient for operations. It was generally the GAF that considered itself most hardly treated; it was very much the junior service.

The allocation of fuel for flying training certainly caused economies to be made through the second half of 1943 but the basic training schedule was accomplished; the fuel allocation was typically 30,000 to 35,000 tons per month. In Feb 44, the allocation was increased to about 45,000 tons per month cope with the greatly expanded fighter aircraft production programme; that increase was accomplished by the expanding outputs from the synthetic oil industry during the spring of 1944. By late summer 1944, as the Allied strategic bombing was targeted on the synthetic industry, the fuel allocation for training reduced to about 20,000 tons per month. From Sep 44 onwards, the allocation declined sharply and by the end of the year flying training had fallen to negligible proportions.

Through that period from late 1943 onwards, the allocation of fuel for the aircraft industry also reduced and this had a direct impact on the flight-testing of new and repaired aircraft. This was reflected in the increasing unreliability of

---

4. Hitler Conferences, Vol. 9, FD 2960/45.

some types as they were delivered to user units and entered combat service. Eventually only one aircraft in five had the proper test and acceptance flights, the others being flown for about 20 minutes and then sent directly to the Fronts.[5]

The German High Command and the GAF had become seriously concerned about aviation fuel shortages and several independent 'strategic reserves' were created, including the 'Fuehrer's Reserve'. These collectively had the effect of at least bridging the impact of industrial output losses and allowed the GAF to maintain operations, albeit subject to various significant restrictions from time to time. For example, Luftflotte 3 had the reserve fuel capacity to operate for four months in anticipation of the Allied landings in Normandy.

The GAF Luftflotte 3 opposition to OVERLORD was not limited to any extent by lack of fuel; a far greater impact was the loss of fighter aircraft in battle. But by Aug 44 the consumption from the fuel reserves was demanding increasing operational restrictions. Reconnaissance operations were limited and air support to the Field Armies by bomber and low-level attack sorties was allowed only under 'decisive situations'.[6] Night-fighter operations were reduced to allow the maximum number of daylight sorties; but by Feb 45, even daylight sorties had to be restricted to conditions where there was a 'most favourable opportunity for interception'.

> The aggregate GAF fuel reserve reached a peak figure of 574,000 tons at the end of Apr 44, a stock position that was stronger than it had been at any time since the summer of 1940.

By Sep 44 Hitler had come to appreciate that there was no good purpose in building larger numbers of conventional fighters if there was no fuel for them. Priority was given to the new German jet and rocket-powered aircraft, typically the Me 262 and Me 163 that were appearing in operations. The benefit that these fighter aircraft types offered was that they did not need high-grade aviation fuel; but their flight performance was outstanding. Perhaps sadly for the Germans, the production rates were not significantly high and their potential was not fully realised.

As the autumn of 1944 drew to a close, the bad weather over much of Germany delivered a much-needed breathing space as the strategic bombing was reduced. That opportunity was seized upon and oil production recovered. Aviation fuel output rose from 18,000 tons in October to 39,000 tons in November. The GAF was therefore able to make sporadic resistance through the first months of 1945 but by the end of Mar 45 the final writing was on the wall.

Effect on the German Navy
The Naval programme that came from the London Naval Treaty of 1935 formed the basis for a number of large, concealed oil storage installations that were

---

5. COS Technical Sub-Committee on Oil, Report AO (46) 1, 8 Mar 46: p. 82, Footnote 6.
6. Hut 3 Archives: CX/MSS/T273/146, 12 Aug 44.

constructed in the later years of the 1930s. These facilities were in the Baltic and North Sea ports, to allow the German naval units to draw fuel from their own bases. The total storage capacity was more than two million tons. The amount of stock at the start of the war was not identified but was believed to have been in excess of one million tons; over 700,000 tons was diesel oil. A large purchase of diesel oil was made from Mexico in 1939, through a firm of cotton importers in Bremen and an American company in New York – Davis & Co. Inc, who had a monopoly agreement for the import of Mexican oil into Germany. Imports in 1939 were believed to have been about 1,300,000 tons, consisting of crude and diesel oils.[7]

The wartime consumption of diesel by the German Navy was initially put at about 20,000 tons per month, but this was far short of actual consumption which increased to about 40,000 tons per month during 1941 to as much as 53,000 tons per month at times through 1943. Supplies of oil for the Navy were fully adequate throughout 1940, but they were then made partly available for the armies in Russia. The supply of diesel for the U-boats was not compromised and remained fully able to support operations; but surface ship operations had to be curtailed. Many of the large German battleships and their escorts spent a great deal of time in harbour, from where they presented a serious threat to British and Allied shipping but rarely realised that threat. The U-boat fleet did not suffer fuel shortages until Mar 45.

The German mercantile marine was of course a vital element of the war economy. Over 600,000 gross registered tons of merchant shipping was laid up before the end of 1942. The pressing need for this cargo capacity forced a costly conversion programme from oil to steam driven power.

Effect on the German War Economy
Within the Reich, as distinct from the occupied countries, shortages of oil did not prevent industrial output from maintaining a high level. There were many other factors that impacted on the war industry. The joint opinion of Speer, Kehrl, Schneider and Buetefisch was recorded as follows:

> There was no reduction in industrial output or in the production of munitions that could be directly attributable to any shortage of oil or of lubricants. The lack of oil did, however, contribute to some extent to transport difficulties which were a retarding factor in maintaining munitions output.

Even after the Allied strategic bombing attacks on oil plants, Speer confirmed that:

> The reduction in the production of motor gasoline and diesel oil for industrial purposes remained within tolerable limits. The rationing of fuel did not produce serious losses in industrial output. From October 1944 production sank in any case owing to difficulties in rail transport and consequently the demands on motor transport diminished also.[8]

---

7. COS Technical Sub-Committee on Oil, Report AO (46) 1, 8 Mar 46: Section XV, p. 84, Footnote (2).
8. ADI(K) Report No. 395/1945.

Airborne Intercept of Enemy R/T

Reference: Air 40/2717: 'Report on Airborne Interception of Enemy R/T Traffic' by HQ Army Air Forces, Washington DC, 1 Nov 44.

The following summary is derived from the reference report, of 20 pages and classified TOP SECRET. It was provided to Air Intelligence DDI 4 by HQ MAAF/CMR dated 5 Dec 44. The author of the report worked as an airborne intercept operator during Apr 44 until Aug 44.

Development
Airborne interception of enemy R/T was carried out in the Mediterranean theatre by the 15th USAAF from Oct 43. Initially only a very few operators were trained and available and combat missions were only monitored on an occasional basis. At that time and for many months afterwards there was limited interest and support for the intercept work within the Bomb Groups. The nature of the work was seen as of direct value to the Intelligence Dept and of no value to the operational bombing missions. However, the 97th and the 99th Bomb Groups became interested, set up their own internal organisation and then with mutual cooperation realised the very real and immediate value of the work. On every major mission into Germany where strong fighter opposition was expected, several intercept operators joined the bomber crews to cover as many R/T frequencies as possible. Their work was highly commended by the Intelligence section for strategic value and by the Bomb Groups for tactical value.

By Mar 44, eleven additional operators were selected and trained and then distributed among the various Bomb Groups of the 15th. They used Hallicrafter S-27 receivers, initially borrowed from the RAF No. 276 Wing.

Immediate Operational Value
On leaving the home base, the intercept operator scanned the frequencies used by the escort fighter formations. The Hallicrafter receiver would pick-up any traffic within roughly a range of 75 miles and the operator could then hear the chatter of incoming escort fighters. That chatter had been used by the enemy to

gain knowledge of where the escorts would join with the bomber force; they then joined up with the bombers before that took place. The Fw-190s were similar to the escort Thunderbolts and the bomber crews only recognised the planes as hostile when they opened fire. The intercept operators could monitor the fighter communications and warn the bomber groups of that risk.

On approaching enemy territory the operator would tune to the R/T frequencies likely to be used by the enemy fighters. The initial traffic was often calls between fighters and their ground controllers to check radios and frequencies. As that traffic grew stronger, the operator was able to gauge the likely range and would alert his bomb crew. A major benefit from that was being able to assess the time when the bomb crews needed to go to a high alert status and to provide an indication of the direction and altitude that the fighters were likely to come from.

When giving an order to the enemy fighters to scramble, the controller would use their code name. That information was often useful to crosscheck on changes in location. The enemy used clear language but with a great deal of code or slang words. The intercept operators had to be completely familiar with those words. There seemed no attempt to avoid or evade airborne interception.

Very often the bombers would claim multiple victories in air-to-air combat. The operators were able to listen to the German reports and identify more accurately the actual losses.

There would often be enemy R/T reports of bomb damage to airfields and the need for fighters to divert to other fields. The connection between unit callsigns and airfield codes was valuable. When enemy fighters were trailing bombers on their return routes, they would often need to divert to forward airfields. The location and use of those forward airfields was also valuable information.

APPENDIX R

Comparison with Dowding

Air Chief Marshal Sir Hugh Dowding (later Lord Dowding) was appointed CinC of Fighter Command when it was formed on 14 July 1936. He was faced with the huge task of creating a new organisation from the ground up, equipped then with aircraft that would not have been out of place in the 1920s. His task would have been forbidding even if he had counted on the cooperation of the Air Staff in Whitehall. Dowding had learnt from previous experience to distrust politicians and their ways; there were many who supported the policy of appeasement and would have favoured seeking terms with Hitler. He was also very sceptical towards some of the senior air marshals.[1] Just one example was the unbelievable attitude of some of those politicians and air marshals who would have discarded the production of the single-seat Spitfire and Hurricane fighters. That school of thought rejected the concept of single-seat fighters with forward firing fixed guns.

In 1940/41 Churchill had habitually cast a critical and disapproving eye at what he called the 'cumbersome machinery' of the Air Ministry. After the Munich crisis in 1938, the rapid expansion of the RAF resulted in an excessive growth and staffing of the Air Ministry. The bureaucracy which grew up became tumescent, with many layers of functionaries that only exacerbated the task of reaching informed decisions. It should be noted that such a rapid expansion of the Ministry was just as bereft of relevant experience as was the Air Intelligence Directorate, discussed in Chapter 6. That experience does not just happen because the number of staff has been multiplied. The real problem was that relevant experience of air operations and equipment for the air war as it was developing did not exist. It was perhaps inevitable that serious fundamental errors would have happened. How sad that the Air Commanders who were doing the real work in the field were largely excluded from the decisions in the Whitehall corridors of power.

If any one man could have been described as the victor in the Battle of Britain during the summer and early autumn of 1940, that one man would have been Dowding. The consequences of that victory are immeasurable. Hitler cancelled the planned invasion of UK under Operation SEALION, when the British Army

---

1. Bib.A32, Pt.1, Chap. 1, p. 15.

was in ruins after the collapse of France and the evacuation of the British Expeditionary Force personnel from Dunkerque. An invasion at that time would surely have sealed the fate of Western Europe. The desert campaigns in North Africa during 1941/42 would surely have been different, if indeed they had continued with the loss of the UK as a home base. The probability of the US subsequently entering into the European war would have been very doubtful with the absence of bases anywhere along the North Atlantic and North African coasts. The outcome of the battles on the Eastern Front could have been different given that Germany would have been able to concentrate on that Front. There must also remain serious doubt as to which nation would have then been the first to successfully develop and use atomic weapons?

So why was Dowding sacked so soon after that incredible victory? He was by no means the only senior officer relieved of command at that time. Air Vice Marshal Park was removed from No. 11 Group, that had been in the thickest of the air battle over south-east England. The circumstances have been well recorded in Bib. A32 but, for the purposes of the argument about Bomber Command and Harris, there is one additional ingredient. That revolves around the use by Fighter Command of both radar and Sigint intelligence to support battle planning and tactical decisions. That Sigint intelligence was the preserve of the RAF Y-Service, Bletchley Park and Fighter Command. Excellent and invaluable though the radar network was, it was often incapable of determining the strength and composition of the German raids that were building over the Pas de Calais. That was where the Sigint provided unique complementary intelligence that was to become available to Fighter Command in something close to 'real time' through the voice reporting system that was created. There was vicious acrimony within Fighter Command about the tactical deployment of fighters and the most vocal critics were Air Vice Marshal Leigh-Mallory from No. 12 Group and some of his squadron commanders. Those critics did not all have access to that Sigint evidence but there was a strong lobby in the Air Ministry, headed by the then VCAS Air Vice Marshal Sholto Douglas, for the 'big wing' tactics. That formed the basis for yet another conflict between Dowding and the Air Ministry. There had been an accumulation of attacks on Dowding from the Under-Secretary of State for Air Harold Balfour supported by senior air marshals such as Sir John Salmond and Sir Philip Joubert. An illuminating and instructive extract taken from Dowding's reply to Churchill on 24 October 1940, in response to the bureaucratic criticisms within the Salmond Report, stated that:

> The system that I have devised (for command and control of Fighter Commands operations) might not be perfect but it cannot be improved by the disruptive criticism on the part of people who do not understand it as a whole.

In Nov 40, when both the Secretary of State for Air Archibald Sinclair and the Air Staff urged Dowding's dismissal, Churchill felt no alternative but to accept their advice, albeit stressing his personal admiration for Dowding's qualities and achievements. When power-brokers such as these are determined to get rid of an outstanding leader who has achieved great things, notably in the face of their contrary advice and opinions, the subsequent analyses reveal that the perpetrators of the dismissal have usually been involved in intrigue and deceit.[2] The crucial key to the enigma of Dowding's dismissal was his unpopularity with the Air Council and that boiled down to personalities and personal aims. It is a common feature of man's nature that there is an inexhaustible resourcefulness in inventing pretexts and 'reasons' for acts and decisions whose motives are unworthy. Those resources were at work in the campaign to dismiss Dowding. They were to be seen later in the continuous criticism and sniping at Harris and Bomber Command, again by people who did not understand the whole issue and – worse – conspired to deny vital intelligence that should have been made available to Harris and his most senior staff. The culmination of that shameful conduct was the failure to acknowledge the achievements of the Command and the massive contribution to the successful outcome of the war in Europe.

---

2. Ibid. Pt.2, Chap. 7, p. 156.

Postscript

The dismissal of Dowding and the campaign to replace Harris, followed by the political erasure of their respective achievements, are consistent with the machinery of power which is most sensitive to criticism and jealously guards its rights and prerogatives.

There is no shortage of such abuse of power within the historical records. A naval court-martial in Portsmouth led to the execution of Admiral John Byng on board HMS *Monarch*. The records show that:

Never did the victim of insensate human rage more richly deserve the martyr's crown, for in that hour of shame and deep degradation he shielded with his blood the Government, which knew that its naval preparations had been criminally postponed and lamentably inadequate; and he satisfied the murderous instincts of those who once more thrust upon the innocent the burden of their own fault.

The date of that tragedy was 14 March 1757.[1] The inscription in the Parish Church of Southill, Bedfordshire, reads:

To the perpetual disgrace of public justice, The Honourable John Byng, Vice Admiral of the Blue, fell a martyr to political persecutors on March 14th in the year 1757, When Bravery and Loyalty were insufficient securities for the Life and Honour of a Naval Officer.

---

1. 'The Portsmouth that has Passed' by William G Gates, pp. 157–158.

Abbreviations and Glossary

ACAS (I)	Assistant Chief of Air Staff (Intelligence)
ADGB	Air Defence of Great Britain (otherwise, Fighter Command)
ADI (Sci)	Assistant Director of Intelligence (Science)
AEAF	Allied Expeditionary Air Force
AI	Air Intercept; also Air Intelligence – depending on the context
Air Cdre	Air Commodore, RAF
AM	Air Ministry
Bib.	Bibliography
BIP	Bomb Impact Point
BMP	Daily Sigint reports by the Air Section at Bletchley Park on the bombing raids; the initials derive from the names of the originators, Bonsall, Moyes and Prior
BS	Bomb Squadron, in USAAF context
BS	Bomber Support, in RAF context
BSDU	Bomber Support Development Unit
BSTU	Bomber Support Training Unit, originally No. 1692 Flight
CAS	Chief of Air Staff (RAF)
CEP	Circular Error Probable
CIU	Central Interpretation Unit (Photographic Reconnaissance (PR)
COA	US Committee of Operations Analysts (previously the Advisory Committee on Bombardment)
COPC	Combined Operations Planning Committee
COS	Chiefs of Staff
CSTC	Combined Strategic Targets Committee
DB (Ops)	Director of Bombing (Operations) – within the Air Ministry
EOU	Enemy Objectives Unit
DCAS	Deputy Chief of Air Staff (RAF)
D of I (O)	Director of Intelligence (Operations)
Dof I (R)	Director of Intelligence (Research)
D of S	Director of Security – within Air Intelligence
DofTels	Director of Telecommunications
FTD	Foreign Technology Division
GAF	German Air Force

GC & CS	Government Codes and Ciphers School (Bletchley Park)
GCI	Ground Controlled Interception
GNP	Gross National Product
Gp Capt.	Group Captain, RAF
HDU	Home Defence Unit (elements of the RAF Y-Service)
HQBC	Headquarters Bomber Command
HF	High Frequency
IFF	Identification Friend or Foe
IIC	Industrial Intelligence Centre (or Committee)
IP	Intermediate Point (prior to a bombing run)
JIC	Joint Intelligence Sub-Committee
JIS	Joint Intelligence Staff
KPR	Key Point Rating
MAAF	Mediterranean Allied Air Force
MAP	Ministry of Aircraft Production
MEW	Ministry of Economic Warfare
MF	Medium Frequency
MSS	Most Secret Source – usually used in the context of ENIGMA and ULTRA material.
NAVTAR	Naval Target (s)
OIC	Operational Intelligence Centre (within the Admiralty, London)
OKW	Oberkommando der Wehrmacht
ORS	Operational Research Section
PRO	Public Records Office
PoW	Prisoner of War
PIU	Photographic Interpretation Unit
POL	Petrol, Oil and Lubricants
PRU	Photographic Reconnaissance Unit
RAF	Royal Air Force
RCM	Radio Counter-Measure(s)
RDF	Radio Direction Finding
R/T	Radio Telephony
SALU	GAF R/T analysis reports generated within GC & CS; the abbreviation SALU derives from the names of the originators, Saltmarsh and Lucas.
Sigint	Signals Intelligence
S/E	Single Engine
SIS	Secret Intelligence Service
SLU	Special Liaison Unit
SOE	Special Operations Executive
Sqn Ldr	Squadron Leader, RAF
Target Set	A number of targets all related to a single object or objective
T/E	Twin Engine
TFF	Target Finding Force
TNA	The National Archives (UK) [Formerly The Public Records Office (PRO).]
TRE	Telecommunications Research Establishment
USAAF	United States Army Air Force
USofS	Under-Secretary of State

USSTAF	United States Strategic Air Forces Europe
VCAS	Vice Chief of Air Staff
VHF	Very High Frequency
Wg Cdr	Wing Commander, RAF
W/T	Wireless Telegraphy
WU	Wireless Unit
WW2	World War 2

German Aircraft Type Designators (as used within the text of this book)

Ar	Arado Flugzeugwerke GmbH
Bf and Me	Bayerische Flugzeugwerke A.G. (Messerschmitt) – changed to Messerschmitt in 1938
BV	Blohm & Voss, Abteilung Flugzeugbau
Do	Dornier Werke GmbH
Fw	Focke-Wulf Flugzeugbau GmbH
He	Ernst Heinkel A.G.
Hs	Henschel Flugzeugwerke A.G.
Ju	Junkers Flugzeug- und Motorenwerke A.G.

Bibliography

The Bombing Offensive

Ref	Title	Author
A1	Despatch on War Operations	Sir Arthur Harris
A2	The RAF in the Bombing Offensive against Germany, Vol V	TNA Air 41/43
A3	The RAF in the Bombing Offensive against Germany, Vol VI	TNA Air 41/56
A4	The Strategic Air Offensive against Germany, 1939–1945	Webster and Frankland
A5	The Planning of the Bombing Offensive and its Contribution to German Collapse	Air 41/57 (Frankland)
A6	Reaping the Whirlwind: Symposium on Strategic Bomber Offensive 1939–1945	RAF Historical Society, March 1993
A7	War in the Ether: An Account of RCM conducted by Bomber Command during the War 1939–1945	Wg Cdr Forsyth, Signals Branch, HQBC, October 1945
A8	Bomber Harris – His Life and Times	Air Cdre Henry Probert
A9	The Hardest Victory	Denis Richards
A10	Instruments of Darkness	Alfred Price
A11	History of the Second World War, Chapter 33	Sir Basil Liddell Hart
A12	ULTRA and the Army Air Forces in World War II	Dr Diane Putney
A13	USAAF Handbook, 1939–1945	Martin Bowman
A14	The Strategic Air War Against Germany 1939–1945	Air 10/3866, British Bombing Survey Unit Report
A15	Royal Air Force / USAF Co-operation, 1941–45	RAF Historical Society, March 1991
A16	The Effects of Strategic Bombing on German Transportation	US Strategic Bombing Survey (TNA Air 48/175)
A17	The Effects of Strategic Bombing on the German War Economy	US Strategic Bombing Survey (TNA Air 48/194)

A18	Point Blank and Beyond	Nigel Lacey-Johnson
A19	Decisive Campaigns of the Second World War	Edited by John Gooch
A20	Zuckerman: Scientist Extraordinary	Bernard Donovan
A21	Operations Analysis in the 8th USAAF in World War 2	Charles W McArthur
A22	The Most Valuable Asset of the Reich: A History of the German Railway, Volume 2, 1933–1945	Alfred C Mierzejewski
A23	The Wages of Destruction	Adam Tooze
A24	The Strategic Air War against Germany, 1939–45: Official Report of the BBSU, published 1998	CASS Studies in Air Power No. 4
A25	The Army Air Forces of World War 2	Craven & Cate, USAF Historical Divn
A26	The Other Bomber Battle	Rex Cording (Thesis for Doctorate)
A27	The Harris Archives	RAF Museum, Hendon
A28	Decision in Normandy	Carlo D'Este
A29	Piercing the Fog; Intelligence and AAF Operations in WW2, USAF History and Museums Program, 1996	John F Kreis, General Editor
A30	Confound and Destroy	Martin Streetly
A31	Bombs Gone: Development of British Air-dropped Weapons	Wg Cdr MacBean & Maj Hogben
A32	Dowding and Churchill	Professor J E G Dixon
A33	Air Publication (AP) 1234 – Air Navigation	HMSO 1941
A34	Target Germany: USAAF Official story of the 8th Bomber Command 1942–43	HMSO, SO Code No. 59–78, 1944

Intelligence Support

Ref	Title	Author
B1	British Intelligence in the Second World War	Hinsley, Thomas, Ransom & Knight
B2	The Official History of British Sigint, 1914–1945	Frank Birch
B3	British Sigint, 1914–1945	TNA HW 43/1-3
B4	A History of the German Air Section, Part III	TNA HW 3/109
B5	A History of the German Air Section, Part I	TNA HW 3/105
B6	The German Air Section	TNA HW 3/110
B7	Air Section and BMP History Notes	TNA HW 50/57
B8	The Secret War of Hut 3	John Jackson
B9	The Hut Six Story	Gordon Welchman
B10	ULTRA Goes to War – The Secret Story	Ronald Lewin
B11	Behind the Battle – Intelligence in the War with Germany	Ralph Bennett
B12	Intelligence Investigations – How ULTRA Changed History	Ralph Bennett
B13	Battle of Wits – Code-breaking in World War 2	Stephen Budiansky
B14	The Code Breakers	Hinsley and Stripp

B15	Most Secret War – British Scientific Intelligence 1939–1945	R V Jones
B16	Action This Day	Smith and Erskine
B17	GCHQ – The Secret Wireless War	Nigel West
B18	The Enemy is Listening: The Story of the Y-Service	Aileen Clayton, MBE
B19	Bletchley Park and the Luftwaffe, Report No 8, October 1997	Peter Wescombe
B20	Electronic Warfare	AVM Browne and Wg Cdr Thurbon
B21	Funkers and Sparkers – Origins and Formations of the Y-Service: BP Report No. 17, Sept 2000)	John Pether
B22	Ultra in the West – The Normandy Campaign of 1944–45	Ralph Bennett
B23	Conduct of the Air War in the Second World War	Edited by Horst Boog
B24	The History of Hut 3 (Jan 1940–May 1945), Vol 1 and 2	TNA HW 3/119–120
B25	Hut 3 – The Western Front from Feb 1942–May 1945	TNA HW 3/99
B26	Hut 3 – Radio Warfare	TNA HW 3/98
B27	The ULTRA Secret	Gp Capt. F W Winterbotham
B28	Bletchley Park Air Section Signals Intelligence support to RAF Bomber Command, 1943–45	Wg Cdr John Stubbington
B29	Very Special Intelligence	Patrick Beesley
B30	The Second World War	Sir Winston Churchill
B31	Figuring It Out at Bletchley Park, 1939–1945	Kerry Johnson and John Gallehawk
B32	Churchill & Secret Service	David Stafford
B33	Eyes of the Royal Air Force	Roy Conyers Nesbit
B34	Top Secret Ultra	Peter Calvocoressi
B35	GC & CS Air and Military History	TNA HW 11/1–11

John Stubbington graduated from the RAF Technical College, Henlow, in 1961 as an Engineer Officer. His career became specialised in the fields of Electronic Warfare and Defence Intelligence. At various times he was with the Bomber Command Development Unit; the Electronic Warfare Support Unit; No 51 Squadron as Engineer Officer; Support Command Signals Headquarters; and the Royal Signals and Radar Establishment. Intelligence appointments were with the UK MoD Directorate of Scientific and Technical Intelligence (DSTI) and the US Air Force Intelligence Division (FTD) at Wright-Patterson Air Force Base.

He retired from the RAF in 1985 and worked for 20 years within the UK Defence Industry, the last 15 years as an independent consultant in Command, Control, Communications, Computing, Intelligence, Surveillance and Target Acquisition (C4ISTAR). For some of that time he was an International Consultant with Raytheon Intelligence and Information Systems.

Index

Note:
Refer to Abbreviations and Glossary as required.

AVM   Air Vice Marshal
App   Appendix
M.P.   Member of Parliament

Admiralty 21, 30, 36, 59, 71, 145, 150, 165, 178, 188, 198, 208, 221, 243, 252, 276, 336, 348
Admiralty Operational Intelligence Centre 34
Airborne Intercept of Enemy R/T App Q
Air Council 325, 332, 347
Air Intelligence:
    Air Intelligence Handbook 63, 172, 176
    Assistant Chief of Air Staff Intelligence 227, 236, 350
    Assistant Director of Intelligence (Science) 44, 204–12, 226, 242
    Established Officer Strength App C
    Organisation App D, E and F
    AI 1 159, 160, 163–4, 169
    AI 2 200, 206, 233
    AI 3 49, 64, 82, 95, 159, 162, 176–86, 192, 202–4, 207, 217, 219, 232
    AI 4 152, 159, 200-04, 233, 274,
    AI (JIS) 213
    DDI 1 158–9, 163
    DDI 2 159, 204
    DDI 3 162
    DDI 4 37, 39, 46, 153–4, 159–60, 204–5, 236–7, 274–5, 349
    Overview of DDI 4 Activity App L
    DAFL 160, 197-198
Air Ministry:
    Director, Bomber Operations 43, 148, 345
    Deputy Director of Signals(Y) 142, 152, 158

Jockey Committee 255, App H
Weekly Intelligence Reports 64, 76, 177, 196, App I
Air Transport Auxiliary 258
Addison, AVM 113, 240, 245
Allen, Gp Capt 153, 205
Anglo-American Oil Targets Committee 53, 343
Appleton, Edward 229
Ardennes Offensive 267, 282, 290, 306, 312, 330, 349
ARGUMENT 258
Arnhem 229, 267
Arnold, Commanding General, USAAF 98, 227, 252–5
Atom bomb 282, 311, 356
Attlee, Clement, M.P. 63, 283, 326, 359
Auckinleck, General 360
AWPD-42 253–4

Babington-Smith, Constance 225
'Baedeker' raids 217
Baker, AVM 43, 148, 273, 344, 346
Baldwin, AVM 118, 242
Baldwin, Stanley, M.P. 84
Ball Bearings 68, 108, 187, 256–7, 288, 291, 295
Barrage Balloon 229, 234
Battle of the Atlantic 43, 48, 67, 71, 89, 141, 145–50, 83, 188, 252, 277, 288, 335–6, 348, 356
Battle of North Cape App B
Bennett, AVM 118

Bennett, Ralph 243, 265, 340
Benson 47
Berrtand, Captain 29
Bevin, Ernest, M.P. 326
BIG BEN 228
Birch, Frank, Commander: Bibliography
BLACK BUCK 140
Blandy, Gp Capt 142, 153, 157, 160, 205
Bletchley Park:
  Hut 3 205–9, 234–6, 243, 250, 261,
    265–74, 349
  Hut 6 37, 144–5, 167
  Bombe 145
  Colossus 265
  Distribution of Air Sigint Itelligence
    reports App M
  Air Section:
    Air Operational Watch 48, 274
    BMP Reports 41–2, 46, 179, 235–8,
      244, 263, 348
    Fighter Sub-Section 39–40
    Hook-Up 234–6, 263
    SALU 179
Blitzkrieg 64–5, 77, 181, 285, 331, 334
Blunt, Anthony 32
BODYGUARD 50–1
BODYLINE 225
Bomb Targets Information Committee 72,
  82
Bombing:
  Accuracy:
    Enemy decoys 121, 129, 333
    Probable bomb-fall ellipse 112, 125,
      223
    Radial Error 116, 127-8, 138
    Systematic Error 128
    Weather effects 130–4, 172, 217,
      220–1, 229, 245
  Area Bombing:
    Cities and Towns 45, 84, 103, 129,
      134–5, 150, 258, 309, 325, 354, 359
    Industrial targets 170–1, 181–5, 188,
      190, 197, 217–20, 231, 245, 257–8, 276
    Large targets 112, 131, 135
    Target acquisition 127–8, 138, 184
    Visual cues 128–138, 168, 184, 226,
      250, 297, 308
  Precision Bombing:
    Required resources 23, 135–6, 251
    Targets 101, 184
    Uninformed use of 22, 85, 106, 122,
      131, 257, 333, 338, 345

Bombsights:
  Mark II Course Setting 117
  Mark XIV 117
  Norden 129, 131
  Stabilised Automatic 117
Bombing Directives 24, 54, 70, 183, 221,
  334, 337
Bombing Survey Reports:
  American (USSBS) 24, 69, 199, Chap 10
  British (BBSU) 24, Chap 10, 32931, 342,
    353, 355
  Bureaucratic humbug App N
  Whitehall and the BBSU App N
Bombing Targets:
  Altenbeken 302
  Amiens 137
  Arnsberg Viaduct 246, 279, 296, 302
  Augsburg 43, 83, 273
  Belloy-sur-Somme 131, 226
  Berlin 51, 124, 134, 184, 195, 232, 282,
    311, 356
  Berchtesgaden 124, 225
  Bielefeld 279, 302,
  Cologne 45–6, 116, 189, 218, 232, 301,
    325, 348
  Cottbus 232
  Dresden 134, 232—3, 302, 359
  Dusseldorf 49, 318, 325
  Essen 49, 113, 119, 127, 197, 317
  Foggia 55
  Freidrichshafen 227
  German Air Force 185
  Hamburg 89, 186, 279, 317
  Hamm 78, 197, 279
  Hildesheim 247
  Kassel 105, 186, 279
  Kiel 88, 239, 317
  Leipzig 232, 261, 303
  Leuna/Merseburg 58, 82, 101, 297, 313,
    319
  Magdeburg 232
  Minden Aqueduct 279, 314
  Mittelland canal 151, 301, 314
  Niemburg 247
  Nuremburg – *see* Preface
  Oppau 58
  Hamm 78, 197, 279
  Oranienburg 184
  Osnabrück 78, 197, 279
  Peenemunde – *see* Preface
  Ploesti 76, 96, 262, 298
  Poelitz 101

Regensburg 256
Remagen bridgehead 279–80, 315
Ruhr 35, 48, 78, 99–106, 115, 121, 196, 223, 239, 247, 269, 276–82
Saumur 124
Schweinfurt 68, 120, 187, 255–6, 260
Schwerte 78
Soest 78
Troglitz 261, 297
Turin 120
Vlotho Bridge 247, 279
Watten 136
Wiener Neustadt 227, 261
Wilhelmshaven 46, 120, 180
Wissant 136
Bomb Types:
Cookie 123–6
General Purpose 123
GRAND SLAM 124, 138, 279, 296, 332
High Capacity 123
Incendiary 124–6
Medium Capacity 123
TALLBOY 124, 136, 138, 227, 279, 296, 332
UPKEEP 332
Bonsall, Sir Arthur 41, 157, 202, 236
Bordeaux 148
Bornholm Island 226
Bottomley, Air Marshal 68, 98, 120, 195, 248, 259, 282
Boyle, Air Cdre 159
Brant, Mr 79–80
Brest 149, 151
British Expeditionary Force, Air Component 35
British Museum 193
Bruneval 244
Bufton, Air Cdre 55, 68, 93–5, 102, 118, 127, 137, 231, 344–7, 359
Bufton Archives, Cambridge 95
Burgess, Guy 32
Bushey Park 86, 166, 260, 268
Butt Report 107, 113, 127, 332
Bylaugh Hall 245
Byng, John, ViceAdmiral of the Blue: App R

Cadell, Gp Capt 153
Caesar 94, 360
Cairncross, John 32
Casablanca Conference 48, 70, 90, 253–5, 276, 308, 333
Card, Wg Cdr 202

Chamberlain, Neville, M.P. 57, 60, 62, 331, 340, 357
Château de Vignolles 29
Cheshire, Gp Capt, V.C. 119, 121
Christiansen, Lt Cdr 226
Churchill, Sir Winston, M.P.
    and Intelligence 18, 25, 33, 52, 56, 66, 85
    and Air Ministry 94, 359
    and Bomber Command 33, 86, 324-25, 359–60
    and Parliament 18, 63, 171, 326
    and US President 93, 254, 308, 325, 334
    and War Cabinet 93, 336
CLARION 102, 269, 279, 302, 314
Clausewitz 69, 283, 323
Coal 48, 55, 58, 67, 76, 79, 82, 102, 105, 191–2, 197, 278, 280, 282, 3004
Cochrane, AVM 119, 346
Cockcroft, Dr. John 229
Coke 58, 67, 82, 91, 278, 300–2, 306, 313, 342
Combined Bombing Offensive 18, 42, 74, 90, 137, 179, 205, 212, 220, 229, 248, 254, Chap 9, 284, 293, 300, 308, 324, 333, 341, 360
Committee of Operations Analysts (US) 253–4, 256
Cooper, Joshua (Josh) 142, 144, 153, 158, 205, 240
COPC 248, 259
Cotton, Sidney 168
CRACKERS 112
Cross, Ronald H., M.P. 61
CROSSBOW 96, 225–7, 267
Combined Strategic Targets Committee 20, 55, 80, 98, 101–5, 224, 230–2, 269, 277, 282, 313–15, 329, 339, 342–3, 360

Dalton, Hugh, MP 61, 80
Daubney, Gp Capt 153, 202
Davies, Wg Cdr 203, 205
De Gaulle, General 38, 93
de Grey, Nigel 349
Defence Committee 82, 93, 226
Denniston, Commander 29, 157
Desert Campaign 76
    Afrika Korps 106, 312
    Alamein 106, 225, 312, 336
Doenitz, Admiral, German Navy 147, 151, 317
Donovan, Colonel, USAAF 38
Doolittle, General, USAAF 86, 251

Dortmund-Ems Canal 151, 190, 196–7, 225, 301, 314
Dowding, Sir Hugh 33, 61, 74, 359, App R
Douglass, Col, USAAF 175, 268
Dunkirk 34–5

Eaker, General, USAAF 23, 86, 131, 133, 236, 248, 253, 259, 333
Eden, Anthony, M.P. 83, 326, 359
Enemy Objectives Unit 91, 251, 360
Eisenhower, General, US Army 50, 9–94, 227, 250, 258, 267, 285, 324
Embry, AVM 260
ENIGMA 19, Chap 2, 64, 86, 114, 167, 173, 255, 261, 265–7, 271–3, 311, 350
Air Ministry 152–3, 206, 242
Battle of the Atlantic 141–2, 146–50, 183, 194, 253
Extracts from Decrypts on Transportation App K
FISH 53, 145
GADFLY 41
RED ENIGMA 41
SCORPION 41
Exchange Officers 261, 345

Falklands Campaign 140
Farnborough 228
Fisher, Sir Warren 60
Fitch, Gp Capt 153, 237
Flak 44, 111, 211, 234, 242, 268
Forster, Lt Col W L 223
FORTITUDE 51
FORTITUDE SOUTH 52
Frankland, Dr Noble 98, 327–28
Freeman, Sir Wilfred 83
Freya 211, 242

Ganzenmuller, Dr 315
Geilenberg 53, 298, 312, 354
Geheimschreiber 42
German Air Force 142, 177–81, 185–6, 193, 198–9, 218, 233, 240, 255, 260, 266–7, 274, 292–4, 306, 309, 319
Luftflotte 3 App B
Fliegerfuhrer Atlantik App B
Ar 234 181
Fw 200 *Kondor* 148, 149
He 280 181
KG40 148, App B
Me 262 181, 267, 294, 311

German Navy 33, 50, 145, 149, 292
Bismarck 151
Gneisenau 33
Prinz Eugen 151
Scharnhorst 33
Tirpitz 124, 138–40
xB-Dienst 150
Goering, Hermann, Reichsmarschall 47, 192, 292, 295

Hankey, Lord 32
Hankey Committee 74–5, 104, 282, 342
Harris, Sir Arthur
As CinC Bomber Command: 22, 85–6, 94, 100, 133, 247, 249, 304, 308, 324, 328, 336, 343, 358
Prior Appointments 84, 107, 341
Bombing Operations 121, 230, 238, 339
With Bufton 94–5, 344–46, 359
With Churchill 85–6, 113, 359
With Portal 85, 122, 344–45, 347, 351
With Target Selection 23, 68–9, 90, 97, 120, 227, 277, 335, 339, 345, 353
Comparison with Dowding App R
Harris Archives 324–5, 340, 344, 351
Hartley Committee 77, 104, 282
Hauschildt, Sgt, USAAF 264
Hitler, Adolf, Fuehrer 35, 50, 60, 64, 76, 147, 191, 214, 226, 285, 289, 291, 309, 315, 320, 331
Houdremont, Professor 317
HURRICANE I 99
HURRICANE II 99
HYDRA 225

Industrial Intelligence Committee 18, 21, 28, 56–7, 64, 74–5, 104, 135, 168, 339
Inglis, Air Cdre 188, 228, 236
Italy 43, 62, 78, 88, 96, 106, 192, 249, 262

Japanese Naval Attaché 51, 165, 195, 270
JERICHO 137
Joint Intelligence Committee 20, 36, 52, 64, 95, 102, 213–15, 256
Joint Oil Targets Committee 77, 104
Jones, Dr RV 208-09, 226, 228

Kammhuber Line 46, 212, 273
Kesselring, Field Marshal 281, 312, 317
Kingston-McCloughry, AVM 94
Knickebein radio beams 113, 117

Knox, Dillwyn 29
Kramer, General, German Army 312

Langer, Colonel 29
Lawrence, O.L., Mr 55, 68, 82
Lease-Lend agreement 329
Leigh-Mallory, Air Marshal 259
Linked Routeing 271–3, 351
Lloyd Committee 75, 104, 342
Longfellow, General, USAAF 249
Lovell, Sir Bernard 83, 115
Ludlow-Hewitt, Sir Edgar 47, 84, 169
Lywood, Air Cdre 164

McDonald, General, USAAF 227, 261, 268, 272
McMullen, Maj-Gen, USAAF 103
MacArthur, General, US Army 88
Maulig, Dr Paul 318
Manifould, Flying Officer 211
MARKET GARDEN 229, 267, 315
Medhurst, AVM 56, 64, 149, 211
Medmenham 169–70, 182, 223, 244, 250
Menzies, Stewart, Colonel 29, 33, 206
Meisel, Admiral, German Navy 51
Mierzejewski, Alfred App O
Milch, Field Marshal 176
MI6 33, 165, 206
Ministry of Aircraft Production 170–1, 176, 208
Ministry of Economic Warfare:
  Responsibilities Chap 3, 276, 339–41
  Black List Committee 59, 61
  Bombers Baedaker 220, 231
  Disregard of ULTRA 55, 106, 196, 282, 341
  Economic Advisory Branch 61–2, 190, 284
  Enemy Branch 62, 65, 196
  General Branch 62
  Key Point Rating 220, 231
  Research & Experiments Dept (RE/8) 49, 217
  Weekly Damage Report 190, 252
  Intelligence reports 196, 213, 351, 358–9
  and Target Selection 23, 28, 43, 45, 65, 68, 69–83, 92, 97, 137, 171, 176–7, 183, 188–9, 231–3, 248, 251, 277, 314, 333–8, 345
Montgomery, Sir Bernard 71, 267, 279, 336
Morley, Wg Cdr 72
Morton, Desmond, Major 56–8, 63, 334
Mount Farm 47, 250

Mueller, Erich 64
Munich Crisis 63, 333, 339
Munich Agreement 57, 60, 340
Napier, Maj Gen, US Army 229
Navigation Aids:
  Dead Reckoning 111–12
  GEE 81–2, 112–15, 117, 127, 135
  G-H 112, 116, 122, 226, 231
  H2S/H2X 114–16, 120, 129–31, 212, 231, 245
  LORAN 115
  Map reading 112
  Oboe 97, 112, 114, 116, 121, 127–8, 131, 135, 231, 245
  Position Lines 111
  Visual 111–17, 120, 126, 128–35, 139, 226, 250, 297, 308, 332–33
Norway 29, 32, 38, 148, 244
Oil Industry:
  Aviation fuel 49, 67, 297–8, 306, 311, 318, 320
  Bergius Plants 67, 191, App. P
  Fischer-Tropsch Plants 67, 298, 306, App. P
  in German War Effort: App P
  Military effects of shortages: App P
  Oil offensive: App P
  Synthetic oil 49, 53, 67, 75, 116, 223, 261, 287, 291, 297–8, 306, 312–13, 342, 352
  Transportation problems: App P
  Underground plants: App P
Oil Lobby 81, 277, 329, 341–2
Orchestral 207
OSLO Report 46, 211, 225, 242
OVERLORD 48, 53, 81, 86, 90–6, 127, 166, 190, 207, 244, 258, 263, 266–7, 274–7, 301, 335, 339
Oxland, AVM 222

Panacea targets 23, 54, 89, 277, 321, 336
Pathfinder Force 89, 114, 117, 245
Paynter, Air Cdre 207, 218, 237, 272, 274
PC Bruno 29
PEARL 42, 237
Pelly, Air Cdre 329, App. N
POINTBLANK 48, 70, 88, 90, 137, 229, 248, 254, 335
Peirse, Sir Richard 33
Philby, Harold 'Kim' 32
Photographic Reconnaissance:
  Central Interpretation Unit 169, 182, 188, 209, 218–19, 223, 244, 250–1

Lockheed XII aircraft 168
No. 106 (PR) Group 47, 170, 244, 251
Photographic Development Unit 169–70
SIS Flight 168
Wild A5 169
Pinetree 170, 243, 248, 251, 259–60
Poland 29, 38, 64, 228, 300
Portal, Sir Charles 47, 85, 92, 94–5, 98,
344–7, 351, 357, 360
Portsmouth 51, 72, 166
POST MORTEM 213
Potsdam Conference 325–6
Power Groups 24, 323, 338, 358
Price, Dr Griffith Baley 134
Putnam, Col, USAAF 236
Pyry Forest 29
Radio Countermeasures:
ASPIRIN 113
BROMIDE 113
CARPET 239
JOSTLE 239–40
MANDREL 239–40
PIPERACK 239–40
WINDOW 213, 239–40
Radio Direction Finding 84, 259
Reichsbahn 191, 280–2, 301–5, 314–16, 341,
App O
Richards, Denis 327
Riddell, Gp Capt 169-70, 244
Romania 29, 49, 75-76, 287, 298, 317, 342
Rommel, General 50, 71, 76, 92, 312, 336
Roper, Trevor 327
Royal Air Force:
No. 100 (Bomber Support) Group 108,
113, 116, 212, 233, 235, 237, 245
No. 192 Squadron 203, 211, 228, 236, 239
No. 51 Squadron 211
No. 80 Wing 113, 238
No. 276 Wing 264
RAF Delegation Washington 87, 162, 164,
198
RAF Wireless Intelligence Service 206
Bomber Command:
Afternoon briefing 224–5, 234, 246
Blue Book 219, 221
Circus Operations 218
Daily Attack Book 223
Despatch on War Operations 308,
327–8, 346–7
Industrial Card Index 218
Final Intelligence Organisation
App G

Intelligence Section 23, 216, 219
Marshalling Yard Blue Book 221
Morning briefing 234, 244–6
Master Bomber 119, 121, 222, 225
Target Attack Cards 223
1,000 bomber raids 218, 241, 348
U-boat Campaign Apr 42–Mar 43
App J
Aircraft:
Beaufighter 110
Catalina 110
Halifax 110, 236, 239
Lancaster 83, 115, 119, 121, 124, 138,
184, 296
Mosquito 110, 114, 119, 121, 124, 137,
151, 228, 234, 239, 245
Spitfire 61, 250
Typhoon 121, 151
Wellington 46, 55
138 (Special Duties) Squadron 38
419 (Special Duties) Flight 38
Coastal Command 42, 44, 47, 147, 153,
201, 206, 274, 300
Fighter Command/ADGB 20, 33, 35,
38–42, 47, 61, 74, 153, 166–7, 206, 208,
218, 227, 249, 259, 274, 348
Royal Navy:
HMS *Glorious* 33
HMS *Hood* 151
HMS *Petard* 149
Naval Intelligence Division 36
Sandys, Duncan, M.P. 226, 228–9
Schmid, Generalleutnant 108, 240
Searchlights 121, 212, 234, 240, 245
Secret Intelligence Service 36–8, 75, 165,
168, 173, 209
Selborne, Lord 43, 61
Sharp, Air Cdre 259
Sheen, Gp Capt 346–7
Sherrington, C.E.R. 77
Simmonds, Flt Lt 264
Sinclair, Sir Archibald 72, 229
Singleton, Lord Justice 45, 66, 113, 127,
332
Spaatz, General, USAAF 23, 86, 88, 90–8,
133–4, 196, 227, 248, 260–1, 267–8
Spanier, Dr Karl Eugen 318
Special Communications Unit 165
Special Operations Executive 61
Special Liaison Units 37, 153, 159, 164–5
Special Liaison Duties 26, 43, 164
Special Signals Units 164–5

Speer, Albert, Reichsminister 49, 53, 55, 65–8, 77, 172–3, 258, 281, 286–94, 304, 312, 317–20, 355
Spoerri, Top Sgt Felix, USAAF 264
Stalingrad 80, 276, 288–9, 298, 356
Stephenson, Colonel 38
Stratemeyer, General, USAAF 87
Student, General 281
Supreme Headquarters (SHAEF) 91, 93–4, 102, 166, 191, 224, 232, 246, 269, 278, 280
Sweden 68, 118, 228, 256
Switzerland 169, 256

Target Finding Force 117
Target Indicators:
  Ground Marking 114, 120
  Low-level Marking 121
  NEWHAVEN 118
  Offset Marking 111, 115, 121
  PARAMATTA 118
  Sky Marking 120
  WANGANUI 118
Tedder, Sir Arthur 71, 92, 94, 98, 122, 248, 267, 277, 329, 336, 343
The Cambridge Four 32, 86
The Iron Curtain 282, 326
THUNDERCLAP 134
Todt, Dr Fritz 64
TORCH 87, 250, 253
Total War 71, 323, 336–7, 357
Transportation Targets: 76, 80, 97, 99–104, 128, 133, 137, 218, 221, 247, 267–9, 276, 282, 300, 305, 310, 341, 343, 352
  Effects of collapse of the Reichsbahn App O
Trenchard Doctrine 107, 323, 332, 335, 358
TRIDENT Conference 334

U-Boats App J
Underground Oil Plant, Porta App O
Upper Silesia 103, 184, 278
USAAF:
  8th AAF: 21, 41, 45–6, 50, 68, Chap 4, 166–7, 183, 199, 213, 222, 230, 233–4, 244, Chap 8, 272, 279, 288, 297, 333, 341, 351, 359
  Bombing Accuracy Sub-Section 129
  Geerlings Maps 250
  Micro-H 131–2
  The Oxford Experiment 131
  Spillage 129, 133, 135

15th AAF 199, 243, 248, 256–8, 261–5, 298, 302, 334, 337
7th Photo Recon Group 250
B-17 Fortress 87, 129, 134, 194, 239, 256
P-51 Mustang 180, 258
B-24 Liberator 87, 131, 226, 261
P-38 Lightning 121, 250
P-47 Thunderbolt 180
USSTAAF: Chap 8
  Bushey 23, 86, 166, 268, 326, 329, 334
  Granville 268
  Rheims 268
  St. Germain 268
US President:
  Roosevelt 93, 219, 254, 283, 308
  Trueman 283
US Advisory Committee 253
US Signal Security Agency 250

Verity, Wg Cdr 217
Versailles 99
Vickers, Colonel 82
Virtz, Dr Ing Gerhardt 318
von Braun, Werner 229
von Rundstedt, Field Marshal 95, 274, 317
V-1 Programme 96, 127, 131, 176, 226-29, 267, 296, 356
V-2 Programme 96, 127, 136, 176, 225–29, 267, 293, 296, 356

Wallis, Dr. Barnes 124, 296, 331
War Cabinet: 20, 48, 70, 80, 83, 93, 113, 134, 137, 149, 183, 198, 213, 221, 226, 334-35, App N, 341–2, 358–9
War Office 37, 59, 152, 164, 167, 192, 340
  Military Intelligence Directorate 34, 37, 152, 350
Wasserfall 228
Watson-Watt, Robert 229
Wavell, General 360
Webster, Sir Charles 327–8
Wheatley, Dennis 160
WIDEWING 23, 260, 262, 268
Winterbotham, Gp Capt 159, 164, 168, 184
Wireless Intercept Committee 30
Woolmer, Viscount 61
Würzburg 211, 239–40, 242
Wycombe Abbey School for Girls 86, 243

X-Gerät 44

Y-Service, RAF: 46–9, 148, 152, 157, 200–1, 203–4, 234, 237, 242, 245, 263–4, 273, 348
Canterbury 223
Cheadle 35, 38, 46, 49, 66, 143, 148, 152, 207, 235, 273
Chicksands 203
Kingsdown 35, 38, 42, 46, 48–9, 143, 152, 202–3, 207, 233-35, 273
Home Defence Units 38, 46, 152, 203, 234, 236, 273

Sigint against KG40/Fw Operations App.B
Young, Col., USAAF 264

ZEPPELIN 51
Zimmerman, Hauptmann 317
Zuckerman, Prof Solly 123, 195, 314, 329